Vienna

Penguin Books

PENGUIN BOOKS

Published by the Penguin Group
Penguin Books Ltd, 27 Wrights Lane, London W8 5TZ, England
Penguin Books USA Inc., 375 Hudson Street, New York, New York 10014, USA
Penguin Books Australia Ltd, Ringwood, Victoria, Australia
Penguin Books Canada Ltd, 10 Alcorn Avenue, Toronto, Ontario, Canada M4V 3B2
Penguin Books (NZ) Ltd, 182-190 Wairau Road, Auckland 10, New Zealand

Penguin Books Ltd, Registered Offices: Harmondsworth, Middlesex, England

First published 2000
10 9 8 7 6 5 4 3 2 1

Colour reprographics by Westside Digital Media, 9 Bridle Lane, London W1
and Precise Litho, 34-35 Great Sutton Street, London EC1
Printed and bound by Cayfosa-Quebecor, Ctra. de Caldes, Km 3 08 130 Sta, Perpètua de Mogoda,
Barcelona, Spain

Edited and designed by

Time Out Guides Limited
Universal House
251 Tottenham Court Road
London W1P 0AB
Tel + 44 (0)20 7813 3000
Fax+ 44 (0)20 7813 6001
Email guides@timeout.com
http://www.timeout.com

Editorial

Editor Kevin Ebbutt
Consultant Editor Geraint Williams
Deputy Editor Helen Van Kruyssen
Researcher Maite Bachero
Proofreader Tamsin Shelton
Indexer Julie Hurrell

Editorial Director Peter Fiennes
Series Editor Caroline Taverne

Design

Art Director John Oakey
Art Editor Mandy Martin
Senior Designer Scott Moore
Designers Benjamin de Lotz, Lucy Grant
Scanning/Imaging Chris Quinn
Picture Editor Kerri Miles
Deputy Picture Editor Olivia Duncan-Jones
Picture Admin Kit Burnet

Advertising

Group Advertisement Director Lesley Gill
Sales Director Mark Phillips
International Sales Manager Mary L Rega
Advertisement Sales (Vienna) Franz-Josef Hartel
Advertising Assistant Daniel Heaf

Administration

Publisher Tony Elliott
Managing Director Mike Hardwick
Financial Director Kevin Ellis
Marketing Director Gillian Auld
General Manager Nichola Coulthard
Production Manager Mark Lamond
Production Controller Samantha Furniss

Features in this guide were written and researched by:

Introduction Kevin Ebbutt. **Key Events** Nicholas Parsons. **History** Nicholas Parsons. **Vienna Today** Katya Adler, Nicholas Parsons. **The Viennese** Nicholas Parsons. **Literary Vienna** Oona Strathern. **Architecture** Rory O'Donovan. **By Season** Geraint Williams, Robin Lee, Sara Moore. **Sightseeing** Geraint Williams. *Taking the flak* Delia Meth-Cohn. **Museums** Cynthia Prossinger, Geraint Williams, Kevin Ebbutt. **Galleries** Jonathan Quinn, Kevin Ebbutt. *The Schiele dealer* Sonya Yee. **Accommodation** George Hamilton. **Restaurants** Katya Adler. **Cafés & Coffeehouses** Katya Adler. **Beisl** Geraint Williams, Katya Adler. **Heurigen** Sonya Yee. **Nightlife** Darim Timimi, Christina Copelli, Dagmar Steidl, Geraint Williams, Kevin Ebbutt. **Shopping & Services** Geraint Williams. **Children** Delia Meth-Cohn. **Film** Adrian Garcia-Lande. *A Hedy cocktail* Kevin Ebbutt. **Gay & Lesbian** Chris Halls. **Media** Deborah Klosky. **Music: Classical & Opera** Robin Lee. **Music: Rock, Roots & Jazz** Geraint Williams. **Sport & Fitness** Deborah Klosky, Peterjon Cresswell. **Theatre & Dance** Richard Hoole, Robin Lee. **Getting Started** Andrena Woodhams. **Wienerwald** Andrena Woodhams. **Lower Austria** Andrena Woodhams. *Poet's corner* Rod Pritchard-Smith. **The Wachau** Andrena Woodhams. **Burgenland** Andrena Woodhams. **Moravia** Andrena Woodhams. **Bratislava** Tom Popper. **Budapest** Chris Condon. *The Sopron shop stop* Dave Rimmer. **Directory** Andrena Woodhams, Geraint Williams, Oona Strathern. *Vienna by numbers* Patrick Bartos.

The Editor must express gratitude to the following:

The main man Geraint Williams, Maite Bachero, Hadley 'Viennese vision' Kincade, Simone Coll, Jonny Gibbons, Robert Knestel, Stefan Jena, the seventh floor support and the designers downstairs, Dave Rimmer, Peterjon Cresswell, Matt McAuliffe, Jason Bold, Mathew Ballard, Herr Doktor Bobby Bennett, Michael Cook, the Lomo crew, Lorenz Seidler, Sophie Blacksell.

Maps by JS Graphics, 17 Beadles Lane, Old Oxted, Surrey RH8 9JG.
Vienna Street Map based on material supplied by APA Publications Gmbh & Co.

Photography by Hadley Kincade except: page 9, 29 Hulton Getty; page 6, 11, 13, 16, 19, 20, 30, 208, 227 AKG; page 12, 18 OFVW; page 17 Bridgeman Art Library; page 22, 23, 217 Associated Press; page 118 Kevin Ebbutt; page 118, 119 Lomo Society; page 211, 241 The Kobal Collection;page 215 Anita-Daniela Krappel; page 231 Weiner Tourismusverband; page 240 Popperfoto; page 249, 252, 253, 254, 257, 258, 259, 260 Andrena Woodhams; page 267, 268 Trip

The following photographs were supplied by featured establishments: pages 124, 237, 255

Contents

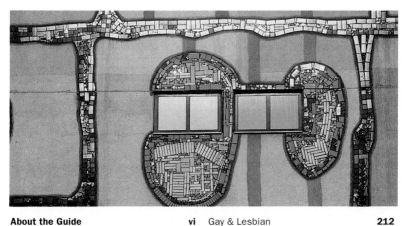

About the Guide

This is the first edition of the *Time Out Vienna Guide*, one of our ever-expanding series on the world's most crucial cities. A dedicated and enthusiastic team of writers who live and work in the Austrian capital sweated and fretted to provide you with everything you might need to know to make a visit to Vienna as rewarding as possible. While detailing the main sights and major attractions, we also direct you to Vienna's coolest cafés, sharpest shopping opportunities and finest new places to lunch and dine.

Postal districts

Vienna is divided into 23 districts. In our listings the first number of each address is the district and the second the street number. So, for example, **Café Central** in the 1st district is listed: *1, Herrengasse 14*. The district number is denoted by the second and third digit in the post code, thus for **Café Central** it is 1010.

To boldly go

Where we mention places that are also listed elsewhere in the guide they are **highlighted in bold** and can be found in the index.

Checked & correct

We've striven to make this Guide as useful and accurate as possible. Addresses, phone numbers, transport details, opening times and admission prices were all checked before going to press. However, please bear in mind that owners and managers can change their arrangements at any time. If you are going out of your way, it's a good idea to phone before setting out.

Prices

In this guide the Austrian Schilling is denoted by an AS. Where we have listed prices, they should be treated as a guideline rather than gospel. Should they vary wildly from those we have quoted, ask for an explanation. If there isn't one, go elsewhere – but please write and let us know.

Spelling changes

We have followed the rule of replacing 'ss' with a 'ß' after a long vowel. So, for example Strasse is spelt Straße. However, bear in mind that over the next two years the powers that be are planning to phase this tradition out of the German language.

Credit cards

Be warned, although most hotels in Vienna take credit cards, many restaurants, cafés and museums do not. The following abbreviations have been used: **AmEx**: American Express; **DC**: Diners' Club; **JCB**: Japanese credit cards; **MC**: Mastercard/Access; **V**: Visa.

Hanging on the telephone

At first glance some phone and fax numbers listed may seem confusing. While there can be as many as 10 or as few as three or four digits to each number, there is also the *Durchwahlen* (direct dial extension numbers) system. This means some numbers are followed by a hyphen and then a digit (usually a 0); this tells you there are a number of extensions. Dialling the main number *plus* those following the hyphen will connect you to an extension. So, if you know the extension you want, dial the relevant digits after the hyphen. Extension 0 will usually get you through to the main desk/operator who will then transfer your call if necessary. Likewise, if you dial all the numbers *up to* the hyphen you will still get through to the same main desk/operator. If there are figures other than a 0 after the hyphen we recommend you dial the *whole* number as that will be the extension you'll need to book a room, make enquires, etc.

Right to reply

It should be stressed that the information we offer is impartial. No organisation has been included because it has advertised in any of *Time Out's* publications, and all opinions given are wholly independent. Rigorous impartiality and cosmopolitan critical assessment are the reasons our guides are so successful. But if you disagree with our opinions, please let us know; your comments are always welcome. You'll find a reader's reply card at the back of the book.

There is an online version of this guide, as well as weekly events listings for over 30 international cities, at **www.timeout.com**

Introduction

Spinning the wheel.

To edit a *Time Out* guide is to produce a snapshot of a city at a certain point in its history – the contemporary climate can be felt throughout the book, from the opening of the latest experimental club night, designer shop or unconventional new gallery to the details of a developing political situation. In editing this first edition of the *Time Out Vienna Guide*, the political situation has proved the thorniest aspect to approach.

The link between our schedules and Austrian political processes has been uncanny. I returned to London for the final stages of producing this guide on the day Vienna went to the polls. As our finished pages went down to design, the front pages of every serious international newspaper were dominated by the electoral success of Jörg Haider and the far-right Freedom Party and their ensuing coalition with the centre-right People's Party. There has been trouble on the streets of Vienna, outcry throughout Europe and the world. We have to ask the same questions as other commentators: Is this just a symptom of an overdue realignment of post-war Austria's smug two-party system? Or is it really the ghosts of a Nazi past coming back to haunt the present?

As nations, as cities, as individuals, we all have to deal with the ghosts of the past. Maybe the crisis unfolding as we go to press will bring past tensions into the present tense, enabling them to be examined and dealt with. Other European voices have been urging cultural boycotts and diplomatic attempts to isolate Austria. But as Peter Brook and Pierre Boulez argued, in a statement published by *Le Monde*: 'Putting the bad boy in the corner won't make him better. On the contrary, it will make him worse.'

Even at the best of times, Vienna's past confronts the visitor at every corner. Sitting in the **Secession** soaking in Gustav Klimt's *Beethoven Frieze* sparks thoughts of Vienna's *fin-de-siècle* artistic greatness. Riding the **Riesenrad** – iconic to Vienna – conjures images of post-war devastation and Orson Welles as Harry Lime, while also providing a metaphor for the cycles of history. And while the **Hofburg** might reverberate with the memory of Hitler's *Anschluß* speech in 1938 being cheered by tens of thousands, it has also more recently been the scene of demonstrations against the current government.

Poking around the **Sigmund Freud Museum** is enough to remind that the prime purpose of the work of this most influential of Viennese

intellectuals was essentially to find out what makes us tick – to isolate the elements that give us our drive. What is driving Haider and company will only become apparent during the lifespan of this edition.

At culture's other extreme, I found myself waiting 20 minutes while the assistants at **Black Market** – one of the city's best music shops and purveyor of all that is cosmopolitan and funky in contemporary Vienna – tracked down the cover to their last copy of the remix of Madonna's 'Nothing Really Matters' by Vienna mixmeisters Kruder & Dorfmeister. As their version played through on the shop's soundsystem, I mused over the fact that of all the original lyrics, these two young Austrians had settled on only one fragment: 'Nothing takes the past away/Like the future.'

The trickiness of the transition between Vienna's twentieth-century past and its twenty-first-century future is no reason to stay away from this thought-provokingly perplexing metropolis, still caught undecided between its ancient role as imperial city-state and its potential role as international world city at the meeting-point of east and west. For now, let's ponder on the fact that Hundertwasser's **Fernwärme** – a huge rubbish incinerator – is the city's most beautiful modern building and certainly its largest work of art. In turn-of-the-century Vienna, there is still plenty to be recycled.

Kevin Ebbutt

SCHÖNBRUNNER TIERGARTEN
since 1752

The world's oldest zoo,
founded in 1752

Modern animal keeping in the
baroque environment of the
emperor's zoological garden.

Open all year,
daily from 9.00 a.m.
U4 Station "Hietzing-Zoo"
Parking area

Tel: 0043-1-877 92 94-0
Fax: 0043-1-877 96 41

SCHÖNBRUNNER
TIERGARTEN

In Context

Key Events

Prehistory

5000 BC Stone Age man working the local hornstone around the Vienna Basin.
800-15 BC Iron Age Celts dominant in the Austrian region. Rise and decline of *Noricum*.
113 BC Kimbern Celts defeat Romans at Noreia.
c15 BC Noricum peacefully absorbed into the Roman Empire.

The Romans

AD 8 *Vindobona* becomes part of the Roman province of Pannonia.
98-117 Under Trajan, a heavily fortified camp is built at Vindobona.
171 Marcus Aurelius in Vindobona.
212 The civil settlement at Vindobona raised to the rank of *Municipium*.
c395 Fire destroys the Roman camp. The legion withdraws.
433 The Eastern Emperor Theodosius II cedes Pannonia to the Huns.

The Dark Ages

482 Death of Saint Severin.
6th Century Avars overrun the Wiener Becken.
9th Century Dedication of Saint Rupert, the first authenticated church in Vienna.
881 'Wenia' appears in the Salzburg annals.
976 Start of Babenberg rule in Austria.
996 First occurrence of the name Ostarrichi (Austria) in an imperial document.

The Babenbergs

1137 Treaty of Mautern between Leopold IV and the Passau bishopric allows the building of a new parish church dedicated to Saint Stephen.
1155 Irish monks found the Schottenstift.
1156 The Margraves of Babenberg become Dukes of Austria. Heinrich IV of Babenberg moves his court to Vienna.
1192 Leopold V inherits Styria and part of Upper Austria.
1193 Leopold V receives his share of Richard the Lionheart's ransom. Some of the money is used to build out the fortifications of Vienna.
1198-1230 Under Leopold VI Vienna becomes a booming commercial and cultural centre.
1246 Last Babenberg, Friedrich II, killed fighting the Hungarians.

The coming of the Habsburgs

1252 Ottokar II, Premysl of Bohemia, marries Friedrich II's widow.
1258 Serious fire in Vienna. Ottokar supports the rebuilding of the city.

1273 Rudolf of Habsburg elected German King.
1276 Rudolf occupies Vienna.
1277 Ottokar II killed at the Battle of Dürnkrut. Rudolf now unchallenged in Austria.
1298 Albrecht I is the first Habsburg to be elected Holy Roman Emperor.

The early Habsburgs

1310 Rising against Friedrich the Handsome.
1320 Vienna's privileges codified in the Eisenbuch.
1338-49 Vienna hit by disasters: locust swarms, plague and fire.
1359 Rudolf IV, 'the Founder', lays foundation stone for south tower of St Stephen's.
1365 Rudolf founds the Vienna University.
1365-1463 Habsburg dynastic struggle between Albertine and Leopoldine lines.
1420-1 The *Wiener Geserah*: the first great pogrom against the Jews under Albrecht V.
1452 Friedrich III is the last Holy Roman Emperor to be crowned in Rome.
1462 Siege of the Wiener Hofburg by Viennese burghers backing Friedrich's rival and brother, Albrecht.
1469 Vienna is made a bishopric.

Renaissance & Reformation

1485-90 The Hungarian King, Matthias Corvinus, occupies Vienna.
1498 Emperor Maximilian I founds the Hofmusikkapelle, forerunner of Vienna Boys Choir.
From 1517 Lutheranism rapidly spreads through the German territories of the Habsburgs.
1521 Ferdinand I takes over the Austrian possessions of Karl V.
1526 Lajos II of Hungary dies fighting the Turks at Mohács. The Habsburgs inherit the Hungarian and Bohemian thrones as a result of Maximilian's marriage pact of 1515.
1529 First Turkish siege of Vienna.
1531-66 Italian-style fortifications are built to help Vienna resist future Turkish attacks.
1551 The Jesuits are summoned to Vienna. The Counter-Reformation begins.
1577 Protestant worship forbidden in Vienna.

Counter-Reformation

1603-38 During the 'monastery offensive' many monasteries and churches are built in Vienna.
1622 Jesuits gain control of the university.
1629 Ferdinand II's Edict of Restitution returns all church properties under control of Protestants to the Catholic Church.

Baroque era
1658-1705 Rule of the 'first Baroque Emperor', Leopold I.
1669 Second expulsion of the Jews from Vienna.
1679 Plague in Vienna. Abraham a Sancta Clara preaching in the city.
1683 Second Turkish siege of Vienna. The city is rescued by an army under Jan Sobieski of Poland and Karl of Lorraine.
1699 The Peace of Karlovitz restores Hungary, Transylvania and Slavonia to Habsburg rule.
1704-11 Hungarian War of Independence against Habsburg hegemony.
1704 The Linienwall erected around the Vienna periphery against Hungarian incursions.

Habsburgs triumphant
1711-40 Building boom in Vienna under Karl VI. Many Baroque palaces and churches built.
1713 Promulgation of the Pragmatic Sanction in an attempt to secure the Habsburg succession in the female line.
1740-80 Maria Theresia reforms government, education, law and the army. The age of enlightened absolutism.
1781 Tolerance Patent offers religious toleration to non-Catholic faiths and later (1782) also to Jews.
1784 Vienna General Hospital founded.
1780-91 Mozart in Vienna.
1791 Première of *The Magic Flute*.

Napoleonic Wars & the *Biedermeier* age
1805-9 Vienna occupied by Napoleonic troops.
1811 The Austrian state is declared bankrupt.
1814-15 Congress of Vienna settles post-war map of Europe.
1835 Population of Vienna reaches 330,000. Poor sanitation causes frequent outbreaks of cholera.
1845 First gas installation in Vienna.
1848 Outbreak of revolution all over the Empire.
1848-9 Franz Josef I becomes Emperor. Defeat of the revolution.

The reign of Franz Josef I
1857 Demolition of city bastions. Building of the Ringstraßen boulevard begins.
1860-1900 Founders' Period (*Gründerzeit*). Liberal hegemony in politics, industrial expansion.
1861 Liberals take over city hall. Infrastructural investment under Mayor Cajetan Felder (1868-78).
1866 Austrian defeat by the Prussians at Königgrätz (Sadowa).
1870 Vienna Tramway Company set up.
1873 World Exhibition in Vienna. Cholera outbreak. Stock Exchange crash.

1881 Ringtheater burns down.
1885 Widening of franchise to include 'Five Gulden Men'. Rise of Karl Lueger.
1888-9 Viktor Adler founds the Social Democratic Party.
1892 Incorporation of the *Vororte* (outer settlements) into Vienna. Population now 1,364,000.
1897-1910 Karl Lueger's term as Mayor of Vienna. Communalisation of public services, anti-Semitic populist politics.
1889 Crown Prince Rudolf commits suicide.
1898 The Vienna Secession is founded.
1900 Freud's *Interpretation of Dreams* published.

End of the Empire to World War II
1914 Franz Ferdinand assassinated in Sarajevo.
1914-18 World War I.
1916 Death of Franz Josef I.
March 1919 Franz Josef's successor, Karl I, resigns and leaves the country.
12 Nov, 1919 Proclamation of the Republic of 'Deutschösterreich'.
1919 Treaty of St Germain fixes the new borders of Austria, shorn of her Empire.
May 1919 Social Democrats take power in Vienna City Council. Period of 'Red Vienna' begins.
1922 The Christian Social Chancellor, Ignaz Seipel, rescues the country from hyper-inflation by means of foreign credits.
1927 The Palace of Justice is burned down.
1934 'Civil War' between Catholic Conservative government forces and the Social Democrats ends in victory for the Conservatives and the founding of the Fatherland Front. Corporate State set up by clerico-Fascist regime.
1934 Attempted Nazi putsch results in assassination of Chancellor Dollfuß.
1938 *Anschluß* with Hitler's Reich. Hitler welcomed in Vienna by jubilant crowds.
9 Nov 1938 *Reichskristallnacht* – Jewish properties burned and looted, Jews beaten up.
1939-45 World War II.

Post-war Austria
1945-55 Occupation by the Allies. Vienna under four-power control.
1955 Austrian State Treaty liberates the country, which becomes neutral.
1956 The Atomic Energy Commission is set up in Vienna.
1965 OPEC offices located in Vienna.
1970 Social Democrats take power under Bruno Kreisky, who remains Chancellor until 1983.
1981 Vienna becomes the third seat of UNO.
1984 Helmut Zilk becomes Mayor of Vienna.
1989 Fall of the Iron Curtain.
1995 Austria joins the European Union.
1999 General election held.

History

Location, location, location... Vienna's position at the commercial and cultural crossroads of Central Europe determined its destiny.

The forces of nature create an opportunity, and man exploits it. Nowhere has this been more true than in Vienna, geographically situated at the crossroads of Central Europe between the Alps and Carpathians, and positioned geopolitically between the heterogeneous East and the gradually hegemonic West. From the very dawn of civilisation there were trade and military routes running east and west along the Danube, while other arteries (notably for the amber trade) ran north and south from the Baltic and North Sea to the Adriatic. The *Wiener Becken* (Vienna Basin) lay conveniently in their paths. In medieval Vienna, Danube shipmen tied up their salt-laden barges below the Ruprechtskirche, merchants from Cologne carried their wares into the Kölnerhof, and in 1196 Crusaders would slake their thirst in the local inns before setting out to perpetrate the first of many recorded massacres of Jews in the city.

Long before this, however, Vienna had already received plenty of transit traffic. Some (the Illyrians and Celts) decided to settle, only to be overwhelmed by the superior weaponry of the Romans; others, like the Avars and Longobards of the Dark Ages, swept through on their way to conquest or defeat elsewhere. Precisely because Vienna was and is a city of a thousand influences, it has seemed to work all the harder at being *sui generis*, at developing an exclusive microculture impenetrable to outsiders, but itself formed by the outsiders of previous eras.

Origins, Celts & Romans

The Vienna Basin, into which Vienna expanded from a few first scrappy settlements on the alpine spurs overlooking the Danube, was formed in the middle tertiary period at a point where the Eastern Alps fall away along a fault-line studded with hot springs (Bad Fischau, Bad Vöslau, Baden bei

Rudolf I vanquishes Ottokar II in the 1278 battle that won Vienna for the Habsburgs.

Wien, Oberlaa). The Basin was once filled with the so-called Miocene Sea, traces of which still mark the hills west of the city. The waters gradually receded, exposing a terraced landscape that took shape 400,000 to 500,000 years ago. Today the city stretches eastward from the sandstone rise of the Hermannskogel (524 metres/1,720 feet) in the *Wienerwald* or Vienna Woods to the low-lying Lobau (149 metres/490 feet), a Danubian water meadow and conservation area. Millennia ago, the mighty Danube itself broke through the Wienerwald hills and, as the ice ages receded, brought with it much of the rubble and detritus on which the oldest part of the city was erected.

As an emblem of Vienna the Danube is as firmly anchored in *kunst*, the city's art and music, as in kitsch. This has obscured its ambivalent reputation before the channelling of the river in the late nineteenth century, when the treacherous arm of the main stream that washed the walls of the old city was tamed into the *Donaukanal* or Danube Canal. Johann Strauß's flattering hymn to the *schönen blauen Donau* ('beautiful Blue Danube'), written three years before major works were initiated (1870) to secure the city from recurrent flooding, was little more than appeasement of an unpredictable Grendel-like menace. A more realistic picture of what the Danube traditionally meant for the Viennese may be seen from a sermon of the seventeenth-century preacher Abraham a Sancta Clara, in which the implied parallels between the river and the wrath of God are by no means accidental: 'Look on the Danube's flood, how great it is! It has no teeth, yet bites away whole areas of fallow… It has no axes or shovels, yet it can undermine palaces and houses… Who can diminish its size? Who can hold back its flow? Great and cruel, cruel and great is the Danube!'

Small wonder that Stone Age man, who arrived in the area in around 5000 BC, kept to the heights above the river, where the first communities engaged in primitive agriculture and worked the local hornstone (an early mine has been discovered in the Mauer district of south-west Vienna). The Late Neolithic Danubian culture appears to have been the product of an intermingling of civilisations, distinguished by differing forms of earthenware decoration: even at this early stage, it seems, Vienna was located at the interface of cultures, although little is known about them.

Much more is known about the La Tène and Hallstatt cultures of the Iron Age Celts (800-15 BC), a branch of whom founded a state known as *Noricum*, whose territory extended over much of modern Austria. Its power was founded on iron and gold panning, as is mentioned by the Greek geographer Strabo. In 113 BC a Roman army was ignominiously defeated at Noreia by the fierce Kimbern tribe; around 15 BC, however, Noricum

seems to have allied itself with Rome voluntarily, and thereafter the whole region from the Alps to the Danube fell under Roman control.

THE CITY IS FOUNDED

Early in the first century AD *Carnuntum*, 40 kilometres (25 miles) east of Vienna along the Danube, became the capital of the Roman province of *Pannonia Superior*. It was probably chosen because the important amber trade route from the Baltic crossed the river here. The settlement of *Vindobona* – probably named after the Vinid tribe of Celts, although several other explanations have been offered – was only a subsidiary outpost of the larger town. It was centred on what is now the **Hoher Markt** in old Vienna, with a squadron of cavalry based nearby in the modern 3rd district. Carnuntum and Vindobona were part of a Roman defensive line, known as the *Limes*, built along the Danube to keep out the Germanic barbarians.

During the reign of Emperor Trajan (AD 98-117) the increasing aggression of the tribes beyond the river necessitated the construction of a substantial fortified camp at Vindobona, with walls 3 metres (10 feet) thick and 10 metres (33 feet) high, on a terrace of ice age rubble above the south bank of the Danube. It must have looked formidable to attackers approaching from the north; it was also well equipped with the necessities of Roman life, including baths, a hospital, and steam-heating in the officers' houses excavated on the Hoher Markt. Nearby (on today's Michaelerplatz) there was a *canabae* or rest and recreation area, with taverns and brothels.

Three other Roman Emperors were significant for Vindobona. The first was Marcus Aurelius, who spent time here in AD 171 during his Pannonian campaign against the Germanic tribes. He did not die in Vindobona, as erroneously reported by a fourth-century Roman historian, but probably did write part of his celebrated *Meditations* there. Fifteen hundred years later the imperial symbolism of the Habsburgs would appropriate the figure of Marcus Aurelius, as a leader combining learning with military prowess. Second was Septimius Severus, a general who was proclaimed Emperor by his legionaries at Carnuntum in AD 193, and whose son granted Vindobona the rank of *Municipium* in 212. The third was Probus (276-82), the first Emperor to allow the growing of vines outside Italy, considered the origin of Vienna's wine trade.

From the end of the third century AD the failure of the Romans to subdue the Germanic tribes, and the constant aggression of Vandals and Goths in particular, made the situation of Vindobona increasingly precarious. At the end of the next century (probably in 395), a fire destroyed the military camp and led to the withdrawal of its Roman Legion. Roman influence lingered on, though, until the Eastern Emperor Theodosius II formally ceded Pannonia to the Huns in 433.

Dark Ages

When the Roman legionaries withdrew southwards, they left behind them a small residue of veterans and Romanised inhabitants. They were now at the mercy of repeated waves of invaders, often themselves in flight from powerful adversaries. We learn of the Vindobonians' fate only indirectly, through the biography of a Romanised monk called Severinus (Saint Severin). Clearly a remarkable personality, in the late fifth century he negotiated on the townspeople's behalf with the all-powerful German chieftains, and founded the first monasteries on the Danube at Favianae (Mautern) and Passau. A group of his followers took the saint's body with them to Italy after his death in 482, a retreat that symbolically marks the final eclipse of Roman influence in Pannonia.

Of the exotic peoples that swept over Vienna in these centuries many left little trace, among them the Langobards or Lombards, who moved on to occupy the north Italian plain that bears their name. They were themselves pursued by the Avars, nomadic warriors from Central Asia, who overran the Wiener Becken in the sixth century. Avar burial grounds have been uncovered around the city at Simmering, Liesing, Mödling and elsewhere. An increasing number of Slavs also pushed into the area, leaving traces in names such as Lainz or Rodaun.

And yet, despite these disruptions, there was evidently some continuity in organised administration. From at least as early as the eighth century a governor dispensed justice from the **Berghof**, which was at the western end of today's Hoher Markt (now recalled by a plaque on the wall). The earliest recorded church in Vienna, the **Ruprechtskirche**, was built just to the east, probably in the ninth century. Its dedication to Saint Rupert indicates its association with the shippers of salt from the Salzkammergut; the missionary Saint Rupert, who died around 710, was the first Bishop of Salzburg, and the patron Saint of salt miners. The eastward spread of Christianity thanks to Rupert and other missionaries also brought with it Bavarian settlers, the ancestors of the German-Austrians who would form the core population of the region. Their numbers swelled, especially as territories that were 'claimed' by the church were granted as feudal possessions to Bavarian nobles.

By the ninth century Vindobona had disappeared from sight, and the city's modern name – which first appeared as *Wenia* in the Salzburg annals of 881 – had become current. It is supposedly derived from the Illyro-Celtic word *Vedunja*, meaning a woodland stream (the *Wienfluß* or River Wien). Wenia was situated at the eastern edge of the Carolingian Empire, in a buffer zone periodically overrun by the Magyars, who appeared from the east in 896. For several decades it was under their control, following the defeat of a Bavarian army at Pressburg (Bratislava) in 907, but the decisive victory of the German King Otto the Great on the Lechfeld, near Augsburg, in 955 marked a turning point. The Magyars would eventually be pushed back to the River Leitha, now in the Austrian province of Burgenland, which became the permanent frontier.

At some time unknown this hotly disputed border territory between 'West' and 'East' – a role to which it reverted during the Cold War over 1,000 years later – came to be known as Austria. The name first occurs in an imperial document of 996 bestowing lands on the Bishop of Freising, described as being 'in a region popularly known as *Ostarrichi'* ('Eastern Realm', the origin of *Österreich*). Even before then, in 976, Emperor Otto II had awarded the 'Ottonian Mark' established by his father, between Enns and Traisen, to the Bavarian Margraves (Counts) of Babenberg. This ambitious dynasty, whose members combined shrewd diplomacy with ostentatious piety, would dominate the expanding territories of 'Austria' for 270 years.

The Babenbergs

When Leopold I of Babenberg (976-94) first took charge of his new possessions the seat of his power was in Melk on the Danube. He managed to extend his lands to the east, probably as far as the Wienerwald, but Wenia itself remained in Magyar hands for some time yet. As in many other areas they controlled, the Magyars contented themselves with occupation of the Berghof and a military presence (a camp was apparently set up on what is now the Schwarzenbergplatz), without establishing any permanent settlement.

The Magyars were finally forced back to the Leitha by Adalbert 'the Victorious' (1018-55). The Babenbergs still had to impose their authority over argumentative local lords, powers in the area since the Carolingian era. Like their successors the Habsburgs, the Babenbergs reinforced their territorial claims by astute marriages into rival dynasties. Their expansionist ambitions were generally projected eastwards, and the Babenberg seat was moved progressively along the Danube from Melk to Klosterneuburg, and then Vienna.

Saint Leopold III of Babenberg (1096-1135) would become the patron saint of Austria (his canonisation went through in 1485). He was a man of genuine piety, a peacemaker who refused an offer of the German crown, devoting himself instead to founding or refounding abbeys and churches (Heiligenkreuz and Klosterneuburg among them). In 1137 his successor Leopold IV (1136-41) agreed with the bishopric of Passau to build a new church in Vienna, just outside the town boundary. Ten years later this Romanesque

The extraordinarily long-lived Friedrich III.

predecessor of the **Stephansdom** cathedral was completed. It was dedicated to Saint Stephen the Martyr in the presence of German Emperor Konrad III, whose knights were gathering in the town for the Second Crusade.

The most significant Babenberg for the history of Vienna was Heinrich II Jasomirgott (1141-77), so-called because of his favourite oath ('So help me God!'). He was prevailed upon to renounce the Dukedom of Bavaria, acquired by his predecessor in 1139, but was handsomely rewarded by the upgrading of Austria itself in 1156 to be a fully fledged dukedom, entirely independent of its western neighbour. Equally important was Heinrich's decision to move his court to Vienna in the same year, to the area still known as Am Hof ('At the Court'). In 1155 Irish monks were summoned from Heinrich's former seat at Regensburg to found the **Schottenstift** ('Monastery of the Scots', so-called because in medieval Latin Ireland was *Scotia Maior*). With Heinrich Vienna thus became a ducal *Residenzstadt*, worthy of his high-born wife, the Byzantine princess Theodora.

The town's economic expansion continued under Heinrich's successor, Leopold V (1177-94), who benefited from two windfalls: he inherited much of Styria and Upper Austria in 1192 when their ruler died childless, and received a handsome share of the huge ransom paid to Emperor Heinrich VI for the release of Richard the Lionheart. The Crusading King of England had insulted Leopold and the Emperor's representative during the siege of Acre in Palestine, and in 1192 was making his way back to England overland after being shipwrecked on the Adriatic coast. He

was recognised in Vienna, and imprisoned in the castle at Dürnstein until March 1193. His ransom was said to have been ten tons of silver, to raise which all the church treasure of England was melted down; Leopold's share was enough to found Wiener Neustadt and extend the fortifications of Vienna and the border town of Hainburg. He was excommunicated for imprisoning a Crusader, but it was only on his deathbed that he promised to pay back some of the money – a promise that his successor easily forgot.

Late twelfth-century Vienna was booming economically and culturally. Under Leopold VI 'the Glorious' (1198-1230), troubadours, known as *Minnesänger*, were prominent at the Babenberg court, singing the praises of noble ladies and celebrating the magnificence and virtue of the Duke. Leopold VI also encouraged trade, making himself popular with the burghers by allowing guilds to be formed and, most importantly, awarding Vienna its 'staple right', in 1221. This obliged foreign merchants trading on the Danube to sell their goods to local traders within two months of their being landed, effectively guaranteeing the lion's share of the downstream trade to the Viennese. This was the nearest thing in the Middle Ages to a licence to print money.

The reign of the last Babenberg, Friedrich II 'the Warlike' (1230-46) saw a decline in the fortunes of the city and the dukedom. After a fierce dispute with the German Emperor, Friedrich was killed in 1246 fighting the Hungarians, leaving no male heirs. The resulting power vacuum was filled by the ambitious Prince Ottokar II of Bohemia, who reinforced his claim by marrying Friedrich II's widow at Hainburg in 1252.

The coming of the Habsburgs

Ottokar cultivated the Viennese burghers – as well as executing a few who tried to oppose him – and most of the town swung behind him. He gave generous support to the rebuilding of the Stephansdom and other buildings after a fire in 1258, and founded a hospital for lepers and the famous **Wiener Bürgerspital** almshouse. He also initiated the building of the **Hofburg**, Vienna's future imperial palace, originally as a fairly simple fortress.

The increased sensibility towards the poor and sick that was revealed in the endowment of hospitals coincided with a great wave of religious fervour – a recurrent phenomenon in Viennese history. The Minorite monastery, which had been initiated under Leopold VI, was rapidly completed, and the energetic priest Pfarrer Gerhard refounded the **Himmelpfortkloster**. The uncertainties of the age were also reflected in outbreaks of religious fanaticism: processions of flagellants appeared in the streets of Vienna, complementing the more orthodox campaigns against impiety by the Dominicans, whose first church in Vienna was consecrated in 1237.

Ottokar's ambiguous position was made precarious by a failed attempt to become King of Germany (there was no set, hereditary succession to the imperial crown, but instead the King-Emperors were elected from among the lesser princes, an essential reason why the title was so insecure). He was further undermined when Rudolf of Habsburg was chosen as King in his place in 1273. Rudolf, whose original, small domain was in modern Switzerland, was initially seen as a compromise candidate deemed harmless by the other electors, but he soon proved himself far-sighted and shrewd. He set out to challenge Ottokar's power, and by 1276 had occupied Vienna. They made a temporary peace, but in 1278 Ottokar was killed in the historic battle of Dürnkrut, on the Marchfeld north-east of Vienna. His embalmed body was displayed in the Minorite monastery, a reminder to the people that those who aspire to climb highest also fall the furthest.

The arrival of Rudolf on the scene began 640 years of virtually unbroken, if sporadically resisted, Habsburg rule in Austria; Vienna was to be the Residenzstadt of every Habsburg ruler except Maximilian I (1493-1519), whose main seat was Innsbruck, and Rudolf II (1576-1612), who preferred Prague. From 1283 Rudolf left the government of Austria in the hands of his son Albrecht, who made himself unpopular by challenging some burgher privileges, and had to put down a rebellion in the city in 1287-8. In 1298 Albrecht I became the first Habsburg to add to the title of German King that of Holy Roman Emperor, which like Vienna would in later centuries also become virtually consubstantial with the dynasty. To accommodate Vienna's new ruling house the Hofburg, going far beyond its modest beginnings under Ottokar, would expand continuously through the centuries, and indeed extensions to it were still being planned when war broke out in 1914.

Problems beset the Habsburgs in the first half of the fourteenth century. In 1310 there was a rising in Vienna against Friedrich 'the Handsome', which had two significant consequences: one of the properties confiscated from the conspirators was handed over to become the first City Hall (**Altes Rathaus**), and the city's rights and privileges were codified for the first time in the so-called *Eisenbuch* (1320). Under Albrecht 'the Lame' (1298-1358), plagues of locusts ravaged the Vienna Basin, in 1338 and 1340; hardly had they disappeared than Vienna was hit by the great plague of the Black Death, at the height of which, in 1349, 500 people were dying each day. The plague was then followed by a terrible fire.

Vienna's Christian population blamed the Jews for the plague (they were said to have poisoned the wells), and Albrecht had to struggle to prevent major violence. A Jewish community had been established in Vienna since Babenberg times, and had reached a considerable size. It was mainly concentrated close to Am Hof, on and around today's Judenplatz. Its location was not accidental, for Jews traditionally enjoyed the ruler's protection; even this, though, was not always enough to spare them from persecution at times of crisis.

DYNASTY BUILDING

Duke Albrecht achieved a shrewd dynastic alliance in 1353, when his son, the future Rudolf IV, married the daughter of Karl IV of Bohemia, Holy Roman Emperor since 1346. Advantageous marriage was thereafter the principal pillar of Habsburg expansionism, as described in a sixteenth-century adaptation of a line from Ovid: 'Others make war; you, fortunate Austria, marry!' The magnificence of the Prague ruled by his illustrious father-in-law was a spur to Rudolf's ambitions: masons who had worked on the great cathedral of Saint Vitus in Prague were summoned to work on the Stephansdom, and Rudolf founded a university in Vienna in 1365, clearly inspired by Karl's earlier foundation of the Prague Carolinum.

In the same year Rudolf died in Milan, aged only 26. He had reigned for a mere seven years, but his ingenious policies ranged from social and monetary reform to the promotion of urban renewal through tax holidays and rent reform. Not for nothing was he known as 'the Founder' (as well as, equally appropriately, 'the Cunning'.

As a moderniser, Rudolf inevitably clashed with vested interests, such as the guilds and the Church. At the same time, though, his attempts to advance the claims of the dynasty over the title of Holy Roman Emperor were ridiculous. His aides produced a forgery known as the *Privilegium Maius*, which invented a picturesque lineage and even more picturesque titles for the earlier Habsburgs. It was magisterially rubbished by the poet Petrarch, who had been asked to verify its authenticity by the Emperor. Even more disastrous was his institution of a system of power sharing among the male Habsburg heirs (the *Rudolfinische Hausordnung*). This resulted in the Habsburg equivalent of a Wars of the Roses between the 'Albertine' and 'Leopoldine' lines (named after Rudolf's two quarrelling brothers and joint heirs), which lasted intermittently for four generations.

In 1411 Albrecht V, of the Albertine line, came of age and entered a Vienna under threat from bands of marauding Moravian knights and the Protestant Hussites of Bohemia, who laid waste parts of Lower Austria for several years running. Disappointing harvests and the loss of the wine trade to German merchants contributed to a rancid atmosphere, in which the Jews were, once again, obvious scapegoats.

Franz Geffel's typically romanticised version of the relief of the 1683 siege of Vienna.

This time the ruler himself was the instigator of a horrifying pogrom, the *Wiener Geserah*. He was enthusiastically backed by the Church, which claimed the Jews were aiding the Hussites. In 1420-1 Albrecht stripped Vienna's poorer Jews of their belongings and despatched them on a raft down the Danube, while richer members of the community were tortured until they revealed where their wealth was hidden, and then burned alive on the Erdberg. Many others opted for mass suicide to escape torture. The centuries-old ghetto by Am Hof was demolished. The exact reasons for Albrecht's ethnic cleansing have never been fully explained, for it represented a break in a long tradition of Jewish protection by rulers, and also removed an important source of ducal finance.

In foreign policy, however, Albrecht V showed the usual Habsburg adroitness. He married the daughter of Emperor Sigismund, and so on the latter's death inherited the crown of Hungary. In the same year, 1438, he was also elected Holy Roman Emperor. Excluding a brief lapse of three years in the eighteenth century, the Habsburgs would retain this title (expensively protected by bribing the other electors) right up until its abolition under pressure from Napoleon in 1806.

Only a year later, though, Albrecht died while fighting the Turks in Hungary. His heir, born after his father's death, was known as Ladislas *Posthumus* (1440-57). His guardian was Friedrich, of the Leopoldine line, and so the dynasty immediately sank back into its chronic inheritance

disputes. Friedrich was crowned Holy Roman Emperor himself in 1452, but his position at home was weak, especially in Vienna. Furious at what they saw as the favouring of other towns by Friedrich, the Viennese merchants forced the release of Ladislas, and declared their loyalty to him. Poor Ladislas, however, died aged only 17 in 1457, whereupon fighting continued between Friedrich and his own brother Albrecht, the latter supported by the Viennese. This culminated in a seven-week siege of the Hofburg in 1462, when Friedrich was holed up in the castle together with his three-year-old son, the future Maximilian I. He was only rescued by the intervention of the Hussite Bohemian King, Jiri z Podebrad, and even then had to agree to share power with Albrecht. Only when Albrecht died in 1463 did Friedrich regain control of Vienna.

Friedrich III's ultimate triumph – he effectively ruled for 53 years, dying in 1493 – is often attributed to the fact that he outlived all his rivals, including the much younger Hungarian King Matthias Corvinus, who occupied Vienna from 1485 to 1490. Moreover, the Emperor's survival, the extinction of the Albertine line and the removal of the Hungarian threat meant that the way was open to a real concentration and expansion of Habsburg power. Friedrich's son, Maximilian, was to take up his inheritance in a context of expanding wealth and power and, at a time when the seeds of humanist learning planted in Vienna in earlier decades were beginning to bear fruit, amid the pan-European cultural blossoming of the Renaissance.

The enlightened Joseph II.

Empire & Counter-Reformation

Maximilian was accorded the nickname of 'the Last Knight', an indication that he lived between two worlds, that of medieval chivalry and that of the Renaissance. Possessed of astonishing energy, he was an enthusiastic participant in tournaments, and performed amazing feats of endurance as a hunter, soldier and athlete. Inspired by the spirit of the Renaissance, he also encouraged the new learning at Innsbruck and Vienna, where it was represented by humanist scholars such as Konrad Celtis and Johannes Cuspinianus. The study of pure sciences, medicine and cartography all began to flourish, although a disproportionate amount of attention was dedicated to studies of the history of Austria and the genealogy of the Habsburgs (which managed to trace the 'House of Austria' back to Noah). In 1498 Maximilian made one of his most memorable contributions to Viennese history, when he founded the *Hofmusikkapelle*, the forerunner of the Vienna Boys Choir.

Maximilian brought Habsburg marriage diplomacy to its apogee. Through his first marriage to Maria of Burgundy one of the richest territories in Europe, including modern Holland, Belgium and Luxembourg, came under Habsburg control. His son, Philip the Fair, married the daughter of Ferdinand and Isabella of Spain, Joanna 'the Mad',

thus acquiring Castile, Aragon, southern Italy and all the Spanish possessions in the New World for the dynasty. In 1515 Maximilian stood proxy for the marriage of his two young grandchildren to the male and female heirs of the joint throne of Bohemia and Hungary, then ruled by the Jagellonian dynasty. These realms too would fall to the Habsburgs after the last Jagellonian King, Lajos II, was drowned fleeing the Turks following the disastrous Battle of Mohács, in 1526.

Philip the Fair died before Maximilian, who was thus succeeded by his grandson Karl V, better known in English as Emperor Charles V. On his accession to the imperial throne in 1519 he ruled over an empire 'on which the sun never set' – much too large for one man to direct, and already beset by a stream of problems. The Ottoman advance in South-east Europe seemed unstoppable, and equally ominous for the dynastic upholders of the true, Catholic, church was the gathering momentum of the Reformation after 1517.

Vienna saw nothing of Karl, who ceded his Austrian possessions to his brother Ferdinand in 1521. The latter was immediately faced with the rapid success of Lutheranism, especially in the towns, coupled in the case of Vienna with demands for more self-government. Ferdinand solved this last difficulty by the simple expedient of executing Mayor Siebenbürger and six councillors in Wiener Neustadt in 1522, and subjecting the Viennese to absolutist control. He was less successful against the Lutherans and the more radical Anabaptists, despite the punishments meted out to leading Protestants (men were burned at the stake and their wives drowned in the Danube). The increasingly Protestant nobility began to make religious freedom a condition of military assistance against the advancing Turks. Having overrun Hungary, the Ottomans were by 1529 at the gates of Vienna, a vulnerable city with old-fashioned defences, and the morale of its religiously divided population lowered by Ferdinand's vicious rule and a major fire in 1525. Only the heroism of the city's defender, Count Salm, and the early onset of winter prevented it from falling.

The Turks left behind much devastation, but important lessons were learned from the siege. Most important was the need to modernise the city's fortifications, which were comprehensively rebuilt in 1531-66 using the well-proven Italian model of star-shaped bastions. Vienna became a heavily fortified imperial seat, entirely subordinate to the court, but it was also cosmopolitan, as functionaries and petitioners came from all over Europe on imperial business.

HEARTS & MINDS

From 1551, when Ferdinand summoned the Jesuits to the city, it also became a testing ground for the Counter-Reformation. Proselytisation was led by scholars and preachers such as Peter Canisius, who compiled the catechisms of the Catholic faith to be used in the struggle for hearts and minds in a Vienna that was still 80 per cent Protestant. This struggle was characterised by dogma and paranoia; the Jewish community, which had gradually re-established itself since 1421, was again a convenient target, suffering prohibitions on property owning and trade, as well as the obligation to wear an identifying yellow ring on clothes. This oppressive atmosphere was relaxed a little under Maximilian II (1564-78), who stuck to the letter of the Peace of Augsburg of 1555, which recognised both the Catholic and Lutheran faiths in the Empire, provided that subjects followed the faith of their princes. Many Lutherans flooded out of Vienna each Sunday to hold services in the chapels of nearby Protestant lords, but as the screw of the Counter-Reformation tightened under Rudolf II (1576-1608) and his brother Matthias, many more migrated to other, more sympathetic parts of Europe.

The dominant figure of the Counter-Reformation in Vienna was Cardinal Khlesl, a Vienna-born convert from Lutheranism, who purged the university of Protestantism, and whose great *Klosteroffensive* (monastery offensive) led to the second great wave of Catholic foundations in the city, from 1603 to 1638. By the time of his death in 1630 the Church could already boast that *Österreich ist klösterreich*: literally, 'Austria is rich in monasteries', but also meaning 'the realm of Austria is a realm of monasteries', a punning expression of the predominance of religious orders in Austrian life.

Protestantism was by no means dead among the nobility, however, and as late as 1619 a group of them forced their way into the Hofburg and delivered a list of demands to Ferdinand II (1619-37). The following year saw the defeat of the Bohemian Protestants at the Battle of the White Mountain, the first major engagement of the Thirty Years War (1618-48). This war and the triumph of Catholicism in southern Germany and Austria would mean the end for Lutheranism in Vienna, even though a Swedish Protestant army threatened the city as late as 1645. In the course of the war, the Jesuits gained control of the university, in 1622, and in 1629 Ferdinand issued his 'Edict of Restitution', restoring to the Catholic Church 1,555 properties under Protestant control since 1552. In Vienna Protestant laymen were also effectively expropriated by an ingenious Catch-22 – only Catholics could become burghers of the city, and only burghers could own property. This was Habsburg religiosity at its most ruthless, with cynical greed and oppression cloaked by a fig leaf of piety.

Neither Queen nor Empress, but canny ruler: Maria Theresia, with husband Franz Stephan.

Baroque Vienna

The positive side of the Counter-Reformation in Vienna is embodied in the great flourishing of the visual arts, architecture, music, drama and literature in the seventeenth and eighteenth centuries. Leopold I (1640-1705), known as 'the first Baroque Emperor', spent millions on huge operas and ballets – the former involving fireworks and artificial lakes, the latter real horses. Leopold and several of his Habsburg relatives were themselves gifted composers, and the Hofoper (Court Opera) and Burgtheater both thrived under imperial patronage. Moreover, the Habsburgs did not differentiate between gifted artists from within the Empire and those from outside it. Leopold's great spectacles were supplied with elaborate machinery and scenery designed by an Italian architect, Lodovico Burnacini, and Italians long held sway in all the fine arts, music and architecture, so that it was only a generation later that local architects such as Fischer von Erlach and Hildebrandt came to the fore – and even they were Italian-trained. The music preferred at court, similarly, was for two centuries Italian-influenced, dominated by a series of Italian composers and librettists from Cesti (1623-69), Caldara (1670-1736) and Metastasio (1698-1782) to Mozart's great rival Antonio Salieri (1750-1825).

Leopold was not an attractive figure: the Turkish traveller Evliya Celebi describes his 'bottle-shaped head', with a nose 'the size of an aubergine from the Morea', displaying 'nostrils into which three fingers could be stuck'. His character was hardly more appealing, even if his deviousness was sometimes dictated by the need to fight wars on two fronts, against the French and the Turks. Educated by bigots, he married an even more bigoted Spanish wife, Margarita Teresa, who blamed her miscarriages on Jews. Egged on by Christian Viennese burghers, in 1669 Leopold ordered a renewed expulsion of the Jews, from their settlement on the Unteren Werd. The area was renamed the Leopoldstadt (now Vienna's 2nd District), and Jewish property was given to Christians. Ironically, this district again became a Jewish quarter in the nineteenth century.

This brilliant move so weakened the imperial and city finances, however, that the richer Jews had to be invited back again, in 1675. Troubles multiplied with a major outbreak of plague in 1679, whereupon the Emperor and nobility scurried off to Prague, leaving the Church authorities to organise relief for the stricken people. A brilliant preacher, Abraham a Sancta Clara, explained in his corruscating tract *Merck's Wien!* ('Take Heed, Vienna!') that the plague was the vengeance of God for the loose living of the Viennese. Abraham's diatribes, combining rhetorical force and earthy vividness, make such good

reading that his admirers tend to overlook the vengeful, paranoid *weltanschauung* from which they spring. His skill was to manipulate his audience by dramatising and exploiting their deepest anxieties, leavening threats of damnation with picturesque stories, like that of *Liebe Augustin*, the drunken bagpiper who escaped unharmed after falling into a lime-pit of plague corpses, and who has come to symbolise Viennese survival skills.

THE SAVING OF CHRISTENDOM

After the plague came the Turks, who besieged Vienna for the second and last time in 1683. The city was rescued only at the last minute, after 62 days, by an army led by Jan Sobieski, King of Poland, aided by the young Prince Eugene of Savoy. 'Christendom' was saved. The Emperor, who had prudently retreated to Passau for the duration, returned to his Residenz to give public, if grudging, acknowledgement to his saviours, and the court artists busily got to work on bombastic depictions of 'Leopold, the Victor over the Turks'.

Leopold's reign lasted 47 years, during which the Empire survived a considerable battering. After a brief interlude under the promising Joseph I (1705-11), who died of smallpox aged 33, and Leopold's younger son Karl became Emperor. By this time, the Habsburgs' enemies were in retreat. After a string of victories by Prince Eugene, the Peace of Karlowitz of 1699 had restored Hungary, Transylvania and Slavonia to Habsburg rule, and in the War of the Spanish Succession the alliance of Austria, Britain and Holland effectively fought Louis XIV's France to a standstill. Even then, however, Leopold's characteristically duplicitous and cynical treatment of the 'liberated' Magyars managed to provoke a Hungarian war of independence (1704-11) led by Prince Ferenc Rákóczi, whose troops devastated the outskirts of Vienna in 1704.

Afterwards, Prince Eugene advised the erection of a new defensive line, the so-called *Linienwall*, along the route today followed by Vienna's beltway, the so-called Gürtel. Vienna began to assume the profile it has today, with outlying villages (*Vororte*) beyond the Gürtel, suburbs (*Vorstadt*) between the Gürtel and the bastions (replaced by the Ringstraßen in the nineteenth century), and finally the medieval core of the *Altstadt*.

After the Hungarian threat had receded, the reign of Karl VI (1711-40) saw a building boom in Vienna: existing churches were Baroque-ised (all thirty Gothic altars of the Stephansdom were replaced), and new Baroque churches were built, notably Hildebrandt's **Peterskirche** and Fischer von Erlachs' **Karlskirche**. The nobility, with new, undisturbed sources of revenue, were determined to compete with the ruling house, and built themselves magnificent winter and summer palaces – at least 15 between 1685 and 1720, the greatest Hildebrandt's **Belvedere**, for Prince

Eugene. It was a time of triumphalism, bombast and conspicuous consumption by both ruling classes and the Church, not especially balanced by job creation for the rest, although Prince Eugene took care to re-employ his war veterans as labourers and gardeners.

The whey-faced Karl VI showed no interest in the plight of the poor. Much of the time that he did not devote to hunting was frittered away on efforts to ensure that one of his daughters could inherit the Habsburg throne, going against all the precedents that allowed only a male heir to succeed (Karl's proclivities were possibly more homo- than heterosexual, and no further children appeared after his two surviving daughters). To bolster the position of his eldest daughter, Maria Theresia, he touted a document known as the 'Pragmatic Sanction' round the courts of Europe, where it was politely signed by princes who had not the slightest intention of honouring it.

As soon as Karl died, to general rejoicing in Vienna, the Empire was attacked by Friedrich II of Prussia, who invaded Silesia and launched 'the War of the Austrian Succession'. Encouraged by Friedrich's initial success, and not wishing to lose out in the expected dismemberment of the carcass of the Habsburg Empire, Karl Albert of Bavaria then invaded Bohemia, with French support. The situation was only saved by good luck, when Karl Albert died in 1745 and Maria Theresia's husband, Franz Stephan of Lothringen, was elected Holy Roman Emperor in his place. Another major factor, though, was the remarkable steadfastness of Maria Theresia herself, which so impressed the Hungarian nobles when she appeared before them to seek support in 1741 that they offered their 'life and blood' for their 'King' – since constitutionally she could officially be neither 'Queen' of Hungary nor 'Empress', even though she has often been described as such.

THE AGE OF ABSOLUTISM

Maria Theresia, one of the greatest of the Habsburgs, had one of the most important qualities in a ruler: an ability to choose wise advisers and able administrators. With her support men like Wenzel von Kaunitz, Friedrich von Haugwitz (a converted Protestant from Saxony), Joseph von Sonnenfels (a converted Jew from Moravia) and Gerard van Swieten (a Dutchman) reformed and reorganised key elements in the ramshackle machinery of imperial government, including the army. This new approach was labelled 'enlightened absolutism' – although some parts were more enlightened than others: Maria Theresia would not tolerate Jews, unless they converted, and was persuaded by Sonnenfels that torturing suspects did not necessarily contribute to law and order only with great difficulty. Motivated perhaps by her Jesuit education she also introduced a risible

City of genius: the grave of Beethoven.

'Chastity Commission' in 1752, which caused Casanova a lot of grief on his visit to Vienna.

Despite such aberrations Maria Theresia was generally held in affection by the Viennese. She abandoned the constant protocol of her forebears and lived relatively informally, if incongruously, in the great Schönbrunn Palace built for her, in emulation of Versailles, by Nikolaus Pacassi. Her encouragement of local manufacturing, the creation of a postal service and even the introduction of house numbering (originally to aid recruiting) were all signs of new thinking. After the death of Franz Stephan in 1765 she ruled jointly with her son, Joseph II (1765-90), who was to take enlightened reforms much further when he ruled alone after Maria Theresia died in 1780.

Joseph had travelled widely, and fallen under the influence of the French Enlightenment and even Masonic ideas. His most lasting achievement was his Tolerance Patent of 1781, granting religious freedom to Protestant and Orthodox Christians, which was followed in 1782 by a more limited Patent for the Jews. In the same year Joseph also dissolved 17 per cent of Austria's monasteries (in Vienna, 11 monasteries and seven convents), on the grounds that they were not engaged in activities useful for the state. Also important for Vienna was his foundation of the **Allgemeinen Krankenhaus** or General Hospital, in 1784, and his opening of the imperial picture gallery and parks such as the **Augarten** and **Prater** to public view.

The age of absolutism had seen the last flourishing of the Baroque style and the transition to a Classicism preoccupied with purity of form, although in architecture this did not really emerge until the following century. The change of direction in music was already evident 40 years earlier, in Gluck's groundbreaking 1762 opera *Orfeo*, considered the first opera to subordinate its music to the requirements of the drama, in place of the florid Baroque operas of the Italians. Gluck was followed by the great names of the *Wiener Klassik* – Haydn (1732-1809) and Mozart (1756-91), who was based in Vienna for the last ten years of his life, which thus almost exactly coincided with the lone reign of Joseph II. Just as Mozart and Haydn learned from each other, so Ludwig van Beethoven, who lived in Vienna from 1792 to his death in 1827, was influenced by both of them, and in turn had a huge impact on Franz Schubert (1797-1828). This unbroken line of genius, nurtured by the patronage of Austrian aristocrats, the dynasty and the Church, and encouraged by the musical enthusiasm of the Viennese, has not been emulated by any other European city.

Napoleon & *Biedermeier*

The nineteenth century began badly for the Habsburg Empire. Joseph's promising successor, Leopold II, died unexpectedly in 1792 after reigning only two years, and was succeeded by his narrow-minded son Franz II (1792-1835). His reactionary views were fuelled by events in France, where his aunt, Marie Antoinette, was

Vienna's most hated: Prince Metternich.

executed by the revolutionaries the year after he ascended the throne. The rise of Napoleon then subjected him to further humiliations, including the occupation of Vienna twice by French troops (in 1805 and 1809), the enforced marriage of his daughter to the upstart French Emperor and finally the bankruptcy of the state.

The French behaved quite graciously as conquerors (a guard of honour was placed outside Haydn's house as he lay dying, and officers crowded in to hear the première of Beethoven's *Fidelio*), but these setbacks inevitably meant that the Habsburgs had lost their aura. Conscious of the absurdity of being titular Emperor of territories that had been overrun by Napoleon, Franz gave himself the new title of 'Emperor of Austria' in 1804, and then, in 1806, a herald on the balcony of Vienna's Kirche Am Hof announced that the title of Holy Roman Emperor, founded by Charlemagne in 800, no longer existed. Napoleon was eventually defeated, however, in 1814, and the Habsburg capital then became the venue for the Congress of Vienna, in which the allied powers – Austria, Prussia, Russia, Britain and many others – sought to agree the frontiers of post-Napoleonic Europe. The shrewd diplomacy of Franz's Chancellor, Prince Metternich – as well as the advantage of being hosts – ensured that, in spite of all the earlier reverses, Austria emerged from the wars with dignity intact and a generous territorial settlement.

On the other hand, though, it now required the repressive apparatus of Metternich's police state to keep the lid on the aspirations unleashed in the wake of the French Revolution. Strict censorship meant that even Franz Grillparzer (1791-1872), Austria's greatest dramatist and a Habsburg loyalist to the core, could get into trouble; disrespect for the authorities could only be voiced indirectly, as in the brilliant ad libbing of the comic genius Johann Nestroy (1801-62). Denied any political voice, Viennese burghers were driven into internal exile. They retreated into a world of domesticity, 'in a quiet corner', the characteristic features of the *Biedermeier* culture, so-called after a satirical figure of a solid, middle-class citizen that was portrayed in a Munich magazine, which predominated from 1814 to 1848.

Painters like Friedrich von Amerling evoked the idealised family life of the bourgeoisie, Ferdinand Raimund conjured an escapist fairytale world on the stage, and Adalbert Stifter cultivated a quietist philosophy of resignation in his celebrated novel *Indian Summer*. In architecture, Josef Kornhäusel designed neo-Classical buildings with a stripped-down, unobtrusive elegance. In music, the revolutionary fervour of Beethoven's *Fidelio* and Ninth Symphony gave way to the melodious romanticism of Schubert's introspective *Lieder*, first performed at intimate soirées with his friends and patrons known as *Schubertiaden*.

Vienna as it looked during the ill-fated World Exhibition of 1873.

While such a life was possible for the property owning and professional class, the burgeoning working-class population of Vienna was at the mercy of the industrial revolution. Overcrowding, unemployment and disease were the lot of most of them, aggravated by a decrepitly inadequate infrastructure and water supply. A cholera epidemic in 1831-2 prompted some remedial measures, but not before typhoid fever from infected water had claimed the life of Schubert, in 1828. Meanwhile, the population of Vienna exploded by 40 per cent between the beginning of the century and 1835, to reach 330,000. Many of the new migrants were former peasants, driven off the land and searching for work.

The desperation of the famine-stricken working class and the frustrations of the politically impotent middle class finally exploded together in the Revolution of March 1848, although its ultimate failure would in good part be due to the inability of these two very different elements to make common cause. At first it seemed as if the old order was doomed: almost the whole Empire was in revolt, the hated Metternich had to flee Vienna and the simple-minded Ferdinand I, who had succeeded Franz in 1835, was forced to concede a new constitution and lift censorship. In Vienna a provisional city council was set up, at last freeing the burghers from noble control, and a Civil Guard recruited from local citizens was formed, with the grudging consent of the authorities.

As elsewhere in Europe in this great year of revolutions, it was the army that put an end to the uprisings. The great Marshal Radetzky won major victories in northern Italy, the Croatian General Jellacic moved against Hungary (helped by the intervention of Russian troops) and Marshal Windischgraetz subdued Vienna. Habsburg authority seemed to have been restored, but not all the achievements of the Revolution could be rescinded: serfdom was abolished throughout the Empire forever, and the mere existence of liberal constitutions, however briefly they had been in force, supplied a new theoretical basis for discussion. Even reactionaries had to contemplate the possible merits of governing by consent rather than force.

Franz Josef

Ferdinand had abdicated, and was succeeded by his 18-year-old nephew Franz Josef I (1848-1916). He began his reign with summary executions and savage repression of former revolutionaries. Yet, by the end of his 68-year rule, he had presided over a gradual emancipation of his peoples, so that by 1900 the seemingly anachronistic Habsburg monarchy was in practice no more oppressive than most Western European states. In 1867 he approved the *Ausgleich* or 'Compromise' with Hungary, granting it equal rights in a new 'Dual Monarchy', to be called Austria-Hungary. Universal adult male suffrage was introduced in 1907, earlier than in Britain. What could not be appeased, however, still less controlled, were the forces of nationalism, which eventually tore his multi-ethnic empire apart and plunged Europe into war.

For Vienna, Franz Josef's most significant measure was the demolition of the old city bastions

Enlightened but anachronistic: Franz Josef.

in 1857, and the approval of a plan for the area beyond them to be occupied by a magnificent boulevard, the **Ringstraße**, on the Parisian model of Baron Haussmann. A symbol of a civil society in rapid expansion, the Ring was to be lined with great public buildings, each built in a Historicist style symbolic of its place in society (*see chapter* **Architecture**). This great project, which took shape over some 26 years, was to be completed with an 'Imperial Forum' linking the last part of the Hofburg to be built (the **Neue Burg**) with the museum quarter. This part of the plan was never carried out, but the Ring, with its new museums, city hall, opera, theatres and stock exchange, still transformed Vienna into a modern metropolis.

Much of the finance for all this came from the high bourgeoisie, whose tastes in the arts were conservative: the greatest patronage was given to Hans Makart, who painted overblown historical canvases, while statues of Habsburg rulers and generals peppered the city. The burghers' preference for the now-entrenched musical tradition of the late Wiener Klassik was satisfied by Johannes Brahms, who lived in Vienna from 1878 until his death in 1897. In contrast, his contemporary Anton Bruckner, who was strongly influenced by Wagner, was subjected to abuse and even ridicule by the critical establishment in Vienna.

The decades from 1860 to 1900 make up the so-called *Gründerzeit* or 'Founders' Period' (also called the Ringstraßen era), a period that saw the first construction of a modern state, economy and society. The administration of Vienna was dominated from 1861 by the rich liberal bourgeoisie, with money made in industrial development, land speculation and finance. The Liberal City Council, elected by a property-based electoral roll of only 3.3 per cent of Vienna's 550,000 inhabitants, naturally followed its own interests, but for a good while these coincided in many respects with those of their fellow citizens.

Enormous investment in the infrastructure resulted in an improved water supply, new bridges across the Danube and the much-needed channelling of the river itself, and in 1870 Vienna acquired its first trams.

Unbridled capitalism had, of course, its downside: in the catastrophic year of 1873 the stock market crashed, and many financiers were ruined or committed suicide. The death toll among businesses was equally dramatic, as 60 companies, 48 banks and eight insurance societies went bust. The crisis ensured that Vienna's World Exhibition of that year was a financial disaster, worsened by a simultaneous outbreak of cholera. For Vienna's Liberals, it was 'never glad confident morning again'; their standing fell, despite the many achievements of the polyglot Mayor from 1868 to 78, Cajetan Felder (he spoke nine languages, including Czech and Hungarian). The catastrophe of 1881, when the Ringtheater burned down killing 386 people, was almost the final straw. Felder's successor was held responsible, and had to resign.

FIN DE SIECLE & END OF EMPIRE

Turn-of-the-century Vienna, as the Habsburg Empire struggled on into what would eventually be seen as its last decades, has become almost a cliché of sensuality, eroticism and an overripe aestheticism. It generated some of the most conflictive movements of the modern era, including both militant anti-semitism and Zionism. It also produced psychoanalysis, and several of the greatest masters of early Modernism in all the arts.

A new star rose in city politics in the 1880s, a renegade Liberal called Karl Lueger, who founded his own Christian Social party and built up a power base by exposing corruption (of which there was plenty) and stirring up anti-semitism, in a first modern systematisation of the vicious scapegoating of Jews that has run like a dark thread through Viennese history. Many of the wealthy Liberal magnates were Jewish, and Lueger adroitly focused popular resentment upon them.

His support was boosted by the extension of the franchise to those who paid only five *Gulden* in taxes, in 1885, and the incorporation of the peripheral settlements (Vororte) into the city in 1892. Vienna more than tripled its area and increased its population by over half a million, to 1,364,000. Immigrants poured into the city (especially Czechs, and Jews from the East), another factor in creating a climate beneficial to Lueger's politics. 'Handsome Karl' was a shrewd populist and gifted administrator, who understood exactly how to turn the envy and discontent of Vienna's petit bourgeois to his advantage. The young Adolf Hitler, living in Viennese dosshouses in the 1900s, enormously admired him. Franz Josef, though, did not. Lueger's faction won a majority on the City Council in 1895, but his election as Mayor was vetoed three times by the Emperor, who among other things feared a flight of Jewish capital if he was elected. The Emperor, though, had to give way in 1897, and Lueger remained in office until 1910.

Lueger was strongly supported by the lesser Catholic clergy, although the hierarchy denounced his radical and anti-semitic views in 1895. Pope Leo XIII, however, upheld Lueger's claim that he was merely adhering to the social doctrines of the Church, and that his objections to Jews were doctrinal, not racial. Papal support was decisive, and the Viennese hierarchy gradually began to appreciate having a Mayor with such a refined understanding of the Jewish 'question'. Lueger's policies may be influencing the world indirectly even today: just as the Christian Social majority was being established in the city, the Budapest-born Viennese journalist Theodor Herzl published the first Zionist agenda, *Der Judenstaat* (1896), arguing that the persistence of anti-semitism in Central Europe showed that Jews, however assimilated, could not be safe without their own state. This was received with incomprehension and even anger by the highly assimilated Viennese Jewish establishment, but it began the process that led to the foundation of Israel.

In contrast to social tensions, the emollient side of the pleasure-loving Viennese of the nineteenth century was revealed in the general passion for theatre and music, which made possible the astonishing careers of musicians such as Josef Lanner and the Strauß dynasty. The Viennese waltz was a commercialised and refined version of folk dances, chiefly the *Ländler* of Upper Austria. Its success made its practitioners the first megabuck earners in music history – Johann Strauß Senior at one time had no less than six orchestras operating in different venues, while so many women wrote to his still more popular son asking for locks of his hair that he resorted to sending them clippings from his poodle. The waltz became emblematic of hedonistic escapism. Its critics pointed out that the Viennese were too busy waltzing to heed the news of the catastrophic defeat of the Habsburg army by the Prussians at Königgrätz (Sadowa) in 1866, a defeat that marked the beginning of the end for the Habsburg Empire. Other commentators complained of its lasciviousness, the dangers it posed to health (enthusiasts were inclined to dance until they dropped), or stigmatised it as a macabre Dance of Death.

Even more censorious things were said about the craze for operetta, which began with an Offenbach-influenced work by Franz von Suppé (*Das Pensionat*, 1860) and continued into the twentieth century (its last major figure, Robert Stolz, died in 1975). For all the abuse heaped on it by intellectuals such as Karl Kraus and Hermann Broch, the operetta was the first, and perhaps the only, successful multicultural product of the Austro-Hungarian Monarchy. Franz Josef's sprawling domains may have been rather unjustly dubbed a *völkerkerker* ('prison of the nations') by the regime's critics, but everyone from Lemberg (Lvov) to Laibach (Ljubljana) could happily whistle the tunes of Strauß, Lehár and Kálmán.

Mayor Karl Lueger, popular with the ladies – but less so with the groups he oppressed.

Gustav Klimt's now over-familiar The Kiss *was considered radical in fin-de-siècle Vienna.*

In the 1890s, Vienna and its peculiar atmosphere generated new trends and the Secession movement displayed a galaxy of talent. One of the most important figures was the architect Otto Wagner, who departed from the ponderous Historicism of his youth to create early-Modernist buildings of great functional integrity; one of his greatest critics, Adolf Loos, rejected Secessionist ornament and carried the idea of functionalism still further. The artist Gustav Klimt broke existing taboos to produce masterpieces of sensual eroticism, combined with a pessimistic emphasis on the inevitability of death, a preoccupation he shared with the next generation of Expressionists such as Egon Schiele. Gustav Mahler took over the Imperial Opera and swept away generations of shibboleths he described as *Schlamperei* (sloppiness), to the great indignation of the players. The most successful playwright was Arthur Schnitzler, whose bleak depictions of sexual exploitation,

societal cynicism and personal trauma won the admiration of Sigmund Freud.

Freud's own *Interpretation of Dreams* appeared in 1900, and caused not a ripple. His novel treatment for 'hysteria' and new-fangled technique of hypnosis were viewed with indifference or suspicion by colleagues in the medical establishment. Moreover, the unwise procedure of 'analysing' people in their absence, employed by the Freud circle, attracted the withering sarcasm of the writer Karl Kraus, who wrote that 'psychoanalysis is the disease of which it purports to be the cure'. Kraus edited the journal *Die Fackel* (The Torch), which was to become an effective counterblast to the belligerent mood that overtook the city after the Empire slithered into war in 1914, while many other Modernist writers, such as Hermann Bahr, the self-publicising leader of the *Jung Wien* literary circle, became ranting war propagandists.

War & 'Red Vienna'

World War I killed off the coffeehouse milieu of turn-of-the-century Vienna, in which Bahr and Kraus had flourished. The brilliant *feuilletons* (meandering cultural essays) perused over the coffee cups, the interminable feuds, the narcissism, the head waiters who acted as unpaid secretaries, the unpaid bills, in short the whole bohemian existence seemed somehow anachronistic after Austria and her allies lost the war and the Empire was dismembered in 1918-19. The assassination of the heir apparent, Archduke Franz Ferdinand, lit the fuse that led to war, and old Emperor Franz Joseph had finally died in 1916. His inexperienced great-nephew Karl I (1916-22) took over the throne, but his inability to end the war on honourable terms sealed his fate, and he went into exile in March 1919.

Vienna's situation was desperate. Deprived of its empire, it had become a *wasserkopf*, a diseased 'hydrocephalus' or head without a body, in a state reduced from over 50 million to three million people overnight. One third of the population was in Vienna, with a huge bureaucracy, many of whose jobs no longer existed, and an added burden of unemployed refugees and ex-soldiers. A 'Republic of German Austria' (*Deutschösterreich*) was proclaimed on 12 November 1918. The name reflected the desire of most Austrians – of all political parties – for an *Anschluß* or union with Germany, since without the Habsburg Empire they could not see any point in Austria continuing as a separate state. This proposal, though, was firmly knocked down by the Allies, who had not fought a war for Germany actually to increase in size, and so the First Austrian Republic began its peculiarly unwanted existence.

In 1919 the Social Democrats swept to power in the Vienna City Council. The party had been founded in 1889 by Viktor Adler, a Jewish doctor with a strong social conscience, and rapidly expanded its support among workers living in horrific conditions in turn-of-the-century Vienna. By 1900 the Socialists were able to win 43 per cent of the votes in local elections, although the absurdly discriminatory electoral system meant they had only two seats on the City Council. After the war, though, the party's moment had come. Adler died in the flu epidemic of 1918, but he and gifted Marxist theoreticians such as Otto Bauer had laid the foundation for the period known as *Rotes Wien*, 'Red Vienna', which followed. It was the first example in the world of a city administered by Socialists.

Potentially a major difficulty was that Vienna was still officially part of Lower Austria, which was conservative dominated. This mismatch was resolved in 1922, when Vienna became a *Bundesland* (Federal Province) in its own right. The Social Democrats were able to embark on one of the most intensive programmes of housing, welfare and cultural initiatives ever seen in Europe. The 63,736 apartments built between 1923 and 1934 naturally had to be paid for, together with the new leisure facilities, schools, colleges and child benefits. The Council's director of finance Hugo Breitner found the money by imposing steeply progressive taxes on unearned income (such as rents), luxuries (such as champagne), property and businesses. His targets called him the 'tax vampire', but few would quarrel with the practical achievements of 'Red Vienna'.

On the other hand, the City Council's Socialist measures and its uncompromising *Kulturkampf* (cultural struggle) with the Church in a traditionally Catholic milieu was also a major factor in the growing polarisation between Socialist Austria (principally Vienna) and Conservative Catholic Austria (much of the rest of the country, outside the cities). For most of the 1920s power was held at national level by a Christian Social government led by a priest, Ignaz Seipel; his greatest achievement was rescuing the country from hyper-inflation in 1922, but differences between right and left widened inexorably during his rule. Both sides had their own militias (the conservative *Heimwehr* and Socialist *Schutzbund*), and a crisis occurred in 1927, when a conservative jury acquitted Heimwehr soldiers who had shot and killed members of the Schutzbund. An enraged mob burned down the Palace of Justice, ignoring pleas for restraint from Socialist leaders. After that things went from bad to worse as the worldwide economic crisis deepened post-1929, and unemployment rose.

Tensions climaxed in a brief civil war in 1934, in which the relatively well-armed forces of the right easily overcame Vienna's Socialist militias. A memorable turning point was the shelling into submission of Karl Ehn's huge housing block the Karl-Marx-Hof, a massive bastion of red support. Afterwards, authoritarian rule was imposed on Austria, and Vienna's administrative independence ended, by the regime of Engelbert Dollfuß, a peculiar combination of extreme reactionary Catholicism and home-grown Fascism.

The Anschluß & World War II

In 1933, though, Hitler had come to power in Germany, and very soon began a drive to increase his influence in the land of his birth, Austria. Shortly after the civil war the Nazis attempted a coup d'état in Vienna, killing Chancellor Dollfuß. He may have been an extreme right-winger, but he had not been ready to follow Hitler's orders. Dollfuß's successor, Kurt Schuschnigg, soon found himself under constant pressure from Hitler and local Nazis to accept the *Anschluß* of Austria to the German Reich (the 'Greater German' solution that

Austrians welcome Hitler to his birthland with an ecstatic rally at Heldenplatz.

most Austrians had wanted at the end of World War I). After abortive and humiliating 'talks' in February 1938, Schuschnigg tried to rally support by calling a referendum on Austrian independence for 13 March; in order to pre-empt this (which would almost certainly have endorsed independence) German troops crossed the border at dawn on 12 March.

In Vienna the Nazis lost no time in hounding their opponents and stigmatising Jews. Hitler was ecstatically received when he addressed a crowd of 200,000 in the Heldenplatz, and the Church hastened to make its accommodation with him – Cardinal-Archbishop Innitzer gave a Nazi salute on his way to meet the *Führer*, and urged the faithful to vote for the *Anschluß* in the subsequent Nazi plebiscite (although, when he later had second thoughts, Nazi thugs trashed his residence). One of the first events of Nazi rule was the *Reichskristallnacht* on 9 November 1938, when mobs attacked Jews, synagogues and Jewish property. Adolf Eichmann – who, like many of the most virulently anti-semitic Nazis, was Austrian-born – opened an office on Prinz Eugen Straße, where Jews were efficiently 'processed': those with sufficient resources could buy their freedom by turning over their assets to the Nazis, while the rest were sent to the concentration camps. Some 120,000 Jews emigrated, while 60,000 were to lose their lives through forced labour or execution. Leading non-Jewish political opponents of the Nazis were also interned in camps. On 1 April

1938 the first transport of prominent Austrian politicians (including Leopold Figl and Franz Olah) left for the camp at Dachau.

The final total of concentration camps in Austria was more than 30. The best known is Mauthausen, on the Danube east of Linz, where 35,318 out of 197,000 prisoners received were executed between 1938 and 1945. The main activity of the forced labour camp was hacking out the stones for the cobbles of Vienna. It is now a memorial.

As the catastrophe of World War II unfolded, a kernel of resistance appeared in Vienna, partly spurred by the Allies' Moscow declaration that Austria's status at the end of the war would depend on her willingness to rebel. This was the origin of the notion of Austria as 'Hitler's first victim', rather than an equal participant in Nazism, which became a stylised political discourse during the post-war four-power occupation of Vienna, the period sharply captured in *The Third Man*.

Because Vienna lay somewhat to the east, quite a lot of war industry was moved to the area during the war — but this proved to be fateful when the Allies began to be able to reach the city with bombers (from 7 March 1944) from Italy. During one air raid over 400 people died in the cellars of the Philiphof, an apartment behind the Opera, and they were never exhumed from the rubble to be buried – an *Against War and Fascism* monument was erected on the site in 1988.

In spring 1945, the Soviet army arrived in Vienna, and the city was taken after fierce fighting.

The war's end saw a devastated city: there had been 8,769 deaths from Allied bombing, and 2,226 from fighting on the ground; 1,184 resistance fighters had been executed, 9,687 died in Gestapo prisons; 36,851 apartments had been destroyed and thousands of other buildings damaged. Over 50,000 Viennese Jews had been slaughtered by the Nazi regime, and a quarter of a million Austrians had died in German uniform.

Some of these statistics could support the notion of Austria as a 'victim' of the Nazis, but on the other hand this idea – politically convenient for all the occupying powers, as they sought to detach Austria from Germany – also meant that in Austria the 'de-nazification' process only penalised and stigmatised the most prominent Nazi criminals, allowing the huge number of passive, opportunistic or enthusiastic participants in the Hitler regime to present themselves as just patriots who happened to lose a war. This confusion between image and reality in dealing with the Nazi era (which was not allowed to exist in Germany) has returned to haunt Austrian post-war politics.

Post-war Austria

In the short term the 'victim' thesis was beneficial, assisting Austrian leaders in their negotiations to end the occupation. This became a real possibility after the death of Stalin, and in 1955 the *Staatsvertrag* (Austrian State Treaty) was signed in the Belvedere. Austria became free and independent, and also neutral, in a manner that was convenient to both the West and the Soviets. Neutrality, vital to Austria's security during the Cold War, is another issue that has become divisive since 1989.

Supported by UN aid and the Marshall Plan, Austrians displayed enormous resourcefulness in rebuilding their devastated country; all the more so considering that the Russians had dismantled most of Austria's industry and shipped it eastwards as war reparations. The rebuilding of Vienna's burned-out Stephansdom was complete by 1952, and by 1955 both the Burgtheater and the Staatsoper reopened. With cultural renewal self-irony also returned and cabaret flourished, notably Helmut Qualtinger's brilliant satirical portrait of the typical Viennese petit-bourgeois opportunist 'Herr Karl', who only joined the Nazis because they offered free sandwiches and a beer. On the other hand, the leading lights of the literature, stage and music of pre-war Vienna – most of whom had been Jews – were conspicuous by their absence.

Vienna voted consistently for Social Democrat mayors, and in 1970 the national government itself became Socialist under the charismatic if somewhat imprudent Bruno Kreisky, Chancellor until 1983. It was his achievement that Vienna became a third seat of the United Nations, when the UN Development Organisation moved to a custom-built **UNO-City** on the north bank of the Danube. The city had already hosted the Atomic Energy Commission since 1956, and was to add OPEC (1965) and the monitoring commission for the Helsinki Agreements (OSCE) to its portfolio. This much sought-after world profile, though, also made hitherto sleepy Vienna a terrorist target: the OPEC conference was stormed by Arab terrorists in 1975, Palestinian terrorists murdered a City Councillor and launched a grenade attack on the Vienna synagogue in 1981, and in 1985 there was a bloody attack on the El Al desk at Schwechat Airport.

Vienna has enjoyed stable government and constant investment in its infrastructure (notably the steadily expanding U-Bahn), even if there have always been mutterings about corruption. The worst case of the latter occurred with the building of a state-of-the-art hospital name, which cost the taxpayer over AS21 billion (£992 million). The new-broom Mayor Helmut Zilk, elected in 1984, made both the political and cultural life of the city more lively, and controversial: the *enfant terrible* of German theatre, Claus Peymann, took over the Burgtheater in 1986, scandalising local audiences with provocative productions of plays by Thomas Bernhard, tackling taboo themes such as Austrian complicity in Nazi rule.

Zilk himself committed the city to a gesture of reconciliation with the Jews, and a new Jewish Museum opened in 1993. Major exhibitions, such as those celebrating *fin de siècle* Viennese culture, have attracted growing numbers of tourists, while among Austrians Habsburg nostalgia and Kaiser-Kitsch have been marketed with ever-greater ruthlessness. The fall of the Iron Curtain, followed by Austria's entry into the EU in 1995, have brought new challenges, and new conflicts. Fears of a flood of cheap labour and 'foreign takeovers' have been ably and notoriously exploited by Jörg Haider's Freedom Party. Vienna thus enters the next millennium with its usual ambivalence, 'moving forwards with its head turned towards the past'.

Socialist Chancellor Bruno Kreisky in 1983.

Vienna Today

A city with a new face.

Just ten years ago, Vienna looked as drab and depressing as any Ostbloc metropolis… several galaxies away from the city's glittering and decadent image at the turn of the last century. This isn't so today. Vienna has been given a massive facelift. Façades in the city centre have been restored and repainted. Modern housing estates have sprung up on the city's outskirts and a few ambitious architectural projects have been attempted.

The consumer experience has also been transformed. Opening hours are now more flexible, ensuring the city's competitiveness with its EU siblings. Designer outlets have moved in around Stephansdom and the Graben, Kohlmarkt and Kärntner Straße – mainly to capitalise on the schillings of the rich Russian or eastern European mafia wives who shop there. Mariahilfer Straße, now virtually indistinguishable from any other western European shopping drag, used to be dubbed 'Magyarhilfer Straße' due to the huge number of Ossis queuing to buy their first colour television in its then dreary selection of shops.

And while many of Vienna's 'city of culture' offerings in its theatres, museums and concert halls are pretty conservative, the avant-garde still makes its presence felt – particularly in the field of new music (*see chapter* **Music: Rock, Roots & Jazz**). Until a few years ago, Palais Liechtenstein and Zwanziger Haus (*see chapter* **Museums**) were Vienna's only concession to modern art, but the 1990s saw such stop-gap solutions as the Kunsthalle before the completion of the Museumsquartier (*see page 38* **Past, present & future**). Helmut Zilk, Vienna's mayor in the 1990s, steered money towards brightening up Vienna. New restaurants and bars appeared throughout the late 1990s and Rathausplatz was transformed into an ice rink by snow and winter and an open-air operatic cinema by sun and summer. The city's summer cultural menu has improved in general – no more school holidays for the bureaucrat artistes at the **Staatsoper** and the state theatres.

Getting out and about in Vienna shouldn't be too hard on your wallet. Prices have plummeted since Austria joined the EU in 1995. Although certain parts of the 1st district can still damage your financial health.

New waves of immigration have helped lower Vienna's cost of living. West Africans and South Americans have joined the Turkish and Yugoslavian communities in the city, adding much-needed cultural colour. Unfortunately, however, many Viennese tend to regard their city's foreign population as a cross to bear, rather than as economic and cultural enrichment. Taxi drivers (when they are not west African) regularly grumble about the Turks and *Tschuschen* (an insulting name for folk from the Balkans), although it's generally recognised they are often the ones doing the jobs many Viennese feel too grand to execute.

Also, it's thanks to Vienna's immigrants that the city doesn't wither away altogether. Vienna has an old population and one of the lowest birth rates in Europe. By the year 2030 the city could have more pensioners than workers.

All the same, relations between the Viennese and their *Ausländer* are often uncomfortable, with a clear distinction made between 'good foreigners' (first worlders) and 'bad foreigners' (everyone else). But provincialism is on the slide and the young Viennese should bring back new attitudes from their many travels abroad. Hopefully.

It's this distrust and dislike of foreigners (with the spectre of hordes of them feeding off Austria's generous welfare state) that the populist Jörg Haider and his anti-immigration Freedom Party exploit for votes.

For many Viennese, though, this political chit-chat is a bit of a bore. *Gemütlichkeit* (comfy cosiness) is their life creed. In Vienna people stand, rather than run up escalators and sit in the city's coffeehouses for hours pondering life, the universe and the latest public scandal.

The Vienna you'll probably see as a tourist is only part of the city's character. The grand buildings and elegant shops exist predominantly within the Gürtel. Outside, blocks of social housing and gloomy shop fronts tell a different story.

Wherever you are in Vienna, though, you are bound to come across sex shops and solariums… they're everywhere. Another common phenomenon is the flash motor. Every inch of Vienna is stuffed with expensive-looking cars. Porsches and Alfa Romeos are two a penny in this town.

The Viennese do have a reputation for dourness and a warm smile can be hard to come by. Service in the city is notoriously rude and although it's slowly improving, the customer still tends to be viewed as klutz rather than king. Yet the Viennese can turn on the charm, *Küss die Hand*, waltz to Strauß, fry a Schnitzel and bake a Strudel so damn well… you may never want to leave.

Sieg Haider!

The October 1999 elections resulted in a stalemate and provoked a serious political crisis. The Social Democrats (SPÖ) remained the largest party with 33.4% of the vote but no overall majority, while the right-wing Freedom Party (FPÖ) and the conservative People's Party (ÖVP) tied for second place with 27.2% and 26.9% of the vote respectively and an equal numbers of MPs.

After the failure of negotiations to re-establish the Grand Coalition of SPÖ and ÖVP that had ruled Austria since 1986, a coalition between ÖVP and FPÖ was hatched instead. This prospect caused uproar, and not only in Austria, since the FPÖ leader Jörg Haider has made statements (later retracted) praising aspects of Nazi rule.

Haider has also consistently courted favour with an easily persuaded sector of the electorate by attacking 'foreigners' (code for immigrant workers) as parasitic on the Austrian state. Fourteen European leaders immediately threatened sanctions against Austria and the country faced the sort of diplomatic isolation it endured between 1986 and 1992, when Kurt Waldheim was President.

The point at issue is similar, namely the dualist approach to Austria's Nazi past, of whose horrors many Austrians were victims, but many others were perpetrators. Waldheim was disingenuous about his wartime record and Jörg Haider had to resign as Governor of Carinthia in 1991 after remarking that 'the Third Reich had a decent employment policy'. He was re-elected Provincial Governor of Carinthia in 1999.

Jörg Haider, both of whose parents were keen Nazis, is a startlingly successful politician, but his rise owes much to the sclerosis in the Austrian political system, whereby ÖVP and SPÖ have carved up the country between them, awarding jobs in the many state and semi-state bodies on a party basis (the so-called *Parteibuch Politik*). By 1999 a coalition of the two 'old' parties had been in power for 13 years and greed and corruption had steadily increased. Opinion polls suggest that disgust with this corruption was the main cause for the Freedom Party's rise in voter esteem from 5.5% of the vote in 1986 to 27.2% in 1999. However a significant proportion of FPÖ voters, estimated at 47%, were attracted by Haider's anti-immigrant rhetoric.

Haider resembles, in presentation and technique, the popular Viennese Mayor and demagogue of the turn of the last century, Karl Lueger. Just as Lueger cynically used anti-semitism as a tactic, so Haider fastens on to any issue which can play to voters' fears and hatreds.

One of the most telling aspects of Haider's success is that it occurred when Austria has been upgraded to the rank of third richest in the EU and around fifth richest (in terms of income per capita) in the world. Comparisons with the Weimar Republic and the rise of Hitler don't stand up on that count. The FPÖ cocktail of thrusting youthful professionalism and reactionary nationalism is not a phenomenon peculiar to Austria: in Bavaria it is described as the politics of 'lederhosen and laptops'. Haider borrows from the American right, imitating Newt Gingrich's posturing social contract and the millionaire-friendly flat tax of Steve Forbes. Good Catholic families are to be seduced with hand-outs, while the less well off, who are hardly to benefit from Haider's tax policies, are encouraged to seek a resolution of their problems in xenophobia. In other words, Haiderism is a modern form of regressive politics, many (but not all) of whose elements stem from the USA and the 14 European countries which proposed to ostracise Austria.

The Viennese

A people of perplexing polarities.

Vienna being a city of many masks and narcissistic self-projections, it is hard to separate its 'image' from the 'reality' – or the performers from their public. Indeed, when the brilliant actor Alexander Girardi was creating Viennese stage characters in the late nineteenth century, the locals obligingly played up to the roles that the Graz-born adoptive Viennese had created for them. This provoked Arthur Schnitzler's dry warning to the uninitiated: 'We Viennese are always play-acting: the wise man understands that.'

In the city where Freud did his fieldwork, the complex interplay between *Sein* (reality) and *Schein* (appearance) has always bewildered outsiders (until and unless, like so many temporary visitors in the past, they become permanent residents and thus part of the self-renewing Viennese identity).

By the same token, there are those who regard the 'discoveries' of the founder of psychoanalysis as more imaginatively insightful than scientific: a mass of recent research has focused on the dubious and even manipulative ways in which the great man obtained his results. Are we dealing with Sigmund Freud or Sigmund Fraud? Or just a typically Viennese mixture of implausible truth and plausible fiction?

AMBIVALENT CHARM

Every self-respecting and role-conscious Wiener is in some respect a frustrated artist, a condition that makes them simultaneously happy and melancholic. Theirs is an ambivalent charm, disguising a highly critical nature that shows itself in humour, self-irony and a talent for malice and intrigue. The poet Franz Grillparzer poignantly catches this ambivalence in his bitter-sweet *Departure from Wien* (he was always pathetically homesick almost as soon as he crossed the city boundary): 'Beautiful you are, but also dangerous/To the apprentice as to the master; /Your summer breath blows enervatingly/You Capua of souls!'

'The Viennese,' he continues, 'live in half-poetry, dangerous to the whole' and embroider 'the picture of truth with fairy tales and wit.' The arts are the key motor of this process.

As Jörg Mauthe puts it 'Music and theatre… are not abstractions… reserved for a social elite in Vienna, but the indispensable attributes of every man's existence…'

Perhaps it is an inevitable consequence of artistic obsessions that the awfulness or even banality of events in the city's past tend to be transmuted into collective myth. For example, the Viennese like to think of themselves as great survivors, and, of course, there is an appealing myth to describe their capacity to cheat the fates. Its protagonist is one Marx Augustin, a drunken bagpiper who fell into a pit of corpses during the plague of 1679, while staggering home from a pub that still exists on the Fleischmarkt. The grim little song about him is almost certainly of a later date, and was probably composed to mock the would-be King of Poland, Augustus of Saxony. No matter: '*O du lieber Augustin*' ('Dear Augustin') is a ditty that is enduringly emblematic of the Viennese *Lebens – und-Überlebenskünstler* (master of the art of living and of survival), whose life combines hedonism with fatalism in roughly equal proportions. Native ironists have given an extra twist to this by calling a local equivalent of *The Big Issue* (the magazine for the homeless) the *Augustin*.

Augustin appears in the fire and brimstone preaching of Abraham a Sancta Clara, the father of the Viennese tradition of Church-sanctioned hatred of the Jews (later of Protestants, later still Liberalism and Socialism). He was no more Viennese than Girardi, but like so many other immigrants before and since, he was instrumental in creating a Viennese flavour that now seems *sui generis*. His diatribes recall Ecclesiastes in their gloomy but beautifully expressed view of human nature and destiny; but it is their aestheticisation of death that so well evokes the *genius loci*. Ever since he discovered the potential for mingling sensuality with apocalyptic menace, the city and its inhabitants have been viewed as practically unrivalled in the sensual Baroque presentation of death and dying.

In his coruscating *Merck's Wien!* (*Take Heed*, Vienna, 1680) Abraham a Sancta Clara brilliantly puns on the street names of the city to create a frisson-inducing image of the omnipresence of the Great Reaper during the plague years: 'In the street of the Lords [Herrengasse], Death is lord of all', 'In the Singerstraße Death has sung Requiems for many', 'On the Graben Death was busy with nothing but burials'.

Even today, Roland Neuwirth, the most colourful protagonist of the music played in the Vienna pubs (*Schrammelmusik*), is no less inventive with his '*Echtes Wienerlied*' ('Genuinely Viennese Song'): it contains 15 suitably convoluted metaphors for death, an experience that is described inter alia as 'putting on wooden pyjamas' and 'viewing the potatoes from underneath'.

Nor should we forget the necrolatry of the Habsburgs, whose hearts are in Augustinerkirche, their entrails in the catacombs of Stephansdom and their bodies in the superb Baroque funerary monuments of the Capuchin crypt.

'He who would know how a Viennese lives must know how he is buried,' wrote Hermann Bahr, 'for his being is deeply bound up with no-longer-being, about which he is constantly singing in countless, half-sad, half-happy songs.'

SENSUAL PLEASURES

The enormous energy the Viennese invest in aesthetic and sensual pleasures is the counterpoint to their absorption with death. Their neuroses, always threatening to burst forth in aggression mixed with subservience, are at the root of their unpredictable behaviour. At any moment they are liable to trigger the oscillations between golden-heartedness and malice that are so disconcerting to the casual visitor. The weight of history lies as heavily upon them as has traditionally the hand of petty and self-serving authority, or that of enlightened but patronising absolutism.

Different dispensations have inspired different strategies for escaping an unacceptable political and social reality: inner emigration in the Metternich era, hedonism in the *Gründerzeit* – recurrently also, as a muffled *leitmotif*, the antinomian response of suicide. The only common thread in all this is defensiveness, for even Viennese aggression is a defence mechanism, as is the inventive *Schmäh* (blarney) and the interminable *Raunzen* (grumbling). Likewise defensive is the opportunistic career of satirist Helmut Qualtinger's memorable creation, der Herr Karl,

whose current allegiance was always such an accurate barometer of existing power relations.

The Viennese reputation for hedonistic escapism has pursued them down the years; it is a weakness they would probably concede, albeit with one eye laughing and one eye weeping, as the local expression has it. If, as so often appeared to be the case, the contemporary situation seemed 'hopeless but not serious', frivolity and sensuality were an effective balm for a people that believed it deserved better of fate, as of its masters.

A line from Johann Strauß's *Die Fledermaus*, 'Happy is he who forgets about that which anyway can't be altered', has been taken to epitomise the shoulder-shrugging attitude of an age deluged in champagne and bad debts; but it is also an expression of stoicism that goes back to Emperor Friedrich III (1440-93), the quintessential Habsburg survivor, who wrote down the same thought in his commonplace book.

SOPHISTICATED AMNESIA

In Vienna it has always been difficult to draw the exact boundaries between ironically heroic endurance on the one hand, and unprincipled opportunism on the other. Many a Viennese cannot make up their own mind about the difference, with the result that (for example, when dealing with the inhabitants' sophisticated amnesia about their behaviour in the Nazi period) someone else often has to make it up for them.

And yet the ability of the city's inhabitants not to be fooled by their own propaganda is one of the things that makes them so delightful (or as Richard Strauss put it, 'People are two-faced all over the world; but in Vienna they are so pleasantly two-faced').

Moreover there is no criticism of their behaviour that the Viennese have not themselves triumphantly trumped. 'They… are an extremely unhappy people,' claimed Hermann Bahr, 'hating Vienna but unable to live without it.' In other words they cannot decide whether theirs is a city of *Träume* (Dreams), as the songwriters would have us believe, or of trauma, as Freud and Schnitzler discovered. Or of both.

It was Johann Nestroy who best understood this, as he also understood the conflicting emotions of his Viennese public; how they wavered between sentimentality and despair, between kindliness and aggression, between blind hedonism and confessional piety. And in all these polarities, he perceived a certain underlying human dignity, a pragmatic capacity for survival and a reconciliation with the choices forced upon the individual by circumstances. It was doubtless this capacity that he was ironically describing to his audience when he delivered himself of a characteristically Viennese aphorism, namely: 'Of all nations, the noblest nation is resignation.'

Literary Vienna

Don't leave home without a good aphorism...

As a conscientious literary traveller to Vienna you will almost inevitably want to spend large amounts of time in Viennese cafés, and probably lesser amounts of time reading Austrian literature itself. For, as you will come to realise, this small but significant body of work wouldn't be what it is without its cafés, and vice versa. This kind of throwaway line is just what you need when asked what you think of Arthur Schnitzler's *Dream Story* (now given an all-new fame as Kubrick's *Eyes Wide Shut*), as it lies largely unread on the table next to your cake crumbs. So feel free. Lounge in one of Vienna's gloriously gloomy cafés in the knowledge that you are following a great literary tradition, exemplified by the poet Peter Altenberg, a dummy of whom has long since replaced him in the **Café Central**. Soak in the melancholy, ponder the Central European preoccupation with death and decline, stare meaningfully into space, but be sure to have a few aphorisms, a pithy phrase or an insightful literary anecdote at the ready. You never know, you could be sitting next to Thomas Bernhard, Franz Grillparzer or Robert Musil, and so you had better know who these figures are.

AUSTRIA'S SHAKESPEARE?

The roots of modern Austrian literature (as distinct from German literature) can be traced back to Grillparzer. He was, if you are feeling generous, the Shakespeare of Austria, although his bust, it must be said, has never been honoured with the most prominent position on the façade of the **Burgtheater**. Byron spoke highly if ambiguously of this dramatist and poet, affirming that 'I know him not; but ages will'. He was born in 1791 on Bauernmarkt in old Vienna, when the city was the cultural capital of the German-speaking world; by the time he died in 1872 the Empire was already in decline. His celebrated 'Shakespearean' feel for tragedy was inspired not just by those turbulent times, but by his own tragic family life. His youngest brother and mother both killed themselves, and he had a long-standing and difficult affair with his cousin's wife, before moving on to fall in love with a 15-year-old girl. On a happier note, Grillparzer was a great frequenter of the long-gone Silbernes Kaffeehaus in Plankengasse, a popular meeting point for writers and artists alike.

Towards the turn of the twentieth century literature fed even more hungrily on the atmosphere of

intoxication and melancholy that was intrinsic to the final apocalyptic spurt of the Habsburg Empire. Georg Trakl (1887-1914) has the dubious honour of being one of the unhappiest poets of this time. He was the Arthur Rimbaud of Austria – a hyper-sensitive alcoholic outsider, with frequent moods of 'frantic intoxication and criminal melancholy'. His training as a pharmacist offered him optimum access to drugs, and the advantage he took of this was clearly reflected in his work: 'The decayed one gliding through the rotting room; Shadows on yellow tapestries; the ivory sadness of our hands is vaulted in dark mirrors…' A tortured sexual relationship with his sister ('the thousand devils whose thorns drive the flesh frantic') didn't help. He died of a cocaine overdose in 1914. His sister shot herself a few years later.

Trakl is notoriously difficult to translate, but he was greatly admired by his contemporaries and countrymen such as the great philosopher Ludwig Wittgenstein (1889-1951), who supported him for a time and hailed him a genius. Another admirer was the Prague-born poet Rainer Maria Rilke (1875-1926), who wrote similarly florid descriptions of Vienna in a 1907 letter to his wife Clara: 'The coherence and the existence of it all is condensed to the point of becoming a fragrance… here too atmosphere has come into being, environment irradiated and darkened from within, in which people are at home and which as a stranger one shares, wards off, touches, tastes with every movement.'

Another colourful Viennese character was the precocious Hugo von Hofmannsthal (1874-1929), or Loris, as he was known, who was already feted in Viennese intellectual circles at the age of 16. Later (like Rimbaud) he gave up poetry following a premature mid-life crisis, and ended up writing libretti for Richard Strauss. Hofmannsthal died suddenly of a heart attack just before the funeral of his son, who had committed suicide. Another, later writer who had an even more miserable life was the novelist Joseph Roth (1894-1939). Rediscovered and newly celebrated in the last few years, he was born on the eastern edge of the Habsburg Empire, in modern Poland, but his work is closely associated with Vienna. Roth's father disappeared before he was born and died in a lunatic asylum, World War I curtailed his education, his wife went mad, and he himself survived on menial jobs and journalism before he died exiled, alcoholic and destitute in Paris. Apocryphal tales abound of him being carried drunk to cafés and even more drunkenly back again. Somehow, however, he also managed to write several extremely readable books, all of them produced during the 1920s and 1930s but dealing with the lost Habsburg world of his youth. Among the most important are *The String of Pearls*, set in Vienna, and *The Legend of the Holy Drinker*, which perhaps says it all.

Alongside alcoholism, the literary '-isms' of the turn of the century were impressionism, symbolism and naturalism. Hermann Bahr (1863-1934) decided he was an expressionist, and became the leading spirit of the *Jungwien* literary circle, which included the likes of Schnitzler and Hofmannsthal and convened at **Café Griensteidl** on Michaelerplatz. Nearby, the Café Central on Herrengasse was the favoured haunt of poet Peter Altenberg (1859-1919), who seems to have spent more time in cafés than out of them, although he probably did so more in pursuit of his other great love, 'ladies noble and very ignoble', than literary stimulation.

HEDONISM & HYPOCRISY

This was also the time, of course, when, as Alan Whicker crudely put it, Freud discovered sex in Vienna. At the same time, writers discovered Freud. The increasing psychologisation of writing in these years is most clearly illustrated by Arthur Schnitzler (1862-1931). Just after his birth, on the Praterstraße in a house adjacent to the Hotel de l'Europe, the baby Arthur lay for a while on his father's writing desk, which gave 'rise to many a facetious prophecy concerning my career as a writer'. Schnitzler became a friend of Freud, visiting him at the home of the world's most famous couch in the Berggasse (now the **Freud Museum**). Freud, however, had first avoided meeting him 'from a kind of reluctance to meet my double'. Schnitzler's 1926 *Dream Story* depends heavily on dream psychology, explores the subconscious, and for its time was, like Freud, a great taboo breaker. Despite its date it is set firmly in *fin de siècle* Vienna, and readers can almost smell the strange atmosphere of hedonism, bourgeois hypocrisy and sexual and psychological frustration from its pages: 'This light banter…led to more serious discussions of those hidden scarcely admitted desires which are apt to raise dark and perilous storms even in the purest, most transparent soul.' His other work known internationally is the 1900 play *Riegen*, best-known in English by its French title *La Ronde*, especially through Max Ophuls' classic 1950 film (it was also the source of the 1990s adaptation *The Blue Room*, another vehicle for Nicole Kidman). Characteristically pessimistic, it portrays a circle of sexual encounters through every class of end-century Vienna, from prostitute to soldier to housemaid to young gentleman and so on back to prostitute again, and can be taken as a gloomy portrayal of the sheer hopelessness of romantic attachments, or perhaps a metaphor for the transmission of sexually related diseases. Schnitzler, a Jew who unlike many at that time denied his Jewishness, also documented the anti-semitic climate of Vienna in the period before World War II in his novel *The Road to the Open*.

Another distinguishing feature of Austrian writing that emerged in the first years of the twentieth century was the use of aphorisms, early-model sound bites. This was the trademark of the Bohemian-born Jewish satirist Karl Kraus (1874-1936), who came out with pompous and self-important phrases such as, 'If I must choose the lesser of two evils, I will choose neither', which became a motto for a whole generation of Viennese. He was the founder, editor and writer of *Die Fackel* (The Torch), the leading satirical magazine of its day. In his paper Kraus famously and tirelessly campaigned against sexual and political hypocrisy, and against war, in his play *The Last Days of Mankind*. All this seemed very radical for its day, but Kraus also had views on women that were dubious to say the least. His defence of prostitutes seemed to revolve around a belief that women are unable to control their sexuality because they lack rationality, unlike, of course, men.

Fellow-countryman Robert Musil (1880-1942) famously said of Kraus that 'there are two things which one can't fight because they are too long, too fat and have neither head nor foot: Karl Kraus and psychoanalysis'. Professional jealousy aside, Musil

Karl Kraus kept The Torch *burning.*

Freud: a major influence on writers of his day.

was a celebrated essayist, and wrote a beautiful if unusual short story *The Temptation of Silent Veronica*, about a psychotic woman who appears to have been buggered by a dog, and, more famously, his huge, unfinished three-volume novel *The Man Without Qualities*. As with the novels of Joseph Roth, it was written after World War I but dealt entirely with the last years of the Empire before 1914, as a kind of epitaph. Like many writers, Musil left Austria after the *Anschluß*, and died penniless and anonymous abroad.

Another casualty of the curse of Vienna was Ödön von Horváth (1901-38), a friend of Joseph Roth who fled to Paris to escape the Nazis and shortly afterwards was killed by a falling branch on the Champs Elysées during a freak storm. Meanwhile, the 'almost over-gifted' Jewish writer Stefan Zweig (1881-1942) fled from the Nazis to South America, to kill himself with his wife in Brazil in 1942. At the young age of 26 Zweig had already seen his work accepted by the Burgtheater, 'the greatest dream of every Viennese writer, because it meant a sort of lifelong nobility'. Utterly cultured, a speaker and translator of several languages, he was a respected figure in literary circles throughout Europe, and for a time in the 1920s his hugely popular biographies and historical books made him the world's most widely-translated author. Reading Zweig's autobiography *The World of Yesterday*, written in a mood of immense sadness and nostalgia in exile, it is easy to see how, as the social and political climate changed, the disillusionment that led to his suicide set in. Referring to the lost Vienna of his youth, he wrote that, 'it was sweet to live here, in this atmosphere of spiritual conciliation, and subconsciously every citizen became supernatural, cosmopolitan, a citizen of the world'.

THE HORROR, THE HORROR

Post-1945, circumstances were completely different. Austrian literature only came to life again after World War II when it 'leapt over its own cultural shadow'. This was not easy. Novelist Heimito von Doderer (1896-1966), who had been a Nazi prior to 1938, wanted, according to one critic 'to be popular and profound and succeeded in neither'. As the full horror of the Nazi death camps emerged, poets such as the Romanian Jewish (but, again, German-speaking) Paul Celan (1920-70) – who lived for a

while in Vienna and has been subjected to a kind of literary *Anschluß* of his own, by being incorporated into Austrian literature – questioned whether it was possible to make the unspeakable speak. His world-famous *Death Fugue* gave the answer, as did a prose text *A Call to Mistrust*, by one of the first Austrian women writers to achieve any prominence, Ilse Aichinger. Interestingly enough it was another woman, Ingeborg Bachmann, whose poems and short prose texts also hit hardest at the nerves of the post-war period. She set fire to herself in her bed in Rome in 1973.

Another important post-war writer is HC Artmann. Intelligent, successful, but daring to be cheerful (only relatively, of course), he was a keen member of the progressive avant-garde *Wiener Gruppe* (Vienna Group), which emerged in the 1950s inspired by Dadaism, futurism, and lots of long sessions in the **Café Hawelka**. Artmann's poems are famously difficult to grasp in German, and we shall spare you the pleasure of trying to read them in English.

If anyone has heard of only one almost contemporary Austrian book (published 30 years ago), it is most likely to be *The Goalie's Anxiety at the Penalty Kick* by Peter Handke, made into a film in 1971 by Wim Wenders.

The most talked-about and successful modern Austrian writer has undoubtedly been Thomas Bernhard (1931-89). Notoriously cantankerous, his mood can be summed up by the dour décor of his favourite coffeehouse, **Café Bräunerhof** on Stallburggasse (you can ask where his favourite seat was, but don't expect a polite reply). A compulsive melancholic, naturally a fan of Trakl, and obsessed by Wittgenstein, Bernhard can be very funny, if you have a Samuel Beckett-ish sense of humour. This 'wilfully repulsive egotist who hates everyone and says so' had a love-hate relationship with his country, following in a great Austrian tradition. In his most readable book, *Wittgenstein's Nephew*, about Bernhard's time spent with the philosopher's clinically insane nephew, he wrote that, 'In the summer we had our regular table on the terrace at Sacher's, and for most of the time lived by nothing else but our accusations. No matter what appeared before us it was accused… We would sit over a cup of coffee and accuse the whole world, accuse it until there was not a shred left of it…' His predecessors were scornful of their countrymen, and yet still wanted their applause; Bernhard went one step further, and in his will banned all productions of his plays in his homeland.

So now, sit back and enjoy your coffee and cake. And if anyone tries to disturb your melancholic peace, just quote Bernhard, who went out of his way to be unpleasant and unfashionable: 'Better the purgatory of loneliness, than the hell of togetherness.'

For a selection of Austrian and Vienna-related books available in English, see **Further Reading**.

Architecture

Baroque opulence, nineteenth-century bombast and an austere array of early modern functionalism.

Two periods stand out in the history of architecture in Vienna – the Baroque age and the late nineteenth/early twentieth centuries, with less prominent styles scattered in between them. Viennese Baroque gained momentum above all in the years following the defeat of the second Turkish siege in 1683, when the city and the Habsburg dynasty breathed a collective sigh of relief and embarked upon a period of general expansion. The first architects of this building boom were the Italians, but the period also produced two Austrian architects of European stature, Johann Bernhard Fischer von Erlach and Johann Lukas von Hildebrandt.

The nineteenth century saw the creation of public buildings on the Ringstraße and the adjoining blocks of apartments that now provide one of the most popular images of Vienna. This second building boom took place following the demolition of the city walls in 1857. It determined much of the present appearance of Vienna, and cemented the city's peculiarly concentric quality, with so much activity and building work clearly focused on the tight perimeter of the Ring, which has proved so problematic in terms of later urban development.

Another Austrian architect of international importance, Otto Wagner, emerged towards the end of this period as the leading figure in the transition from Historicism to Modernism. Adolf Loos, who followed a little later, did not leave such a strong physical impression on the city as Wagner, but as a thinker, polemicist and writer he was one of the central figures in the development of modern Viennese architecture.

BEGINNINGS TO GOTHIC

The oldest existing church in Vienna is the little **Ruprechtskirche**, on the Ruprechtsplatz, which, following the destruction of the Roman military camp, formed the core of what remained of the small riverside settlement. The church, begun in the eleventh century or earlier, has both Romanesque and Gothic elements, and the oldest stained glass in Vienna.

Stephansdom, Saint Stephen's Cathedral, now the centre of the 1st district, was begun in the 1140s at a crossing point of busy north-south and east-west trade routes, which was then outside the city walls. Added to and altered many times in subsequent centuries, the cathedral as we see it today is a Gothic hall-style church that was built around an earlier Romanesque building of which the west (entrance) façade survives. It has a very fine late-Romanesque portal. The cathedral was badly damaged by bombing at the end of World War II, which explains the lack of stained glass in the interior. Inside, the most important work of art in the cathedral is the Late Gothic pulpit, from c1500, by Anton Pilgram. The sculptor depicted himself at the base of the pulpit, beneath the steps, leaning out of a window. The balustrade of the staircase up to the pulpit is decorated with intricately carved figures of toads and lizards, symbolising evil, and a dog, a symbol of goodness.

Vienna is not rich in intact Gothic churches, since most were rebuilt or redecorated in the Baroque period. The fourteenth-fifteenth-century **Maria am Gestade** at Salvatorgasse 1, however, despite having many nineteenth-century additions and fittings, has a most elegant Gothic tower capped by a pierced stone helmet.

Ruprechtskirche – *the oldest in Vienna.*

Imperial aspirations – **Karlskirche**.

Baroque building boom

The seventeenth and eighteenth centuries were years of unprecedented building activity and expansion in Vienna. For decades the Turks posed a constant threat to the city, but they were driven back in 1529, and following this victory the city was encased in a new, modernised ring of defensive walls that would stand until 1857. In 1533 the Habsburgs chose Vienna as their main residence in their eastern territories, a decision with fundamental consequences for the city's development. The future 1st district, within the ring of walls, became an unquestioned centre of ecclesiastical and temporal power. It was not, however, until the second victory over the Turks in 1683 and the burst of confidence that stemmed from it that Vienna began to see truly rapid development and a full-scale building boom. The architecture of this expansive era was strongly influenced by Italian developments, and indeed most of the architects of the initial phase of Viennese Baroque were Italians.

Herrengasse, which now runs (under different names) from behind the **Staatsoper** to the Freyung, was laid out at this time, and is lined with a series of Baroque aristocratic palaces, interrupted halfway along the avenue by the main entrance to the Hofburg, the sprawling complex that was the Habsburgs' main residence.

The southern section of Herrengasse, between the **Hofburg** and Albertinaplatz, is now called Augustinerstraße. Heading north from Albertinaplatz, the first important building is the Palais Lobkowitz on Lobkowitzplatz, an early Italianate

building from 1685-7, probably by Giovanni Pietro Tencala, with a later portal by JB Fischer von Erlach, perhaps the most important architect of this era. It now houses a theatre museum, and concerts are sometimes held in the *Festsaal*, where Beethoven's *Eroica* was first performed. Further on along Augustinerstraße Herrengasse towards the Hofburg there is one of Fischer von Erlach's masterpieces, the **Nationalbibliothek** (National Library) at the rear of Josefsplatz, a U-shaped square opening off Herrengasse. Visitors often miss out the library, and in particular its magnificent *Prunksaal*, which has been called 'one of the finest Baroque interiors north of the Alps'. The hall is based on examples in Rome, where Fischer had spent some time during his training as an architect, and consists of a long gallery interrupted at the middle by a transverse vaulted oval.

The library forms part of the **Hofburg**. This palace complex was altered and expanded almost continually from the thirteenth to the early twentieth centuries, and its main Baroque elements are in the largest courtyard, *In der Burg*. The Leopoldine wing on the west side, which now contains the offices of the Austrian President, is one of Vienna's earliest Baroque buildings, designed 1660-9 by Philiberto Lucchese and extended by Domenico and Martino Carlone. Opposite it is the Reichskanzlei wing, by Johann Lukas von Hildebrandt, the Genoa-born Austrian architect who was Fischer von Erlach's great rival.

Of the surviving palaces in the Herrengasse area built for the aristocracy rather than the Habsburg monarchy the most interesting is Palais Kinsky, which is actually on Freyung (No.4). Recently restored, it now houses an art auctioneers, and so is accessible to the public. Also designed by Hildebrandt (in 1716), it has a marvellous Baroque staircase with ceiling frescoes by Marcantonio Chiarini. Palais Mollard-Clary at Herrengasse 9 has a delightful Baroque façade from the 1760s; Palais Batthyany (No.19) and Palais Trautmannsdorf (No.23) are less important but still good examples of Viennese palatial buildings.

Prior to the major developments of the nineteenth century the Herrengasse axis extended beyond the circle of the Ring. At its southern end it was neatly terminated by another major work by JB Fischer von Erlach, **Karlskirche**, which stands outside the 1st district across the (underground) River Wien. Perhaps Vienna's most important Baroque church, it was built in fulfilment of a vow made by Emperor Karl VI that he would erect a church dedicated to Saint Carlo Borromeo, the saint especially associated with relief of the plague, if Vienna's last great plague receded in 1713. The broad façade was designed to create an impact from a distance; the church itself is an oval, with its long axis at right angles to the façade. The complex mix of iconography and stylistic elements used in this building gives an indication of the Habsburgs' imperial aspirations and their desire to establish their position in European history (the Greek portico, the twin columns with spiral sculptural reliefs reminiscent of Trajan's column in Rome, the curiously oriental caps to the side towers, and so on). For those who sometimes find Baroque architecture too ornate the interior of this church is cooler than those of many Viennese churches, even almost Classical. Following the death of the elder Fischer in 1723 work on the Karlskirche was continued by his son, Josef Emanuel Fischer von Erlach, and finally completed in 1739.

There are many other Baroque ensembles in central Vienna, generally located off major commercial streets such as Kärntnerstraße, Graben and Kohlmarkt which themselves are largely nineteenth century in character. One such cluster of Baroque buildings is in the streets around Annagasse, just to the east of Kärntnerstraße. **Annakirche** itself was originally a Gothic building, but the present interior is a small, gleaming Baroque jewel, with frescoes by Daniel Gran and fine side altars. The pews and organ loft balustrade are mid-eighteenth-century.

STAIRWAYS TO HEAVEN

Two streets further down Kärntnerstraße and parallel to Annagasse is Himmelpfortgasse and the **Winter Palace of Prince Eugene of Savoy**. This building, on which the two rivals JB Fischer von Erlach and Hildebrandt both worked, boasts one of Fischer's finest achievements – a staircase in a relatively restricted space, which exudes Baroque vitality and strength. The palace now houses the Ministry of Finance, but the porter generally allows tourists to have a look at the staircase, moving from relative gloom up a single flight of stairs that then splits into two flights, both leading to an upper landing that is carried by mighty atlantes.

Just one block further north is another ensemble of buildings centred around Franziskanerplatz, one of Vienna's most charming and intimate squares. As its name suggests, it is dominated by a Franciscan church, **Franziskanerkirche**, in a curious South German Renaissance style but with an interesting interior. It has many Baroque features, notably the plaster 'curtain' above the first side chapel to the left as you enter the church, the illusionistic high altar by the Jesuit painter Pozzo (*see below*), and the sculpture commemorating the martyrdom of Saint Johannes Nepomuk. Nearby too on Singerstraße is the **Deutschordenshaus** (House of the Teutonic Knights), built in 1667 by Carlo Canevale and redesigned between 1720 and 1725 by Domenico Martinelli, which contains a series of delightful courtyards.

Just north of the Wollzeile is one of the oldest parts of the city, the Bäckerstraße Sonnenfels-gasse-Schönlaterngasse area, which, again, contains some fine Baroque façades and courtyards. On Schönlaterngasse is the relatively inconspicuous entrance to the **Heiligen-kreuzerhof**, a generously dimensioned courtyard that was originally a 'branch' house of the Cistercian Monastery of Heiligenkreuz, outside Vienna (*see chapter* **Wienerwald**). The nearby Dr Ignaz-Seipel-Platz, flanked by the Universitätskirche, **Alte Universität** (Old University) and Akademie der Wissenschaften (Academy of Sciences), is a smaller but equally impressive square, with a feel rather like an outdoor room. The recently restored Universitätskirche, now better known as the **Jesuitenkirche** or Jesuit church, is an early Baroque building begun in 1627 by an unknown architect, but both the façade and more importantly the interior were greatly altered in 1703-5 by the Jesuit lay brother and painter-architect Andrea Pozzo, famous for his *trompe l'oeil* effects in the Gesù, mother church of the Jesuit order, in Rome. The interior is High Baroque in style, with a painted false 'dome'; a white stone in the floor of the nave marks the point from where this illusion works best. The main altar is a highly dramatic illusionistic piece, the altar painting being lit from the side by hidden windows that are visible from the lane behind the church. The church also has fine Baroque pews. Pozzo himself is buried in the crypt.

Near the Jesuit church in Postgasse is the Dominican church, known as the Dominikaner-kirche or Santa Maria Rotonda. The present church is the third on the site, and was built in the 1630s by Italian architects; it has a powerfully articulated façade that clearly shows the influence of early Roman Baroque. The interior was restored in the nineteenth century. The high altar dates from 1840, as do several of the paintings, but the impression conveyed is in general still that of a typical early Baroque *Saalkirche* or hall-church, with side chapels.

To the west of the axis of Kärntnerstraße and Rotenturmstraße there is a further district of Baroque building in the Judenplatz-Kurrentgasse-Am Hof area. At Kurrentgasse 2, on the first floor, there is the tiny Stanislaus Kostka Kapelle, a real Baroque gem. This is the room where the teenage Polish Jesuit saint (1550-68) lived while in Vienna, which was later converted into a chapel. Its present appearance dates from 1742. The chapel is hard to get in to, but worth the effort. Schulhof, off Kurrentgasse, is a tiny street with several fine Baroque houses.

The church of the Nine Angelic Choirs or **Kirche Am Hof** on the large square of Am Hof is, like many Viennese churches, essentially a Gothic structure, as the interior still reveals. However, the early Baroque façade, possibly by Carlo Carlone and dating from 1607-10, completely screens the earlier church. This was the first Jesuit church in Vienna, built before the Universitäts-kirche, and is very much in the style of Roman Jesuit churches, with strong references to the Gesù. In another corner of the same square, bordering the Färbergasse, is the Bürgerliches Zeughaus (Citizens' Arsenal), which has an interesting three-bay gabled façade by Anton Ospel from 1731-2 based on Spanish or French models.

On Judenplatz is the **Böhmische Hofkanzlei** (Bohemian Chancellery), once the centre of admin-istration of the Czech lands in Vienna. The main façade on the square was added by Matthias Gerl in 1751-4, but the building still owes much to the original 1714 design of JB Fischer von Erlach, especially the eastern section of the 20-bay façade on Wipplingerstraße. Here Fischer introduced Palladian Classicism to Austria for the first time, combining it, however, with French and Italian High Baroque motifs. The **Altes Rathaus** or Old Town Hall, on the other side of Wipplingerstraße, was rebuilt in 1699-1706 on the base of a medieval building. It is in the style of Fischer von Erlach, and has some interesting interiors.

Other Baroque churches in the 1st district include the Schottenkirche on Freyung (at the northern end of Herrengasse), which is attached to **Schottenstift**, a Benedictine monastery founded by Irish monks. This is another early Baroque church, built in the mid-seventeenth century over an earlier Gothic church under the direction of Carlo Carlone and Marco Spazzo. Like the Dominican church this three-bay, vaulted hall with deep side chapels was extensively renovated in the nineteenth century, but it still has some fine Baroque memorials to members of aristocratic fam-ilies. **Peterskirche** on Petersplatz, off Graben, is another oval Baroque church, largely the work of Hildebrandt, with a High Baroque façade from 1702. The interior is highly atmospheric, with colouring (ochre and gold) darker than the Karlskirche. After Ruprechtskirche this was the second church founded within the walls of Vienna, but its present appearance reveals nothing of this fact. The crypt, though, has a gargoyle from the thirteenth century and two sandstone altars from the early sixteenth century.

OUTSIDE THE RING: THE BELVEDERE

For all the wealth of Baroque buildings within the old city, visitors have to leave the 1st district to find perhaps the most impressive Baroque palace (or rather palaces) of all in Vienna – the **Belvedere**. This huge estate is made up of two buildings, the Oberes and Unteres (**Upper** and Lower) Belvedere, with outbuildings and a park between the two palaces. The whole complex was the garden palace of Prince Eugene of Savoy, the great hero of the campaigns against the Turks after the siege of 1683, whose winter residence in Himmelpfortgasse has already been mentioned.

Prince Eugene's summer palace was designed by Hildebrandt, who had previously served the Prince as a military engineer. The park was laid out first, followed by the Lower Belvedere, in 1714-16, and finally the Upper palace, which stands on a much higher point and was designed to be seen from a distance, in 1721-3. The views over Vienna from the first floor of the Upper Belvedere or the terrace in front are spectacular, and can be com-pared with Canaletto's painting of the same view, which is now in the Kunsthistorisches Museum. Both palaces have fabulous, richly decorated inte-riors, and the Upper Belvedere now houses the nineteenth-twentieth-century sections of the Öster-reichische Galerie, while its Baroque and medieval collections are displayed in the Lower Belvedere. The grand park, originally laid out by the French-Bavarian garden designer Dominique Girard, is still a very attractive place for strolling, even though it has lost some of its original Baroque appearance (there are plans to restore it).

Adjoining the Belvedere gardens is the park of the **Palais Schwarzenberg**, which still domi-nates Schwarzenbergplatz even though since 1945 it has been somewhat obscured by the curious Russian war memorial in front of it. This 1720 palace, still owned by the Schwarzenberg family but now the Im Palais Schwarzenberg hotel, was begun by Hildebrandt and then finished by Fischer von Erlach and his son. Although heavily damaged in World War II it has been restored, and still boasts some fine interiors.

There are also, naturally, many fine Baroque buildings outside the central districts. Most of the inner suburbs have Baroque churches – **Mariahilferkirche** in the 6th district, Saint Ulrich in the 7th and, particularly worth a visit, **Piaristenkirche** and its adjoining square in the 8th district, a complex building reminiscent of Baroque churches in Prague. The Habsburgs' sum-mer residence at **Schönbrunn** is also Baroque in parts, although it is largely the decoration that impresses, while the room lacks any real Baroque excitement. The Baroque gardens are very fine, however, and in winter have a truly Viennese melancholy.

DOMESTIC VIRTUES: *BIEDERMEIER*

The years that followed the huge upheaval of the Napoleonic Wars saw great changes in the atmos-phere of Vienna, including the beginnings of indus-trialisation. During the *Vormärz* (Pre-March) period prior to the Revolution of March 1848 – the time of Schubert, and also of Chancellor Metternich – the dominant style in architecture and many other fields was known as *Biedermeier*, so-called after a satirical figure of a solid middle-class citi-zen portrayed in a Munich magazine. Emphasis was laid on calm domesticity, and the most favoured style was a simple, restrained Classicism.

Houses are plain, with windows that often have lunettes above them containing classical reliefs. The Biedermeier period is more famous, however, for its furniture, which is elegant, functional and unpretentious, and so well suited to modern homes. The **Kaiserliches Hofmobiliendepot** in the 7th district has a series of rooms decorated with this furniture, using curtains and chair coverings with patterns dating from the time, which might surprise those who think of the style as tastefully subdued.

Public buildings from the Biedermeier era tend to be plain and functional. Examples include the Hauptmünzamt (Central Mint) 3, Am Heumarkt 1 by Paul Sprenger, from 1835-8, and the Technisches Universität on Karlsplatz. One of the best architects of this time was Josef Kornhäusel, who designed a sequence of rooms in the **Albertina**, next to the Staatsoper, the 1826 Synagogue on Seitenstettengasse (the only synagogue in Vienna to survive the Nazis) and, alongside the latter, the architect's own house, at Seitenstettengasse 2.

The Ringstraßen era

The defeat of the revolution of 1848 was the prelude to Vienna's second great period of expansion, the era of the *Gründerzeit* ('Founders' Period'). The city acquired a much stronger position as central capital of the monarchy, and in 1850 the old, inner city was combined with the 34 suburbs to form a unified administrative area. The population grew dramatically, leading to an acute housing shortage and a rapid rise in rents. By 1857, so many homeless people were sleeping in the open that the authorities tried to accommodate them in jails, stables and underground cellars.

It was against this background that in the same year of 1857 the Emperor Franz Josef I signed a decree ordering the demolition of Vienna's city walls and the initiation of a planned development and extension of the city. A competition was convened for plans to give a set shape to the growth of the city on to the *glacis*, the strip of open land that had always been maintained – to give guns a free field of fire – between the walls and the old suburbs, and to connect old Vienna with the outer districts. The schemes submitted were influenced by the existing, concentric form of the old city, and by the then-fashionable example of the reconstruction of Paris and its boulevards under Haussmann. The development plan that was finally approved in 1858 by Franz Josef was the product of numerous reworkings, and incorporated the work of all of the three main prize-winners – Ludwig von Förster, the duo van der Null/Sicardsburg and Friedrich Stache. Its central feature, which has left a permanent stamp upon the city, was the construction of two concentric

rings around old Vienna – the inner, wide Ringstraße as a *via principalis* with the adjoining Franz Josefs Kai along the Danube, and an outer major traffic artery, Lastenstraße (the Zweierlinie), which runs along the line of Landesgerichtstraße, Auerspergstraße and Museumstraße. Along the Ring and through the former glacis the city was to be dignified with new, monumental public buildings and equally impressive private properties, also in accordance with the overall plan.

The next three decades saw the creation of over 90 new streets and squares, and the construction of more than 500 public and private buildings. The new public buildings around the Ring were arranged not in line with any traditional religious or political hierarchies, but simply one after the

Café Karl-Otto im Wagner Pavilion. *Pg164.*

other. This layout has often been criticised, but was in fact an expression on the ground of a new social reality, the emerging power of the bourgeoisie.

Significantly enough, the **Staatsoper**, the Opera House, was the first monumental building completed on the Ringstraße. It was planned by Eduard van der Nüll and August von Siccardsburg, and built from 1861-9. Like many of the major buildings on the Ring it was badly damaged in World War II; post-war, the auditorium was restored in a simplified fashion, and with the long rooms on either side – still used for promenading during the intervals – makes a curious, but interesting, 1950s impression. The monumental staircase, the Schwind foyer, the loggia facing the Ringstraße and the staircase and *Teesalon* survive in their original state.

Going on from the Opera around the Ring in a clockwise direction, the next large edifice is the **Neue Burg**, which is only a fragment of the envisaged Kaiserforum (Emperors' Forum), which was to have included a central building, masking the Baroque Leopoldine wing of the Hofburg, connected on either side to semicircular wings extending towards the Ringstraße . Each of these wings was to be linked in turn to the twin museums across the Ring by triumphal arches. However, only one of the curving wings, the Neue Burg, was

Golden rule: Austria's **Parlament**.

ever built, between 1881 and 1913, as the last element in the Hofburg to be erected.

The two museums on the outer side of the Ring – the **Kunsthistorisches** and the **Naturhistorisches**, for arts and sciences – were both conceived in the context of the Kaiserforum project. The exterior features of both were the work of Gottfried Semper – chief architect of the whole Kaiserforum scheme – while Carl Hasenauer designed their interiors. The vestibule and staircase in the Kunsthistorisches, with Canova's sculpture of Theseus conquering the Centaurs and ceiling frescoes of the *Apotheosis of the Renaissance* by the Hungarian Mihály Munkácsy make up a fine example of a nineteenth-century monumental interior.

The Ringstraße and its eclectic collection of buildings are prime examples of nineteenth-century Historicism in architecture. In this current, which picked and borrowed erratically from a whole variety of preceding eras, the particular style chosen for a building was intended to reflect its specific function. Thus, the two museums were designed in an Italian High Renaissance style, as was another 'art palace', the Akademie der Bildenden Künste (Academy of Fine Arts) on nearby Schillerplatz, built 1872-6 and designed by one of the leading architects of Historicism, Theophil Hansen. Just north of the main museums, however, the same architect built Austria's **Parlament** as a neo-Classical structure, completed in 1883. The choice of Classical columns for the parliament was intended to refer to the origins of democracy in Greece, and to link them to the Austrian constitutional monarchy. This is one of the largest and architecturally more successful Ringstraße buildings, for Hansen handled the grouping of masses with skill and restraint. It's another that suffered war damage, but some fine interior features have survived: the vestibule, with 24 monolithic Corinthian columns with richly gilded capitals, and the *Abgeordnethaus* (house of the members of parliament), modelled on a Greek theatre.

The parliament is followed by the **Rathaus** or town hall, built by Friedrich Schmidt in a Flemish Gothic style – considered emblematic of municipal self-esteem – opposite which across the Ring is the 1888 **Burgtheater** (National Theatre), with a well-articulated façade by Semper and interior by Hasenauer. The auditorium was rebuilt in a simplified fashion after war damage. The **Universität** (1873-83) by Heinrich Ferstel follows. This is another 'cultural' building that followed Italian Renaissance styles, and has the usual monumental reception rooms and staircases.

The next major construction near the Ring was actually the first to be begun around the boulevard, the **Votivkirche**, built as an act of thanksgiving for the failure of an assassination attempt on the Emperor in 1853. Set back a little from the

Ring, on the modern Rooseveltplatz, it is modelled on thirteenth-century French Gothic churches. Heinrich Ferstel won the competition to design it aged only 26 in 1856, but recurrent problems and his own perfectionism delayed its completion until 1879. The Börse (Stock Exchange) by Theophil Hansen, from 1874-7, and the bizarre 1865 pastiche-Renaissance Roßauer Kaserne barracks are the last monumental buildings on this stretch before the boulevard ends at the Franz Josefs Kai and the Danube Canal.

In the opposite direction around the Ring, anticlockwise from the Staatsoper, the first large monument is the 1865-8 **Künstlerhaus**, by August Weber, which, like the nearby art museums, is Italian-Renaissance in style. Next door to it is the **Musikverein** (1867-9), another building by Theophil Hansen, and the home of the Vienna Philharmonic Orchestra. It has Vienna's best-known nineteenth-century interior, the *Großer Saal*, an orgy of Historicist decoration familiar from the Strauß concert broadcast worldwide each New Year's Day. Further north in the same direction, beyond the Stadtpark, is the **Museum für Angewandte Kunst** (Museum of Applied Arts), designed 1866-71 by Heinrich Ferstel, which is also an excellent showcase for artefacts from all Vienna's stylistic periods. The adjoining School of Applied Arts was also by Ferstel. The last large building on Stubenring, as this section of the Ring is called, is the Regierungsgebäude, built between 1909 and 1913 by Ludwig Baumann as the War Ministry of the Habsburg Empire, in a heavy, neo-Baroque style with all sorts of bombastic decorative flourishes.

WAGNER & JUGENDSTIL

Opposite the ponderous Regierungsgebäude, set back from the Ringstraße and fronted by a small, grassy square, there is a radically different building, the 1904-12 **Postsparkasse** or Post Office Savings Bank, perhaps the most famous creation of Otto Wagner (1841-1918). A figure of European importance, Wagner can by himself represent the transition from nineteenth-century Historicism to Modernism, and had a lasting impact on Vienna. The Postsparkasse is one of his most seminal works, reflecting his aim to combine 'need, function, construction and sense of beauty', with a façade that is dramatically plain, especially when contrasted with the overkill of the War Ministry. Wagner's façade was made of sheets of marble screwed to the substructure, and inside the building the cash hall, with its glass roof, aluminium warm air blowers and glass block floor is one of the most important works of modern architecture and ought not be missed (open only during normal bank hours).

Wagner was not politically in favour – he had bid to build the War Ministry, but Baumann's

The magnificent **Kirche am Steinhof**.

heavy traditional style was preferred – but nevertheless left another indelible mark on Vienna by designing what is still the basis of the public transport system: the Stadtbahn. Most of the stations on what are today the underground lines U4 and U6 and the Vororteline S45 are by him, as well as the railings, bridges and original light fittings. At **Kettenbrückengasse** there is a kind of Wagner ensemble: the U4 station, and diagonally opposite, two apartment blocks on the Wienzeile, the **Majolikahaus**, with its ornamental tiled façade, and Linke Wienzeile 38/Köstlergasse 3, with gold decoration, elegantly resolved corners and dramatic roof sculptures. Comparing them with other blocks nearby, one can see that Wagner retained the traditional separation of his apartment buildings into base, main floors and cornice, but eliminated heavy bombastic ornament. Among the many other fine Wagner buildings in Vienna are the delightful little 1906-7 **Schützenhaus** or sluice-gate building by Augartenbrücke bridge on the Donau Canal (near Schottenring U-bahn stop), the magnificent **Kirche am Steinhof**, built in the grounds of a mental hospital with a wonderfully modern interior, his own two houses the Villa Wagner I and II on Hüttelbergstraße and the imposing block at Rennweg 3 (1889), which for many years housed the Yugoslav embassy, built in his earlier, more Historicist style.

Past, present & future

Certain key projects, perhaps not always realised as originally intended, mark the development of architecture in the city. Due to the compact nature of central Vienna such projects, although spread across the centuries, often deal with the same areas – lending weight to the contention of architectural critic Friedrich Achleitner that Viennese architecture is a reflection on its past.

Perhaps the most radical and extensive of these projects was the decision to demolish the city walls and lay out the Ringstraße in 1857. Photographs of the city before this time reveal an almost magical walled town with a broad strip of open space surrounding it. The image is that of a town as a complete, unfragmented entity. One of the last, highly symbolic Ringstraße projects represents the very opposite. Only one wing (the **Neue Burg**) of the proposed Kaiserforum linking the Hofburg and Gottfried Semper's battleship-like museums was built. As early as 1907 the idea of building the second, symmetrical wing had been dropped and various proposals were made by the Historicist Ludwig Baumann and the Jugendstil architect Ohmann to complete Heldenplatz. But World War I and the collapse of the Habsburg empire made the completion of the project in the new Austrian Republic senseless and lends the surviving fragment a particular historical significance and identity.

Loos Haus is a seminal project which provoked an uproar in Vienna. Looking at the building today it is hard to understand the fuss. This is, however, the point. Loos believed an urban building should have a civilised, restrained exterior which did not 'shout' – looking at the pompous entrance to the palace or the neighbouring nineteenth-century building at the corner of Schauflergasse what he meant becomes clear. His rejection of ornament was regarded as dangerously radical. His 'building without eyebrows'

– due to the lack of cornices above the windows – is one of the key works of modern architecture.

Hans Hollein's **Haas Haus** on Stephansplatz may not occupy such an important role in the history of modern architecture. But the architect's arduous battle to have his design built resulted in a key victory for the right to build modern architecture in the inner city.

Ortner & Ortner's Museum Quarter is one of the most significant building projects in Vienna since the turn of the century. This museum complex is placed within Fischer von Erlach's eighteenth-century Imperial Stables complex which was to form the rear of the nineteenth-century Kaiserforum. Ortner & Ortner won the design competition in 1990 but their design became the subject of ba heated debate. The project was reduced in height and size and modified (a tower which would have served as an external symbol of the complex was eliminated), construction has started, the opening is planned for 2001. This project with its two new museum buildings (the Leopold Museum will be home to one of the most significant art collections in the country and a Museum of Modern Art – currently split between Palais Liechtenstein in the 9th district and Zwanziger Haus), a new Kunsthalle and the converted winter riding school as a multi-purpose hall represents a direct intervention in Vienna's imperial past linking the residential 7th district with the twin monumental nineteenth-century museum buildings (how the quarter is expected to look is pictured below).

The attempt to create a modern architecture which interprets and respects its surroundings while avoiding pastiche or wheedling 'good manners' is important for the future of modern architecture in Vienna's inner city and may go some way to opposing the tendency to create a kind of 'Old Vienna' architectural theme park.

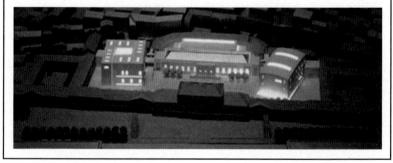

Many other architects – less significant than Wagner, but also innovative – were active in the vibrant artistic atmosphere associated with the Jugendstil and turn-of-the-century Vienna. Joseph Maria Olbrich designed the **Secession** building at Friedrichstraße 12, built to house the exhibitions of artists who walked out and so 'seceded' from the reactionary Akademie der Bildenden Künste in 1897, and the name of which was extended to an entire movement. Max Fabiani designed the 1901 Artaria Haus, Kohlmarkt 9, the ship-like 1910 **Urania** building (Uraniastraße 1) and the Portois & Fix building (1898-1900) at Ungargasse 59-61. Josef Plecnik, later to design fascinating buildings in his native Slovenia, built the Zacherlhaus (1903-5) at Brandstätte 6 and the Heilig Geist Kirche at Herbststraße 82.

The most important architect to follow after Wagner, however, was Adolf Loos, equally influential as a theorist, polemicist and designer. His most important work in Vienna, originally built in 1912 for the Goldmann & Salatsch tailors' company but now generally known as the **Loos Haus**, stands on Michaelerplatz, right opposite the main entrance to the Hofburg. Loos detested what he saw as the vulgar, meaningless decoration of the Ring's Historicist buildings: the façade of the Michaelerplatz block is radically devoid of ornament, and even the window boxes were added against Loos' initial wishes to quieten some of the ferocious criticism the building aroused. It is said that Emperor Franz Josef, whose own tastes in architecture were predictably conservative, refused to use this entrance to his palace after the Loos Haus appeared. Its interior has been expertly restored, although it suffers somewhat from the fact that it is now not a gentlemen's tailors but a bank branch, and so the display cases are no longer filled with rolls of fine materials. Loos' 1909 **American Bar**, at Kärntnerdurchgang 108, is a tiny, cleverly planned gem of an interior – a curious early European homage to American civilisation as a model of modernity – and the exclusive tailors Knize, Graben 13, has preserved its 1910-13 Loosian interior almost unaltered. Loos also built a number of villas in the suburbs of Vienna, but none is open to the public. The only Loosian domestic interior that is easily viewable is a reconstruction of his own sitting room in the **Museum der Stadt Wien**.

Red Vienna

The years following World War I and the collapse of the Habsburg Empire saw the establishment of Austria's First Republic, great poverty and intense social problems. From the end of the war until 1934 Vienna was under the control of a Social Democrat administration, whose ambitious radical programmes led to the city being labelled 'Red Vienna'.

Karl-Marx-Hof: *representative of Red Vienna.*

A central part of these policies was the construction of public housing for the city's working class.

This programme was extremely successful, and some 56,000 apartments were constructed within a decade. In their layout these 'superblocks' were often modelled on the traditional structure of the city's palaces, with central courtyards like a *cour d'honneur*, or continued in modified form the existing structures of Viennese apartment blocks. This drew criticism from the more aggressive Modernists of the Frankfurt School, who favoured white-block architecture.

Nevertheless, the Viennese housing programme was one of the most productive in Europe of its time. Best-known of the 'Red Vienna' blocks is the 1926-30 **Karl-Marx-Hof**, a huge block, extending for a kilometre along Heiligenstädterstraße, designed by Otto Wagner's pupil Karl Ehn.

DAMAGE & DESTRUCTION

Vienna was more severely damaged in World World II than is often appreciated – 523 air raids from 1943 damaged or totally destroyed over 21,000 buildings, including monuments such as the Stephansdom, the Staatsoper, the Volkstheater and the Albertina. The reconstruction period after the war led to some 'improvements' typical of the time, such as underground pedestrian passages, but, due to lack of funds or a traditional Viennese tendency to move behind developments in the rest of Europe,

Haas Haus – *a modern breakthrough.*

the city was not adapted to suit the demands of the car as was the case in many German cities.

The renovation of historic and war-damaged districts in Vienna got under way in the late 1950s. Since then almost all the damaged areas of the 1st district have been restored, giving them something of a Disney-ish quality. Beginning in 1978 the underground U-bahn system was constructed – incorporating lines of Wagner's Stadtbahn – which has led to major changes in the life of the city. Further schemes to regulate the flow of the Danube (an issue in Vienna for centuries) created the **Donauinsel** (Danube Island), which now forms a kind of leisure paradise with noisy, lively bars and restaurants, quiet nudist areas and wildlife sanctuaries.

CONTEMPORARY CREATION

Austria, and Vienna above all, has an excellent international reputation in modern architecture. Whether this is deserved, however, or if it's just a case of the work of a few architects being promoted while the mediocre productions of the majority are ignored is open to question.

During the 1980s, a local cliché ran that major projects were awarded to politically well-connected big offices, while the city's most talented designers expended their energies on small-scale projects such as bars or shops. Examples of such projects

are Hans Hollein's **Reti** candle shop (his first complete design, 1964-5) at Kohlmarkt 8-10, the **Kleines Café** (1970-7) by Hermann Czech on Franziskanerplatz, the Reis bar by Coop Himmelblau (1977) off Kärntnerstraße, the **Kiang** restaurant (1984-5) by Helmut Richter, Hollein's Schullin jewellers (1972-4) at Graben 26, the 1985-7 **Café Stein** by Gregor Eichinger and Christian Knechtl at Währingerstraße 6 and the adjoining 1993 **Stein's Diner**, by the same architects.

Hollein's **Haas Haus** on Stephansplatz, completed in 1990, is a project on a very different scale, which has represented a significant breakthrough for modern architecture in Vienna. Right opposite the cathedral, this is obviously a hyper-sensitive site, and previous planning policy had allowed scarcely any new buildings in the museum-like 1st district. However, the building that stood here was a nondescript 1950s block, dating from the early post-war reconstruction of Stephansplatz. Political support from the Mayor at that time, Helmut Zilk, was important in pushing Hollein's project through. There's much to criticise in the building – it represents a last flourish of 1980s Postmodernism, and there's nothing more out of date than yesterday's fashions. Also, it's disastrous as a shopping centre, so much so that it's currently due to undergo major internal alterations. The important thing for modern architecture in central Vienna is, however, that it was built.

Another project that has had an even more tortuous history is Ortner & Ortner's project for a 'Museum Quarter', to be located within the imperial stables complex facing the rear of the Hofburg, which was once intended to be incorporated into the Kaiserforum scheme. Ortner & Ortner's design envisaged preserving the Fischer von Erlach stables, but demolishing most of the nineteenth-century accretions inside them. The project met with strong opposition from Vienna's (and Austria's) best selling daily newspaper, *Krone Zeitung*, and has been trimmed down, modified and reduced, but a start has been made on construction and the project is to be completed by 2001. Another partial victory for modern architecture. *See page 38* **Past, present & future.**

Outside the 1st district modern architecture is encouraged, for example as part of Vienna's move towards and across the Danube (an area referred to as Transdanubien). The most prominent example is the site in the 22nd district known as the 'Donaucity' originally planned for an Expo in 1995 that the Viennese rejected in a referendum. The intention is to develop here, along the prominent Wagramer Straße axis, a new centre that will help to finally eliminate Vienna's mono-centric quality. On this site in front of the monumental bureaucratic ensemble of the UNO city housing blocks, schools and office towers are shooting up. The lucid severity of the original development plan has been diluted (a typically Viennese occurrence) but there are some interesting buildings by younger Austrian architects to be seen here.

Vienna has experienced a rash of tower building in recent times: the tallest is the **Millennium Tower**, not in the Donaucity expansion area but further upstream on the city side of the Danube in a run-down area at Handelskai. The 50-storey tower by Peichl/Podrecca/Weber, which has a total height of 202 metres (663 feet) is based in plan on two intersecting cylinders and experienced several typically Viennese modifications during the design process. It is swivelled at an angle to the river and projects above a surrounding shopping and housing complex. A bridge spanning the busy Handelskai and the railway line provides a link to the Danube.

There's also the Vienna Twin Tower project by Italian architect Massimiliano Fuksas, who teaches in Vienna. This building, currently under construction, stands in the Wienerberg area of the 10th district where Vienna's nineteenth-century grid structure starts to break down. It's in the extensive grounds of a former brickworks, transformed to create a golf course, park and 'business park'.

Fuksas' building is made up of two blocks, rectangular in plan, placed at an angle to each other and connected by glass bridges. This is the first completely transparent office building in Europe to employ an air displacement heating and ventilation system.

Dramatic developments have also taken place in school building, with a 'Programme 2000' that has led to the erection of many completely new schools, often by well-known or emerging architects. They are generally quite far removed from the city centre, but for aficionados of modern architecture they are well worth visiting. Particularly interesting is Helmut Richter's school on Kinkplatz, in the 14th district, a high-tech structure inspired by Western European examples, as this kind of building is almost unknown in Vienna. It represents a triumph of perseverance on the part of the architect, who has refused to admit the word compromise.

It would be untrue and misleading to present Vienna as an architectural paradise. It has its grim tower blocks, housing estates that still have that strong Eastern Bloc atmosphere that the former Communist countries themselves are doing everything to eliminate, and suburbs made up of single houses in monotonous 1950s styles or with a misconceived, inappropriate alpine-hut look. Nevertheless, architects in Vienna are often celebrities, the term 'star architect' is used without a trace of irony to describe successful designers, and politicians and business people are beginning to recognise the potential of good design. And, despite its over-restoration, the old city still possesses an unmistakable magic: architecturally, it is easily legible, providing clear reflections of the most significant eras of its fascinating past.

Helmut Richter's school on Kinkplatz: a triumph of perseverance.

By Season

Vienna's cultural calendar.

Befitting a city so anchored in tradition, Vienna has a hefty programme of annual events, ranging from the high arts to the high kitsch. Classical music, in the form of the **Klangbogen**, the **Osterklang** and a host of summer events, occupies a vast chunk of the calender. Other musical tastes are represented by the extensive but slightly lame **JazzFest Wien** and the avant garde/new classical **Wien Modern**.

Vienna is blighted by extremely harsh winters, but this does not deter it from organising New Year festivities that attract thousands of tourists each year. The ball season extends through the winter (*see page 230* **Having a ball**), and **Fasching**, the German-speaking world's version of Carnival, runs until Ash Wednesday.

Once the snow has melted things really get going with a major music, dance and theatre festival, the **Wiener Festwochen**, the **Vienna Marathon** and a rather cheesy reply to Berlin's Love Parade, the Rainbow Parade, which takes to the streets in June (*see page 215* **Colourful co-ordination**).

Sturm *goes down a storm in Vienna.*

The summer sees Vienna's largest single open-air event, the SPÖ sponsored **Donauinselfest**, when up to half a million people congregate on the Danube Island over a weekend.

Vienna has a lucrative congress and trade fair industry which keeps hotels booked up and ensures an almost permanent presence of wealthy foreigners throughout the year. To what extent this will be affected by attempts to isolate the country after the entrance of Haider's FPÖ into the governing coalition remains to be seen.

Regardless of the number of foreign visitors in Vienna, the Viennese will continue with their idiosyncratic seasonal activities, which are one of the most fascinating and enjoyable aspects of city life here. There can be few cities where the changing seasons are so visible. Christmas is pleasantly old fashioned with advent markets and mulled wine on sale throughout the city. Easter too has its street markets and during the hot summers the locals head for pools and the woods.

Wine is a big deal around Vienna. In September the first grape juice (*Most*) goes on sale, followed by a pleasant semi-fermented variety (*Sturm*) in October. Autumn also sees the shops and markets flooded with myriad varieties of pumpkin and in November everyone sits down to the St Martin's Day goose (*Martinigansl*), traditionally served with red cabbage and potato dumplings.

Public holidays

New Year's Day (1 Jan); **Epiphany** (6 Jan); **Easter Monday**; **Labour Day** (1 May); **Ascension Day** (sixth Thursday after Easter); **Whit Monday** (sixth Monday after Easter); **Corpus Christi** (second Thursday after Whitsun); **Assumption Day** (15 Aug); **Austrian Public Holiday** (26 Oct); **All Saints' Day** (1 Nov); **Immaculate Conception** (8 Dec); **Christmas Day** (25 Dec); **St Stephen's Day** (26 Dec).

Spring

Frühlingsfestival

Spring Festival
Konzerthaus, 3, Lothringerstraße 20 (712 1211). U4 Stadtpark/tram D. **Office open** *mid Mar-mid Apr* 9am-7.45pm Mon-Fri; 9am-1pm Sat. **Tickets** AS160-800. **Date** *mid Mar-mid Apr.* **Credit** AmEx, DC, JCB, MC, V.

The **Music Film Festival** *lights up the night on* **Rathausplatz**. *See page 44.*

This famous spring festival held in the **Konzert-haus**, with concerts by the Vienna Philharmonic and other major ensembles, has a different theme each year: the 2000 festival was dedicated to Bach to mark the 250th anniversary of his death, with complete performances of his entire cello and organ repertoire, the Brandenburg Concertos, and the *Saint Mark's Passion*.

Easter Market

Freyung. U3 Herrengasse. **Date** Mar or Apr.
A traditional Easter market in the centre of Vienna. Stalls sell food, drink, Easter eggs and knick-knacks.

Osterklang

Easter Festival
Information & tickets: 1, Stadiongasse 9 (42 717). U2 Rathaus/tram J. **Office open** *during festival* 10am-6pm Mon-Fri. **Tickets** AS150-1,250.
Date Mar or Apr. **Credit** AmEx, DC, JCB, MC, V.
Vienna's Easter festival generally includes concerts by the Philharmoniker at the **Musikverein**, an Easter concert at **Stephansdom** and tours of the city. The festival is promoted by the same group as the **Klangbogen** festival (*see below*).

Vienna Marathon

Information: Enterprise Sport Promotion, 10, Keplerplatz 12/1/5 (606 9510/fax 606 9540). **Registration** AS480-580. **Date** May. **Credit** MC, V.
Starts at Schönbrunn palace and finishes at Rathausplatz. The race has a limit of 8,000 runners; about 2,000 are usually foreigners. Other activities on the day include a half marathon and a kids' 2.5km run. Internet registration starts in December.
Website: www.vienna-marathon.com

JazzFest Wien

Information (503 5647). **Tickets** from Libro (319 0606) & Kurier-Corner (Opernpassage; 587 5789).
Date *Jazz-Club Festival* May-June; *Jazz Film Festival* June; *Main Jazz Festival* June-July.
Vienna's largest jazz festival is divided into three parts: the main Jazz Festival, the Jazz Film Festival and Jazz-Club Festival. Big name acts perform in the Opera House, Sofiensäle, Radiokultur-haus or the Stadthalle; lesser known performers are staged in small to medium-sized clubs; and a jazz film festival is held at the Opernkino.

The festival has been a rather conservative affair in recent years, hauling in guaranteed hall-fillers such as Bobby McFerrin and Al Jarreau and even people who have nothing to do with jazz, such as the REM/Patti Smith extravaganza at the Staatsoper in 1999. The official excuse is that anything more challenging would encroach on the Saalfelden Jazz Festival, held near Salzburg in August. The sheer size of the programme, however, guarantees that there is something for all tastes.
Website: www.jazzfestwien.at

Wiener Festwochen

Vienna Festival
Main Festival office: 6, Lehárgasse 3a (589 220/info 589 2222/fax 589 22 49/kartenbuer@festwochen.at). **U1, U2, U4 Karlsplatz (exit Secession)/bus 57a.** **Office open** *during festival* 9am-5pm Mon-Thur; 9am-4.30pm Fri.
Beethoven events: Musikverein, 1, Karlsplatz 6 (505 8190/fax 505 8190-94). U1, U2, U4 Karlsplatz/tram 1, 2, D, J. **Tickets** *for all events* AS350-1300.
Date May-June. **Credit** AmEx, DC, JCB, MC, V.

*Streetside strutting at **Hallamasch.***

A smorgasbord of international orchestras, opera and dance companies converge on Vienna for two months of performance madness, with events in all the city's main venues. Predictably, Beethoven and other Viennese classics always figure prominently. A fixture on the international music scene. Note the different contact details for Beethoven events. At other times of year information about the festival can be obtained from 6, Lehárgasse 11. *Website: www.festwochen.or.at/*

Summer

One of the most consistently popular of Vienna's summer musical events is the Mozart season presented each year by the **Kammeroper** against the backdrop of the artificial 'Roman ruins' of Schönbrunn palace, although lately renovation work has meant that they have moved indoors to the **Schloßtheater Schönbrunn.**

In July and August the city has two open-air cinemas – the **Freiluftkino Krieau** and **Kino unter Sternen**. *See chapter* **Film.**

Wiesen

Music Festival
By car: A2 motorway, dir. Graz. Exit Wiener Neustadt, then S4 dir. Mattersburg-Eisenstadt. Exit Sigleß. Follow signs to Wiesen (3km).
By bus: Eurolines (712 0453) from Wien Mitte/ Landstraße (tickets: AS100 single; AS170 return).

Tickets from Libro; Virgin Megastore (Mariahilfer Straße); Kurier-Corner (Opernpassage; 597 5789). **Dates** *Spring Vibration* June; *Forestglade* July; *JazzFest* July; *Two Days A Week* Aug; *Wiesen Sunsplash* Aug.

If the weathers fine, a trip out to Wiesen to catch some good sounds in well-equipped yet utterly rural surroundings cannot be recommended too highly. Wiesen was initially a three-day Jazzfest, which throughout the 1980s attracted the crême de la crême. Today, in addition to the jazz, there are also a number of other weekends dedicated to pop, rock and reggae. Facilities have been improved too, and the stage area is now covered by a giant dome to pre-empt the unpredictable Austrian summer.

The 1999 festival featured the likes of Pharoah Sanders, Burning Spear and the Red Hot Chilli Peppers. As you approach the festival area from the main road, it becomes clear that Wiesen is a rallying point for Austrian hippiedom, with the sound of bongos and ritual chants emanating from the dense woodland.
Website: www.wiesen.at

Im Puls Tanz

Festival for Contemporary Dance
7, Neustiftgasse 3/12 (info 523 5558/tickets 71 696/ fax 5231 6839/office@tanzwochen.at). U2 Volkstheater/bus 48a. **Office open** 9am-6pm daily; *telephone enquiries* 9am-8pm daily. **Date** July-Aug. **Credit** AmEx, DC, JCB, V.
Staged at the **Burgtheater** and the **Sofiensäle** (*see chapter* **Music: Rock, Roots & Jazz**). The festival attracts dance groups from around Europe, including the Jonathan Burrows Group, Merce Cunningham Dance Company and Compagnie Marie Chouinard as well as individuals such as Susanne Linke and Reinhild Hoffmann, to perform their new interpretations of dance.
Website: www.impuls-tanz.at or www.tanz2000.at

Klangbogen

Vienna Summer of Music
1, Stadiongasse 9 (42 717/fax 40009 98410). U2 Rathaus/tram D. **Office open** *July-Aug* 10am-6pm Mon-Fri. **Tickets** AS150-1,200. **Date** July, Aug. **Credit** AmEx, DC, JCB, MC, V.
Just because the Philharmoniker goes off to Salzburg for the summer, it doesn't mean that Vienna rolls up its streets. Guest orchestras perform at the Musikverein, while opera and operetta take over the Theater an der Wien, all under the capable guidance of festival director Roland Geyer. The same Klangbogen organisation also provides a ticket service and promotion for other groups throughout the year, most importantly the Wiener Opernszene.

Rathausplatz Music Film Festival

Rathausplatz. U2 Rathaus/tram 1, 2, D, J. **Tickets** free. **Date** July, Aug.
Every evening at twilight, opera and classical music films are shown for free on a giant screen in the square in front of the city hall. Decent films and music bring culture buffs out in droves; food stands bring everyone else. Make sure you get there early to get a seat.

Donauinselfest

Donauinsel. U1 Donauinsel. **Tickets** free.
Date weekend in Aug.
The whole island is invaded for one weekend by around half a million revellers for this massive party organised by the Social Democrats. The Donauinselfest is one of the largest free events in Europe and usually features some cheesy old has-beens like the remaining Beach Boys or Bonnie Tyler at the top of the bill.

Seefestspiele Mörbisch

Mörbisch am Neusiedlersee, Burgenland (mid June-Aug 02685 8181-0/fax 02685 8334).
By car: A2 dir. Graz, to the A3 at Neusiedlersee exit, then Eisenstadt Süd to Mörbisch.
By bus: departs 6pm from Reisebüro Blaguss, Wiedner Hauptstraße 15 (501 800).
Office open *July-Aug* 8am-4pm Mon-Thur; 8am-1pm Fri. **Tickets** AS280-880. **Date** July-Aug.
Credit AmEx, DC, MC, V.
One of the hits of the summer season, this operetta festival is held on the shores of Neusiedler See (*see chapter* **Burgenland**). Director Harald Serafin combines high production values with operetta stars of yesterday and tomorrow, including his daughter Martina, an operetta diva. Bring at least a pint of mosquito repellent.

Tickets for the festival can also be obtained through Österreich Karten Express (96 096; open 9am-9pm Mon-Sat; 10am-9pm Sun). For information about the festival at other times of year, call 02682 66210 or fax 02682 66210-14.

Autumn

Hallamasch is a weekend street festival that takes place in September, with a procession down Mariahilfer Straße and musical events in front of Karlskirche. Also in September, skaters and wheelchair athletes take to the streets for the **Vienna Inline Marathon**. The Viennale film festival runs for two weeks from mid-October (*see chapter* **Film**).

Wien Modern

Vienna Modern Music Festival
Konzerthaus, 3, Lothringerstraße 20 (712 1211). U4 Stadtpark/tram D. **Office open** 9am-7.45pm daily.
Tickets AS160-800. **Date** Nov. **Credit** AmEx, DC, JCB, MC, V.
Founded by Claudio Abbado, Wien Modern was awarded the International Classical Music Award in 1992 and continues to present a dynamic programme of modern work.

Winter

Silversterlauf

Information: Lauf-und Conditions-Club Wien or Roadrunners Club Vienna, Dr Peter Pfannl, 20 Wallensteinplatz 3-4 (330 3412).
Registration: Ringstrassengalerien, 1 Kärntner Ring 5-7. U1, U2, U4 Karlsplatz/tram 1, 2, D, J/bus 3a.
Registration (from 26 Dec) AS150. **No credit cards.**
A 5.4km run around the Ring, open to all ages, every New Year's Eve at 3pm.

Walking's for wimps: the **Vienna In-line Marathon** *(www.inline-marathon.at).*

CITYRAMA

YOUR PARTNER FOR VIENNA

CITY SIGHTSEEING & EXCURSIONS
HOTEL ROOM RESERVATIONS
INDIVIDUAL CITY PACKAGES
TRANSFER- & PRIVATE CAR SERVICE
SPECIAL INTEREST- & STUDY TOURS

visit our homepage
www.cityrama.at

CITYRAMA
phone   ++43/1/534.13/0
fax...++43/1/534.13.22
e-mail   office@cityrama.at

OPERA - OPERETTA - MUSICAL
THEATRE - CONCERT
SPANISH RIDING SCHOOL

call
++43/1/534.17/0
fax   ++43/1/534.17.26
e-mail   office@viennatickets.at

Sightseeing

Sightseeing

Vainglorious, verdant and periodically vilified. This is Vienna.

Chances are your first impression of the centre of Vienna will be via the in-your-face grandiloquence of the city's main boulevard, the Ringstraße. Such is the concentration of monumentalism, 'the heavy public buildings and prancing statuary' as Graham Greene saw it, that many visitors experience an overwhelming feeling of oppression when confronted with this veritable Vegas of architectural styles. Do not fret. Vienna is one of the few European cities that still retains a pre-automobile quality of life, blessed with an abundance of parks and green areas, an eminently walkable city centre and an almost eerie lack of noise pollution.

With sights concentrated within and around the Ringstraße, you are unlikely to feel the need to use the splendid public transport system until you have finished with the attractions of the Innere Stadt, the city centre. When you tire of the asphalt, take any of the trams heading north and west and you will find yourself in the legendary Vienna Woods (*see chapter* **Wienerwald**) or among the vineyards that line the city's northern fringe. In Vienna the city blends seamlessly into the countryside – no vacant lots or industrial scars, just a gradual intensifying of the greenery until the last trace of imperial pomp has faded.

The Innere Stadt

Vienna's Innere Stadt or City, as it is referred to on the name of the most central U-Bahn station, Stephansplatz City, in a rather self-conscious attempt at cosmopolitanism, contains the greatest density of sights in the city. There is more than enough to keep the inquisitive long weekender busy within its neatly delineated 360 hectares (890 acres). When you tire of the pomp, turn to the organic embellishments of *Jugendstil* or to the polemical austerity of an Adolf Loos façade. Or just enjoy the serenity of bucolic silence in the centre of a major European capital.

Since the Romans founded the garrison town Vindabona in 15 BC along the banks of the Danube, the present inner city developed through the patronage of first the Babenberg dukes and then the Habsburgs. And owing to the latter's fear of the invader and general distaste for modernity, the Innere Stadt remained a neatly defined kernel long after other European cities had expanded and integrated their historic centres with the burgeoning suburbs.

The Danube has long since been banished to the east of the city in an attempt to forestall constant flooding and has to be actively sought out by those who wish to set eyes on the inspiration for Vienna's most universal melody.

In its place the Danube canal (Donaukanal) now forms the northern limit of the Innere Stadt, with the south, east and west limits encased by the nineteenth-century Ringstraße, the broad boulevard symbolising the birth of Austrian democracy and a life beyond the Habsburgs.

Bisected by the lively, pedestrian Kärntner Straße and its continuation, Rotenturmstraße, the city's nerve centre is Stephansplatz and the Gothic bulk of the city's cathedral, **Stephansdom**. West of Stephansplatz is Graben, a broad, elegant thoroughfare eventually leading to the vast, rambling **Hofburg**, the Imperial Palace, headquarters to the Habsburg Empire up to World War I. These are the most transited streets of the Innere Stadt, where tourism is most palpably present. North of Graben and to the east of Rotenturmstraße, the crowds thin out and a fascinating network of medieval and Baroque streets ensues. Here you can appreciate the peaceful co-existence of an affluent modern lifestyle within the incomparable framework of recent antiquity that is Vienna today. The city breathes a pavement-café ambience more akin to the Catholic Mediterranean than to the land of Luther whose language the Austrians share after a fashion.

Stephansplatz

Situated at the junction of two U-Bahn lines (U1 and U3) and two of Vienna's most famous pedestrian streets, Kärntner Straße and Graben, Stephansplatz is a useful landmark for exploring the Innere Stadt as well as a good vantage point for getting an impression of Viennese street life. Visitors are often struck by the sheer emptiness of Vienna's streets, yet whenever a door is pushed open, bars and restaurants are packed, the clientele seemingly having been beamed in. But Stephansplatz, dominated by the imposing bulk of the cathedral, is rarely empty. Street performers, political protesters, office workers, tourists, Baroque-clad students hawking tickets for dodgy Strauß evenings throng the square, providing a variety of visual entertainment. The buildings surrounding Stephansdom on three sides are a mixture of Baroque and nineteenth-century housing various agencies of the Church.

Stephansplatz: *square it's at.*

On the north side of Stephansplatz is the **Dom-und Diozesanmuseum** (Cathedral and Diocese Museum). Facing the main entrance to the cathedral the buildings are nondescript post-war efforts, with some, such as the corner of Rotenturmstraße, frankly shoddy. The demolition of one such monstrosity made way for Hans Hollein's **Haas Haus** (1990), once the most polemical of modern buildings in the city, whose ground floor is now home to a mishmash of not-so-prestigious shops that belie the luxury of its materials and location. The upper floors, with two restaurants and a bar owned by Attilla Dogudan, Vienna's society gastronome and best mate of Niki Lauda, give the place a bit of much-needed glamour.

For all the fuss, the Haas Haus is not in fact situated on Stephansplatz at all but on the adjacent and often overlooked Stock-im-Eisenplatz (approximately 'iron in wood') where journeymen would hammer a nail into a log to ensure safe passage home after a trip to Vienna. A glass case protecting a stump of larch studded with nails is on the side of the Equitable Palace building, on the corner of Kärntner Straße, the neo-Baroque nineteenth-century seat of the famous insurance company. It's

worth taking a peek inside at the sumptuous marble cladding of the entrance hall and the courtyard tiled in Hungarian Zsolnay ceramics. To gain access to any locked palatial building in Vienna it suffices to ring the bell of any corporate-sounding address and push the door open.

Stephansdom
St Stephen's Cathedral
1, Stephansplatz (5155 23767). U1, U3 Stephansplatz. **Open** 6am-10pm daily.
Although originally located beyond the medieval city walls, Stephansdom forms the epicentre of the present Innere Stadt and dominates the city's skyline. No other building is so unanimously loved and revered by the Viennese as their dear *Steffl* (little Stephen in the local dialect). It is certainly a symbol of endurance, having undergone numerous phases of building and repair due to the ravages of the Turks, the Napoleonic French and the Allies. The last restoration was finished in 1948 after fire, reputedly started by hungry looters sacking nearby shops, destroyed the roof of the nave. From the outside the cathedral appears divided into three distinct parts. On a sunny day the geometrically designed tiled roof of the nave, depicting the Habsburg crown protected by chevrons, is magnificent. Dating from the late thirteenth century, the oldest existing feature is the romanesque **Riesentor** (Giants' Gate), the main entrance to the cathedral. The origin of the name is unclear but the most attractive explanation is that mammoth bones dug up during the building work were taken by the good burghers of Vienna for the remains of a race of giants killed in the Biblical flood. The entrance is flanked by the impressive **Heidentürme** (Pagan Towers), so-called because of their tenuous resemblance to minarets, forming a façade peppered with references to the city's history past and present.

Look out for the circular recess to the left of the entrance, which enabled citizens to check their local bakers were not peddling undersized loaves, and on the other side the inscription O 5 (*pictured below*) – capital O and the fifth letter E – representing the first two letters of Oesterreich, a symbol of the Austrian resistance in World War II. This symbol is regularly highlighted in chalk whenever prominent Nazi collaborator and ex-Austrian president Kurt Waldheim attends Mass. The icing on the cake is undoubtedly the 137m (450ft) high south tower, a

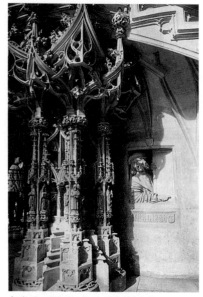

*A gloom with the view – **Stephansdom**.*

magnificently hoary Gothic finger completed in 1433 after 74 years of work. A north tower of similar dimensions was projected in the early sixteenth century but austerity measures imposed during the first Turkish siege of 1529 sadly put paid to the idea.

The interior with its beautiful high vaulting is surprisingly gloomy and often packed with visitors. Still, it very much remains a place of worship, and during Mass, access is denied to most of the nave. It is worth going inside to see the extraordinary carving of the Pilgram pulpit at the top of the nave, where the sculptor, contravening the usual stonemasons' code of practice, has depicted himself looking out of a window to admire his own work. This motif is repeated under the organ loft on the north side of the nave. Other highlights include the tomb of war hero Eugene of Savoy in the Tirna Chapel also located to the north of the nave just inside the main entrance. Visibility is, however, poor. The cathedral's catacombs are home to the entrails of the principal Habsburgs, while, bizarrely, their hearts dwell in the **Augustinerkirche** and what was left of their bodies in the **Kaisergruft**. Unless you have an overriding interest in contemplating piles of bones and skulls, the catacombs can be given a fairly wide berth.

A lift operates from the north side of the nave to the top of the north tower where the cathedral's enormous bell, the *Pummerin* (Boomer), is housed. For the sense of achievement and to enjoy the splendid views, it is probably more worthwhile to take on the 553 steps that lead to the top. Access is from the outside on the south side.

East of Stephansdom

The two principal streets to the east of Stephansdom, Singerstraße and Domgasse, lead to Vienna's only remaining medieval quarter. Due to the lack of first-order monuments, this small but charming labyrinthine network of streets is practically free of tourists and must be one of the most desirable residential areas of any European inner city. The area is known as the Blutviertel (Blood Quarter), which supposedly derives from a massacre of renegade Templar Knights in 1312 on Blutgasse, which connects Singerstraße and Domgasse. In contrast the house at Blutgasse 7 is a fine example of the tranquil, airy inner courtyards that abound in this area.

Look out for the exterior walkways that access the flats, at Blutgasse 3 for example, a so-called Pawlatschenhaus (gallery house – deriving from the Czech *pavlač*, existing throughout the city. On Singerstraße there are a number of seventeenth-century palaces such as the Neupauer-Breuner at number 16 housing the Vienna branch of Sotheby's and the Woka lighting company responsible for repros of classics by Josef Hoffmann and Adolf Loos.

One block east at the junction of Singerstraße and Grünangergasse is the imposing Palais Rottal, and in the delightful Grünangergasse itself at number 4, Palais Fürstenberg with two finely carved stone greyhounds over the portal. If you're looking for refreshment, good stops to try are **Santo Spirito**, a café-bar with a distinctly ecclesiastical theme and classical music in the nearby Kumpfgasse, or for a taste of Mozart visit the **Figarohaus** on Domgasse.

Schatzkammer des Deutschen Ritterordens

Church and Treasury of the Teutonic Knights
1, Singerstraße 1 (512 1065). U1, U3 Stephansplatz. **Open** *Church* 7am-6pm daily. *Treasury May-Oct* 10am-noon Mon, Thur-Sat; 3-5pm Wed, Fri, Sat; Sun by appointment. *Nov-Apr* 10am-noon Mon, Thur, Sat; 3-5pm Wed, Fri, Sat. **Admission** AS50; AS30 concs; free under-11s. **No credit cards**.
The building on Singerstraße and those of the adjoining courtyard belong to one of the most powerful orders to emerge from the Crusades. The fearful sounding Teutonic Knights in fact had the present buildings constructed in the fourteenth century to house their facilities for caring for the sick and needy, good works that had begun during the Crusades and continue to this day. The church is recognisibly Gothic but apart from the sixteenth-century altarpiece and the coats of arms and the tombstones of its illustrious members, it is more interesting to have a look at the eclectic collection in the Treasury – everything from arms and armour to bizarre household objects picked up during the Crusades. Not to be missed is the tiny, beautifully painted eighteenth-century **Sala Terrena**, Vienna's earliest concert hall, where Mozart reputedly played, located at the foot

of the staircase to the Treasury (*see also chapter* **Music: Classical & Opera**). The two cobbled inner courtyards are also worth strolling through and there is a shady terrace bar, a godsend in the summer heat.

In & around Kärntner Straße

A pedestrian street since the 1970s, Kärntner Straße takes its name from being the start of the main road south to the province of Kärnten (Carinthia) and beyond to the Habsburg port of Trieste. Connecting Stephansplatz with another of Vienna's major tourist attractions, the **Staatsoper** (Opera House), it is always clogged with visitors. Once a street of luxury shops, it has been considerably downgraded over the last few years and is now awash with pavement cafés, chain stores and takeaways. An occasional glimpse of former glories is offered by such establishments as Lobmeyer at number 26, a famous glassmaker with a museum containing some original items by the Wiener Werkstätte design firm. Nevertheless it is a fun street to walk along with plenty of street performers and opportunities for people-watching. Near the corner of Stock-im-Eisenplatz is the Kärntnerdurchgang with the fabulous Adolf Loos **American Bar** (1908). This tiny bar was restored in 1990 and the play of mirrors and superb materials – Skyros marble, mahogany and brass – give it an amazing air of palatial cool. It is now open to the public again and worth the rather over-inflated price of the drinks. Weihburggasse leads down to one of the most pleasant squares in Vienna, the Italianate Franziskanerplatz.

The square is probably better known in Vienna for the **Kleines Café** than for the good works of the Franciscans. This superb little café owes a little to Loos for its use of lateral mirrors to create space. It is a pleasant spot to sit in summer and admire the Baroque houses of Weihburggasse and delightful Moses Fountain (1798) by JM Fischer.

The other streets to the east of Kärntner Straße – Himmelpfortgasse, Johannesgasse and Annagasse – all have a number of splendid Baroque houses and a sprinkling of minor sights, the most notable being the Winter Palace of Prince Eugène of Savoy (*see chapter* **Architecture**) in the first of the three, at number 8. This fine Baroque palace was conceived by Fischer von Erlach and completed by von Hildebrandt in 1709; it is now used by the Ministry of Finance. The rooms are out of bounds, but its most arresting features, the vestibule and the staircase propped up by four atlantes and the statue of Hercules on the landing, can be seen during office hours.

Franziskanerkirche

Church of the Franciscans
1, Franziskanerplatz (512 4578). U1, U3 Stephansplatz.

The Habsburgs were always big fans of austere orders such as the Franciscans and Capuchins, a tradition that goes back to Rudolf of Habsburg, the founder of the dynasty. The present church dates from 1611 but the Franciscans were given possession of the neighbouring house some 20 years earlier, itself an establishment for the reform of the city's prostitutes, where the townsmen were encouraged to take them as wives. Today the church operates a more contemporary version of good works in the form of giving meals to the homeless. The church itself is a rather weird mixture of Gothic and German Renaissance dotted with curious roundels that used to contain portraits of the saints. The interior is rather more luxurious than one would expect from the Franciscans and the *trompe l'oeil* by Andrea Pozzo (1707) surrounded by an arched high altar is worth a look. Also check the enormous green curtain with fleurs-de-lis rendered in stucco that hangs from the north wall.

West of Kärntner Straße

Directly west of Kärntner Straße lies Neuermarkt, a large traffic-clogged rectangular square, formerly the medieval flour market. Architecturally, the square is a dreadful hotch-potch of old and new; however, amid the parked cars is a copy of Donner's splendid Providentia Fountain (1739). The naked figures of the original – allegorical representations of the four main Austrian rivers – proved too much for Maria Theresia's Chastity Commission and were removed in 1773. Since 1921 they have been in the **Barockmuseum** in the Lower Belvedere (*see chapter* **Museums**). Shops, cafés and restaurants abound here, but apart from the curious façade of Wild, something approaching Vienna's Fortnum and Mason, there isn't much to recommend it. To the south however, behind an unassumingly grim façade is the **Kapuzinerkirche** and the **Kaisergruft**, the crypt where the Habsburgs rest in peace despite the constant stream of tourists trudging past their spectacular tombs. The influx of visitors is fully justified as the crypt gives an entirely new meaning to the word coffin.

Kaisergruft & Kapuzinerkirche

Imperial Crypt & Church of the Capuchin Friars
1, Neuermarkt (512 6853-12). U1, U2, U4 Karlsplatz, U1, U3 Stephansdom/tram 1, 2, D, J/bus 3a. **Open** 9.30am-4pm daily. **Admission** AS40; AS30 concs; AS10 under-14s. **No credit cards.**
From 1633 onwards, the Habsburgs have been laid to rest in the crypt of the Church of the Capuchins, an offshoot of the Franciscans whose austerity appealed to successive Emperors. So much so that each funeral was preceded by a belittling ritual consisting of the reigning Emperor announcing his name to the waiting prior who then proceeded to deny knowledge of his person and refuse him entry. Finally the Emperor was forced to identify himself as 'a humble sinner who begs God's mercy' and the cortège would be granted permission to enter. Today

AS50 and silence (*Silentium!* reads the inscription over the entrance) is all they ask. To see the coffins in chronological order, turn right on entering then double back when you reach the end of this tract, the Founders' Vault, which contains the remains of Matthias and wife Anna who originally conceived the idea of the crypt. Many of these early tombs are decorated with skulls and crossbones, weapons and bats' wings, progressively increasing in size until you reach the gigantic iron double tomb of Empress Maria Theresia and her husband, Franz Stephan. For sheer size and representational extravagance – above the tomb the couple appear to be sitting up in bed embroiled in a marital tiff – this has to be the highlight of the show. In stark contrast, their son Josef II, whose reforms tried and failed to popularise the drop-bottom reusable coffin, lies in a simple copper casket. Further along is the New Vault with its bizarre, diagonal concrete beams where major Habsburgs like Maximilian I of Mexico and Napoleon's second wife, Marie Louise, are accommodated. Their son, the Duc de Reichstadt, was moved from here to Paris in 1940 by the Nazis in a rather pathetic attempt to ingratiate themselves to their new subjects. In the Franz-Josef Vault people tend to dwell a little longer as here lie the Habsburgs who still touch hearts. Franz Josef I, the last Emperor, his wife, the eternally popular Empress Elisabeth, and their son, the unhappy Prince Rudolph, victim of the Mayerling suicide pact. 'Sissi's' tomb is invariably covered in flowers and small wreaths with ribbons in the colours of the Hungarian flag commemorating her sympathy for that country's national aspirations. The vault itself is simple with elegant wall lights in the Jugendstil manner. The last room contains the remains of Empress Zita, buried with full pomp in 1989, and a bust of her husband, Emperor Karl I, who died in exile in Madeira where he remains to this day.

West of Neuermarkt

The area bounded by Neuermarkt to the east, Graben to the north and Hofburg to the west is made up of a network of narrow streets ideal for strolling and replete with numerous antique shops and galleries, unmissable *Kaffeehäuser* such as the **Bräunerhof** and **Hawelka** and places to visit such as the **Jüdisches Museum**.

Dorotheum

Dorotheum Auction House
1, Dorotheergasse 17 (515 600). U1, U3 Stephansplatz. **Open** 10am-6pm Mon-Fri; 9am-5pm Sat. **Admission** free. **Credit** AmEx, DC, MC, V.
In the past, a 'visit to Auntie Dorothy's' was a popular euphemism for hard times. Set up in 1707 by Emperor Josef I as a pawn shop for the wealthy, the Dorotheum is now Vienna's foremost auction house with small branches throughout the city. The building itself is a bit of neo-Baroque bombast built in the late 1890s with entrances in both Dorotheergasse and the parallel Spielgelgasse. Auctions are held daily, with regular specialised sales. For those on a

budget, try the Glashof on the ground floor, which is full of interesting affordable bric-a-brac. Affluent fans of Modernist furniture are well advised to try the Franz-Josef Saal on the second floor, a veritable Jugendstilfest.

Graben & Kohlmarkt

The famous streets of Vienna do not so much have a buzz to them as an air of stately permanence. Graben and Kohlmarkt are remarkable in that they are entirely made up of nineteenth- and turn-of-the-century buildings, without a single post-war prefab besmirching either. Running into the Stock-im-Eisen-Platz, Graben (ditch) today is a broad pedestrian thoroughfare built along what was the southern moat that defended the Roman camp established a few streets to the north. Commerce harks back to imperial times with innumerable shops bearing the k.u.k. (*kaiserlich und königlich*) royal warrant, among them gentlemen's outfitters announcing branches in Prague and Karlsbad. Their patrons gather on the café terraces sipping their melanges and spritzers, the genteel atmosphere occasionally disturbed (or maybe enhanced) by busking music students, chanting Krishna monks or designer-clad New Russians barking into their mobile phones.

Architecturally, the buildings on Graben are either Historicist or Jugendstil. In the first camp the most noteworthy are the neo-Classical Erste Österreichisches Spar-Casse (First Austrian Savings Bank) (1836) on the corner of Tuchlauben, with an enormous gilded bee symbolising thrift and hard work, and the only remaining Baroque building at number 11, the Bartolotti-Partenfeld Palace (1720). Jugendstil is represented by the monumental Grabenhof (1876) at numbers 14-15 built by Otto Wagner to another architect's plans, and the Ankerhaus at number 10 which Wagner designed, built and for a time used as his studio. Where Habsburgergasse crosses Graben there are some delightful Jugendstil-inspired public conveniences, occasionally the scene of a one-man show featuring the works of Charles Bukowski, that master of toilet humour. There are two fine fountains, the Josef Fountain to the west, right between the two flights of steps leading to the ladies and the gents, and the Leopold Fountain to the east, built by JM Fischer on the orders of Franz I to celebrate his predecessors.

Pestsäule/Dreifaltigkeitssäule

Plague Monument/Trinity Column
1, Graben. U1, U3 Stephansplatz/bus 1a, 2a, 3a.
Between Fischer's two fountains soars the centrepiece of the Graben, the Pestsäule or plague monument. Dating from 1692, this is probably the finest example of the many that were erected throughout the Empire to mark the end of the plague of 1679 and also to celebrate deliverance from the spiritual 'plagues' of the Turks and the Reformation.

Bottoms up in the Neuermarkt – a downtown cyclist's chillout spot.

The Baroque stone carving, primarily by Fischer von Erlach, depicts a gorgeously ephemeral mass of cherubs and saints swathed in clouds, slightly obscured by the wire mesh that protects it from the pigeons.

Peterskirche
Church of Saint Peter
1, Petersplatz, 6 (636 433). U1, U3 Stephansplatz/bus 1a, 2a, 3a.
Built on the site of what was probably Vienna's oldest Christian temple dating from the late fourth century and tucked into the little square just off Graben that bears the same name, the present church was built by Lukas von Hildebrandt and completed in 1733. Undoubtedly the finest Baroque church of the Innere Stadt, its green copper dome echoes the more bombastic Michaelertor in the Hofburg. The dome's fresco has faded badly but the interior remains spectacular due to a wealth of *trompe l'oeil* effects around the choir and the altar. Today the church is a focus of Opus Dei activity in Vienna and visitors can help themselves to some rather fetching cards with the image and life story of the cult's Catalan founder, Escrivá de Balaguer, in a variety of languages.

DESIGNER OR DESIGNED SHOPS
Often it's not so much what's in the window display but the building or shopfront itself. The Graben-Kohlmarkt axis is dotted with minor modern masterpieces of the genre. From the magnificent Klimt-like mosaic angels on the Engel Apotheke, a chemist in the adjoining Bognergasse, through Loos' exercise in minimal clarity for the

Manz bookstore at Kohlmarkt 16 to Hollein's designs on both Kohlmarkt and Graben, shops can be enjoyed as simple artefacts. Knize, a bespoke outfitters for ladies and gents at Graben 11, was designed by Loos too, and still has many of its original fittings in the interior.

In the early 1970s the jewellers Schullin had Hans Hollein render the façade of their premises at Graben 26 with bluish marble and a trickle of gold running through it. Hollein was given another opportunity on their shop at Kohlmarkt 7, where he came up with a striking axe-like form in sheet metal over the door supported by thin wooden uprights. Turnover was obviously on the up for Messrs Schullin as in the mid-1990s they had designer Paolo Piva convert a small shop space in the **Loos Haus** at Kohlmarkt 18 into their specialised watch department. Piva's work must have struck a chord as his designs were later selected for the extensions to the Knize store.

But if it's designer shops you're after, they're all around here: Hugo Boss (Bognergasse 4); Escada (Graben 26); Versace (Trattnerhof 1); **Helmut Lang** (Seilergasse 6), and a little further afield, Prada (Weihburggasse 9).

Off Graben to the west the pedestrian zone continues and assumes the name Kohlmarkt, formerly the city's coal and charcoal market. This is Vienna's Bond Street with Cartier, Dunhill and Gucci all plying their trade. There are also a number of eye-catching indigenous establishments such as the Jugendstil furniture makers **Thonet** at number 6 (though probably not for much longer

*Anybody seen Adolf? The **Neue Burg** is where Hitler announced the Anschluß. See page 59.*

as Louis Vuitton intends to move in here), map-makers **Freytag & Berndt** in Max Fabiani's Jugendstil building, the Artaria Haus, at number 9 and, of course, **Demel** at number 14, pastry cooks to the Habsburgs and still one of the most ornate cakes 'n' coffee outlets in the city. Although the elegance of the shopfronts is distracting, it is the view of the Michaelertor and its magnificent dome that dominates the street, leading you inexorably towards the labyrinth of the Hofburg.

Loos Haus

Loos House
1, Michaelerplatz 3. U3 Herrengasse/bus 2a.
The stir caused by the Haas Haus was a storm in a teacup in comparison to outrage unleashed by the building of Adolf Loos' Modernist masterpiece right opposite the Baroque Hofburg. Built between 1909 and 1911, the building immediately received the nickname of 'the house without eyebrows' in reference to the absence of window cornices. Work was even stopped at one point until Loos agreed to add ten window boxes. The story goes that the Emperor was so appalled by the unseemly nakedness of its façade that he ordered the curtains to be drawn on all the palace windows overlooking its new neighbour. Art critic Robert Hughes sees in Loos' abandoning of ornamenation the seeds of German architect Mies van der Rohe's now-popular dictum 'less is more'. In the words of the architect himself: 'The evolution of culture is synonymous with the removal of ornamentation from utilitarian objects.' Today the building is a bank and has exhibition space on the upper floors.

Hofburg

The vast area of the Imperial Palace and its adjoining parks and gardens occupies most of the south-eastern part of the Innere Stadt, from the **Burgtheater** round to the **Staatsoper**. Within its confines are two of Vienna's most universally known institutions – the **Spanische Reitschule** and its famous Lipizzaner horses and the **Burgkapelle,** which holds regular concerts by the Vienna Boys' Choir. Both are vastly overrated and given the not-insignificant entrance costs, time and money are best invested in simply wandering around the palace's squares and alleyways and visiting its more rewarding museums, especially the **Weltliche und Geistliche Schatzkammer** and the **Völkerkundemuseum** (Ethnological Museum). It is probably best not to attempt to 'do' the Hofburg in one long session but to revisit whenever you find yourself in its vicinity.

An important public thoroughfare connecting the Ringstraße to Kohlmarkt and Graben, Hofburg is open 24 hours a day and is particularly atmospheric after dark. It represents the achievements of a building programme that spanned seven centuries and then came abruptly to a halt with the fall of the Empire after World War I, leaving one major project unfinished.

Whereas the Habsburgs' predecessors, the Babenbergs, had their court on Am Hof, the new rulers set up shop in 1275 in the Burg, a fortress originally built by King Ottokar II of Bohemia on the site of what is today the Schweizerhof. Under

HIS · AEDIBVS
ADHAERET · CONCORS
POPVLORVM · AMOR

The eagle has landed.

Ferdinand III (1521-64) two separate entities, Stallburg and Amalienburg, were added and eventually joined together in the 1660s by the Leopoldinischer Trakt during the reign of Leopold I (1657-1705). The name Schweizerhof comes from the time of Maria Theresia (1740-80) when Swiss guards were billeted here. However, it was under her father Karl IV (1711-40) that some of Hofburg's greatest Baroque architecture was built, namely the Hofbibliothek and the Winterreitschule by Fischer von Erlach, father and son. The square of In der Burg was finally completed in 1893 with the construction of the Michaelertrakt. If the façades of these buildings seem rather dowdy, the Neue Burg, built under Franz Josef's reign, more than makes up for them in terms of sheer pomp and monumentality.

The sprawling seat of the Habsburgs can be roughly divided into four parts – the **Alte Burg**, the oldest section containing the Schatzkammer (treasury) and the Burgkapelle (chapel); **In der Burg**, where Franz Josef and Elisabeth's apartments are located; **Josefsplatz**, access point to the Spanish Riding School, the National Library and numerous minor museums; and finally the **Neue Burg** on Heldenplatz.

For maximum dramatic effect, there are two main approaches to the Hofburg – from the Ringstraße through the Burgtor or from Kohlmarkt by means of the Michaelertor. The former gives you the

The magnificent Michaelertor.

grandiose vista of the immense neo-Classical Neue Burg, the spot where Hitler announced the *Anchluß* to crowds of cheering Viennese. The latter offers a view of the immense copper-domed Michaelertor. Both are overwhelmingly spectacular at night.

ALTE BURG
The core of the palace is the Alte Burg, built around the original fortress (1275). The oldest remaining part is the section of moat running beside the Schweizertor, the entrance to this part.

Weltliche und Geistliche Schatzkammer
The Secular and Sacred Treasuries
1, Schweizerhof (533 7931). U3 Volkstheater, Herrengasse/tram 1, 2, D, J. **Open** 10am-6pm Wed-Mon. **Admission** AS100; AS70 concs. Free English audio-visual guides upon deposit of ID. **No credit cards**.
Undoubtedly the most important of Hofburg's museums, it contains the great treasures of the Holy Roman Empire, fine examples of gold and jewellery and a number of fascinating totemic artefacts. The entrance is beneath the steps to the **Burgkapelle** and is best reached through the Schweizertor. Most of the exhibits were amassed by Ferdinand I (1521-64) but assembled in the Hofburg under the reign of Karl IV in 1712. There are 20 smallish rooms with extremely subdued lighting and labelling entirely in German; however, the entrance price includes the use of a device that gives an English commentary. In the secular section top exhibits include the crown of Rudolph II (room 2) made in 1602 and festooned with diamonds, rubies, pearls and topped with a huge sapphire; the ornate silver cot of Napoleon's son, the Duc de Reichstadt (room 5); an amazing agate bowl once thought to be the Holy Grail, though more likely stolen from Constantinople in 1204, and opposite, the 'horn of the unicorn', a 2.4m (8ft) long narwhal's horn, a gift to Ferdinand I in 1540 from Sigismund II of Poland (room 8, categorised as 'inalienable heirlooms' of the Habsburgs). Room 7 has a massive 2,680-carat Colombian emerald as the centrepiece of the Habsburgs' private collection of sparklers. In the twilight and confusing layout of the rooms be sure not to miss the star attraction: the Byzantine octagonal crown of the Holy Roman Empire, studded with jewels and pearls with a cross protruding from the brow-plate and a bejewelled arch behind. Thought to be the work of a German goldsmith, it was first used at the coronation of Otto I, the first Holy Roman Emperor, in 962. Finally, room 12 contains a number of relics – Karl IV was an inveterate collector – including supposed bits of wood off the Cross, a shred of the tablecloth from the Last Supper and a tooth of John the Baptist!

Burgkapelle
Palace Chapel
1, Schweizerhof (533 9927-71). U3 Volkstheater, Herrengasse/tram 1, 2, D, J. **Open** *Jan-end June, mid-Sept-end Dec* 11am-3pm Mon-Thur; 11am-1pm Fri. **Mass with Boys' Choir** *3 Jan-27 June, 12 Dec-26 Dec* every Sunday incl 25 Dec at 9.15am. **Tickets** cannot be reserved by phone but fax 533

*It's difficult to get your head round the whole of the **Hofburg**.*

9927-75; or try the Palace Chapel's box office, open 11am-1pm, 3-5pm daily.

Dating from the late 1440s, the original Gothic features of the Palace Chapel have been considerably tampered with over the years but the vaulting and wooden statuary are still intact and visible. Unfortunately you can only visit by going on a guided tour or by nursing your hangover with a performance of the execrable Vienna Boys' Choir at 9.15 on Sunday mornings when they are accompanied by members of the Staatsoper.

IN DER BURG

This part comprises the buildings around the large square of the same name opposite the Schweizertor. This is probably the most transited part of the Hofburg with buses, taxis and fiacres all allowed through and groups of tourists swarming near the entrance to the Schatzkammer. The buildings are uniformly Baroque and the square is empty but for the lone statue of Emperor Franz – the first Austrian Emperor and the last of the Holy Roman Empire.

To the south is the Leopoldischer Trakt, now out of bounds as part of the Austrian President's official residence, and opposite is the Reichskanzleitrakt, the section that houses Franz Josef and Sissi's apartments, which are open to the public, though unless you are a serious Habsburg nostalgic, they may seem dull and samey. The passageway beside the Leopoldischer Trakt takes you into Ballhausplatz, scene of the initial disturbances following the announcement of the coalition between the ÖVP and Haider's FPÖ.

Kaiserappartements/Hofsilber- und Tafelkammer

Imperial Rooms and Court Silver and Porcelain Collection

1, Innerer Burghof Kaisertor (533 7570). U3 Volkstheater, Herrengasse/tram 1, 2, D, J. **Open** 9am-4.30pm daily. **Admission** AS80, AS95 combination; AS60 students, AS75 combination; AS40 6-15s, AS50 combination; AS60 OAPs, AS75 combination Wed, Thur. **Credit** AmEx, DC, MC, V.

The Silver and Porcelain Collection gives a pretty good idea of how the Habsburgs liked to entertain, and the 290-piece Sèvres dinner service given to Maria Theresia by Louis XV goes a long way towards explaining why this type of extravagance is no longer tolerated except in a handful of constitutional monarchies and banana republic dictatorships. If you are a serious porcelain fanatic, you'll be in seventh heaven; if not, you could give it a go as it only means a small supplement on the ticket to the Imperial Rooms. The latter only show the rooms of Franz Josef and Sissi – part of the reason for the size of Hofburg was each new tenant's refusal to occupy the rooms of their predecessors – and these are in stark contrast to the opulence of the crockery section. In particular Franz Josef was a frugal old dog whose daily routine consisted of a cold wash at 4am, a spartan breakfast of a bread roll and coffee and then down to affairs of state, while 'his cities snored from the Swiss to the Turkish border', in author Frederic Morton's memorable phrase. Access to the rooms is by means of a splendid marble staircase, which then leads first to Franz Josef's centre of operations, a series of chambers of more or less identical decoration but with the recent helpful addition of informative plaques in English that help bring the rooms to life. The Audienzsaal (Audience Chamber) has a number of paintings by the Biedermeier painter Krafft showing the ups and downs of Franz I's reign – his return to Vienna after defeat by and victory over Napoleon (1809 and 1814 respectively).

Next door in the Audienzimmer you can see the raised desk where Franz Josef stood to receive petitions, a favourite pastime of his. His readiness to award titles to the middle classes, especially to Jews, was always galling to the traditional aristocracy. In his study hangs a portrait of Sissi by Franz Winterhalter, which her husband would occasionally glance at as he assiduously went through his paperwork. He was after all 'the first bureaucrat of the Empire', in popular parlance. His bedroom gives an inkling as to the Emperor's austere lifestyle – no running water, just a bathtub and a fold-away washstand. In the Grand Salon there are pictures and a bust of Field Marshall Radetzky, whose victories in Italy represent the last major Habsburg military successes. Here too is Winterhalter's larger, oft-reproduced portrait of Sissi, exuding a glamour that is difficult to detect in her chambers, which come next. Here any parallel with Princess Diana grinds to a halt in spite of the superficial common ground of marital difficulties, an obsession with the body beautiful and a violent death. In her bedroom and boudoir the fittings are just as spartan as Franz Josef's – simple iron bed, copper bathtub. The paintings, however, are all landscapes and hunting scenes, more in common with Prince Charles than Di. A quirkier note is given by the set of wooden exercise bars, suggesting that Sissi was a forerunner of the modern fad of working out.

Once past the Sissi section there are four rooms known as the Alexander apartments, where Alexander I, Czar of Russia, stayed during the Congress of Vienna in 1815, but bereft of any memento of his passing. Fans of the drama of Mayerling (*see chapter* **Wienerwald**) will enjoy the Small Drawing Room where there are portraits of Prince Rudolf and the lesser known but equally tragic Karl Ludwig (1833-96), Franz Josef's younger brother who died from drinking the contaminated waters of the River Jordan.

JOSEFSPLATZ

Named after Josef II, one of the more progressive of the Habsburgs, who in 1783 ordered the demolition of the wall that encased the square within Hofburg, thus converting it into a public thoroughfare. A large equestrian statue of the iconoclastic Emperor (1807) stands in the middle of the square. Josefsplatz is the scene of one of the key moments in *The Third Man*, when Harry Lime stages his death in a motor accident in front of the Palais Pallavicini – his sumptuous place of residence. The Pallavicini (1784) and the nearby Palais Pálffy are examples of fine 1st district Baroque aristocratic palaces, and the former has an impos-

ing marble staircase adorned with tapestries and a beautiful ivy-covered Hof. Star attractions on Josefsplatz include the **Augustinerkirche**, the **Nationalbibliothek**, the Winterreitschule (home of the Spanish Riding School) and the nearby **Albertina**, one of the world's finest collections of graphic art.

Directly opposite the Albertina in the triangular point of Albertinaplatz is the highly controversial *Monument against War and Fascism* by the Austrian sculptor Alfred Hrdlickla. It consists of four separate elements – two marble blocks symbolising the Gate of Violence; a representation of Orpheus entering Hades; the Stone of the Republic engraved with fragments of an Austrian Declaration of Independence published in 1945; and in the middle, the origin of the outrage, a small bronze statue of a kneeling Jew scrubbing the street clean.

Albertina

Graphische Sammlung Albertina
Main building: *1, Augustinerstraße 1*
Temporary exhibition hall: *Akademiehof, 1, Makartgasse 3 (581 3060/info @albertina.at). U1, U2, U4 Karlsplatz/tram D, J, 1, 2, 62, 65.* **Open** 10am-5pm Tue-Sun. **Admission** AS70; AS35 concs; free under-10s, ICOM members. **No credit cards**.
As you head south from Josefsplatz along Augustinerstraße, the Albertina looks out from its

Monument against War and Fascism.

Palais-a-go-go

With the Habsburg Empire spreading its tentacles throughout Central Europe over seven centuries, it is hardly surprising that the aristocrats of subject nations should have found the need to build some stupendous *pieds-à-terre* in the vicinity of the Court. Vienna has palaces like most cities have cinemas and after years of neglect, the majority have been renovated, usually by the government, cash-rich multinationals and local real estate firms in search of prestige premises. Many are located on and around Herrengasse (Lords' Lane), which as the name suggests, has always been a hotbed of aristocratic activity. Apart from chic office space, these extravagant locations are often used for congresses and corporate entertaining, but some have galleries and restaurants. Here are some of the most prominent and user-friendly.

Palais Harrach

1, Freyung 3. U2 Schottentor.
Housing a branch of the **Kunsthistorisches Museum**, this seventeenth-century palace, designed by Domenico Martinelli, has a couple of galleries, some interesting shops, especially Kalash, and a pricey Italian restaurant. Check the display of Roman antiquities found during restoration work in the window of the latter. Its location on the historic Freyung makes it one of the most transited city palaces.

Palais Ferstel

1, Freyung 2. U2 Schottentor.
Next door to the Harrach, this Renaissance-style palace is the work of Heinrich Ferstel, architect of the **Votivkirche** and the **Universität**. Finished in 1860, Palais Ferstel is perhaps best known as the home of the **Café Central**. Its stoutly columned entrance leads into an Italian-style arcade lined with gift shops. Formerly the seat of the Vienna Stock Exchange, these first floor rooms are now used as corporate entertaining halls.

Palais Esterhazy

1, Wallnerstraße 4. U3 Herrengasse.
The most recently renovated, this enormous late seventeeth-century pile has offices, shops and an Italian restaurant, **Regina Margherita**. Once the home of the Hungarian Esterhazy family whose coat of arms blazes in gold above the entrance, the most interesting part of their complex is the **Esterhazykeller**, a bier keller with vaulted ceilings, dark and conspiratorial in the best Central European tradition. Settle down in an alcove with a Krügel and plan your putsch.

raised emplacement above the old Hofburg ramparts on to the rear of the **Staatsoper**. Dogged by financial difficulties, the restoration of the Albertina, visibly the most dilapidated building of the Hofburg complex, is a long-running saga. During the excavations for the new study rooms and the depository, a medieval tower from the old city wall was discovered – the building plans have been changed to incorporate this tower. Although it has the reputation of being 'one of the world's great collections of graphic art', most of the 1.5 million prints and 50,000 drawings, watercolours and etchings are hidden away in archives with only a small number of facsimiles on show. Now with the opening of a branch of the Albertina in the glass-and-steel Akademiehof, its treasures and those of other collections are finally being exhibited. Even when the Albertina reopens, only special exhibitions will take place because graphics are extremely sensitive to light. The Albertina is also home to Austria's cinématèque, the **Filmmuseum** (*see chapter* **Film**).
Website: www.albertina.at

Augustinerkirche

Church of St Augustin
1, Augustinerstraße 3 (533 7099). U1, U2, U4 Karlsplatz, U3 Herrengasse/tram 1, 2, D, J. **Open** ask about concert times.
The Gothic Church of St Augustin, dating from the early fourteenth century, is an important stop for those on the quest of the Habsburgs' entrails, for here in the Herzgrüftel (Little Heart Crypt) lie their hearts, part of a Spanish imperial tradition to create several focal points of devotion to the Crown. Viewing is only by appointment, though. Free for all to see is Canova's impressive marble memorial to Maria Theresia's daughter Maria Christina and the rococo organ on which Brückner composed his memorable Mass no.3 in F minor. The musical tradition continues and Sunday morning Mass is celebrated with a full orchestra. The church is also famous as the venue for numerous Habsburg weddings such as those of Maria Christina and Franz Stefan, Elisabeth and Franz Josef and Prince Rudolf and Stefanie.

Nationalbibliothek

National Library
1, Josefsplatz (53410-0). U1, U2, U4 Karlsplatz, U3 Herrengasse/bus 2a, 3a. **Open** *Jan-May, end Oct-end Dec* 10am-2pm Mon-Sat. *May-Oct* 10am-4pm Wed, Fri, Sat; 10am-7pm Thur; 10am-2pm Sun.
Entrance to Austria's largest library is through the western side of Josefsplatz and the main reason for going in is to see Fischer von Erlach's Baroque Prunksaal, completed by his son in 1735. An immense tract, it is adorned with marble pillars, an enormous frescoed dome showing the *Apotheosis of Karl IV* by Daniel Gran and gilded wood-panelled bookcases containing over 200,000 works. These include a fifteenth-century Gutenberg Bible and the 15,000 volumes of Prince Eugene of Savoy's collection, which his spendthrift niece sold

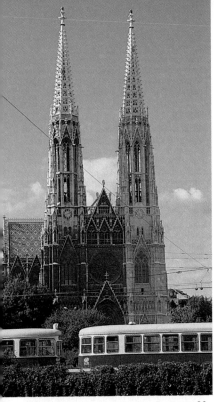

Votivkirche's soaring steeples. See page 60.

to the Habsburgs. Once inside you can also visit the Museums of Globes, Theatre and Esperanto as well as checking out the collections of papyrus and musical scores.

Spanische Reitschule

Spanish Riding School
1, Winterreitschule, Josefsplatz (533 9031). U1, U2, U4 Karlsplatz, U3 Herrengasse, U1, U3 Stephansplatz/bus 2a, 3a. **Open** *Mar-June, Sept, Nov-Dec* 10am-noon Tue-Sat. **Admission** AS100; AS30 children; free 3-6s; no under-3s.
No credit cards.
The world-famous Spanish Riding School and its Lipizzaner horses are in the top five of Vienna's classic tourist attractions, but the exorbitant ticket prices only make it worthwhile for those with a serious interest in dressage. Once inside, though, the splendid Baroque setting and the unnatural posturing of this rare breed give an insight into how divorced from reality the Habsburgs had become. These graceful white horses are a cross between Spanish, Berber and Arab horses and the name commemorates the imperial stud in Lipizza, near Trieste, where they have been bred from 1570 onwards. Built by the son of Fischer von Erlach in 1735, the initiative for the school came from Karl IV whose portrait hangs over the imperial box when the riders enter

the arena they still doff their bicorne hats to him in gratitude. The horses are stabled in the Stallburg (Stables) at Reitschulgasse 2, where there is the **Lipizzaner Museum**, detailing the breed's history with exhibits of riding-related artefacts. On a non-equestrian note, the building is also famous as the scene of the meeting of Austria's first Constitutional Assembly in 1848 and earlier, during the 1815 Congress of Vienna, Beethoven conducted a mammoth concert for the benefit of the delegates.
Website: www.spanische-reitschule.com

NEUE BURG

The monumental Neue Burg overlooking the vast emptiness that is Heldenplatz (Heroes' Square) is the last section of Hofburg to be constructed. Not completely finished until 1926, it was never occupied by a Habsburg. Its monumental neo-Classicism gives Vienna the same air that circulates in all major seats of power, past and present. One can only wonder how it would have looked had Gottfried Semper's plans to construct an identical edifice on the opposite side of the square come to fruition. Of the square's original features, it's worth taking a close look at Anton Fernkorn's two equestrian statues, which face each other – Prince Eugène of Savoy, nearest the Neue Burg, and Karl IV, defeater of Napoleon at Aspern in 1809. The building today houses the main reading room of the National Library and four interesting museums – the collections of weaponry, ancient musical instruments and the Ephesus Museum accessible with a single ticket, and the **Volkerkündemuseum**, which has a separate entrance and ticket. *See chapter* **Museums**. There is no access to the balcony where Hitler actually stood but a good view can be had from inside. Memorable too is the view of the Ringstraße buildings across the Volksgarten, especially the sight of the **Rathaus**, flaunting its municipal power at the moribund monarchy. Some mutations have taken place in the short history of the Neue Burg. The triumphal Burgtor on the Ringstraße side (incorporated within the city walls in 1820) was transformed into a monument to the Austrian dead in World War I by the Austro-Fascists in 1934. The latter also built two entrances to the square either side of the Burgtor, whose stylised eagles represent one of Vienna's rare examples of truly fascistic architecture. Inseparable from the memory of Hitler's triumphal declaration of Austria's incorporation into the Third Reich, it is instructive that the greatest dramatist and enfant terrible of postwar Austria, Thomas Bernhardt, should have titled his most scathing attack on his country's past *Heldenplatz*. On a slightly more positive note, the flags fluttering on the north side of the square mark the headquarters of the Organisation for Co-operation and Security in Europe (OCSE), a hive of diplomatic activity during the 1990s due to the reappearance of genocide in the former Yugoslavia.

In & around Herrengasse

On Michaelerplatz is **Café Griensteidl**, a reconstructed version of what was once one of Vienna's most famous literary cafés and second home to Arthur Schnitzler, Hugo von Hofmannsthal and others. Closed at the turn of the century, it was reopened in 1990. On the opposite side of the square is the Michaelerkirche. A neo-Classical façade hides the church's Gothic origins and these can be seen from a pretty courtyard by entering Kohlmarkt 11, beside the Zsolnay glass and ceramics shop. Notice here too the well-conserved Baroque carriage houses. In the middle of the square there are also some rather nondescript Roman ruins, considered by locals to be the remains of a brothel, which are displayed in a designer recess by Hans Hollein.

West of Michaelerplatz runs Herrengasse – Lords' Lane – lined with innumerable palaces that are today primarily used to house government agencies. The Landhaus at number 13 was until recently the seat of the Lower Austrian regional government. A new administrative centre has been built in the regional capital St Pölten. More interestingly, the building was the scene of the outbreak of the 1848 Revolution when troops fired on a crowd demanding the resignation of the arch-reactionary Prince Metternich. Opposite the Landhaus is the **Palais Ferstel** and **Café Central**.

Schottentor & the Mölker Bastei

As Herrengasse runs to the west it narrows into Schottengasse leading on eventually to the Ringstraße at Schottentor, a busy junction overlooked by the imposing **Votivkirche**. To the north there is a network of fine but rather lifeless nineteenth-century streets, but to the south there is the rare opportunity to see a chunk of the old city walls, the miniscule but picturesque Mölker Bastei. Take the Mölkerstieg steps beside the Julius Meinl store, near the corner of Schottengasse that leads into Schreyvogelgasse. It is here that Harry Lime makes his first appearance in *The Third Man*, in the doorway of number 8. A lot has been made of the house at number 10, the Dreimädlerhaus (1803), where it was purported that Schubert had a carnal interest in the three daughters who lived there. Today it is probably of more interest as the premises of Ludwig Reiter, one of Vienna's finest shoemakers with his finger on the pulse of understated modernity (*see chapter* **Shopping & Services**).

Follow the cobbled street round and you are now on the Mölker Bastei, the old rampart that looks out towards the Neue Universität on the Ringstraße. At number 8 is the **Pasqualatihaus** (1798), where Beethoven lived for a time. The house is a small museum which gives little idea of the chaos of daily life for the tormented genius, certainly nothing of the plates of rotting food and unemptied chamberpots described by his visitors. The museum is open 9am-12.15pm and 1-4.30pm Tuesday to Sunday (535 8905).

Freyung

The name Schottentor (Scots' Gate) refers to the supposedly Scottish Benedictine monks who the Babenbergs invited to run the church and monastery they had founded in 1155. The monks in fact came from Scotia Major (the medieval name for Ireland). One of the many ersatz Irish pubs that flourish in Vienna now (and throughout Europe for that matter) has led a rather absurd campaign to have the name changed. **Schottenstift** (Monastery of the Scots) offered asylum to fugitives in the Middle Ages, which is the origin of the name of the broad tract that runs past the monastery, the Freyung or Sanctuary. Ignore the church and pass through the adjacent entrance to the Schottenhof, a spacious neo-Classical courtyard. There used to be a pleasant café terrace here, but it now belongs to Pizza Hut. On the opposite side is the **Museum in Schottenstift**, a fairly recent creation installed in the rooms of the Prelacy. It has some good seventeenth- and eighteenth-century Dutch, Flemish and Austrian painting, but it is most famed for the Schottenaltar, a fifteenth-century winged altarpiece with its superb painting of *The Flight to Egypt*, with a view of Vienna in the background.

Freyung itself, its broad cobbled pavements flanked by the palaces Harrach and Ferstel to the south and the so-called Schubladlkastenhaus (Chest of Drawers House) (1774), is transformed on Fridays into an impromptu market of organic farmers, apiarists, schnapps distillers and various back-to-the-landers. Further along on the north side is the **KunstForum**, a Bank Austria-sponsored space hosting prestigious itinerant exhibitions of modern painting (*see chapter* **Galleries**).

Running north alongside the KunstForum is the Tiefer Graben, the former bed of the Alserbach, a tributary of the Danube, diverted to avoid flooding. The **Hotel Orient** is located in this street, where luxurious themed rooms can be rented by the hour. Further down the street a raised bridge with Jugendstil railings and streetlights carries Wipplingerstraße over the old river valley, which emerges in Concordiaplatz in the shadow of **Maria am Gestade** (Our Lady of the Riverbank), Vienna's finest Gothic church.

Am Hof

Freyung slopes gently upwards to Am Hof, the biggest square in the Innere Stadt. Formerly the power centre of the Babenberg dynasty and scene of jousts and executions, today it is a little windswept and lifeless except on Fridays and

People's playground: Rathauspark. Page 67.

Saturdays when there is an antique and antiquarian book market. In summer nearby restaurants set up open-air terraces.

Am Hof is dominated by the **Kirche am Hof** from whose balcony the end of the Holy Roman Empire was effectively announced in 1806 when, on the orders of Napoleon, Emperor Franz II proclaimed himself Franz I of Austria. The Gothic core of the church is only seen from the lanes at the back as the façade (undergoing renovation) is resoundingly Baroque and crowned with a host of angels in honour of the Nine Choirs of Angels to whom the church is dedicated.

Other buildings of interest on Am Hof include the Feuerwehr Zentrale, surely the grandest fire station in Christendom, with its Firefighting Museum, the Bürgerliches Zeughaus (the Citizens' Armoury) (1732) at number 10 and a couple of fine Baroque houses at numbers 12 and 13. In the basement of the former is the tenebrous Urbani Keller, the most elaborate and possibly the gloomiest of Vienna's beer cellars, and in the latter, the Palais Collalto where Mozart played his first public concert in Vienna in 1762.

Just past Am Hof, at Bognergasse 9, is the Engelapotheke whose façade adorned with mosaics of two angels and some fine ironwork by pupils of Otto Wagner, is a small masterpiece of Jugendstil decoration. Naglergasse, a narrow street

running parallel to Am Hof, is the natural continuation of Graben. The street was an extension of the same Roman fortifications and has some well-conserved Baroque façades hiding original Gothic houses. It's fairly lively with antique shops, boutiques and pavement cafés and restaurants.

Judenplatz

Leaving Am Hof to the north, an attractive network of ancient lanes and alleyways leads to Judenplatz. In the corner are two more of the small museums that abound in Vienna – the **Uhrenmuseum** (Clock Museum) and the **Puppen- und Spielzeug Museum** (Doll and Toy Museum). The magnificent Baroque Kurrentgasse also has an intriguing plaque at number 4, announcing the soon-to-be-opened First Viennese Museum of Body Art and Video Art.

Kurrentgasse leads north into Judenplatz, the centre of Vienna's first Jewish ghetto, dating back to the twelfth century. Today there is nothing palpably Jewish about it apart from the stars of David on the window panes of the Torah school at the west end, which is currently being renovated. In fact the square has been something of a building site for the last few years since excavations revealed the charred remains of the main synagogue, burnt down in the ferocious pogrom of 1421. Work was undertaken to erect a memorial to Austrian victims of the Shoa by British sculptor Rachel Whiteread.

True to her reputation for controversy, her plans for a monolithic concrete cast of a library have not been to the taste of local residents or the Jewish community, but it seems that it will be unveiled in 2000, some 60 years after the Kristallnacht. Facing Whiteread's monument is a statue of Gottfried Lessing (1729-81), a major figure of the German Enlightenment whose work *Nathan the Wise* was a paean to tolerance towards the Jews. Destroyed by the Nazis, the sculptor Siegfried Charoux, made a new cast after World War II but it was not re-erected until 1982.

At number 2 is Zum Großen Jordan (The Great Jordan), the oldest house in the square. The relief on its façade dates from the sixteenth century and could not be further from the spirit of Lessing, by actually celebrating the events of 1421. Depicting the baptism of Christ, its Latin inscription reads: 'By baptism in the River Jordan bodies are cleansed from disease and evil, so all secret sinfulness takes flight. Thus the flame rising furiously through the whole city in 1421 purged the terrible crimes of the Hebrew dogs. As the world was once purged by the flood, so this time it was purged by fire.'

Apart from the fine apartment buildings, the most spectacular part of the square is the **Böhmische Hofkanzlei** (Bohemian Chancery) from which the Habsburgs ruled over the Czechs

Taking the flak

For an Austrian with a yen for monumental architecture and a love-hate relationship with Vienna, Adolf Hitler left little concrete in the city to remember him by.

His plans for a grandiose extension of Vienna across the Danube never got off the drawing board, and he was too busy with destruction to build mundane things like houses. That leaves the Viennese free to forget their city's role in Hitler's life – were it not for six enormous flak towers, built by forced labourers in 1943-4 to defend Vienna from air-raid attacks.

Arranged in pairs in a triangle around **Stephansdom** the flak towers are about the size of Paris's Arc de Triomphe and speak a far more naked language of power. Their nine-storey windowless towers – some square, some round – are topped by four protruding ears, designed to hold anti-aircraft guns. Inside the reinforced concrete thick walls were air-raid shelters, field hospitals and even a munitions factory.

Their location, always along important axes in the middle of a park close to the city centre, was chosen personally by Hitler. The two most dramatic towers are in the Augarten (2nd district). The first two to be built are in Arenberg Park (3rd district). The pair in the 6th district are separated by a few streets. One is in the centre of the Stiftskaserne barracks and, reportedly, used to store top secret army communications equipment. The other dominates the tiny Baroque Esterházypark and houses the aquatic zoo (*see below*).

The towers were built to last 4,000 years, Hitler boasted. Over 55 years on, they're still going strong. Many Austrians argued for razing the uncomfortable reminders of a past they were doing their best to forget or reinvent. But it soon became clear that would be impossible. Some children playing in one of the flak towers in the **Augarten** ignited several thousand pieces of munition. The massive explosion lifted the roof slightly, leaving an impressive crack

in the wall, now home to hundreds of nesting pigeons. Otherwise it did nothing but break windows in all the houses around the park.

If the towers were to stay, the new thinking went, they should be converted into useful buildings, like the smaller versions that were built in Berlin and Hamburg. There has been no shortage of suggestions. Dozens of architects, including the young Hans Hollein, came up with designs for everything from apartment buildings, to space-age skyscrapers, swimming pools, coffeehouses and museums. The artist Christo wanted to wrap them like he did the Berlin Reichstag, and Friedrich Hundertwasser (famed for his brightening up of incinerators and council housing) wanted to decorate them with some glittering tiles.

The discussions continue to this day, stifled as much by bickering over ownership rights between the federal and city authorities, as by a sense that the flak towers are a healthy reminder of an era most prefer to forget. Incredibly in a city where every second building has its history inscribed on a plaque, festooned with red and white flags, there is nothing to say what these monstrosities are.

Only one tower, so far, has been opened to the public. Handed over to the city of Vienna in 1980, the Esterházypark flak tower houses the **Haus des Meeres** (587 1417; open 9am-6pm daily; admission AS85), an aquatic zoo with a so-so display of sharks, tropical fish and eels on four of the nine storeys. Inside, it's dour.

The city is doing its best to cut the walls down to size. One side is covered in childrens' drawings, for the kindergarten children who use the park's playgrounds. One side has been turned into a practice climbing wall (*see* **Kletterwand am Flakturm** *in chapter* **Sport & Fitness**). And in 2000, the Esterházy flak tower will become the first to be adapted in any major way – the zoo is adding an aquarium, jutting out of one wall.

for almost 300 years. Now the seat of the Constitutional and Administrative Courts, the façade of Fischer von Erlach's Baroque palace that is seen from Judenplatz is actually the rear. As a result of the ravages of the wars of 1809 and 1945 the building had to be patched up and now the main entrance on Wipplingerstraße is obscured by an arched walkway.

Maria am Gestade & around

The recently cobbled Jordangasse leads round into Wipplingerstraße and the **Altes Rathaus**, the Old Town Hall, now a restaurant and home to the interesting **Museum of Austrian Resistance**. Its courtyard encloses a beautiful fountain by Donner, the *Andromeda Brunnen* (1745), and the Gothic Salvatorkapelle, the town hall chapel, whose fine Renaissance portal is best viewed from Salvatorgasse directly behind.

Wipplingerstraße is a bit too traffic-ridden for comfort so it's best to walk east, taking in the enormous sign showing a chimney sweep (a much-loved figure in Viennese mythology) and turn into the cobbled Himmelgasse and follow Salvatorgasse to where **Maria am Gestade** looks over a flight of steps leading down into Concordiaplatz. A curiously narrow edifice, the church originally looked over the Alserbach, a tributary of the Danube, hemmed in on the other side by the houses of Salvatorgasse. The church was always associated with the Danube fishermen and now the Czech community in Vienna. Work began on the church in 1414, around the time **Stephansdom** was being built.

Hoher Markt

You would never think the Hoher Markt, the site of Vindabona's Roman forum, was actually the oldest square in Vienna. To get an idea of what it looked like before the bombs of 1945 and the New Brutalists transformed it, have a look at the engravings in the shop on the corner of Jordangasse and Schultergasse. At midday tourists congregate around the Jugendstil Ankeruhr, an elaborate mechanical clock encrusted into a sort of bridge between the two monumental edifices belonging to the Anker insurance company. The figures that trundle out on the hour include Marcus Aurelius, Roman governor of Vindabona, and composer Josef Haydn. The full list and a history of the clock are given on a plaque in various languages on the insurance building. Beneath the clock there are stone brackets depicting Adam, Eve, an angel and a devil with a pig's snout. Bauernmarkt, which passes underneath, is a swish shopping street with a number of designer stores and eateries. The centrepiece of Hoher Markt is Fischer von Erlach the Younger's *Vermählungsbrunnen* (Marriage Fountain) dramatising Mary's marriage to Joseph, presided over by a high priest – undoubtedly a figment of the sculp-

Take time to clock the Ankeruhr.

tor's Baroque imagination. In the shopping arcade on the south side there is usually access to the Roman ruins – officers' quarters with baths and underground heating – but they are closed to the public at present.

Judengasse & Ruprechtskirche

This area of the Innere Stadt is the focal point of the Jewish history of Vienna and north-east of Hoher Markt is still the city's textile quarter. In spite of the pogroms of the Middle Ages, it was not until the Nazis that the Jewish presence was eradicated from the area. Today the community is located predominantly over the Donaukanal in the 2nd district, but Judengasse and the adjoining streets will forever be associated with the Jews. Photos from the turn of the century show Judengasse as a street full of second-hand clothes dealers and today the rag trade is still visible in the form of small boutiques.

However, in the early 1980s the area comprising Judengasse, Seitenstettengasse and Rabensteig turned into Vienna's main nightlife scene, receiving the moniker of 'The Bermuda Triangle' – the place you can never find your way out of. Today the scene is post-teenie and distinctly untrendy, but there are shedloads of bars and restaurants catering for a fairly well-heeled crowd. During the day the streets are sleepy, often the only presence are the armed police who patrol permanently since the 1983 attack on the Stadttempel, which left three dead.

Built in neo-Classical style by Josef Kornhäusel in 1826, the Synagogue is one of the few that escaped destruction in the Nazi years, probably due to the fact that setting it on fire would have endangered the neighbouring houses. At number 2 is the so-called Kornhäusel-Turm, built by the architect as a studio and, according to local legend, a refuge from his nagging wife. It has some pleasant floral designs on the façade but its sheer size can best be appreciated from behind in Judengasse.

Sterngasse runs off Judengasse to the west, and is worth checking out for the splendid English bookshop **Shakespeare & Co**. At the end of the street a flight of steps named after Theodore Herzl, the Viennese founder of Zionism who dreamt of an Israel full of *Kaffeehäuser* and intellectuals, leads down to Marc-Aurel-Straße.

Walk to the end of Judengasse and you're on a sort of balcony overlooking the busy Franz-Josefs-Kai and the Donaukanal. Among the high-rises of the 2nd district, an area especially punished by bombing, you see the very modest-looking HQ of OPEC, scene of one of Carlos the Jackal's most daring one-man kidnappings in the 1970s. While you're admiring the cityscape from here you may well overlook the ivy-clad **Ruprechtskirche** to your right, the oldest church in the city, whose existence is documented from 1137. Squat and Romanesque, it is a great tonic after Vienna's Baroque excesses. The steps take you down on to a broad concourse, which to the south leads to Schwedenplatz. It's all 1970s cement but the human traffic descending into its busy U-Bahn station or waiting for trams makes it one of those transited zones that Vienna often seems to lack. The ice-cream salon Am Schwedenplatz at number 17 is a local legend.

For a dark twentieth-century-type chill head east from the steps and in Morzinplatz is the *Monument to the Victims of Fascism* (1985) on the site of the old Hotel Metropole, Gestapo HQ during the war and bombed to bits in 1945. The text states: 'For patriotic Austrians, it was a hell. For many others, the forecourt to death. It is in ruins, like the thousand-year Reich. But Austria is resurrected and with Austria, her dead, the immortal victims.' West of here the streets follow a grid-like pattern, full of monumental apartment buildings, but with a rather deserted moribund air. There are a number of lively bars and restaurants along Salzgries, but only dedicated music fans need plod through here to the temple of Viennese nu-beat science, the **Black Market** record store on Gonzagagasse.

In & around Rotenturmstraße

Rotenturmstraße, named after the red tower that capped the city wall, cuts through the northern sec-

tion of the Innere Stadt. Lively and commercial, it is a good pointer for those unfamiliar with the city. At its most northerly point it divides the Bermuda Triangle zone from the medieval streets around Fleisch Markt, the old meat market. The latter is a hotch-potch of old and new, but with a little careful observation. There are some minor sights to enjoy. At number 7 for instance, film fans will get a buzz out of the plaque marking Billy Wilder's home when he was a schoolboy in Vienna. Opposite at number 14 there is a fine Jugendstil façade and next door leads to a pleasant Hof, home to Vienna's first vegetarian restaurant **Siddhartha** (*see chapter* **Restaurants**) and HQ of the Austrian Buddhist Society. The street widens at number 11 where the narrow Griechengasse descends towards Schwedenplatz.

Facing the staircase is the late eighteenth-century Greek Orthodox church. No longer in use, services are now held at Hansen's flamboyant Griechische Kirche (1861), full of gilt and decorative brickwork, on Fleisch Markt. Built for Greek subjects of the Habsburgs, this Byzantine fantasy is the most arresting edifice on the street, but with two carpet stores on its ground floor, it is hard to believe it is still a place of worship. Sunday is the best day to get inside as during the rest of the week it's hard to get beyond the dark yet ornate arcaded hallway.

Adjoining the church at number 11 is another of those veritable Viennese institutions, the **Griechenbeisl**, one of Vienna's oldest restaurants, with connections to the Greek community and famous patrons like Beethoven, Brahms and Schubert (*see also chapter* **Beisln**). Needless to say, it's a bit of a tourist trap.

Fleischmarkt runs directly into Postgasse (there is a 24-hour post office at number 8-10) and winds its way round into the beautiful Schönlaterngasse with its fine Baroque façades, such as the Basilikenhaus at number 7. At number 5 is the enormous **Heiligenkreuzerhof**, a fine courtyard bounded by mid-eighteenth century outbuildings which was the city premises of the Cistercian monks of Heiligenkreuz (*see chapter* **Wienerwald**). Originally an outlet for the monastery's produce, the buildings are now to-die-for apartments with the occasional gallery on the ground floor. The courtyard's delightful Berhardskappelle is popular for society weddings. Schönlaterngasse, the street of the Beautiful Lanterns (check the one on number 6) comes out on Sonnenfelsgasse, which, along with the parallel Bäckerstraße, run from the Altes Universität (or now Dr-Ignaz-Seipel-) Platz to Lügeck, on Rotentürmstraße.

Apart from the Renaissance portal at number 15 and the excellent Kunstbuchhandlung (one of the best art bookshops in Vienna) at number 8, the most noteworthy building in Sonnenfelsgasse is the massive Baroque Hildebrandthaus at number

*It's all Greek to me: the statuary of the **Parlament**. See page 67.*

3. In its entrails is the **Zwölf-Apostelkeller** (Twelve Apostles Cellar), Vienna's largest and best-loved bierkeller *(see chapter* **Heurigen***)*.

Bäckerstraße also has a handful of remarkable houses with interesting façades and courtyards, such as the marvellous Renaissance Hof at number 7, the premises of violin and piano manufacturers. The **Alt Wien** *(see chapter* **Nightlife***)* at number 19 is a place worth remembering for later in the day. Note also the bizarre patch of mural that was unearthed during restoration work at number 12, showing a bespectacled cow playing backgammon with a wolf. This is supposedly a parody of the tension between Catholics (the cow) and Protestants (the wolf) in seventeenth-century Vienna.

To the east Bäckerstraße opens out into Dr-Ignaz-Seipel-Platz and the buildings of the Alte Universität, the Academie der Wissenschaft (Academy of Sciences) and the Jesuitenkirche. The square is remarkable for its absence of modern buildings, but once you're through the tunnel on the southern side, it's back to the spaciousness of the Ringstraße.

The Ringstraße heavyweights

Well into the 1850s, unlike other European cities of a similar stature, Vienna still conserved its city walls beyond which lay a vast area of greenbelt known as the *Glacis*, principally used as a military parade ground but to some extent converted into a recreational area by the 'people's emperor' Josef II. In an edict pronounced on Christmas Day 1857,

Emperor Franz Josef initiated a building pro-gramme that gave the city the face it bears today. The broad, horseshoe-shaped Ringstraße con-structed along this tract of land was to Vienna what the *grands boulevards* were to Paris – a thor-oughfare designed to quell revolt by ensuring the rapid movement of troops to scenes of unrest. Nevertheless its very existence is a testimony to the democratisation of public life in nineteenth-cen-tury Vienna, following the 1848 Revolution.

While the first Ringstraße building, the **Votivkirche**, was built to reaffirm imperial abso-lutism, the military defeats of 1859 and 1866 and the advent of a constitutional monarchy in 1867 forced a reassessment of the aims of the whole pro-gramme, gradually leading to an emphasis on buildings of public utility – the city hall, the uni-versity, the parliament, the museums, the opera house, the Burgtheater and the numerous parks and gardens. The array of buildings takes some beating when it comes to sheer pomp and imperi-al ostentation. 'A martian coming to earth would unhesitatingly land at Vienna, thinking it to be the capital of the planet.' Bill Bryson's remarks are close to the mark. Athough heralding a new age, the architects of the Ringstraße, apart from Otto Wagner's **Postsparkasse**, contributed nothing in the way of innovation, preferring the models of the past to express the aspirations of the bur-geoning Viennese middle classes, a style baptised as Historicism.

Think of a day along the Ringstraße as a way to refresh your knowledge of the principal

European architectural styles. Each section of the Ringstraße has its own name, such as the Burgring for the stretch that passes the **Hofburg**. Apart from the civic buildings there are also an enormous number of palatial apartment buildings, which, according to dissident architect Adolf Loos, enabled Viennese landlords to fulfill their wish to own a palace and their tenants' to live in one. It is often alleged that the nouveau riche were encouraged to buy plots on the Ringstraße in return for aristocratic titles, bestowed by Franz Josef himself. No longer the des res they once were – the traffic has put paid to that – they now tend to be used as offices. Shops located on the Ringstraße are also on the decline as high rents dissuade retailers and draconian parking restrictions make access difficult.

GETTING AROUND THE RINGSTRAßE

The best way to familiarise yourself with what is actually on offer and get an idea of the dimensions of the inner core of Vienna is to take a tram ride round the whole Ring, which takes in the canal embankment too, not strictly speaking a part of the Ringstraße. Tram 1 goes round clockwise and number 2 anticlockwise and the drivers of both take a five-minute fag-break in front of the Stadtpark. Just wait patiently.

Generally the tram is a better bet than the U-Bahn, as stations tend to be located further away from the sights. Although a bit of a slog, the whole thing could be walked in less than an hour. Care should be taken to avoid cyclists, especially messenger services, who speed along the cycle paths on the pavement with a zeal that recalls the worst excesses of motorists.

Donaukanal to Schottentor

The Schottenring (the Scots' Ring) is probably the least interesting stretch of the Ringstraße and is best negotiated by tram. Named after the Benedictine monks who established a church and monastery just inside the city walls in the late twelfth century, it does, however, have a number of remarkable buildings and Vienna's only inner city high-rise, the Ringturm (1955), which looks over the Donaukanal, cutting quite a dash with its night time illumination.

On the opposite side of the Ringstraße, between two apartment buildings, you get a glimpse of the Roßauer Kaserne, a bizarre red-brick barracks, one of three built in the wake of the 1848 Revolution and still occupied by forces of coercion – the police this time. The finest public building along here, at Schottenring 20, is the Börse (stock exchange), built by one of the major Ringstraße architects, Theophil Hansen. The subdued red of the brickwork (Hansenrot as it is often referred to) and the white stone of its cornices make it one of the Ringstraße's most elegant edifices.

Schottentor to Oper

Two of the major visual attractions along this section of the Ring are the **Kunsthistorisches Museum** and the **Naturhistorisches Museum** and the gardens that separate them. Described by Jan Morris in her readable but damning essay on Vienna as 'the most museumy museums' she had ever clapped eyes on, there can be little doubt as to their purpose. The work of Gottfried Semper, brought in from Germany when Ferstel and Hansen's plans were turned down on account of their primacy of form over function, was part of a grandiose plan to link these museums to the planned extension to the Imperial Palace by means of two triumphal arches across the Ringstraße. The building of this monumental Kaiserforum was interrupted by World War I and finally ditched after the fall of the House of Habsburg. Vienna is left with one of the world's finest collections of paintings, in the most part from the sixteenth and seventeenth centuries. Particularly astounding is the collection of Dutch and Flemish painting, which includes the largest number of Brueghels in the world. It is difficult to work up a lot of enthusiasm for the sombre Museum of Natural History with its moth-eaten taxidermy and scant interest in following the worldwide trend of interactive museums combining fun and learning.

Votivkirche

9, Rooseveltplatz. U2 Schottentor/tram 1, 2, D.
The Votivkirche is built on the spot where Franz Josef survived an assassination attempt by a Hungarian nationalist in 1853. Work began in 1854 before the edict to demolish the city walls was even published, and was finally completed 25 years later, owing to the exacting standards of craftsmanship demanded by the 27-year-old architect Heinrich Ferstel. Set in Rooseveltplatz with the Sigmund Freud Park in front, the Votivkirche is an impressive sight – its two monumental steeples rendered with elaborate stone carving recall the great Gothic cathedral of Chartres. However, there is something moribund about it, possibly because it never had any real parishioners apart from the soldiers of the nearby barracks, the similarly monumental Roßauerkaserne. It is also beset with restoration problems and often draped in screen-printed advertising hoardings in a desperate attempt to raise funds.

Universität

1, Karl-Lueger-Ring. U2 Schottentor/tram 1, 2, D.
If the Votivkirche was built at the direct behest of the Emperor, its neighbour the new university is probably the Ringstraße building that had to fight the hardest to gain a frontline position on the boulevard. Due to its decisive role in the events of 1848, the university was very much out of favour with the forces of reaction and it was not until 1870 that the site was secured and work begun in 1873. With that master of pastiche Heinrich Ferstel in command once again, he received the brief to build in

*Burgher me – the **Rathaus**.*

Renaissance style echoing the secular universities of Italy, much to the chagrin of teaching staff who favoured a more rational style for the furtherance of the natural sciences. It is easy to gain access to the university in term time and a walk around the arcades of the inner courtyard is very pleasant. It is also worth attempting to get into the Grosser Festsaal, the main hall, to see Klimt's ceiling frescoes depicting the seven pillars of wisdom. If you go in through the main entrance on the Ringstraße, the Festsaal is clearly marked, but it is not officially open to the public. With a bit of luck you may coincide with one of the graduation ceremonies frequently held there.

Rathaus

1, Rathausplatz. U2 Rathaus/tram 1, 2, D.

Forming the centrepiece of Rathausplatz and its gardens (something of a cruising zone at night), the town hall is undoubtedly the most imposing edifice on the Ringstraße. Inspired by Flemish Gothic and bearing more than a passing resemblance to the Hôtel de Ville of Brussels, Friedrich Schmidt's building is clearly visible from the Hofburg and was a constant reminder to the court that the burghers were now running the show. Spare a moment for the poor functionaries who had to work in its gloomy labyrinthine offices before the advent of electric light. Visitors are free to wander through the seven inner courtyards, but must join a guided tour to see the elaborate interior decoration and numerous frescoes illustrating

scenes from Vienna's past. Open to the public too is the vast Rathaus Keller, a rather touristy cellar serving beer and roast pork, one of many such establishments in and around the 1st district. Flanked by the Universität to the north, the Parlament to the south and the Burgtheater opposite on the other side of the Ringstraße, the Rathausplatz has become something of a people's playground since the early 1990s when the popular Socialist mayor Helmut Zilk took it upon himself to liven up the city's rather dreary nightlife. Throughout the summer filmed operas are shown on a giant screen in front of the town hall and the square is inundated with stands offering eats and drinks. If opera isn't your bag, you may find the atmosphere a tad conventional and the prices mildly abusive. Still, Zilk's initiative had a domino effect and numerous public spaces are now used in summer for everything from alfresco dining to open-air cinemas.

Parlament

1, Karl Renner-Ring 3. U2, U3 Volkstheater/tram 1,2, D.

Like the Rathaus, the neo-classical Danish architect Theophil Hansen's Parlament stares across the Ring at the Imperial Palace to the east. Bristling with Hellenic statuary and bronze chariots for want of home-grown democratic symbolism, the façade of the building appears obscured by the two lateral ramps and the rather splendid statue of Athena, set in a fountain representing the Danube, Inns, Elbe and Moldau. Architecturally as problematic as the birth of Austrian democracy itself, seen face on from pavement or tram-window level it looks pitifully small. In a practical sense too, it suffered from indifferent acoustics. Nevertheless it is worth a walk up the ramp to take a closer look at the recently restored frontal frieze of Franz Josef I granting the first, highly limited democratic constitution.

Messepalast

Beyond the park that separates the two museums and the busy road running parallel to the Ringstraße lies the Messepalast, originally the imperial barracks and stables and later converted into a trade fair centre (the origin of its present name). With trade fairs now held in a section of the Prater, this complex is the monumental building site of the projected Museumsquartier, intended to replace the temporary solution of the Portakabin-like **Kunsthalle** on Karlsplatz. For many years this complex of overgrown dilapidated buildings was very pleasant to stroll through and food and drinks were, and still are, available at the bucolic **S'glacisbeisl**, located right at the back of the complex (and heavily signposted). Some parts of Fischer von Erlach's original building are being used as additional exhibition space by the Kunsthalle as well as housing the Public Net Base, a state initiative that was designed to promote the cyber-world as a panacea for the planet's ills.

The Ringstraße Parks

On the southside of the Ringstraße there is no shortage of inviting green areas where the weary walker can rest away from the hubbub of the traffic. In all there are three major parks or gardens, each offering a variety of curiosities from statues and Graeco-Roman temples to rare plants and purveyors of controlled substances. Some of the buildings are increasingly becoming the hottest nightspots in town due to their attractive locations and the fact that they are out of earshot of Vienna's extremely grumpy residents. There is also a good selection of kiosks, terraces and even a converted botanical garden serving food and drinks.

Volksgarten

People's Garden

Main entrance: Heldenplatz (opposite the Neue Burg).
U2, U3 Volkstheater, U3 Herrengasse/tram 1, 2, D,
J/bus 2a. **Open** *Apr-Oct* 6am-10pm daily. *Winter*
6am-8pm daily.

In-spite of its egalitarian-sounding name, the Volksgarten was originally a playground for Vienna's beau monde at the turn of the nineteenth century. Built after Napoleon's troops demolished the southern section of the city walls, it is slightly ironic that the gardens were later laid out in such a frenchified manner. The centrepiece is the Doric Theseus-Tempel, commisioned by Napoleon as a replica of the Theseion in Athens to house Canova's statue of Theseus and the Minotaur. This statue was moved to the staircase of the **Kunsthistorisches Museum** when it opened in 1890 and the temple has lacked a raison d'être ever since.

Dear to the hearts of many Austrians is the statue of Empress Elisabeth (1837-98) at the northern corner. Today the name **Volksgarten** (*see chapter* **Nightlife**) is synonymous with the large semi-open air discotheque over the Ringstraße from the museums and the superb **Pavilion** next door, a sleek 1950s construction where the tuned-in and turned-on of Vienna drink Caipirihnas to dope beats in the shadow of the Neue Burg.

Burggarten

The Palace Gardens

Main entrance: Burgring. U1, U4 Karlsplatz/tram 1,
2, D, J. **Open** *Apr-Oct* 6am-10pm daily. *Winter* 6am-8pm daily.

The Burggarten is almost the polar opposite of the Volksgarten, leafy, informal, with great expanses of lawn ideal for summer frolicking. With the completion of the restoration work on the magnificent turn-of-the-century **Palmenhaus** (*see chapter* **Nightlife**) the gardens now attract a good crowd. Previously the place was the preserve of tourists who come to photograph the marble **Mozart Denkmal**. This statue of the boy-wonder, set on a plinth depicting scenes from *Don Giovanni*, was moved to its present location in 1953 from Augustinerplatz where it was originally unveiled in 1896.

Schmetterlinghaus

Butterfly House

(533 8570/fax 532 2872). U1, U4 Karlsplatz/tram
1, 2, D, J. **Open** *Apr-Oct* 10am-4.45pm Mon-Fri;
10am-6.45pm Sat, Sun. *Nov-Mar* 10am-3.45pm daily.

Admission AS65; AS45 concs; AS30 3-6s. **No credit cards.**

Situated beside the Palmenhaus in the Burggarten is the Schmetterlinghaus, which was opened in 1999. Originally built in steel and glass with Jugendstil decoration in 1901 by Friedrich Ohmann, it lay in disuse for years. Now it is home to around 40 different species acquired from butterfly farms in Thailand, Costa Rica and Brazil, none of them rare or endangered. Several hundred butterflies fly freely in 85% humidity amid a welter of tropical vegetation, large trees and a waterfall.

Stadtpark

City Park

Main entrance: Johannesgasse (beside Stadtpark U-
Bahn station). U2 Stadtpark, U3 Stubentor/tram 1,
2. **Open** 24 hours a day, all year.

The largest of the Ringstraße parks, the Stadtpark stretches from just east of Schwarzenbergplatz to Stubentor going beyond the causeway of the Wien river, itself notable more for an aesthetic approach to public works than to its natural beauty. The main entrance is flanked by superb stone-carved Jugendstil colonnades, just south of the most emblematic building in the park, the neo-Renaissance Kursalon, a venue for rather tacky Strauß concerts. Apart from tourists and kipping office workers, it is also the stomping ground of benign dope dealers. Music is very much the theme of the park and the schmaltzy but nonetheless finely executed statue of Johann Strauß junior draws as many amateur photographers as Mozart's in the Burggarten. Scattered around the park are also busts of Schubert, Bruckner and Lehár, he of *The Merry Widow*. The tradition continues today just across the river at the **Meierei**, an OAPs meeting point during the day and several nights a week another DJ temple where Vienna's finest, Kruder & Dorfmeister, regularly spin the discs.

The Ringstraße & the high arts

Trouble and strife in the world of theatre, opera and classical music are virtually affairs of state in Austria and it is not uncommon for even the local tabloids to lead with such stories. Naturally the vast majority of Vienna's temples to high art are located on the Ringstraße itself or a stone's throw away. The world-famous **Staatsoper** (State Opera House) was the first public building to be opened on the hallowed street in May 1869. Due to its location between the highly transited Kärntner Straße and Karlsplatz, it is probably the single Ringstraße building Viennese citizens see most often on a daily basis.

For many years the **Opernball** (*see page 231* **Having a ball**) with its ostentatious show of wealth and monarchic nostalgia, was the focus of virulent left-wing/anarchist demonstrations, culminating in a massive pitched battle on the visit of Franz Josef Strauß (the Bull of Bayern) in the early 1990s. Things have calmed down consider-

Kunsthistorisches Museum – *a 'most museumy museum'. See page 66.*

ably in recent years but the police still maintain almost absurdly tight security on the night. Spirits also run high both in and around the **Burgtheater**, possibly the most important theatre in the German-speaking world (*see chapter* **Theatre & Dance**).

Down a side street off the Ringstraße behind the **Imperial Hotel** lies Vienna's foremost concert hall, the **Musikverein**, home to the illustrious Vienna Philharmonic and venue of the annual New Year's Day concert. The Musikverein is Theophil Hansen's most extravagant work, for some the culminating work of Historicist decoration. The elaborate gilded ornamentation of the suspended ceiling is best appreciated by attending a concert. Getting tickets, however, is complicated as most go to subscription holders, a privilege in Vienna akin to being a season ticket holder at Barcelona. The Philharmonic has recently had its fair share of scandal due to some less than satisfactory performances, and only in 1999 did it finally abandon its ridiculous policy of only contracting male musicians. *See also chapter* **Music: Classical & Opera**.

Oper to the Donaukanal

South-east of the **Staatsoper** the Ringstraße takes the name Kärntnerring, acknowledging the historic route south to the province of Kärnten that bisects it at this point. This is the Ringstraße at its most bustling and commercial – opera-goers dressed to the nines, loose-jawed substance abusers emerging from the underground precinct leading to Karlsplatz and Asian newspaper sellers dressed in fluorescent jackets advertising the names of Austrian dailies are among the pavement fauna. Here too are the big names of Vienna's hotel trade – the **Sacher**, the **Bristol** and the **Imperial**, with the presence of armed police advertising the visit of some international dignitary.

From the Staatsoper to the next major junction at Schwarzenbergplatz, shoppers spill out of recently inaugurated **Ringstraßen Gallerien**, a squeaky-clean upmarket shopping centre that extends almost the full length of the block.

Schwarzenbergplatz

Where Kärntnerring turns into Schubertring the Ringstraße opens out into a vast rectangular concourse named after Karl von Schwarzenberg, hero of the Battle of Leipzig (1813) and member of one of the Empire's most influential aristocratic families. His equestrian statue stands amid the constant stream of today's iron horses that make the square a nightmare to cross on foot. The square is lined with monumental buildings such as the seat of the Austrian Employers Association and the **Kasino am Schwarzenberg**, a small auditorium belonging to the Burgtheater. At the far end of the square stands the *Russen Heldendenkmal* (Russian Heroes' Monument), a gift from the Soviet people commemorating their soldiers' role in the liberation of Vienna. This enormous column topped with a standard-bearing soldier holding a gilded shield has had various nicknames since it

The redesigned **Vienna Museum of Technology** is one of the oldest technology museums in the world, ranking alongside the major museums of technology in Paris, London and Munich.

The Museum wants to be a place where various perceptions of the nature and meaning of technology can be examined. It offers a wide range of information in following areas: "Nature and Knowledge", "Images of Technology", "Heavy Industry", "Energy", "Musical Instruments", Innovation Forum", "Transportation" and the "Mini-TMW" (for children aged between 3 and 6).

For its presentation the Museum utilizes different forms of media, such as images, models, video displays, and audio-based stations which are accompanied by the necessary information.

Address: **Mariahilfer Straße 212, 1140 Vienna**
Open: daily
Tel. **++43-1-89998-6000 (Information)**
Mail: mbox@tmw.ac.at
Internet: www.tmw.ac.at

Art at the Turn of the Century-Collection
Klimt–Schiele–Kokoschka

Special Exhibition, 09 | 20 | 2000 – 01 | 07 | 2001
Klimt–Painter of Women

Visit the Jewish Museum Vienna!

The museum is located in the historical centre of the city, at Palais Eskeles in Dorotheergasse 11. Besides from the permanent exhibitions the museum offers temporary exhibitions relating to a diversity of Jewish topics in the domains of literature, architecture, photography, and modern art.

Jewish Museum Vienna
A-1010 Vienna, Dorotheergasse 11

Opening hours:
Sunday to Friday 10 a.m. to 6 p.m.
Thursday 10 a.m. to 8 p.m.

Information and guided tours:
Phone +43-1-535 04 31, ext. 25
Fax: +43-1-535 04 24
E-mail: info@jmw.at
Internet: http//www.jmw.at

*Saving grace: Otto Wagner's **Postsparkasse**, a beacon of modernity on the Ringstraße.*

was erected in 1945, which range from the quaint *Erbsenpepi* – an allusion to the *Erbsen* (dried peas) handed out by the Russians as rations and to Pepi, the Viennese diminutive of Josef (Stalin) – to the 'unknown rapist', a reference to abuses on the civil population during the liberaton of Vienna. Aware of its unpopularity, the Soviets had a clause written into the 1955 Austrian State Treaty obliging the Austrians to pay for its upkeep. In front of the column is the *Hochstrahlbrunnen* (Tall Fountain), built in 1873 in honour of Vienna's first mains water supply and tall enough to block it from view.

On the west side is the elegant art nouveau French embassy (1912), whose vaguely oriental façade gave rise to the rumour that the building plans for France's embassy in Istanbul had been mistaken for those of Vienna. On nearby Zaunergasse is the recently inaugurated **Arnold Schönberg Center**, an archive, library and concert hall dedicated to the King of Klanger.

Back on the corner of Schwarzenberggasse stands one of the Ringstraße's poshest cafés, the **Café Schwarzenberg**, whose terrace is a magnet for the Euro-trash holed up in the nearby five-star hotels. Like **Café Landtmann** beside the Burgtheater, the pricey Schwarzenberg has suffered from over-scrupulous renovation and is best avoided.

Parkring & Stubenring

Beyond Schwarzenbergplatz the north side of the Ringstraße is lined with more top-of-the-range hotels overlooking the **Stadtpark** to the south. On foot it is more enjoyable to cut through the park and check out its memorials to Strauß et al, or in summer, stop and listen to the free concerts held in the afternoon in front of the Kursalon, the temple of the waltz. At Stubentor things pick up a little and on this last stretch of the Ringstraße there are a couple of top-class sights. Those in need of a little rest and refreshment before taking on the nearby **Museum für Angewandte Kunst** (MAK) and Otto Wagner's **Postsparkasse** are well advised to visit the most attractive Ringstraße Kaffeehaus, the **Café Prückel** on the corner of Karl-Lueger-Platz. With high ceilings and decorated with discreet 1950s tat, the Prückel has an understated bohemian ambience and a small flea-market in the basement next to the toilets.

Directly opposite the Postsparkasse is the ex-Kriegsministerium (Ministry of War), which today houses less bellicose sections of the civil service. This neo-Baroque monster was only completed in 1912 and demonstrates how little had changed ideologically and architecturally since the first Ringstraße building, a barracks, was erected in the 1850s. Walk 500 metres east and you reach the Donaukanal with its characteristic green railings. Overlooking the canal is the curious **Urania**, an observatory completed in 1910 by Max Fabiani and now a cinema and children's puppet theatre.

Postsparkasse
Post Office Savings Bank
1, Georg-Coch-Platz 2. U3 Stubentor/tram 1, 2.
Open 8am-3pm Mon-Wed, Fri; 8am-5.30pm Thur.

Built over an eight-year period from 1904-1912 and slotted into a narrow gap between apartment buildings, Otto Wagner's Postsparkasse, the most monumental of Vienna's Modernist buildings, would benefit from a more spacious emplacement. However, its conception as an alternative home for middle-class savings to the powerful Jewish-dominated banking houses of the late nineteenth century shrouds Wagner's building in an unpleasant cloud of anti-Semitism. With that in mind perhaps it's not such a tragedy that the building was denied first-line status. Quite unlike anything else along the Ringstraße, the Postsparkasse shines like a beacon of modernity with its economy of ornamentation and radical choice of materials – the façade, with its slabs of grey marble held in place by aluminium studs (17,000 in all), is crowned by the institution's name rendered in unmistakable Jugendstil lettering overseen by stylised angels of victory wielding laurel wreaths. Still functioning as a bank, the Postsparkasse and its wealth of elegant functional details can be seen during normal business hours.

Landstraße

One of Vienna's largest inner city districts, the 3rd, takes its name from Landstraßer Hauptstraße, the busy street that heads south-east from the **Stadtpark** in the direction of Hungary. The district itself is bordered to the east by the Donaukanal and reaches as far south as Erdberg, at the end of the U3 U-Bahn line. Sights are spread out over the whole area so some kind of public transport pass is recommended.

When Count Metternich, a resident of the area for many years (his home is now the Italian embassy at Rennweg 27), coined his famous phrase *In Wien fängt die Orient an* ('The Orient starts in Vienna') it is commonly thought that he was referring to the 3rd district. Alternately chic residential and Ostbloc grim, Landstraße has a variety of sights appealing to all tastes. Top of the list has to be the magnificent **Belvedere Palace** just south of Schwarzenbergplatz.

In the vicinity of the palace there are two interesting museums – the **Heeresgeschichtliches Museum** and the **Museum des 20.Jahrhunderts** – the area of Rennweg with the city's main diplomatic quarter and a number of fine buildings and churches. Down towards the canal, east of Landstraßer Hauptstraße, are two curious buildings by the dippy-hippy Austrian artist Friedensreich Hundertwasser, which, despite the disapproval of the city's intelligentsia, are fast becoming some of Vienna's most popular tourist attractions.

Further afield still tram enthusiasts may want to check out the **Straßenbahnmuseum**, Mozart fanatics and cemetery freaks the ancient **St Marxer Friedhof** and architecture aficionados the Gasometern, three nineteenth-century gas

deposits currently being converted into a residential/leisure centre by the much celebrated Coop Himmelb(l)au team.

Located in a godforsaken part of the 3rd district, complete with adjacent motorway flyover, St Marxer Friedhof was the first of Vienna's outer-limits cemeteries, built on the orders of the reform-minded Josef II, when he decided to close all the cemeteries of the Innere Stadt for hygienic reasons in the 1780s. No one has been buried here since 1874. By far the most illustrious corpse to be laid to rest in St Marx was Mozart, given a pauper's burial in a mass grave in 1791. For many years his untimely end fuelled the myth that in Vienna more than anywhere, no one is a prophet in their own land. The truth is more prosaic. Mozart's death coincided with Josef II's diktat, making mass burial the norm. His wife Constanze's later attempts to pinpoint the exact place of burial, an impossible quest, eventually led to the erection of the so-called *Mozartgrab*, featuring an angel in mourning and a truncated pillar representing his early death. A plan of the graves is available at the entrance. In the summer you could tie in an early evening visit to St Marx with a night at **Szene Wien**, one of Vienna's best live music venues.

Belvedere

The palace consists of two separate entities – the **Unteres** (Lower) and **Oberes** (Upper) **Belvedere**, located at either end of an expanse of French gardens on three levels.

The upper part is by far the most impressive and is considered to be one of the finest secular Baroque buildings in Europe. Approaching from the north, the sight of the façade is marvellous, but the main entrance to the palace is actually on the southern side. Building was commissioned by Prince Eugene of Savoy, master strategist of the defeat of the Turks, which eventually led to Vienna embarking on a construction boom that produced the jewels of the city's Baroque era. Having acquired the land in 1697, Prince Eugene had to wait until 1714, by which time he had received his share of the booty from the Emperor, to actually start building. With Fischer von Erlach's great rival Lukas von Hildebrandt at the helm, the two palaces were completed in record time – the Unteres Belvedere in two years (1714-16) and the Oberes Belvedere, amazingly, in only one (1721-2). While the lower palace became the Prince's residence and offices for the administration of his estates, the monumental Oberes Belvedere served as a representational palace for receptions, negotiations and feasts. Eugene was something of a Renaissance man with a keen interest in botany and zoology as well as military strategy. He established various gardens on the eastern side of the grounds, which contained his aviary and

Belvedere – *the gardens separating upper and lower afford magnificent views of Vienna.*

menagerie – once home to the first giraffe to survive in captivity in Central Europe. The Alpine Garden further to the south can be visited but the rest is occupied by the University Botanical Gardens, with no public access. After the Prince's death the Belvedere passed to his niece Viktoria, an extravagant fool who ended up selling the contents of the library to the Habsburgs and the picture collection all over Europe. In 1752 Maria Theresia bought the Belvedere itself and in 1776 Josef II had the imperial picture collection moved there. Three years later the gardens were opened to the public.

The last resident of the Belvedere was Archduke Franz Ferdinand, later of Sarajevo fame, who set up a rival court there. The Belvedere returned to the political limelight in 1934 when Schuschnigg, Chancellor of the Austro-Fascist government, used it as his residence, and again in 1955, when it was the scene of the signing of the Austrian State Treaty that established Austria as an independent neutral state by sanctioning the withdrawal of the occupying powers.

Rennweg

Rennweg slopes up the eastern side of the Belvedere from Schwarzenbergplatz. During the week there are usually enormous queues outside number 3, an early Otto Wagner house with fine reliefs at the top hinting towards Jugendstil, now the Yugoslav embassy. The queuers are applying for visas or waiting to pay the exorbitant sum of around AS30,000 for the privilege of giving up Yugoslavian citizenship in order to get an Austrian passport.

Number 5 is also a Wagner house where Gustav Mahler lived from 1898 to 1909. Opposite the entrance to the Unteres Belvedere there's an even bigger crowd filing in and out of the Gardekirche (1763) where the Polish community celebrates Mass every Sunday. Although the façade has been given a neo-Classical dressing down, the interior remains exuberantly rococo. It's worth taking a stroll down Salesianergasse (named after the Salesianerkirche on Rennweg with its splendid green dome) and along Jaurèsgasse, the heart of the diplomatic area. The British, German and Russian delegations are all located here, but the real treat is the rather badly conserved onion-domed Russian Orthodox church at number 2. Beyond the S-Bahn line is Ungargasse where at number 59-61 is the Max Fabiani Portois & Fix building (1900) with an Otto Wagneresque tiled façade in shades of green with Jugendstil ironwork on the top floor. Further north is the Neulinggasse where there are two of Vienna's six World War II *Flaktürmen* (anti-aircraft towers) in the adjacent Arenberg Park (*see page 62* **Taking the flak**).

Prinz-Eugen-Straße

Running parallel to the Belvedere on the western side, Prinz-Eugen-Straße, dividing the 3rd and 4th districts, has its fair share of imposing edifices, many of which are today embassies. Near

A masterpiece of Baroque: **Karlskirche**.

the corner with Schwarzenbergplatz is the discreet entrance to **Palais Schwarzenberg** (1720), now a five-star hotel but originally built by Fischer von Erlach and son for Adam Franz von Schwarzenberg, Chief Equerry to Emperor Karl VI. Its present owner reputedly thanked Elizabeth II for 'bombing my palace into a profitable hotel'.

A block further south of the entrance to the Upper Belvedere is Goldeggasse where at number 19 you can visit, albeit by prior appointment, the **Bestattungsmuseum** (Burial Museum), worth seeing alone for the wrought-iron grille over the entrance from a nearby cemetery depicting a crowned grim reaper. At the end of Prinz-Eugen-Straße, across the hellish Gürtel, the inner city ring road, is the depressing sight of the post-war Sudbahnhof. Vienna is a disappointment for railway enthusiasts as all its splendid nineteenth-century stations were bombed out of existence.

It is worth the trek up beyond the station to the **Heeresgeschichtliches Museum** just to admire Theophil Hansen's fantastic synthesis of Byzantine (the dome), Moorish (brickwork and window arches) and late medieval Italian elements, completed in 1856 – certainly a broader definition of Historicism than that of the Ringstraße. Once inside star attractions include spoils from the Turkish wars up the stairs in the vestibule; Franz Ferdinand's car and blood-stained tunic from the Sarajevo assassination; and Albin Egger Linz's powerful anti-war painting *To the Unknown Soldier. See chapter* **Museums**.

By the Donaukanal

On Untere Weissgerberstraße is **KunstHaus Wien**, the work of local artist and architecture guru Friedensreich Hundertwasser. *Falter* actively dissuades people from visiting this place. Its reason: its fear that any increase in its popularity will inevitably lead to the whole of the city being remodelled in a similar fashion.

Exaggerated maybe, but Hundertwasser imagery is omnipresent in Vienna and throughout Austria, tying in with the nation's predisposition towards anything ecological. The artist's declaration of war on the straight line and belief that building is an aggression against nature and must be remediated by planting trees and grass on roofs reaches many hearts. So make what you will of the KunstHaus Wien, a conversion job on the old Thonet furniture factory, the whole façade given a chequerboard exterior and repointed with brightly coloured ceramics.

Inside, once you have negotiated its most disconcerting feature – undulating brick floors – there is a permanent collection of Hundertwasser's work and space for some of the most high-profile (in the colour supplement sense) itinerant exhibitions that tour Europe.

On the ground floor there is a shop pumping out Hundertwasser repros and souvenirs and a splendid café/restaurant heaving with vegetation. His work is a hybrid of Chagall, Gaudi and eco-warrior symbolism. He claims to follow in the footsteps of the Viennese oddballs like Schiele and

Klimt, but apart from the shared enthusiasm for mosaic and beards, the buck stops there.

There are some good models of his work for the **Fernwärme** and various housing projects but you are left with the feeling of how come I've never heard of him before? A big fish in a small pond. If you've developed a taste for it though, very nearby on Löwengasse is the housing project that brought him into the public eye. Very similar to the KunstHaus, the residents are now heartily sick of tourists pestering them to see the interiors. So much so that Hundertwasser took it upon himself to build the Kalke Village directly opposite, a dreadful shopping complex done out in the same way, which at least takes the heat off the flats.

Wittgenstein-Haus

3, Parkgasse 18 (713 3164). U3 Rochusgasse. **Open** 9am-5pm Mon-Fri. **Admission** AS20. **No credit cards**.

Philosopher Ludwig Wittgenstein designed this house as a home for his sister Gretl. Carrying on in his father's tradition of funding new architecture, he conceived a series of concrete cubes in the minimalist spirit of Loos, which was finished in 1926. In 1970 the place was acquired by the Bulgarian government for its embassy. Its presence is indicated by the statues of the Orthodox saints, Cyril and Methodius, in the garden. The house can only be visited while exhibitions or literary events are being held there.

Karlsplatz

Heading south across the Ringstraße from the Staatsoper, there is a bleak scenario of post-1945 buildings that opens out into the amorphous mass of Karlsplatz. This is where Vienna stops being user-friendly to the visitor.

An illogical series of pedestrian non-sequiturs makes you wonder whether you're still in the walkable city where you started. By far the best way to navigate this chaos is to take the underpass on the corner of Kärntner Straße and the Staatsoper and follow the signs. This underground causeway, apart from the recent apparition of Pizza Hut, is wonderfully free of global commerce, mixing the traditional with the hip – takeaway sushi and tramezzini side by side with purveyors of Alpine hats, scale-model railway accessories and newsstands offering everything from *La Gazzetta dello Sport* to *Asian Babes*.

Walking the whole precinct is an opportunity to witness Vienna's dysfunctional at first hand as this is a favourite meeting place of the city's substance abusers. The signs direct you to what should be the top-priority **Secession**, the kicking **Kunsthalle** or the tranquillity of Resselpark and the majestic **Karlskirche**. In an undistinguished modern building virtually next door to Karlskirche is the **Museum der Stadt Wien**.

Also on Karlsplatz is the neo-Renaissance **Künstlerhaus**, built in 1868 and commissioned by the Viennese Society of Fine Arts, a bastion of academic painters from whom the Secessionists split in 1897. The exterior is peppered with life-size statues of Leonardo, Raphael, Michelangelo and many others and inside there are regular exhibitions of contemporary Austrian painters. It also houses a theatre/cinema inside with splendid Modernist decoration, but films here are generally shown in German-language versions.

Karlskirche

4, Karlsplatz (504 6187). U1, U2, U4/tram 1, 2, D, J.

Visible from all sides of the rambling Karlsplatz, this masterpiece of Baroque ecclesiastical architecture has more than a hint of Rome and even a touch of Byzantium about it, with its two decorated Trajan frontal pillars adorned with roosting Habsburg eagles, setting off the divine oval dome. Emperor Karl IV commissioned Fischer von Erlach to build a church that would celebrate the passing of the 1713 plague, dedicating the whole thing to the memory of San Carlo Boromeo, renowned for his role in tending victims of the 1576 plague in Milan. Thus Karl could celebrate the work of his selfless namesake by having the events of his life depicted on Fischer's splendid columns and then topping them with his own imperial eagles. The columns can be interpreted variously as plague columns, the pillars of Hercules (symbolising Karl's unsuccessful claim to Spain) or as the pillars of the Temple of Solomon in Jerusalem. The church was finally completed in 1737 by Fischer's son, at the time a surreal sight indeed, standing alone on the meadows of the Glacis. The exterior is a hard act to follow but inside it is all light and airiness, showing off Rottmayr's immense fresco and Fischer's sunburst above the altar to great effect. In front of the church is a large shallow ornamental pond with a Henry Moore sculpture (*Hill Arches*, 1978) reflecting the church's impressive façade.

Kunsthalle

4, Karlsplatz (52 189-0). U1, U2, U4 Karlsplatz/tram 1, 2, D, J. **Open** 10am-6pm Fri-Wed; 10am-10pm Thur. **Admission** AS80; AS60 concs. Combination ticket with Museumsquartier AS100; AS80 concs. **No credit cards**.

Vienna's scale-model response to the Pompidou Centre resembles a building site lock-up apart from its perspex walkway over one of Karlsplatz's many traffic arteries. Intended as a stop-gap measure until the Messepalast project came to fruition, it seems likely that delays over the latter will mean that the Kunsthalle's days are far from numbered. And when that day dawns, more than a few young *Wiener* will shed a tear at the passing of this tin shed, scene of some of the best curated-in-Vienna exhibitions of cutting-edge contemporary art. Furthermore its café and terrace, serenaded by fine DJs, has become one of the places to hang on a summer's night. From the Kunsthalle via the Karlsplatz underpass there is access to the Resselpark, an oasis of tranquillity named after the unfortunate Czech inventor of the

*Cabbages and kings: the superb **Secession** houses Klimt's Beethoven Frieze.*

screw propellor, Josef Ressel, who unsuccessfully patented his invention and remained in obscurity, apart from in Vienna, of course.

Otto Wagner's Stadtbahn Pavilions

1, Karlsplatz (505 8747). U1, U2, U4 Karlsplatz/tram 1, 2, D, J. **Open** *Apr-Oct* 1.30-4.30pm Tue-Sun. **Admission** AS25; AS10 concs. **No credit cards**.

Were it not for a sit-down protest by students from the nearby Technisches Universität, these splendid pavilions might have been demolished during a bout of U-Bahn construction in the late 1960s. Originally located on either side of the busy Akademiestraße, they were reconstructed in their present emplace-ment with only a few slabs of discoloured Carrara marble being replaced. Rendered in modernissimo materials for the time – cast iron, copper, bronze and concrete – the two stations represent a distillation of Wagner's contribution to *fin-de-siècle* Vienna.

Their curved copper roofs indicate a mark of respect for the nearby Karlskirche and the lyre-like grilles on the doors nod in the direction of Hansen's decorative work on the neighbouring Musik vereingebäude. Organic motifs of sunflowers peace-fully coexist with the peculiar Jugendstil reseda green of the ironwork, a colour seen throughout Vienna. By placing them side by side their func-tionality has been neutered and they look a little out on a limb amid so much traffic. Only one offers access to the U-Bahn. The other has cafés on different levels (*see* **Café Karl-Otto** *in chapter* **Cafés & Coffeehouses**) – the one on the upper level has many original fittings such as the clock, ceiling and wall decorations. The downstairs café hosts **Klub Shabu** (*see chapter* **Nightlife**) in the evenings.

Secession

1, Friedrichstraße 12 (587 5307). U1, U2, U4 Karlsplatz. **Open** 10am-6pm Tue-Wed, Fri-Sun; 10am-8pm Thur. **Admission** AS60; AS40 concs. **No credit cards.**

The temple of modernity or the golden cabbage, the Viennese Secession building (1898) has just celebrated its centenary and to relive the radical break that the building and its followers represented, it was completely sponge-painted in red. Now restored to pristine white, its sumptuous details can once again be appreciated, albeit a reasonable perspective of its façade means running the gauntlet of passing traffic. Here, unlike with Karlskirche, the thoughtless planning of Karlsplatz works to the detriment of one of its finest tenants. Once the extravagance of its gilded globe has sunk in, turn to the legend above the entrance, which reads: 'To the age its art, to art its freedom.' Principally financed by Karl Wittgenstein, father of Ludwig, and designed by Josef Olbrich, the building was severely damaged by bombing in World War II and only restored to its present form in the mid-1980s. Even though space is very much at a premium in the Secession, today it is used for exhibitions and installations. There are usually two or three exhibitions at one time hierarchically divided between the main space, the grotty little graphics cabinet upstairs and the cellar. A lot of the shows alternate between local heroes such as Clemens Stecher or Johanna Kandl (who is on the committee) and big names on the international circuit.

It is the permanent home of Klimt's controversial *Beethoven Frieze*, conceived as a homage to the composer as part of the Secession's fourteenth exhibition, visualising the choral movement to his Ninth Symphony. It has a bizarrely unfinished look to it, with vast tracts of blank white, but the three painted sides contain startling images, especially the front wall, where on either side of the monster – a slightly absurd pre-Hollywood King Kong – there are two groups of female figures, one representing

Sickness, Madness and Death, and the other, Voluptuousness, Debauchery and Wantonness. All this symbolism is well documented in the excellent English commentary on offer and glass cabinets in the ante-room display Klimt's preliminary sketches and original copies of the Secession journal, *Ver Sacrum* (*Sacred Spring*). A tempting but pricey range of Secession merchandise is available in the vestibule. *Website: www.t0.or.at/secession*

Wienzeile

No stay in Vienna is complete without a Saturday stroll along the bustling concourse of Vienna's principal food market (*see also chapter* **Shopping & Services**) that runs for a couple of kilometres along the Wienzeile, the course of the Wienfluß, the river that emerges beside the Stadtpark after a lengthy underground trajectory. In the last century the market was held in Karlsplatz alongside the site of the Secession, as Carl Moll's beautiful naturalistic study of the Naschmarkt in the Belvedere clearly shows. However, when the river was built over in the 1890s, the market was moved to this new esplanade, which divides Vienna's 4th and 6th districts. On both sides there are a number of sights worth taking in. At Linke Wienzeile 6 is the **Theater an der Wien**, today home of the Lloyd Webber-style musical but with a long history that stretches back to 1801 when it opened under the directorship of Emanuel Schikaneder, author of the libretto for Mozart's *Magic Flute*. He is depicted as Papageno, the bird-catcher in the opera, in a statue above the main portico. Schikaneder was also one of Beethoven's most loyal protectors, allowing him to live in the theatre for a time. *See also chapter* **Music: Classical & Opera**. More interesting than the modern façade is the backstage area down the adjacent side street, which eventually leads west to the **Café Sperl** on Gumpendorfer Straße – one of Vienna's most atmospheric coffeehouses. The market's name derives from *naschen*, literally 'to scoff', and apart from the enormous variety of produce on offer – from Pecorino to Patak's Pickles – there are kebab stalls, curry houses, sushi bars and Schnitzel dispensaries to satisfy the most whimsical. Although the market operates throughout the week, Saturday has the added attraction of a large flea market located in the space south of the Kettenbrückengasse U-Bahn station. When you've passed the last covered stall, the stupendous façades of the two Otto Wagner houses at Linke Wienzeile, numbers 38 and 40, come into view – for *fin-de-siècle* fans one of the most breathtaking sights the city has to offer.

Otto Wagner Houses

5, Linkewienzeile 38, 40. U4 Kettenbrückengasse.
Built between 1898 and 1899, these houses are the culmination of Wagner's welding of Secessionist decorative vernacular with his own belief in the use of

modern materials. At number 38 the gorgeous two-dimensional floral designs of the façade's majolica tiles – it is known as the **Majolikahaus** – and the clear distinction between commercial premises and dwelling make these two buildings the antithesis of the Ringstraße palace. The gilded organic embossing of number 40 is by Secessionist Kolo Moser. As if to accentuate their Modernist *cri de coeur*, Wagner has placed two female figures on the roof of the latter, their hands cupped around their mouths in an exuberant proclamation of times to come.

Mariahilf

Vienna's 6th district, Mariahilf, rises from the hollow of the Wien river valley via various steep lanes and flights of steps to Mariahilfer Straße, the Viennese equivalent of Oxford Street. Sights are pretty thin on the ground here, but its uneven geography, human bustle and varied architecture make it pleasant to stroll.

To get an idea of the lie of the land and a marvellous view south-east, head for the Gerngross shopping centre on the corner of Mariahilfer Straße and Kirchengasse and take the high-speed lift to the top floor. From the café terrace looking north, there is an excellent view of the hills of the Wienerwald, and to the south, the onion domes of the Baroque Mariahilferkirche with one of this district's two monolithic Flaktürmen behind. Often decried as unsightly, these gigantic anti-aircraft towers with 5m (16ft) thick reinforced-concrete walls capable of housing thousands of troops are simply impossible to demolish without severely endangering nearby buildings. A good view of the other Flaktürm, resplendent with dozens of satellite dishes, inside the Stiftskaserne (1749), an ex-barracks, can be had from the first floor of the New Yorker shop at Mariahilfer Straße number 22-24. In a city whose history is so closely linked to World War II yet has little to recall those terrible times, the Flaktürmen, with their stout permanence, fulfill the important 'Lest we forget…' function (*see page 62* **Taking the flak**).

In a city where shopping is resolutely low-key, Mariahilfer Straße comes as a bit of a shock with its numerous international franchises and chain-stores. The scene of frenzied buying by Czechs and Hungarians after the fall of the Wall when TVs and fridges were piled high on its pavements, the street now resembles any other Western European shop-till-you-drop zone.

Mariahilfer Straße is also home to the **Tabakmuseum** and the **Hofmobiliendepot** (*see chapter* **Museums**).

Neubau

North of Mariahilfer Straße lies Neubau, the 7th district, currently one of the most kicking areas of Vienna as far as nightlife, original shops and alternative lifestyle goes. All the streets within the zone bounded by the Neubaugasse to the west and the Kirchengasse to the east are pleasant to walk but for peace, tranquillity and heterogenous Biedermeier architecture, the Spittelberg quarter north of Siebensterngasse is a must. Once a red-light district catering for the urges of soldiers at the nearby Stiftskaserne, its cobbled pedestrian streets have become something of a des res in recent years and the proliferation of restaurants and antique dealers specialising in Jugendstil testify to the gentrification of the area. In summer the Hof of the Amerling Beisl at Stiftgasse 8 or the terrace of Lux in Schrankgasse are very relaxing. Before Christmas the whole network of streets is transformed into an advent market, with stalls purveying the wares of artesans and *Glühwein*, the delicious local mulled wine.

If the traffic on the Siebensterngasse doesn't bother you, the terraces of **Shultz** (*see chapter* **Nightlife**) and Siebenstern (a swish bar owned by the Communist Party), on the corner of Kirchengasse, are great places to hang and be seen. Attempts have been made to establish a Viennese Speakers' Corner in the square but as yet nothing regular takes place.

Take a look at Mondscheingasse round the corner and the splendid apartment building with three monumental lion's heads and a stucco tree whose branches spread over the doorway. Further down Kirchengasse beyond Burggasse to the south is the fine Ulrichsplatz with its Baroque church, sloping down to Neustiftgasse. At number 40 there is one of Otto Wagner's most austerely functional apartment buildings and round the corner at Döblergasse 4 is the house – it is closed to the public at the moment – where he lived and worked until his death in 1918.

Josefstadt

The genteel 8th district of Vienna takes its name from Josef I (1705-11), during whose reign plans for this new residential area were laid out, one of the earliest examples of urban planning beyond the city walls.

Its southern limit is Landesgerichtsstraße, which runs directly behind the **Rathaus**, and these first streets of the lower part such as Lenaugasse are fine intact examples of Biedermeier building. Its principal street, Josefstädter Straße, cuts through the district from the Gürtel to the north offering a fine vista of the main tower of Stephansdom. Given its proximity to the city centre, the area is popular with both the traditional middle class and students and is a pleasant mix of *Tracht* and New Age. Sights are scarce, but strollers and window shoppers will enjoy the antique and second-hand stores, mostly

A lot of Otto

As is the case with Gaudí in Barcelona, one of the best excuses for a visit to Vienna is the chance to track down and enjoy the buildings and civil engineering of Otto Wagner – the architectural kingpin of turn-of-the-century Vienna. Having honed his trade on the Ringstraße, Wagner found himself in the position of being able to dictate his own terms to the city's rich and powerful. A firm believer in the parity of beauty and function, without Loos' scary Freudian rooted loathing of ornamentation, Wagner's buildings and public infrastructure literally adorn the city.

Few architects have left their imprint on a city like Wagner has in Vienna. He was born in 1841 to a family that encapsulated the bourgeois aspirations of the Ringstraße era, wealthy enough to have him trained as an architect and later fine-tuned at the Academy of Fine Arts by the Staatsoper duo Siccardsberg and Van der Nüll. By the late 1860s he was building apartments along the Ringstraße and demonstrating himself to be a shrewd businessman in this time of unfettered speculation.

However, in the 1890s through his involvement in urban engineering projects and his exposure to the Secession movement, his functionalist vein came to the fore. Having advocat-

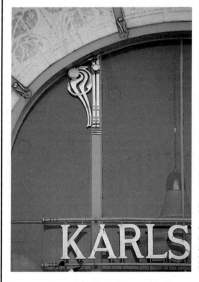

ed a public transport network as the key to modern urban planning, he was appointed chief architect of the new Vienna City Railway System, and between 1894 and 1901 designed 30 stations and was instrumental in the planning and design of tunnels, viaducts and bridges. Today these are still in use, as a trip along the overground stretch of the present U6 from Spittelau to Längenfeldgasse illustrates. The U4 too is very much Wagner's baby. Out of town in Hietzing he designed the rather bombastic Kaiser Pavilion – the Emperor's own metro station. The stations have an understated elegance with their delicate floral stucco and proud ironwork at the forefront, from the stanchions of the platform canopies to the railings between each station.

Another example of Wagner's aesthetic approach to civil engineering can be seen on the Nußdorfer Wehr- und Schleusenanlage – the weir and lock gates at the start of the Donaukanal in Nußdorf. Completed in 1898, the most noteworthy feature are the two huge bronze lions on pillars either side of the lock gates. He had hopes of transforming the whole of the Wiental into a rival to the Ringstraße but beyond the Gürtel little was completed apart from the railway.

Wagner lionised his contemporary Gustav Klimt as 'the greatest artist who ever walked the earth', sharing his messianic desire to do away with the dead wood of Historicism, while both owed a considerable part of their fame to their participation in the shenanigans of the Ringstraße.

Unlike the tortured and obsessive painter, however, Wagner was a paradigm of the hyperactive rational artist-engineer, perfectly at home with the trappings of wealth and fame. His villas in the Hütteldorf district and above all the revolutionary **Kirche am Steinhof** built for the patients of a psychiatric hospital are worth the trek to the woods of the western suburbs. Wagner died in 1918 and is buried in a tomb of his own design – one that's disappointingly free of Jugendstil iconography, in the Hietzing cemetery.

in Langegasse, Piaristengasse and Lederergasse. Look out for numerous plaques denoting illustrious residents such as Fritz Lang (Langegasse) and Stefan Zweig (Kochgasse). Two theatres attract crowds to the area of an evening – the **Vienna's English Theatre** in Josefsgasse and the famous **Theater in der Josefstadt** where Harry Lime's girlfriend in *The Third Man* performs (*see chapter* **Theatre**). Recommended places for a drink and a rest are **Café Hummel**, the busiest bar/café in the area (with possibly the rudest waiters in Vienna) on the corner of Josefstädter Straße and Albertgasse, the Jugendstil **Café Florianihof** on Florianigasse opposite Schlesingerplatz and in the summer the two terraces of the Maria Treu Kirche on Piaristengasse.

The section of the Gürtel that traces the northern boundary of Josefstadt is the city's latest hip nightlife zone with a number of new bars built into the arches of Otto Wagner's Stadtbahn, today the route of the U6. Places like **rhiz** and **B72** have had a lot of exposure as temples of Vienna's burgeoning digital underground. With its numerous peepshows, sex shops and concomitant prostitution, the Gürtel is about the nearest Vienna gets to inner city deprivation.

However, with EC cash flowing in, a whole range of projects is planned to make the area more palatable, the new bars being just the aperitif. During the day it's worth crossing the Gürtel into the 16th district to check out one of Vienna's most colourful street markets – the **Brunnenmarkt** (*see chapter* **Shopping & Servcies**) – piles of fruit and veg and excellent kebab houses in the heart of the Turkish and Yugoslav communities, between Thaliastraße and Yppenplatz.

The **Museum für Volkskunde** is on the corner of Langegasse and Laudongasse, a short walk from Alser Straße and the start of the 9th district. At number 17 is the Dreifältigkeitskirche (Church of the Holy Trinity), of special interest to classical music buffs as the scene of Beethoven's funeral in 1827, which attracted a multitude of mourners stretching as far as the composer's last place of residence in Schwarzspanier Straße. Here too is a plaque commemorating the hymn *Faith, Hope and Charity,* which, shortly before his death, Schubert composed for the consecration of the church.

A short walk away is **Piaristenkirche** on Jodok-Fink-Platz. In the centre of the square is a gilded plague column commemorating deliverance from the 1713 plague. On the eastern side of the square is the Piaristengymnasium, one of the city's top grammar schools. If you sit at either of the terraces in the square, bear in mind that they belong to the restaurant diagonally, not directly opposite. It could mean the difference between a pizza and a goulash. Avoid the ghoulish, touristy Piaristenkeller to the east of the square.

Piaristenkirche

8, Jodok-Fink-Platz (4204 2513). U2 Rathaus/tram J.

Josef I included in his plans some land to be set aside for the Order of the Piarists to found a monastery. The Maria Treu or Piaristenkirche (1753) stands majestically between the monastery outbuildings, its newly painted convex façade flanked by two elegant towers. Its original design was traced by Von Hildebrandt as early as 1716 but it was not entirely completed until the nineteenth century. The coat of arms over the entrance is that of the church's patron Sigismund, Count Kollonitsch, the first Archbishop of Vienna after it finally became an independent archbishopric in 1722. The interior is notable for Franz Maulbertsch's magnificent ceiling frescoes and for its organ on which Anton Brückner took his examination for the Academy. While he played, one of the examiners was heard to say, 'He should be examining us!'

Alsergrund

The 9th district occupies a large area stretching as far as the Danube canal and is principally known as the medical and university district of the city. In fact directly opposite the Church of the Holy Trinity is the **Altes Allgemeines Krankenhaus**, one of Europe's oldest hospitals now transformed into an attractive university campus with a seemingly endless number of inner courtyards,. It is home to some curious sights such as the Narrentürm, an eighteenth-century lunatic asylum that has been converted into the fascinating yet slightly grotesque **Pathologisch-anatomische Bundesmuseum** (Museum of Pathological Anatomy).

To the north a couple of dark monolithic towers denote the presence of the AKH (Allgemeines Krankenhaus), the largest hospital in Europe, whose construction was shrouded in the most serious corruption scandal of the Bruno Kreisky era. Its ultra-modern installations can be visited on guided tours. Infamous inmates have included Nico, son of Ceaucescu, who died of liver cancer there in the mid-1990s.

Nearby on Währinger Straße is the **Josephinum**, Josef II's academy for military surgeons – nowadays a medical museum. However, the district is probably most famous for Berggasse 19, where Sigmund Freud lived and did most of his pioneering work on psychoanalysis. The **Sigmund Freud Museum** is of great interest, both for those of an academic bent and as a chronicle of the social and intellectual history of late nineteenth and early twentieth century Vienna.

The area around Berggasse, the Servitenviertel, is the most pleasant strolling area in the 9th district, having the only extra-muros church to survive the Turkish siege, the late seventeenth-century **Servitenkirche**. Nearby too is the small Jewish cemetery of Seegasse and a little further the **Palais Liechtenstein**, a wonderful Baroque summer

A load of rubbish? Hundertwasser's designs on the **Fernwärme**.

palace that houses part of the Ludwig Foundation's modern art collection (*see chapter* **Galleries**). It was built to a design by Domenico Martinelli between 1691 and 1711 and is still the property of the Princes of Liechtenstein, but no longer inhabited by foppish aristocrats. Since 1979 it has been a rather bizarre home to a collection of works by everyone from Picasso to Yoko Ono. How long this arrangement will continue depends on the completion date of the Museumsquartier where this lot will eventually hang. Hemmed in by imposing wrought ironwork, the palace is also on a giant scale with a grandiose entrance hall flanked by two gigantic marble staircases. These lead to the Ceremonial Hall with a ceiling fresco by Andrea Pozzo depicting the *Apotheosis of Hercules* and eventually to the collection.

A place worth calling in on for classical music fans is **Schuberthaus** (*see chapter* **Museums**), the birthplace of Schubert on Nußdorfer Straße.

The Seegasse Jewish cemetery is often overlooked. Access is through the old people's home at Seegasse 9-11, built on the site of the old Jewish hospital. It's a bit rough on the residents to live their last years with a cemetery for a garden. Like all Jewish cemeteries in Vienna, this one bears the scars of rabid anti-Semitism, with virtually all the tombs desecrated. Look out for the curious mound of stones with a carved fish on top – it's not clear whether it's actually a gravestone.

Take a stroll along the Donaukanal upstream, dodging the cyclists, rollerbladers and joggers to get a fantastic view of one of Vienna's most singular buildings, the **Fernwärme**, a municipal rubbish incinerator embellished by the love-him-or-hate-him Friedrich Hundertwasser, with the vineyards of Kahlenberg in the background.

Altes Allgemeines Krankenhaus (AKH)
Old General Hospital
9, Alser Straße/Spitalgasse. Tram 5, 33, 43, 44.
There is not a great deal to see within this labyrinth of 15 or so inner courtyards, opened in 1784 as the Allgemeines Krankenhaus (General Hospital), but since the mid-1990s it has become a model conversion of existing public buildings into an inner city university campus. In summer it's a delightful place to hang out, with numerous bars and terraces as well as a regular open-air cinema programme. Check in *Falter*. Before it became part of the university and the buildings were transformed into faculty rooms, bookshops and admin space, parties and raves were held in the old operating theatres and labs. From the Alser Straße entrance head east across the tree-lined main courtyard, which eventually brings you to the Narrentürm, the peculiar cylindrical building that now houses one of Vienna's strangest museums.

Fernwärme
9, Spittelauer Lände 45 (3132 62030). U4, U6 Spittelau. Guided tours by appointment.
There can't be many cities where the municipal rubbish incinerator features in the sightseeing section, but with some justification Hundertwasser's 1989 remodelling of a hideous industrial building is now one of Vienna's great visual surprises. This is mainly due to the enormous smoke stack, wrapped in vitro-ceramic tiles and crowned with a large golden mosaic bulb. His treatment of the plant buildings and offices beneath correspond to the usual

Hundertwasser iconography that decorates his projects in the 3rd district. In eco-minded Vienna the debate between landfill and incineration was fiery and the latter was adopted not without considerable dissent since the plant is located inside the urban area. Assurances that cutting-edge filter systems (housed within the mighty bulb) would reduce emissions to a minimum and the favourable prevailing winds finally won the day.

The other argument in its favour is the use of the hot water generated by incineration as a cheap, effective means of central heating. The system now provides heating for over 180,000 homes and 4,000 large consumers. The plant is best observed from the U6 line or from the banks of the Donakanal, but two guided tours are available – one 'artistic' and the other technical.

Servitenkirche

Church of the Servites
9, Servitenplatz. U4 Roßauer Lände/tram D Porzellangasse.
Servitenviertel is a charming, villagey network of streets around Servitenplatz. Belonging to the Serviten Order, the church's oval-shaped nave is said to have influenced the builders of Karlskirche. Baroque to the marrow, the church has a fine interior with impressive stucco, a pulpit by Moll (1739) and a relief showing the martyrdom of John Nepomuk, a popular Czech saint often venerated in Vienna, being drowned in the Vltava. Unless you make it for Mass, the church has to be viewed through iron railings.

Leopoldstadt

The physical and psychological barrier of the Donaukanal, with its neo-Brutalist skyline, often makes the 2nd district seem grey and distanced from the Innere Stadt. It was probably this that Ferdinand II had in mind when in 1624 he sanctioned the creation of a Jewish ghetto in this area.

The name of the district has its origin in Leopold I's decision to expel the Jews in 1670 and demolish their synagogue, replacing it with the Leopoldkirche. By the late eighteenth-early nineteenth century Jews escaping from the Russian and Polish pogroms flooded into Vienna, with the majority taking up residence in Leopoldstadt. Photos from the last century show Taborstraße and Prater Straße, the area's two main commercial arteries, to be thriving Jewish areas full of shops and theatres with a marked Orthodox presence. With the collapse of the Eastern Bloc the process is repeating itself and today's Jews are overwhelmingly from ex-Soviet republics, mingling with the Turkish and Yugoslav communities long established in the area.

Max Fabiani's Urania, venue for the Viennale, overlooks the Donaukanal.

Of all the city centre districts, however, it is probably the greyest, most punished by Allied bombing, with minimal interest for the visitor. That said it does have two fine parks, the **Augarten** with its two flak towers, the **Augarten Porzellanmanufactur** and the Palais Augarten, built by Fischer von Erlach the elder at the end of the seventeenth century. The palace cannot be visited as it serves as the boarding school for the infamous **Wiener Sängerknaben** (Vienna Boys' Choir). Behind the palace is the Kaiser-Josef-Stöckl (1781), now a residence for the boys who can no longer hit the high notes, the school of the Vienna Boys' Choir and, in summer, Vienna's most popular open-air cinema, **Kino unter Sternen**.

There's also the **Prater**, whose gigantic nineteenth-century Ferris wheel, the **Reisenrad**, was immortalised during Orson Welles' 'Five hundred years of democracy...' speech in *The Third Man*. More a forest than a park, the Prater today is the city's premier leisure zone with a permanent funfair, stacks of bars and restaurants, the **Ernst-Happel-Stadion**, horse racing, acres of space for lounging, kilometres of tarmac for cycling, jogging and rollerblading and an Olympic-size swimming pool. *See also chapter* **Sport & Fitness**.

The commercial centre of the 2nd district can be reached on foot or by tram from Schwedenplatz, taking you along the busy Taborstraße. The area around Karmeliterplatz has some charming streets and a good open-air food market.

Further along Taborstraße at the junction with Obere Augarten Straße are some pleasant cafés to stop and rest. To the north lie the 50 hectares (124 acres) of the Augarten, the oldest Baroque garden in Vienna. Established by Ferdinand III in 1650 and laid out in its present form in 1712, the park was opened to the public by Josef II in 1775.

A bit bleak in winter, the Augarten comes into its own in the summer with all the chestnuts in bloom and the injection of life given by the open-air cinema and the various outdoor restaurants set up at its entrance. The cinema is located between two more of Vienna's monumental anti-aircraft towers. It also has a number of second division sights that, depending on your tastes, may well be of interest.

The other major causeway of the 2nd district, Prater Straße, runs from the Donaukanal to the Praterstern, a railway/U-Bahn station and traffic junction serving the nearby amusement park and providing a bit of street life with its crowds and general shabbiness.

The Prater is the main reason for descending on this part of the city, but there are a few other attractions like the Tegetthoff column at the end of Prater Straße, commemorating the Habsburgs' most glorious admiral, and a couple more of Vienna's eclectic museums – the **Johann Strauß Haus** and the **Kriminalmuseum**.

Augarten Porzellanmanufactur

2, Schloß Augarten (21 124-0). Tram N, 5.
The works of the Wiener Porzellanmanufactur, Austria's foremost manufacturer of posh crocks, has been around since 1718. Its current premises, the Schloß Augarten, have a chequered history. Built on the ruins of Leopold I's summer palace after it was destroyed during the Turkish siege in 1683, the building became an important venue for society events at the end of the eighteenth century, which included concerts by Mozart, Beethoven and Schubert. Augarten's florid designs will probably not appeal to fans of cool understatement, but it does have a small line in Modernist designs amid all the rococo. Temporary exhibitions are held in the foyer and wares can be purchased on the premises or at Augarten's flagship store on Graben.

Schützenhaus

2, Obere Donaustraße 26. U1, U4 Schwedenplatz.
Architecture is not a strong point of Leopoldstadt, but Otto Wagner's Schützenhaus (Defence Tower), built 1906-7, is a charming example of Jugendstil functionalism. Built on the site of an old defensive fortification, Wagner's building contained the machinery of a now-defunct lock that was popular with bathers in the early twentieth century. It has all the characteristics of Wagner's work – wall cladding sustained by large metal rivets and an upper façade reflecting the waterway by means of blue tiles with a wave motif. The Schützenhaus is probably best observed from the Schwedenplatz side of the canal.

Prater

Derived from the Spanish *prado* (meadow), the vast area of the Prater is a mixture of fairly untamed woodland, sports and leisure facilities and a funfair, operating 365 days a year. The Prater has become synonymous with the funfair whose gigantic **Riesenrad** (big wheel) is as much a symbol of the city as Stephansdom itself. Originally an area of woodland and water meadows traversed by numerous branches and meanders of the then-uncontrolled Danube, it was given its spinal column – the chestnut-bordered Hauptallee – by Ferdinand I in the mid-sixteenth century. At this time the whole area was a royal hunting ground and in 1560 Maximilian II had a hunting lodge built, known by the suggestive name (to English ears anyway) of the Lusthaus. The present day Lusthaus, resplendent in Schönbrunner yellow, marks the furthest point of the Hauptallee, some 5km (3 miles) from where it starts by the funfair. At this south-east end of the Prater there are a number of old overgrown tracts of the Danube that can be explored by rowing

boat. Here too is the Freudenau, Vienna's only racecourse, with a magnificent nineteenth-century grandstand with beautiful decorative ironwork. Races are held most Sundays throughout the summer (*see chapter* **Sport & Fitness**).

Funfair

The Wurstelprater is the Viennese name for the funfair section of the Prater. The name does not have anything to do with *Wurst* (sausage) in spite of the fact that hot dogs, frankfurters and so on are widely available, but rather harks back to the Punch-like character Hanswurst who appeared in all the park's puppet shows. There is no entrance fee as the booths, rides and restaurants are run by a number of different operators.

Attractions range from old-fashioned merry-go-rounds to the cutting edge of fairground technology for today's thrill-obsessed public. The latter includes the Spaceshot, which catapults 12 riders up a 50m (164ft) tower at 90 kph (56mph), and the totally nauseating Space Shuttle, a two-seater capsule connected to elastic cables that is flung into the air and then bounces and turns at random. Riders can purchase a video of their tortured faces and screams.

Riesenrad

A ride on the world-famous Riesenrad is one of Vienna's quintessential experiences. Orson Welles fans will thrill at the opportunity to relive one of cinema's most famous scenes and the rest of us can enjoy the superb views. Built in 1898 by Walter Basset, the Riesenrad is the only surviving example of his curious trade – the ones he built for Blackpool, Paris and London no longer exist.

The wheel was damaged in World War II and rebuilt in 1945 with only half of the wooden gondolas (15 in all) being replaced. The accent is very much on the visual as the wheel moves slowly, taking around 20 minutes to complete one circle. At its highest point you are 65m (213ft) above the ground and the fading cityscape photographs inside the gondolas help you discern the various landmarks. If you want to do it in style, there is a 'luxury cabin' with mahogany panelling and Jugendstil curtains seating up to 12 that can be rented for a mammoth AS3,500 an hour, with a half-hour ride possible.

*Over a century old, the infamous **Riesenrad**.*

Vienna International Centre – *home to the UN and many a conference. See page 85.*

The Danube

When you talk about the Danube in Vienna it's important to be specific as three waterways bear the name. Most familiar to the visitor is the Donaukanal, an artificial construction that divides the main part of the city from the 2nd and 20th districts. Beyond the 2nd district lies the Donau, properly speaking, an enormous mass of water divided by the Donauinsel, a man-made island some 40km (25 miles) long.

Once you reach the eastern bank, it's a relatively short walk to the Alte Donau (Old Danube), an arm of the river's original course akin to an oxbow lake that has been preserved for the leisure opportunities it offers. It is by far the most attractive stretch of the river, whose weeping willows and rowing clubs resemble the Thames at Eton.

Donauinsel

Danube Island

Over the centuries the Danube has been a major source of flood danger to the city, so to ensure the river's safe passage through the city, the main causeway was dug out between 1870 and 1875, with the help of steam excavators used on the Suez Canal. The rectilinear course of the Danube today is rather bleak and distanced from the exuberance of Strauß' famous waltz. In the 1970s another bed was dug on the eastern side to channel floodwater, creating a new slower-moving arm – the Neue Donau. This left a long narrow stretch of land dividing it from the main part of the river. For years the

Donauinsel was an inhospitable, windswept tract, but with tree planting and natural growth of vegetation it has been transformed into a massive leisure zone rivalling the Prater. While it still falls short of being an authentic Arcadia, the sheer space and the relative cleanliness of the water make it ideal for cycling, skating, bathing and picnicking during the summer months. Nude bathing and sunbathing are also permitted.

The area adjacent to the Donauinsel U-Bahn station has become a major nightlife area during the summer, known as the **Copa Cagrana** after the nearby Kagran district. It is all very brash and commercial, but popular with young Viennese and the South American community wanting to live a bit of *la vida loca* when the temperatures rise. In August the whole island is taken over for a weekend by the Social Democratic Party's **Donauinselfest** (*See chapter* **Vienna by Season**).

Vienna International Centre

From the fleshpots of the Copa Cagrana a foreboding cluster of grey semi-cylindrical towers comes into view. This is the Vienna International Centre or **UNO City** – a combination of conference centre and HQ number three of the United Nations. Bruno Kreisky succeeded in making Vienna the third seat of the UN in the early 1970s, running the operation from the Hofburg. The need for larger premises led to the construction of the present complex, which was finished in 1979 and houses the offices of the International Atomic Energy Authority (in a no-nukes country!), the Commission for Infectious Diseases and the High Commission for Refugees (UNHCR). UNIDO, the threatened industrial organisation, is located elsewhere in the city. Although its construction almost bankrupted the city, it ensures a badly needed international presence in the city and is a godsend for the city's hotels and restaurants. Guided tours of the complex take place at 11am and 2pm Monday to Friday (26060 3328/fax 26060 5899). Remember to bring your passport as security is extremely tight.

Alte Donau
Old Danube

Two stops further on the U1 and you are in the picturesque old Danube, a pleasant area to stroll and have a few drinks or dinner at the water's edge. On the western side is the Gänsehäufel, one of the city's most popular bathing areas, with pools as well as the river. Numerous sections are the private domain of certain public workers, so you see bizarre signs like Polizeibad (Policemen's Baths) and Straßenbahnerbad (Tram Drivers' Baths)! Be sure to take plenty of insect repellent as mosquitoes can be a real problem in summer.

On the north-west side of the Alte Donau, adjacent to the UNO buildings, is the Donau Park, an area of attractive modern gardens built around the Donauturm (Danube Tower), for years the tallest building in Vienna, complete with high-speed lift and revolving restaurant.

West of Vienna

The main attraction on the western side of Vienna is the Habsburgs' summer palace, **Schönbrunn**, and its delightful gardens and parkland. The trip can be combined with a look round the neighbouring suburb of Hietzing, which is a treat for architecture freaks – Otto Wagner, Adolf Loos and various other Viennese Modernists built here. However, for those with a particular interest in Wagner's contribution to Jugendstil Vienna, a trip to the far-flung 14th district in the west of the city is a must. In reasonably close proximity there are two of his villas and the outstanding **Kirche am Steinhof** – Wagner's one and only stab at ecclesiastical architecture.

Kirche am Steinhof
Otto Wagner Church
14, Baumgartner Höhe. U2, U3 Volkstheater/bus 48a. **Open** 3pm Sat. **Admission** free; AS40 guided tour in German.

A trek out here is highly recommended to anyone with an interest in Wagner's work, Modernism in general or the development of mental health institutions. For Wagner's church is located within the grounds of Steinhof, a pioneering experiment in the care of the mentally ill, set in hectares of beautiful parkland, and intended for use by inmates and staff alike. Built in 1902, Wagner designed the layout and many of the 61 pavilions that make up the centre. In 1904 he received the commission to build the church and completed it in 1907. Obscured by the main entrance to the hospital, take the path that runs up

the hill to the left of the admin buildings and slowly the immense copper cupola (32m/105ft high) of the church comes into view, suggesting some kinship with Karlskirche. Set upon a huge stone plinth and clad in white marble with four Jugendstil angels by Othmar Schimkowitz aloft, the Kirche am Steinhof must be one of the world's few examples of ecclesiastical functionalism. For Wagner never lost sight of the church's raison d'être – a place of worship for the mentally ill. Inside it is all light and clean surfaces. With the altar to the north sunlight pours in through Kolo Moser's magnificent stained-glass windows depicting a procession of saints. Moser started the work on the mosaic of the altar fresco, which features St Peter with Franz Josef's head, but his conversion to Protestantism led to him being dropped from the team, despite Wagner's intervention on his behalf. The architect had no truck with denominational in-fighting, envisaging his church for all religions and specifically as a place of worship for the patients of Steinhof. With their needs in mind, the pews were deliberately shortened to facilitate access to distressed patients, the floor has a 30cm (12in) drop from the altar to the entrance to help wash the floors, toilets were located in the right-hand side of the sacristy and a small clinic on the right. Wagner oversaw all the details, even designing special robes for the priests. While he received the blessing of the Bishop of Lower Austria, Archduke Franz Ferdinand, who officially opened the church, made no attempt to hide his contempt for it, saying in his inaugural address that the architecture of Maria Theresia's time was far superior. Since the 1980s Steinhof has been an open centre with patients free to leave of their own acccord. With the constant stream of visitors to the church and to performances at the Jugendstil theatre on the grounds, Steinhof has an air of normality that other such institutions would do well to copy. Below the church there is a memorial to the mentally ill victims of the Nazis.

Otto Wagner Villas
14, Hüttelbergstraße 26, 28 (914 8575). Tram 49 to terminus. **Open** 10am-4pm Tue-Sat. **Admission** AS120. **Credit cards** AmEx, DC, JCB, MC, V.

The villa at number 26 is the only one of the two that can be visited, as it is now home to the Ernst-Fuchs Museum, a lamentable piece of egomania by the 'Magic Realist' painter of the same name who has filled the house with his gaudy oeuvre and cluttered the garden with his fertility goddess sculpture and a fountain. Some credit must be given to Fuchs and his contemporary and soulmate Hundertwasser who, in 1968, squatted the house in order to save it from the Council's demolition order. He purchased it in 1972 and set about its restoration and transformation. It is an early work of Wagner's, completed in 1888 and more reminiscent of his Ringstraße work with Ionic pillars and a touch of the Palladian about it. The colourful cornices were added by Fuchs but the odd bit of Jugendstil shines through in the ceilings and the windows of the pergola on the left. The cube-like villa at number 28, however, is much more in the familiar Otto Wagner Jugendstil tradition: a simple steel and concrete structure, completed in 1913 and intended, typically Viennese this, as a home for his wife once she became a widow. As fate should have it, she died three years before him. Sparsely adorned with characteristic blue tiles and aluminium rivets, there is also some Kolo Moser glass work over the two entrances. The houses are a ten-minute walk from the tram terminus on Linzer Straße. It's best to follow the path alongside the Halterbach stream and avoid the busy Hüttelbergstraße.

Schönbrunn

After the **Hofburg**, the Habsburgs' summer palace **Schönbrunn** is the major destination of the thousands of tourist buses that descend into Vienna every year. The immensity and rococo overkill of the palace and its interior will not be to everyone's taste, but the adjoining Schloßpark, with its zoo, palm house and acres of Baroque gardens can be safely recommended. If it's hot, bring swimming things as there's one of Vienna's best open-air baths, Schönbrunner Bad, to the east of the park with an Olympic-size pool and nude sunbathing zone.

Access to Schönbrunn is quick and fuss-free from the city centre with the U4 to Schloß Schönbrunn, where you should take the exit marked Grünbergstraße and enter through the Meidlinger Tor on this street. If you want to head directly for the main entrance and access to the state rooms, leave via the other new exit. Alternatively you could travel a stop further to Hietzing and enter the park through the Hietzinger Tor near the zoo and botanical gardens. The latter enables you to take a quick look at Otto Wagner's **Hofpavilion Hietzing**, Franz Josef's private U-Bahn station, before embarking on Schönbrunn.

The Baroque era in Vienna is characterised by the enthusiasm of aristocrats and architects alike for building summer residences on a dramatic scale. The Belvedere, Palais Liechtenstein and Schloß Schönbrunn are the three most well-known products of the building boom that followed the defeat of the Turks. The Habsburgs' connection with what is today Schönbrunn dates back to 1569, when fear of the crescent moon was still a reality. Maximilian II acquired the land, then known as Kattenburg, in order to build a hunting lodge, which used to stand near what is today the Meidlinger Tor. At this time a natural spring was discovered on the estate, the origin of the name Schönbrunn (beautiful spring). After the siege of 1683, Leopold I went full speed ahead, commissioning a summer palace for his son, the future Josef I, from Fischer von Erlach, who also tutored the young Crown Prince on architecture. His original plans envisaged a palace on the scale of Versailles on the hill where the Gloriette stands today and are considered to be one of the great unrealised works of Baroque architecture. Economic considerations ruled the day and in 1696 work began on the present site where Josef himself lived for a time in an unfinished structure whose completion was interrupted by the Spanish Wars of Succession (1701-14).

The present form of the palace owes its existence to the intervention of Empress Maria Theresia, the monarch most closely associated with Schönbrunn. In order to accommodate her ever-expanding brood (she had 16 children, ten of whom lived to adulthood), she had her architect Nikolaus Pacassi add another floor to the two wings, and also supervised the work on the rococo interiors and the layout of the gardens.

Her son Josef II inherited rather more of Maria Theresia's thrift than her enthusiasm for Schönbrunn and had huge uninhabited sections of the palace boarded up. He was, however, a keen gardener – completing the classical layout of the gardens and commissioning their most impressive monument, the Gloriette, in commemoration of the victory over the Prussians at Kolin in 1775, which returned Prague to Habsburg rule. Napoleon occupied Schönbrunn in 1805 and 1809, and his son, the Duc de Reichstadt, spent most of his short life within the confines of the palace.

The reign of Franz Josef is intimately connected to the palace as the Emperor was born and died in Schönbrunn (1830 and 1916 respectively) but his wife Elisabeth had no fondness for the place – probably due to the fact that they spent their wedding night there: reputedly she staved off her husband's advances for all of two nights. What was actually consummated in Schönbrunn's Blue Chinese Salon in November 1918 was the dissolution of the Austro-Hungarian Empire when Karl I signed away any chance of the monarchy's survival.

During the four-power occupation of Vienna, Schönbrunn was first HQ to the Russians and then to the British until it returned to the Austrian state in 1947. In 1961 it briefly returned to centre-stage when Kennedy and Khrushchev met for the first time at the palace and put the word détente on everyone's lips.

Schloß Schönbrunn

13, Schönbrunner Schloßstraße 47 (811 130/info & booking 811 13-239). U4 Schönbrunm, Hietzing/tram 10, 58/bus 15a. **Open** Palace *1 Apr-31 Oct* 8.30am-5pm daily. *1 Nov-31 Mar* 8.30am-4.30pm daily. Gardens 6am-dusk daily. **Admission** Grand Tour AS120; AS105 concs; AS60 children. Guided tours for Grand Tour AS145; AS130 concs; AS75 children. Imperial Tour AS90; AS80 concs; AS45 children. Prices include audio-guides. Parks and gardens free. **No credit cards.**

Painted in the ubiquitous but slightly nauseating tone of yellow known as *Schönbrunnergelb*, the gigantic palace lies close to the banks of the Wien river and the main urban freeway to the west. It is the focal point of a gorgeous extension of parkland

I should rococo: the money-spinning **Schönbrunn**, *a summer palace fit for the Habsburgs.*

larger than the Principality of Monaco, much favoured by the Viennese for Sunday strolls and summer lounging. Nowadays the administration and exploitation of the palace is in the hands of a semi-private company that extracts as much financial mileage out of this historic monument without caring unduly for its actual upkeep. In summer concerts are held in the grounds and the outbuildings, Christmas sees the **Great Court** swamped with the stalls of Vienna's largest advent market and product presentations regularly take place in its hallowed rooms. Add to all this the many thousands of tourists who pass through the turnstiles every year and it becomes clear that Schönbrunn is an absolute money-spinner.

Architecturally Schönbrunn is not particularly distinguished, but the Great Court with its impressive iron gates and obelisques topped with imperial eagles is quite a sight. Entrance to the state rooms is by way of the Blauerstiege (blue staircase) on the west wing but tickets are sold at the front of the east wing. For those who are determined to go inside, the Grand Tour covering 40 rooms (of a total of 1,441)

is the best option as the Imperial Tour of 22 rooms does not include access to Maria Theresia's west wing, meaning you miss out on probably the most impressive section, from an interior decoration angle. The ticket includes the use of a hand-held device with a commentary in English so there is really no need to go for the guided tours unless you enjoy being frogmarched from one room to another. Bear in mind that due to the hordes of visitors it can get mighty crowded and that you are given an exact entrance time. In summer you will probably end up having at least an hour to kill, which is no problem as all the best bits are on the outside.

THE INTERIORS

The circuit begins at the west wing. At the top of the blue staircase are Sissi and Franz Josef's nine private rooms, which are as dowdy as those of the Hofburg. Beginning with the billiard room, which served as a waiting room for petitioners, you pass into the actual audience chamber, the **Nußbaumzimmer** (Walnut Chamber). Next come the Emperor's study and the bedroom containing his simple iron death bed com-

Gloriette – standing grand in the grounds of **Schönbrunn**.

plete with a painting by Makart recreating the sombre scene of his passing away. After the shared bedroom, a joyless chamber, things pick up a little with the **Maria Antoinette Room** and the nursery, which have the original décor from Maria Theresia's time, and the **Breakfast Room** with lovely views over the park.

Here the State Apartments begin with the **Spiegelsaal** (Hall of Mirrors) where the child Mozart played a duet with his sister Nannerl in 1792 for Maria Theresia and her daughters. This leads into the largest of the three rooms dedicated to the landscapes of the Polish court painter Josef Rosa and then out into the highly impressive **Große Galerie** aflame with the lights of chandeliers and wall appliqués illuminating three huge ceiling frescoes by Guglielmo Guglielmi to the glory of the House of Habsburg. The most easterly of the three, *The Glories of War*, is a copy, the original ironically destroyed by a bomb in 1945. Used as a ballroom during the nine-month long Congress of Vienna in 1815 (the Congress danced but didn't advance, it was observed at the time), it was also here that Kennedy and Khrushchev met in 1961. Off the Great Gallery on the park side is the Small Gallery, which also contains a fresco by Guglielmi and access to the two chinoiserie rooms. This part is under renovation, but at some point in 2000 it should be possible to see the Round Chinese Room to the west where Maria Theresia used to hold secret meetings with her foremost adviser Prince Kaunitz.

Beyond the Great Gallery you pass through the **Carousel Room**, whose name derives from the painting showing the amazonian Maria Theresia mounted on a Lipizzaner in a ladies' tournament held at the Winter Riding School in 1743, to the

Ceremonial Hall with Van Metyens paintings of Josef II's wedding to Isabella of Parma in 1760. Here the cheapskates who opted for the Imperial Tour are ushered out of the building.

The last section – the **Audience Rooms** – are only included in the Grand Tour and are undoubtedly the most worthwhile. Starting with the airy chinoiserie Blue Chinese Room where Karl I abdicated in 1918, visitors pass into the rather stultifying Vieux-Lacque-Zimmer whose black lacquered panelling adorned with Japanese landscapes was designed by Canavale around 1770. Here too is Batoni's portrait of Maria Theresia's husband Franz I. In the walnut-panelled Napoleon Room, the diminutive Corsican is thought to have slept during his two sojourns at Schönbrunn and evidence also suggests that here Maria Theresia sweated through the birth of her 16 children.

The elaborate Porcelain Room, the work of Isabella de Parma, with its *trompe l'oeil* criss-cross parasol motifs, has more painted woodwork than actual Meissen porcelain. However, no expense was spared in the subsequent Millionenzimmer where Maria Theresia reputedly spent a million silver florins on its rosewood panelling and priceless Persian and Indian miniatures.

After the Gobelinsalon with its eighteenth-century Brussels tapestries, you get to the Memorial Room dedicated to 'L'Aiglon' (the Little Eagle), the Duc de Reichstadt, Napoleon's son by Archduchess Marie Louise, who was virtually kept prisoner in Schönbrunn after his father's fall from grace in 1815 until his untimely death at the age of 21. After Maria Theresia's Bedroom, the remaining rooms used to be the domain of Franz Josef's father Archduke

Franz Karl and contain innumerable portraits of sundry Habsburgs.

It is a shame that no access is allowed to the **Bergl Rooms**, which the Dutch botanist Jacquin decorated with magnificent colourful frescoes depicting a variety of tropical birds and plantlife on idealised classical backgrounds. Outside you have the opportunity to visit two sets of outbuildings, the Orangery and the **Wagenburg** (*see chapter* **Museums**) for which there is an extra charge. A rest in the gardens is probably the most advisable course of action after the overkill of the interiors.

THE PARK

While the Habsburgs had done everything in their power to avoid the pernicious rationalist influence of France (Maria Theresia was the first monarch to speak French) and remain true to the Catholic ideal and Spanish court manners, the Baroque gardens of Schönbrunn were their first espousal of the fashions of Paris. After this there was no going back and from Maria Theresia's time onwards the language at court was Schönbrunner Deutsch, upper-class twitishly nasal and peppered with French expressions – the Viennese still call their milky coffee a *melange* and refer to the pavement as the *trottoir*.

The first gardens at Schönbrunn had been laid out at the beginning of the eighteenth century by Jean Trehet according to Fischer von Erlach's plans, but these were greatly extended under the joint monarchy of Maria Theresia and Josef II, creating the network of avenues that intersect at two central points either side of the broad parterre that runs from the palace to the *Neptunbrunnen* (Fountain of Neptune, 1781). In the distance on the brow of the hill rises the majestic form of the Gloriette – today the rather snooty **Café Gloriette** (*see chapter* **Cafés & Coffeehouses**) with the best view of the palace and gardens. To the east of the fountain lie most of the park's follies amid the encroaching woodland: Von Hohenberg's superb Roman ruins (1778) and his Obelisk Fountain (1777), as well as the *Schöner Brunnen* from which the palace's name derives and later set in a grotto by Canavale with the statue of a nymph pouring its waters into an enormous scallop basin.

Like the Prater and the Augarten, it was during the reign of Josef II in 1779 that the gardens of Schönbrunn were also opened to the public. He reputedly countered complaints at court with the remark that if he wanted to spend all his time among equals, he would have to dwell in the Kaisergruft among the tombs of the dead Habsburgs.

Tiergarten und Palmenhaus
Zoo and Palm House
13, Hietzinger Tor (Zoo 877 9294/Palmenhouse 877 5087-406)). U4 Hietzing. **Open** Zoo Oct-Apr 9am-4.30pm daily. *May-Sept* 9am-6.30pm daily. Palm House *Oct-Apr* 9.30am-5pm daily. *May-Sept* 9.30am-6pm daily.
Admission Zoo AS95; AS45 concs; AS30 children. *Palm House* AS45; AS40 OAPs; AS30 students; AS20 children. *Combination ticket* AS120; AS105 concs; AS60 students; AS40 children.
No credit cards.

A large section of the western side of the gardens is taken up by the Tiergarten (zoo) built on the site of Franz Stephan's royal menagerie (1752), making it the world's oldest zoo. The first animals came from Prince Eugene's menagerie at the Belvedere. Many of the original Baroque buildings and cages are still in use but most of the zoo's 750 or so species now have more modern quarters. These are laid out radially in 12 units around the central octagonal pavilion (1759), all the work of Jean Nicholas Jadot. The pavilion was originally used as a breakfast room by the imperial family and today it is a restaurant catering for visitors to one of the most aesthetically pleasing zoos in existence. Apart from the usual selection of animals, there is also a *Streichelzoo* (petting zoo) where children can get up close to more harmless species and stroke them. Also, on the sloping area to the south, there is the Tirolergarten with a reconstructed timber Tyrolean farmhouse and numerous farmyard animals, where the royals could get back to the land.

The main entrance to the zoo is the Hietzinger Tor but you can also enter near the Neptune Fountain and to the south of the park behind the Tirolergarten. It's worth getting one of the so-called KombiKarte, which includes access to the Palmenhaus, situated near the Hietzinger Tor entrance beside the botanical gardens (1754). Maria Theresia's husband Emperor Franz was a keen botanist and gardener, financing expeditions to Africa and the West Indies

'Is that fur real?' **Schönbrunn***'s zoo.*

Grave danger: **Zentralfriedhof**, *where tombstones go bump in the night.*

to collect rare species and bring them back to Vienna. To oversee the whole process he had Dutch experts such as the botanist Jacquin and the gardener Van Steckhoven brought in. The magnificent iron and glass construction of the Palmenhaus, a replica of the one in Kew Gardens, is the work of Segenschmid and dates from 1882. The space is separated into three different climatic zones.

Hietzing

With the presence of the monarchy at Schönbrunn, the process of gentrification started early in the neighbouring village of Hietzing, and today, along with the 19th district around Grinzing, it is one of the poshest areas of the city with astronomical house prices. With a rapid U-Bahn connection to the city centre and a vast area of the Wienerwald on its doorstep, Hietzing was already a des res area in the nineteenth century, home to the business elite and successful bohemians such as Egon Schiele, who from 1912 had his studio at Hietzinger Hauptstraße 101, the area's main drag. Today the street is not particularly charming, but once you wander into the side streets and see some of the magnificent Modernist and Biedermeier villas, it has some of the leafy gentility of Hampstead. Hietzing institutions include the Café Dommayer where Johann Strauß

To Hell with steeples – **Wotruba Kirche**. *See page 94.*

gave his first public concert in 1844. The clientele, young men with rosy cheeks and cravats, are first cousins to the typical English public schoolboy. Much more recommendable for food, drinks and public is the slightly shabby Jugendstil Café Wunderer on Hadikgasse, the opposite side of the U-Bahn line from Hietzing village. Round the corner from the Dommayer is the imposing edifice of the Parkhotel Schönbrunn (1907) where the Emperor's guests used to hole up.

Hofpavilion Hietzing
13, Schönbrunner Schloßstraße (877 1571). U4 Hietzing. **Open** 1.30-4.30pm Tue-Sun. **Admission** AS25; AS10 concs. **No credit cards**.
If you take the U-Bahn to Hietzing, you emerge through a station that has all the concrete charm of Birmingham's Bullring. Look east and Otto Wagner's Hofpavilion, a private station for the imperial family, comes into view. Built in 1899 on Wagner's own initiative (probably to ingratiate himself to the monarchy), this copper-domed cube adorned with decorative ironwork is a reminder of the golden years of the railway, but maybe a tad too ornate to form part of the Jugendstil pantheon.

Complete with a wrought-iron awning for the imperial carriage and a magnificent mahogany-panelled octagonal waiting room heated by a marble fireplace, this little extravagance was used by Franz Josef on precisely two occasions. His allergy to technological advance was legendary. Like Wagner's Karlsplatz pavilions, this one also looks a bit obsolete amid all the roaring traffic, but the interior, fine work from the Wagner/Olbrich tandem with a superb asymetric Wiener Werkstätte carpet by the

Backhausen firm (*see chapter* **Shopping & Services**), photos of Wagner's work and original posters for his Stadtbahn project make it well worth the price of entrance.

Hietzing's villas

Architecture fanatics will have a field day wandering through Hietzing's residential streets. There are houses by Josef Hoffmann, Friedrich Ohmann and Adolf Loos, but unfortunately none of them is open to the public. The individual villas are also widely dispersed so be prepared for some hefty walks.

However, there is a high concentration on Gloriettegasse to the west of the Schloßpark where at number 9 Katherina Schratt, Franz Josef's lover was installed in a rather modest Biedermeier villa, enabling the Emperor to pay her morning visits. Further west along the street at number 21 is the Villa Schopp, Friedrich Ohmann's fine Jugendstil house built in 1902 with floral motifs and superb decorative iron-work.

At number 18 is Josef Hoffmann's monumental Skywa-Primavesi Villa (1913-5), a rather neo-Classical reading of Modernism with four imposing central pillars on a symmetrical frontage with two large triangular pediments each housing a relief of a male and female figure. Commissioned by a wealthy landowner, it now serves as a training centre for the ÖGB, the Austrian Trade Union Confederation. Walk further west up the Gloriettegasse and on the brow of the hill you get a stupendous vista of the **Kirche am Steinhof** with the woods in the background.

There are five Adolf Loos villas in Hietzing. Three of them are located in the area bounded by Lainzer Straße and Hietzinger Hauptstraße (bus 58 and 60): Villa Scheu at Larochegasse 3; Villa Straßer at Kupelwiesergasse 28; and Villa Steiner at St-Veit-Gasse 10. Beyond Hietzinger Hauptstraße and close to the Kai is Villa Rufer at Schließmanngasse 11 and a great deal further west is the Villa Horner at Nothartgasse 7.

A good kilometre up the nearby Veitingergasse is the Werkbundsiedlung, a wedge-shaped housing project of 70 individual homes built between 1930 and 1932 by a group of Modernist architects including Loos and Hoffmann under the direction of Josef Frank. These small geometric Bauhaus-style homes were originally intended for sale, but even after following strict economic criteria for their construction, they proved too expensive for prospective purchasers and were bought by the City Council in 1934 and rented out. Four were destroyed in World War II, but today, after renovation in the early 1980s, there is something almost idyllic about the whole estate. In the house Frank himself designed at Woinovichgasse 32 there is a small documentation centre with information about the project.

Hietzinger Friedhof

Hietzing Cemetery
13, Maxingstraße 15. U4 Hietzing, then 10-minute walk. Bus 56b, 58b, 156b. **Open** *Mar, Apr, Sept, Oct* 8am-5pm daily. *May-Aug* 8am-6pm daily. *Nov-Feb* 9am-4pm daily. **Admission** free.
The graves of many illustrious Viennese reside in this picturesque cemetery located south of the Tirolergarten on the south side of the Schloßpark: a testimony to Hietzing's popularity among both the wealthy and the artistically inclined. Top tombs include Gustav Klimt and Otto Wagner, though the latter's is disappointingly Jugendstil-free and frankly quite pompous. Also buried here are the composer Alban Berg, Austria's greatest nineteenth-century dramatist Franz Grillparzer, the leader of the Austro-Fascists Engelbert Dollfuß, and Klimt and Wagner's friend and collaborator Kolo Moser.

Lainzer Tiergarten & Hermesvilla

13, Lainzer Tiergarten (entrance on Lainzertor) (804 1324). Bus 60b. **Open** *Apr-Sept* 10am-6pm Tue-Sun. *Oct-Mar* 9am-4.30pm Tue-Sun. **Admission** AS50; AS25 concs; AS20 schoolchildren; AS75 family card. **No credit cards**.
To the west of Hietzing lies a vast tract of countryside bordering the Wienerwald known as the Lainzer Tiergarten, literally zoo, but referring more than anything to the large number of wild boar and deer that roam freely throughout its woods and meadows. The Lipizzaner horses also graze here during the summer months, so for kids with an animal-bent the area is paradise. Karl VI (1685-1740), Maria Theresia's father, used to enjoy a spot of hunting here and under Josef II a 40km (25mile) long perimeter wall was built around the whole estate. It's a bit of a trek from the city centre but for those in need of greenery and peace and quiet it can't be beat. The only major sight, apart from the wildlife, is Hermesvilla, a brick-built mansion commissioned by Franz Josef as a gift to Sissi in an attempt to save their floundering marriage. It's a gentle ten-minute walk from the Lainzer Tor. Hermesvilla was named by Sissi herself after her favourite Greek god, but in spite of interiors by Klimt and Makart and a purpose-built gymnasium she never developed any great fondness for the place.

Wotruba Kirche

13, Georgsgasse/Rysergasse (888 5003). S-Bahn 1, 2 Atzgersdorf-Mauer/bus 60a Kasernegasse. **Open** 2-4pm Thur-Fri; 2-8pm Sat; 9am-5pm Sun. Guided tours by appointment.
To the south of Lainzer Tiergarten near the village of Mauer lies another of Vienna's ecclesiastical eccentricities – the Church of the Holy Trinity by Austrian sculptor Fritz Wotruba (1907-75), a curious conjunction of rectangular slabs of concrete illuminated by narrow, vertical glass panels. The general effect is that of a voluminous Brutalist sculpted mass, tempered by the bucolic surroundings of the Wienerwald. Its attempt to create the atmosphere of a sanctuary within these foreboding forms has been unanimously applauded by the Viennese.

Red or dead? Rotes Wien*'s socialist designs.*

Southern Vienna

The southern districts of Vienna hold little of specific interest for the visitor, but for anyone wishing to get off the beaten track and see something of the city's main working-class districts there are a handful of minor sights. The main reason people head south is to visit the vast **Zentralfriedhof**, Vienna's main cemetery with over two million tombs – far more than the city's present population.

Vienna's 10th district, Favoriten, is the city's largest with a population of around 170,000. It was the focus of emigration for Czechs in the nineteenth century, and a *Favoritner* today is something like the Viennese equivalent of a cockney Londoner and Reumannplatz is the Bow Bells of Vienna. Named after labour leader and Socialist politician Jacob Reumann, it is a lively square with a market on the nearby pedestrian Favoritenstraße and Vienna's best-loved ice-cream salon Tichy, with a fast connection to the city centre via the U1. Right on the square is the imposing **Amalienbad** (1926), Vienna's largest public baths with room for 1,300 bathers. The main pool has an arched glass roof that can be opened and the facilities are decorated throughout with fine colourful mosaics in designs reminiscent of Jugendstil. From Reumannplatz you can take bus 68a to Urselbrunnengasse to visit the Böhmischer Prater (Bohemian Prater), a curiously old-fashioned mini-version of Vienna's premier fairground with antiquated rides, beer gardens and sausage stands, much loved by local inhabitants.

Zentralfriedhof

Central Cemetery
11, Simmeringer Hauptstraße 234 (760 410). Tram 71, 72. **Open** *May-Aug 7am-7pm; Mar, Apr, Sept, Oct 7am-6pm; Nov-Feb 8am-5pm.* **Admission** free.

The Zentralfriedhof is up there with Père Lachaise and Highgate in the European graveyard itinerary. Opened in 1870 by the City Council, when the St Marx cemetery had reached its capacity, this enormous cemetery has somewhere in the region of 2.5 million tombs, pantheons and memorials laid out over an area larger than the Innere Stadt. As you arrive on the tram one side of the Simmeringer Hauptstraße is taken up with an endless line of undertakers and stonemasons (there are none on the city's high streets), as well as a fair share of cafés and restaurants catering for mourners and visitors. If you are in need of refreshments, be sure to visit the bizarre candlelit Schloß Concordia at number 283, a mixture of café, restaurant and summer terrace with literary events, musical performances and interesting clientele.

Given its scale, the cemetery has three different tram stops: the first leaves you near the old Jewish cemetery and Schloß Concordia; the second at the main entrance; and the third by the entrance to the Protestant and new Jewish sections. The main entrance is probably the best bet as there you can pick up a guide in English (AS50) and go straight to the Ehrengräber (the tombs of honour) where many well-known Viennese lie. Follow the main avenue past the semicircular line of tombs encrusted into arches – don't miss the memorial to mining baron August Zwang resembling the entrance to a mine guarded by lamp-wielding dwarves –

and in sector 32A you will see the tombs and memorials to Austria's most famous composers.

The centrepiece is a monument to Mozart although he is in fact buried in an unmarked grave in **St Marxer Friedhof**. Beethoven and Schubert were moved here from the Währing cemetery in 1899, but among those actually laid to rest here are Brahms, Hugo Wolf and most of the Strauß clan. On the opposite side of the avenue are the extravagant tombs of influential Viennese such as the Ringstraße architect Hansen (Danish in fact) and the painter Makart. Back on the avenue heading towards the main church in a circular recess is the Prezidentsgruft, with the remains of the Presidents of the Second Republic. Nearby in section 33C there are a number of interesting graves, such as those of Bruno Kreisky and Arnold Schönberg who lies under an extraordinary cube-like form crafted by sculptor Fritz Wotruba, himself buried in the same area.

The central monument of the cemetery is the Dr-Karl-Lueger-Kirche (1910), the work of Otto Wagner's pupil Max Hegele with more than a nod in the direction of his mentor's **Kirche am Steinhof**. The whole thing is a mausoleum to Vienna's populist Mayor, 'der schöne Karl', anti-Semite extraordinaire Karl Lueger.

Beyond the church visitors thin out, but for those with an interest in the cruel history of the twentieth century there are several fascinating sections, such as the Soviet war cemetery with the graves of soldiers who died during the 1945 liberation of Vienna directly behind the church.

Further on there is a monument to the victims of World War I, the graves of 7,000 Austrians who died fighting the Nazis (sector 97) and those of the victims of the 1934 Civil War and Austrian members of the International Brigade who fell in the Spanish Civil War (section 28).

Numerous sections of the Zentralfriedhof are given over to non-Catholics. South of the main gate near the outer wall is the Russian Orthodox sector laid out around an onion-domed temple, and sectors 26 and 36 contain Moslem graves. However, the old Jewish section to the north near the first gate should not be missed. Overgrown and desecrated, the sheer size (over 60,000 graves) gives an idea of the importance of Vienna's Jewish community before the Nazis. Among those buried here are members of the Austrian branch of the Rothschild family and the novelist and playwright Arthur Schnitzler.

Northern Vienna

The hills of the northern part of the Wienerwald are visible from various points along the western side of the Ringstraße. These hills, ending abruptly at the Danube are in fact the continuation of the foothills of the Alps away to the south-west. This L-shaped expanse of forest is the lung of the city, offering the Viennese myriad opportunities for leisure and relaxation, and inspiration for the city's writers and musicians. From Schottentor you can take any number of trams to explore the four wine-growing villages that now form part of urban Vienna. Nußdorf, Grinzing, Sievering and Neustift am Walde used to be separate entities that became wealthy by supplying the city with the slightly acid white wine the Viennese drink with so much relish. With olde worlde architecture surrounded by vines and forests and impressive views over the whole city, they rapidly became home to the city's wealthier denizens.

Unlike Hietzing in the west, this area has no U-Bahn connection, so tram's the word and count on at least 30 minutes to reach the various termini. Although the area is peppered with sights of an architectural/historical nature such as the monumental Karl-Marx-Hof housing complex, the Jugendstil villas of Hohewarte or numerous Beethoven memorials, the main reason why visitors head up here is to get a head full of young white wine in one of the many Heurigen or wine taverns. While the *Heurigen* of this area are almost universally decried as commercial or touristy by self-respecting *echte Wiener* (real Viennese), the combination of wine and views is a must for any visitor, and anyway there are still plenty of establishments that are not rip-offs. *See also chapter* **Heurigen**.

Karl-Marx-Hof

19, Heiligenstädter Straße 82-92. U4 Heiligenstadt/tram D.

If you're heading towards Nußdorf, it's worth breaking the journey to see this imposing salmon pink kilometre-long housing complex, which has become a symbol of the so-called *Rotes Wien* (Red Vienna) period of municipal Socialism between 1919 and 1933. The most durable legacy of this period are the *Gemeindebauten*, gigantic council housing projects, erected throughout Vienna's suburbs and financed by the *Wohnbausteuer* (Home Building Tax), levied on wealthier citizens. While they are not that architecturally innovative, they did provide thousands of decent dwellings and facilities for working-class families in the city and have weathered considerably better than similar post-1945 projects.

Built between 1926 and 1930, the Karl-Marx-Hof originally consisted of 1,325 flats, some as small as 26sq m (280sq ft), as well as a laundry, kindergarten, library, post office, clinic, shop premises, public baths and gardens. During the 1934 Civil War that brought the Austro-Fascists to power, Karl-Marx-Hof was a bastion of left-wing resistance and the building was almost destroyed by heavy artillery fire.

In 1989 a full restoration programme involving the modernisation of the flats and the building's connection to the Fernwärme district heating system was completed. The very name Karl-Marx-Hof, emblazoned on its frontage alongside allegorical reliefs depicting Child Welfare, Liberation, Physical Culture and Enlightenment, is such an affront to late twentieth-century global capitalism that this building's place in the pantheon of social experimentation is fully assured.

Nußdorf & Leopoldsberg

The nearest of the wine villages to the Danube, Nußdorf lies in the shadow of Leopoldsberg (425m/1,395ft), the second highest point of the Wienerwald, overlooking the Danube valley. Leopold of Babenberg had built a fortress on top of the hill in the eleventh century and 500 years later in 1683 an assortment of princes loyal to the Habsburgs descended on Vienna to break the Turkish siege. The summit can be reached by bus 38a from Heiligenstadt U-Bahn along the impressive cobbled Hohenstraße (*see also chapter* **Wienerwald**) built by a public works scheme during the Austro-Fascist regime of the 1930s. Walkers can choose between a hefty 3km uphill walk from Nußdorf or the shorter, more intense zig-zag footpath that begins in Kahlenbergerdorf.

Next to Leopoldskirche (1693) and the ramparts there is a shady courtyard where you can have a drink and enjoy the views. Inside the church there is a display about the Turkish siege, and the main lookout point has a memorial to Austrian POWs imprisoned in the USSR until the 1950s.

Nußdorf's reputation is built around its wine industry and numerous Heurigen, especially along the narrow picturesque Kahlenberger Straße. The Eroicagasse on the south side of the Kahlenberger Straße takes you to the popular Mayer am Pfarrplatz, more a restaurant than a Heuriger, located in a fine Biedermeier house where Beethoven lived for a time. Here too you are a stone's throw from Otto Wagner's sluice gate system for the Donaukanal, but access is a little complicated as you have to wind your way across the railway and through the industrial estate.

Heiligenstädter-Testament-Haus

Heiligenstadt Testament House
19, Probusgasse 6 (375 408). Tram D, 37/bus 38a. **Open** 9am-12.15pm, 1-4.30pm Tue-Sun. **Admission** AS25; AS10 concs. **No credit cards.**

Virtually next door to Mayer am Pfarrplatz is the so-called Heiligenstädter-Testament-Haus, one of Beethoven's many residences in this area where, in 1802, he wrote his famous testament or letter to his brothers in which he bequeathed them his fortune, apologising for his misanthropy and spoke frankly of his oncoming deafness. Here too he wrote his Second Symphony. The house is now one of Vienna's three museums dedicated to the composer and exhibits include a copy of the Testament, Beethoven's death mask and a lock of his hair. Across the courtyard is the rival Beethoven Austellung, belonging to the Beethoven Society but with little to recommend it apart from the chance to see inside another wing of the house.

The area is positively bristling with Ludwig van memorabilia – the street names such as Eroicagasse and Beethovengang as well as a Beethoven monument (1910) by Robert Weigl in the Heiligenstädter Park on the south side of Grinzinger Straße. On this street too number 64 is the house that Beethoven shared for a time in 1808 with the dramatist Franz Grillparzer. If you head back towards the city with tram 37 along Döblinger Hauptstraße, you can visit the Eroicahaus at number 92 where he composed his Third Symphony, the *Eroica*. This is the third Beethoven Museum, with identical opening times.

If you have the energy, follow Kahlenberger Straße uphill out of Nußdorf to the north for about

2km through the vineyards and at number 210 is the Sirbu, a Heuriger with magnificent views of the Danube and an excellent roast pork-oriented buffet (open Apr-mid-Oct, 3pm-midnight Mon-Sat). If you feel like further exertions, you could try making it up to the Kahlenberg (or bald mountain), the highest point of this section of the Wienerwald at 484m (1,588ft) or the more gentle option of walking downhill to Kahlenbergerdorf beside the Danube where there are buses back to the city.

Grinzing & Kahlenberg

The village of Grinzing is the quintessence of Viennese rural kitsch, ably manipulated by innkeepers and restaurateurs to keep the cash registers ringing. The most famous of Vienna's wine villages, virtually all tour groups are bussed into Grinzing for a night of tart white wine and *Schrammelmusik* at any one of the establishments along Grinzing's picturesque main drag. The combination of villagey atmosphere and countryside has proved irresistible to Vienna's wealthier denizens for over a century now and Grinzing, like the other lesser-known nearby villages, is the des res of the diplomatic community and others with money to burn.

Mahler fans may well consider a visit to Grinzinger Friedhof to visit his austere Jugendstil tomb by Josef Hoffmann. Other famous residents include Ringstraße architect Ferstel and formidable art groupie Alma Mahler, wife to Gustav, writer Franz Werfel and Bauhaus luminary Walter

Gropius, while also finding time for flings with Kokoschka and Klimt.The daughter she had by Gropius, Manon, is also buried here. The cemetery is located on Mannagettagasse off Straßergasse.

If you tire of the sickly prettiness of Grinzing, a trip on the 38a bus is one of the most spectacular routes in the city, along **Höhenstraße** (*see also chapter* **Wienerwald**) taking in fine views of the forest and the city. The first possible stop is Am Cobenzl, a look-out point with bar and restaurant with views of Grinzing's vineyards. Further up you could descend at Krapfenwaldgasse and have a swim at the Krapfenwaldbad, the city's posh-totty swimming baths. Although the pools are fairly small, the parkland is magnificent with some of the most northerly Mediterranean pines in Europe and, of course, superb views. The whole place is a paean to state intervention in the leisure industry.

The 38a chugs on up Höhenstraße to the highest point on the range, Kahlenberg, which for many years was thought to be the rallying point of the victors over the Turks until historians finally decanted for the neighbouring Leopoldsberg. Today the hill has a restaurant from whose terrace you can probably see as far as Hungary on a clear day.

Back down in Grinzing, recommended Heurigen in this area are **Weingut Reisenberg**, but more for the views than anything. The wine can be dodgy, the clientele obnoxious, but the food is excellent. By far the best in the area is **Zawodsky**, which has a beautiful garden full of apple trees, good simple food and drinkable wine (*see also chapter* **Heurigen**).

Museums

From crime to composers, burial to Baroque.

After an initial glimpse at Ringstraße Vienna, it is tempting and plausible to see the whole city as a gigantic museum or waxworks, staunchly rejecting innovation and modernity. The city's two monster museums, the **Kunsthistorisches** and the **Naturhistorisches**, are paradigms of nineteenth-century museum architecture with little in their interiors to suggest that modern notions of interactiveness and user-friendliness have taken much of a hold here. Peter Noever's renovation of the **MAK**, Vienna's temple to the arts and crafts, was internationally praised for being a step in the right direction, but until the Museumsquartier project is completed (*see page 38* **Past, present & future**), Vienna will remain short of modern exhibition space and open to the charge of being fossilised.

What should be said of Vienna's museums, however, is that they are unparalleled in the eclectic nature of their contents and their choice of locations. They deal with the strange, often sublimated aspects of human activity and society: crime, pathology, funeral rites, alcohol and tobacco. In a city where collecting is a hobby undertaken with semi-spiritual fervour, it is hardly surprising to

find museums to dolls, teddy bears and clocks. Vienna's musical heritage is also well represented by a large number of memorial rooms, of varying degrees of interest and authenticity, dedicated to famous composers associated with the city. All of these are installed in a bewildering variety of villas, Baroque townhouses, summer palaces and, of course, monolithic nineteenth-century colossi.

TICKETS & INFORMATION

As a rule, the smaller the museum the fewer the concessions made to visitors. Opening times can be baffling and labelling in English a rarity. On the plus side, you are likely to get the undivided attention of overseers so don't hesitate to ask them to make clocks chime or re-run videos.

If you're intending to take in more than a couple of museums, the Vienna Card is a worthwhile purchase as museums don't come cheap here. Admission may well change in 2000 as museums are now independent financial entities and are, therefore, able to specify their own prices.

Although the Vienna Card holder may take any underground, tram or bus for a period of 72 hours

*The overwhelming **Kunsthistorisches Museum** – one of the finest in Europe. Page 101.*

and enjoy reductions in some shops, restaurants and sightseeing events, it is advisable beforehand to weigh the advantages for museum visits. Upon purchase, the card holder receives a 64-page booklet of the museums that offer reductions ranging from 10% (Kunsthistorisches Museum) to 55% (Albertina). The three-day ticket costs AS210. There is an added advantage for families: a child up to 15 years may ride the public transport free. The Vienna Card is sold at hotels, the tourist information office (*see chapter* **Directory**), 14 sales counters (all over the city) and the Vienna Transport information offices (Stephansplatz, Karlsplatz, Westbahnhof, Landstraße/Wien Mitte) or with a credit card by phone (7984 40028).

1st district

Akademie der bildenden Künste

Academy of Fine Arts

1, Schillerplatz 3 (1st floor on the right) (5881 6225/ GemGal@akbild.ac.at). U1, U2, U4 Karlsplatz. **Open** 10am-4pm Tue-Sun. **Admission** AS50; AS20 concs; AS30 Vienna Card holders. **No credit cards.**
Set back from the Ring behind a statue of Friedrich Schiller, Theophil von Hansen's Academy of Fine Arts houses a fine, but largely forgotten picture gallery. A friendly porter points the way to the star of the show – Hieronymus Bosch's *The Last Judgement*. Room 1 is darkened to enhance the impact of Bosch's only monumental triptych (1504-6) outside Spain. The academy also has a lot to answer for by turning down the 18-year-old Adolf Hitler's application to study here in 1907. Egon Schiele was accepted, but had a miserable time. The collection includes work such as *Tarquin and Lucretia* by Titian, Botticelli's *Madonna Tondo*, and Rembrandt's early *Unknown Young Woman*, but the bulk are Flemish and Dutch paintings. Admirers of Rubens will delight in the numerous oil sketches for his frescoes of the Jesuit Church in Antwerp (lost in an eighteenth-century fire) and Whitehall in London. Room 4 is dedicated to neo-Classicism and works by the academy's professors, who are contractually obliged to contribute at least one work.

Archiv des österreichischen Widerstands

Austrian Resistance Archive

1, Wipplingerstraße 8 (Altes Rathaus, stairway 3) or Salvatorgasse 7 (53 436/01 779/fax 53 436/990 1771/docarch@email.adis.at). U1, U3 Stephansplatz, U1, U4 Schwedenplatz/tram 1, 2. **Open** 9am-5pm Mon-Thur (telephone in advance). **Admission** free.
This permanent exhibition in the Old Town Hall was set up to educate the country's youth about the consequences of Austria's loss of self-identity and freedom after Nazi annexation in March 1938. Once past the dusty door (you must telephone first as the place is often closed), there are various displays (with German and English labelling) on subjects such as the rise of Austro-Fascism, Civil War in 1934, persecution of the Jews, neo-Nazi activities after WWII and 'Fascism is not Dead'. As pertinent as ever.

Dom- und Diozesanmuseum

Cathedral and Diocese Museum

1, Stephansplatz 6 (523 560). U1, U3 Stephansplatz. **Open** 10am-5pm Tue-Sat. **Admission** AS70; AS50 concs; AS30 groups of 7 or more. **No credit cards.**
Located in the Baroque Archbishop's Palace, this pricey museum can only be truly recommended to devotees of Baroque painting, with works by Austrian masters such as Anton Kraus, Franz Maulbertsch and Michael Angelo Unterberger. However, there is a hotch-potch of curiosities typical of ecclesiastical museums: the first European portrait on panel, that of Rudolph IV (1360); a Giotto-esque stained-glass window (1340) with *Jugendstil* ornamentation (restored 1900); and the blackened remnants of the cathedral's Gothic carved choir stalls (destroyed 1945 in a bombing raid). Another attraction, however, is the massive Nürnberg iron treasure chest (1678), displayed open to reveal the mechanics of its complex multi-lock system. The artist's inscription reads: 'The art [of construction] I have from God the Highest so I can mock my enemy', dating from the days of the Turkish onslaughts. The lock itself was never broken.

Figarohaus

Mozart Museum

1, Domgasse 5/Schulerstraße 8 (513 6294). U1, U3 Stephansplatz. **Open** 9am-6pm Tue-Sun.
Admission AS25; AS10 concs. **No credit cards.**
Mozart lived here between 1784 and 1787, his happiest years in Vienna, when he wrote *The Marriage of Figaro*. The house contains none of his personal effects – those that exist are all in his home town of Salzburg – only copies of famous manuscripts and a few prints of the man himself and his illustrious chums. Visitors can refresh their memories by listening to his works on the headphones provided, but this is only really for absolute devotees.

Jüdisches Museum

Jewish Museum of the City of Vienna

1, Dorotheergasse 11 (535 0431/fax 535 0424/info@jmw.at). U1, U3 Stephansplatz. **Open** 10am-6pm Sun-Fri; 10am-8pm Thur.
Admission AS70; AS40 concs. **No credit cards.**
Vienna has the distinction of being home to the world's first Jewish museum, opened in 1895 and closed, its exhibits confiscated, by the Nazis in 1938. Housed in the Palais Eskeles since 1993, the building was given the once-over in 1995 by ultra-trendy architects Eichinger oder Knechtl, and now serves as a study centre, archive and library, with three floors of exhibition space. The ground floor has an important collection of Judaica, displayed amid fragmented frescoes by Nancy Spero reworking images such as those of a medieval matzo bakery, Gustav Mahler conducting and the smoking remains of a synagogue razed by the Nazis. The first and second floors hold temporary exhibitions, often linking general historical, political and artistic themes of the city with the role of Jews and their interaction with the Gentile community. The second floor also has a permanent historical exhibition using 21 holograms to depict aspects of Jewish culture in Vienna. The

coffee served at the **Café Teitelbaum** was hailed the best in the city by *Falter* in 1999.
Website: www.jmw.at

Kunsthistorisches Museum

Museum of Fine Arts
1, Burgring 5 (entrance Maria Theresian-Platz) (52 524/info@khm.at). U2 Babenbergerstraße, U2, U3 Volkstheater/tram 1, 2, D, J. **Open** 10am-6pm Tue-Sun; 10am-9pm Thur. English lecture tours *Easter-1 Nov* 11am, 3pm, Tue-Sun. **Admission** AS100; AS70 concs; AS30 per person English lecture tours, minimum of ten. **No credit cards**.

One of the finest museums in Europe with a huge collection of the art treasures amassed by the Habsburgs. Indeed, more than a day is needed to appreciate these imperial galleries in full. The architectural and decorative programme of the building with its granites, marble and stucco interspersed with murals by Makart, Matsch, Gustav Klimt and his brother Ernst in the vestibule produces an almost overwhelming effect upon entry. The main galleries on the first floor are arranged in a horseshoe plan with Flemish, German and Dutch paintings in the east wing and Italian work in the west. Most visitors begin their tour in Room X, the busiest in the museum, with its almost unrivalled collection of work by Pieter Bruegel the Elder, acquired by Rudolph II. The nature theme of Bruegel's work can be seen in pictures such as *Hunters in the Snow* (1565). *The Peasant Wedding Feast* (1568-9) echoes repercussions of the Reformation and was the source of inspiration for Jacob Jordaens' boisterous and bawdy Baroque *The Feast of the Bean King* (c1656) in Room XI. Side-tracking to the smaller rooms (XVI), Albrecht Dürer's *The Adoration of the Trinity* (1511) illustrates his resplendent use of colour. Continuing to Room XVIII, Holbein's *Jane Seymour* (1536), his first portrait executed as Henry VIII's court painter, is crisply objective in characterisation and costume. The Flemish painter Anthony van Dyck's (Room XII) *Portrait of a Young Man in Armour* (c1624) is a subtle psychological study contrasting hard, shiny metal with the softness of white lace and pale facial features. Mannerist Giuseppe Arcimboldo's unusual, composite heads (Room XIX), allegories of the Seasons and Elements (1562-87), are not witticisms but imperial metaphors. The depiction of Fire incorporates symbols of the Order of the Golden Fleece into its facial profile. Rooms XIII and XIV contain the museum's collection of Peter Paul Rubens, depicting himself as a nobleman, but with tiny, tired lines around his eyes (*Self-Portrait*, 1638-40). Nearby *The Little Fur* (Room XIII), the name Rubens gave to the portrait of his second wife Helene Fourment, is a sensitively painted statement of the love of an older man for a younger woman (Helene was only 16 when she married the 53-year-old Rubens). She also stood model for the voluptuous girl captured by a lurid satyr in the *Worship of Venus*. Some of the facets of Dutch seventeenth-century life are visible in Jan Steen's humorous *Topsy-Turvy World* (1663) and Jan Vermeer's reflective *Art of Painting* (1665-6) (Rooms XXIII-IV). The three Rembrandt self-portraits (1652,

1656 and 1657) in Room XV have withstood the critical survey of experts and de-attribution. The intimate and personal portrait of his son *Titus* (1656) was painted during a time of insolvency. Crossing through the café takes you to Room VII and Bernardo Bellotto. He was taught by his uncle, the Venetian Antonio Canal, known as Canaletto. There are several of Bellotto's views of Vienna, commissioned by Maria Theresia, here. Caravaggio's major work *Madonna of the Rosary Feast* (1606-7), in Room V, was purchased by Rubens and his friends after the artist's death in 1610. The intense red drapery reappears later in Rubens' *Holy Family beneath an Apple Tree* in Room XIII. Three large rooms (I-III) are dedicated to the Venetian school: the works of Tintoretto, Veronese and Titian. The Titian collection covers 60 years of his development. Room II has one of the few authenticated works by Giorgione, *The Three Philosophers*. Raphael's *Madonna in the Meadow* (1505) in Room IV is a serene piece, its composition influenced by Leonardo da Vinci.

On the ground floor, the east wing (the Kunstkammer) is a chamber of curiosities and exotica (Rooms XIX-XXXVII) with ornaments, glassware, clocks, globes and astrolabes. Benvenuto Cellini's gold and enamel salt cellar (1540) was a present to Archduke Ferdinand of Tyrol. The Egyptian and Near Eastern collections (I-VII) of the west wing have large-scale wall paintings, pottery, the remains of mummified bulls' heads, crocodiles and cats and examples of Books of the Dead on papyrus. Room VII has the blue-green ceramic hippopotami that smile at you from every corner of the museum shop. The Greek and Roman collection in Rooms IX-XV includes the famous Gemma Augustea, a two-layered onyx cameo that commemorates the military victories of the first Roman Emperor.
Website: www.khm.at

Lipizzaner Museum

1, Stallburg/Hofburg, Reitschulgasse 2 (533 7781). U1, U3 Stephansplatz, U3 Herrengasse/tram 1, 2, D, J/bus 2a. **Open** 9am-6pm daily. **Admission** AS70; AS50 concs; combination ticket with Riding School morning exercise AS140; AS60 concs. **Credit** AmEx, DC, JCB, MC, V.

Only for those with an equestrian bent. The Lippizaner industry in Vienna milks unsuspecting tourists with exorbitant ticket prices and the museum is no different. Enter through what is a souvenir shop next to the imperial stables in the Renaissance Stallburg, run the gauntlet of the trinkets and you are in a fairly respectable display showing the history of the famous breed of white horses complete with Baroque paintings, saddles, liveries and uniforms. Through a couple of windows you can get a glimpse of the nags themselves in their stables.
Website: www.lipizzaner.at

Museum für Angewandte Kunst (MAK)

Museum of Applied Arts
1, Stubenring 5 (712 8000). U3 Stubentor, U4 Landstraße/tram 1, 2. **Open** 10am-6pm Tue-Wed, Fri-Sun; 10am-9pm Thur. **Admission** AS30; AS15

*Thoroughly modern **MAK**: Vienna's temple to the arts and crafts. See page 101.*

concs; free under-10s. For special exhibitions AS90; AS45 students, OAPs; free under-10s. **No credit cards**.

This is to Austria what the Victoria & Albert Museum is to England. The building dates from 1872 and is another neo-Renaissance work of Ferstel's. It was later extended to house the Arts and Crafts School that both Klimt and Kokoschka attended and later a wing was added, with access from the Weiskirchnerstraße, to house temporary exhibitions. In the course of a thorough revamping completed in 1993 many of the more interesting and younger artists with a footing in Vienna were invited to devise concepts for the various rooms. Some of these are excellent (Franz Graf's blue room, Gang Art's installation for the carpet collection, Barbara Bloom's presentation of the chair collection in silhouette) and make the collection truly remarkable despite the controversy surrounding such stagy presentation. The director is an architect, Peter Noever, which is starting to show in the new acquisitions (there being several architects' models among them), and the two larger spaces dedicated to temporary exhibitions tend to concentrate on the work of his pals such as Vienna-based art professor Bruno Gironcoli or American minimalist Donald Judd. For Jugendstil fanatics, the highlight is undoubtedly Klimt's *Stoclet Frieze*, originally commissioned in 1904 for the Palais Stoclet in Brussels.

The MAK Gallery tends to show the work of younger Vienna-based artists, for example Beatrice Stähli's grim trophies of unattractive pets and Flora Neuwirth's furniture installations. The interior of the MAK Café in the same building was designed by local star architect Herman Czech and is worth seeing for the reworked Thonet bentwood chairs. *Website: www.MAK.at*

Naturhistorisches Museum

Natural History Museum
1, Wien, Burgring 7 (52 177/oeff.arbeit@ nhm-wien.ac.at). U2 Babenbergerstraße, U2, U3 Volkstheater/tram 1, 2, D, J. **Open** 9am-6.30pm Mon, Thur-Sun; 9am-9pm Wed. **Admission** AS30; AS15 concs. **No credit cards**.

One of the largest natural history museums in the world and the scientific counterpart to the Kunsthistorisches Museum across the square. It was opened in 1889 and little has changed since then – some of the display cases are over a century old, the labelling is in German and little effort has been made to make the museum more interactive or even modern. The upper floor did get electric lighting in 1988. The basis of the collection is the work of Emperor Franz Stefan, Maria Theresia's husband, an amateur scientist who collected skulls, fossils, precious stones, meteorites and rare stuffed animals. It also includes items acquired by Rudolph II and Prince Eugene of Savoy. The most valuable piece has only recently been put on display: the 'Venus of Willendorf' (found in the Wachau) – a curvacious 11cm (4in) high limestone fertility symbol believed to be over 25,000 years old. When the figurine was moved from the museum for an exhibition in

Schönbrunn, she was transported in an Austrian Army armoured personnel carrier and insured to the tune of £50 million. The museum has minerals, meteorites, casts of dinosaurs and zoological exhibits. The range of meteors is considered valuable and members of staff work closely with NASA in comet research. It also has the world's largest collection of human skulls (some 43,000 – from 40,000 BC to the present), and is sometimes jokingly referred to as the second-largest cemetery in Austria; the largest single topaz known (110kg/243lb); and an ostrich given by Maria Theresia to her husband Franz Stephan with 761 precious stones and over 2,000 diamonds. The museum stores the oldest human sculpture, 'Fanny' from Stratzing (dated 32,000 BC), in a vault – photographs of it are on display.
Website: www.nhm.at

Neidhart-Fresken

Neidhart Frescoes
1, Tuchlauben 5 (535 9065). U1, U3 Stephansplatz. **Open** 9am-12pm Tue-Sun. **Admission** AS25; AS10 concs; free Fri. **No credit cards**.
This private house/museum contains the oldest secular frescoes in the city (1400-20), a chance find during the renovation of eighteenth-century Baroque stucco walls of a private home in 1979. A cloth merchant, Michel Menschein, commissioned this Four Seasons cycle depicting scenes of lively medieval jollity inspired by the songs and verse of Neidhart von Reuental (1180-1240), an aristocratic minstrel.

Österreichisches Theatermuseum

Austrian Theatre Museum
1, Palace Lobkowitz, Lobkowitzplatz 2 (512 8800/fax 512 8800-45/info@theatermuseum.at).

U1, U2, U4 Karlsplatz/tram 1, 2, D, J. **Open** 10am-5pm Tue, Thur-Sun; 10am-9pm Wed. *Children's museum* 10-10.30am, 2-2.30pm Tue-Sun.
Admission AS40; AS20 children; AS32 Vienna Card holders. **No credit cards**.
Housed in the Baroque Lobkowitz Palace, this museum will be reopening its permanent collection of costumes, stage models and theatrical memorabilia in February 2000. Special exhibitions have centred around great composers, directors and artists: Alfred Roller, Gustav Mahler, Mozart and Johann Strauß. Currently on display are various items from the Old Burgtheater (Altes Burgtheater), closed one day before the opening of the new Burgtheater on 14 October 1888: a stone counterweight for scenery changes, a seat from the stalls and a wooden model of the stage. The Jugendstil artist Richard Teschner designed an innovative convex mirror-stage as a puppet theatre, in which performances are held with his original figures and the original music score. Inquire about performances at the ticket booth. Open to visitors is the upstairs festival hall, where Beethoven's *Eroica* had its première in 1803: Beethoven had dedicated it Napoleon, later scratching out the dedication on learning of Napoleon's imperialistic ambitions.

Gedenkräume des österreichischen Theatermuseums

Memorial Rooms of the Austrian Theatre Museum
1, Hanuschgasse 3 (near Albertinaplatz) (512 2427). U1, U2, U4 Karlsplatz/tram 1, 2, D, J. **Open** 10am-noon, 1-4pm Tue-Fri; 1-4pm Sat. **Admissison** AS40; AS20 concs. **No credit cards**.
These are memorial rooms for the great and famous

Late nineteenth-century monolith, the **Naturhistorisches Museum***.*

Max Reinhardt, Hugo Thimig, Emmerich Kalman, Fritz Wotruba, Herman Bahr and others. Interesting for music and theatre students.

Puppen- und Spielzeugmuseum
Doll and Toy Museum
1, Schulhof 4 (tel/fax 535 6860). U1, U3, Stephansplatz, U3 Hertrengasse/bus 1a, 3a. **Open** 10am-6pm Tue-Sun. **Admission** AS60; AS30 concs; AS20 children over 6; AS40 for groups of 10 or more. **No credit cards.**

An eighteenth-century Viennese house, adjacent to the **Uhrenmuseum** (*see below*), adapted into a private museum in 1989 for 600 dolls and toys from the last two centuries – mostly of French and German origin. *Biedermeier* dolls with porcelain faces follow Empire ancestors of wood or wax, the oldest a Queen Anne doll (1750). Gaultier fashion dolls model exquisitely tailored robes. One-room doll's houses (*Puppenstuben*) are thematically arranged: stores, salons, kitchens, school rooms and even a doll shop – dolls selling dolls! There are also locomotives and some imperial toy soldiers, including a figure of Emperor Franz Josef (1900).

Sammlungen des Kunsthistorischen Museums in der Hofburg
Collections of the Fine Arts Museum in the Hofburg
1, Neue Burg, Heldenplatz (52 524). U1, U2, U4 Karlsplatz/tram 1, 2, D, J. **Open** 10am-6pm Wed-Mon. **Admission** AS60; AS30 concs; AS50 Vienna Card holders. **No credit cards.**

These three collections are an excuse to enter the imposing edifice of the Neue Burg, forever associated with Hitler's *Anschluß* addresss from the building's central balcony. Unfortunately there is no access to the actual spot. The museums are located on either side of the Neue Burg's monumental central staircase.

Ephesus Museum
Housed in the Neue Burg since 1978, this collection displays the spoils from nineteenth-century Austrian archaeological digs in Ephesus and Samothrace with architectural fragments, statues, a scale model of the site in Turkey and a 40m (131ft) frieze commemorating the victory of Lucius Verus over the Parthians.

Collection of Arms & Armour
Originally the collection of ceremonial arms acquired by two Habsburgs – Archdukes Ernst of Styria and Ferdinand of Tyrol, this is now one of the world's most extensive displays of arms and armour from the fifteenth to the seventeenth centuries. The collection follows the development of armour from late-Gothic tournaments to late-Renaissance wedding festivities, with items such as the costume suit for Albrecht of Brandenburg (1526) and the delicately fluted and tuckered version for Elector Otto Henry (1516). Bellicose followers of fashion indeed. Archduke Ferdinand of Tyrol (1547) was the other major contributor to the collection and his 87-piece eagle armour, which could be assembled in a variety of combinations, is one of the most impressive exhibits. Ferdinand's leather and blue embroidered

parade armour (1550-5) was repeated in four other colours: ash grey, red, black and white. The silver portrait head of Philip II of Spain, Ferdinand's gift of a gold rapier to Maximilian II and the embroidered saddle of Kara Mustafa, the besieger of Vienna in 1863, are among the collection's other highlights. The rows of Milanese, Turkish, Spanish and Flemish suits of armour, with fantastic visors, bird-like, dog-like, nightmare-like, give the collection a rather carnivalesque air.

Collection of Ancient Musical Instruments
Set up in the longest corridor of the Neue Burg, adjoining the Armoury Collection, this chronologically arranged collection was also started by Ferdinand of Tyrol. The German audio-guide is worth taking as it provides an atmospheric soundtrack played by the likes of Christopher Hogwood's Academy of Ancient Music. Renaissance instruments are the collection's forte and, together with the initiative of the conductor Nikolaus Harnoncourt, it has helped to rekindle an interest in early music played on original instruments. A reproduction of Maximilian's woodcut Triumphal Procession by his court artists Burgkmair, Beck and Dürer illustrates the period. In Room X, tiny models of instruments, toys for Ferdinand of Tyrol's children, his own lute with an ivory back (1580) and a cister with his coat-of-arms (1574) display an interest in rare and high-quality instruments. A Celestini virginal, loved by the 15-year-old Mozart, an Italian Baroque fish-form harp, 12 recorders in five sizes tuned in fifths, a quartet note-stand, a Schentz pianoforte, a composing table with notes for the blind Maria Theresia Paradis, six silver trumpets – outstanding specimens – purchased by Maria Theresia and paintings of musical soirées enhance the composers' rooms. Mozart, Haydn, Liszt and Brahms; a row of Bösendorfers, a portrait of the 13-year-old Beethoven and Haydn's wax bust with real hair and clothing are also present. The Romantic Age has a magnificent historicist Neo-Classical piano (prize-winner at the Paris World Exhibition in 1867) and designs from the modern movement, illustrated with pianos by Josef Hoffmann and Josef Frank, end with a synthesiser. The original four rock crystals whose form Josef Matthias Hauer used as a basis for the 12-tone system are also to be seen.

Teddybärenmuseum
Teddy Bear Museum
1, Drahtgasse 3 (tel/fax 533 4755). U1, U3 Stephansplatz/bus 1a, 3a. **Open** 10am-6pm Mon-Sat; 2-6pm Sun. **Admission** AS45; AS20 students, school children; AS10 under-6s. **Credit** AmEx, DC, MC, V.

Mechanical bears, antique bears, bears on wheels, drumming bears whose eyes light up – in fact, this museum, opened in 1996, has just about every type of teddy bear (and some other tin toys) to either provoke some childhood memories or interest your children. There's a shop too.
Website: www.teddybear.org

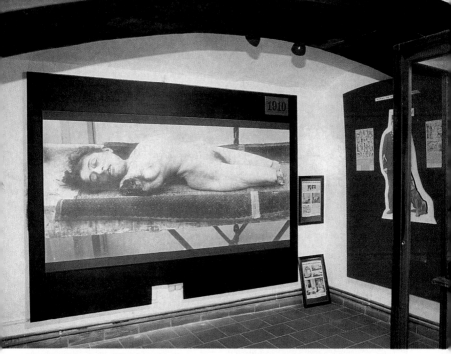
*Gruesome displays of heinous deeds on show at the **Kriminalmuseum**. See page 106.*

Uhrenmuseum

Clock Museum

1, Schulhof 2 (533 2265). U1, U3 Stephansplatz, U3 Herrengasse. **Open** 9am-4.30pm Tue-Sun. **Admission** AS50; AS25 concs; AS20 over-6s; AS75 family with two children under 15; free on Fri morning (except holidays); free tours every first/third Sun of the month (guides will speak English if requested). **No credit cards.**

Covering three floors of the Baroque Obizzi Palace, this museum houses clocks and chronometers from the fifteenth to the twentieth centuries (the most recent piece is a 1992 computer clock). This collection of over 3,000 timepieces ranges from tower, astronomical and novelty clocks to grandfathers and period pieces. There's a doorman on each floor to open the door when a visitor rings the bell. These bells, combined with the ticking and chiming of the clocks as time passes inexorably by, create a lilting soundtrack to your horological musing.

Völkerkundemuseum

Ethnological Museum

1, Neue Burg, Heldenplatz (534 30-0/fax 535 5320/vö@ethno-museum.ac.at). U1, U2, U4 Karlsplatz/tram 1, 2, D, J/bus 2a. **Open** 10am-4pm Wed-Mon. **Admission** AS50; AS80 families with two children under 15; AS25 for schoolchildren, groups of ten or more; AS50 Vienna Card holders; free entry on 16 May; 26 Oct; 10 & 24 Dec. Makeshift disabled access (wooden ramps). **No credit cards.**

While the Austro-Hungarian Empire dominated most of Central Europe and the Balkans, it never got a foothold in more far-flung places. Nonetheless it managed to assemble a more than respectable collection of exotica, now housed in the part of the Neue Burg nearest the Ringstraße. Divided into geographical sections with China, Korea and Japan on the ground floor and Polynesia and the Americas on the first floor, with a hunter/gatherer department in a separate wing, the anthropologically minded will enjoy its varied exhibits. Its most celebrated exhibit is the crown of Montezuma, a unique feathered headdress, the most valuable specimen on display in the Central America section. How it actually reached Europe is a contentious issue but the claim that it came to Vienna via a gift by Cortés to Karl V has raised the hackles of a group of Mexicans, who regularly hold protests in Stephansplatz, complete with drummers, dancers and nick-nack stalls, to demand its return. So far there has been no official petition on the part of the Mexican government. The crown itself is in a glass case at the end of a long corridor of stone gods and goddesses with unpronounceable names – Machuilxochitl and Quetzalcoatl – as if it were the grail of a long and arduous pilgrimage. A darkened adjoining room shows further outstanding feather mosaics, the best-preserved collection of these fragile objects in the world. Highlights of the Chinese section (Room IV) include a 375cm (12ft 4in) high bronze incense burner of the Q'ing period (1660) in front of a red lacquer carved screen (1760), celebrating the Mother of the West's birthday party. The room is dominated by a demon paper kite of the slayer spirit Zong Kui. Room VI has a colourful Japanese Doll Festival depicting Emperor and Empress reigning over rows upon rows of court ladies, musicians, generals and servants. The modernised Polynesian and Americas sections, much of it nabbed by Captain Cook and bought at auction by Franz I, use videos, sound and slides to recreate the perceived horrors of such things as Polynesian cannibalism. Look out for itinerant exhibitions too.

Website: www.ethno-museam.ac.at

2nd district

Ambrosi Museum

2, Scherzergasse 1a (216 4022). Tram N. **Open** 10am-5pm Tues-Sun. Closed until autumn 2000.
The atelier of Austrian sculptor Gustinus Ambrosi (1893-1975), converted into a museum and sculpture garden is run by the Österreichische Galerie, so a ticket to the Belvedere is valid here too. Located on the eastern side of the Augarten in a wooded zone known as the Englischen Park, the museum shows numerous works by the sculptor, but best of all are the bronze busts of various political and artistic personalities such as Otto Wagner and a surprising rendition of Mussolini with hair.

Johann Strauß Haus

2, Praterstraße 54 (214 0121). U1 Nestroyplatz. **Open** 9am-12.15pm, 1-4.30pm Tue-Fri. **Admission** AS25; AS10. **No credit cards**.
Unlike most of Vienna's myriad of music museums, this one at least has a go at period décor and actually has exhibits belonging to the 'King of the Waltz', such as his grand piano, organ and stand-up composing desk. There is also a vast collection of ball-related memorabilia including posters, invitation cards and pendants given out as keepsakes of events. Strauß lived in the house from 1863 to 1878 when his first wife died.

Kriminalmuseum

Crime Museum
2, Grosse Sperlgasse 24 (214 4678/fax 2144 6784). Tram 21, N. **Open** 10am-5pm Tue-Sun. **Admission** AS60; AS50 students, groups, OAPS; AS30 children. **No credit cards**.
It is hardly surprising that a city remarkable for the safety of its streets and absence of petty crime should have a museum dedicated to the heinous deeds committed within its confines. Exhibits are mostly photographs and press cuttings so this is only really for those with a good understanding of German. The museum oscillates between lionising villains such as Breitwieser, Vienna's greatest safebreaker whose funeral in 1919 was attended by hundreds of admirers, and offering interesting social background to cases such as Josephine Luner who tortured her maid, Anna Augustin, to death. The displays of Theresa Knoll murdering her husband with a hatchet (1808), of the first non-publicly executed robber/murderer Francesconi (1876), and of the husband who killed his bride on their wedding night (1932) are so gruesome that the feeling of many

visitors is best summed up by the entry in the visitors' book by a Scotsman: 'I'm glad I don't understand German.'

3rd district

Heeresgeschichtliches Museum

Museum of Military History
3, Hauptgebaude, Arsenal Objekt 18 (information 79 561/79 561-17 707). U1 Südtirolerplatz/tram D, O, 18/bus 13a, 69a. **Open** 9am-5pm Mon-Thur, Sat, Sun. **Admission** AS70; AS45 children; AS100 family. **No credit cards**.
Vienna's first purpose-built museum (commissioned by Franz Josef I and completed in 1856) was designed by the Danish architect Theophil Hansen as part of the Arsenal complex – one of the four large barracks built post-1848 to quell possible further unrest. Of these, only the Arsenal and the Roßauer Kaserne (*see chapter* **Sightseeing**) remain. Hansen's design broadens the range of Historicist devices to include Byzantine, Venetian Gothic and Moorish elements. Access to the museum is through the Feldherrenhalle (Hall of the Generals), lined with statues of pre-1848 Austrian military leaders. The museum is on two floors with courtyards given over to tanks and armoured vehicles. The first floor contains militaria from the Napoleonic Wars, the Austro-Prussian War as well as artefacts from the Renaissance, the Thirty Years' War (1618-48) and the second siege of Vienna (1683), which led to the defeat of the Turks and Habsburg dominion of the Balkans. The trophies captured in these campaigns are among the finest in the museum – Turkish standards, tents and the Great Seal of Mustafa Pasha. The west wing of the ground floor assembles all the uniforms of the armies of the Crown Lands after the reform of 1867. The sheer size and diversity of the Imperial Army, at one time protecting an empire of over 54 million subjects, is illustrated by the contents of a display showing the handbooks issued to all soldiers – including the oath of allegiance to Franz Josef I, in 11 different languages and three different scripts. The fascinating room covering the assassination in Sarajevo on 28 June 1914 of Archduke Franz Ferdinand contains the car he was shot in and his blood-stained tunic. A recent acquisition is the Mayor of Sarajevo's settee on which the Archduke bled to death, brought to Vienna in 1997 during the siege and bombing of Sarajevo by the Serbs. Further displays on World War I and its aftermath show all the tragedy of nationalism, particularly ironic being a Red Crescent poster requesting donations – via the Austro-Hungarian Imperial Army – for the Turkish Army: 200 years earlier, they had been foes on the battlefield. Albin Egger Linz's painting *To the Unknown Soldier*, in a style reminiscent of Stanley Spencer, encapsulates the mechanical lambs-to-the-slaughter butchery of World War I. The east wing of the ground floor, recently renovated, follows the history of the Austrian Navy. For a land-locked country, it's fairly impressive, with a good display on the 1872 expedition to the North Pole, which discovered and named Franz-Josef-Land.

Oberes Belvedere & österreichische Galerie

Upper Belvedere & Austrian Gallery
3, Prinz-Eugen-Straße, 27 (7955 7134/belvedere @belvedere.at). Tram D, O, 18. **Open** 10am-6pm Tue-Sun. 'English Insights' (short talks presenting selected highlights of the Upper Belvedere) 11am Tue-Fri.
Admission AS60; AS40 concs (includes entrance to Lower Belvedere museums). **No credit cards.**

The façade of the Upper Belvedere is one of Vienna's great sights and the view it commands of the city one of the best. Add to this the contents of the Austrian Gallery and it becomes clear why this is one of Vienna's biggest crowd-pullers. If you only get to one gallery during your stay, make it this one. Its attraction resides in its collection of paintings by Vienna's great Modernist triumverate – Klimt, Schiele and Kokoschka. The Austrian Gallery is the country's major collection of nineteenth-and early twentieth-century painting, both Austrian and European, divided into nine major categories. Among the Classical collection highlights are Caspar David Friedrich's *Sea-Shore in Mist* (1807) and David's *Napoleon on the St Bernhard* (1801). The Biedermeier/Romanticism section is full of pious family portraits in comfy bourgeois living rooms but also some interesting cityscapes of Vienna. For those unfamiliar with Austrian Realism, this section has the superb *Naschmarkt in Wien* (1894) by Carl Moll, later an influential member of the Secessionist movement, and Emil Jakob Schindler's (Alma Mahler's father) *Steamer at Kaisermühlen* (1872). Here there are also works by Courbet, Daumier, Delacroix and Corot. Impressionism is also present with Renoir's *After the Bath* (1876) and Van Gogh's *The Plain at Auvers* (1890), but the collection is patchy. The Historicist nudes of Hans Makart in *Bacchus and Ariadne* and the *Five Senses* series are a sensual treat, in stark contrast with Egon Schiele's disturbing emaciated human forms in the Austrian Expressionism section. Here there are some of the most famous paintings by the world's most tortured yet accessible Expressionist. Subject matter apart, you just cannot ignore the quality of his draughtsmanship while shuddering at a warts 'n' all 'dissatisfied self-scrutiny' in the words of Robert Hughes. *Death and the Maiden* and *The Embrace* are two of the most striking pictures by this Mapplethorpe of Mitteleuropa. Also to the fore among the Expressionist exhibits are Oscar Kokoschka's more animated, twisted brushstrokes. Another of these morbidly sensitive *fin-de-siècle Wiener*, he at least reduces the libidinous pressure for a time with a few bucolic landscapes and his superb *Tiger-Lion* (1926), painted after being scared out of his wits in front of a lion's cage at London Zoo. Before you reach these treasures you will have passed before *The Kiss* and the *Portrait of Adele Bloch* by the man who got the ball rolling in the first place, Gustav Klimt.

Straßenbahnmuseum

Tramway Museum
3, Ludwig-Koeßler-Platz (7909 44900/tour tickets 7909 44026). U3 Schlachthausgasse/tram 18, 73.

Open *May-Oct* 9am-4pm Sat, Sun. Sightseeing tours on vintage tram: *May-Oct* 9.30am, 1.30pm Sat, Sun. Departs from Karlsplatz. **Admission** AS20; free under-15s, Vienna Card holders. **No credit cards.**

Trams are omnipresent in Vienna. Not the most speedy mode of transport but clean, silent and, with their numerous stops, ideal for exploring the city. Housed in three brick sheds, this museum contains every conceivable form of carriage that has graced the rails of Vienna's vast network, including horse-drawn trams, a working steam tram and a number of buses too. The Viennese love endearing nicknames and the ubiquitous red and white tram is known as the 'Bim', aping the sound of the tram's bell. The newest Siemens-built, Porsche-designed ultra-low platform model is also on display – the 'Porsche-Bim' is gradually being phased into the present tram network. Hiring vintage trams for a spin round the city is a popular way of celebrating weddings and other festivities, and throughout the summer there are regular vintage tram rides departing from Karlsplatz beside the Otto Wagner Pavilions.

Unteres Belvedere & Barockmuseum

Lower Belvedere & Baroque Museum
3, Rennweg, 6a (7955 7134). Tram 71.
Open *Gardens* dawn till dusk daily. *Museums* 10am-6pm Tue-Sun. English highlights tour 4pm Sun. **Admission** AS60; AS40 concs (includes entrance to Upper Belvedere and Austrian Galleries). **No credit cards.**

Entering the Belvedere from Rennweg, you pass the Lower Belvedere and the signs direct you into the Baroque Museum. If you're feeling a bit Baroque-saturated, give it a go anyway as you get the full monty for one ticket and the lower part has a lot more of Prince Eugene of Savoy's original décor than the upper. As for the Baroque Museum, it contains a good range of works by the principal Austrian Baroque painters, the original lead castings from the fountain on Neuer Markt and plenty of *trompe l'oeil* effects. The latter make the Marmorsaal the highlight of the visit – a two-floor extravaganza celebrating the Prince's military career and, in a fresco by Martino Altamonte, transforming him into the god Apollo! Next comes the Groteskensaal (Hall of Grotesques), housing some incredible busts of faces distorted in a wide variety of grimaces by the oddball sculptor Franz Xavier Messerschmidt (1732-83) on a background of painted animals and birds in the manner of Roman wall decoration. After the Marmorgalerie, where the Prince's three statues from Herculaneum would be today were it not for the poor housekeeping of his niece (they are now in Dresden), you reach the Goldkabinett – an authentic Baroque freakout, fuelled by oriental vases, 23-carat gold panelling and a lot of mirrors. The Museum of Medieval Art is in the Orangery and highlights include the magnificent colours of the early fifteenth-century Znaimer Altar attributed to a Viennese workshop. The work of Michael Pacher, a fifteenth-century Tyrolean painter and sculptor best known for his Gothic altar in St Wolfgang near Salzburg, is represented here in the form of five pictures that mark the transition towards a more perspective-based Renaissance art. *Website: www.belvedere.at*

4th district

Bestattungsmuseum

Burial Museum
4, Goldeggasse 19 (50 195/4227). Tram D. **Open** noon-3pm Mon-Fri, or by appointment. Group tours on request. **Admission** free.

This museum is a fitting testimony to the local obsession with the ceremonies and paraphernalia of burial, and some of the exhibits are frankly comical – a coffin with a bell pull for those mistakenly buried alive and a packet of undertakers' cigarettes bearing the legend *Rauchen sichert Arbeitsplätze* 'Smoking protects jobs'. The museum attempts to clarify and substantiate this Viennese obsession not only with historic photographs of Emperor Franz Joseph's and Archduke Franz Ferdinand's funerals or the touching documentary of a couple pushing their son's coffin on a simple cart in 1945. Everything, from a practical, reusable coffin with trapdoor to pallbearers' livery and a stiletto (stabbed into the corpse before the coffin was closed to ensure that the body was indeed dead), is on display here.

Museum der Stadt Wien

Museum of the City of Vienna
4, Karlsplatz (505874 784021). U1, U2, U4 Karlsplatz/tram 1, 2, D, J/bus 3a. **Open** 9am-6pm Tue-Sun. **Admission** AS50; AS25 concs; AS20 Vienna Card holders; AS75 per family; free every Fri morning; AS160 ticket for ten entrances. Access for disabled persons. **No credit cards**.

This museum, though a little patchy, documents Vienna's history and has everything from scale models of the city, artefacts from the time of the Turkish siege, reconstructions of interiors like Adolf Loos' living room and Franz Grillparzer's Biedermeier apartment to works by Makart, Klimt and Schiele. Numerous pieces by Wiener Werkstätte collaborators like Kolo Moser and Josef Hoffmann are also on display, as well as the façade of Otto Wagner's *Die Zeit* telegraph office (1902), which used to be on Kärntner Straße.

6th district

Museum für Mittelalterliche Rechtsgeschichte: Die Geschichte der Folter

Museum of Medieval Legal History:
The History of Torture
6, Fritz Grünbaumplatz 1 (595 4593/fax 595 4577). U3 Neubaugasse/bus 57a. **Open** 10am-6pm daily. **Admission** AS85; AS70 concs; AS45 under-16s; AS75 Vienna Card holders; AS150 guided tours (to book, phone five days in advance). Disabled access on request. **No credit cards**.

This recently opened museum – in a former air-raid shelter beneath the Esterházypark – was founded on private initiative. The booths with staged torture scenes from medieval to modern times are meant to be pedagogical and not too alarming. Visitors should shudder – but not faint. The founders seek to educate and warn against any use of torture by focusing on its history in a manner viewable by schoolchildren. Medieval bakers who cheated in the weight of bread would be placed in a vat filled with human excrement, ironically placed on the Neuer Markt, where flour was sold. Bickering women would be confined face-to-face in shrew fiddles, highway robbers left to starve in hanging cages and adulteresses forced to push carts of manure through the streets. Most of the displays emphasise the intimidating and humiliating aspect of torture bent on public ridicule. Background sounds add to the atmosphere: gurgling water (water torture) or deep sighs (witch burning). On the other hand, severe punishments did accompany severe crimes: a convicted murderer hangs, open-mouthed, from his gibbet after having his legs broken by the wheels of a cart. A further indication of the pedagogical intent of this museum is the former classroom booth. The blackboard lists the punishments meted out by the teacher during his 51-year career: no less than 911,527 times did he brandish his stick. *Website: www.folter.at*

7th district

Hofmobiliendepot

Imperial Furniture Collection
7, Mariahilfer Straße 88, Andreasgasse 7 (524 3357-0/fax 524 3357-666). U3 Zieglergasse. **Open** 9am-5pm daily. **Admission** AS90; AS60 concs; AS45 children over 6, OAPs. **Credit** AmEx, DC, MC, V.

Recently reopened and restored, this gigantic lock-up for the monarchy's unwanted furniture and fittings is an entertaining sight for anyone with an interest in interior decoration. Maria Theresia founded the institution in 1747 as a storehouse for household furniture of the imperial abodes. With reconstructions of bedrooms from the palace at Laxenburg, Jugendstil salons and some amazingly colourful ceramic toilets, it gives a far more lively insight into how the privileged lived than the aseptic state apartments of Hofburg and Schönbrunn.

Tabakmuseum

Tobacco Museum
7, Mariahilfer Straße 2 (526 1716). U2 Babenbergergasse. **Closed** until 2001 when it will form part of Museumsquartier.

An impressive collection of tobacco tins, ornamental carved pipes, snuff boxes and cigarette packets, mostly from the nineteenth century, put together by Austria Tabak, the state tobacco monopoly, founded by Josef II in 1784. This maintains an iron grip on distribution, limiting sale of the wicked weed to official outlets, the Trafik, or in bars and restaurants, which can apply a whopping 20% mark up. The museum has notes in English to help you round the exhibits and, naturally, smoking is permitted throughout the building. The museum is currently closed awaiting new premises in the Museumsquartier.

*Maria Theresia's storehouse of imperial furnishings, the **Hofmobiliendepot.***

8th district

Museum für Volkskunde

Museum for Folklore
8, Laudongasse 15-19 (406 8905/fax 408 5342).
Tram 5, 33, 43, 44/bus 13a. **Open** 9am-5pm Tue-
Sun; 9am-12pm Sat. **Admission** AS45; AS30 concs;
AS15 children under 16; AS75 family ticket.
No credit cards.
In Von Hildebrandt's early seventeenth-century
Palais Schönborn on the corner of Langegasse and
Laudongasse, this museum deals with the customs,
religious rites and secular celebrations of the
Austrians. Founded in 1895, its purpose was to
emphasise the multicultural character of the
monarchy, evident from the large ethnographic map
of the Empire. Two walk-in *Bauernstuben* (farmhouse parlours) and a pair of magnificent ceramic
stoves are the highlights of the furniture collection.
Temporary exhibitions are normally excellent, dealing with a wide range of aspects of human habita-
tion, architecture and lifestyle.

9th district

Josephinum

Museum of Medical History
9, Währinger Straße 25/1 (4277 63401). Tram 37,
38, 40, 41, 42. **Open** 9am-3pm Mon-Fri.
Admission AS20; AS10 concs. **No credit cards.**
Named after Josef II, the Josephinum is Canevale
building dating from 1775. Fronted by impressive
wrought iron-work, the institution was intended as a
school for military surgeons after the Emperor had
witnessed first hand the butchery that passed for
surgery in field hospitals. The museum's exhibits
include a through-the-ages look at surgical instruments displayed in fine rosewood cabinets, but the
main attraction is the Wachspräparate Sammlung, a
collection of life-size wax anatomical models made by
Florentine craftsmen in 1780. The scale model of the
AKH is also interesting, as is the neo-Classical library
with Corinthian columns.

Pathologisch-anatomische Bundesmuseum

Museum of Pathological Anatomy
9, Spitalgasse 2 (Courtyard 13) (406 8672). Tram 5,
33, 43, 44. **Open** 3-6pm Wed; 8am-11am Thur;
10am-1pm first Sat in the month. **Admission** free.
No credit cards.
The so-called Narrenturm (Fool's Tower) is in the
last courtyard of the former General Hospital.
Commissioned by the Emperor, this house of intern-
ment for the mentally ill was built by Canevale in
1784 and was used as such until 1866. Its stone
façade is dotted with bullet holes and miniscule windows. Inside there are five floors, each with 28 cells
off circular corridors. The present museum is a medical house of horrors, including wax models of TB
sufferers and an exhibit showing Dr Robert Koch's
discovery of the bacillus in 1882, an enormous collection of kidney and gall stones and a vast array of
deformities preserved in formaldehyde. Its most

occasion they confiscated a substantial amount of money, and later he was heard to remark that he had never charged so much for a house call. On arriving the visitor is offered a guide to the exhibits in a choice of languages and is then let loose in the various rooms of Freud's apartment, whose walls are filled with glass cases containing photos, letters, first editions and bits of the ethnic bric-a-brac the good doctor so assiduously collected. The divan is in London and only the waiting room furniture remains. The guide, however, is superbly documented and some of the items such as a photo of the house daubed with swastikas are quite chilling. In one room there is a video set-up showing super-8 films of Freud and family. The scenes of him chatting to Viktor Adler, founder of the Austrian Socialist Party, show an impressive gesticulator, seemingly unaware of the camera. Another room is set aside for small exhibitions of contemporary art related to the theme psychoanalysis, which are often not as bad as they sound. The staff are obviously aficionados and extremely helpful (by Viennese standards). Books and several eye-catching souvenirs are on sale and visitors are allowed the not-inconsiderable privilege of using the old man's toilet.
Website: www.freud.to.or.at

12th district

Hetzendorf Fashion Museum
12, Schloß Hetzendorf, Hetzendorferstraße 79 (802 1657). Tram 62/bus 63a. **Open** 9am-12pm Tue-Sun. **Admission** AS50; AS25 concs. **No credit cards**.
This 18,000-plus object collection of nineteenth-and twentieth-century clothing and accessories, including hats, handbags, shoes, shawls and jewellery, is part of Vienna's fashion school. Some showrooms were opened to the public in 1991 and the library with its 12,000 volumes may be used by visitors upon presentation of ID.

Schnapsmuseum
12, Wilhelmstraße 19 (815 7300/fax 815 7300). U6 Philadelphiabrücke. **Open** 9am-7pm daily. **Admission** AS90 (includes a tasting). **Credit** AmEx, DC, MC, V.
This distillery, founded by the Fischer family in 1875, still produces brandies and liqueurs – including Schönbrunner Gold (enriched with 23-carat gold leaf). Members of the family act as guides to visitors and offer the chance to taste and buy their products.
Website: www.schnapsmuseum.com

13th district

Wagenburg
Imperial Coach Collection Schönbrunn
13, Schönbrunner Schloßstraße (877 3244). U4 Schönbrunn, Hietzing/tram 60, 10, 58/bus 10a. **Open** *Apr-Oct* 9am-6pm daily. *Nov-Mar* 10am-4pm Tue-Sun. **Admission** AS60; AS40 concs; free under-10s. **No credit cards**.
The collection has been housed in the former winter riding school of Schönbrunn Palace since the demise

Pathologisch-anatomische Bundesmuseum.

notorious piece – the preserved head of Sissi's assassin – is not on display. Not for the faint-hearted.
Website: www.pathomus.ac.at

Schuberthaus
9, Nußdorferstraße 54 (317 3601). Tram 37, 38. **Open** 9am-12.15pm, 1-4.30pm Tue-Sun. **Admission** AS25; AS10 concs. **No credit cards**.
Schubert was born in this house as the son of a schoolteacher and lived here until he was a child of five, when he boarded as a Vienna choir boy. Noteworthy is the usual size of a Biedermeier apartment – just one room and a kitchen (for a family of 13). Decorated with contemporary drawings of his chamber music performances, it is used today for concerts. There is also a Schubert memorial room at Kettenbrückengasse 6, where he died and composed his last string quartet, his last piano sonatas and his last song, *Der Hirt auf dem Felsen*.

Sigmund Freud Museum
9, Berggasse 19 (319 1596/fax 317 0279). U2 Schottentor/tram 37, 38, 40, 41. **Open** *Oct-June* 9am-4pm daily. *July-Sep* 9am-6pm daily. Archive, library by appointment. **Admission** AS60; AS40 concs; AS25 schoolchildren. **Credit** MC, V.
Opened in 1971 on the initiative of Freud's daughter, Anna, the museum is located in the apartment where Sigmund lived and worked from 1898 to 1938, when he was forced into exile by the Nazis. His legendary sense of humour survived the ignominy of having the Gestapo search his home. On one

of the Habsburgs after World War I. The wealth of the Empire is amply illustrated by the variety of horse-drawn carriages and sleighs the family had at their disposal, the most extravagant being Emperor Franz Stephan's gold-plated coronation carriage with Venetian glass windows, weighing over 4,000kg. By way of contrast, the tiny gilt garden carriage built for Napoleon's son, the Duc de Reichstadt, is a poignant reminder of his lonely existence at Schönbrunn. On the funereal side there is Franz Josef's hearse (drawn by eight horses), which was buffed up for the last major Habsburg funeral, that of Empress Zita in 1989.

15th district

Technisches Museum Wien

Technical Museum
15, Mariahilfer Straße 212 (8999 86000/ fax 8999 86666). U4 Schönbrunn, then a 10-minute walk through park/tram 52, 58. **Open** 9am-6pm Mon-Tue, Thur-Sat; 9am-9pm Wed; 10am-6pm Sun. **Admission** AS95; AS45 children; AS75 over-65s; AS190 family; free under-6s. **Credit** AmEx, MC, V.

Reopened in 1999 after years of renovation (Prince once used it for one of his famous after-show gigs), it now houses a collection of work by many of the Empire's most gifted engineers, innovators and inventors: Ressel (inventor of the screw propellor), Etrich (inventor of the stable wing for aircraft), Madersberger (inventor of the typewriter), Marcus (the debate rages on whether he or Benz invented the automobile – in any case, the oldest still functioning automobile, his from 1875, is on display here), Ghega (builder of the first mountain-crossing railway) and Porsche. The Jugendstil building was finished in 1908 and is divided into three large, glass-roofed courtyards with two storeys of balconies surrounding them. There are sections on automobiles (most of the world's four-wheel drive assemblies are produced in Austria), ships (before World War I, the Austrian Empire had the sixth largest navy in the world) and railroads. The left courtyard contains mineralogical exhibits. The building is also home to an IMAX cinema. *See also chapter* **Children**.
Website: www.tmw.ac.at

18th district

Geymüller Schlößl

Geymüller Mansion
18, Khevenhüllerstraße 2 (479 3139). Tram 41, then bus 41a. **Open** *Mar-Nov* 10am-5pm Thur-Sun. **Admission** AS30; AS15 concs. **No credit cards**.

Built for Viennese banker Johann Geymüller in 1808, this summer villa in Pötzleinsdorf is used by the MAK (Museum of Applied Arts) as an annexe for its collection of fine Biedermeier furniture, whose impressive period workmanship will interest antique furniture buffs. Make the trip worthwhile, especially if you're with kids, by strolling around the delightful Pötzleinsdorfer Schloßpark with its wild deer and domestic animal zoo.

Something to think about: the father of analysis at the **Sigmund Freud Museum***.*

Galleries

'To the age its art, to art its freedom.'

Think pink: Freie Klasse Wien's rebel yell.

The contemporary arts scene in Vienna is moving. Fast. It is experiencing a boom, the likes of which have not been seen here since the art market years of prosperity in the 1980s. Many galleries moved into smarter premises in the last years of the twentieth century, initiatives are being launched and there are plenty of temporary art spaces and projects to see. The general standard of contemporary art to be seen in Vienna is high and the mix of fare is thoroughly cosmopolitan.

The art scene in Vienna has a strange middle-of-nowhere, but thoroughly networked feel to it – strengthened by a lively amount of activity on the Internet. The overriding feeling is that the real opportunities (and cash) are elsewhere, so artists are ferreting away and hoping to get noticed outside of Austria.

In the 1960s Viennese artists did hit the international headlines with Actionism – an extreme art movement that involved self-mutilation, the slaughtering of animals, faecal demonstrations,

anti-Papal iconography and deliberately antisocial taboo-breaking. And, of course, Gustav Klimt and the Secessionists lit up and revolutionised a conservative art world at the end of the nineteenth century. 'To the age its art, to art its freedom', is the legend over the entrance to the **Secession** (*see chapter* **Sightseeing**) – it should still apply today. Although not if the Freedom Party's Jörg Haider has his way. 'There is a limit to the freedom of art,' he has said. His party has threatened to cut state subsidies to the art world, a move which would have serious repercussions for Austrian artists with little private sector support.

WHERE & HOW

The gallery scene has moved from the heart of the 1st district towards the Museumsquartier (*see page 38* **Past, present & future**) on the boundary between the 1st and 8th districts. All galleries, arts centres and museums are listed in the monthly *Vienna Art Guide* (free) and the Verband Österreichischer Galerien Moderner Kunst (Austrian Society of Contemporary Art Galleries) also produces a quarterly of its members' showings around the country. Both pamphlets can be found at most galleries and museums. The *Kunst* (art) section in *Falter* will also keep you abreast of events and shows.

For viewing it makes sense to divide the nights from the days. Check out the (mostly) static visuals during the daytime. Get your information and a sense of what is going on after dark. Places such as **Klub Shabu**, **Schikaneder**, **Blue Box**, **rhiz**, **Jenseits**, **B72**, **Flex**, **Meierei**, **Roxy** and **Café Kunsthalle** carry flyers and are popular with the arts crowd.

Despite bringing in big names (even the German fashion megastar Karl Lagerfeld did a stint here) to teach for one- or two-year periods, Vienna's art colleges have struggled with their teaching programmes. This led to a number of rebel students (under the name Freie Klasse Wien) to establish their own classes and curriculum – it was headline stuff in the domestic media for the three years their course lasted. They disbanded at the end of December 1999 – the last demonstrative action being the erection of a long, pink Portakabin

Wall ball: **KunstForum** *concentrates on the big names of the art world. See page 114.*

on the Ring as an alternative education space. With their tough admissions procedure, though, the art colleges are still considered prestigious. The atmosphere is generally relaxed and there are occasional bursts of contemporary relevance on the public interface. Both the University of Applied Arts, on Oskar-Kokoschka-Platz, and the **Akademie der bildenden Künste** (Academy of Fine Arts), on Schillerplatz (*see chapter* **Museums**), hold graduation shows for four days around the last week in June. Check *Falter* for the exact dates.

LINKS

www.basis-wien.at/db has a database in English on contemporary art in Austria.
www.austriaculture.net is an amusing if trite site with a strong focus on the visual arts.
The following sites are in German, but are still worth a browse: **www.t0.or.at**; **www.black box.at**; **www.thing.at**; **www.evolver.at**

Public galleries & collections

See also **Albertina** (*chapter* **Sightseeing**), and **MAK** (*chapter* **Museums**).

KunstForum
1, Freyung 8 (537 3311). U4 Herrengasse.
Open 10am-6pm daily; 10am-9pm Wed (whenever there's an exhibition). **Admission** AS95; AS60 concs; AS190 family; AS70 per person for groups. **No credit cards.**
Exhibitions at this Bank Austria-sponsored space seldom offer strictly contemporary art, tending instead to concentrate on work by the likes of Monet, Picasso or Turner.

Kunsthalle Wien
Karlsplatz: *4, Treitlstraße 2 (521 8933). U1, U2, U4 Karlsplatz.* Museumsquartier: *7, Museumsplatz 1 (521 8933). U3 Volkstheater/tram 49.* **Open** 10am-6pm Fri-Wed; 10am-10pm Thur. **Admission** AS80; AS60 students; AS40 OAPs. **Credit** AmEx, DC, MC, V.
As the official art space for the City of Vienna, this is a well-funded facility. It has two sizeable spaces, one in the big (formerly bright yellow) box at Karlsplatz and another in the Museumsquartier (both with the same opening times and admission prices). However, the whole operation is moving into the Museumsquartier when it is completed at the end of 2001. The well-loved tin box and its popular café will continue to be used for smaller scale exhibitions, workshops and for chilling on summer evenings. Occasionally highly recommendable fare such as thematic exhibitions on angels, visions of the future and art and literature, based on the work of several artists using everything from photography and painting to video installations. *Website: www.kunsthallewien.at*

KunstHausWien
3, Untere Weissgerberstraße 13 (712 0491/ fax 712 0496). Tram N, O. **Open** 10am-7pm daily.
Admission AS95; AS70 concs; AS30 children; half-price Mon. **Credit** AmEx, DC, MC, V.
Popular names show here: usually photographers, invariably male. In 1999 there was an exhibition of the School of London artists (without Lucian Freud,

Glossing over the cracks: the venerable **Künstlerhaus**. *See page 116.*

The Schiele dealer

A trip to the **Kunsthistorisches Museum** was the humble beginning of what became one of the world's most important collections of Austrian art. In 1947, a young Viennese ophthalmology student, Rudolf Leopold (born 1925), was so impressed by the museum that he decided to collect art. With little money or formal training in art, Leopold went on to amass the biggest private collection of works by turn-of-the-century Expressionist artist Egon Schiele (1890-1918). Leopold is now widely regarded as one of the world's leading Schiele experts and is about to have a museum of his own in the Museumsquartier (*see page 38* **Past, present & future**).

The construction of the **Leopold Museum** is expected to finish in October 2000 and its opening in summer 2001 will mark the first time Leopold's collection, comprising 5,266 works by Schiele and other Austrian luminaries such as Gustav Klimt, Oskar Kokoschka, Josef Hoffmann and Adolf Loos, can be seen in its entirety by the public.

Leopold first came across a catalogue of paintings and sketches by Schiele at a book auction in 1950 and was immediately struck by the intensity of his work. He began to attend Vienna art auctions, and met one of Schiele's greatest patrons, the art critic Arthur Roessler, who also owned a number of Schieles. Roessler told the 25-year-old student that he could buy an early work, *Sonnenuntergang* – if he could provide a sufficient interpretation of the painting. The art critic was impressed enough by the amateur that he allowed him to buy another, more valuable painting, *Tote Stadt,* on the spot.

While running an ophthalmology practice, Leopold devoted his spare time to adding to his collection. The lack of regard for Schiele in post-war Austria kept prices low and Leopold, financing his purchases by giving private lessons in Latin and maths, took advantage.

Prices began to rise during the 1960s and 1970s as art critics began to recognise the importance of Schiele's work; Leopold borrowed from Austrian banks, leveraging works he already owned so he could buy more. He acquired 150 oils, gouaches, watercolours and drawings by Schiele, including works such as *Dead Mother* (1910), *Portrait of Wally* (1912) and *Reclining Woman* (1917).

The collection was valued at some AS6.5 billion in 1993, and although he was deeply in debt, Leopold didn't want to sell. The Austrian National Bank and the government didn't want the collection to leave the country. So in 1994 they struck a complicated AS2.2-billion deal that awarded Leopold some cash, established a museum for the collection and paid Leopold a salary to run it.

who removed his work from the travelling exhibition when it came to Vienna).

The building is the work of Friedensreich Hundertwasser and includes his museum and a gift shop. Hundertwasser has a foible for marketing the dinkily esoteric and a hatred of straight lines (he calls them 'the Devil's work'). The first two floors house a collection that covers Hundertwasser's development from early boyhood drawings to his Spiral paintings.
Website: www.kunsthauswien.com

Museum moderner Kunst Stiftung Ludwig Wien

Museum of Modern Art Ludwig Foundation Vienna
Palais Liechtenstein
9, Fürstengasse 1 (317 6900). Tram D.
Open 10am-6pm Tue, Wed, Fri-Sun; 10am-8pm Thur. **Admission** AS60; AS40 concs. Ticket for both locations AS80; AS60 concs. **Credit** MC, V.
20er Haus
3, Arsenalstraße 1 (799 6900).Tram D/bus 13a.
Open 10am-6pm Tue-Wed, Fri-Sun; 10am-8pm Thur. **Admission** AS60; AS40 concs.
No credit cards.

The largest museum of modern art in Central Europe. Its collection is housed in two buildings. The Baroque Palais Liechtenstein houses a cross-section of twentieth-century international art. Rooms are dedicated to art movements from Expressionism (Alexej Jawlensky, Oskar Kokoschka), Cubism (Albert Gleizes, Fernand Leger) and Futurism (Giacomo Balla) to Surrealism (Max Ernst, René Magritte), Vienna Actionism (Hermann Nitsch, Arnulf Rainer) and Pop Art (Jasper Johns, Andy Warhol). And there are about five special shows annually. The 20er Haus is housed in a pavilion originally constructed for the World Exhibition in Brussels in 1958. The architect's signature is on the front of the building. Alternating exhibitions are held on the first floor. The international collection, expanded in 1991, is on the second floor. There's work by such artists as Joseph Beuys, Donald Judd, Sol LeWitt and Bruce Nauman. The Austrian avant-garde is represented by the likes of Peter Kogler, Hartmut Skerbisch and Franz West. Its sculpture garden has works by Alberto Giacometti, Henry Moore and Fritz Wotruba.
Website: www.Austria.EU.net/MMKSLW

Art in action: **Georg Kargl**, a star of the gallery scene. See page 121.

EA-Generali Foundation

4, Wiedner Hauptstraße 15 (504 9880). U1, U2, U4 Karlsplatz. **Open** 11am-6pm Tue-Wed, Fri; 11am-8pm Thur; 11am-4pm Sat, Sun. **Admission** AS60; AS40 concs. **No credit cards**.

Known among some observers as the 'institution for institutional critique', this is the smartest art space in town. The germ warfare lab-style space is owned by the Generali Insurance Company, which prides itself on its collection (heavily featuring Heimo Zobernig, Franz West, Dan Graham and Valie Export). It is dedicated to sculpture and new media work (with video often featuring).
Website: www.gfound.or.at

Künstlerhaus

1, Karlsplatz 5 (587 9663). U1, U2, U4 Karlsplatz/ tram 1, 2, D, J. **Open** 10am-6pm Fri-Wed; 10am-9pm Thur. **Admission** AS90; AS60 concs; AS25 children; AS180 family card. **No credit cards**.

This institution is the public face of the Kunstverein (Artists' Society), one of a staggering number of such societies in Vienna (others include the Secession, Galerie Station 3 and the Wiener Kunstverein). The Künstlerhaus had been degenerating rapidly in terms of content as the result of mismanagement and internal bickering, before Doris Rothauer (curator) and Ecke Bonk (graphic designer and artist) moved in to try to restore the venerable establishment's reputation. It remains to be seen whether a new logo and a certain amount of hype will do the trick. Expect large and ambitious presentations with a smooth gloss. The nearby Passagegalerie at the end of the underpass between the Künstlerhaus and Resselpark shows some well-thought of younger artists.
Website: www.k-haus.at

Sammlung Essel

Essel Collection
An der Donau Au, 1 3400 Klosterneuburg (02243 37050). S4 from Spittelau to Weidling-Klosterneuburg/bus 239 from U4 Heiligenstadt. **Open** 10am-7pm Tue-Sun; 10am 9pm Wed. **Admission** AS80; AS60 concs. **No credit cards**.

Opened in December 1999 to house a collection often criticised as having a priority on size rather than the significance of the work, the Sammlung Essel is nonetheless a significant improvement in Vienna's contemporary art panorama. And, in a country where private initiative is rare, the venture is refreshing. Curated by the internationally respected Rudi Fuchs, the collection features a who's who of post-1945 Austrian art – Maria Lassnig, Arnulf Rainer, Nitsch and Hundertwasser and others. There is also work by Gilbert & George, Georg Baselitz, Julian Schnabel, Antonio Saura and Antoni Tàpies.
Website: www.sammlung-essl.at

Private galleries

1st district

Galerie Charim Klocker

1, Dorotheergasse 12 (512 0915). U1, U3 Stephansplatz. **Open** 11am-6pm Tue-Fri; 11am-2pm Sat.

Having moved out of an apartment-cum-gallery, Klocker is now housed in a smart, *Jugendstil* space and shows Austrian and German post-war and contemporary art – such as pieces by Rudolf Schwarzkogler (whose work is the epitome of what Actionism and Body Art were about) and John

Bock's almost childish, ironic representations of systems. The gallery's main focus is on conceptual photography.
Website: www.charimklocker.at

Galerie Ernst Hilger
1, Dorotheergasse 5 (512 5315). U1, U3 Stephansplatz. **Open** 10am-6pm Tue-Fri; 10am-4pm Sat.
Shows paintings (demonstrating some kind of an art historical adherence to what is Austrian) that appeal to informed local taste.
Website: www.hilger.at

Galerie Grita Insam
1, Kölnerhofgasse 6 (512 5330). U1, U3 Stephansplatz or U4 Schwedenplatz. **Open** noon-5pm Tue-Sat.
Grita Insam's operation is being realigned with established, but no longer sensational names such as Medical Hermeneutics or Art and Language, complemented by a new generation of local artists such as Manfred Erjautz and Gerol Tagewerker.

Galerie Heike Curtze
1, Seilerstätte 15 (512 9375/fax 513 4943). U1, U3 Stephansplatz. **Open** 11am-6pm Tue-Fri; 11am-4pm Sat. *Downstairs* 3-6pm Mon-Fri; 11am-4pm Sat.
Contemporary Austrian art with a focus on Actionism. The downstairs space is for newcomers.

Galerie HS Steinek
1, Himmelpfortgasse 22 (512 8759). U1, U3 Stephansplatz or U4 Stadtpark. **Open** 11am-6pm Tue-Fri; 11am-4pm Sat.
Low key, once well placed but now being abandoned as the serious spaces move out of the immediate centre of town. For many years this was the place to see good applied photography. A steady repertoire space showing reliable, no-frills local talent such as Isle Haider. Shows are often co-ordinated to complement what is going on at the Secession if one of the artists it represents is showing there.
Branch: 9, Pramergasse 6 (310 3930).
Website: www.kunstnet.at/steinek

Galerie Julius Hummel
1, Bäckerstraße 14 (512 1296). U1, U3 Stephansplatz or U3 Stubentor. **Open** 3-6pm Tue-Fri; 10am-1pm Sat.
Regional fare with a strong leaning towards work influenced by artists who hit the headlines in Austria in the 1970s.

Galerie Kalb
1, Bäckerstraße 3 (512 9720). U1, U3 Stephansplatz. **Open** 2-6pm Tue-Fri.
Body Art and Actionism are Kurt Kalb's mainstay and he is still considered significant on a local level. The space tends to support former students of the two Viennese art colleges who have been trained in the gestural mannerisms of their teachers.

Galerie Krinzinger
1, Seilerstätte 16 (513 3006). U1, U3 Stephansplatz. **Open** 10am-6pm Tue-Fri; 11am-4pm Sat.

Shows established names of the 1960s and 1970s (Hermann Nitsch, Arnulf Rainer, Ludwig Attersee), proponents of Neue Malerei (new painting) and other artists (including some BritArt). Even work by Modernist Meret Oppenheim (famed for her fur-lined teacup and saucer) has made an appearance.
Website: www.netway.at/krinzinger

Galerie Krobath & Wimmer
1, Eschenbachgasse 9 (585 7470). U2 Babenbergerstraße. **Open** 11am-6pm Tue-Fri; 11am-3pm Sat.
Having moved from a small art-shop-cum-gallery, this place is ready to enter the big league with names such as Octavian Trauttmansdorff (a former Aperto contributor and exhibitor at the Secession in 1999).

Galerie Lang Wien
1, Seilerstätte 16 (512 2019). U1, U3 Stephansplatz. **Open** noon-6pm Tue-Fri; 11am-4pm Sat.
Nothing snazzy, but a reliable if rather conservative space showing (mostly local) artwork on paper.
Website: www.kunstnet.at/lang-wien

Rocking: **Galerie Hubert Winter**. *Page 121.*

It's a Lomo thing

Austrian student Matthias Fiegl found an old Russian camera in a shop in Prague in 1991. He brought it back to Vienna and, with his friend Wolfgang Stranziger, experimented with it. The blurred, distorted shots with fantastic colours that they produced with their Lomo camera inspired them to start the world of Lomography.

They started bringing more Lomos back from Eastern Europe and formed the Lomographic Society. As more people bought the camera the society held its first exhibition in Vienna.

The producers of the Lomo camera in St Petersburg (Lomo is an acronym for Leningradskoye Optiko-Mekhanicheskoye Ob'edinyeniye) were about to stop production in 1994, until the Lomographers convinced them not to and kept them busy with orders.

The reputation and popularity of the camera grew throughout the 1990s. Lomo ambassadors opened embassies everywhere from London to Los Angeles, Hanoi to Havana. The Lomo Society International now numbers more than 80,000 people 'bound together by a zealous love to snapshot every static and moving object that hits their way and a passionate addiction to celebrate fun,' according to Stranziger. With this increase in popularity has come more acceptance from the mainstream – the Vienna tourist office commissioned a Lomo city guide; the Lomographers have also produced a brochure for Ferrari.

'Ultimately Lomographers are heavily soul connected to their home town: they are crazy about Vienna's wild blend of east-west, south-north cultural explosion, their hot Lomoblood is stimulated by both the lascivious flair of foregone centuries and the current exertions of a hedonistic lifestyle,' says Stranziger.

With this in mind, we asked the Lomographers for a selection of images they felt best illustrated the spirit of Vienna.

Lomo HQ

7, Stiftsgasse 15-17 (524 8488/lomo@lomo.com) U3 Neubaugasse. **Open** 10am-5pm Mon-Fri.
Credit AmEx, DC, MC, V.
Nerve centre of Lomo activity.
Website: www.lomo.com

Lomo Factory

15, Siebeneichengasse 2 (899 4421) U4 Meidlinger Hauptstraße. **Open** 10am-5pm Mon-Fri.
Credit AmEx, DC, MC, V.
Central depot where you are welcome to see (zillions of images), touch (dozens of lomographers) or just purchase your object of desire. A Lomopackage is AS1,390; an ActionSamplerKit costs AS299.

Galerie Meyer Kainer

*1, Eschenbachgasse 9 (585 7277). U2 Babenberger-
straße.* **Open** 11am-6pm Tue-Fri; 11am-3pm Sat.
Christian Meyer and Renate Kainer ran the first-rate
Galerie Metropol with **Georg Kargl** (*see below*), but
that operation fizzled out in the mid-1990s. The two
newer operations initially split the flock of artists
(Walther Obholzer, Mark Dion, Renee Green,
Gerwald Rockenschaub, Raymond Pettibon) they
were working with, but they are now expanding in
directions of their own – a prime example being
Heimo Zobernig (whose work plays on the idea of
'exhibiting' rather than what is being shown).

Galerie Nächst St Stephan Rosemary Schwarzwälder

*1, Grünangergasse 1 (512 1266).
U1, U3 Stephansplatz.* **Open** 11am-6pm Mon-Fri;
11am-4pm Sat.
An attractive, well-lit *Gründerzeit* apartment on the
site of the first commercial gallery in Vienna (opened
in the 1950s by the still lively, long-retired Christa
Hauer). The owner Rosemary Schwarzwälder has a
reputation for being difficult: a number of good artists
have worked with her, a few still do. Considered to be
the only serious space devoted to contemporary
abstract painting in Vienna – with work by Imi
Knöbel and Gerhard Richter (big names in Germany)
and Robert Mangold and Brice Marden from the US.
Website: www.kunstnet.at/st-stephan

Galerie Ulysses

1, Opernring 21 (587 1226). U1, U2, U4 Karlsplatz.
Open 10am-6pm Tue-Fri; 10am-1pm Sat.
A prestigious gallery of over 25 years standing.
Shows the likes of Arnulf Rainer and one of the few
Austrian female painters to have established herself
on an international level, Maria Lasnig.

Galerie V & V

*1, Bauernmarkt 19 (535 6334). U1, U3
Stephansplatz.* **Open** 11am-6.30pm Tue-Fri; 11am-
5pm Sat. **Credit** AmEx, DC, MC, V.
The emphasis here is not on the intrinsic market
value of the materials employed, but the design
concepts behind the work. A wonderful browse.
Website: www.spinst.co.at/v+v

Hoffmann & Senn

*1, Dominikanerbastei 19 (535 9930).
U1, U3 Stephansplatz.* **Open** 11am-6pm Tue-Fri;
11am-3pm Sat.
Gabi Senn and Suzanna Hoffmann opened the first
of the wave of smart galleries in the late 1990s. They
have created a gallery of cosmopolitan dimensions
with a large window frontage in a former car
showroom. To help finance the project, they have a
small annexe selling end-of-line prêt à porter. The
programme varies from well-established names
such as Cosima von Bonin (sculpture), to young local
painters (Marco Lulic) or the newcomers from the
Hamburg-based Akademie Isotrop.

Portfolio Kunst AG

1, Fichtegasse 5 (512 6788). U1, U3 Stephansplatz.
Open 10am-7.30pm Mon-Fri; 11am-5pm Sat.

Shows and works with some good local talent. All
very clean, but a bit passé in terms of content.
Website: www.kunstag.at

Raum Aktueller Kunst Martin Janda

*1, Eschenbachgasse 11 (585 7371/fax 585 7372).
U1, U2, U4 Karlsplatz.* **Open** 2-6pm Mon-Fri; 11am-
3pm Sat.
The owner Martin Janda has used his connections
well to move rapidly from small, more personal
initiatives to excellent, if often unexciting work by
artists (usually under 40) from Austria and elsewhere.
Website: www.thing.at/RAK

4th district

Christine König

*4, Schleifmuhlgasse 1a (585 7474). U1, U2, U4
Karlsplatz/bus 59a.* **Open** 1am-7pm Tue-Fri;
11am-3pm Sat.
Having moved into swish new premises, König is
about to re-establish herself as one of the mainstays
in the gallery world. Documenta and Biennale
participants (to which an astonishing number of
Viennese artists get invited) have long been regulars
here. Artworks by some of the more enigmatic, big
local names of the older generation such as Arnulf
Rainer are shown here, as is the work of newer stars
on the scene like Erwin Wurm (clothing distorted to
fit objects) or Peter Kogler (wallpapering of large
spaces with screen printed tubes in gaudy colours).
In the former premises (an apartment in the 1st

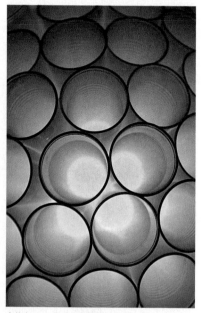

A light touch: **kunstbüro 1060.** *Page 122.*

district) Christine König was the first in Vienna to show work by the likes of Janis Kounellis, Rebecca Horn and Gilbert & George.
Website: www.kunstnet.or.at/koenig

Galerie Johannes Faber
4, Brahmsplatz 7 (505 7518). U1, U2, U4 Karlsplatz. **Open** 2-6pm Tue-Fri; 11am-3pm Sat.
Czech, Austrian (and some American) photography.
Website: www.jmcfaber.at

Galerie Trabant
4, Schleifmuhlgasse 13 (587 5265). Tram 62, 65 Schleifmuhlgasse/bus 59a. **Open** 2-7pm Tue-Fri; 11am-3pm Sat.
This place used to be a bar with a flourishing gallery tagged on to the back – the owners dropped the bar in the latter half of the 1990s. Work by big names has been shown here (Gilbert & George) and it produces regular editions of videotapes with serious content, but the space is dingy and something appears not to be gelling with the operation. A clear focus on new media, but seems to be on its way out.

Georg Kargl
4, Schleifmuhlgasse 5 (585 4199). Tram 62, 65/bus 59a. **Open** 1-6.30pm Tue-Fri; 1-7.30pm Thur; 11am-2pm Sat.
A shocking space: at first glance it looks like a smart shopfront, but go downstairs for a surprise (it's vast). Kargl is probably the star among the gallery owners in town, both as a personality and for his work at the now-defunct Galerie Metropol (*see* **Galerie Meyer Kainer** *above*). This gallery was the first to open in this area and provided the incentive for the two neighbouring spaces (*see* **Christine König** *above* and **Kerstin Engholm Galerie** *below*). Seriously sellable contemporary art by Gerwald Rockenschaub, Mark Dion and Elke Krystufek (one of the most credible contemporary perpetrators of Actionism – having masturbated publicly in the Kunsthalle).

Kerstin Engholm Galerie
4, Schleifmuhlgasse 3 (585 7337/fax 585 7338). Tram 62, 65/bus 59a Schleifmuhlgasse. **Open** 1-7pm Tue-Fri; 11am-3pm Sat.
This space only opened recently, but so far the presentation has been levelled at a cosmopolitan and wealthy clientele.

6th, 7th & 8th districts

Cult
7, Bandgasse 19 (526 0974). U3 Neubaugasse/bus 13a. **Open** 4-7pm Tue-Fri; noon-2pm Sat.
Cult is an alternative 1980s project that is still going. The space fails to attract much attention despite showing some interesting local artists.
Website: www.kunstnet.at/cult

Galerie Hubert Winter
8, Breitegasse 17 (524 0976). U3 Volkstheater. **Open** 11am-7pm Tue-Fri; 10am-2pm Sat.
Having specialised in Land Art and similar, and coming from Surrealism, Winter is an oddball who has started to take off after over a decade of highs

The minimal **mezzanin**. *See page 122.*

and lows. His original gallery in the 1st district has now become the subsidiary space and the whole (expanding) operation – which includes a branch in Berlin – has moved its headquarters into smart premises with a sexy 1970s façade. Peter Weibel and Lawrence Weiner are among the more established artists of various generations regularly on show in this gallery.
Branch: 1, Sonnenfelsgasse 8 (512 9285).
Website: www.kunstnet.at/winter

Galerie Knoll
6, Esterházygasse 29 (587 5052). U3 Neubaugasse/bus 13a. **Open** 2-6.30pm Tue-Fri; 11am-2pm Sat.
In an attractive, secluded setting with a focus on conceptual art with a strong aesthetic edge. Hans Knoll also has a gallery in Budapest and has been instrumental in forging artwork links between Central Europe and the former Eastern Bloc.
Website: www.kunstnet.at/knoll

Galerie Peter Lindner
6, Schmalzhofgasse 13/3 (913 4458). U3 Zieglergasse/bus 59a Gumpendorfergürtel. **Open** 2-6.30pm Tue-Fri.
This gallery has been in existence for over ten years, but is still not exactly high profile. Semi-academic aesthetics in a variety of media by mostly Austrian artists is what Peter Lindner has regularly been showing in what started out as an extension to his own studio.
Website: www.kunstnet.at/lindner

Anyone for coffee? **Projektraum Viktor Bucher**'s *apartment gallery.*

Galerie Station 3

7, Mariahilfer Straße 82/I/3 (524 0909).
U3 Zieglergasse. **Open** 10am-6pm Tue, Wed; 10am-
4pm Thur, Fri; 11am-3pm Sat.
An eyesore really. This is the GHQ of the Society of
Austrian Fine Artists, and nine out of ten of the
presentations here have been a total waste of time.
However, a new generation of 'Fine Artists' has
moved into the boardroom and things may change.

kunstbüro 1060

6, Schadekgasse 6 (585 2613). U3 Neubaugasse/
bus 13a. **Open** 4.30-8.30pm Wed-Fri; 11am-4pm Sat,
or by appointment.
A small space. The shows here are excellent, and
often feature as recommended arts viewing in *Falter*.
In 1998 local masters of trash Gelatin filled the place
with old furniture, but arranged it with routes to
crawl through and gave tours inside the labyrinth.
Owner Amer Abas has also opened an annexe,
kunsthalle 1060, in the same house.

mezzanin

7, Mariahilfer Straße 74a (526 4356).
U3 Neubaugasse/bus 13a. **Open** 2-7pm Tue-Fri;
10am-2pm Sat.
After a seriously hyped start in the local media as a
one-woman show presenting a new generation of
local artists, the owner Karin Handelbauer is now
getting down to the serious work of establishing an
agenda for the space. Contemporary video by hot
new contenders seems to be providing the focus.

Sehsaal

6, Luftbadgasse 13 (587 6721). Bus 13a
Gumpendorfer Straße. **Open** 2-7pm Thur-Fri;
11am-2pm Sat, and by appointment.

Painfully 'sensitive' fringe. Sehsaal is a newish
initiative that may lose its current aura of naïvety.
The owners have founded an artists' society and
the project smacks of self-edification rather than
serious intent.
Website: www.sehsaal.at/hoeller-rautter/

2nd & 3rd districts

Galerie Freund/Wind

3, Ungargasse 27/I/2 (718 8711). Tram 0.
Open 10am-6pm Sat, or by appointment.
Esther Freund has slowly been establishing her
well-hidden space on the gallery scene in the studio
of Abstract Expressionist painter Herbert Brandl
and former main exhibition space of the now-
defunct, legendary Galerie Peter Pakesch. The line-
up here is in an Austrian (and Pakesch-ian) tradition
of contemporary Baroque and tends to favour the
work of forceful male personalities, despite the
owner's gender. Turn right in the archway, go up
the stairs to the first floor and out along a 1980s
metal ramp and staircase.

Projektraum Viktor Bucher

2, Praterstraße 13/I/3 (212 6930). U1 Nestroyplatz.
Open 2-7pm Tue-Thur; 10am-3pm Fri,
or by appointment.
In the tradition of apartment galleries, the
Projektraum is now housed in its second premises.
The current site is a live-in exhibition space, which
operates on a low budget and features some
innovative if not quite optimised architectural
approaches to interior fittings. The programme itself
has a heavy focus on drawing. The staff speak
fluent English and you're almost guaranteed an
excellent cup of coffee.

Consumer

Accommodation

There's plenty to choose from – but book well in advance.

Former US military headquarters, the **Bristol** is now one of the world's top hotels.

If there's an accommodation problem in Vienna, it's likely to be one of choice – from a sumptuous palace to a simple pension. The decision is yours, governed, of course, by how much you want to spend on lodging. Vienna is not exactly cheap, but if you pick and choose and follow the usual tips for European cities (such as the areas around the railway stations), you won't have to take out a loan to cover the cost of a decent room. One obstacle in Vienna, however, is the abundance of congresses and conventions that take over great chunks of hotel space in the mid-price category. Last minute rooms are always available but not necessarily in the price category or neighbourhood you'd prefer. The centre of the city fills up first, starting with the 1st district (postal code 1010) and going on to districts two to nine (1020-1090). After that you may have to sacrifice convenience, so it pays to book in advance for choice of location as well as price.

You'll find hotels scattered throughout Vienna, even well out into the suburbs. The choicest locations generally are those in the 1st district, for walking-distance convenience to museums, shopping, restaurants, music and nightlife. But the closer-in hotels in districts two to nine also offer fine accommodation generally below 1st district rates.

The larger international chains arrived late in Vienna, led by the InterContinental in the 1960s. This means that many hotels are small by today's standards; but it also means that hotels tend to be individually run and offer more personal service than many of the massive 'rooms factories'.

Vienna's hotels are classified according to a star rating reflecting amenities and services. The five categories are also a guide to room rates. Our listings follow the following categories: **The sky's the limit** (over AS3,500 for a double); **Expensive** (AS3,000-3,500); **Moderate** (AS1,500-3,000); **Budget** (AS1,000-1,500); **Very cheap** (under AS1,000); **Seasonal hotels**; **Hostels**; **Camping** and **Long-term accommodation**. A single room or single occupancy will usually cost 15-20 per cent more than half the double room rate. Note that higher rates due to special events such as New Year may push a hotel into a higher price category. Nor are hotel rates as solidly fixed as innkeepers would like you to believe. Much depends on season and what's going on in town to boost room demand. It pays to ask about special offers, particularly if you plan to stay for a week or longer.

Since some of the traditional hotels have been around for many years, if not centuries, air-conditioning is a luxury limited mainly to the top houses. In recent years Vienna has suffered spells of hot, humid days and nights when the usual Viennese solution of opening the windows is no answer. If you're sensitive to heat and expect to be in the city from mid-July to early September, you'd do well to consider air-conditioned accommodation.

Many of the older hotels have difficulty dealing with the needs of the handicapped. We have listed those with special rooms for the disabled. You can also check with the tourist office for specific information on accessibility and services.

Unless you're planning on a number of excursions out of town, a car is more of a complication than a convenience. Street parking is limited to overnight (8pm-8am) and to a maximum of two hours with a parking ticket during the day in all of the inner districts. Relatively few hotels have garages or parking; we note these under 'Hotel services' but be sure to ask about parking charges.

ADVANCE BOOKING

Early bookings are advised for Vienna since there's nearly always something going on that keeps the hotels filled. If you arrive without accommodation, there are helpful offices at the Westbahnhof (west) and Südbahnhof (south) railway stations and at Schwechat airport. In town, the tourist office on Albertinaplatz, behind the **Staatsoper**, will make bookings for you for a small fee.

Unless otherwise noted, rates are for a double room with an en suite bathroom and will include breakfast. Breakfast offerings may vary widely and are included at most hotels and pensions but not at the top luxury hotels.

The sky's the limit

Bristol
1, Kärntner Ring 1 (515 16-0/fax 5151 6550/ hotel_bristol@sheraton.com). U1, U2, U4 Karlsplatz/ tram 1, 2, D, J. **Rates** *single* AS3,950- 5,800; *double* AS5,200-7,200; *suites* AS9,000-43,000. **Credit** AmEx, DC, JCB, MC, TC, V.
Even if location were the only deciding factor, the Bristol would still rank among the world's top hotels. On the Ringstraße across Kärntner Straße from the Staatsoper, this hotel offers nearly every amenity and service a guest could demand; the concierge is outstanding. The 140 rooms are furnished to reflect Viennese tradition but the contemporary requirements – communications, elegant modern bathrooms – have not been overlooked. The Bristol bar is a traditional and intimate meeting place going back well before the 1945-55 era when the Bristol was US military headquarters. The

Corso restaurant behind the lobby is rated one of the city's best. *See chapter* **Restaurants**.
Hotel services *Air-conditioning. Babysitting. Bar. Business services. Concierge. Conference facilities. Continental breakfast. Currency exchange. Fax. Interpreting services. Kitchenette. Laundry. Limousine service. Multilingual staff. No-smoking rooms. Parking. Restaurant.* **Room services** *Hairdryer. Minibar. Modem line. Radio. Rooms adapted for disabled. Room service (24 hours). Safe. Telephone. TV: cable/satellite. Video. Voicemail.*

Im Palais Schwarzenberg
3, Schwarzenbergplatz 9 (798 4515/fax 798 4714/palais@schwarzenberg.via.at). U1, U2, U4 Karlsplatz/tram D, 71/bus 4a. **Rates** *single* AS3,000-4,800; *double* AS3,400-5,800; *suites* AS5,800-12,800. **Credit** AmEx, DC, JCB, MC, TC, V.
Don't let the car park in front of the Schwarzenberg distract you from the elegance of the hotel itself. At the back are formal gardens more like a country estate, great for jogging or strolling. The 44 rooms and suites easily sustain the designation as a palace, built in 1720 and still owned by the Schwarzenberg family (*see chapter* **Sightseeing**) whose art and antique furnishings contribute to the authenticity and style. For the ultimate in luxury, take one of the duplex suites overlooking the gardens. Newly converted rooms in the wing to the back are somewhat more contemporary but appealing. Baths throughout are modern. For a special treat, arrange dinner

Im Palais Schwarzenberg.

The impeccable **Hotel Imperial** *– as preferred by visiting heads of state.*

in the glass-enclosed or outdoor terrace; the restaurant is excellent.
Hotel services *Air-conditioning. Babysitting. Bar. Breakfast buffet. Business services. Concierge. Conference facilities. Currency exchange. Fax. Garden. Interpreting services. Laundry. Limousine service. Parking. Multilingual staff. Restaurant.* **Room services** *CD player. Hairdryer. Minibar. Modem line. Radio. Rooms adapted for disabled. Room service (24 hours). Safe. Telephone. TV: Cable/satellite. Video. Voicemail.*

Imperial

1, Kärntner Ring 16 (501 230/fax 5012 3410/ hotel_imperial@sheraton.com). U1, U2, U4 Karlsplatz/tram 1, 2, D, J. **Rates** *single* AS4,400-4,900; *double* AS5,500-6,100; *suite* AS6,700-45,000.
Credit AmEx, DC, JCB, MC, TC, V.
Probably more luxurious today than when it was built as a town palace in 1869, the Imperial on the Ringstraße is the first address for state visitors or anyone else seeking the ultimate in discretion, service and accommodation. Expect the staff to address you by name. Most of the 128 rooms are high-ceilinged, spacious and meticulously appointed with antiques and comfortable furnishings; baths are elegant, many as big as bedrooms in other establishments. The bar, done up in red velvet, is cosy if sometimes noisy; the restaurant is erratic but the café is a popular favourite for lunch, afternoon tea or a post-concert snack.
Hotel services *Air-conditioning. Babysitting. Bar. Breakfast buffet. Business services. Conference facilities. Concierge. Currency exchange. Interpreting services. Laundry. Limousine service. Multilingual staff. Restaurant. Valet parking.*

Room services *CD player. Hairdryer. Minibar. Modem line. Radio. Rooms adapted for disabled. Room Service (24 hours). Safe. Telephone. TV: cable/satellite. Video. Voicemail.*

Radisson SAS Palais

1, Parkring 16 (515 170/fax 512 2216 sales@viezh.rdsas.com). U4 Stadtpark/tram 1, 2, D. **Rates** *single* AS2,300-3,900; *double* AS3,900-4,700; *suite* AS5,900-9,800 **Credit** AmEx, DC, JCB, MC, TC, V.
Take two turn-of-the-century townhouses and a clever architect and the result can be as enticing as the 247-room Radisson SAS Palais. The former open inner courtyards are now glassed over as atrium lobby and open café areas with touches of greenery. Rooms and baths have been cleverly incorporated into the basic structures. Décor is an effective combination of Scandinavian modern and Viennese traditional, retaining a comfortable old-world feeling while offering efficiency. Views are best out over the park from the upper front rooms. Service is generally good but the front desk occasionally does get harried. You're about a five-minute walk from the centre of the city.
Hotel services *Air-conditioning. Babysitting. Bar. Breakfast buffet. Business services. Conference facilities. Concierge. Currency exchange. Fitness room. Interpreting services. Kitchenette. Laundry. Limousine service. Multilingual staff. No-smoking rooms. Parking. Restaurant. Sauna. Solarium.* **Room services** *Hairdryer. Minibar. Modem line. Radio. Rooms adapted for disabled. Room service (24 hours). Safe. Telephone. TV: cable/satellite. Video. Voicemail.*

Sacher

*1, Philharmonikerstraße 4 (514 560/fax 514 57-810/
hotel@sacher.com). U1, U2, U4 Karlsplatz/tram 1, 2,
D, J, 62, 65/bus 3a.* **Rates** *single* AS2,500-2,700;
double AS3,900-4,550; *suite* AS6,900-39,000. **Credit**
AmEx, DC, JCB, MC, TC, V.

Countless films have been made here, books written
about the Sacher and its legends, and the venerable
107-room hotel continues to uphold both tradition
and reputation. Emperor Franz Josef dined here
almost daily and invariably had the same meal each
day, the famous *Tafelspitz* (boiled beef). The location immediately behind the Staatsoper is superb
but so is the service, which all but anticipates your
specific wishes in advance; the concierge can work
miracles with tickets to sold-out events. Guest rooms
are opulent to the last touch with attractive furnishings and modern baths while retaining authentic flavour. The art on corridor walls rivals many
museums. The lounge bars are very popular.
Hotel services *Air-conditioning. Babysitting. Bar.
Breakfast buffet. Business services. Concierge.
Conference facilities. Currency exchange. Interpreting
services. Laundry. Limousine service. Multilingual staff.
No-smoking rooms. Parking. Restaurant.* **Room
services** *Hairdryer. Minibar. Modem line. Radio.
Rooms adapted for disabled. Room service (24 hours).
Safe. Telephone. TV: cable/satellite. Video. Voicemail.*

*The **Sacher**, star of screen and legend.*

Expensive

Europa

*1, Neuer Markt 3/Kärntner Straße 18 (515 94-0/fax
513 8138/europa.wien@austria-trend.at). U1, U3
Stephansplatz.* **Rates** *single* AS1,800-2,200; *double*
AS2,500-4,000. **Credit** AmEx, DC, JCB, MC, TC, V.

Recent renovation has swept this superbly central
hotel into the twenty-first century with the most modern of room décor and furnishings, in colours and
styles quite the opposite of traditional Vienna. Of the
113 moderately sized rooms, those on the Neuer
Markt side are the quieter but lack the excitement and
view of the busy, pedestrian-zone Kärntner Straße;
rooms on the corners are more spacious and have
angled windows that give a partial panorama out-
look. The staff will look after your needs fairly well.
Hotel services *Air-conditioning. Babysitting. Bar.
Breakfast buffet. Conference facilities. Currency
exchange. Interpreting services. Laundry. No-smoking
rooms. Parking (AS300 day). Multilingual staff.
Restaurant.* **Room services** *Hairdryer. Minibar.
Radio. Room service (6.30am-11pm). Telephone. TV:
cable/satellite.*

Hilton Vienna

*3, Am Stadtpark (717 00-0/fax 713 0691/
rm_vienna@hilton.com). U3, U4 Landstraße.*
Rates *single* AS3,200-3,800; *double* AS3,700-4,300;
suite AS4,900-29,000. **Credit** AmEx, DC, JCB, MC,
TC, V.

A favoured choice for convenience: the terminal
where airport buses finish is at the back of the hotel
and across the street are the U3 and U4 U-Bahn lines,
which will scoot you into the city centre faster than
the ten minutes it would take on foot. The public
areas have been redone to erase most of the pseudo-
art deco décor, which dated quickly; the 600 rooms
are better than standard Hilton style and service too
is superior. Views from rooms on the upper floors out
over the **Stadtpark** are spectacular. The reopened
Prinz Eugene restaurant is regaining its reputation.
If the Vienna Hilton is full, there's the 218-room Plaza
Vienna, also a Hilton group hotel, at the same prices
across the city centre at Schottenring 11.
Hotel services *Air-conditioning. Babysitting.
Bar. Breakfast buffet. Business services. Concierge.
Conference facilities. Currency exchange. Interpreting
services. Kitchenettes in some of the suites.
Laundry. Multilingual staff. No-smoking rooms.
Parking. Restaurant.* **Room services** *Hairdryer.
Minibar. Modem line.Radio. Room service.
Telephone. TV: cable/satellite. Safes in the suites.
Video. Voicemail.*

InterContinental Wien

*3, Johannesgasse 28 (711 22-0/fax 713 4489/
vienna@interconti.com). U4 Stadtpark.* **Rates** *single*
AS2,500-3,600; *double* AS3,300-4,800; *suite* AS5,200-
9,200. **Credit** AmEx, DC, JCB, MC, TC, V.

The 453-room InterContinental was Vienna's largest
and first chain hotel when it went up in the mid-1960s.
It has worn well, from the velvet and crystal lobby to
the more modern but still comfortably individual
style of the rooms. For service and accommodation,
the hotel remains one of InterContinental's flagships.

enjoy the city feeling!

Welcome to Austria's leading hotel group

with 15 hotels in Vienna and another 8 hotels in St. Pölten, Linz, Salzburg, Graz and Villach as well as 4 resort hotels in Geinberg, Kitzbühel, Fieberbrunn and Rust. Each with a unique character, ideally situated with a wide range of services.

Arrive and feel at home.

Despite the variety and individuality of the hotels there is one thing they have in common: sincere Austrian hospitality, friendly and skilled service and the intention of making your stay at any Austria Trend Hotels & Resorts a memorable one.

Choose from one of 15 hotels in Vienna.

AUSTRIA TREND
HOTELS & RESORTS

SERVICE INSIDE

service to feel w

AUSTRIA TREND HOTELS & RESORTS
Lehárgasse 9 A-1060 Vienna Tel.: 0043/1/58800-680 Phone: 0043/1/58800-6
e-mail: office@austria-trend.at http://www.austria-trend.at

You're about a ten-minute walk to the city centre. Rooms on the back overlook the city, those on the front the Stadtpark. The bar is pleasant if hardly intimate, the brasserie somewhat standard, but the main restaurant retains a high reputation.
Hotel services *Air-conditioning. Babysitting. Bar. Breakfast buffet. Business services. Concierge. Conference facilities. Currency exchange. Fitness room. Interpreting services. Laundry. Multilingual staff. No-smoking rooms. Sauna. Solarium. Restaurant. Valet parking.* **Room services** *Hairdryer. Iron. Laptop. Minibar. Modem line. Radio. Room service. Telephone. TV: cable/satellite. Safes in the suites. Video. Voicemail.*

Marriott Vienna

1, Parkring 12a (515 18-0/fax 515 18-6736/ mhrs.vieat.gm@marriott.com). U4 Stadtpark, U3 Stubentor/tram 1, 2/bus 1a. **Rates** *single* AS2,300-2,800; *double* AS2,800-3,400. **Credit** AmEx, DC, JCB, MC, TC, V.

The glasshouse impression you get from the outside of the Marriott Vienna carries over into the atrium lobby and lobby bar, replete with greenery and waterfall. There are few intimate corners. The atmosphere is somewhat busy and businesslike and definitely American, but that translates into efficient yet friendly service as well. The 313 rooms are spacious and attractively furnished in modern if somewhat standard style. Rooms on the front offer a restful view over the Stadtpark; upper rooms on the back look toward **Stephansdom** and the centre of the city with the Vienna woods in the distant background. Inner court rooms are quiet, though viewless.
Hotel services *Air-conditioning. Babysitting. Bar. Breakfast buffet. Business services. Conference facilities. Concierge. Currency exchange. Fitness room. Interpreting services. Laundry. Multilingual staff. No-smoking rooms. Sauna. Solarium. Indoor pool. Restaurant.* **Room services** *CD player. Hairdryer. Minibar. Modem line. Radio. Room service. Telephone. TV: cable/satellite. Safe. Video. Voicemail.*

Moderate

Pension Altstadt Vienna

7, Kirchengasse 41 (526 3399-0/fax 523 4901/hotel@altstadt.at). U2, U3 Volkstheater. **Rates** *single* AS1,380-1,480; *double* AS1,780-2,480. **Credit** AmEx, DC, MC, V.

A one-time residential building close to the main museums has been lovingly converted into a personal, intimate pension with a long list of guests who return regularly. Each of the 25 rooms and suites is individually decorated, mostly in period style, with quaint touches such as an antique cradle. Upper rooms and suites look out over the city centre. Management is unusually personable and helpful.
Hotel services *Airport service (AS400). Bar. Bike storage room (AS150/day). Breakfast buffet. Currency exchange. Day permit (AS50) for parking in the street. Laundry. Restaurant. Small conference room.* **Room services** *Hairdryer. Minibar. Radio. Telephone. TV: cable/satellite. Safe.*

König von Ungarn: *see page 131.*

Am Schubertring

1, Schubertring 11 (717 02-0/fax 713 9966/ hotel.amschubertring@teleweb.at). U4 Stadtpark. **Rates** *single* AS1,450-1,850; *double* AS1,750-2,500. **Credit** AmEx, DC, JCB, MC, V.

The upper floors of two turn-of-the-century office buildings have been attractively converted into a friendly, central hotel. The 39 rooms have varying views, outward and inward. The rooms are appealingly decorated in light colours with dark wood and fabric accents. Service is good and there's an intimate bar adjoining.
Hotel services *Air-conditioning. Bar. Breakfast buffet. Currency exchange. Kitchenette in some rooms. Laundry. No-smoking rooms.* **Room services** *Hairdryer. Minibar. Radio. Room service (6am-11pm). Telephone. TV: cable/satellite.*

Am Stephansplatz

1, Stephansplatz 9 (534 05-0/fax 534 05-711/ hotel@stephansplatz.co.at). U1, U3 Stephansplatz. **Rates** *single* AS1,490-1,560; *double* AS2,160-2,360. **Credit** AmEx, DC, JCB, MC, TC, V.

You couldn't be more central than this location directly opposite Stephansdom. Rooms on the front have a magnificent view although you'll also not easily overlook the Pummerin, the huge bell in the stubby north tower that peals at noon and 6pm. Despite renovations, the hotel still suggests its 1950s origins, somewhat utilitarian in style. The 60 rooms are comfortable enough if not luxurious and baths are quite adequate. Service may be variable

The family-owned **Wandl**, ideally placed near the city's most elegant shops. See page 132.

depending on the amount of hassle at the front desk, but you're here as much for convenience as anything. **Hotel services** *Bar. Breakfast buffet. Currency exchange. Laundry. Parking (AS300/day).* **Room services** *Hairdryer. Minibar. Radio. Room service (6am-12pm). Telephone. TV: cable/satellite.*

Astoria

1, Kärntner Straße 32-34/Fürichgasse (51 577-0/ fax 515 77-82/astoria@austria-trend.at). U1, U2, U4 Karlsplatz/bus 3a. **Rates** *single* AS1,800-2,200; *double* AS2,500-4,000. **Credit** AmEx, DC, JCB, MC, TC, V.

The Astoria is one of the grand old hotels dating to the last century, which accounts for the large high-ceilinged rooms along with the slightly musty atmosphere. Renovations have brought facilities and décor up to date. The trade-off for a superb location and views out over the busy pedestrian Kärntner Straße is street noise, less evident on the upper floors or those looking on to the side streets. The upstairs somewhat formal restaurant is rather good. Front desk management is helpful.
Hotel services *Air-conditioning. Babysitting. Bar. Breakfast buffet. Conference facilities. Currency exchange. Laundry. No-smoking rooms. Restaurant.* **Room services** *Hairdryer. Minibar. Radio. Room service (6am-12pm). Telephone. TV: cable/satellite.*

Austria

1, Wolfengasse 3/Fleischmarkt 20 (51 523-0/fax 51 523-506/hotelaus@eunet.at). U1, U4 Schwedenplatz/ tram 1, 2, 21, N/bus 2a. **Rates** *single* AS960-1,240; *double* AS1,420-2,470. **Credit** AmEx, DC, JCB, MC, V.

This older hotel is located on a blissfully quiet cul-de-sac yet convenient for the city centre and transport.

Furnishings, décor and new baths of the 46 rooms have been brought up to a modern standard, but the hotel still has a few rooms without bath or toilet that are in our budget price range. Despite such touches as oriental carpets and crystal chandeliers, the general atmosphere is one of informal relaxed comfort. Personnel is particularly friendly and helpful.
Hotel services *Babysitting. Bar. Breakfast buffet. Currency exchange. Laundry. No-smoking rooms.* **Room services** *Hairdryer. Minibar. Radio. Room service (6am-12pm). Telephone. TV: cable/satellite.*

Biedermeier im Sünnhof

3, Landstraßer Hauptstraße 28 (71 671-0/fax 716 71-503/hotel.vienna@dorint.rogner.com). U3, U4 Landstraße, then bus 74a Weyrgasse. **Rates** *single* AS1,550-2,100; *double* AS2,000-2,650. **Credit** AmEx, DC, JCB, MC, TC, V.

This jewel of a hotel resulted from the skilful conversion of last-century residential buildings into modern accommodation; the name 'Biedermeier' refers to the 1830s when in Vienna civil servants and the upper-working class public got a sense of domestic contentment. The 203 rooms are done in a period style and décor that emphasises comfort with simplicity. The only problem here for individual travellers is the tour groups that are also drawn by the recreated Viennese charm. The location is about 20 minutes' walk from the centre, although transport is convenient and frequent. The picturesque narrow alley that divides the hotel houses boutiques and galleries.
Hotel services *Air-conditioning. Babysitting. Bar. Breakfast buffet. Conference facilities. Conservatory. Currency exchange. Laundry. No-smoking rooms.*

Parking (AS180/day). Restaurant. **Room services** *Hairdryer. Minibar. Radio. Safe. Telephone. TV: cable/satellite.*

Capricornio

1, Schwedenplatz 3-4 (533 3104-0/fax 533 7671-4/capricorno@schick-hotels.com). U1, U4 Schwedenplatz. **Rates** *single* AS1,320-1,760; *double* AS1,580-2,420. **Credit** AmEx, DC, MC, TC, V.

Location is the feature here, overlooking the Danube canal and busy Schwedenplatz, the U-Bahn literally at the door and only five minutes on foot from the city centre. The lively 'Bermuda Triangle' with its varied bars and restaurants is a couple of blocks around the corner. The 46 rooms are smallish, particularly singles, and décor is of an acceptable but undistinguished period evoking Vienna tradition. Rooms at the back are quieter but the trade-off is no balcony or view. The City Central Hotel with identical rates but slightly more upmarket facilities and larger rooms belongs to the same group and is across the canal at Taborstraße 8, as is the slightly more expensive 130-room Stefanie at Taborstraße 12. **Hotel services** *Air-conditioning. Babysitting. Breakfast buffet. Currency exchange. Laundry. Parking (AS220/day).* **Room services** *Hairdryer. Minibar. Radio. Room service (6am-6pm). Telephone. TV: cable/satellite.*

K+K Hotel Maria Theresia

7, Kirchberggasse 6-8 (521 23-0/fax 521 23-70/ kk.maria.theresia@kuk.at). U2, U3 Volkstheater/ tram 49/bus 48a. **Rates** *single* AS1,580-1,890; *double* AS2,080-2,520. **Credit** AmEx, DC, MC, TC, V.

This Best Western affiliate is ideally located for the museums and has convenient transportation to the city centre, about 20 minutes' walk away. Nearby is the quaint Spittelberg district with narrow streets and eighteenth-century houses now home to restaurants, artists and galleries. The hotel is spacious and informal, its 123 rooms standard in décor and furnishings. You may find tour groups here. Staff are friendly and helpful. **Hotel services** *Air-conditioning. Babysitting. Bar. Breakfast buffet. Conference facilities. Currency exchange. Laundry. Multilingual staff. Parking (AS120/day). Restaurant.* **Room services** *Hairdryer. Minibar. Modem line. Radio. Room service (6am-6pm). Safe. Telephone. TV: cable/satellite.*

Kaiserin Elisabeth

1, Weihburggasse 3 (515 26-0/fax 515 26-7/ kaiserin@ins.at). U1, U3 Stephansplatz/tram 1, 2. **Rates** *single* AS1,000-1,500; *double* AS2,200-2,850. **Credit** AmEx, DC, JCB, MC, TC, V.

The venerable Kaiserin (Kaiserin Elisabeth was Emperor Franz Josef's wife) belongs to Viennese hotel tradition, although fortunately from time to time renovations and updating have been undertaken. Notwithstanding, the small red velvet and crystal reception lobby exudes a slightly decadent imperial atmosphere. The location is superb, on the edge of a pedestrian zone just off Stephansplatz. The 63 rooms are adequate in décor and furnishings slightly reminiscent of the 1950s. The front desk is a plus, with very helpful staff.

Hotel services *Air-conditioning. Babysitting. Bar. Breakfast buffet. Currency exchange. Laundry.* **Room services** *Hairdryer. Minibar. Radio. Telephone. TV: cable/satellite.*

König von Ungarn

1, Schulerstraße 10 (515 84-0/fax 515 84-8). U1, U3 Stephansplatz. **Rates** *single* AS1,650; *double* AS2,350. **Credit** AmEx, DC, JCB, MC, V.

The King of Hungary is tucked into a charming sixteenth-century house with a history: Mozart lived next door. Conversion into a hotel turned the central courtyard into a captivating informal atrium lobby/lounge/bar complete with tree. Access is retained to the 33 medium-sized rooms on the upper floors via the galleried hallways. Each room is individually decorated, with emphasis on antiques and country furnishings, stripped wood and colourful fabric accents. New management is reliable, but to be on the safe side, get written confirmation of bookings. **Hotel services** *Air-conditioning. Babysitting. Bar. Breakfast buffet. Conference facilities. Currency exchange. Laundry. Multilingual staff. Parking (AS200/day). Restaurant.* **Room services** *Hairdryer. Minibar. Radio. Room service (6.30am-8pm). Telephone. TV: cable/satellite. Safe. Voicemail.*

Mailberger Hof

1, Annagasse 7 (512 0641-0/fax 512 0641-10). U1, U2, U4 Karlsplatz/U1, U3 Stephansplatz/bus 3a. **Rates** *single* AS1,200-1,800; *double* AS1,900-2,900. **Credit** AmEx, DC, MC, V.

Tucked away in an engaging Baroque townhouse on a pedestrian side street from the busy Kärntner Straße, the Mailberger Hof is a favourite with opera stars, who welcome its discreet, quiet location. The lobby lounge is quiet for informal relaxation and there's a business corner with desk and modem. The 40 rooms are splendidly decorated in co-ordinated homely style, most tending toward Laura Ashley without being overdone. For longer stays, small suites with kitchenettes are available. The family management is accommodating and helpful. **Hotel services** *Babysitting. Breakfast buffet. Business services. Conference facilities. Currency exchange. Laundry. Multilingual staff. Restaurant.* **Room services** *Hairdryer. Minibar. Radio. Safe. Telephone. TV: cable/satellite. Voicemail.*

Opernring

1, Opernring 11 (587 5518-0/fax 587 5518-29). U1, U2, U4 Karlsplatz/tram 1, 2, D, J. **Rates** *single* AS1,500-1,900; *double* AS1,900-2,900; *suite* AS2,900-3,800. **Credit** AmEx, DC, MC, V.

Front rooms at the Opernring, a Best Western affiliate, look diagonally through the trees across the busy Ringstraße to the traditional view of the Staatsoper. The hotel shares its building with offices, but the 35 spacious rooms and baths are imaginatively integrated. Furnishings and décor have been redone in classic modern to lend a fresh, lighter look. Rooms on the inner courtyard are quieter but view only the plain back of another block. **Hotel services** *Babysitting. Breakfast buffet. Currency exchange. Laundry. Multilingual staff.*

No-smoking rooms. Parking (AS280/day).
Restaurant. **Room services** *Hairdryer. Minibar.*
Radio. Room service (6.30am-2pm). Telephone. TV:
cable/satellite.

Rathauspark

1, Rathausstraße 17 (40 412-0/fax 404 12-761/
rathauspark@austria-trend.at). U2 Rathaus.
Rates *single* AS1,100-1,650; *double* AS1,590-2,400.
Credit AmEx, DC, JCB, MC, TC, V.
A turn-of-the-century upmarket apartment house
has been painstakingly restored and converted into
this attractive 117-room hotel. Elegant touches are
still evident in the plaster-ornamented ceilings of
rooms on the lower floors. Rooms are welcoming,
decorated in light colours and light wood accents
and furniture. The American-style full breakfast
buffet is highly praised.
Hotel services *Babysitting. Breakfast buffet.*
Conference facilities. Laundry. Fax. Multilingual staff.
No-smoking rooms. Parking (AS220/day). **Room**
services *Hairdryer. Minibar. Radio. Room service*
(6.30am-12pm). Telephone. TV: cable/satellite.

Römischer Kaiser

1, Annagasse 16 (512 7751-0/fax 512 7751-13/
info@rkhotel.bestwestern.at). U1, U2, U4 Karlsplatz/
U1, U3 Stephansplatz/bus 3a. **Rates** *single* AS1,390-
2,390; *double* AS1,990-3,290. **Credit** AmEx, DC, JCB,
MC, TC, V.
The 'Roman Emperor' name refers to the early
Roman settlement of what today is Vienna. The
hotel, now a Best Western affiliate, is set in an old
townhouse centrally located on a quiet side street off
Kärntner Straße. The 24 rooms are on the smallish
side as are the baths, but décor is a pleasant mix of
friendly fabrics and lighter colours. Staff are cour-
teous and helpful.
Hotel services *Air-conditioning. Babysitting. Bar.*
Breakfast buffet. Currency exchange. Laundry. Fax.
Multilingual staff. No-smoking rooms. Parking
(AS220/day). **Room services** *Hairdryer. Minibar.*
Radio. Room service (6.30am-2pm). Safe. Telephone.
TV: cable/satellite.

Starlight Suites

1, Renngasse 13 (533 9989/fax 533 9989-11/all
locations: starlighthotel.co.at). U2 Schottentor/tram
1, 2, D. 1, Salzgries 12 (535 9222/fax 535 9222-11).
U1, U4 Schwedenplatz/tram 1, 2, 21, N/bus 2a.
3, Am Heumarkt (710 7808/fax 710 7808-11). U4
Stadtpark. **Rates** *single* AS1,680; *double* AS2,080.
Credit AmEx, DC, MC, V.
These three suite hotels offer a welcome variation to
the Vienna scene. All are new and similar in concept,
with living room, bedroom and tiled bath, working
area and minibar. The décor is modern in natural
woods and bright colour fabric accents. The locations, totally renovated former apartment buildings,
are relatively quiet yet convenient for transport and
the city centre. Staff are friendly and helpful with
services such as theatre tickets.
Hotel services *Air-conditioning. Babysitting. Bar.*
Breakfast buffet. Currency exchange. Fax. Laundry.
Multilingual staff. No-smoking rooms. Parking
(AS180/day). **Room services** *Hairdryer. Minibar.*
Radio. Telephone. TV: cable/satellite.

Wandl

1, Petersplatz 9 (534 55-0/fax 534 55-77/
reservation@hotel-wandl.com). U1, U3
Stephansplatz. **Rates** *single* AS1,080-1350;
double AS1,700-2,200. **Credit** AmEx, DC, JCB, MC,
TC, V.
If location is everything, the Wandl has it, centrally
situated just off the pedestrian Graben, the
heart of the city's most elegant shopping. This has
been a family-owned hotel for over 150 years.
Renovations have added baths to most but not all
rooms. Rebuilding also accounts for the bright, wide
corridors. Décor in most rooms is on the simpler
side but acceptable; for a treat take one of the rooms
done up in period style. Ask for special rates for a
longer stay.
Hotel services *Breakfast buffet. Bar. Currency*
exchange. Fax. Laundry. Multilingual staff.
Parking (AS250/day).
Room services *Minibar. Radio. Telephone. TV:*
cable/satellite.

Zur Wiener Staatsoper

1, Krugerstraße 11 (513 1274-0/fax 513 1274-15/
office@zurwienerstaatsoper.at). U1, U2, U4
Karlsplatz/tram 1, 2, D, J/bus 3a. **Rates** *single*
AS1,050-1,200; *double* AS1,400-1,750. **Credit** AmEx,
MC, V.
The colossi supporting the bay above the entry door
give the outward impression of more elegance than
this hotel offers. The trade-off inside is smallish yet
comfortable rooms with undistinguished décor. But
rates are remarkable for a location just off Kärntner
Straße and literally within a baton's throw of the
Staatsoper. Don't expect much in the way of facili-
ties or support assistance, but the tourist office is
only a block away.
Hotel services *Bar. Breakfast buffet.*
Currency exchange. Fax. Multilingual staff.
Parking (AS220/day).
Room services *Hairdryer. Radio. Safe.*
Telephone. TV: cable/satellite.

Budget

Carlton Opera

4, Schikanedergasse 4 (587 5302/fax 581
2511/carlton@ping.at). U1, U2, U4 Karlsplatz/U4
Kettenbrückengasse/bus 59a. **Rates** *single* AS800-
1,300; *double* AS1,080-1,800. **Credit** AmEx, DC, JCB,
MC, TC, V.
The façade reveals the 1904 origins of this hotel,
which has happily preserved many of the art deco
touches inside as well. The 52 rooms are mostly
high-ceilinged, many with parquet flooring.
Furnishings are comfortable if undistinguished, the
white tiled baths likewise. Single rooms are com-
pact but adequate. The location, about a 15-minute
walk from the city centre, puts you close to the
Naschmarkt.
Hotel services *Bar. Breakfast buffet.*
Currency exchange. Fax. Multilingual staff.
Parking (AS150/day). Internet/e-mail room.
Room services *Hairdryer. Minibar. Radio.*
Safe. Telephone. TV cable/satellite.

Hotel Orient: *for illicit encounters by the hour.*

Pension Christina

*1, Hafnersteig 7 (533 2961-0/fax 533 2961-11/
christina@pertschy.com). U1, U4 Schwedenplatz/
tram 1, 2, 21, N.* **Rates** *single* AS710-860; *double*
AS1,160-1,480. **Credit** DC, MC, V.

The 33 rooms are somewhat on the small side but
attractively decorated and comfortably furnished.
Amenities are few, but the feature here is a quiet yet
central location on a tiny side street just steps away
from Schwedenplatz. The Christina is part of the
local Pertschy group, so if the pension here is full,
there may be rooms either at the slightly more expensive **Pension Pertschy** (*see p134*) or the slightly
cheaper Pension Baronesse at Lange Gasse 61.
Hotel services *Breakfast buffet. Currency
exchange. Day permit (AS50) for parking in the
street. Fax. Multilingual staff.* **Room services**
Minibar. Radio. Safe. Telephone. TV: cable/satellite.

Fürstenhof

*7, Neubaugürtel 4 (523 3267-0/fax 523 3267-26/
reception@hotel-fuerstenhof.com). U1, U6
Westbahnhof.* **Rates** *single*s AS880-1,320; *doubles*
AS1,320-1,600. **Credit** AmEx, DC, MC, V.

Walk diagonally left out of the Westbahnhof, across
the thick traffic on the Gürtel (or better, take the
pedestrian tunnel to Mariahilfer Straße) and you're
at this hotel's door. The historic façade identifies the
building as about a century old. Most of the 58
rooms are large with comfortable if undistinguished
furnishings and décor. Rooms on the side have less
traffic noise than those on the front. If you can cope
with facilities down the hall, the few rooms without
baths are about half the price of the others.
Hotel services *Breakfast buffet. Currency
exchange. Fax. Parking (AS340/day). Laundry.*

Multilingual staff. **Room services** *Minibar. Modem
line.Radio. Telephone. TV: cable/satellite.*

Hotel Orient

*1, Tiefer Graben 30 (533 7307/fax 535 0340/
www.nethotels/domicile). U1, U3 Stephansplatz.*
Rates for a maximum of three hours *double* AS650;
suite AS790-950; *night double* AS1,200; *suite* AS2,200.
Credit AmEx, DC, MC, V.

Suites are sold by the hour and the night (only
Saturdays and Sundays) for furtive philanderers
and clubbers who want to keep up the party in this
'love hotel', a seventeenth-century tavern. Choose
from the Kaisersuite, the new Rosa Rosa Rosa room
with whirlpool, the Red Room, Mona Lisa or Taste
of Africa room. Orson Welles and Kenneth Anger
have stayed. The Orient has a sister, family-orient-
ed hotel behind Stephansdom.
Branch: Domicile; 1, Schulerstraße 14 (513 3199).

Ibis Wien Mariahilf

*6, Mariahilfer Gürtel 22-24 (59 990-0/fax 597 9090/
mariahilf@hotel-ibis.co.at). U1, U6 Westbahnhof/U6
Gumpendorferstraße.* **Rates** *single*s AS890; *doubles*
AS1,090. **Credit** AmEx, DC, MC, TC, V.

If you'll settle for a standard room – and these are
of an excellent standard – the newish Ibis is one of
the best value in town. You're about eight minutes
on foot from the Westbahnhof. The 341 rooms are
bright and contemporary, if furnished on the simpler side. Rooms on the upper floors of the Wallgasse
side have magnificent views out over the city. You
will have to fight tour groups at breakfast and
check-in/check-out.
Hotel services *Bar. Breakfast buffet. Conference
facilities. Currency exchange. Parking (AS130/day).*

*Quiet and comfortable, the **Pension Pertschy** is just off the Graben.*

Laundry. Multilingual staff. Restaurant.
Room services *Air-conditioning. Minibar.*
Radio. Telephone. TV: cable/satellite.

Kärntnerhof

*1, Grashofgasse 4 (512 1923/fax 513 2228-33/
kaerntnerhof@netway.at). U1, U4 Schwedenplatz/
tram 1, 2, 21, N.* **Rates** *single* AS880-1,140;
double AS1,160-1,790. **Credit** AmEx, DC, MC,
TC, V.
A small cul-de-sac only three blocks from
Schwedenplatz hides this hotel from general notice.
But the guests who have discovered it return regu-
larly for the attractive modernised rooms and
exceptional personal service. The location is won-
derfully quiet, despite the fact that Kärntnerhof is
also central to public transport, restaurants, shop-
ping and nightlife.
Hotel services *Bar. Breakfast buffet.*
Currency exchange. Fax. Parking (AS200/day).
Laundry. Multilingual staff.
Room services *Hairdryer. Radio. Telephone.*
TV: cable/satellite.

Pension Nossek

*1, Graben 17 (533 7041/fax 535 3646). U1, U3
Stephansplatz.* **Rates** *single* AS800-850; *double*
AS1,250-1,600. **No credit cards.**
The family-owned and managed Pension Nossek on
the three middle upper floors of a turn-of-the-
century apartment/office block has been a favourite
for generations, both for its friendly service and its
superb location in the heart of the city. The pedestrian area ensures relative quiet. The 26 rooms
range from fairly spacious to compact and there are
crystal chandeliers and furnishings in period style.
Many guests regularly book their stay up to a year
in advance.
Hotel services *Breakfast buffet. Fax. Parking
(AS150/day). Laundry. Multilingual staff.*
Room services *Hairdryer. Minibar. Radio.
Telephone. TV: cable/satellite.*

Pension Pertschy

*1, Habsburgergasse 5 (534 49-0/fax 534 49-49/
pertschy@pertschy.com). U1, U3 Stephansplatz.*
Rates *single* AS770-940; *double* AS1,160-1,660.
Credit DC, MC, V.
You might easily overlook the fact that this town
palace just off the Graben is now a friendly pension,
but the once-elegant stairway (which you hardly
notice when you take the lift to the first floor reception) gives away the secret. The inner rooms look on
to a quiet central courtyard. Most of the 47 rooms are
spacious, done up in comfortable period furniture
including some antiques; a couple still have their
original tiled heating stoves as showpieces. Baths, of
course, were later additions, not luxurious but generally satisfactory. Staff are unusually helpful.
Hotel services *Breakfast buffet. Fax. Parking
(AS180/day).* **Room services** *Hairdryer. Minibar.
Radio. Telephone. TV: cable/satellite. Voicemail.*

Post

*1, Fleischmarkt 24 (515 83-0/fax 515 83-808). U1,
U4 Schwedenplatz/tram 1, 2, 21, N/bus 2a.* **Rates**
single AS840-960; *double* AS1,200-1,480. **Credit**
AmEx, DC, JCB, MC, TC, V.
The location's main feature here, steps from
transport at Schwedenplatz and convenient for
shopping and nightlife. The 107 rooms are a bit on
the old-fashioned side with standard furniture and
occasional oriental rugs on the parquet floors. The
few rooms without baths are real bargains. Staff are
accommodating.
Hotel services *Breakfast buffet. Fax. Parking
(AS220/day).* **Room services** *Hairdryer. Minibar.
Radio. Telephone. TV: cable/satellite. Voicemail.*

Pension Suzanne

*1, Walfischgasse 4 (513 2507/fax 513 2500). U1,
U2, U4 Karlsplatz/tram 62, 65/bus 3a.* **Rates** *single*
AS790-890; *double* AS1,090-1,390. **Credit** MC, V.
Most of the 25 rooms in this 1950s building were
originally small efficiency apartments, so they are

complete with mini-kitchenettes; some even have small outside balconies. Décor is of varied period but comfortable; baths are compact. Inside rooms or those in the back building are quietest. The Suzanne has a host of regulars so book early.
Hotel services *Breakfast buffet. Currency exchange. Day-permit (AS50) for parking in the street. Fax. Internet/e-mail at the front desk.* **Room services** *Hairdryer. Radio. Telephone. TV: cable/satellite.*

Pension Zipser

8, Lange Gasse 49 (40 454-0/fax 408 5266-13/zipser@netway.at). U2 Rathaus. **Rates** *single* AS790-860; *double* AS1,090-1,480. **Credit** AmEx, DC, JCB, MC, V.
This one-time apartment house dates to 1904 but the 47 fair-sized rooms inside, like the lobby/reception, are fresh and inviting in contemporary restful colours and furnishings. Some rooms on the back have splendid tree-shaded balconies. The staff are friendly and helpful.
Hotel services *Bar. Breakfast buffet. Currency exchange. Day-permit (AS50) for parking in the street. Fax. Parking (AS180/day).* **Room services** *Hairdryer. Radio. Telephone. TV: cable/satellite.*

Very cheap

Kugel

7, Siebensterngasse 43 (523 3355/fax 523 3355-5/hotel.kugel@netway.at). U2 Volkstheater, then tram 49 Neubaugasse. **Rates** *single* AS500-640; *double* AS800-820. **No credit cards**.
This is in a shopping neighbourhood with ample restaurants and you're only a couple of tram stops right from the door of this older apartment house to the main museums. The 38 attractively decorated rooms are a real bargain and there are rooms without bath which are cheaper yet. The breakfast room is rather dull but offerings are ample, or you can start your day instead at one of the nearby coffeehouses.
Hotel services *Bar. Bike storage room. Breakfast buffet. Day-permit (AS50) for parking in the street. Fax.* **Room services** *Radio. Telephone. TV.*

Pension Lehrerhaus

8, Lange Gasse 20 (403 2358/402 7435/fax 403 2358-69). U2 to Rathaus. **Rates** *single* AS520; *double* AS900. **No credit cards**.
Several floors of an apartment house dating to the early part of the nineteenth century have been adapted into this modest 40-room hotel. The high-ceilinged rooms are of various sizes and toilet and bath facilities vary accordingly, but rooms are welcoming and immaculate. Décor is mainly in lighter colours with light wood furniture. Rates vary depending on facilities; rooms without bath or toilet are real bargains. Breakfast is not included; pay for what you want from coin machines in the breakfast room or head for any of the many excellent Viennese cafés in the neighbourhood.
Hotel services. *Day-permit (AS50) for parking in the street. Fax. TV room.* **Room services** *Hairdryer. Radio. Telephone.*

Rathaus

8, Lange Gasse 13 (406 0123/fax 408 4272). U2 Lerchenfelderstraße. **Rates** *single* AS660-760; *double* AS870-1,170. **Credit** AmEx, DC, MC, TC, V.
Here you're convenient for museums and transport. The 43 rooms in this one-time noble apartment building are spacious and attractively furnished in a light, contemporary style. Baths are modern. A few rooms without baths are cheaper still. The staff are helpful. Under the same management as the **Zipser** (*see above*) up the street.
Hotel services *Fax. Garage (AS170/day). Day-permit (AS50) for parking in the street. Laundry.* **Room service** *Hairdryer. Radio. Telephone. TV.*

Pension Wild

8, Langegasse 1 (406 5174/fax 402 2168 info@pension-wild.com). U2 Lerchenfelderstraße. **Rates** *single* AS490-690; *double* AS590-990. **Credit** AmEx, DC, MC, V.
Combine a friendly, relaxed family environment in a converted apartment house located conveniently and it's not surprising that this pension is usually fully booked. The 19 rooms are attractively modern with colour co-ordinated fabrics as accents against the lighter walls and light wood furniture. Most rooms are recently redecorated. Rooms without toilet or shower are cheaper. Buffet breakfast is offered in a cheerful front room and small kitchenettes on each floor are handy for snacking or light meals. *See also chapter* **Gay & Lesbian.**
Hotel services *Fax. Breakfast buffet. Day-permit (AS50) for parking in the street.* **Room service** *Hairdryer. Radio. Telephone. Minibar and TV only in the most expensive rooms.*

Seasonal hotels

During the July-September season, student residences are turned into reasonable if modest hotels. All have single or double rooms, with bath or shower. Furnishings are what you'd expect in a better-class dorm, adequate but nothing fancy. There's central booking via **Academia** (40176-0/fax 40176-20/acahot@academia-hotels.co.at) for four hotels grouped in Pfeilgasse; **Albertina** group (512 7493/fax 512 1968/office@albertina-hotels.at) with five scattered locations; and **Rosen-Hotel** (597 9475/fax 597 9475-9/headoffice@ rosenhotel.com) for three seasonal hotels plus others around the city.

Academia

8, Pfeilgasse 3a (40176-0/fax 40176-20/acahot @academia-hotels.co.at). U2 Lerchenfelderstraße, then tram 46 to Strozzigasse/Neubaugasse. **Rates** *single* AS680; *double* AS820. **Credit** AmEx, DC, MC, V.
With 300 rooms, this is one of the larger and better of the seasonal hotels and headquarters of the Academia group.
Hotel services *Bar. Cable/satellite TV room.* **Room services** *Telephone.*

Accordia

2, Grosse Schiffgasse 12 (212 1668/fax 212 1668 697/office@albertina-hotels.at). U4, U4 Schottenring/tram 1,2. **Rates** *single* AS575; *double* AS900. **Credit** AmEx, DC, MC, V.
Newest of the seasonal hotels and belonging to the Albertina group, this 90-room three-star accommodation is across the Danube canal but fairly close to the city centre.
Hotel services *Bar. Garden. TV room.* **Room services** *Phone.*

Aramis

19, Döblinger Hauptstraße 55 (369 8673/fax 369 2420/office@albertina-hotels.at). U2 Schottentor/ tram 1, 2, D, then tram 37 Gatterburggasse. **Rates** *single* AS575; *double* AS900. **Credit** AmEx, DC, MC, V.
Set back in a quiet park-like area from the street, this 58-room Albertina group hotel offers three-star facilities in a suburban environment surprisingly convenient to the city centre.
Hotel services *Bar. Garden. TV room.* **Room services** *Telephone.*

Atlas

7, Lerchenfelder Straße 1-3 (521 78-0/401 7655/ fax 401 7620/acahot@academia-hotels.co.at). U2 Lerchenfelderstraße. **Rates** *single* AS780; *double* AS1,080. **Credit** AmEx, DC, MC, V.
Location makes the difference at this 182-room three-star Academia group facility; museums are nearby and the U-Bahn is literally at the door.
Hotel services *Bar. Bike storage room. TV room.* **Room services** *Telephone.*

Auersperg

8, Auerspergstraße 9 (406 2540/fax 406 2549-13/office@albertina-hotels.at). U2 Lerchenfelderstraße. **Rates** *single* AS375-520; *double* AS620-860. **Credit** AmEx, DC, MC, V.
This 75-room facility is an older and more modest two-star member of the Albertina group but well located for museums, shops and transport. The lower rates are for rooms without toilet or shower.
Hotel services *TV room.* **Room services** *Telephone.*

Auge Gottes

9, Nussdorfer Straße 75 (319 4488/fax 319 4488-11). U2 Schottentor/tram 1, 2, D, then tram 37, 38 Währinger Gürtel/U6 Nussdorferstraße. **Rates** *single* AS290; *double* AS470-570. **No credit cards.**
The 80 rooms in this former apartment block converted to modest student house are about the cheapest clean and decent accommodation to be found; a few of the double rooms have showers but for all, the toilets are down the hall. Transport services are excellent and you're halfway out to the wine suburbs.
Hotel services *Cable/satellite TV room.* **Room services** *Telephone.*

Burgenland 3

6, Bürgerspitalgasse 17 (597 9475/fax 597 9475-9/ headoffice@rosenhotel.com). U3, U6 Westbahnhof. **Rates** *single* AS590-665; *double* AS980-1,130. **Credit** AmEx, DC, MC, V.

Pension Zipser. *See page 135.*

You're within three blocks of the Westbahnhof at this 120-room three-star Rosen-Hotel accommodation.
Hotel services *Bar. TV room. Garden.* **Room services** *Telephone.*

Niederösterreich

2, Untere Augartenstraße 31 (331 14-0/fax 331 14-80/headoffice@rosenhotel.com). U2, U4 Schottenring/tram 1, 2, then tram 31 to Obere Donaustraße. **Rates** *single* AS550-630; *double* AS910-1,060. **Credit** AmEx, DC, MC, V.
This fairly recent two-star Rosen-Hotel member with 68 rooms has easy access to the city centre and is close to the vast Augarten park.
Hotel services *Bar.* **Room services** *Telephone.*

Hostels

The city's *Camping* leaflet will give you the addresses and critical details of the youth hostels and other similar ultra-low-cost no-frills accommodation. The most elegant hostel is **Schlossherberge am Wilhelminenberg,** but it's a long bus ride from the city centre to reach the 41-room, 164-bed hilltop castle.

Closest to the centre is the 68-room, 241-bed **Jugendherberge Myrthengasse** 7, Myrthengasse 7 (523 6316/fax 523 5849/oejhv-wien-jgh-neustiftg.@oejhv.or.at). U2, U3 Volkstheater, then bus 48a to Neubaugasse. Rates per person AS165-180. No credit cards.

The location is on the fringe of the city but transport is easy to the 285-bed **Jugendgästehaus der Stadt Wien/Hütteldorf-Hacking** 13, Schlossberggasse 8 (877 1501/fax 87702-632/jgh @wigast.com). U4 Hütteldorf. Rates per person AS156-170 with continental breakfast, AS179-200 with American breakfast. Credit MC, V.

Camping

Campingplatz der Stadt Wien/ Wien West
14, Hüttelbergstraße 80 (914 2314/fax 911 3594). Tram 49 Hüttelbergstraße, then bus 148, 152. **Rates** per person AS67-73; 4-15s AS38; per tent AS37-42; per camper van AS62-69; electricity hook-up AS40. **Open** Mar-Jan. **Credit** AmEx, DC, MC, V.
The site is on the edge of the Wienerwald 8km (5 miles) west of the city centre. Facilities include lounges, kitchen with cooking facilities, supermarket, buffet, washing machines and drier. Disposal facilities for chemical toilets and motor van service centre. This fairly large location nevertheless gets packed in midsummer.

Camping Neue Donau
22, Am Kaisermühlendamm 119 (202 4010/fax 202 4010). U1 Donau International Centre, then bus 91a to campsite Kleehäufel. **Rates** per person AS67-73; 4-15s AS38; per tent AS37-42; per camper van AS62-69; electricity hook-up AS40. **Open** mid-May-mid-Sept.
This location is just north of the 'New Danube' recreation area parallel to the main Danube, offering hiking, cycling, swimming, boating and nude bathing areas nearby. About 4km (2.5 miles) north-east of the city centre, facilities include lounges, kitchen with cooking facilities, supermarket, buffet and washing machines. Disposal facilities for chemical toilets and camper van service centre. Understandably a popular area.

Camping Rodaun
23, An der Au 2, Vienna-Rodaun (888 4154). Schnellbahn to Liesing, then bus 253, 254, 255 Willergasse, then walk. **Rates** per person AS73; 3-13s AS45; per tent AS60; per camper van AS69. **Open** late Mar-early Nov.
This site about 10km (6 miles) west of the city centre in the Rodaun suburb is on the fringes of the Wienerwald, adjacent to an artificial lake created by a dam across the Liesing river. Facilities include electricity outlets and a restaurant.

Campingplatz Schloss Laxenburg
Münchendorfer Straße, 2361 Laxenburg/Lower Austria (02236 713-33). **Rates** per person AS67-73; 4-15s AS38; per tent AS37-42; per camper van AS62-69; electricity hook-up AS40. **Open** Apr-Oct.
The Laxenburg campsite is set in a vast park area with its own lake, part of the grounds to Laxenburg castle, about 15km (9 miles) south-west of Vienna city centre. Facilities include a restaurant, supermarket, heated swimming pool and children's pool.

Long-term accommodation

Kaiser Franz Joseph
19, Sieveringer Straße 4 (329 00-0/320 7355/ appartementhotel@kaiserfranzjoseph. co.at). U2 Schottentor/tram 1, 2, D, then tram 38 to Sieveringer Straße/U4 Heiligenstadt, then bus 39a to Obkirchergasse. **Rates** single AS1,230-2,110; double AS1,560-2,090; monthly rates by agreement. **Credit** AmEx, DC, MC, TC, V.
Kaiser Franz Joseph is a newish 96-room hotel with apartments. The décor is attractively modern with comfortable furnishings. Though it's close to the wine-growing suburbs, the location nevertheless has good transport to the city centre.
Hotel services *Air-conditioning. Bar. Business services. Fax. Fitness room. Hairdresser. Currency exchange. Parking (AS150/day). No-smoking rooms. Kitchenette. Laundry. Massage. Sauna. Solarium. Supermarket. Bank. Multilingual staff. Restaurant.* **Room services** *Minibar. Modem line. Refrigerator. TV: cable/satellite. Telephone. Voicemail.*

Sacher Appartements
1, Rotenturmstraße 1 (533 3238/fax 533 3238/ sacher.apartments@netway.at). U1, U3 Stephansplatz. **Rates** single AS630-1,100; double AS900-1,350; monthly rates by agreement. **No credit cards**. TC.
This eight-room apartment hotel occupying the upper floor of a post-war office block offers compact but comfortable apartment accommodation. It's in the very heart of the city and there is bus and subway transport (and even horse-drawn carriages) literally at the door.
Hotel services *Air-conditioning. Fax. Kitchenette. Laundry.* **Room service** *Hairdryer. Microwave. Modem line. Radio. Refrigerator. Safe. Telephone. TV. Voicemail.*

Singerstrasse 21-25
1, Singerstraße 21-25 (51 449-0/fax 513 1617/ apartments@singerstraße2125.at). U3 Stubentor/ tram 1, 2/bus 1a. **Rates** studio, weekly/monthly AS7,700-9,100/AS27,496-32,796; executive suites, weekly/monthly AS11,900-13,300/AS43,980-49, 998. (Reception available 8am-8pm Mon-Fri.) **Credit** AmEx, DC, JCB, MC, V.
The 77 apartments in this multi-floored purpose-built complex look as good as new in their attractive livery of light grey walls and contrasting natural wood floors. The furniture is modern. Two sizes each of studio and two-room executive accommodation offer every convenience a longer-term guest could want, from elegantly outfitted bathrooms to compact full kitchenettes complete with glassware, tableware, dishes, pots and pans, toasters, coffee machines and even a dishwasher. The sitting room areas include a stereo system with CD player.
Hotel services *Air-conditioning. Fax. Kitchenette. Laundry. Parking (AS130/day). Designer furniture.* **Room services** *Phone. Radio. CD player. Safe. Laptop. TV: cable/satellite. Voicemail.*

Restaurants

Dumplings, pig's knuckle, cream sauces, sausage stacks, bread puddings and plum jam: welcome to a nutritionist's nightmare.

Catholicism may be Austria's official religion, but you could argue the real one is actually food. Austrians eat a lot, and take their food (and wines) very seriously. They also love their traditions, but even so the Viennese are gradually changing their food habits. The vast but unimaginative menus of yore offering huge portions of heavy meat dishes and calorific desserts are shrinking in size, and at the same time increasing in flavours and variety. Vienna's status as a seat of the United Nations has ensured that international cuisine now flourishes in the former capital of boiled beef and dumplings, and it's no longer a rarity to see an Italian, French or vegetarian dish in local restaurants.

The Viennese are also increasingly health conscious, so that the old stereotype of a red-faced pork and strudel-stuffer is well out of date. There are gyms and solariums around every corner, wholemeal breads in every bakery and herbal teas and muesli packing supermarket shelves.

Despite the world-food boom, though, Austria remains proud of its own national cuisine. One can quibble over the definition of 'Austrian' food. Most of the country's 'national' dishes can be traced back to foreign lands, which were not quite so foreign under the multi-national Austro-Hungarian Empire: goulash and *Palatschinken* (pancakes) from Hungary, *Knödel* (dumplings) from the Czech lands, grilled pork from Dalmatia. However, they are now all part and parcel of Austrian cuisine.

'Austrian cooking' also varies from province to province. The Waldviertel, bordering the Czech Republic, is famous for its poppy seed specialities – from *Mohnzelten* (poppy seed-filled pastries) and *Germknödel* (huge sweet dumplings, filled with plum jam and covered in hot butter and poppy seeds) to poppy seed oil for salads and cooking. The skiing provinces of Carinthia, Vorarlberg and Tirol are famed for heavy, hearty, greasy dishes such as *Käsespätzle* (baby dumplings drowned in cheese and served in a black pan resembling a mini-wok) and the similar *Kärntner Kasnudeln* and *Tiroler G'röstl* (potato cubes in a greasy mix with onions and bacon). Green Styria, often described as the Austrian Tuscany, is celebrated for its fresh farm produce, delicious *Kernöl* (pumpkin seed oil) and *Kürbiskernsuppe* (cream of pumpkin soup, topped with roasted pumpkin seeds). Styria is also known for simple eats such as *Brettljause* (a selection of cold cuts served on a crude wooden platter) and more sophisticated dishes, often involving Styrian beef, such as *saueres Rindfleisch* (thin-sliced beef in an apple vinegar and pumpkin oil dressing). Many top restaurants in Vienna are run by Styrians or influenced by Styrian cuisine, such as the **Steirereck** (literally, 'Styrian corner') and the **Schnattl**.

Styrian wines are also among Austria's best. Grapes for the celebrated Schilcher wine from western Styria are grown nowhere else in Austria, or the world, for that matter. It's officially a red, but looks more like a rosé, and, as its name promises, shimmers in the glass.

FROM *BEISL* TO WURST

Vienna boasts a wide variety of traditional Austrian eateries, from top-category restaurants to the simple *Beisl*. This word comes from the Yiddish for 'little house', and that's what it is – an informal, homely local place with heavy wooden furniture, where you might go as much to drink beer or wine as to eat sturdy local dishes (*see chapter* **Beisln**). At a more sophisticated point on the dial, the city has also been hit by *Neu Wiener Küche* fever. 'New Viennese cooking' is Vienna's answer to nouvelle cuisine. Portions are smaller, prices are higher and food presentation generally more attractive than in the slab-of-meat-on-a-plate style still frequently encountered in Vienna's simpler restaurants.

Speaking of simple, things don't get more basic than at your local *Wurstelstand* (sausage stand), where you can witness first hand (or rather, first bite) the Austrian obsession with sausages. There are hundreds of them: from the simple hot dog-type Frankfurter – usually served as a *Wurstel mit Senf*, with a splodge of mustard on a paper platter and accompanied by a *Semmel* (Austrian white roll) – through the *Käsekrainer* (otherwise known as an *eitriger*, 'pus-filled' sausage, because the cheese filling oozes out when you take a bite), the spicy, peppery *Debreziner*, the chunkier *Bratwurst*, favoured at barbecues, the even fatter Bavarian *Weisswurst* (white sausage) and many more.

The Viennese are also extremely fond of streetside snacks in general. On cold winter days you can catch the *Maronimänner* (chestnut men), selling paper cones filled with hot chestnuts or roast potatoes, or stop at a *Punschstände* (hot punch stand) – even better for warming the cockles. Take-away pizza is available across town, or, if you'd rather sit down, most coffeehouses offer *kleinigkeiten* ('small eats'), such as slices of brown bread with different toppings, *Gulaschsuppe* (a bowl of goulash) or *Wurstel mit Senf*.

Across Austria, the changing seasons are celebrated with suitable dishes. *Martini Gansl* (goose season) comes around Saint Martin's day, in mid-November, and late autumn also brings *wild Wochen*, the game season. *Weinachtsbäckerei* (Christmas biscuits) are made throughout Advent and the Christmas season, and *Faschingskrapfen* (Carnival doughnuts) are eaten at Carnival time, which officially starts on the 11th day of the 11th month but is essentially celebrated in February. *Heringschmaus* ('Herring feast') is the special food for Ash Wednesday and the whole of Lent, and with May comes *Spargel Woche* or 'asparagus week' (look out especially for those from the Marchfeld region). In early summer there is a tribute to fresh strawberries, with strawberry wine, punch, cakes and sweet dumplings.

RESTAURANT CUSTOMS

Prices at Viennese restaurants are generally reasonable and locals eat out a lot, so it's advisable to book a table in advance when you can. Wine lists are pretty extensive and often include international labels; however, since you're in Austria, it would be a shame to ignore native vintages. Wines are also relatively cheap, and quality wines are often available by the glass. Asking for a *viertel* will order a quarter-litre glass, an *achtel*, half a litre.

One aspect of dining that is not great in this city, however, is service. Those familiar with Parisian waiters may well recognise the unfriendly and arrogant air, the patronising stare and erratic timing. Also, the widespread assumption that smarter restaurants will provide better service cannot be relied on in Vienna. Thankfully, however, many Viennese waiters are learning that throwing plates at customers across the table perhaps doesn't encourage them to come back, and things are improving.

However awful the service, it's the done thing to tip, even through gritted teeth. How much you leave is up to you, but there are some rough lines to follow. In cheap eating places, round up your bill to the next zero; in more upmarket restaurants, aim for ten per cent. In between, you can maybe arrive at an average.

Restaurants are listed and divided up here by districts, and by the price of an average meal (main course plus two glasses of house wine) into Expensive, Moderate and Budget.

Pigging out

Veggies beware: the principal dish in a typical Austrian meal is invariably meat. And it's usually pig, pig, pig and a bit more pig, although you often come across the odd cow or two as well. Macho eaters can test themselves on *Blunzen* (black pudding) or even *Beuschel* (chopped offal covered in sauce). *Tafelspitz* (boiled beef) and *Wiener Schnitzel* (breaded veal) are two most ubiquitous meat dishes, and restaurants often compete to rustle up the most succulent of the former and the largest of the latter. Boiled beef apparently originated in the reign of Emperor Franz Josef, who liked it for his midday meal.

The names of many traditional dishes give some indication of the kind of cholesterol bomb they represent for your digestive system. *Bauernschmaus* (peasants' treat) consists of mounds of meat and/or sausages, and the *Grossglockner* (the name of Austria's highest mountain) is a similar dish served with sauerkraut and dumplings. The romantically titled *Schlachtplatte* (slaughter platter) will see you munching through mounds of game. Also common on traditional menus, in season, are giant, opulent game dishes, to be followed by Baroque desserts; don't be surprised, either, to see the Viennese tuck into a huge dessert served piping hot as their main lunchtime meal. Health food? Who mentioned health food?

The Viennese diet may be traditionally meat-obsessed, but the city does have some all-vegetarian eating places:
Moderate: Siddhartha, for Indian-based meat-free cooking, or Wrenkh, for contemporary vegetarian food, *both in 1st district*
Budget: Nice Rice, again for Asian-style vegetarian dishes, *6th district*
In addition, the following restaurants, while not fully vegetarian, feature a better-than-average range of vegetarian dishes in their menus:
Moderate: Guess Club, Haas Haus Do&Co, *both in 1st district;* Cuadro, Motto, *both in 5th district;* Kiang Noodles, *7th district;* Stomach, *9th district;* Villa Aurora, *16th district*
Budget: BIO.K, Palatschinkenkuchl, *both in 1st district;* Die Wäscherei, *8th district*

From the well-stocked larder of **Steirereck.**

Expensive (above AS600)

1st district

Corso

1, Hotel Bristol, Mahlerstraße 2 (5151 6546). U1, U2, U4 Karlsplatz/tram 1, 2, D, J/bus 3a. **Open** noon-3pm, 7pm-1am, Mon-Fri, Sun. **Credit** AmEx, DC, JCB, MC, V. **Average meal** AS1,000.
The Steirereck (*see below*) has the name and the fame, but this is the place to find the current peak of cuisine in Vienna. The Corso took over from the traditional restaurant in the Hotel Bristol in 1984. From *amuse-guele* appetisers to the final coffee, chef Reinhard Gere spoils diners with his Viennese *haute cuisine.* He worked in Munich and several other Vienna restaurants before arriving here, and his buttered fish tartare, *Tafelspitz* with *Semmelkrenn* (boiled beef with horseradish) and fried perch in red pepper cream sauce are all superb. The emphasis is on fresh ingredients and subtle dishes without the customary Vienna stodge, except when it comes to dessert – such delights as sweet cream cheese and nougat dumplings with pumpkin cracknel.

Drei Husaren

1, Weihburggasse 4 (5121 0920). U1, U3 Stephansplatz/tram 1, 2. **Open** noon-3pm, 6pm-1am, daily. **Credit** AmEx, DC, MC, V. **Average meal** AS900.
One of Vienna's oldest continuously running restaurants, dating back to 1933, and a tribute to Viennese noble cuisine in the good old bad days of the Austro-Hungarian Empire. A menu of delicacies fit for a king (or emperor) means that it's always full of Habsburg-hungry Austrians, and wealthy tourists seeking atmosphere. The 'Three Hussars' hors-d'oeuvres trolley is justly renowned: choose from over 30 delicacies, including calves' brains in a mustard sauce on a bed of spinach. For dessert, don't miss the *Husarenpfannkuchen,* the house crêpes.

Kervansaray-Hummerbar

1, Mahlerstraße 9, first floor (512 8843). U1, U2, U4 Karlsplatz/tram 1, 2, D, J/bus 3a. **Open** noon-midnight Mon-Sat. **Average meal** AS600.

Vienna's most renowned fish restaurant, specialising in lobster. Classic starters are the hors-d'oeuvres 'Kervansaray', a selection of smoked salmon, trout, eel and giant shrimps, or the piquant Saint Michel fish soup. Pasta fans can indulge in lobster tagliatelle, or own-made ravioli stuffed with fresh lobster and salmon. There's a whole array of lobster variations for main courses, or poached salmon fillets, sole, mini-turbots and other fish delicacies. It's possible, however, to chicken out on fish at the Kervansaray, as the menu also includes lamb, veal, chicken, goose liver and even the house döner kebab. Luxury louses can try the caviar menu, available on request. On the ground floor in the *Hummerbar* (Lobster Bar), diners can have a (slightly) more modest meal of Turkish and international delicacies.

3rd district

Palais Schwarzenberg

3, Hotel Schwarzenberg, Schwarzenbergplatz 9 (798 4515/600). Tram D. **Open** noon-3pm, 6pm-midnight, daily. **Credit** AmEx, DC, JCB, MC, V. **Average meal** AS900.
Part of the luxurious early eighteenth-century palace still owned by Prince Schwarzenberg, this is a terribly smart, but tranquil, dining venue, and the restaurant's gardens are the most spectacular in the city. The menu offers a mixture of outrageously opulent Viennese and international dishes, with seasonal variations. If they're available, try the wild duck cannelloni or the fillet of rose fish with chicory in red wine butter. Fine Austrian wines are available by the glass.

Steirereck

3, Rasumofskygasse 2 (713 3168). Tram N. **Open** noon-3pm, 7pm-midnight, Mon-Fri. **Credit** AmEx, DC, MC, V. **Average meal** AS1,000.
For most Viennese the yardstick of success and social standing is a meal at the Steirereck. The wine list is impressively comprehensive: among labels most worth trying are the full-bodied whites from FX Pichler in the Wachau, the sumptuous reds from Rust in Burgenland or Austria's most distinguished sweet wines, from Alois Kracher of Illmitz, Burgenland. The seasonally changing menu highlights Austrian cuisine with a Styrian slant, but there are some international dishes, and the list is spiced with interesting combinations such as lobster and courgette on a bed of saffron rice, or caviar on red cabbage jelly. Service is unusually good, even sometimes too attentive. Check out too the powerfully smelling larder filled with maturing cheeses – the Steirereck also makes its own. If you don't want to splash out quite so much but still want a taste of the experience, try the set brunch for AS100, the *Wiener Gabelfrühstück* (literally, 'Viennese Fork Breakfast') served from 10.30am to noon – an elegant selection of smaller dishes. The Steirereck is also unusually child-friendly, with a separate children's menu and toys available on demand.

15th district

Altwienerhof

15, Herklotzgasse 6 (892 6000). U6 Gumperdorfer Straße. **Open** noon-2pm, 6.30pm-2am, Mon-Sat. **Credit** AmEx, DC, JCB, MC, V. **Average meal** AS1,200.

If you take your food seriously and have money to spare, this place is worth the trek. Rudi Kellner is one of Austria's most respected chefs, well versed in the arts of several culinary cultures. His foremost speciality is what he calls his 'grande cuisine', with a bias towards *la belle France*, a gastronomic experience not to be missed – delicacies include goose liver pralines, or lightly boiled pheasant covered in an exquisite goose liver sauce. For an extra pleasure, book a table in the conservatory.

Moderate (AS130-600)

1st district

Aioli

1, Stephansplatz 12, third floor of the Haas Haus (532 0373). U1, U3 Stephansplatz. **Open** 10am-1am daily. **Credit** V. **Average meal** AS300.

A Mediterranean oasis in the heart of Vienna's 1st district, created by two young Barcelona designers. Fresh ingredients – seafood, ham, delectable cheeses, *pimientos de padrón* (Spanish small sweet peppers), Catalan onions – are flown in daily from Barcelona and Milan. Fish and pasta dishes are wonderful, and don't even think of missing out on the Aioli (fresh garlic mayonnaise). The staff are rather less authentic, and the atmosphere is also not truly Mediterranean – and not just because of its Pizza Hut-style self-service antipasti bar. Aioli remains unmistakably Viennese, filled with smart Austrian businessmen and women in suits.

Barbaro's

1, Kärntner Straße 19 (513 1712). U1, U3 Stephansplatz. **Open** noon-3pm, 6pm-midnight, daily. **Credit** DC, MC, V. **Average meal** AS400.

A breathtaking view – from the top floor of the Steffl shopping centre – with prices to match. Luigi Barbaro is the king of Italian cooking in Vienna, and the opening of this showcase was awaited with baited breath by Vienna's yuppies. The menu is extensive, and dishes are made with the freshest ingredients. Fish is especially good: barbecued scallops are a speciality, served with courgettes and thinly sliced chips. For meat eaters, the veal steak with truffle tagliatelle and steamed vegetables is a great choice, while for vegetarian pasta fans the pumpkin ravioli with pepper sauce is a must. Barbaro's also has fine Italian red wines and Austrian whites. Book a table by the window for an up-close and personal view of **Stephansdom** by night.

Cantinetta Antinori

1, Jasomirgottstraße 3-5 (533 7722). U1, U3 Stephansplatz. **Open** noon-2pm, 6pm-midnight, daily. **Credit** AmEx, DC, MC, V. **Average meal** AS350.

Vienna's oldest large-scale Italian restaurant, owned by the Marchese Antinori, is always full. The essentially Tuscan food is very good, beginning with the olive bread placed on the table. Outstanding among first courses is the balsamic vinegar soup; of mains,

Figlmüller: *for the hotel concierge's favourite Schnitzel. See page 144.*

Restaurant meets florist at the singular **Hansen**.

sea bass with white truffles and rosemary roast potatoes, or saddle of lamb with vegetables in lamb gravy. The Antinori family produce their own Tuscan wines and olive oil, all naturally used in the restaurant. The downside of the Cantinetta is its layout, with too many narrow tables cramped together, which, coupled with the cigarette smoke, can make eating here a claustrophobic experience.

Da Conte
1, Kurrentgasse 12 (533 6464). Bus 1a, 3a. **Open** noon-3pm, 6.30pm-1.30am, daily. **Credit** AmEx, DC, MC, V. **Average meal** AS220.
Luxurious Italian cuisine in comfortable surroundings. Charming Sr da Conte is the Ischian proprietor, and sometime cook; his fish and seafood are excellent, especially in the mixed grill with sea bass, monkfish, prawns and calamari (AS300-350 per portion) or pasta with octopus. Cheeses are also worth examining, and betray his soft spot for truffles, as in Parmesan with truffle oil, or warm Gorgonzola with truffles. The Contes can advise you on which wine to choose; for dessert, if you have a Viennese appetite, try the profiteroles oozing with cream.

David & Ruven's
1, Seittenstettengasse 2 (535 2530). U1, U4 Schwedenplatz/tram 1, 2, 21/bus 2a. **Open** noon-3pm, 5.30-11pm, daily. **No credit cards.** **Average meal** AS250.
A kosher restaurant in the middle of the Bermuda Triangle, with Viennese arched ceilings, red velvet upholstery and a stone-paved entrance. Classics of German-Jewish food such as *Gefiltefisch* (stuffed carp) and *Kigel* (potato strudel) are almost as good as home-cooking, but David & Ruven's also offers a

wide variety of healthier Middle Eastern Jewish cuisine as well – grilled meats and fish, salads and delicious houmous and tahina dips.

Figlmüller
1, Wollzeile 5 (512 6177). U1, U3 Stephansplatz/bus 1a. **Open** 11am-10.30pm daily. **Credit** AmEx, DC, MC, V. **Average meal** AS225.
If you're staying in the city centre and want to eat traditional Schnitzel, your host or hotel will very probably direct you to Figlmüller. But think twice about it. The Schnitzel are certainly tasty and said to be the largest in Vienna, but the restaurant is touristy, overpriced and self-important. Wines all come from the owner's own vineyards in Grinzing; no beers or coffees and other hot drinks are served.

Gösser Bierklinik
1, Steindlgasse 4 (535 6897). U1, U3 Stephansplatz/bus 1a. **Open** 10am-11.30pm Mon-Sat. **Credit** DC, MC, V. **Average meal** AS160.
An ancient inn with big wooden tables, stone walls and standing-only booths for serious beer drinking. The restaurant is in a more formal room at the back, and serves Schnitzels, dumplings and other traditional Austrian food.

Guess Club
1, Kärntner Straße 44 (585 6349). U1, U3 Stephansplatz. **Open** 7pm-4am daily. **Credit** AmEx, DC, MC, V. **Average meal** AS300.
A modernistic den of crossover pop cuisine. Weird and wonderful multi-national dishes are served up in super-cool surroundings, with a Star Trek-type bar, a video wall and Net access. If you just fancy a snack, try roast beef sandwiches (AS45), udon soup

with surimi (AS50) or glass noodles with tofu (AS75), and hang cool in the fake cowhide-decorated Media Lounge. For serious eats, head for the Shining and Dining room, with its weird lighting effects: dishes to go for include suckling pig, shark with spicy stuffing and beef carpaccio served with rocket and Parmesan pastry pockets, with Thai basil sorbet to follow. And that's not all: breakfasters should hike upstairs to the sickly coloured Peach Room, the winter garden or the wood-panelled Nut Room, also used for private parties and events. *See also chapter* **Nightlife**.

Gulaschmuseum

1, Schulerstraße 20 (512 1017). U1, U3 Stephansplatz/bus 1a. **Open** 9am-midnight Mon-Fri; 10am-midnight Sat, Sun. **Credit** MC. **Average meal** AS146.

Kitschy Gasthaus décor and a five-language menu with enough mistakes to provide a full evening's entertainment are just some of the attractions of this long-running tourist favourite. There are always at least 15 types of goulash to choose from on the daily changing menu: forget the normal beany goulash thing and go for chicken liver goulash, fish goulash or even chanterelle goulash, for vegetarians. If you have a stomach for heavy food and a sense of humour, there are worse places to spend an evening.

Haas Haus Do&Co

1, Stephansplatz 12, seventh floor (535 3969). U1, U3 Stephansplatz/bus 1a, 2a, 3a. **Open** noon-3pm, 6pm-midnight, daily. **Credit** V. **Average meal** AS300.

International cuisine from Austria's trendiest catering service (clients include Grand Prix racers and the private jets of the glitterati). Their central Stephansplatz venue offers a popular but expensive lunchtime sushi bar, and weird and wonderful stir-fries for veggies; seafood and meat eaters should try the king crab and Uruguayan steak combo.

There's a spectacular view of **Stephansdom**, so it's worth booking a window table in winter, and balcony space in summer. It's also famed for having the youngest, best-looking waiters and waitresses in all Vienna.

Hansen

1, Wipplingerstraße 34 (532 0542). U2 Schottentor/ tram 1, 2, D/bus 1a, 3a. **Open** 9am-9pm Mon-Fri; 9am-5pm Sat. **Credit** AmEx, DC, JCB, MC, V. **Average meal** AS230.

One-of-a-kind in Vienna, and a feast for the eyes as well as the taste buds. A combination of restaurant and elegant flower shop, ideally placed in the Roman market hall underneath the Vienna stock exchange. The location means it fills up with trendy executives at lunchtime, but the atmosphere remains surprisingly fresh and unstuffy. Young Viennese cook Christian Voithofer's menu is modern and creative – to the point of being a tad pretentious – but efforts like the pasta and noodle variations with sauces influenced from all over the world are fresh and enjoyable. Drawbacks are a) the hall acoustics and b) the early closing times, due to inflexible Austrian shopping laws. Reservations are essential.

Hoshigaoka Saryo

1, Führichgasse 10 (512 2720). U1, U2, U4 Karlsplatz/tram 1, 2, D, J/bus 3a. **Open** noon-3pm, 6pm-midnight, daily. **Credit** AmEx, DC, JCB, MC, V. **Average meal** AS400.

Many consider this to be Vienna's best Japanese restaurant, just around the corner from the **Staatsoper**. The upstairs room is a feast for the eyes as well as the stomach, as the teppan yaki cooks juggle shrimps, knives and pepper mills as they prepare your meal before your eyes. For a more relaxed gastronomical experience stay on the ground floor, where there's sushi, a big à la carte menu and a range of set-price menus featuring sashimi and tempura.

Schnitzel-free zones

If you feel like a break from Austrian fare:
American
Livingstone, *1st district*; Bayou, *2nd district*
Chinese
Kiang Noodles, *6th district;* Jumbo, Lucky Buddha, *7th district*
Croatian
Kornat, *1st district*
French
Bordeaux, *9th district;* La Crêperie, *21st district*
Greek
Taverna Lefteris, *3rd district*
Indian
Siddhartha, *1st district;* Demi Tass, Indian Pavilion, *both in 4th district*
Italian
Barbaro's, Cantinetta Antinori, Da Conte, Novelli,

Regina Margherita, A Tavola, *all in 1st district;* Trattoria l'Ambasciata della Puglia, *18th district*
Japanese & Korean
Hoshigaoka Saryo, *1st district;* Toko Ri, *2nd district;* Midori, *6th district*
Jewish
David & Ruven's, *1st district*
Latin American
Saci, *4th district;* Rincón Andino, *6th district*
Multi-national
Haas Haus Do&Co, Guess Club, *in 1st district;* Cuadro, Schlossgasse 21, *5th district;* Salz and Pfeffer, *6th district*
Spanish/Mediterranean
Aioli, *1st district;* Bodega Española, *4th district*
Thai/East Asian
Wok – Asia Cuisine Restaurant, *4th district*

Kornat

*1, Marc-Aurel-Straße 8 (535 6518). U1, U4
Schwedenplatz/tram 1, 2, 21/bus 2a, 3a.*
Open 11.30am-3pm, 6pm-midnight, Mon-Sat.
Credit DC, MC, V. **Average meal** AS250.
A Croatian restaurant specialising in Dalmatian cuisine, this is one of the best places in Vienna for fresh fish, which is flown in every day from the Dalmatian coast, and has great pasta dishes as well. Tonka is as passionate about cooking as her husband Djelko is about his wines: the impressive list includes Dalmatian, Italian, Spanish, French and Austrian labels. When in the mood, he also bursts into Croatian folk songs, and loves it if you hum along.

Livingstone

*1, Zelinkagasse 4 (533 4565). U2, U4
Schottenring/tram 1, 2/bus 3a.* **Open** 5pm-4am daily. **Credit** AmEx, DC, V. **Average meal** AS200.
A vaguely Victorian-colonial-looking restaurant that brings to Vienna Californian crossover cuisine – Mexican/Italian/Asian, to be precise. The swordfish and mahi mahi are as good as you'd get in Santa Monica, and the burgers with a full choice of side orders are pretty impressive too.

MAK

1, Stubenring 5 (714 0121). U3 Stubentor/tram 1, 2.
Open 10am-2am Tue-Sun. **No credit cards.**
Average meal AS180.
This spacious restaurant/café in the Museum of Modern Art (*see chapter* **Museums**) welcomes a fashion- rather than culture-conscious clientèle, with designer-ish food to match. House speciality is *piroghi* – pastry pockets stuffed with assorted fillings, such as beef or cream cheese; for something

larger, have the succulent duck in red wine sauce with red cabbage and dumplings, or king-sized prawns with potato gratin. To finish off, go for fluffy orange parfait, or calorie-crammed sweet-nut dumplings in vanilla and apple cream. Wines are mainly dry whites. There's also an elegant courtyard, the place to book a table in summer.

Neu Wien

*1, Bäckerstraße 5 (513 0666). U1, U3 Stephansplatz/
bus 1a, 3a.* **Open** 6pm-2am daily. **Credit** AmEx, DC, JCB, MC, V. **Average meal** AS250.
As the name suggests, this is the taste of 'New Vienna'. Here the trendy and traditional intermingle; in the décor (candles on tables and walls, modern paintings on the walls) and in the eclectic menu, where nouvelle cuisine meets the Habsburgs. The menu changes frequently, but among the best of the regularly appearing dishes are the *Zanderfilet*, a crispy pike with cream beet sauce, and veal with tagliatelle in truffle sauce. The smooth Vranac wines from Montenegro make an ideal accompaniment.

Novelli

*1, Bräunerstraße 11 (513 4200-0). U1, U3
Stephansplatz/bus 1a, 2a.* **Open** 12-2pm, 6-11pm, Tue-Sun. **Credit** AmEx, DC, MC, V. **Average meal** AS350.
To eat at this modern Italian citadel is a real indulgence. The dining room is open-plan, with an elegant yet comfortable feel; soft lighting is provided by spectacular chandeliers, and seating is in big brown leather chairs. Diners can go directly to a table, or sit for a while to ogle the fresher-than-fresh antipasti while posing at the discreetly sleek bar. Modern Italian dishes such as poached sea bass in

Franz Josef's favourite dish: the ubiquitous Tafelspitz.

Wrenkh *serves vegetarian food with a difference. See page 149.*

tarragon cream or steak fillet with sage gnocchi and onions soaked in balsamic vinegar are beautifully prepared and presented; from the dessert menu, dive straight in for the chocolate mousse, in three tiers, divided by wafer-thin dark chocolate and served on a swirl of exotic fruit. There's also a lengthy, relatively expensive list mostly of fine Italian wines. The clientèle reflect the classy prices, but staff, perhaps confident of juicy tips, are pleasantly helpful.

Oswald & Kalb

1, Bäckerstraße 14 (512 1371). U1, U3 Stephansplatz/bus 1a, 3a. **Open** 6pm-2am daily. **Credit** AmEx, DC, JCB, MC, V. **Average meal** AS280.

A restaurant that's extremely pricey for the kind of food it offers, for no good reason except that it's in with Vienna's headline makers and shakers. Service is also correspondingly snotty, although soft lighting gives the place a conspiratorial air. The menu features traditional Austrian fare with Viennese and Styrian specialities: *Tafelspitz* (boiled beef), Wiener Schnitzel, roast calves' trotters and the like.

Palmenhaus

1, Burggarten (entrance Goethegasse) (533 1033). U1, U2, U4 Karlsplatz/tram 1, 2, D, J. **Open** 10am-2am daily. **Credit** AmEx, DC, MC, V. **Average meal** AS202.

This former glasshouse in the Burggarten was turned into a modern café/restaurant in 1998. The 'Palmhouse' is urban trendy, but has a natural touch too: with high-reaching glass walls and curving ceilings that give it a spacious feel, it's full of palm trees, and is right next door to Vienna's Butterfly House. The menu is modern and relatively short;

antipasti, fish dishes or tomato goulash are all prepared with fresh ingredients and attractively presented. The cheese selection is predominantly Italian, the wine list mainly Austrian (bottles to try are the Grüner Veltliner or Pinot Blanc whites, or Zweigelt or Blaufränkisch reds). It's popular for long, relaxed brunches: book to avoid disappointment, but if you forget, wait for a table at the glitzy bar with its extensive array of flashy bottles. *See also chapter* **Nightlife.**

Plachutta

1, Wollzeile 38 (512 1577). U3 Stubentor/tram 1, 2/bus 1a. **Open** 11.30am-midnight daily. **Credit** AmEx, DC, MC, V. **Average meal** AS350.

Smart, modern and quite pricey, Plachutta offers traditional fare amid green and yellow décor, with waiters in matching uniform. It's a mecca for beef enthusiasts, as the chef, Plachutta Junior, specialises in Styrian beef dishes. *Kruspelspitz* enables you to sample two boiled beef varieties in one go.

Regina Margherita

1, Wallnerstraße 4 (533 0812). U3 Herrengasse/ bus 2a, 3a. **Open** noon-3pm, 6pm-midnight, Mon-Sat. **No credit cards. Average meal** AS250.

A smart-looking Italian restaurant in a quiet leafy courtyard in the heart of old Vienna. This is Luigi Barbaro's less pricey alternative to the celebrated **Barbaro's** (*see above*), specialising in pizza, baked by Neapolitan chefs. The pizza oven is a work of art in its own right: it was created out of stones collected in Santa Maria Cappovetere, sand from the Neapolitan seaside and earth from Mount Vesuvius. Standards like Pizza Margherita take on new life

here, adorned with fresh tomatoes and basil, chunks of buffalo mozzarella and slithers of Parma ham.

Santo Spirito
1, Kumpfgasse 7 (512 9998). U1, U3 Stephansplatz/tram 1, 2. **Open** 11am-2am Sun-Thur; 11am-3am Fri-Sat. **No credit cards. Average meal** AS170.
'Famed' for its loud classical background music, particularly opera, the 'Holy Spirit' has a dark, bistro-like interior with red velvet curtains and golden cherubs on the walls. Especially popular are its excellent brunches, named after composers, such as the Händel (English breakfast, with ham and eggs) or the Bach (raw vegetables, muesli with yoghurt, a fresh apple and carrot juice). For lunch or evening meals there's lovely tapas-style food, or more filling choices such as chicken breasts with saffron rice or pork medallions with parsley potatoes. To finish off, make for the sinful profiteroles. Reservations are necessary in the restaurant, which attracts a mixed clientèle. *See also chapter* **Gay & Lesbian**.

Siddhartha
1, Fleischmarkt 16 (513 1197). U1, U4 Schwedenplatz/tram 1, 2, 21/bus 2a. **Open** 11.30am-11pm daily. **Credit** AmEx, MC, V. **Average meal** AS140.
A smart vegetarian restaurant with a bit of an identity crisis: it's situated on the Fleischmarkt ('meat market'), and has red leather upholstery. However, it also offers a good choice of Indian-based vegetarian food, such as curry soya steak or, even better, Indian Dream – a spicily moreish blend of curries served with samosas and chapatis.

A Tavola
1, Weihburggasse 3-5 (512 7955). U1, U3 Stephansplatz/tram 1, 2. **Open** noon-3pm, 6pm-midnight, Mon-Sat. **Credit** AmEx, DC, MC, V. **Average meal** AS150.
It's been hard to get a table at this Tuscan restaurant ever since it opened. The atmosphere is casual, and Italophiles especially feel at home. While looking at the menu, dunk the great chunky bread into the bowls of thick olive oil provided on each table. The antipasti and own-made soups are delicious, and pasta dishes include an unusual spaghetti with curry, black olives and chicken breasts; there's also a plentiful choice of beef, chicken, fish and game.

Walzerschiff Johann Strauß
1, Kleine Donau, Schwedenplatz (533 9367). U1, U4 Schwedenplatz/tram 1, 2, 21. **Open** Wed-Sun 8pm-4am Wed-Sun; *Apr-Oct* 8pm-4am daily. **No credit cards. Average meal** (includes boat trip) AS400.
A Viennese experience for kitsch queens. Wine, dine and waltz down the Danube aboard a boat, which could only be called the Johann Strauß. The river cruise is quite fun, but the menu is bland and unimaginative (carp, pike or boiled beef) and the waltz programme even less inspired – they could find something else to play from the JS repertoire as the ship wobbles from side to side, apart from repeating *The Blue Danube*. Even so, a tacky but pleasurable experience, especially on a clear summer's night.

Wrenkh
1, Bauernmarkt 10 (533 1526). U1, U3 Stephansplatz. **Open** *Restaurant* 11.30am-2.30pm, 6pm-midnight, Mon-Sat. *Bar* 11am-midnight Mon-Sat. *Summer* closed Sat. **Credit** AmEx, DC, MC, V. **Average meal** AS180.
An alternative to the usual grungy, studenty veggie joint, Wrenkh provides vegetarian food for the young and elegant, serving imaginative bar and restaurant menus. The restaurant is comfortable, if a little more formal than the bar; among the best dishes to be found on the menu are an enjoyable miso soup, wild rice risotto with mushrooms, and Greek fried rice with vegetables, sheep's cheese and olives. There's also a generous buffet brunch which is served on Sundays.

Zum Kuckuk
1, Himmelpfortgasse 15 (512 8470). U1, U3 Stephansplatz/tram 1, 2. **Open** noon-2.30pm, 6pm-midnight, Mon-Sat. **Credit** AmEx, DC, JCB, MC, V. **Average meal** AS280.
A traditional haunt of Viennese epicures. However, if the sight and sound of cuckoo clocks gives you the horrors, don't set foot in this tiny, vaulted-roof restaurant. Inside you leave modern Vienna behind: also around the walls are prints from Emperor Franz Josef's time, and there are masses of fresh flowers on the tables. Sip a glass of *Sekt* with blood-orange juice while perusing the generous menu, which, for all the place's renown, offers good, honest traditional cooking, from beef roulades marinated in red wine to roast duck in honey-green pepper sauce. It also has excellent fish and game dishes.

Zum Schwarzen Kameel
1, Bognergasse 5 (533 8967). U1, U3 Stephansplatz/bus 1a, 2a, 3a. **Open** 9am-8pm Mon-Fri; 9am-3am Sat. **Credit** AmEx, DC, MC, V. **Average meal** AS130.
Extremely Viennese, with an old world, gentleman's club-type atmosphere, this is a charming lunch restaurant where you can also stand at the bar and munch delicately prepared sandwiches. Red cabbage spread, the divine *Matjesherring* or even more godly smoked ham sandwich are all great, especially washed down with a full-bodied red wine such as the Blau Portugieser. The adjoining delicatessen opened in 1618, and is a Viennese institution: rumour has it Beethoven used to shop there.

2nd district

Bayou
2, Leopoldgasse 51 (214 7752). Tram 21, N/bus 5a. **Open** 4pm-midnight Mon-Sat; 11am-midnight Sun. **Credit** DC, MC, V. **Average meal** AS218.
A Creole/Cajun mecca, in the heart of Vienna's old Jewish district. The various Gumbo stews are as hot as you can handle, prepared with gusto by manager Erich Dirnwöber, and the garlicky grilled chicken with coriander, the olive oil and vodka salad dressing and seafood gumbo can all be recommended. Leave room for a Dirnwöber favourite: New Orleans bread pudding with butterscotch cream.

What's on the menu

Useful phrases

Do you have a table for... (number) people?
Haben Sie einen Tisch für... Personen?
I want to book a table for (time) o'clock
Ich möchte einen Tisch für... uhr bestellen
I'll have (name of food)
Ich nehme ...
I'll have (name of food) without (ingredient)
Ich nehme... ohne...
I'm a vegetarian
Ich bin Vegetarier
Can I/we have an ashtray, please
Einen Aschenbecher, bitte
The bill, please
Zahlen, bitte
Waitress/waiter
Fräulein, Herr Ober

Basics

Die Speisekarte Menu
Das Menü Fixed-price menu
Die Tageskarte Menu of the day
Couvert/Gedeck Cover charge
Die Weinkarte Wine list
Das Glas Glass
Das Messer Knife
Die Gabel Fork
Der Löffel Spoon
Die Vorspeise Starter
Die Hauptspeise Main course
Die Nachspeise Desert
Das Frühstück Breakfast
Das Mittagessen Lunch
Das Abendessen Dinner

Menu

Apfelsaft (-gespritzt) Apple juice (mixed with soda water)
Almdudler Herbal lemonade
Banane Banana
Brot Bread
Durch Well done (as in steak)

Ei (Spiegelei; Rührei; pochiertes/ verlorenes Ei; weiches Ei; hartgekochtes Ei) Egg (fried; scrambled; poached; boiled, hardboiled)
Eis Ice cream
Eiswürfel Ice cube
Englisch Rare (as in steak)
Fisch Fish
Fisolen Beans
Fleisch Meat
Garnelen Prawns
Gebacken Baked/fried
Gebraten Roast
Gekocht Boiled
Gemüse Vegetables
vom Grill Grilled
Goulasch Gulash/stew
Gurke Cucumber
Hendl/Hahn/Huhn Chicken
Kaffee Coffee
Kartoffel/Erdäpfel Potatoes
Käse Cheese
Knoblauch Garlic
Knödel Dumplings
Kotelett Chop
Leitungswasser Tap water
Marillen Apricots
Meeresfrüchte Seafood
Medium Medium-rare (as in steak)
Mehlspeise Patisseries
Milch Milk
Mineralwasser Mineral water
Nachspeise Dessert
Obst Fruit
Öl Oil
Oliven Olives
Orangensaft Orangejuice
Frischgepresster Orangensaft Freshly squeezed orange juice
Paradeiser Tomatoes
Pfeffer Pepper
Pommes frites Chips
Reis Rice

Lusthaus

2, Freudenau 254 (at the end of the Praterhauptallee) (728 9565). U1 Praterstern, then bus 82a. **Open** noon-6pm Sat, Sun; *May-Dec* noon-11pm Mon, Tue, Thur, Fri; *Oct, Apr* noon-6pm Mon, Tue, Thur, Fri. **Credit** AmEx, DC, MC, V. **Average meal** AS215.
A charming pavilion set in the Prater. In contrast to the noisy, cheap and cheerful fairground part of the park (the site of the **Schweizerhaus**, *see*

below), this restaurant and its surroundings have a nostalgic, elegant air. The menu is regularly updated according to the chef's mood and the season, and traditional Viennese food – for example boiled beef with cream of chives and roast potatoes – is always beautifully presented here. Game and lamb dishes are excellent too, although fish can be disappointing – often either cooked or sauced to death. Desserts, however, are another high point. The wine list is respectable, if a little overpriced. The place is not to be recommended to vegetarians or

Rind Beef
Rostbraten Steak
Rotwein Redwine
Salz Salt
Sauce/Saft sauce/gravy
Schalentiere shellfish
Schinken/Speck Ham
Schlag Whipped cream
Schnecken Snails
Schokolade Chocolate
Schwein Pork
Semmel White roll
Senf Mustard
Serviettenknödel Sliced dumplings
Sulz Brawn
Suppe Soup
Tee Tea
Topfen Cream cheese
Torte Cake
Vollkorn Wholemeal
Wasser Water
Weinessig Vinegar
Weisswein White wine
Wurst Sausage
Zucker Sugar
Zwetschke Plum
Zwiebel Onion

Savoury dishes

Leberknödelsuppe Clear beef broth made with liver; includes small dumplings
Fritatensuppe Clear beef broth with floating slivers of pancake
Rindsgulasch Beef stew spiced with paprika and served with dumplings (originally a Hungarian recipe)
Erdäpfelgulasch Potato stew; often includes pieces of frankfurter sausage
Tiroler g'röstl Hash served in a blackened skillet
Tafelspitz mit g'röste Boiled beef served with fried, grated potatoes, covered in an apple and horseradish sauce. (Emperor Franz Joseph used to eat this every lunchtime, apparently)
Beuschel chopped offal covered in sauce
Bauernschmaus Means 'peasants'treat'. A plate of hot meats including smoked pork, roast pork or pork cutlet, frankfurters and a selection of ham. It's usually served with dumplings
Blunzn Black pudding
Gefüllte Kalbsbrust Veal breast filled with several types of meat or vegetable
Wienerschnitzel Veal or pork escalope fried in breadcrumbs
Gefüllte Paprika Green peppers stuffed with mince meat and rice; cooked in a tomato sauce
Käsespätzle Baby dumplings, covered in a powerful cheese sauce
Eierschwammerln Chanterelle mushrooms (seasonal in autumn). Served in meat sauces or over salad
Eierspeise Scrambled omlette served in a pan, sometimed with ham
Heringsalat Pickled herring salad; traditionally served on Ash Wednesday
Gemischter Salat Tomatoes, potato salad, green beans, lettuce and lots of onions, covered in gooe-pimple inducing wine or apple vinegar

Dessert

Salzburger Nockerl Sweet Salzburg Dumplings Basically a huge cloud of empty-tasting egg-white
Palatschinken Thicker than the French crepe; served sweet or savoury
Mohr im Hemd Rich chocolate pudding. Steamed and served with a hot chocolate sauce and whipped cream.
Topfen/Marillenknödel Curd cheese or apricot dumplings, covered in breadcrumbs and fried in butter. Served with a hot fruit puree
Reisauflauf Rice pudding
Kaiserschmarrn Thick fluffy pancake, chopped into small pieces and covered in icing sugar. Usually served with a plum compôte

dieters, but service is friendly, and in summer, the candlelit tables on the circular terrace offer a view worthy of landed gentry. Watch out, however, for the mosquitoes.

Toko Ri

2, Franz-Hochedlingergasse 2 (214 8940).
Tram 31. **Open** noon-3pm, 6pm-midnight, Mon-Sat; 6pm-midnight Sun. **Credit** AmEx, DC, JCB, MC, V. **Average meal** AS200.
Vienna's sushi experts all agree: if Oscars were awarded for the best raw fish in the city, Toko Ri would snap up the prizes . The quality and choice at this restaurant is really outstanding – there are over 20 choices among the starters (such as salmon teriyaki in a caramel sauce with baby gherkins and tiny onions) a similar range of sushi (prices start at AS135 for a small portion) and equally good sashimi and tempura. All the main courses are accompanied by a small salad and followed by a serving of fresh fruit. All this can be washed down with Japanese beer.

Stop off at a branch of **Trzesniewski** for budget snacks on the go. See page 157.

3rd district

Im KunstHaus

3, Weissgerberlände 14 (718 5152). Tram N.
Open 10am-midnight daily. **Credit** AmEx, DC, MC,
V. **Average meal** AS200.
Wacky café/restaurant that's part of the Kunsthaus
gallery, which houses a permanent exhibition on the
Austrian modern artist, architect and philosopher
Friedensreich Hundertwasser. True to his style the
restaurant is arrayed in bright colours, has undulating floors and is lined from wall to ceiling with
fresh flowers, but it's independent of the gallery, so
you can eat without paying to see the exhibition.
Compared to the setting the menu is a little disappointing – a rather unimaginative mix of soups, salads and meats that varies with the seasons (beef
soup in winter, gazpacho in summer). It's still a fun
place to eat, though, and in summer you can sit outside in a *Midsummer Night's Dream*-like garden. See
also chapter **Galleries**.

Taverna Lefteris

3, Hörnesgasse 17 (713 7451). U3 Rochusmarkt/bus
4a. **Open** 6pm-1am Mon-Sat. **No credit cards**.
Average meal AS160.
Employees of the Greek embassy declare this the
best Greek restaurant in town. The menu has a
Cretan slant, with several Turkish-influenced
dishes. It's also pretty, with beautiful wooden floors,
and walls that are a rather too light blue; in summer,
you can eat outside under the trees. Greek musicians
play live every Tuesday and Thursday from 8pm.

4th district

Bodega Española

4, Belvedergasse 10 (504 5500). Tram D. **Open**
6pm-1am Tue-Fri. **Credit** V. **Average meal** AS250.
The taste, sounds and smells of Spain, in the heart
of Vienna's 4th district. Tapas such as *pinchos de
pollo con arroz* (small skewers of grilled chicken on
rice) are delicious, as is the *crema catalana* dessert
(similar to crème brûlée). There's also a wonderful
selection of Spanish wines, expertly selected by

manager Walter Steltzer, with a particularly impressive choice of Riojas. Reserve to be sure of a table.

Demi Tass

4, Prinz-Eugen-Straße 28 (504 3119). Tram D.
Open 11.30am-2.30pm, 6-11.30pm, Mon-Sat.
Credit AmEx, DC, MC, V. **Average meal** AS150.
Indian specialities, especially from northern India:
good chicken, lamb and fish, as in murghi shajahani
(chicken cooked with hazelnuts, raisins, pineapple
and bananas) and machi bengali (grilled salmon
baked with tomatoes, onions and an array of Indian
spices). To follow up there are Indian sweetmeats
such as the house dumplings, of sweet cream cheese
fried in syrup and cardamom. Exotic cocktails are
another attraction, headed by the Demi Tass itself
(mango liqueur, Grand Marnier, cognac and soda).

Saci

4, Mühlgasse 20 (587 7036). Bus 59a. **Open** 6pm-
2am Mon-Sat. **Credit** V. **Average meal** AS150.
A bright, modern Brazilian bar and restaurant. It
hosts frequent exhibitions by young Brazilian
artists; the food range is limited but high-quality,
courtesy of the Brazilian chef. A great option for
winter is the *Feijoada*, a rich, thick bean stew. The
house coconut milk and Brazilian cocktails are
equally well worth the indulgence.

Wok – Asia Cuisine Restaurant

4, Operngasse 20b (585 2102). U1, U2, U4
Karlsplatz/bus 59a. **Open** 11.30am-2.30pm, 5.30-
11pm, daily. **Credit** MC. **Average meal** AS190.
The taste of Asia, yes, but not much sign of a wok.
Maybe it went missing in the chaotic kitchen.
Nevertheless, this mainly Thai restaurant offers a
wonderful choice of Asian dishes: starters like tom-
yam gung (Thai spicy-sour soup with prawns),
mouth-watering mains such as nyonya curry (chick-
en curry with lemongrass and coconut milk) and
desserts like the 'coppa Thai' (coconut ice-cream
with palm seeds and mango). The set menu includes
soup or spring rolls, a choice of main courses and
dessert, all for AS200. There's also a good choice of
Austrian white wines. Staff are ever smiley.

5th district

Cuadro

5, Margaretenstraße 77 (544 7550). Bus 13a, 14a, 59a. **Open** 7.30am-11pm Mon-Fri. **Credit** V. **Average meal** AS130.

A futuristic ethno diner/café in an elegant Biedermeier building. The sandwiches, strudels and burgers taste great, and – true to the restaurant's name – are all square-shaped. Forget straightforward burgers: instead there are bali burgers (with curry sauce), a chilli burger with roast ham, and burgers mixed with special herb concoctions (14 herbs and spices, in the tandoori and bali burgers). Everything is own-made, including the square-shaped rolls for the sandwiches (sample the fisherman special, with smoked salmon, cream cheese and a mouth-watering honey, mustard and dill dressing). Veggies should try the nachos, soups or tapas; coffee is excellent too. The ultra-modern steel interior could create a sterile atmosphere, but it's saved by the constant presence of a young, lively crowd.

Motto

5, Schönbrunner Straße 30 (entrance Rüdigergasse) (587 0672). U4 Pilgramgasse/bus 59a. **Open** 6pm-4am daily. **No credit cards. Average meal** AS217.

Outrageously posy and *Les Liaisons Dangereux* in atmosphere, Motto has been in among Vienna's gay community for years, but is now catching on fast among trendy heteros. To go with its bitchy and very camp staff, there's a correspondingly camp candles-and-shadows atmosphere. Specialities include Frau Helene's steak flambés, every Sunday, Monday and Tuesday, such as the Dr Roschitz, with chanterelle and truffle mushrooms flambéd in brandy and a rich, creamy sauce, or the Moskwa, with caviar rice and flambéd in vodka. It also serves vegetarian dishes, such as spinach lasagne. Sip a cocktail at the Motto Bar while waiting for a table.

Schlossgasse 21

5, Schlossgasse 21 (544 0767). Bus 13a, 59a. **Open** 11.45am-2am daily. **Credit** V. **Average meal** AS175.

A very fashionable place that offers a multi-ethnic range of foods (Indonesian, Thai, Indian) mixed with traditional Viennese cooking. Also popular is its drinks range, with four types of beer on tap, a respectable selection of wines available by the glass or bottle and innumerable types of schnapps. There's a fabulous garden for eating out in summer.

6th district

Hungerküstler

6, Gumpendorferstraße 48 (587 9210). Bus 57a. **Open** 11am-2am daily. **Credit** MC, V. **Average meal** AS140.

Reasonably priced, enjoyable food served in relaxed, candlelit surroundings, with classical music in the background. The *Spinatspätzle* (baby dumplings covered in spinach, cream and cheese), red wine goulash or *Schinkenfleckerl* (farfalle pasta fried with ham in a creamy sauce) all hit the spot. A good place to come if you're alone, and enjoy a glass of wine, although you should be ready to wait for your meal.

Kiang Noodles

6, Joanelligasse 3 (586 8796). U4 Kettenbrückengasse. **Open** 11.30am-3pm, 6-11.30pm, daily. **Credit** AmEx, DC, JCB, MC, V. **Average meal** AS180.

The first Chinese restaurant in Vienna to specialise in noodle soups of all sorts, in a brightly lit cellar with long, wooden tables for communal eating (design ideas were borrowed from the London-based Wagamama noodle chain). Noodles come in all forms – fried (such as the Singapore fried noodles with dried shrimps and mushrooms), spicy (tan-tan noodles in soya and sesame sauce with peanut butter) or the delicious Tza-Kiang noodles with pork and garlic sauce, and there are also good vegetarian options. Service is friendly.
Branches: 1, Rotgasse 8 (533 0856); 8, Lederergasse 14 (405 3197).

Midori

6, Gumpendorferstraße 29 (corner of Köstlergasse) (586 3673). U4 Kettenbrückengasse/bus 57a. **Open** noon-3pm Mon-Sat; 6pm-midnight Sun. **Credit** AmEx, DC, MC, V. **Average meal** AS185.

Japanese/Korean cuisine, served amid sparse décor. The sushi, sashimi and tempura are all fresh and beautifully done, and the Korean staff are friendly.

Rincón Andino

6, Müzwardeingasse 2 (587 6125). U4 Pilgramgasse/bus 13a. **Open** 10am-2am Mon-Fri; 10am-4am Sat. **No credit cards. Average meal** AS135.

Down a tiny cobbled street is one of Vienna's best-loved – and most fashionable – places, offering Latin American food and music. Dishes such as *pavo a la crema de naranjas* (turkey in a Cointreau cream sauce, with wild rice) or *papas rellenas con espinacas y queso* (potato croquettes filled with cheese and spinach) are full of flavour. The atmosphere is always kicking, and the staff sometimes stressed, but it's great for group eats. Tuesday is salsa night, while on Thursday there's a salsa/merengue evening. It also has a garden terrace for the summer.

S'frackerl

6, Brückengasse 11 (597 3840). Bus 57a. **Open** 11.30am-2.30am Mon-Sat. **Credit** MC, V. **Average meal** AS190.

Traditional Austrian food in cosy and charming surroundings – wooden beams, open fireplaces and generous portions of stodgy stuff such as *Mohr im Hemd* (a sticky chocolate speciality).

Vinissimo

6, Windmühlgasse 20 (586 4888). Bus 57a. **Open** 11am-11pm Mon-Sat. **Credit** MC, V. **Average meal** AS228.

A hybrid of winery and bistro. A weekly changing selection of 15-20 wines is available by the glass, and the full list includes some 400 different labels (half of them Austrian), which can be sampled in situ or taken away. The restaurant offers Italian cuisine with a strong Viennese influence, in starters such as the *Weinbeisserteller* ('wine nibble platter' – basically antipasti) and mains such as own-made pastas like basil and cream cheese ravioli with tomato butter, or tagliatelle with baby limes and fresh water crabs. To follow there's an excellent selection of cheeses, such as soft French Explorateur or Vorarlberger Bergkäse (a hard mountain cheese).

7th district

Jumbo

7, Stuckgasse 6 (524 5997). Tram 49. **Open** 6-11.30pm Mon; 11.30am-2.30pm, 6-11.30pm, Tue-Sun. **Credit** V. **Average meal** AS250.

A rather humble interior can create a false impression that belies the culinary delights lying ahead at this, Vienna's finest Chinese restaurant. Lamb cutlets, or the roast tongue covered in a heavenly black pepper and honey sauce, are superb, and the crab, served in a black-bean and coriander concoction, is unforgettable. It's accordingly more pricey than most of the city's Chinese restaurants.

Das Kulinarisches Mysterium

7, Apollogasse 20 (524 6690). U3 Zieglergasse. **Open** 5pm-midnight Mon-Sat. **Credit** DC, V. **Average meal** AS250.

A must for hungry esoterics. Britt Valtsanidis is an astrologer, her husband Nikolaus a chef, and the Kulinarisches Mysterium their love child. You can have your astrological chart read in a bright pink room, and then move next door to tuck into 'Mars' love food' (Styrian entrecote), 'Jupiter's seduction' (roast lamb cutlets from the Waldviertel) and dessert 'à la Venus' (mandarin parfait with chocolate butter and white guarana sauce, which tastes as confusing as it sounds). A place you love, or find infuriating. A sign in the toilet reminds you to put the seat down to avoid disturbing the Feng Shui.

Lucky Buddha

7, Kaisergasse 13 (526 1681). U3, U6 Westbahnhof/ tram 5. **Open** 11.30am-2.30pm, 5.30-11.30pm, daily. **No credit cards**. **Average meal** AS150.

The Lucky Buddha has some of Vienna's best dim sum, lovingly prepared by chefs from Hong Kong, as well as equally impressive duck and seafood dishes. You can choose your lobster fresh from the aquarium, and Canton duck is baked in a delicious house sauce the ingredients of which are a jealously guarded secret. Desserts include great Cantonese coconut, mango or almond puddings, and service is pleasant.

8th district

Schnattl

8, Lange Gasse 40 (405 3400). Tram J. **Open** 11.30am-2.30pm, 6pm-midnight, Mon-Fri; 6pm-midnight Sat. **Credit** AmEx, DC. **Average meal** AS320.

One of Vienna's best restaurants, serving Austrian dishes with an unmistakeable Styrian influence,

prepared with a French cook's attention to detail. Potato and blue-cheese soufflé, or veal steak with artichoke risotto, are exquisite; the cheese platter is limited in size, but every cheese is ripened to perfection. The wine and schnapps lists feature Austria's best. Service, however, can be so slow that you end up munching the wallpaper.

9th district

Bordeaux

9, Servitengasse 2 (315 6363). Tram D. **Open** 6pm-1am Mon-Sat. **Credit** V. **Average meal** AS300.

A very designerish-bistro, right down to the snotty service, which offers elegant French cuisine from a short seasonal menu. French classics such as snails, coq au vin and boeuf bourguignonne are always a safe bet, as are the cheeses, crème brulée or pears dunked in red wine. People are lured to Bordeaux by its long and refined wine list, boasting some 130 French labels, concentrating, as the name suggests, on Bordeaux. They range drastically in price, between AS220 and AS6,000, and there are usually seven or eight red and white wines available by the glass. Wine samplers should choose the 'trilogy' – three pre-selected glasses of different reds or whites.

Servitenstüberl

9, Servitengasse 7 (317 5336). Tram D. **Open** 10am-11pm Mon-Fri. **Credit** MC, V. **Average meal** AS130.

Edible evidence of Austrian cuisine's Hungarian roots. Pal and Szuzsa Szakall greet diners in broken German, and bicker among themselves in Hungarian while preparing your feast – *Schmankerl* (delicacies) such as *Ziegeunerbraten* (Gypsy Roast), Hungarian dumplings or thick broth-type 'wedding soup'. The AS75 set menu is a real bargain.

Stomach

9, Seegasse 26 (310 2099). Tram D. **Open** 4pm-midnight Wed-Sat; 10am-10pm Sun. **Credit** MC, V. **Average meal** AS200.

If you enjoy your meat but can't bear another round of Schnitzel and fatty pork, then hither thee to Stomach. It has some of the best cuts of beef in town, thanks to the restaurant's Styrian origins, but also offers a good vegetarian menu. Modern cuisine Austrian-style: innovative, style-conscious dishes, and portions that are still large by European standards, but small to Austrian traditionalists.

11th district

Schloß Concordia (Kleine Oper Wien)

11, Simmeringer Hauptstraße 283 (769 8888). Tram 71. **Open** 10am-2am daily. **No credit cards**. **Average meal** AS170.

A morbidly fantastic turret-restaurant straight out of imperial Vienna. Directly opposite the main gate to the largest city cemetery, the Zentralfriedhof, it has a huge stone crucifix by its entrance; inside, there's a glass summerhouse in a garden, and a gallery, small living room and library. The menu

Loud, sweaty and beery – the thirst-quenching **Schweizerhaus**. *See page 158.*

offers a predictable mix of Viennese and international dishes, but the house speciality is Schnitzel. The popcorn Schnitzel is one of a kind – a sausage wrapped in cheese and thin Schnitzel, covered in smashed pieces of popcorn and served with cranberries and salad.

16th district

Villa Aurora
16, Wilhelminenstraße 237 (489 3333). Tram 44, then bus 46b. **Open** 10am-midnight daily. **No credit cards**. **Average meal** AS176.
Decent food and surreal surroundings make this a popular venue for private parties. Perched up in the hills of the 16th district (at the top of the hill on Wilhelminenstraße), the restaurant is crammed into the rooms of what looks like an old Victorian home. Sit outside in summer to catch a spectacular view of Vienna and the huge home-made wooden sailing boat, sitting in the restaurant grounds. In the glass outhouse, meanwhile, there's a piano and swimming pool. House specialities include different types of Schnitzel and game dishes; there's a limited choice for vegetarians. One warning – trying to park a car here can be a frustrating experience.

18th district

Trattoria L'Ambasciata della Puglia
18, Währinger Straße 170a (479 9592). Tram 40, 41. **Open** 11am-3pm, 6-11pm, Mon-Sat. **Credit** V. **Average meal** AS230.
Simple, loud and deliciously Italian, the 'embassy' offers a great selection of hearty wines and fresh pastas from owners Gino and Giuseppe's native Puglia: linguine with tuna, aubergine and mint, or *orecchiette* with sardines, broccoli, tomatoes, baby peppers and lots and lots of garlic. Puglia is essentially known for its dry red wines, and the Primitivo 97 and Castel del Monte are delightful; if you insist on a white, go for the dry and elegant Felicitá.

19th district

Das Saletti
19, Hartäckerstraße 80 (479 2222). Tram 37, 38, then bus 40a. **Open** 6.30am-2am daily. **No credit cards**. **Average meal** AS148.
In the hills of Vienna's snobby 19th district, the Saletti is a haunt of the city's aristocratic young. It's a fun place to come for breakfast, when you can choose from the substantial *Kaiserfrühstück* (imperial breakfast, with everything from croissants to fruit salad, ham and cheese, AS195), the *Sektfrühstück* (champagne breakfast, AS175) or a traditional Viennese breakfast (AS78). Main meals are pretty artery-clogging: chilli con carne, meat ratatouille or *Krautfleckerl* (farfalle pasta fried with white cabbage in a creamy sauce). Although it's a glass pavilion in the midst of greenery, be sure to take in lungfuls of oxygen before entering: the restaurant gets cramped, packed and smoky.

21st district

La Crêperie
21, An Der Oberen Alten Donau 6 (270 3100). U1 Alte Donau. **Open** 10am-midnight daily. **Credit** AmEx, DC, MC, V. **Average meal** AS130.
Crêpes, crêpes and more crêpes; sweet or savoury, and generally overpriced, but the setting beside the Danube, perfect for a romantic dinner, can make up

for it. In summer, you can watch your choice of fresh fish being grilled in the garden, or have a *Mondscheinpicknick* (moonlight picnic), which includes the hire of an electric boat (AS650) or rowing boat or pedalo (AS500), a bottle of *Frizzante* and a baguette filled with ham, camembert, salad and fresh fruit (available 8-11pm).

Cheap eats

Although there is a branch of the IQ organisation in the city, the word Mensa in Vienna is synonymous with cheap eating: this city-wide network of university canteens is open to the general public, but cheaper still for student ID holders. Expect to pay in the region of AS50 for two courses.

Afro-asiatisches Institut

9, Türkenstraße 3 (310 5145-122). U2 Schottentor. **Open** 11.30am-2.30pm Mon-Fri.
As the name suggests, this is the most exotic as far as Mensas go. Some veggie options.

Katholische Hochschulgemeinde

1, Ebendorferstraße 8 (408 3585). U2 Schottentor. **Open** 11.30am-2pm Mon-Fri. **Closed** Easter & Aug to mid-Sept.
A couple of meat-oriented set menus. Central.

Mensa Markt

9, Wirtschaftsuniversität, Augasse 2-6 (310 5718). U6 Spittelau/tram D. **Open** 7.30am-7.30pm Mon-Thur; 7.30am-6.30pm Fri. *Jul-Aug* 7.30am-3.30pm Mon-Fri.
Modern Mensa with a good AS50 breakfast buffet, vegetarian specials and non-smoking area.

Musikakademie

1, Johannesgasse 8 (512 9470). U1, U3 Stephansplatz. **Open** 7.30am-2pm Mon-Fri.
Small, centrally located with splendid al fresco eating in the courtyard. The strains of novice violinists fill the air.

Neues Institut Gebäude (NIG)

1, Universitätsstraße 7 (427729-841). U2 Schottentor. **Open** 11am-2pm Mon-Fri.
Set in the dreadful new university building (already in an advanced state of decay), you reach the top-floor Mensa via a bizarre paternoster lift. The food is rather average, but the atmosphere lively with roof terrace and splendid views of the **Votivkirche**.

Technische Universität (TU)

4, Wiedner Hauptstraße 8-10 (586 6502). U1, U2, U4 Karlsplatz. **Open** 11am-2.30pm Mon-Fri.
On the first floor with entrances on Wiedner Hauptstraße and Operngasse. Food is better than most. Daily veggie dishes.

Budget (below AS130)

1st district

BIO.K

1, Reichsratsstraße 11 (5010 6129). U2 Rathaus/tram J. **Open** 8am-midnight Mon-Sat; 10am-10pm Sun. **No credit cards**. **Average meal** AS102.
A health-food, vegetarian-friendly alternative to McDonald's – offering everything from burgers to breakfasts, and tucked away next to the Rathaus.

Brezlg'wölb

1, Ledererhof 9 (533 8811). U3 Herrengasse/bus 1a, 2a, 3a. **Open** 11.30am-1am daily. **Credit** AmEx, DC, JCB, MC, V. **Average meal** AS125.
An atmospheric medieval cellar within the old city walls very popular with students, serving hefty old-fashioned Viennese cuisine to an accompaniment of classical music. Austrian classics such as *Tiroler G'röstl* (a hash of potato cubes with onions and bacon, served in the pan used to cook them) or *Kasnockerl Spätzle* (baby dumplings in a powerful cheese sauce) are delicious here.

Lustig Essen

1, Salvatorgasse 6/corner of Marc-Aurel-Straße (533 3037). Tram 1, 2. **Open** 11.30am-midnight daily. **Credit** MC. **Average meal** AS100.
Wait before you jump for joy at the prices here: the idea is small prices for small portions, of which you are then encouraged to eat as many as you possibly can. *Lustig Essen* means 'fun eating' and it is, if you go with a group and load the table with a whole assortment of little dishes – everything from prosciutto rolls filled with mascarpone, house smoked salmon, beef carpaccio with fresh basil and olive oil, *Holzhackernockerl* (baby dumplings baked in ham, cheese and cream), mini-Schnitzel and gorgeous Gorgonzola with berries or goat's cheese and pesto. There are also similar mini-style desserts.

Markt-Restaurant Rosenberger

1, Maysergasse 2 (512 3458). U1, U2, U4 Karlsplatz/tram 1, 2, D, J. **Open** 7.30am-11pm daily. **Credit** AmEx, DC, JCB, MC, V. **Average meal** AS100.
This self-service, cheap and cheerful restaurant offers reasonably priced eats in a rather plastic looking, food-court-style fake market place. You go from stall to stall to choose your food, and then pay at the main cash desk. Stalls offer everything from spaghetti with a choice of sauces, to fresh fruit juices, a variety of cooked meats and vegetables, salads, cheeses and cakes. The food is quite fresh and prices are pretty low, but Rosenberger is not much frequented by the Viennese, who associate the chain with motorway service stations.

Palatschinkenkuchl

1, Kölnerhofgasse 4 (512 3105). U1, U4 Schwedenplatz/tram 1, 2, 21/bus 2a. **Open** 10am-midnight Mon-Sat; 5pm-midnight Sun. **Credit** AmEx, DC, MC, V. **Average meal** AS100.
Palatschinken are Austrian pancakes: they're thicker than French crêpes but, like their cousins, come in

Pack a classic and join the studious types at the medieval **Brezig'wölb**.

savoury and sweet varieties. Favourites here are the *Topfenpalatschinken* (with sweet cream cheese), the *Nuss* (with nuts) or the *Marillenmarmeladepalatschinken*, with apricot jam. Adventurous souls head for the *Schlemmerteller* (feast platter) and concoct their own Palatschinken delight. There's also a special Palatschinken menu for kids, and great milkshakes. Sit downstairs in the roomy cellar to avoid reeking of cooked butter.

Trzesniewski

1, Dorotheergasse 1 (512 3291). U1, U3 Stephansplatz/bus 3a. **Open** 8.30am-7.30pm Mon-Fri; 9am-5pm Sat. **No credit cards. Average meal** AS50. Viennese snack bars in the old tradition, and ridiculously cheap. The huge assortment of daintily sliced open-face sandwiches is startling, running through egg varieties on black bread (AS9 per slice) and crab, herring or lobster options, to be washed down with mini-mugs of beer (Pfiff). There's nowhere to sit down and so none of the usual Viennese cosiness, but they're charming just the same. The most central branch is around the corner from **Stephansdom**. **Branches**: 3, Galleria, Landstraßer Hauptstraße 97-101 (712 9964); 6, Mariahilfer Straße 95 (596 4291); 15, Am Meiselmarkt (982 2975); 21, Shopping Center Nord, Top 12 (278 8178); 22, Donauzentrum, Top 159 (203 0126); Shopping City Süd, Top 271 (699 5215).

Wurstelstand Albertina

1, Corner of Goethegasse. U1, U2, U4 Karlsplatz/tram 1, 2, D, J. **Open** 8am-2am daily. **No credit cards. Average meal** AS55.
You can find these sausage stands on street corners all over Vienna, but this one, just behind the **Staatsoper**, is one of the most famous because of its location. The prices and range are the same as at any other Wurstelstand, yet elegantly dressed theatre- and opera-goers flock here after performances to tuck into Bratwurst, Käsekrainer or Frankfurter.

2nd district

Schweizerhaus

2, Straße Des 1. Mai 116 (728 0152). U1 Praterstern, then tram 21. **Open** Mar-Oct 10am-midnight daily. **Credit** DC, MC, V. **Average meal** AS125.
Popular with raucous lads and lasses of all ages and nationalities, this place on the edge of the Prater is loud, sweaty and beery. The restaurant is housed in what was the Swiss Pavilion of the 1873 Expo and is the only surviving edifice from that blighted event, coinciding as it did with a stock market crash and a cholera epidemic claiming 3,000 lives. Run since 1920 by the Kolarik family, the Schweizerhaus is famous for its huge portions of specialities such as *gegrillte Steltzen* (grilled pigs' trotters, 600 of which are guzzled every day), tripe soup and other country fare.

4th district

Indian Pavilion

4, Naschmarkt, Stand 74-75 (587 8561). U1, U2, U4 Karlsplatz, U4 Kettenbrückengasse. **Open** 10.30am-6.30pm Mon-Sat. **No credit cards. Average meal** AS110.
A wonderful bargain Indian restaurant crammed into a stall at Vienna's largest open-air fruit and vegetable market. The mild curries and tasty lentil dishes are great, and Indian beer and traditional Indian music make a perfect accompaniment to a meal.

6th district

Nice Rice

6, Mariahilfer Straße 45/Raimundhof 49 (586 2839). U3 Neubaugasse. **Open** 9am-midnight Mon-Sat. **No credit cards. Average meal** AS100.
A likeable and unpretentious vegetarian restaurant, with only six tables. The cooking is creative, with an oriental touch, as in the fresh samosas or basmati rice with Persian *gheimeh* (a stew of yellow peas, courgettes, aubergine and soya in a saffron sauce). Those with a big appetite should order the oriental

platter, an assortment of all the main dishes. To drink there's organic beer. The staff are friendly.

7th district

Centimeter II

7, Stiftgasse 4 (524 3329). U3 Neubaugasse/tram 49. **Open** 10am-2am Mon-Fri; 11am-2am Sat; 11am-midnight Sun. **Credit** AmEx, DC, MC, V. **Average meal** AS85.
Popular with students, this is a basic pub that serves snacks. Its name stems from the food: you order black bread covered in a spread of your choice, and pay by the centimetre. If you're after a truly Austrian experience, try *liptauer* spread (savoury cream cheese mixed with paprika, garlic and herbs).

Plutzer Bräu

7, Schrankgasse 2 (526 1215). U2 Volkstheater/tram 49. **Open** 11.30am-2am daily. **Credit** MC, V. **Average meal** AS120.
A modern beer bar with wooden benches and tables, in the heart of the Spittelberg district. The traditional pub-style food is decent – wash down Plutzerbräu spare ribs with Styrian beer, or the house Plutzerbier – and there's also American cocktails, a video wall showing live sports on satellite TV and a terrace for sitting outside in summer.

Schnitzelwirt

7, Neubaugasse 52 (523 3771). Tram 49/bus 13a **Open** 10am-11pm Mon-Sat. **No credit cards. Average meal** AS120.
This city institution is distinctly scuzzy as well as cheap, and loved by the Viennese because of it. Hence, it's always packed in the evening. To eat there's a comprehensive Schnitzel menu, promising Schnitzel as it was meant to be: huge slabs of meat, fried golden brown in breadcrumbs and accompanied by a serving of potato salad. Service is rough.

8th district

Die Wäscherei

9, Albertgasse 49 (corner of Laudongasse) (409 2375-11). U6 Josefstädter Straße/tram J, 43, 44. **Open** 5pm-2am daily. **Credit** DC, MC, V. **Average meal** AS100.
A newish and trendy *Bierlokal*, 'the Laundromat' seems out to evoke visions of sexy men and women taking their clothes off, as in that Levi's commercial – it opened in 1998 with a startling exhibition of black and white photos of naked women posing rather uncomfortably in and around the washing machines. Each month new works by young, Austrian artists are exhibited, often for sale. Die Wäscherei can also boast a good range of beers, including Die Weisse, a Salzburg brew difficult to find in Vienna, and the food is good and cheap, with better-than-average choices for vegetarians. Favourites include the Wäscherei-sandwich (roast chicken, ham, green salad and a cocktail dressing), *feurige Nockerl* (fiery dumplings with chilli peppers, onions, red peppers, tomatoes and ham) and the regular vegetarian stir-fries.

Cafés & Coffeehouses

Full of people who want to be alone… in company.

Vienna is known the world over for its coffeehouse tradition and the good news is that, unlike on gondolas in Venice, cable cars in San Francisco and safaris in Kenya, you're as likely to meet a local in a *Kaffeehaus* as a fellow tourist. The Kaffeehaus is to the Viennese what the pub is to the British: refreshment, social life, home. Austrians consume twice as much coffee as beer. In the past *Stammgäste* (regulars) at a coffeehouse would have their post and laundry delivered there. Today, the Viennese meet in coffeehouses to lunch with friends, exchange intimacies, clinch business deals, read the paper or play chess and billiards. Each coffeehouse has its individual style, ambience and price range, but every one is as likely to host the hoi polloi as a member of Vienna's high society.

Whether you get served or not is one of the first wait-and-sees of your visit to the coffeehouse. Of course, you'll be served – eventually – but part of the Viennese coffeehouse tradition is for your (tuxedoed) waiter to be grumpy and irritable and to specifically not look in your direction if you're making desperate signs to a) order something or b) pay. The customer is not king. Still, that in itself is charming… after you get used to it. And the saying goes that if you've three times proclaimed in a loud voice that you wish to pay and the waiter still ignores you, you can leave without paying. Not many dare to try it out, though. The Viennese yell out 'Zahlen, bitte' (pay, please) in blood-curdling tones rather than endure the waiter's tardy and condescending arrival at their table.

Coffee was first introduced to Vienna (and Western Europe) by the Turks in 1683. Vienna was besieged by the Turks and legend has it that Herr Kolschitsky, a merchant, dressed up as a Pasha to spy out the Turkish camps. Thanks to him, the imperial army conquered the Turks and Kolschitsky was rewarded with the imperial permission to open Vienna's first official coffeehouse. Kolschitsky's Kaffee Schrank (Coffee Cupboard) was a roaring success and became a focal point of the city.

Vienna's coffeehouses took the form we know today in the late eighteenth century, but their true moment of glory came in the late nineteenth century, when dandies wrote, read and debated in the

Kaffeehäuser. Vienna's intellectuals cosied at their favourite café; the literary circle *Jung Wien,* for example, met regularly at **Café Griensteidl** from 1890. When the café closed for refurbishment seven years later, critic Karl Kraus mused that the movement would probably die out. In fact, they hopped over to **Café Central** instead. Josef Stalin and Leon Trotsky played chess in Café Central in 1913. Doctors Sigmund Freud and Viktor Adler bickered in **Café Landtmann** as youngsters and, years later, composer Gustav Mahler engaged Freud as his shrink in the same coffeehouse.

Vienna's Kaffeehäuser won't disappoint those in search of *The Third Man* ambience either. The 1950s were the next landmark in Vienna's coffeehouse history. Faded glamour and smoke-stained

*The august **Café Central**, now tourist central.*

walls are as much part of the cafés' charm as *Jugendstil* light fittings and tables.

The coffee isn't cheap (and it isn't always that good, despite all the tra-la-la surrounding it), but it's brought to your table in style. It arrives on a silver tray with a small glass of water – to dilute stomach acids and bid you welcome. Pick up one of the many newspapers on offer or simply sit back and enjoy Vienna's laid-back coffeehouse experience. To quote nineteenth-century writer Alfred Polgar, 'Vienna's coffeehouses are full of people who want to be alone… in company.'

Coffeehouses

The cost of a *Melange* (see page 166 **Wien caffeine szene**) is included in all listings.

1st district

Café Bräunerhof

1, Stallburggasse 2 (512 3893). U3 Herrengasse/ bus 2a, 3a. **Open** 7.30am-8.30pm Mon-Fri; 7.30am-6pm Sat; 10am-6pm Sun. **No credit cards**. Melange AS36.

Dubbed 'the literature café', Bräunerhof has one of the best Kaffeehaus selections of international newspapers in the city. It's one of Vienna's oldest cafés. Famous Stammgäste include opera diva Maria Jeritza and turn-of-the-century playwright Hugo von

Hofmannsthal (when he wasn't in Café Griensteidl, *see below*). Blood-and-guts performance artist Hermann Nitsch was also a regular. It is very generous with the *Schlagobers* (whipped cream). Check out the selection of melt-in-the-mouth pastries and catch the Bräunerhof trio (piano, violin, cello) on Saturdays and Sundays, 3-6pm.

Café Central

1, Herrengasse 14 (5333 76326). U3 Herrengasse/bus 1a, 2a, 3a. **Open** 8am-8pm Mon-Sat; 10am-6pm Sun. **Credit** AmEx, DC, JCB, MC, V. Melange AS39.

When Café Griensteidl (*see below*) was demolished at the turn of the century the literary set moved to the Central, converting it into Vienna's number one intellectual hangout. Trotsky, or Bronstein as he was known in his clandestine years before World War I, was such an assiduous regular at the Central that an Austrian minister, on being informed of imminent revolution in Russia, supposedly remarked, 'And who on earth is going to make a revolution in Russia? I suppose you're going to tell me it's that Bronstein who sits all day at the Café Central!' Today it would require a considerable feat of imagination to mentally recreate those heady days of the Central, with its predominantly tourist clientele. It's worth popping in, though, to admire the decorated pseudo-Gothic vaulting and pay your respects to the dummy of the penniless poet Peter Altenberg that sits just inside the door reading the paper. If you're impressed by the pastries, pop across the road to the **Café Central Konditorei** (*see chapter* **Shopping & Services**).

Demel

1, Kohlmarkt 14 (535 1717). U3 Herrengasse/bus 2a, 3a. **Open** 10am-7pm daily. **Credit** AmEx, DC, JCB, MC, V. Melange AS52.

This 200-year-old former k.u.k (kaiserlich und königlich – imperial and royal) bakery has a magnificent choice of cakes and biscuits and outrageously steep prices to match (see cost of a Melange). It's set in suitably grand, chandelier-laden surroundings and is loved by those seeking a taste of imperial Vienna. A hot chocolate here is a must, as is the *Sachertorte*. Demel and Sacher (*see below*) are the only bakeries in possession of the real recipe (so they say). A great place to buy traditional Viennese confectionery as gifts to take home. You'll have to fight your way through a bevy of grannies to get to the counter, though.

Diglas

1, Wollzeile 10 (512 8401). U1, U3 Stephansplatz/bus 1a. **Open** 7am-midnight daily. **Credit** AmEx, DC, JCB, MC, V. Melange AS39.

Plush red velvet booths give this Biedermeier café an air of intimacy. No surprise, then, that Viennese *grandes dames* come here to chat with their friends. Renowned for its coffee menu and good selection of teas served in bird-bath cups. One of the best *Apfelstrudel* in the city. German speakers may be able to fathom the *Wiener Schmäh* (Viennese ironic, sometimes biting, sometimes charming humour); the waiters here are oozing with it.

Café Engländer

1, Postgasse 2 (512 2734). U3 Stubentor/tram 1, 2.
Open 7am-1am Mon-Sat; 10am-1am Sun. **No credit
cards.** Melange AS35.
A sombre café with a highbrow reputation. Order a
cup of coffee or two to drink as you plough your way
through the Engländer's fine selection of newspapers. There are three choices of breakfast, which cost
from AS40 to AS118.

Café Frauenhuber

*1, Himmelpfortgasse 6 (512 4323). U1, U3
Stephansplatz/tram 1, 2.* **Open** 8am-midnight Mon-
Sat; 10am-10pm Sun. **No credit cards.** Melange
AS39.
Vienna's oldest café, operating since 1824, with a
Baroque façade by Johann Lukas von Hildebrandt,
and one of its most charming. Mozart reputedly per-
formed here, but now the café is filled with shoppers
and tourists visiting the nearby **Stephansdom**.

Café Griensteidl

*1, Michaelerplatz 2 (535 2693). U3 Herrengasse/bus
2a, 3a.* **Open** 8am-11.30pm daily. **Credit** AmEx, DC,
V. Melange AS40.
The present Café Griensteidl is built on the site of
the original café, demolished in 1897, and reopened
in 1990. True to its literary reputation, it has a couple of bookshelves (filled with real books, rather than
the fake covers seen in Parisian cafés) and an excellent choice of international newspapers. Unusually
for a Viennese Kaffeehaus, it's child-friendly and
even has several high chairs.

Café Hartauer 'Zum Peter'

*1, Riemergasse 9 (512 8981). U3 Stubentor/tram 1,
2.* **Open** 8pm-2am Mon-Fri; 7pm-2am Sat. **No credit
cards.** Melange AS38.
One for opera-lovers. Photos of opera stars new and
old adorn this quirky Jugendstil café. Peter, the manager, will gush if you're male and possibly ignore
those of the fairer sex.

Café Hawelka

*1, Dorotheergasse 6 (512 8230). U1, U3
Stephansplatz/bus 3a.* **Open** 8pm-2am Mon, Wed-Sat;
4pm-2am Sun. **No credit cards.** Melange AS37.
Immortalised in Kraftwerk's *Transeurope Express*
video, this café is dark, smoky and another of
Vienna's 'intellectual' hangouts. If single, the
charming 80-plus proprietress will seat you next to
a lonely member of the opposite sex and feed you
home-made pastries. She says the secret of her long-
lasting marriage is that she and hubby Leopold only
bump into each other for a couple of hours each day.
He's at the Hawelka at the crack of dawn baking the
pastries and she spends all night selling them.
Leopold has become such a familiar figure in the
city that he recently featured on advertising posters
for the water authority.

Heiner

*1, Wollzeile 9 (512 2343). U1, U3 Stephansplatz/bus
1a.* **Open** 8.30am-7pm Mon-Sat; 10am-7pm Sun. **No
credit cards.** Melange AS36.
An enticing patisserie turned café that has a wood-
panelled room with a dolls' house feel. The Heiner

Master pâtissier and unlikely cult hero – Leopold, proprietor of **Hawelka.**

has a stack of sinfully good home-made chocolates and pastries, and diabetics are also catered for.

Café Imperial
1, Hotel Imperial, Kärntner Ring 16 (5011 0389). U1, U2, U4 Karlsplatz/tram 1, 2, D, J. **Open** 7am-11pm daily. **Credit** AmEx, DC, JCB, MC, V. Melange AS45.
Elegant and imposing, with gold-coloured wallpaper and brocade draperies. Vienna's nobility and powerful businessmen meet here to close deals. Famous Stammgäste include composer Richard Wagner and Karl Kraus. Piano music tinkles in the background from 3.30pm to midnight daily (except on Mondays and in July and August).

Café Kunsthistorisches Museum
1, Burgring 5 (526 1361). U2, U3 Volkstheater/tram 1, 2, D, J. **Open** 10am-6pm Tue-Sun; until 10pm Thur. **Credit** AmEx, DC, JCB, MC, V. Melange AS38.
A traditional Kaffeehaus in the sumptuous surroundings of the **Kunsthistorisches Museum**. The mosaic floors, marble pillars and grand, painted ceilings will take your breath away. The cakes and canapés aren't bad either. Thursday is late night viewing at the museum, which the café calls 'night of art and enjoyment'. Now the bad news: you have to pay the AS100 entrance to the museum to get near the place. It has beer on tap (a café rarity).

Kursalon Hübner
1, Johannesgasse 33 (Stadtpark) (713 2181). U4 Stadtpark/tram 1, 2. **Open** 11am-11pm daily. *Nov-Mar* closed. **Credit** AmEx, DC, JCB, MC, V. Melange AS45.
Café/restaurant in the lush **Stadtpark** cluttered with non-matching chairs and threadbare upholstery. From May to August there are open-air Strauß and Vienna Waltz concerts, featuring a full orchestra and ballet dancers. Great terrace, but a rather stiff and granny-ish ambience.

Café Landtmann
1, Dr-Karl-Lueger-Ring 4 (532 0621-0). U2 Schottentor/tram 1, 2, D. **Open** 8am-midnight daily. **Credit** AmEx, DC, JCB, MC, V. Melange AS44.
This elegant café, opposite the **Rathaus** and the old university, was a favourite of Sigmund Freud. A traditional Kaffeehaus where hats and coats must be surrendered to the frowning cloakroom dame and the deejayed waiters refuse to smile. Landtmann has suffered from an over-scrupulous renovation, killing off any authenticity. Popular with theatre-goers, Austrian businessmen and politicians.

Café Mozart
1, Albertinaplatz 2 (513 0881). U1, U2, U4 Karlsplatz/tram 1, 2, D, J/bus 3a. **Open** 9am-midnight daily. **Credit** AmEx, DC, JCB, MC, V. Melange AS44.
Although grand in name and situated temptingly close to the **Staatsoper**, this Kaffeehaus is best left out of your top ten places to visit. For one thing, it has plastic cake imitations in the window, and for another, it's packed full of tourists. The Japanese company Mitsukoshi bought Café Mozart

Café Mozart: *soon to be big in Japan.*

in 1985 and plans sister establishments in every major city in Japan. Not many Viennese to be seen here. The café's claim to fame is its role as Café Old Vienna in *The Third Man*.

Café Museum
1, Opernring 21 (586 5202). U1, U2, U4 Karlsplatz/tram 1, 2, D, J. **Open** 8am-midnight daily. **No credit cards.** Melange AS36.
Designed by Adolf Loos, Café Museum used to have a stylish interior, but no longer. It's still popular among students, artists and chess players.

Neuhaus Chocolatier
1, Ringstraßengallerien (512 5414). U1, U2, U4 Karlsplatz/tram 1, 2, D, J. **Open** 10am-7pm Mon-Fri; 10am-5pm Sat. **Credit** AmEx, DC, JCB, MC, V. Melange AS33; Schoko AS38.
A chocoholics' delight. A Belgian chocolate shop with an ornate, miniature Kaffeehaus, inside the glitzy Ringstraßengallerien. There is a handful of tables and a *Schmuseeck* (snogging corner) with a grand upholstered sofa for two.

Café Prückl
1, Stubenring 24 (512 4339). U3 Stubentor/tram 1, 2. **Open** 9am-10pm daily. **No credit cards.** Melange AS39.

The best of the Ringstraße cafés, attracting bridge players, *grandes dames* and trendies. Its 1950s décor, with magnificent Venetian chandeliers and six-metre (19 feet) high ceilings, has just been renovated. It offers a good choice of international press, plus home-made cakes and children's menus. There's a small flea market in the basement and live piano music on Fridays from 7pm to 10pm. Ideal after a visit to the nearby **MAK**.

Café Sacher

1, Philharmonikerstraße 4 (512 1487). U1, U4 Karlsplatz/tram 1, 2, D, J, 62, 65/bus 3a. **Open** 8am-11.30pm daily. **Credit** AmEx, DC, JCB, MC, V. Melange AS43.

It is said that if tourists want a taste of imperial Vienna, they should stay a night at the **Sacher** hotel. However, if you want a taste of a true Viennese Kaffeehaus, avoid the Sacher at all costs. The locals hardly ever frequent this establishment – misguided tourists do. The atmosphere is claustrophobic: walls filled with imperial portraits and ceilings heavy with chandeliers. Better to buy the famous Sachertorte in all shapes and sizes at the hotel's shop on the pedestrian Kärntner Straße round the corner. It also delivers abroad.

Café Schwarzenberg

1, Kärntner Ring 17 (5128 99813). Tram 1, 2, D. **Open** 7am-midnight Sun-Fri; 9am-midnight Sat. **Credit** AmEx, DC, JCB, MC, V. Melange AS42.

Slap bang on the Ring and perfect for posing on the summer terrace, this is Viennese café tradition at its best. There is a pompous Jugendstil interior with mirrors gleaming from every wall. Snooty waiters dressed in tuxedos condescendingly bring your coffee and expect a generous tip. Piano player 8-10pm Tue-Fri; 4-7pm, 8-10pm Sat, Sun.

Café Segafredo

1, Am Graben (533 5025). U1, U3 Stephansplatz/bus 1a. **Open** 8am-midnight Sun-Thur; 8am-1am Fri-Sat. **No credit cards**. Melange AS33.

The place for wannabes to see and be seen on a summer's day or night. Out of the many outdoor cafés on the Graben this overcrowded establishment is undoubtedly the posiest. Watch Vienna's world and their designer dogs pass by. Very good coffee.

Café Silberkammer

1, Innerer Burghof (533 3113). U3 Herrengasse/bus 2a. **Open** *May-Sept* 9am-8pm daily; *Oct-Apr* 9am-6pm daily. **No credit cards**. Melange AS38.

An ideal spot from which to contemplate the two eras for which Austria is renowned – the Austro-Hungarian Empire and the Third Reich: the café is in the Habsburgs' Hofburg, just by Heldenplatz where Hitler spoke to an entranced audience of 500,000 Viennese admirers in 1938. Indulge in a *Hofburgjause* (Hofburg snack at AS69), consisting of a Melange and a piece of *Hofburg Guglhupf* (traditional Austrian marble cake baked in a dome-like shape). Or if you're yearning for an afternoon tea, it'll cost you AS125 (a light feast of little salmon rolls, muffins and cake). Choose from a rich assortment of black, green, white, aromatic, fruit and herbal teas.

*The interior may have had one refit too many, but the **Café Museum** still pulls 'em in.*

Let them eat cake

Café Teitelbaum

*1, Dorotheergasse 11 (512 5545). U1, U3
Stephansplatz/bus 3a.* **Open** 10am-6pm Sun-Fri;
10am-8pm Thur. **No credit cards.** Melange
AS30.

A Kaffeehaus in Vienna's renovated **Jüdisches
Museum.** The Teitelbaum isn't strictly kosher, but
it does serve one of the best cups of coffee inn town,
along with some very fine *Mohnstrudel* and
Linzertorte. The coffee won the 'best in the city' prize
from *Falter* in 1999. There is also good vegetarian food
and a selection of Jewish newspapers.

Out of the Innere Stadt

Café Karl-Otto im Wagner-Pavilion

*4, Karlsplatz U-Bahn station, Karlsplatz (505 9904).
U1, U2, U4 Karlsplatz/tram 1, 2, D, J/bus 3a.* **Open**
9am-2am daily. **Credit** AmEx, DC, JCB, MC, V.
Melange AS34.

A Kaffeehaus in a disused Jugendstil underground
station pavilion designed by Otto Wagner. Gilt patterns, including Wagner's beloved sunflowers, are
stamped on to the white marble walls. An identical
pavilion next door is used for exhibitions; both have
recently been renovated. In summer, you can sit on
the terrace and admire **Karlskirche** over the
flower-filled Ressel Park.

Café Savoy

*6, Linke Wienzeile 36 (586 7348). U4
Kettenbrückengasse/bus 59a.* **Open** 5pm-2am Mon-
Fri; 9am-2am Sat. **No credit cards.** Melange AS34.

Gilded glamour, Baroque-style, with full-length mirrors and carved reliefs on the ceiling. Popular among
shoppers at the Naschmarkt on Saturday. Otherwise
the Savoy is frequented by an arty/camp crowd, with
some outrageously dressed night-time customers. It
also has a garden and some tables outside in the summer, but the traffic noise can be a bit much. *See also
chapter* **Gay & Lesbian.**

Café Amacord

*5, Rechte Wienzeile 15 (587 4709). U1, U2, U4
Karlsplatz/bus 59a.* **Open** 10am-2am daily.
No credit cards. Melange AS30.

Half-café, half-restaurant just off the Naschmarkt.
Good Italian-inspired Austrian cooking. Chatty,
friendly waiters with great music and Guinness, this
is a rare combination in Vienna. Very busy, voluble
crowd. Lots of foreign press available.

Café Rüdigerhof

*5, Hamburgerstraße 20 (586 3138). U4
Pilgramgasse/bus 13a, 14a.* **Open** 10am-2am
Mon-Fri, Sun; noon-2am Sat. **No credit cards.**
Melange AS28.

The cakes in Vienna's coffeehouses are often baked by the Kaffeehaus itself and usually displayed in a glass cabinet. Here are some of the more common calorie-busters:

Sachertorte the most famous Viennese cake. Rich chocolate sponge cake covered in apricot jam and a thick, dark chocolate layer. Hotel Sacher and Café Demel claim to be the only establishments with the authentic recipe

Guglhupf supposedly Freud's favourite. It can be jazzed up with pieces of candied fruit or chocolate drops, but at its most basic this is a marble cake baked in a fluted ring mould and cut into slices

Apfelstrudel cooked apples and raisins in pastry and sprinkled with icing sugar. Usually served hot with lashings of whipped cream or a generous portion of vanilla ice-cream

Topfenstrudel like apple strudel, but with a sweet curd cheese filling

Linzertorte nutty sponge cake with a strawberry jam filling. Also try the Linzerauge: it's less sickly sweet, but similar to a jam tart

Mohnkuchen sponge cake made of poppy seeds. It melts in the mouth

Imperial Torte rich blend of chocolate and marzipan with a nut and butter-cream filling

Esterházy Torte layers and layers of sponge and cream, covered in white icing and crowned with a feather emblem

Located in a magnificently restored Jugendstil house a stone's throw away from U4 Pilgramgasse. For the summer there's a wooded terrace where you can sit and stare at the curves of the building's stucco. Inside, the Rüdigerhof is virtually a museum of retro fittings (mostly 1950s) with especially wacky fluorescent lamps. Small eats available but most people come for a beer or a coffee.

Bar Italia

6, Mariahilfer Straße 19-21 (585 2838). U2 Babenbergergasse/bus 2a. **Open** 8.30am-2am Mon-Sat; 10am-2am Sun. **No credit cards.** Melange AS32.

Drop in while shopping on the Mariahilfer Straße. A choice of hearty, healthy or fatty breakfasts is served until 11.30am on workdays; 3.30pm on Sundays. The bar is modern and cool. The latest pair of sunglasses is the unofficial entrance ticket, regardless of weather or time of day. Excellent coffee. Warm up with a café *corretto con grappa* (AS47) on a blustery afternoon. The brioches and focaccia sandwiches are fresh and delicious.

Café Jelinek

6, Otto-Bauer-Gasse 5 (597 4113). U3 Zieglergasse. **Open** 8am-8pm Mon-Fri. **No credit cards.** Melange AS36.

Quiet, relaxing Kaffeehaus without any historical or mythological nonsense. The old couple who run it do not allow mobile phones and frown on tipping. Loyal youthful to 30-something clientele. Only children of regulars are tolerated. There are cakes and snacks, but no substantial meals.

Café Ritter

6, Mariahilfer Straße 73 (587 8238). U3 Neubaugasse/bus 13a. **Open** 7.30am-11.30pm daily. **No credit cards.** Melange AS35.

The Ritter is a curious mixture between a Jugendstil and a 1950s café. In fact, it was originally opened at Prince Esterházy's summer palace in 1867. Now it lies on the bustling Mariahilfer shopping street and noise is just part of the fare.

Café Servus

6, Mariahilfer Straße 57-59 (587 6392). U3 Neubaugasse. **Open** 10am-midnight Mon-Sat. **No credit cards.** Melange AS32.

Jugendstil interior. Popular among shoppers and cinema-goers. There's an excellent choice of freshly prepared dishes and a great banana milkshake. Cheerful piano player on Tuesdays, Thursdays and Saturdays 8-11pm.

Café Sperl

6, Gumpendorfer Straße 11 (586 4158). U2 Babenbergergasse/bus 57a. **Open** 11am-11pm Mon-Sat; 3-11pm Sun. **Credit** AmEx, DC, JCB, MC, V. Melange AS38.

A true Viennese Kaffeehaus. Faded grandeur with a cosy touch (and no mobile phones allowed, either). Most Viennese have a soft spot for this place with its tuxedoed and grumpy waiters. The velvet booths are fine spots for a touch of tranquillity. It also has two billiards tables. Café Sperl, more than any other Viennese coffeehouse, plays 'the Kaffeehaus' in national and international film productions, so don't be surprised to catch it on celluloid – or to see a film crew outside. Approach the uncovered home-made cake display with care: it gets as much attention from flies as from Sperl's clientele.

Das Möbel

7, Burggasse 10 (524 9497). U2 Volkstheater. **Open** noon-1am daily. **No credit cards.** Melange AS27.

Minimalist interior with wild and wacky designer couches and chairs – from S&M to k.u.k – all available for purchase. Sunday brunch 10am-4pm. Internet access noon-1am Mon-Fri; 10am-1am Sat-Sun (AS20 for half an hour).

Café Westend

7, Mariahilfer Straße 128 (523 3183). U3, U6 Westbahnhof. **Open** 7am-11pm daily. **No credit cards.** Melange AS32.

Vienna's inner city ends with this grand old Kaffeehaus. From here on out, Vienna tells quite a different story from the grandeur you get used to in town. Some say Hitler used to hang out here during his time as a student in Vienna. If it's your first time in the city and you arrive by train at Westbahnhof, this café across the road will give you your first taste of Vienna's cakes, coffees and charm.

Café Prückl: the Ringstraße's best (p162).

Café Eiles
8, Josefstädter Straße 2 (405 3410). U2 Rathaus/tram J. **Open** 7am-10pm Mon-Fri; 8am-10pm Sat-Sun. **Credit** AmEx, DC, MC, V. Melange AS34.
A favourite haunt for lawyers and politicians because of its location near several government offices. Also practical if you're strolling through the theatre-filled 8th district. It has booths and high tables. Eiles serves a hearty Viennese breakfast from 7am to 11.30pm (AS68).

Café Florianihof
8, Florianigasse 45 (402 4842). Tram 5, 33, J. **Open** 8am-2am Mon-Fri; 10am-2am Sat-Sun. **Credit** MC, V. Melange AS30.
Recently renovated Jugendstil coffeehouse and restaurant offering good food, international press and magnificent décor. Light and airy, it's an ideal spot to sit and read or write a letter.

Café Hummel
8, Josefstädter Straße 66 (405 5314). Tram 5, 33, J. **Open** 7am-2am Mon-Sat; 8am-2am Sun. **Credit** AmEx, DC, JCB, MC, V. Melange AS30.
Extremely busy bar/restaurant/coffeehouse, the focal point of Josefstadt. Waiters are notoriously rude and do not take kindly to people who consume their Big Macs from the nearby McDonald's on their terrace. Great for people-watching.

Further afield

Café Dommayer
13, Auhofstraße 2 (877 5465). U4 Hietzing. **Open** 7am-midnight daily. **Credit** AmEx, DC, JCB, MC, V. Melange AS38.

Wien caffeine szene

In a Viennese Kaffeehaus you don't simply order 'a coffee' – it comes in a list of variations to put Starbucks to shame. Know your brew:

Grosser Brauner a large cup of coffee with a dash of milk
Kleiner Brauner as above, but in a smaller cup
Grosser Schwarzer/Mocca large black coffee
Kapuziner a Schwarzer with a shot of cream
Kurz Viennese version of an espresso
Melange most people's favourite; a milky coffee served with milk foam on top (like an Italian cappuccino)
Cappuccino confusing, but this isn't like the Italian version. A Viennese cappuccino has whipped cream on top
Verlängerter Brauner like the Brauner, but with a little more water in the coffee
Verlängerter Schwarzer a watered-down Schwarzer (black coffee)

Türkische served with grounds and sugar in a copper pouring pot
Einspänner a Schwarzer served in a long glass with whipped cream
Kaffee verkehrt more milk than coffee
Milchkaffe milkier than a melange
Kaisermelange with an egg yolk and brandy
Café Maria Theresia with orange liqueur and a dash of whipped cream
Mazagran cold coffee with rum and ice. To be downed in one go
Franziskaner made with hot milk and a topping of whipped cream
Fiaker Austrian-German for the horse and carriage you can take around town. The coffee is a Verlängerter with rum and whipped cream
Biedermeier Grosser Brauner with a shot of Biedermeier liqueur
Pharisäer strong black coffee with whipped cream on top, served with a glass of rum

You can admire the **Café Rüdigerhof**'s fine Jugendstil lines from its leafy terrace. See p164.

One of Vienna's best-known traditional Kaffeehäuser, a stone's throw away from **Schönbrunn Palace**. Johann Strauß Junior debuted here in 1844. Concerts still take place on the third Saturday in every month. The restaurant has a huge garden where different theatre companies perform on the third Sunday in the month, from May to September. Strauß concerts by the Vienna Strauß Ensemble 2-4pm every Saturday from May to October. The café holds a Christmas market in its garden throughout December.

Café Gloriette

13 Gloriette, Schönbrunn (879 1311). U4 Schloß Schönbrunn. **Open** *May-Sept* 8am-8pm daily; *Oct-Apr* 8am-5pm daily. **No credit cards.** Melange AS38.

Although beautifully situated, this café is a wasted opportunity. The Gloriette itself is an impressive neo-Classical arcade, designed by Ferdinand von Hohenberg in 1775 – it's the crowning glory of the hill behind Schönbrunn Palace. The café itself is a disappointment: unimaginatively decorated and generally lacking in charm or flair. Redeeming features include the fantastic view and Sunday brunch with live classical music (AS175 for adults and AS75 for children) from 9am to 11.30am.

Wiener Konzertcafé Schmid Hansl

18, Schulgasse 31 (406 3658). Tram 40, 41. **Open** 8pm-4am Tue-Sat. **Credit** V. Melange AS35.

A cross between a café and a small *Heuriger*. Original owner Schmid Hansl was renowned for bursting into song in front of his clientele. He became so famous that professional singers flocked to the café to accompany him in a duet. Hansl's son, a former Vienna choir boy, now runs the café and

opera stars still perform here unannounced. True to the plaque outside the café that reads 'Home of the Viennese song', so-called *Wienerlieder* and operetta are played here every evening.

Blaustern

19, Döblingergürtel 2 (369 6564). U6 Nußdorfer Straße/tram 37, 38. **Open** 9am-2pm daily. **No credit cards.** Melange AS28.

Located on the Gürtel, close to Spittelau and Hundertwasser's **Fernwärme**, this large, modern café/restaurant has Becks on tap, own-brand coffee and great snacks. There's a large terrace in summer, but the traffic is a drawback.

Cobenzl

19, Am Cobenzl 94 (320 5120). U4 Heiligenstadt, then bus 38a. **Open** 10.30am-10pm daily. **Credit** V. Melange AS29.

This pavilion café offers a fantastic view over Vienna from the top of Cobenzl hill from its round terrace or window seats. Excellent hot chocolate.

Tearoom

If you're dying for a cup of tea:

Haas & Haas

1, Stephansplatz 4 (513 1916). U1, U4 Stephansplatz. **Open** 9am-8pm Mon-Fri; 9am-6.30pm Sat. **No credit cards.** Melange AS35.

Haas & Haas calls itself an English *Teehaus*. It serves afternoon tea, English breakfast and, even better, a champagne breakfast. It also has a tea shop with a fine array of Austrian fruit and herbal teas – try the *Kaminfeuer* (fireplace tea).

Beisl

Satiate a big appetite...

Throughout the German-speaking world the terms *Gasthaus* or *Wirtshaus* are both used to describe any large no-frills eating house and watering hole. In Vienna, however, such establishments go by the name *Beisl*, from the Yiddish for 'little house'. Good Beisl are usually family run, typically with wood-panelled interiors, a fondness for early formica and an easygoing atmosphere provided by a host of regulars sipping at a *Krügel* or *Spritzer*.

All Beisl offer the gamut of Austrian cuisine. Meat dominates, with pork at the fore and beef and offal bringing up the rear. Potatoes (the best are *Rösti*, grated and baked) and *Knödeln* (dumplings of various types) are the standard accompaniment. Many meals are served with salads but beware of overly sweet dressings. The wonderfully nutty, camouflage-green pumpkin seed oil occasionally crops up on Beisl potato salads. Desserts are usually on the heavy side too (*see chapter* **Restaurants**) so the typical Beisl meal consists of a main course without starters, to leave room for an apricot dumpling or two.

A smattering of German is a big plus when it comes to ordering in a Beisl. However, Austrian idiosyncrasies can be disheartening for those keen to practise what they learnt at school. Tomatoes are no longer the familiar sounding *Tomaten*, but the confusingly exotic *Paradeiser*, and potatoes go under the French-sounding *Erdäpfeln* (*pommes de terre*) not the German *Kartoffeln*. The irascible Karl Kraus claimed that Austria and Germany were two countries divided by a common language. Handwritten menus or their total absence can also provoke comical or exasperating situations.

The wholesome tradition of the Beisl exerts a fascination on foodies and the word often gets tagged onto newly opened restaurants to gain extra kudos. Thus, the sophisticated media-haunt **Oswald & Kalb** (*see chapter* **Restaurants**) is often described as a Beisl despite serving excellent innovative food at prices way above those of the traditional establishments listed below.

Beim Czaak

1, Postgasse 15 (513 7215). U1, U4 Schwedenplatz. **Open** 8.30am-midnight Mon-Fri; 11am-midnight Sat. **No credit cards. Average meal** AS130.
Although the Czaak has been massively renovated, it still retains its Beisl feel. The food is consistently good but without great surprises and the clientele a bit glitzier than that of the average Beisl. Top Czech beer on tap and friendly young staff.

Gasthaus Wickerl

9, Porzellangasse 24a (317 7489). Tram D. **Open** 11am-11pm Mon-Fri. **No credit cards. Average meal** AS110.
A classic Vienna Beisl, Wickerl is a favourite with students, and, apparently, the city's top chefs can be spotted here, wolfing down the dumplings. It offers cheap lunch menus at around AS70, big-screen footie and a particularly atmospheric backroom.

Griechenbeisl

1, Fleischmarkt 11 (533 1941). U1, U4 Schwedenplatz. **Open** 11.30am-11.30pm daily. **Credit** AmEx, DC, MC, V. **Average meal** AS250.
Griechenbeisl is a small, cosy old Beisl made up of a maze of panelled rooms. It's never empty and the atmosphere is always bustling, mainly because of its association with the *Liebe Augustin* legend (*see chapter* **History**). The traditional food is not quite as good as the story. As you go in, don't forget to give a wave to the iron figure of Augustin that hangs over the entrance.

Perauer

7, Zieglergasse 54 (526 1108). Tram 49. **Open** 11am-11pm Mon-Fri. **No credit cards. Average meal** AS150.
A brand-new Beisl, yet still in the age-old tradition: simple wooden furniture, rusty-red walls and an unpretentious atmosphere. Susanne Perauer's cooking, however, is more new Vienna than old (even if portions are still traditionally huge). Fresh ingredients such as beef, cheeses and vegetables come from farms in the Waldviertel, and are used in imaginative takes on traditional fare such as fried goat's cheese on a bed of salad in a poppy seed oil dressing, or roast suckling pig with potato and cabbage dumplings. There's also a daily vegetarian option. Perauer's previous restaurant was in the village of Dürnstein in the Wachau, and she's brought some of the region's best white wines with her to Vienna, as well as excellent Burgenland reds.

Reinthaler

1, Gluckgasse 5 (512 3366). U1, U2, U4 Karlsplatz/ tram 1, 2, D, J. **Open** 9am-11pm Mon-Thur; 9am-10pm Fri. **No credit cards. Average meal** AS130.
Located behind the **Staatsoper**, Reinthaler is becoming a bit of a rarity in the Innere Stadt – an authentic, affordable Beisl. Its wood-panelled rooms and green formica tables are nearly always crowded. The colourful mixture of OAPs, students and workers in overalls make it a great place for people-watching. There's all the usual fare with excellent *Schweinsbraten*, a stinging goulash and plenty of offal.

Pork out on a prime piece of Schnitzel.

S'glacis Beisl

7, Museumsplatz 1 (526 6795). U2 Babenberger Straße or U2, U3 Volkstheater/bus 57a. **Open** 10pm-midnight daily. **Credit** AmEx, DC, JCB, MC, V. **Average meal** AS146.

A bit hard to find, as it's situated in the grounds of the sprawling **Messepalast**, this is rather like a city *Heuriger*, with a vine-covered terrace filled with leafy alcoves. As in many out-of-town Heurigen, the food is disappointingly bland and unimaginative.

Steman

6, Otto-Bauergasse 7 (597 8509). U3 Zieglergasse. **Open** 10am-midnight Mon-Fri. **No credit cards.** **Average meal** AS100.

Renovated in 1999, but has kept its old-world charm and dark wooden interior, with a clouded glass wall separating the bar from the tables. Feast here on well-prepared, well-priced local classics: Schnitzel, *Zwiebelrostbraten* (onion roast), *Kalbsgulasch mit Butterknockerl* (calf goulash with butter dumplings), *Lauchstrudel* (leek strudel) and *Erdäpfelschmarren* (fluffy potato pancakes). To go with these calorie bombs, try the Salzburg red wine, Chateau Cascadais.

Stiegen-Beisl

6, Gumpendorfer Straße 36 (587 0999). Bus 57a. **Open** 6pm-2am Mon-Sat; 6pm-midnight Sun. **Credit** V. **Average meal** AS140.

A wonderful example of a Viennese Beisl: simple, cosy and comfortable. Very Austrian, so not good for vegetarians: specialities include roast pork covered in cheese sauce served with potato strudel and broccoli, or *Mühlviertel* beer roast with potato dumplings and boiled cabbage with diced ham. You can't help wondering who has sat and plotted what with whom on the Stiegen-Beisl's dark wooden benches during its 108-year history.

Ubl

4, Pressgasse 26 (587 6457). U4 Kettenbrückengasse. **Open** noon-2.30pm, 6pm-midnight daily. **No credit cards. Average meal** AS140.

With its ancient panelling, wood-burning stove and atmospheric sedateness, the Ubl is a great Viennese social institution. While it features the usual staples

such as fine *Schwiebelrostbraten*, Ubl has brought more Italian influenced cooking to the menu; side orders of braised fennel and other veg make a change from all that pork. The summer terrace is a good spot to relax after a visit to the nearby Naschmarkt.

Zu den Drei Buchteln

5, Wehrgasse 9 (587 8365). U4 Kettenbrückengasse/bus 59a. **Open** 6pm-midnight Mon-Sat. **No credit cards. Average meal** AS150.

From the outside this looks like just one more Beisl, but look inside and you'll find it unusually packed with Viennese from all walks of life, in search of excellent traditional Czech-style or Viennese fare. The cooking is heavy but excellent; portions have lately become just a little smaller, and so more manageable for those who intend to eat again in their lifetime. This is the place to come to finally get your mouth around things like *Fleischknödel* (meat dumplings), *Blunzen mit Kraut* (blood sausage with greasy cabbage) and the Buchtel pudding, after which the place is named: sweet bread with plum jam filling, smothered in hot vanilla sauce.

Zu den Zwei Lieseln

7, Burggasse 63 (523 3282). Bus 48a. **Open** 10am-10pm Mon-Sat. **No credit cards. Average meal** AS125.

Viennese food heaven in this century-old Beisl. Fans can indulge in Schnitzel in all its variations – try the cordon bleu and the Serbian Schnitzel. With huge portions and matronly waitresses, the Zwei Lieseln is a city legend, and everyone from builders to TV personalities can be found here.

Weinhaus Wild

3, Radetskystraße 1 (712 5750). Tram N, O. **Open** 8am-11pm Mon-Sat; 10am-11pm Sun. **No credit cards. Average meal** AS100.

Wild is a popular establishment with a lot of boozy regulars and the odd tourist recovering from a visit to the nearby Hundertwasser buildings. The food is Beisl fodder, cheap and cheerful with zero finesse. Wild is best suited to a few Krügeln with friends soaking up the Mitteleuropa vibes that resound in its murky interior.

Heurigen

Escape from the city and enjoy a Viertel or two of wine.

A visit to the *Heurigen*, or wine taverns, in Vienna's outer suburbs is a fine way to pass a sunny afternoon. The word Heuriger refers to wine from this year's grape production as well as the establishment at which it is served.

During Heurigen season tavern operators hang a sprig of pine, or *Busch'n*, outside the door to signal that they are *ausg'steckt* (literally hung out, meaning open). The tradition dates back to the reign of Emperor Joseph II, who decreed in 1784 that wine-growers could sell their produce from their own premises for a maximum of 300 days a year. Today, this law only applies to the *Buschenschank*, taverns which exclusively sell their own vintage and close when supplies are finished. The term Heurigen is now used more loosely, referring to any establishment which sells wine.

Mostly located in the outer reaches of Vienna's suburbs, Heurigen usually offer courtyards and gardens, often alongside their own vineyards. The emphasis at most Heurigen is on quantity, not quality – but the wine is cheap.

The typical measure is a quarter of a litre (*Viertel*), served in a glass mug, though it is also possible to order an eighth of a litre (*Achtel*). Wine is also often mixed with mineral water (*Gespritzt*). White wine is the most popular, and represents 80 per cent of Austrian wine production. Heurigen also sell wine by the bottle.

In addition to the wine itself, Austrians also like to drink at all the stages that come between the grape and the wine, including the unfermented must (*Most*), and the partially fermented *Sturm*. A popular time to visit a Heuriger is in the Sturm season (early autumn) when the quality of the drinks varies wildly as the new vintage slowly progresses to the wine stage. Sturm is not to everyone's taste – some love it, while others claim that it tastes like bad grape juice.

Most Heurigen serve a moderately priced buffet of hot and cold foods. Typical offerings include bread with a variety of cold meats, cheeses and spreads, fried chicken (*Backhendl*), roast pork (*Schweinsbraten*), sausages, dumplings and a wide variety of pickled salads. Traditionally, a maudlin strain of accordion and fiddle music (*Schrammelmusik)* accompanied the copious wine drinking, but now such performances are mostly reserved for the more touristy venues.

The most popular Heurigen destination for tourists is Grinzing. The taverns in this area feature Schrammelmusik and often have full restaurant service, but be warned that the Viennese seldom frequent them and at night the winding streets are clogged with tourist buses. The area's biggest virtue is that unlike other more authentic Heurigen areas, it can be easily reached by public transport.

Although the other taverns are more out of the way, they are always located near each other, so it is easy to have a night of Heurigen-hopping in one of the major areas – Heiligenstadt, Neustift am Walde, Nußdorf or Sievering in the 19th, or Stammersdorf or Strebersdorf in the 21st district.

Most of the Heurigen open from March to October or November depending on the weather and the owner's inclination.

If you're short of time or haven't the inclination to venture out of the city but want to experience the atmosphere of the Heurigen nevertheless, check out the *Stadtheurigen*. Located centrally – usually in the cellars of Vienna's old monasteries – these are, strictly speaking, not real Heurigen. However, they are convenient, open all year round and can be fun places to try Austrian vintages.

Heurigen

Grinzing

Reinprecht
19, Cobenzlgasse 22 (320 1471/1389). U2 Schottentor, then tram 38 to end terminus. **Open** from 3.30pm daily.
A popular spot in the heart of the tourist district, this Heuriger has a terraced garden and is housed in a beautiful yellow building. It offers grill specialities as well as a buffet, Schrammelmusik and decent wines by the bottle – the Pinot Blanc is recommended. Though it is in the tourist ghetto, Reinprecht does have a fun, lively atmosphere and is arguably the best of the Cobenzlgasse Heurigen. A good starting point for a night of Heurigen-hopping.

Weingut Reisenberg
19, Oberer Reisenbergweg 15 (320 9393). U2 Schottentor, then tram 38 to end terminus, then bus 38a. **Open** 4pm Mon, Wed-Sun.
With a spectacular view over Vienna, Weingut Reisenberg is one of the prettiest Heurigen in the Grinzing area, and is just a short bus ride away from the main tourist establishments on Cobenzlgasse. The kitchen is headed by one of the top chefs from the Vienna Marriott Hotel, Peter Haidbauer.

Kahlenberger Dorf

Hirt

19, Eisernenhandgasse 165 (318 9641). S-Bahn from Franz-Josefsbahnhof to Kahlenberger Dorf. **Open** *Apr-Oct* from 3pm Wed-Fri; from 12pm Sat, Sun. *Nov-Mar* from 12pm Fri-Sun.

Difficult to reach without a car – the village is just north of the Nußdorf Heurigen area. But even with your own transport, you still have to walk up a steep hill through the vineyards for about 15 minutes to get to your destination. The view of the city and the Danube, however, is breathtaking and the terrace is certainly one of the most scenic places to sit in late summer. The inside is cosy, and the service is friendly. Located near the Kahlenberg (*see also p96* **Sightseeing**) in the Wienerwald, it is a popular place for Viennese to take guests for a drink and bite to eat after a walk.

Heiligenstadt

Zimmermann

19, Armbrustergasse 5 (320 9393). U2 Schottentor/ tram 37. **Open** from 5pm Mon-Sat.

Zimmermann is something of a posh Heuriger, with few tourists and a reputation for attracting a more upper-class clientele. It has beautiful outdoor seating under the fruit trees and a pet zoo with rabbits and guinea pigs for the kids. The classic Viennese dishes, such as *Schinkenfleckerl* (noodles with ham) and *Butterschnitzerl*, are a cut above the usual buffet fare, but are also more expensive (up to AS380 for one person). The restaurant holds up to 200 guests and can be rented out for parties.

Neustift am Walde

Schreiberhaus

19, Rathstraße 54 (440 3844). U6 Währinger Gürtel, then bus 35a. **Open** from 11am daily.

Located in the middle of the Neustift am Walde area, Schreiberhaus offers great Viennese food and is a well-known spot for family parties and corporate events. The big terraced garden is pretty, and the interior is comfortable and stylish, without the usual Austrian kitsch. A visit to the area could also include another Heuriger down the street, Buschenschank Wolff, which is well-known for its wines.

Obersievering

Zawodsky

19, Reinischgasse 3 (320 7978). U2 Schottentor, then tram 38. **Open** from 4pm Mon-Fri; from 3pm Sat, Sun.

One of the best-kept secrets of Vienna Heurigen culture, Zawodsky offers one of the finest views of the city and a relaxed, rough-and-ready atmosphere – there's no décor to speak of, just picnic tables and benches. Few tourists seem to know of its existence. The food selection of cold meats and cheeses is less extensive than at most places, and it is really only worth coming here in the warmer months when you can sit outside. Opening times can be unpredictable, so call ahead.

Stammersdorf

Wieninger

21, Stammersdorfer Straße 78 (292 4106). Tram 31 to the last terminus. **Open** from 3pm Wed-Fri; from 2pm Sat; from 1pm Sun.

Stammersdorf is Vienna's biggest wine-producing district. This tavern features bottled wines from Fritz Wieninger, who is considered to be one of Austria's top vintners. Its Chardonnay and Cabernet-Merlot come highly recommended. The establishment is run by Fritz's mother and brother and features a well-prepared, rustic Viennese menu.

Strebersdorf

Weingut Schilling

21, Langenzersdorfer Straße 54 (292 4189). Tram 32 to end terminus. **Open** from 3.30pm daily.

A big place with a friendly atmosphere and a large garden at the foot of the Bisamberg, Weingut Schilling has a good reputation for its wines – try the Cuvée Camilla. There is a copious buffet, which offers such Austrian specialities as blood sausage (*Blutwurst*) and grilled pork knuckle (*Stelze*). The service is fast and efficient.

Stadtheurigen

Esterhazykeller

1, Haarhof 1, near Naglergasse (533 3482). U3 Herrengasse. **Open** 11am-11pm Mon-Fri; 4pm-11pm Sat, Sun.

Around since 1683, Esterhazykeller offers cheap, but still drinkable wine (under AS20 for an Achtel) and moderately priced food and snacks. The brick-vaulted cellar is pleasant enough, and there is a *Bierhof* conveniently located in the same courtyard in case you feel like switching from wine to beer.

Specht

1, Bäckerstraße 12 (512 2637). U1, U3 Stephansplatz. **Open** 5pm-2am daily.

Located near the **Café Alt Wien** (*see chapter* **Nightlife**), Specht is housed in a vault dating from the Middle Ages. The wines by the glass are good (AS19-35 for an Achtel), and there is a buffet and à la carte offerings (*Wiener Schnitzel* AS95). There is also live accordion music on Thursday, Friday and Saturday evenings. Specht is possibly one of the least interesting of the Stadtheurigen, but it is an acceptable place to spend the evening if **Zwölf Apostelkeller** (located just one street up from Bäckerstraße) is full.

Zwölf Apostelkeller

1, Sonnenfelsgasse 3 (512 6777). U1, U3 Stephansplatz. **Open** 4.30pm-midnight daily.

Tucked away in one of Vienna's most charming cobbled alleyways, this neo-Gothic, vaulted den is one of the better examples of the traditional cellar restaurants. The cuisine and wines are nothing exceptional. Ordering is made easier by a choice of buffets or an all-inclusive Heurigenbuffet (AS248). Music is played daily from 6.30pm.

Nightlife

Boozing and grooving.

*A happy Monday at **Flex**'s Dubclub. See page 235.*

Vienna is catching up. While the nightlife options don't compare to Europe's bigger capitals – there's enough going on to keep nightowls amused.

Relaxed licensing laws and the variety of watering holes offer a multiplicity of opportunities for the itinerant boozer. Prices, too, are fairly reasonable with half a litre of top-grade, high-octane lager rarely costing more than AS45, AS38 being about the average. Spirits, however, are a different game of soldiers and a mean two-centilitre measure of bog-standard Scotch often reaches an astronomical AS50. Wine depends greatly on where you choose to consume it, but unlike at the *Heurigen*, where the tart-tasting local white wine retails at around AS90 a litre, city-centre wine drinking has considerable kudos attached to it and is no bargain. Wine, however, is sold by the initially confusing measure of the *Achtel* (eighth of a litre) or by the *Viertel* (quarter of a litre). Beer comes your way in half litres by yelling *Krügel* (pronounced 'crew-gull', with the accent on the 'crew') or in thirds at the shout of *Seidl*. Hardly worth mentioning is the *Pfiff*, which sounds as derisory as the measure itself.

The heat generated by DJs such as Patrick Pulsinger, Erdem Tunakan, Kruder & Dorfmeister, the Sofa Surfers and the Vienna Scientists have had an undeniably positive effect on the city's nightlife scene. Having a team of resident DJs has now become *de rigueur* whenever a new bar or restaurant opens in the city. Even Austria's premier mind-numbing tabloid, the *Neue Kronen Zeitung*, religiously lists DJ events. The truth is, however, the Viennese seem to prefer nodding their heads to the music while seated rather than dancing the night away.

To keep abreast of what's on where, Vienna has two listings weeklies, *City* and *Falter*. The latter is infinitely superior on the critical/political front, but, if your German's not up to it, *City* costs half the price. Vienna has also fully embraced the flyer as the nightlife bush telegraph. They litter the bars and clubs and vie for space among the merchandise in record stores such as **Black Market**, **33.45** and **Rave Up**.

While the Bermuda Triangle zone of the 1st district near Schwedenplatz was the first concentrated nightlife zone in the city, the cobblestoned clubbers area is very clean teen dominated today. Other club-studded patches include the Spittelberg/Neubau area where the 20-something clubs such as **Wirr** and **Blue Box** are located. On the opposite side of Mariahilfer Straße in the 6th district are **Piper's Ballroom** and **Guess**. Along the redeveloping Gürtel in the 8th distric places such as **rhiz**, **Chelsea** and **B72** have filled this red light zone with some life. While around Karlsplatz **Roxy**, **Klub Shabu**, **Meieri** and **Schikaneder** are all worth checking out. The most recommendable city-centre locations are the splendid **Volksgarten Pavilion** or the Stadtpark with the **Meierei**.

In the summer the scene switches outdoors. 1999 favourites included the Summer Stage, a **Café Stein** project encouraging numerous other bars and restaurants to open al fresco branches along the Roßauerlände section of the Donaukanal, the patio of the old AKH (*see chapter* **Sightseeing**), or the eternal Copa Cagrana or Sunken City, a string of clubs and bars located on either side of the Donauinsel.

Trams and the U-Bahn grind to halt around 12.45am, but there's a pretty comprehensive night bus service between 1am and 5am. The buses leave from Schwedenplatz in the 1st district. Taxis are not exorbitant, but a AS28 supplement is charged when you order one by phone. In general though, if the weather's okay and the energy's there, don't think twice about walking home: you're in the safest capital city in the world.

Design of the time: **American Bar.**

1st district

Café Alt Wien

1, Bäckerstraße 9 (512 5222). U1, U3 Stephansplatz. **Open** 10am-2pm Mon-Thur, Sun; 10am-4am Fri, Sat. **No credit cards.**

A fine late-night drinking establishment with a small selection of eats. Despite its nicotine-stained ceilings, poster-covered walls and general air of Paris circa 1968, it serves the best goulash in Vienna. The clientele is a mixture of students and elderly bohemians. It can get very crowded.

American Bar

1, Kärntnerdurchgang (512 3283). U1, U3 Stephansplatz. **Open** noon-4am daily. **Credit** AmEx, DC, MC, V.

Designed by Adolf Loos in 1908, it's a tiny bar with pricey drinks. The *trompe-l'oeil* effect of the mirrors makes it feel bigger and the luxurious atmosphere of its marble and darkwood interior make it a memorable spot to set the evening's activities in motion.

Dino's

1, Salzgries 19 (535 7230). U1, U4 Schwedenplatz/tram 1, 2, 21, N/bus 2a. **Open** 6pm-3am Mon-Thur; 6pm-4am Fri, Sat; 8pm-3am Sun. **Credit** AmEx, DC, MC, V.

Dean Martin would have approved. *Falter* rates Dino's as one of Vienna's top six American Bars – as these plush-quality-booze-serving entities are known from here to Paris. Owner/barman Rene will

It's not always this empty in **Café Alt Wien**. Honest. See page 173.

mix you anything from a Long Island Ice Tea to a Rob Roy (AS80 to AS110). There's a good variety of whiskeys too. The music is jazz and American mainstream.

Flanagan's
1, Schwarzenbergerstraße 1-3 (513 7378). Tram 1, 2, D. **Open** 1pm-2am Mon-Thur, Sun; 1pm-4am Fri, Sat. **Credit** AmEx, DC, MC, V.
This spacious pub is said to have stood in Churchtown County Cork before being dismantled and transported to Vienna. Owner Alan Field and his staff are all Irish. There are, of course, Guinness and Kilkenny on tap, but they're expensive (AS63 for a pint); the Austrian beers are reasonably priced. It's expat central and many come for that taste of home – there's fish and chips, egg and bacon butties and Irish stews, occasional quiz nights and big-screen sport entertainment.

Fledermaus
1, Spiegelgasse 2 (513 1418). U1, U3 Stephansplatz. **Open** 10pm-4am daily. **No credit cards**.
Up until 1998 the home of the Porgy & Bess jazz club, now it's a magnet for a chic crowd who enjoy slumming it under its subterranean brick arches. Various DJs churn out house and funk at weekends, but the place is very much in its infancy and may change its sonic policy. Exude photogenic importance at the door and don't come in groups.

Havana Club
1, Mahlerstraße 11 (513 2075). U1, U2, U4 Karlsplatz/tram 1, 2, D, J/bus 3a. **Open** 8pm-4am Tue, Wed; 8pm-5am Thur; 8pm-6pm Fri, Sat. **Credit** AmEx, DC, MC, V.

Only for serious Latin American fanatics, with rum and rhythms energising a devoted crowd of locals and expats. The Havana Club is the latest jewel in Dominican Mario Castillo's bar empire. Each day has its own motto. Tuesday is Absolut Salsa night, Friday is Fiesta de la Rumba night. Dance instructors and guest DJs generate a lot of (sometimes unwanted) body contact.

Hot Pepper
1, Friedrichstraße 12 (in the Secession) (586 9396). U1, U2, U4 Karlsplatz/tram 1, 2, D, J/bus 59a. **Open** 6pm-2am Tue-Thur; 6pm-4am Sat. **Admission** AS30-80. **Credit** MC, V.
Lurking beneath the historic confines of the **Secession**, this aptly named small basement club is like a sauna when full. Run by Percy, a Barbadian, and his Austrian wife Barbara, it's one of Vienna's most popular African hangouts. There is reggae every night except Sundays (hip hop & soul night). DJs Rebell and Natti Hossi provide the dancehall on Thursdays and Fridays. Roots and Culture nights with DJs Ras Jahka and Me Cultjah are Tuesdays and Wednesdays. On Saturdays there are always live bands, but be warned, it gets ridiculously full and hot and women can be pestered to dance – it's harmless, but occasionally irritating. Apart from the dancehall with the DJ stand and bar, there is a smaller space for chilling. You can sit outside near the entrance when it's warm.

Kleines Café
1, Franziskanerplatz 3 (no phone). U1, U3 Stephansplatz. **Open** 10-2am daily. **No credit cards**.
Owned by Hanno Pöschl, whom you may recognise

from appearances in films ranging from the dire (*Before Sunrise*, 1995) to the legendary (*Querelle*, 1982). With the latter in mind, don't come here looking for a spot of rough trade, as the toilets aren't big enough to unwrap a condom. As the name suggests, the whole place is tiny, though architect Hermann Czech's design makes great use of the space with mirrors placed à la **American Bar** (*see p173*), whose restoration he undertook in 1985. The clientele, like some of the staff, are an eccentric mix of arty-intellectual and proto-bohemian types, prone to occasional tantrums. Good small eats and one of Vienna's best summer terraces on the beautiful Franziskanerplatz.

Mosaique

1, Postgasse 2 (512 7446). U3 Stubentor/tram 1, 2. **Open** 9pm-4am Mon-Sat. **Admission** AS30-80. **No credit cards.**
Hidden in the tunnel next to Café Engländer – this is the name taxi drivers are familiar with. It's a large basement club with high arched ceilings and a stone floor. Fridays and Saturdays are reggae nights run by two Ghanaians, Bishop and Mike. The crowd is a mixture of teenagers, hip hop fans and Africans. Regular DJs Galactic Lion (UK), Dread G, Pablo and Kodak spin the tunes. When the mood is right (and it often is), the place can be buzzing and the dance-

Small but perfectly formed: **Kleines Café.**

floor full. The downside is that the sound system is not as loud and the bass is not as heavy as it could be, due to a limiter on the amp enforced by the local magistrates.

Palais Eschenbach

1, Eschenbachgasse 11 (587 3633-26). U2 Babenberger Straße/tram 1, 2. **Open** from 9pm Fri. **Admission** AS90. **No credit cards.**
When the temperature heads for zero, the Havana nights in this spectacular Historicist palace help Vienna's substantial Latin American community survive the winter. Definitely worth a visit for its monumental pillared and frescoed interiors; however the music is commercial salsa and merengue with virtually no quality control. Free dance lessons, live acts and a decent selection of cocktails. It can be a bit of meat market. Moves to open-air locations in the summer.

Palmenhaus

1, Burggarten/entrance Goethegasse (533 1033). U1, U2, U4 Karlsplatz/tram 1, 2, D, J. **Open** 10am-2pm daily. **Credit** AmEx, DC, MC, V.
Expensively renovated palmhouse with a restaurant and bar. In the summer you can sit outside – if you can find a table. Not bad for sipping a variety of Austrian wines at the long bar, amid the smartly turned out; however the building itself is really the star of the show. Look out for the DJ nights, staged from time to time.

Planter's

1, Zelinkagasse 4 (533 3393). U2, U4 Schottenring/tram 1, 2/bus 3a. **Open** 5pm-4am daily. **Credit** AmEx, DC, MC, V.
Large airy colonial-style bar with luxurious furnishings and magnificent teak panelling, attracting a similar clientele to the Palmenhaus. Cigars and rum are the attraction here – the whole bar area is decorated with glass cabinets housing hundreds of bottles. There is a small dancefloor where you can groove to Latin sounds of all varieties, but somehow it's just too smart.

Volksgarten

1, Burgring 1 (533 0518). U2, U3 Volkstheater/tram 1, 2, D, J. **Open** *May-Sept* 10pm-5am Thur-Sun. **Admission** AS80-180. **No credit cards.**
One of the city's most established party zones, with 1970s ambience and a decent sound system conveying a varied mix of soul, funk, hip-hop and house, with the action spilling outdoors into the garden in summer. The punters are a mixture of party animals, fun-searching out-of-towners, and a regular handful of Eastern European women of dubious virtue. It's essential to check the listings and flyers as new nights are always cropping up. Sunday's Soul Sugar Club is a reliable event for those in search of satisfaction-guaranteed groove and funk from accomplished DJs Samir and Arno. The Saturday night hip hop session with DJ Chinaman is also still going strong. Drinks are rather expensive so it's worth getting fuelled up in advance. How it will be affected by Joe Zawinul's plans to open his 'Birdland' jazz club here in 2000 remains to be seen.

Volksgarten Pavilion

1, Burgring 1 (533 0518). U2, U3 Volkstheater/tram 1, 2, D, J. **Open** *June-Sept* 11am-midnight daily.
The 1950s Pavilion has become the place to hang on a summer night in Vienna. Admission is usually free, but in 1999 it began charging for (the oversubscribed) Tuesday night, Techno Café. Good weather is the key as it all revolves around a splendid garden with tables lit by dinky lamps. At night laid-back tunes drift out over Heldenplatz and there's a fine view of the illuminated Neue Burg. Floodlit boules too.

Bermuda Triangle

Although there are a large number of bars in this area, the name is utterly exaggerated – you'd have to be a bit of a dope to actually get lost here. Nonetheless, were you to ask the average Austrian where to go for a night on the town, the reply would be here. On Fridays and Saturdays the place is heaving with teenagers and office workers out getting pissed, but unlike in Britain, it's fight free – like most of Vienna in fact. During the week it's a tad more relaxed with a number of nice bars and places to eat, the best of them being:

First Floor

1, Seitenstättengasse/Rabensteig (512 7123). U1, U4 Schwedenplatz/tram 1, 2, 21, N/bus 2a. **Open** 8pm-3am daily. **Credit** AmEx, DC, MC, V.
This elevated – literally – bar (above the 'Ron con Soda') is not what one would expect in the Bermuda Triangle. Designed by dude architects Eichinger oder Knechtl with original fittings taken from the Mounier Bar, a 1930s bohemian hangout on Kärntner Straße. The staff are unusually capable and the lighting from the aquarium is subdued. The crowd is mixed (28-60).

Krah Krah

1, Rabensteig 8 (533 8193). U1, U4 Schwedenplatz/tram 1, 2, 21, N/bus 2a. **Open** 11am-2am Mon-Sat; 11am-1am Sun. **No credit cards**.
In the heart of the Bermuda Triangle opposite the **Roter Engel** (*see below*) this big, noisy place has occasional live jazz events on Sundays – arrive early to get a table. It has one of the largest selections of beers in the city and serves Austrian food including a great assortment of chunky open-faced sandwiches. Always packed. Terrace open in the summer.

Ma Pitom

1, Seitenstättengasse 5 (535 4313). U1, U4 Schwedenplatz/tram 1, 2, 21, N/bus 2a. **Open** 5pm-3am Mon-Thur, Sun; 5pm-4am Fri, Sat. **No credit cards**.
Nice place, boring youthful clientele, but gorgeous waitresses. Ma Pitom would be divine were it not on the main drag of the Bermuda Triangle, the relentless piped pop and inefficient ventilation making it impossible to enjoy the good food on offer.

Roter Engel

1, Rabensteig 5 (535 4105). U1, U4 Schwedenplatz/tram 1, 2, 21, N/bus 2a.
Open 5pm-4am daily. **Admission** free, but AS50 with live music. **No credit cards**.

Designed by Coop Himmelb(l)au, this place caused a bit of a sensation at first. Now it's just another Bermuda bar, packed at the weekends, with pretty uninspiring jazzoid live music. More enjoyable in summer when there's outdoor seating.

Zum Finisteren Stern

1, Sterngasse 2 (535 8152). U1, U4 Schwedenplatz/tram 1, 2, 21, N/bus 2a. **Open** 4pm-midnight Mon-Fri; noon-9pm Sat. **No credit cards**.
Away from the bustling end of the Triangle, this laid-back wine bar/shop has excellent wines and antipasti. Ideal for an early evening tipple sitting outside in one of Vienna's most picturesque corners. Heavily recommended by *Falter*, whose offices are a stone's throw away in Marc-Aurel-Straße.

2nd district

Bricks

2, Taborstraße 38 (216 3701). Tram N.
Open 8pm-4am daily. **Admission** free-AS40.
No credit cards.
Small, dimly lit basement club/bar with no plaster on the walls – hence its name – split into three rooms. One has a large horseshoe-shaped bar where the music is quiet enough for conversation. The middle room has a dancefloor, while the smallest room has table football and a couple of arcade games. The place has a lot of potential, but the owners Bertl and Marcus don't seem prepared to spend money on the aesthetics or the sometimes defective equipment. Having said that, there's something going on every night of the week so it's worth checking out. Among the best are Amour on Saturdays with hip hop, swing and soul, and Wednesdays with DJ Elk (one of Vienna's best loved) playing 1960s classics.

3rd district

Meierei

3, Stadtpark (Heumarkt entrance) (710 8400). U4 Stadtpark. **Open** 10pm-late Wed, Fri, Sat (check posters and listings). **Admission** AS80-100. **No credit cards**.
Set in the bucolic surroundings of the Stadtpark with no neighbours to annoy, the Meierei transforms itself at night from an OAPs' coffee-and-card-games spot into one of Vienna's most frequented clubs. Heaving at weekends, it's nicer in summer, when you can pop out into the park for a breath of fresh air. The whole thing runs under the auspices of the Sunshine Club, which has a roster of Vienna's finest DJing talent such as soulman Samir, Jürgen Drimal as well as Pulsinger & Tunakan and Kruder & Dorfmeister. Goldie, 4 Hero and various Wall of Sounders have also passed through here. In late 1999 it started to put on live acts such as Brazilian funksters Azymuth and Heinz Tronigger's excellent Madrid de los Austrias. However, so much international exposure of the Wien DJ scene has taken its toll and drawbacks here include shirty doormen and excessive bar prices.

Great or godawful? Opinions are divided over the **Guess Club**. *See page 178.*

4th district

Café Anzengruber
4, Schleifmühlgasse 19 (587 82979). U1, U2, U4 Karlsplatz/bus 59a. **Open** 11am-2am Mon-Sat. **No credit cards.**
At first sight just another Vienna coffeehouse, the Anzengruber is a favourite of the city's switched on, both for afternoon intimacies and more boisterous evening entertainment. A lot of charming if rather crusty art covers the walls and the atmosphere is pleasantly old world. The food is also good, especially the mean Gulaschsuppe. Another feather in the cap of the Freihaus Viertel (*see below*).

Freihaus
4, Margaretenstraße 11/Schleifmühlgasse 7 (587 1665). U1, U2, U4 Karlsplatz/bus 59a. **Open** 5.30pm-2am Mon-Sat; 10am-2am Sun. **Credit** MC, V.
A large early-evening hangout with reasonable food, but it's primarily for boozers. Mozart enthusiasts may thrill to the fact that the place is named after the large tenement, the Freyhaus, which used to stand in the nearby Margaretenstraße where the young Amadeus premièred *The Magic Flute*. This section of the 4th district is now marketed under the label 'Freihaus Viertel'. Popular with the art crowd from the nearby galleries, it has curious vending machines selling second-hand English books (from **Shakespeare & Co**) at around AS20 a hit.

Klub Shabu
4, Künstlerhauspassage (505 9904). U1, U2, U4 Karlsplatz/tram 1, 2, D, J. **Open** 9pm-2am Mon-Thur, Sun; 9pm-4am Fri, Sat. **Credit** AmEx, DC, MC, V.
The dingy '70s atmosphere seems charming in the

orange lighting. The DJs spin anything from country to electronic to one of Vienna's more eclectic and arty crowds. Note: the entrance is hard to find – it's beneath one of Otto Wagner's pavilions – and may be threatened by the proposed U-Bahn extension.

Café Kunsthalle
4, Treitlgasse 2 (586 9864). U1, U2, U4 Karlsplatz/tram 62, 65/bus 59a. **Open** 10am-2am daily. **No credit cards.**
A relaxing oasis on Karlsplatz, despite the traffic. The spacious open-air café is a popular meeting point in summer and the tunes spun inside vary from drum 'n' bass to house and jazz.

Roxy
4, Operngasse 24 (587 2675). U1, U2, U4 Karlsplatz/tram 1,2, D, J/bus 59a. **Open** 10pm-4am Mon-Sat. **Admission** AS60. **No credit cards.**
Useful central late-nighter, the Roxy has been given a new lease of life and a minor face-lift by the Sunshine crew. Best of all is the increased quality control on the music front, with DJ Samir principally to thank. While it's difficult to say what you're likely to hear in the Roxy, early 2000 was full of Brazilian beats, poppy house and killer jazz-tinged grooves. Recommended.

Schikaneder
4, Margaretenstraße 22-24 (585 5888). U1, U2, U4 Karlsplatz/bus 59a. **Open** 8am-2am daily. **No credit cards.**
In late 1999 the foyer of the Schikaneder Kino (a small re-run cinema) was extended to form an attractive space for having a few drinks to the sound of DJs various. The regulars are a young arty set, who often

have the seats removed from the cinema in order to hold larger-scale events. The Schikaneder is pumping a bit of much needed life into an attractive part of the city that has gone a bit downhill in the last few years.

6th district

Barfly's

6, Esterhazygasse 33 (586 0825/3899). U3 Neubaugasse. **Open** 6pm-3am Mon-Thur; 6pm-4am Fri, Sat. **Credit** AmEx, DC, MC, V.

The first of Mario Castillo's expanding bar empire, Barfly's has been around since the early 1990s, attracting a slightly ritzy, moneyed crowd for its smooth r'n'b and decent, though pricey, drinks. Enter through the door to the Fürst Metternich Hotel.

Café Einhorn

6, Joanelligasse 7 (586 3212). U4 Kettenbrückengasse. **Open** 3pm-4am Mon-Fri, Sun; 10am-4am Sat. **No credit cards.**

Come in here with your flea market trophies. Café Einhorn stays open later than almost anyone, and its oddball clientele and cosy atmosphere make it one of the city's best-kept secrets. Previously owned by Vienna jazz legend Utzi Förster, jazz is the theme here and in the basement there's a small museum dedicated to Utzi, with clippings, photos and musical bric-a-brac. German speakers will find the captions amusing.

Guess Club

6, Kaunitzgasse 3 (585 5108). Bus 57a. **Open** *Bar* 3pm-2am Mon-Wed, Sun; 3pm-4am Thur-Sat. *Restaurant* 6pm-1am daily. **Credit** AmEx, DC, MC, V.

Ultra-modern 'concept' bar with weird lighting, cool decor and elaborate web pages, with numerous cams to give you a taste of the place. Various bars, various cocktails and various visually delightful eats, the Guess Club elicits a variety of reactions, ranging from 'cold, pretentious shite' to 'this is exactly what Vienna needed'. Make what you will. *See also chapter* **Restaurants**.
Branch: 1, Kärntner Straße 44 (585 6349).
Website: www.guessclub.com

Jenseits

6, Nelkengasse 3 (587 1233). U3 Neubaugasse. **Open** 9pm-4am Mon-Sat. **No credit cards.**

One of Vienna's finest. Ring to enter. Reputedly an ex-brothel, the chintz and velvet interior appears to back up the legend. Whatever used to go on there, today it is an excellent spot to while away part of an evening, boozing in incomparable retro surroundings to the sound of top DJs such as Amina Handke, daughter of the author of *The Goalie's Anxiety at the Penalty Kick*. Get there early because it heaves from 11pm on and the door man habitually loses his cool and yells 'Es hat keinen Sinn!' – it's totally pointless (for you to come in) – at unsuspecting punters.

Piper's Ballroom

6, Hofmühlgasse 23 (596 9380). U4 Pilgramgasse/bus 57a. **Open** 8am-2am daily.
Admission AS30-120. **No credit cards.**

A recently renovated and reopened former ballroom that had closed for a while due to noise pollution

Inside out: **Piper's Ballroom.**

problems. It's the brainchild of Sigi, the man behind one of Vienna's hottest club nights, Soul Sugar, but also some of its biggest flops. Piper's is huge with a spacious dancefloor and two bars (one for cocktails). It does have beer on tap, but this seems to stop at peak times, forcing you to buy the expensive bottled beer. Pot plants and 1970s sofas abound, a PlayStation and good food (usually vegetarian) is available. Top Vienna DJs like Marcello, Gü-Mix and Jürgen Drimal as well as reggae dudes Kodak and Cutty Mello perform regularly and there are also occasional visits from Germany's finest: Rainer Trüby and the genial Compost/Jazzanova crews.

Titanic

6, Theobaldgasse 11 (587 4758). U2 Babenbergerstraße/bus 57a. **Open** 7pm-4am daily. **Credit** AmEx, DC, MC, V.
After more than 17 years of existence, a part of the Titanic has been given a badly needed restyle. Cashing in on what *Falter* accurately described as the post-Buena Vista 'Cuba virus', the entrance floor now consists of the Mango restaurant with Panamerican cuisine, the Cohiba cigar lounge (cigar smoking is a current obsession in Vienna) and the Azucar Bar for cocktails. Downstairs, however, it's the same old dingy labyrinth with two dancefloors playing Latin and various strains of funk/groove/hip-hop. Popular with the South American crowd, the Titanic is usually packed and although it is a bit of a pick-up joint, the vibe is almost always good.

7th district

Blue Box

7, Richtergasse 8 (523 2682). U3 Neubaugasse/bus 13a. **Open** 6pm-2am Mon; 10am-2am Tue-Thur, Sun; 6pm-4am Fri, Sat. **Credit** MC, V.
The Blue Box has been around for years, making it one of the most popular and durable bars in the city. However, the place is starting to look extremely tatty and in need of a good scrub. When it gets late, thick clouds of smoke and the relentless music, often with a hammer-like bass, can make it a bit nightmarish. It does an excellent breakfast buffet, which is most enjoyable in summer when you can sit outside.

Camera

7, Neubaugasse 2 (523 3218). U3 Neubaugasse. **Open** 9pm-4am daily. **Admission** AS50. **No credit cards**.
This 1970s-style den of iniquity is better suited for scoring rather than for hangin' out. Expect rock, funk and groove.

Europa

7, Zollergasse 8 (526 3383). U3 Zieglergasse. **Open** 9am-5am daily. **No credit cards**.
Attracts a young, club-fashionable crowd day and night. The look is modern and minimalist, with window booths where you can watch girls and boys go by. A breakfast buffet is served at weekends 9am to 2pm (AS110), and there's everything from vegetarian to children's grub to hangover specials. A back room has now been opened for DJ nights, thankfully reducing the often ear-splitting volume in the main room.

Pulse

7, Schottenfeldgasse 3 (523 6020). U3 Zieglergasse. **Open** 8pm-2am daily. **No credit cards**.
If you like a drink with a variety of beats booming out at top volume, Pulse is a good choice. Youngish crowd, good drinks and cool minimal interior. DJs change daily and there are flyers aplenty.

Shebeen

7, Lerchenfelder Straße 45 (524 7900). Tram 46. **Open** 5pm-2am Mon; 5pm-4am Tue-Fri; 1pm-4am Sat; 10am-2am Sun. **No credit cards**.
Calls itself 'the international pub'. It is run by a South African – check the Nelson Mandela picture and cricket kit. Very popular with expats and always full for major televised sport events on its big screen in the backroom. On Sundays it offers a wonderful brunch till 2pm – AS145 for an eat-as-much-as-you-want selection of cereals, English breakfast goodies and pancakes. There are plans to open the large basement in spring 2000 for live bands and DJs.

Shultz

7, Siebensterngasse 31/Kirchengasse (522 9120). U3 Neubaugasse/tram 49. **Open** 9am-2am Mon-Sat; 5pm-2am Sun. **Credit** AmEx, DC, MC, V.
A spacious bar housed behind plate glass in the ground floor of a splendid Jugendstil building, Shultz is one of the rare breed of Barcelona-style designer boozers in Vienna. Cocktails are the mainstay and the seemingly cloned and highly competent bar staff will assemble a mean Caipirinha, but only serve you small beers. Stefan, the boss, is a bit of a patron of the (modern) arts and large canvases and sculptures are displayed to good effect outside. Music is a listenable blend of cool funk and nu-beats. If the terrace is packed in summer, it's worth moving next door to have a large draught Budweiser at Siebenstern, the stylish boozer belonging to probably Austria's wealthiest political party – the Communists.

Sub Zero

7, Siebensterngasse 27 (522 0208). Tram 49. **Open** 9pm-4am Tue-Sun. **Admission** AS80. **No credit cards**.
Newly opened underground club with a young crowd. A tad claustrophobic, but once you get your bearings it's good fun. Playstation, ancient pac-man consoles and an amazing foot massage machine (AS5 well spent) are dotted in various nooks and crannies. Two small dancefloors with Jason KingSize spinning house and various possees of drum 'n' bassers on Saturdays and ragga & dancehall on Tuesdays.
Website: www.subzero.at

Wirr

7, Burggasse 70 (524 6825). Bus 48a. **Open** 10pm-4am Mon, Fri, Sat. **Admission** free-AS80. **No credit cards**.
A new place and already the extended front room of the alternative crowd. It's easy to feel at home in the comfy, mismatched sofas and chairs, enjoying a cup of herbal tea or a tasty meal on the ground floor before going downstairs to check out the lounge music.

8th district

B72

8, Hernalser Gürtel, Stadtbahnbögen 72-73 (409 2128). U6 Alser Straße/tram 44. **Open** 8pm-4am Mon-Thur; 8pm-6am Fri, Sat. Concerts up to AS200. **No credit cards.**

Part of the kicking Gürtel scene, but it doesn't take itself quite as seriously as the philosophy-touting **rhiz** (see below). Housed in a railway arch, the limited space is well planned with a relatively quiet bar area, a main dancefloor/stage and an overhead gallery. Entrance is free except when bands play – a mix of local talent and indie/post-rock acts from Europe and the US. Other nights feature a variety of DJs spinning everything from obscure soul to Britpop via reggae and drum 'n 'bass. Drink prices are moderate – the excellent Czech Staro Brno is on tap.

Chelsea

8, Lerchenfelder Gürtel 29-32 (407 9309). U6 Josefstätter Straße/tram J. **Open** 7pm-4am daily. **Admission** AS60-140 concerts. **No credit cards.**

The Gürtel's longest-standing resident a couple of doors down from **rhiz**. There's an all-pervasive atmosphere of Brit adoration so it shouldn't be hard to strike up conversation with the regulars. The booze is comforting for the homesick, with Guinness and Strongbow on tap and live British football on Sunday afternoons. Bands from Blighty are regular performers and they often appear here before they reach the heights of fame (Cornershop and Space, for instance). Generally acts are of the guitar-toting variety. Not much design or home-spun philosophy here, just boozing and foot tapping. Flat surfaces creak under the weight of flyers.

Enrico Panigl (Triest, Wien, Marienbad)

8, Josefstädter Straße 91 (406 5218). U6 Josefstädter Straße/tram J. **Open** 6pm-2am daily. **No credit cards.**

Panigl is a reliable establishment for superb wines and appetisers with a distinct Italian touch, as its name suggests. These days Panigl only actually operates in Vienna, but retains a classy pan-Mitteleuropa feel, down to the beautiful old marble bar and solid wood panelling. Foxy waitresses too. **Branch**: 1, Schönlaterngasse 11 (513 1716).

Gerard

8, Lederergasse 11 (402 0786). Tram J Piaristengasse. **Open** 8pm-4am. **Admission** free-AS80. **Credit** AmEx, DC, MC, V.

Another ex-brothel whose splendid fin-de-siècle fittings were ripped out by foolish youngsters and replaced by a cheesy pseudo-blaxploitation interior in an attempt to cash in on the Tarantino boom a few years back. The wonderful old separés still exist so you can have a smooch when the funk gets too much.

rhiz

8, Lerchenfelder Gürtel, Stadtbahnbögen 37-38 (409 2505/rantasa@rhiz.org). U6 Josefstätter Straße/tram J. **Open** 6pm-4am Mon-Sat; 6pm-2am Sun. **Admission** performances up to AS100. **No credit cards.**

A ten-minute walk from **B72** (see above), rhiz is a similar set-up, with two railway arches shut off by huge plate-glass windows and visible original brickwork. Inside, the ceiling is covered in a mesh of ventilation ducts and wiring à la Pompidou Centre and metallic projection screens hang from the walls.

Putting on the **rhiz**.

Meierei: *something to smile about. See page 176.*

The selection on the CD jukebox would make any reader of *The Wire* moist, but it's rarely operational. Musically, rhiz offers one of the city's most aurally challenging programmes, with the accent firmly on electronica, turntablism and other millennial mutations. Regulars include Dorfmeister and Huber's duo Tosca and Mego folk such as Pita (with whom rhiz often collaborates on CD projects) and occasionally there are multimedia events such as a reading with sounds by David Toop from his book, *Exotica*. The atmosphere is often quite earnest and anoracky. Internet access is available (AS30 an hour) and drinks, especially whisky, are reasonable by Vienna standards. Check rhiz's website to get an idea of where it stands on the ideas front and what they're putting out on the rhiz label. The summer terrace is a soundscape in itself – cars roar by, the tram clatters round the corner and the U-Bahn roars overhead.
Website: www.rhiz.org

9th district

Café Stein

9, Währinger Straße/Kolingasse 1 (310 9515/319 7241). U2 Schottentor/tram 1, 2, D. **Open** 7am-1am Mon-Sat; 9am-1am Sun. *Stein's diner* 7pm-2am Mon-Sat. **No credit cards**.
By day full of students (the university is just diagonally across from it) studying, smooching or surfing the Internet (10am-11pm; a rip-off AS65 per half hour). By night, still students, media people and models frequent this multi-level (3 floors) café. Proprietor Ossi Schellmann, the man behind the original U4 disco (*see below*), and a bit of a nightlife guru in Vienna, has succeeded in giving the Stein a

big city feel (rare in Vienna) and visitors usually feel at home here. The food is generally excellent, but the drinks are a little overpriced. There is always decent background music being played in the café, the nature of which depends on the staff, who vary between masters of the art and incompetent trendies unable to smile. Stein's Diner, with a separate entrance on Kolingasse, boasts a typical American diner atmosphere, with a lot of red leather and low lights. There are often DJs, but no fixed nights. Check the flyers found in the café.

Charlie P's

9, Währinger Straße 3 (409 7923). U2 Schottentor/tram 1, 2, 37, 38, 40, 41, 42, D. **Open** 10am-2am Mon-Thur; 10am-3am Fri, Sat; 10am-1am Sun. **No credit cards**.
The Irish pub vogue has invaded Vienna and this is one of the more popular, particularly with expats. It's normally hopelessly full with a boisterous crowd by 10pm at the latest.

12th, 16th & 18th districts

Paddy's

18, Anastasius-Grün-Gasse 6 (478 6744). U6 Nussdorferstraße. **Open** 6pm-1am Mon, Sun; 6pm-2am Fri, Sat. **No credit cards**.
Small Irish pub run by Roland, an Austrian who harbours a tremendous fondness for the Emerald Isle. It has dartboards, one of the cheapest pints of Guinness in Vienna (AS54) as well as Kilkenny, Harp, Strongbow and other local and imported beers. Food is served – including an approximation of fish and chips. At weekends there are live Irish

Café Stein: *step up for surfing, studying, smooching and scoff. See page 181.*

folk bands, made up of Austrian musicians with the odd Irish member. The Roadie Rowdy Piper Band are said to be the best.

U4

12, Schonbrünner Straße 222 (815 8307). U4 Meidlinger Hauptstraße. **Open** 10pm-5am daily. **Admission** AS60-100. **Credit** AmEx, DC, MC, V.

The grande dame of Vienna's disco scene, this likeable club is occasionally a live music venue, featuring German hip hop acts such as Fettes Brot. Club mythology talks of aftershow gigs by Prince, Sade and Falco, but now the tonic is very much theme nights – the popular but dodgy-sounding Notte Italiana (Italian pop and disco), Boogie Nights (part of the current tiresome obsession with funk and porn cf. **Piper's Ballroom**'s Hustler night) and the unimaginatively named Heaven Gay Night on Thursdays (*see chapter* **Gay & Lesbian**). It has had the same bouncer (Conny de Beauclair) guarding the door for the past 20 years.

Vorstadt

16, Herbststraße 37 (493 1788). U6 Burggasse. **Open** 11am-2pm Mon-Sat; 10am-midnight Sun. **No credit cards.**

A Beisl-style attraction beyond the Gürtel, the Vorstadt is an oasis in the the grim west end of the 16th district. There is a regular programme of live bands, affordable and tasty food (plenty for veggies) and a shady inner yard. It's a long trek from the U-Bahn, but a decent welcome is assured.

Munchie mansions

Café Drechsler

6, Linke Wienzeile 22 (587 8580). U1, U2, U4 Karlsplatz, U4 Kettenbrückengasse/bus 59a. **Open** 3am-8pm Mon-Fri; 3am-6pm Sat; closed Sun. **No credit cards.**

Sunrise on the Naschmarkt is best viewed from this old coffeehouse, a renowned asylum for sleepwalkers, Naschmarkt stall-holders, tramps and ball-goers. The food is good and served by an old, friendly waiter. Like the **Salz & Pfeffer** (*see below*), this place is frequented by everyone looking for a bite to eat, coffee or one last beer after the clubs/party.

Gräfin vom Naschmarkt

4, Linke Wienzeile 14 (586 3389). U4 Kettenbrückengasse. **Open** 4am-2am daily. **Credit** AmEx, DC, MC, V.

Kitschy interior and full of the strangest characters. A good place for a reconstructive goulash after a night on the town.

Robert Goodman

4, Rechte Wienzeile 23 (586 3496). U4 Kettenbrückengasse. **Open** noon-10am Mon-Thur, Sun; noon-late Fri, Sat. **No credit cards.**

Eating until 8am, dancing until 10am to anything from Schlager (German crooners) to commercial hip hop and reggae, depending on the DJ. After your meal, watch your step on the steep descent to the cellar, where the club is.

Salz & Pfeffer

4, Joanelligasse 8 (586 6660) U4 Kettenbrückengasse/bus 57a. **Open** 6pm-8am Mon-Thur, Sun; 6pm-9am Fri, Sat. **Credit** AmEx, DC, MC, V (only above AS300).

Where post-clubbers head for food or further refreshment. The heavy curtain at the door (mind the step) protects the guests from daylight. In the next room (mind the step), stomachs growl on the foam sofas. The restaurant at the back (no step) has a large selection of good-value Viennese dishes. Water and bowls of snacks are provided on request for canine guests. You might want to close your eyes to the kitsch decor, but the mixed clientele and the open fire make it cosy in winter.

Shopping & Services

Big high-street names are moving in, but away from the numbers traditional businesses still survive.

There is something wonderfully understated about the commercial life of Vienna, with high-street shopping parked in clearly defined areas such as Mariahilfer Straße and Kärntner Straße. The rest of its streets seemingly turn their backs on sales potential. You can wander through charming streets where all that can be found are a couple of junk shops and the odd bakery, where window dressing consists of pinning a few shirts on to a panel and not dusting for a decade. Opening hours, with Saturday early closing, are reminiscent of 1960s Britain. For those with an ardent dislike of conspicuous consumption, Vienna will be a godsend. Big designer names are just starting to arrive in Vienna – Gucci and Prada have only been here since the late 1990s. The same goes for global high-street names. It seems the Austrians have more desire to ski and ramble than to shop.

While Austria and the Alpine region as a whole has a reputation for being pricey, the pound or dollar in your pocket will protect you. Vienna is certainly not dear in comparison with other capital cities, but as Austria is a fairly small market, food prices, for example, may seem steep.

Opening times are gradually getting longer and now the *Langer Samstag* (when shops open till 5pm on the first Saturday of the month) only operates outside the main purchasing precincts. Most shops are open from around 9am to 6pm Monday to Friday, with some open until 7.30pm on Thursdays. On Saturdays 5pm is the absolute max and Sunday opening is virtually unknown. Service isn't always the friendliest and uppity shop assistants and waiters are legendary in Vienna.

Vienna's greatest commercial attraction is the vast number of antique/bric-a-brac/junk emporia and concomitant flea markets (*Flohmarkt*), in spite of the tourist board's attempts to sell the city as a high-street shopping paradise. Much of the stuff you come across in the junk shops is the legacy of the fine craft tradition that flourished in Vienna under the patronage of the Habsburgs and many shops still sport the stamp of quality, the royal k.u.k (*kaiserlich und königlich*) warrant.

So what is there to spend your dosh on in Vienna?

Commercial centre: Kärntner Straße.

Many of the products touted in the city are not actually Viennese – the famous chocolate *Mozart Kügeln* (Mozart balls, to translate crudely) are a speciality of Salzburg and Loden's traditional dark green weaves and the nauseating Swarovski glass figures both originate from the Tyrol. Chocolate is not an Austrian speciality but the pâtisserie is excellent. The most disappointing, however, is the world-famous *Sachertorte* whose apricot jam filling destroys an adequate but rather dry chocolate cake. The strudels are far superior and the *Marillenknödel* (apricot dumplings) are to die for. Those with extra cash to splash can acquire a **Woka** lamp, a **Thonet** chair or a pair of **Reiter** trainers.

Antiques

Austrians have a fondness for the old and antiquated and a corresponding reluctance to throw it
away. Throughout the city you will see many junk
shops (*Altwaren*), upmarket antique shops
(*Antiquitäten*) and stamp, coin and postcard emporia. In the 1st district the streets around the
Dorotheum (*see chapter* **Sightseeing**) are dotted with purveyors of antique furniture and fine
art. Those with an interest in *Jugendstil* and
Modernism should check out the 7th district
around Siebensterngasse. The streets around
Josefstädter Straße in the 8th district have a good
mix of antiques and more affordable Altwaren.

Es Brennt

1, Freisingergasse 1 (532 0900). U1, U3
Stephansplatz. **Open** 3-6pm Mon-Fri; 11am-5pm Sat.
Credit AmEx, DC, MC. V.
Similar to **RaumInhalt** (*see below*), but considerably
more expensive. There's plenty of Bakelite jewellery,
ceramics and fine old office furniture. The Lichterloh
branch has more 1970s design and in the 17th district Es Brennt has an enormous warehouse, the
Glasfabrik, with furniture and fittings needing
restoration. Knowledgeable staff with an eye for a
stylish window display.
Branches: *Lichterloh* 6, Gumpendorfer Straße 17 (586
0520); *Glasfabrik* 17, Lorenz-Mandel-Gasse (494 3490).

Das Kunstwerk

6, Laimgrubengasse 24 (0664 121 8414). Bus 57a.
Open 2-8pm Mon-Fri; 10am-2pm Sat. **Credit** DC,
MC, V.
Viennese and Hungarian art deco furniture and
objets d'art along with 1960s and 1970s design in
laid-back surroundings in a quiet street just off the
Naschmarkt (*see page 196*). Wolfgang is always
delighted to show people round, and if you hit it off,
he may start mixing his excellent Amaretto cocktail.
Branch: 4, Operngasse 20 (0664 121 8414).
Website: www.daskunstwerk.at

RaumInhalt

8, Langegasse 19 (4090 9892). U2 Lerchenfelder
Straße. **Open** noon-7pm Mon-Fri; 10am-3pm Sat.
Credit AmEx, DC, MC, V.
One of the many great little shops offering modern
design from the 1920s to the 1970s. It specialises in
1950s Scandinavian design and plastics from the
1950s and 1960s. The guys will give you lots of tips
about the market scene in Vienna and their stock.

Bicycles

Cycling is a religion in Vienna. There are lots of
excellent shops and a Sunday market in the square
in front of **Karlskirche** from May to October.

Bike Attack

2, Praterstraße 25 (214 5381). U1 Nestroyplatz. **Open**
10am-9pm Mon-Fri; 9am-1pm Sat. **Credit** DC, MC, V.
Emphasis on mountain bikes, but also plenty of
tourers and racers.

Cooperative Fahrrad

6, Gumpendorfer Straße 111 (596 5256).
U6 Gumpendorfer Straße. **Open** 10am-1pm, 2-6pm,
Mon-Fri; 10am-1pm Sat. **No credit cards.**
Co-operative with its own workshops.

Shakespeare & Co – *chock-full of literary and academic titles.*

Bookshops

Amadeus

6, Mariahilfer Straße 99 (595 4550). U3 Neubaugasse. **Open** 9.30am-7pm Mon-Fri; 9.30am-5pm Sat. **Credit** AmEx, DC, JCB, MC, V.
Austria's most chic, large-scale bookstore with four floors of books and a small music department with a reasonable selection of jazz and classical. English books are present with an ever-growing choice of fiction. Nice café on the top floor with a massive range of foreign magazines (for sale). The basement has six touch-screen computers with free Internet access, as do all the other branches.
Branches: 6, Mariahilfer Straße 37 (586 2392); 1, Kärntner Straße 19 (513 1450) (in Steffl store).

British Bookshop

1, Weihburggasse 24 (512 1945/fax 512 1026). U3 Stubentor/tram 1, 2. **Open** 9.30am-6.30pm Mon-Fri; 9.30am-5pm Sat. **Credit** AmEx, DC, MC, V.
English-language shop associated with Blackwell's with stacks of novels, history and Viennesia. It's also the best EFL shop – teachers ply their trade on the notice board at the back. Bargains can be found in the summer when it sells off stock.

Comic-Treff Steiner

6, Barnabitengasse 12 (586 7627). U3 Neubaugasse. **Open** 10am-7pm Mon-Fri; 10am-2pm Sat. **Credit** MC, V.
The best comic emporium in Vienna, run by young, clued-up English speakers. It has a decent line in quirky American productions. Good on peripheral items, with a vast selection of *The Simpsons* and *Star Trek* merchandising.

Freitag & Berndt

1, Kohlmarkt 9 (533 8685). U3 Herrengasse. **Open** 9am-6.30pm Mon-Fri; 9am-5pm Sat. **Credit** AmEx, DC, MC, V.
If maps are your bag, don't miss the chance to visit this fine store located in Max Fabiani's Jugendstil Artariahaus. Serious ramblers should call by to get the excellent maps of the Wienerwald. There's a large selection of travel books too.

Kuppitsch

1, Helfersdorfer Straße 3 (533 3268-0/fax 535 2729). U2 Schottentor/tram 1, 2, D. **Open** 9am-6.30pm Mon-Fri; 10am-5pm Sat. **Credit** MC, V.
This rather unattractive-looking store has masses of English paperbacks hidden in its large basement. A bit of a lottery, but definitely the largest selection of such wares in Vienna.
Branch: 9, Alserstraße 4 (Old AKH) (409 1311).

Shakespeare & Co

1, Sterngasse 2 (535 5053). U1, U4 Schwedenplatz. **Open** 9am-5pm Mon-Fri; 9am-1pm Sat. **Credit** AmEx, DC, MC, V.
This tiny shop is Vienna's most reliable address for literature and academic titles in English. Shakespeare is great on contemporary and classic literature, fine arts and music, sociology and Vienna-related themes. In the back room there's a hefty travel and poetry section. The atmosphere is sedate with photos of some of the luminaries who have done readings on the premises.

Carpets

Metternich's adage that the Orient begins in Vienna remains true. The abundance of carpet and rug stores run by Iranians, Turks and Afghans is one prime indicator.

Adil Besim

1, Graben 30 (533 0910). U1, U3 Stephansplatz. **Open** 9.30am-6pm Mon-Fri; 10am-5pm Sat. **Credit** AmEx, JCB, MC, V.
The most reputable address in the city and more a gallery than a shop. Sumptuous Persian carpets, some in gigantic sizes, at prices few can afford.

Kalash

1, Freyung 3 (533 7027). U2 Schottentor/tram 1, 2, D. **Open** 10am-6pm Mon-Fri; 10am-1pm Sat. **Credit** AmEx, DC, JCB, MC, V.
Located just inside the **Palais Harrach**, Kalash is more a museum exhibit than a shop with its superb display of antique brass and bronze figures from Bangladesh, Pakistan, Afghanistan and Nepal.

Philosophie im Boudoir. *See page 186.*

Teppich-Galerie

1, Kochgasse 26 (403 6622). Tram 43, 44. **Open** 10am-6pm Mon-Fri; 10am-noon Sat. **No credit cards**. This store is typical of those you find throughout Vienna, stocked to the ceiling with rugs and off-cuts. Persian is the thing here and bargains are to be had.

Cosmetics

Bipa

1, Kärntner Straße 1 (512 2210). U1, U3 Stephansplatz. **Open** 8am-6.30pm Mon-Fri; 8am-5pm Sat. **No credit cards**.
Bipa, **Billa**'s (*see page 193*) cosmetics and cleaning products outlets, are present in every shopping street and are the best places to stock up on essentials. They also have cheap photo developing.
Central branches: 1, Fleischmarkt 26 (513 2771); 6, Mariahilfer Straße 7 (581 8870).

Impo Diskont Dufter

1, Graben 7 (512 9692). U1, U3 Stephansplatz. **Open** 9am-6.30pm Mon-Fri; 9am-5pm Sat. **Credit** AmEx, DC, JCB, MC, V.
Cheapest address in town for top-of-the-range cosmetics and perfumes with branches all over the city.
Central branches: 1, Kärntner Straße 30 (512 3368); 6, Mariahilfer Straße 113 (596 0788).

Karen Van Vliet

1, Köllnerhofgasse 4 (513 1155/fax 0260 22122). U1, U4 Schwedenplatz. **Open** 10am-6pm Mon-Fri; 10am-5pm Sat. **Credit** DC, MC, V.
No relation to Captain Beefheart, Karen's establishment has a beautiful frontage and offers its own non-animal tested products. Treat yourself to a make-up session (AS280-580); one-hour course (AS1,360).

Nanadebary

1, Bauernmarkt 9 (533 1111). U1, U3 Stephansplatz. **Open** 10am-6pm Mon-Fri; 10am-5pm Sat. **Credit** DC, MC, V.
Exclusive fragrances from Hard Candy, Bumble & Bumble and Dementer. Nanadebary is Vienna's only outlet for L'Artisan Parfumeur.

Design & household

Backhausen

1, Kärntner Straße 33 (51 404-0). U1, U2, U4 Karlsplatz. **Open** 9.30am-6.30pm Mon-Fri; 9.30am-5pm Sat. **Credit** AmEx, DC, JCB, MC, V.
Backhausen is Vienna's best home furnishings store, combining contemporary design with over 3,500 patterns by artists of the Wiener Werkstätte movement. Very starchy staff, but lovely stuff.

Philosophie im Boudoir

9, Berggasse 14 (319 1079). Tram D. **Open** 2-7pm Tue-Fri; 11am-3pm Sat. **No credit cards**.
A stone's throw from Freud's house, one cannot help thinking that Sigmund would have tittered at the idea of sleeping on sheets and pillow cases decorated with winged phalli. All this was dreamt up by

Something for the weekend sir?

Renate Christian, ex-pupil of Vivienne Westwood (and it shows).

Thonet

9, Bergasse 31 (310 2002). Tram D. **Open** 9am-6pm Mon-Thur; 9am-1pm Fri. **No credit cards**.
Bespoke furniture manufacturers since the turn of the century, it still produces Wiener Werkstätte and Adolf Loos classics. Simple bentwood dining chairs were always its forte, but later it branched out into other realms of furniture with varying success.

Woka

1, Singerstraße 16 (513 2912/fax 513 8505). U1, U3 Stephansplatz. **Open** 10am-6pm Mon-Fri; 10am-5pm Sat. **Credit** AmEx, DC, MC, V.
Since 1978 Wolfgang Karolinsky and his firm Woka have been making superb reproductions of lamps and light fittings designed by members of the Wiener Werkstätte set as well as by Adolf Loos. By acquiring many of the original tools, moulds and presses, Woka's lamps are as close to the real thing as you are likely to get.

Erotic

All along the Gürtel there are countless sex shops, peep shows, titty bars and prostitutes. Sex shops are present throughout the city and this is a selection of the more imaginative.

Condomi

6, Otto-Bauer-Gasse, 24 (581 2060). U3 Zieglergasse. **Open** noon-6.30pm Mon; 10am-6.30pm Tue-Fri; 10am-4pm Sat. **Credit** MC, V.

Condoms are the shop's forte – over 250 varieties in all as well as lubricants, ether oils and lots of jokey articles. There is also a separate room where women can inspect the range of vibrators and dildos away from the gaze of the male clientele.

Love and Fun

7, Lerchenfelder Straße 59 (523 1720). Tram 46. **Open** 9am-10pm Mon-Sat. **Credit** AmEx, DC, JCB, MC, V.
Friendly assistance and a wide range of magazines, erotic undies and S&M accoutrements. Large selection of made-by-women erotic videos – all in German.

Tiberius

7, Lindengasse 2 (tel/fax 522 0474/leather@tiberius.at). U6 Gumpendorfer Straße. **Open** 3-6.30pm Mon-Fri; 10am-3pm Sat. **Credit** AmEx, DC, MC, V.
Vienna's foremost address for leather, rubber and S&M articles. Michael and Karl's dominatrix service run from their flat became so popular they decided to open a shop. Massive selection of harnesses, cockrings, handcuffs and other peripherals. They also run events under the moniker of Pervs in Paradise.

Esoteric & headshops

Bush Planet

7, Kirchengasse 19 (524 0440). Bus 13a/tram 49. **Open** 10am-7pm Mon-Fri; 10am-5pm Sat. **No credit cards**.

A grow-your-own emporium with a bewildering selection of bulbs, fertilisers, soil and plants. Plenty of cannabis-related literature in German and English as well as a range of skins and pipes. Window display includes a fine White Widow and the ubiquitous Howard Marks signed photograph.

CIA (Cannabis in Austria)

8, Piaristengasse 38 (402 6729/cia@hurra.de). Tram J. **Open** 11am-7pm Mon-Fri; 11am-5pm Sat. **No credit cards**.
CIA are Bertl and Tom, friendly English speakers who can fill you in on all aspects of wicked weed cultivation and supply you with the necessary growing gear. For the idle, there are take-away plantlets.

GLW Shop

3, Erdbergstraße 15 (769 8905). U3 Rochusgasse. **Open** 2-7pm Mon-Thur; noon-7.30pm Fri; 10am-5pm first Sat in month. **No credit cards**.
GLW stands for *Gesundheit Lebensfreude Wohlbefinden* – health, happiness and feeling good. After a visit to the GLW Shop there's no telling what state you're likely to be in, having picked up a Psilocybin mushroom growing kit (AS590), a Peyote cactus bristling with buttons (AS190 for a young plant) or the slightly more lightweight San Pedro cactus (a snip at AS90). All completely legal here. Owner Susanne also has a selection of herbal teas and therapeutic herbs and oils as well as an arsenal of smoking devices. Various potions can be consumed on the premises at the Space Bar. Mail order sale too.
Website: www.come.to/glw

Master of minimalism: **Helmut Lang***'s flagship shop, see page 190.*

Trading places – the markets of Vienna are full of character and characters.

OM Esoterik

7, Neustiftgasse 77 (526 5223). Bus 13a, 48a.
Open 9.30am-6pm Mon-Fri; 9.30am-5pm Sat.
No credit cards.
Crystal-clutching dolphin worshippers will have a field day in this bookshop-cum-nick-nack outlet. In fact, the 7th and 8th districts are hives of esoteric activity and bastions of Green Party voters.

Flea markets

Flea market burrowers can have the time of their lives in Vienna. Bargaining is de rigueur.

Autokino

22, Autokinostraße. Bus 26a from U1 Kagran.
Open dawn-2pm Sun.
A long trek out east and only recommended for those with a real flea market problem. It's held on the lot of a drive-in cinema and has all the usual stalls, but far more junk than genuine antiques.

Kettenbrückengasse

5, Kettenbrückengasse. U4 Kettenbrückengasse.
Open dawn-5pm Sat
This market has something for everyone, with the bargain basement stalls located beside the U-Bahn

and the more specialised dealers further towards the Linke Wienzeile. There are stands selling furs (happily worn by many Viennese), leathers and Loden stuff, lamps and lighting fittings, tin toys and dolls, antique watches and jewellery and loads of crocks. Look out for the attractive pastel-coloured Austrian Lilianporzellan from the 1950s. The atmosphere is quite unlike the flea markets of most European cities. The extraordinary babble of languages is something to behold – Russians flogging icons and Soviet memorabilia, Romanian gypsies plying (possibly fake) Roman coins and figures and peoples of the Balkans selling more or less anything.

Flowers

Florists are excellent in Vienna. Seasonal specialities such as sunflowers, sticky buds and berries inundate the stands. The best place to see what's on offer is the far end of the Naschmarkt just before the Kettenbrückengasse U-Bahn station. Most U-Bahn stations also have good flower stands at reasonable prices. Cheap but often uninspiring are the wares of the Holland Blumenmarkt chain with branches all over the city, which are open Sundays.

*The **Reiter** place for shoes.*

Manic Botanic

6, Mollardgasse 3 (tel/fax 585 3428). U4 Kettenbrückengasse. **Open** 7.30am-7.30pm Mon-Fri; 10am-3pm Sat. **Credit** DC, MC, V.
Serves lots of offices in Vienna. The 24-hour, seven days a week service has a minimum charge of AS200 for delivery.

Natur Blumen

8, Florianigasse 19 (405 9531). Tram 5, 33, 43, 44. **Open** 8am-7pm Mon-Fri; 8am-3pm Sat. **Credit** AmEx, DC, MC, V.
Natur Blumen goes for rustic styles, using whatever springs up in the countryside to great effect.

Fashion

Buying clothes in Vienna used to be a fairly nightmarish experience, but with the arrival of major European chains local entrepreneurs have cleaned up their act and prices are more reasonable and the variety greater. Still, you may be surprised to see how many Austrians are in traditional costume. In recent years the *Tracht* (traditional Alpine clothing) has almost become acceptable again and the truly hip occasionally mix a bit of Loden in with their Kangol berets. Apart from **Helmut Lang**, no other Austrian designers have really managed to cut the mustard on the international scene, but Gerald Tomez, whose collection is available at **Chegini Check-Out** is tipped to go places.

Helmut Lang

1, Seilergasse 6 (513 2588). U1, U3 Stephansplatz. **Open** 9.30am-6.30pm Mon-Fri; 9am-5pm Sat. **Credit** AmEx, DC, JCB, MC, V.
Long-time exile in New York, Helmut Lang's flagship shop in Vienna has his characteristic checkerboard floor and minimal window displays. There are lots of strange synthetics, but not much colour. You'll also find a large stock of his legendary distressed denim.

Loden-Planck

1, Michaelerplatz 6 (533 8032). U3 Herrengasse. **Open** 9am-6pm Mon-Fri; 9am-4pm Sat. **Credit** AmEx, DC, JCB, MC, V.
If the Loden look gets your mojo rising, this is where you should go. The dark green fabrics do not come cheap. Very good repros are available from the Peek and Cloppenberg store on Mariahilfer Straße.

Modus Vivendi

6, Schadekgasse 4 (587 2823). U3 Neubaugasse. 1-7pm Mon; 10am-7pm Tue-Fri; noon-4pm Sat. **Credit** DC, MC, V.
Gorgeous knitwear for men, women and children, both off-the-peg and made-to-measure.

Rag

1, Sterngasse 4 (533 1961). U1, U4 Schwedenplatz. **Open** 10.30am-6.30pm Mon-Fri; 10am-5pm Sat. **Credit** AmEx, DC, MC, V.
Where Vienna's youth come for their arse around the knees trousers and other surf 'n' skate wear. A good place to pick up flyers.
Branches: 1, Judengasse 4 (5331 9616); 6, Mariahilfer Straße (581 3006).

Designer discounts

Chegini Check-Out

1, Kohlmarkt 4 (Courtyard) (535 6108-14). U3 Herrengasse. **Open** 2-6.15pm Mon; 10am-6.15pm Tue-Fri; 10am-5pm Sat. **Credit** AmEx, DC, MC, V.
A snooty designer boutique with two branches in the Innere Stadt. It's worth trawling through the Check-Out store, however, which offers discounts on some labels.
Branches: 1, Plankengasse 4 (512 2231); 1, Kohlmarkt 7 (533 2058).

Pan

6, Mariahilfer Straße 77 (Generali Center) (585 2283). U3 Neubaugasse. **Open** 10am-7pm Mon-Fri; 10am-5pm Sat. **Credit** AmEx, DC, MC, V.
The best reason for visiting the declining Generali Center is to pick up a bargain here. Massive stock of

Helmut Lang for men with weird parkas and washed-out denim. For women the accent is more on Italian brands.

Markenschuh-Diskont
4, Rilkeplatz 3 (505 6104). Tram 62, 65. **Open** 9am-6pm Mon-Fri; 9am-12.30pm Sat; 9am-5pm first Sat in month. **Credit** AmEx, DC, JCB, MC, V.
This is a pretty chaotic-looking place, but it offers hefty discounts on the likes of Hugo Boss, DKNY and Bruno Magli.

Lingerie

Palmers
1, Kohlmarkt 8-10 (533 9204). U3 Herrengasse. **Open** 9am-6.30pm Mon-Fri; 9am-5pm Sat. **Credit** AmEx, DC, JCB, MC, V.
Palmers, Austria's number one undies manufacturer and retailer, runs one of the most high-profile billboard advertising campaigns in the country and its images of scantily clad models are everywhere. Its shops have everything from thermals to basques at reasonable prices.
Central branches: 1, Kärntner Straße 4 (512 9341); 1, Tuchlauben 3 (533 7188).

Wein & Wäsche
1, Lobkowitzplatz 3 (512 9034). U1, U2, U4 Karlsplatz. **Open** 10am-7.30pm Mon-Fri; 10am-5pm Sat. **Credit** DC, MC, V.
Local wine-diva Christina Fieber hit upon the clever idea of a shop combining top-of-the-range lingerie with a fine selection of Austrian and Italian wines. This sensual alliance seems to be working as she moved into plusher premises in spring 1999.

Wolford
1, Gonzagagasse 11 (535 9900). U2, U4 Schottenring. **Open** 9am-6pm Mon-Fri; 10am-5pm Sat. **Credit** MC, V.
Its tights and stockings have a worldwide reputation. The company is 50 years old in 2000. This cool branch, its communication office, is next door to the **Black Market** (*see page 196*) record store.
Central branch: 1, Freyung 2 (535 4363).

Second-hand

Glamorous
6, Gumpendorfer Straße 66 (587 0340). U3 Neubaugasse/bus 13a, 57a. **Open** 1-7pm Mon-Fri; noon-5pm Sat. **No credit cards**.
Enthusiastic anglophile Birgit sells a wide range of new 1970s clobber with a bit of second-hand thrown in. She also rents stuff out for theatre and film projects such as the recent hit comedy *Sonnenallee*, a German 1970s teen drama set in the former GDR.

Jimmy
7, Neubaugasse 72 (523 4477). U3 Neubaugasse/bus 13a. **Open** 9am-6.30pm Mon-Fri; 9am-4pm Sat. **No credit cards**.
Large second-hand selection of leather jackets and sheepskins. Some 1970s stuff and an interesting selection of bizarre Bavarian leatherwear.

Kamikaz Paris
7, Neubaugasse 55 (0699 1028 7057). U3 Neubaugasse/bus 13a. **Open** 10am-7pm Mon-Fri; 10am-5pm Sat. **No credit cards**.
Laurent has been importing 1970s gear from his native Paris and the US for two years.

Shoes

GEA
1, Himmelpfortgasse 26 (512 1967). U1, U3 Stephansplatz. **Open** 10am-6pm Mon-Fri; 10am-5pm Sat. **Credit** DC, MC, V.
Slightly hippyish well-made shoes. The accent is on comfort and natural materials. Its Waldviertler ankle boots are part of the mythology of Austria's alternative scene.

Humanic
1, Kärntner Straße 1 (512 9101). U1, U3 Stephansplatz. **Open** 9.30am-7pm Mon-Fri; 9.30am-5pm Sat. **Credit** AmEx, DC, JCB, MC, V.
The flagship store of Austria's leading shoe chain. Stocks a wide range of international brands.

Reiter
1, Mölkersteig 1 (533 4204). U2 Schottentor. **Open** 10am-6.30pm Mon-Fri; 10am-5pm Sat. **Credit** AmEx, DC, JCB, MC, V.
Vienna is full of bespoke shoemakers but Ludwig Reiter has made an international name for himself especially in the US. His superb bowling shoes (based on regulation Austrian army issue) are a fine example of understated modernity.

Sport

Der Fan-Shop Strobl
8, Strozzigasse 18-22 (4060 61813). Tram 46, J. **Open** 9am-6.30pm Mon-Fri; 9am-1pm Sat. **Credit** AmEx, DC, MC, V.
If you have to have that shiny, green and white Rapid Vienna shirt, this is the place to acquire it.

Food & drink

Delicatessens

Grimm
1, Kurrentgasse 10 (533 1384). U1, U3 Stephansplatz. **Open** 7am-6.30pm Mon-Fri; 7am-noon Sat. **No credit cards**.
Bread is invariably excellent in Austria with a bewildering range of cereals, seeds and spices used in its manufacture. Many find the presence of caraway seed unpleasant, so ask if things have *Kummel* in them. Grimm is said to be the best in Vienna, but with quality running so high, you have nothing to lose by trying any old bakery.

Haas&Haas
1, Haas Haus, Stephansplatz 4 (512 9770). U1, U3 Stephansplatz. **Open** 9am-6pm Mon-Fri; 9am-5pm Sat. **No credit cards**.
Has a magnificent range of teas and coffees. The

COUNTRY-ROCK STAR JOANNA ATTACKS PREGNANT WOMAN

DIESE

FOR SUCCESSFUL LI

Is this only the begin The Luxury of Dirt Te

BY **KEITH REINHARD**

Country-rock star Joanna, who reached number world's country-rock charts with "Dirty Country summer, has had a remarkable career. Her new Luxury of Dirt" has been climbing the charts ra everything seems to be falling to pieces. IT'S REA full story. Wednesday night as Joanna was trying to club The Twitty Twit, she was denied entry. "She wa dirty clothes" the bouncer Mikey Bündefeldt According to anonymous witnesses, Joanna then argued has become a luxury in this shiny, flashy world.

Joanna then raised her right hand as if she was about to hit the bouncer who then professionally avoided the assault which caused Joanna to fall. In her fall she violently grabbed another woman who was queuing for the club which caused them both to fall. The innocent woman who, it appeared, could have been pregnant, had to seek medical advice the following morning, a spokesman from the law-firm Suit & Case told It's Real.

o one is goin to talk dirty to m says victim bouncer Mikey

Inside report by **BOB SCARPELLI**

"Joanna laughed and said her dirt were a luxury, but I've been work door for 5 years and noone is going dirty to me", Mikey Bündefeldt, the l at the club The Twitty Twit says a know he's honest about it. "Whe been in this business business. If som you don't

Get the story in your free copy of It's R At your local Diesel dea or at www.diesel.u

IT'S REA

TOMORROW'S TRUTH TO

Number 105 in a series of Diesel "How to..." guides to successful living.
For more information: call Diesel U.K. 0171-8332255 www.diesel.com
This advertisement is pure fiction. The characters, names, incidents, dialogue and plot are used fictitiously.
Any resemblance to actual persons or companies is purely coincidental.

Macadamia roast coffee is fantastic. Cool, black marble interior with a small, non-smoking espresso bar.

Janele
1, Kohlmarkt 4 (535 8434). U3 Herrengasse. **Open** 7am-6.30pm Mon-Fri; 7am-1.30pm Sat. **No credit cards.**
With branches all over the city, Janele has great bread and good sandwiches to take away. Try its tomato strudel and an excellent *Topfen Kolatsche*, a sort of Danish pastry with lemon curd cheese. **Central branches**: 1, Tuchlauben 22 (535 8933); 1, Laurenzerberg 3 (533 2968).

Kecks
1, Herrengasse 15 (533 6367). U3 Herrengasse. **Open** 10am-10pm Mon-Fri; 10am-3pm Sat. **Credit** DC, MC, V.
A designer deli specialising in Austrian products with customer-friendly opening hours. It also has an attractive lunchtime menu. Top Austrian hams and cheeses are supplied from small producers and there's a range of organic products. Good place for bottles of fruit schnapps.

Organic produce & health food

Although the Austrians are terribly high-minded about healthy living, they remain enthusiastic smokers and meat eaters. Organic products are not widely available and are not stocked by the major supermarkets apart from the Ya! Natürlich range of products, whose reliability as organic has been questioned. Look for shops that sell *Bio* (organic) products or those labelled *Reformhaus* (health food store).

Reformhaus Verde
8, Josefstädter Straße 27 (405 1329). Tram J. **Open** 8.30am-6.30pm Mon-Fri; 8.30am-noon Sat. **Credit** AmEx, DC, MC, V.
Well-stocked health food store with organic veg, bread and over 200 varieties of tea. English spoken.

Willi Dungl
1, Schottengasse 9 (533 9512). U2 Schottentor/tram 1, 2, D. **Open** 7.30am-6pm Mon-Fri. **No credit cards.**
Willi Dungl is one of the prime movers in the Vienna healthy living scene. His store has a bakery, organic fruit and veg and an excellent range of pulses and other staples. You can also pick up info about his fatfarm/spa hotel in Gars-am-Kamp.

Pâtisserie

Look out for the magic word *Konditorei* (pâtisserie) for the largest selection, but most bakers have the basic strudels and *Kolatschen* (like Danish pastries).

Café Central Konditorei
1, Herrengasse 17 (535 9905). U3 Herrengasse. **Open** 10am-6pm Mon-Sat. **Credit** AmEx, DC, JCB, MC, V.
The cake division of the famous café is a rather stuffy, luxurious establishment purveying some divine chocolate truffles. The star product is the Imperial Torte – the king-size version (4lb) costs AS530.

Demel
1, Kohlmarkt 14 (535 1717). U3 Herrengasse/bus 2a, 3a. **Open** 10am-7pm daily. **Credit** AmEx, DC, JCB, MC, V.
The mother of all pastry shops, the Demel is an authentic k.u.k establishment sporting an incredibly extravagant interior where you can purchase its vast array of cakes and chocolates. It's a little too swarming with tourists for comfort, though. *See also chapter* **Cafés & Coffeehouses.**

Lehmann
1, Graben 12 (512 1815). U1, U3 Stephansplatz. **Open** 9am-7pm Mon-Sat. **No credit cards.**
A genteel coffeehouse/restaurant in a prime spot on Graben. Lehmann deals in all the principal Viennese sweets and cakes as well as serving light meals.

Supermarkets

Austria's supermarkets leave a lot to be desired. They tend to be small and cramped with little consideration for their customers. The big two – **Billa Corso** (abbreviation of *Billig Laden* – cheap shop) and **Meinl** – have both been taken over by the large German concern Rewe, making a bit of a mockery of Billa's pathetic 'Buy Austrian' campaigns that disturbingly recall Haider's filthy 1999 electoral propaganda. In short, the great unwashed shop at Billa and the wealthy at Meinl. There are competitors, but none deserves a mention here. The two listed below are flagship stores bearing little resemblance to the often shabby suburban branches.

Billa Corso
1, Kärntner Ring 11-13, Ringstraßengallerien (512 6625). U1, U2, U4 Karlsplatz/tram 1, 2, D, J/bus 3a. **Open** 7.30am-7pm Mon-Thur; 7.30am-7.30pm Fri; 7.30am-5pm Sat. **No credit cards.**
The best thing about the Ringstraßengallerien. While some Billas resemble a shop in a Warsaw suburb in the early 1980s, this one has a good Italian deli, fresh fish and attractive fruit and veg.

Meinl am Graben
1, Kohlmarkt (532 3334). U3 Herrengasse. **Open** 8.30am-7pm Mon-Fri; 8am-5pm Sat. **Credit** AmEx, DC, MC, V.
Reopened in December 1999 after extensive renovation, Julius Meinl is the Marks & Sparks food department of Austria. The irony is that Rewe, the firm that bought Billa, now owns this noble establishment too and the classic logo with its taste of the Orient. According to the terms of the buy-out, Meinl's name will disappear except for in a handful of stores such as this that the Meinl family were obliged to maintain by the monopolies commission. Everything costs a few schillings more here, but you can get fresh herbs, and buy from a proper butcher and fishmonger. Meinl cock a snook at the eco-minded Austrians by giving away carrier bags.

Wine

Wein & Co
*6, Linke Wienzeile 2 (585 7257). U1, U2, U4
Karlsplatz.* **Open** 9am-midnight Mon-Sat. **Credit**
AmEx, DC, MC, V.

Wein & Co's flagship store on the corner of the
Naschmarkt opened in November 1999 and will probably prove to be a bit of a test case for entrepreneur-
ial attempts to circumvent Austria's restrictive retail
legislation. By creating a mix of shop and wine bar
with small exquisite eats, it opens until midnight.
This is the best affordable wine establishment and
the informed staff should be able to orient you. It sells
the stupendous Riedl range of wine glasses and a
selection of international titbits such as pimientos de
piquillo, vinegars and top-grade pasta.

Unger & Klein
1, Gölsdorfgasse 2 (532 1323). U2, U4 Schottenring.
Open 2-10pm Mon-Fri; 11am-2pm Sat. **Credit** MC, V.

Magnificent 'theatre of drinking' designed by
Eichinger oder Knechtl in 1992. A wine bar and
store, Unger & Klein is a favourite of media bods,
but don't let that put you off. With 20 wines by the
glass starting at a reasonable AS25 per *Achtel.*

*Sort your head out at **London Underground**.*

Jeroboam
4, Schleifmühlgasse 1 (585 6773). Tram 62, 65. **Open**
9am-2pm Tue, Sat; 3-8pm Wed-Fri. **Credit** MC, V.

Specialist shop dealing exclusively in *Sekt*, Spumante
and all things sparkling. Stocks over 50 different
types of champagne.

Hairdressers

Grecht
*9, Spitalgasse 33 (406 4118). Tram 37, 38, 39, 40,
41.* **Open** 1-7pm Mon; 10am-7pm Tue-Wed; 9am-7pm
Thur-Fri; 9am-3pm Sat. Phone for appointments.
Credit V.

One of Vienna's most ritzy hairdressers, Grecht has
been blow-drying the city's wealthy for over a decade.

GmbHaar
7, Kirchengasse 39 (523 3763). Bus 48a. **Open**
11am-9pm Mon-Fri; 11am-4pm Sat. **Credit** AmEx,
DC, MC, V.

Ron and the rest of the staff are Toni & Guy-trained
and have been doing basic cut and colour (no perms)
for Vienna's club scene for about ten years. The pseu-
do-oriental décor resounds with trip hop and dope
beats. A drinks machine serving two of Austria's
best beers will help you get over that pre-cut angst.

London Underground
8, Josefstädter Straße 29 (407 1607). Tram J. **Open**
1-6pm Mon; 9am-6pm Tue, Wed; 9am-8pm Thur, Fri;
8am-1pm Sat. **No credit cards**.

Run by the extremely talkative expatriate Brit Kurt,
this salon caters for all ages, and its English-speaking
staff are a godsend at moments of follicular anxiety.
Excellent scalp massage included in the deal.

Herbalists

Herbena
*6, Köstlergasse 10 (961 0636). U3 Neubaugasse/bus
57a.* **Open** 9am-6pm Mon; 9am-7pm Tue, Wed;
10am-4pm Thur, Fri; 9am-noon Sat. **No credit
cards**.

Herbs and spices of all varieties for therapeutic ends
as well as for cooking.

Die Kräuterdrogerie
*8, Kochgasse 34 (404 522/fax 409 1727). Tram 43,
44 Skodagasse.* **Open** 8.30am-6pm Mon-Fri; 8.30am-
1pm Sat. **No credit cards**.

Healing herbs and ether oils (Birgit is a trained pharmacist) as well as ayurvedic products. It also has a
food section with regular deliveries of organic veg.

Jewellery

Galerie Slavik
*1, Himmelpfortgasse 17 (513 4812). U1, U3
Stephansplatz.* **Open** 10am-1pm, 2-6pm, Tue-Fri;
10am-5pm Sat. **Credit** AmEx, DC, MC, V.

Renate Slavik is a jolly lady who has been running
her gallery to show off the work of international
jewellery designers for over ten years – bangles,

Limited choice: late-night shopping, Vienna-style.

necklaces, chains and rings in precious metals and even paper. Exhibitions change regularly every six weeks so it's worth checking her website.
Website: www.galerie-slavik.com

Kaufhaus Schiepek

1, Teinfaltstraße 3 (533 1575). U2 Schottentor/tram 1, 2, D. **Open** 10am-6pm Mon-Sat. **Credit** AmEx, DC, MC, V (on purchases over AS300).
Brightly coloured jewellery and lots of beads 'n' stuff to make your own. Cheap and cheerful.

Wiener Interieur

1, Dorotheergasse 14 (512 2898). U1, U3 Stephansplatz. **Open** 10am-6pm Mon-Fri; 10am-1pm Sat. **Credit** AmEx, DC, JCB, MC, V.
Dorotheergasse and environs are full of antique jewellers. This small establishment deals in art nouveau/ deco and 1950s costume jewellery.

Late night shopping

Getting your hands on virtually anything outside normal opening hours is tough in Vienna – 24-hour establishments are non-existent and Sundays are like they used to be in Britain in the 1950s. However, there are a number of life-savers such as the vending machine in the U-Bahn passage at Karlsplatz, the so-called Shop 24, which dispenses everything from fresh milk and bread to Mars bars and tampons. It's near the Kunsthalle exit. The **Billa** (*see above*) supermarkets at two railway stations, Wien Nord (U1 Praterstern) and Franz-Josefs-Bahnhof (tram 5, 33) are open on Sundays till 7pm, but the crowds can induce claustrophobia. One town-centre life-saver is Drugstore Kaunitzgasse, opposite the **Apollo** (bus 13a, 14a), open 5am-9pm, with a bit of everything, including cigarettes at normal prices.

Markets

Brunnenmarkt

16, Brunnengasse. U6 Josefstädter Straße. **Open** 6am-5pm Mon-Fri; 7am-2pm Sat.
Not as spectacular as the Naschmarkt and more limited in its range of wares, the Brunnenmarkt is nevertheless a bustling, colourful market with a distinctly Balkan/Turkish flavour. All along Brunnengasse there are stalls and shops offering fruit and veg, halal meat, kitsch decorative stuff and sticky Turkish pâtisserie. At the east end of the street is Yppenplatz, which comes alive on Saturdays when farmers descend on the area to sell their produce. After years of neglect, local pressure blocked a plan to build houses in the square and forced improvements such as better facilities for children and market traders as well as a partial pedestrianisation of the area. Take a coffee on the terrace of Club International, a café/resource centre that has done more than most to improve the lot of immigrants in the area. If you're hungry, head for the Kent on Brunnengasse – Vienna's finest and cheapest kebab house.

Karmelitermarkt

2, Karmeliterplatz. Tram 21, N. **Open** 7am-5pm Mon-Fri; 7am-1pm Sat.
Located in the heart of Vienna's Jewish district, the

*Tucking into the joys of the **Naschmarkt**.*

Karmelitermarkt is on a much smaller scale than the Naschmarkt or the Brunnenmarkt. Apart from all the usual market produce, it has a number of kosher shops and some good flower stalls.

Naschmarkt
4, Linke und Rechte Wienzeile. U1, U2, U4 Karlsplatz. **Open** 6am-5pm Mon-Sat.
A visit to Vienna's premier open-air fruit and veg market should be on everyone's itinerary. Located on a long esplanade covering the course of the Wien river, this superb market can satisfy the most demanding culinary requirements as well as being an ideal spot to eat, drink and hang. Saturdays are busy. Approaching from Karlsplatz, the first section is taken up with fishmongers, pork butchers and the market's priciest and most exotic greengrocers. Other highlights here include a number of excellent juice bars and the famous *Sauerkraut* stall run by the biggest mouth on the market. Further along there are several Chinese and Indian shops and a pagoda-shaped bar called Zur Eisernen Zeit ('In the Iron Age'), which has one of the most eccentric clientele in the city. Here the market is bisected by Schleifmühlgasse and from then on the stalls are of the more workaday fruit and veg variety, all at far more reasonable prices than on the first stretch. Further on, the market narrows and you run the gauntlet of a number of fine kebab stalls. This last section opens out on to a broad tract where, on Saturdays, country dwellers ply honey, veg, cheeses, wine and flowers.

Organic Market Freyung
1, Freyung. U2 Schottentor. **Open** 9am-5pm first & third Fri & Sat in month.
This market sells exclusively organic products directly from the growers. Some stalls also sell non-edible wares – such as basketware, candles and wooden toys.

Mountaineering & rambling

Mörtz
6, Windmühlgasse 9 (587 5787). U2 Babenbergergasse. **Open** 8.30am-1pm, 2-6pm, Mon-Fri; 8.30am-noon Sat. **Credit** V.
Specialists in mountaineering and rambling footwear.

ÖTK – Alpinsport
1, Bäckerstraße 16 (512 3844). U1, U3 Stephansplatz. **Open** 9am-5pm Mon, Wed, Fri; 9am-7pm Tue, Thur; 11am-5pm Sat. **No credit cards.**
Everything you need for mountaineering plus advice on locations. Also runs climbing courses.

Music

Vienna is not badly served for music emporia and new establishments are constantly opening. If classical music is your bag, beware of the shops in the 1st district, such as EMI Austria on Kärntner Straße, as they abuse tourists by cashing in on their proximity to temples of high art. The best classical selection at the most competitive prices is in the Virgin Megastore on Mariahilfer Straße 37-39, with a reasonable selection at **Teuchtler Alt&Neu**.

Audio Center
1, Judenplatz 9 (533 6849). U1, U3 Stephansplatz. **Open** 10am-7pm Mon-Fri; 10am-5pm Sat. **Credit** AmEx, DC, JCB, MC, V.
An excellent jazz store with CDs and vinyl. It has a good selection of world music and is not afraid to stock crazier improv and crossover jazz stuff. Headphones available for inspecting the wares, plenty of knowledgeable advice and loads of jazz flyers.

Black Market
1, Gonzagagasse 9 (533 7617). U2, U4 Schottenring. **Open** 10am-7pm Mon-Fri; 10am-5pm Sat. **Credit** AmEx, DC, JCB, MC, V.
The best hip hop/funk/dance store in town, run by Alexander Hirschenhauser, one of the original motors behind the current Vienna scene. The clothes part has tons of Stüssy-type stuff, astronomically priced. There's a café where you can hang and enjoy the sounds. You can listen to CDs and vinyl on headphones and get switched-on tips from the knowledgeable and helpful staff.

Teuchtler Alt&Neu
6, Windmühlgasse 10 (586 2133). U2 Babenbergergasse. **Open** 1-6pm Mon-Fri; 10am-1pm Sat. **Credit** AmEx, DC, JCB, MC, V.
A long-standing Aladdin's cave selling used and new CDs and vinyl. Jazz and classical are its strong points. Prices are the best in Vienna, but the categorising is slightly chaotic. Staff are smiley, but don't bother enquiring after that elusive disc as stock turnover is huge.

Rave Up
6, Hofmühlgasse 1 (596 9650). U4 Pilgramgasse/bus 13a, 14a. **Open** 10am-6.30pm Mon-Fri; 10am-6pm Sat. **Credit** MC, V.
Popular with local DJs on the hunt for beats, reggae, electronica and hip hop. It's a good place to come to for flyers. It also has a fairly comprehensive selection of Viennese stuff from the most upfront labels like Mego, Klein, Cheap and Spray. Friendly staff and a chance to listen on headphones.

Using the **Black Market** – where the best sounds can be found.

Ton um Ton

7, Lindengasse 32 (523 8286). U3 Neubaugasse.
Open 11am-7pm Mon-Sat. **No credit cards.**
The place to find that Edgar Broughton Band album you need to complete your collection. Total emphasis on 1960s and 1970s obscure British rock and folk, American jingle-jangle and European stuff you've never heard of. Large selection of vinyl in the basement, often at giveaway prices.

33:45

3, Krummgasse 1 (713 6004). U3 Rochusmarkt.
Open 2-7pm Mon-Thur; noon-8pm Fri; 11am-5pm Sat. **No credit cards.**
Specialised DJ shop with lots of vinyl. Good for flyers – staff know what's going on club-wise.

Record Store

4, Operngasse 28 (581 2053). U1, U2, U4 Karlsplatz. **Open** 1-6pm Mon-Fri. **No credit cards.**
The address for vinyl recidivists as it stocks nothing else but second-hand singles and LPs from jazz to prog rock. Has been expanded to house the shipments it receives from the US. Kruder & Dorfmeister are regulars here and their Simon and Garfunkel-pastiche sleeve hangs in the window next to the original.

One-stop shopping

Generali Center

6, Mariahilfer Straße 77. U3 Neubaugasse. **Open** 10am-7pm Mon-Fri; 10am-5pm Sat.
It's looking a bit shabby these days after a grand opening when Austrians such as Arnie left their handprints for posterity in a parochial parody of Hollywood. The shops are mostly of the jeans and

surf wear variety with a sports shop and café also. The latest addition is Coming Home, a sort of Habitat. The best reason for nipping in here is the **Pan** store (*see p190*).

Gerngross

7, Mariahilfer Straße 38-40 (52 180-0). U3 Neubaugasse. **Open** 9.30am-7pm Mon-Fri; 9am-5pm Sat. **Credit** varies.
What was previously Vienna's Dickens & Jones has now been transformed into a five-floor complex of various franchises. The Akakiko sushi bar and the rooftop terrace bar have superb views of the city. The basement has an excellent supermarket – Merkur – and direct access to the U3 Neubaugasse station.

Ringstraßen Gallerien

1, Kärntner Ring 11-13. U1, U2, U4 Karlsplatz/tram 1, 2, D, J/bus 3a. **Open** 7.30am-10pm Mon-Sat. **Credit** varies.
A massive shopping/office complex on three floors. Shops are mostly fashion outlets, with the best Billa supermarket in town in the basement and a number of cafés and bars. Expensive and a bit soulless.

Steffl

1, Kärntner Straße 19 (523 1756). U1, U3 Stephansplatz. **Open** 9.30am-7pm Mon-Fri; 9.30am-5pm Sat. **Credit** AmEx, DC, JCB, MC, V.
The latest shopping mecca in the city and probably the most chic. The former, dowdier Steffl was gutted and plexi-glass lifts installed, taking you to various floors full of Ralph Lauren, DKNY, Boss et al. There is a whole floor of cosmetics and a Mozart-orientated chocolate section. On the fourth floor there's a branch of **Amadeus** (*see p185*) and the Media Café with free touch-screen Internet (and long

queues). At the top is an Italian restaurant and the posey Skybar, both owned by local society restaurateur, Luigi Barbaro.

Photographic

Photobörse
8, Lerchenfelder Straße 62-64 (406 7916). Tram 46.
Open 9am-6pm Mon-Fri; 9am-1pm Sat. **Credit** AmEx, DC, MC, V.
Vast selection of second-hand and new cameras as well as trade-in possibilities. The guys specialise in Contax, but also have shelves full of Leica, Rollei, Pentax, Canon and Nikon.

Services

In a country blessed with high salaries, contracting services, especially repairs, can prove expensive. Ask for an estimate.

Computers

Apple Center
5, Schönbrunner Straße 121 (545 5251/fax 544 7513). U4 Margaretengürtel. **Open** 10am-6pm Mon-Fri. **No credit cards.**
The place to call for Apple queries. However, it only does repairs on machines up to two years old.

Der Computer Doctor
18, Gentzgasse 9 (470 7005). U6 Volksoper. **Open** 9.30am-noon, 2-6pm, Mon-Fri. **No credit cards.**
The good doctor will repair your PC, but it's best to ring in advance.

Maximum
6, Stumpergasse 3 (597 5010). U3 Zieglergasse. **Open** 10am-6pm Mon-Fri. **No credit cards.**
Apple specialists with a quick repair service and sale of second-hand and new machines.

Key cutting

Mister Minit
1, Helfersdorferstraße 2 (535 9862). U2 Schottenring/tram 1, 2, D. **Open** 9am-6pm Mon-Fri **No credit cards.**
Your global partner for key cutting and shoe repairs. For services on a Saturday, head for the branch in the Gerngross centre.
Branch: Gerngross 7, Mariahilfer Straße 38-40.

Laundry & dry cleaning

Bendix Laundrette
7, Siebensterngasse 52 (523 2553). Tram 49/bus 13a. **Open** 8am-6pm Mon-Thur; 8am-1pm Fri. **No credit cards.**
Self-service or service washing – AS95 for 4kg.

Hartmann
1, Jasimirogottstraße 6 (533 1584). U1, U3 Stephansplatz. **Open** 9am-1.30pm, 2.30-6pm, Mon-Fri. **No credit cards.**

Reliable, centrally located dry cleaners which also do wonders with leather and suede.
Branch: 6, Linke Wienzeile 164 (597 0208).

Miele
8, Josefstädter Straße 59 (405 0255). Tram J. **Open** 7.30am-7.30pm Mon-Fri. **No credit cards.**
Will wash laundry at AS130 for 5kg.

Opticians

Melitta Kleemann
1, Tuchlauben 12 (533 0098). U1, U3 Stephansplatz. **Open** 9.30am-6pm Mon-Fri; 9.30am-5pm Sat. **Credit** AmEx, DC, JCB, MC, V.
Lots of designer frames and branches throughout the city. Does small repairs and adjustments for free.
Branch: 6, Mariahilfer Straße 81 (587 2400).

Optiker Maurer (See Me)
8, Josefstädter Straße 8 (405 0788). U2 Rathaus/tram J. **Open** 9.30am-1.30pm, 3-6pm, Mon-Fri; 9am-noon Sat. **Credit** MC, V.
Friendly service, reasonable prices. Top frames too.
Branch: 7, Siebensterngasse 40 (523 6494).

Stationery

Basic stationery requirements can be obtained cheaply at any branch of Libro, Austria's WH Smith, which also sells some English books.

Huber & Lerner
1, Kohlmarkt 7 (533 5075). U3 Herrengasse. **Open** 9.30am-6pm Mon-Fri; 9am-5pm Sat. **Credit** AmEx, DC, JCB, MC, V.
Vienna's elite have been acquiring their calling cards here since 1901. Vast range of fine handmade paper, envelopes and pens. Snooty and expensive.

Theyer & Hardtmuth
1, Kärntner Straße 9 (512 3678-0). U1, U3 Stephansplatz. **Open** 9.30am-6pm Mon-Fri; 10am-5pm Sat. **Credit** AmEx, DC, JCB, MC, V.
The best address for top-of-the-range fountain pens, diaries, organisers and handmade paper.

Travel

Das Bestplatzcenter
1, Opernpassage 1/7 (581 1808/fax 587 7142). U1, U2, U4 Karlsplatz. **Open** 10am-7pm Mon-Fri; 9am-noon Sat. **Credit** AmEx, DC, JCB, MC, V.
Friendly service. Usually has the best charter prices in the city and lots of bargain last-minute deals.

Mitfahrzentrale
8, Daungasse 1a (408 2210). Tram 43, 44. **Open** 3-7pm daily. **No credit cards.**
At 19 Groschen per kilometre this is the cheapest way of travelling bar conventional hitch-hiking. The Mitfahrzentrale is in touch with hundreds of long-distance drivers, particularly those heading for Germany. A trip to London will set you back AS1,000 (AS300 to the office, the rest to the driver).

Arts & Entertainment

Children

The old define the young, but they're learning to love them.

The Viennese are discovering the joys of youth. Politicians vie with each other to shower mothers with promises of money to persuade them to produce more offspring. And the city keeps sprouting new ideas to make Vienna fun for children.

Thank God. Somewhere along the line, following its turn-of-the-century boom, Fascism, Hitler and war, Vienna had grown old and grumpy. Its population shrank for almost a hundred years before picking up again in 1986 (mainly thanks to immigration). And that left the city to grow older and older, until it was clear that the Viennese really did prefer their dogs to their children as critics claimed.

In the 1970s, the City Council decided it was time to reassert the right of children over canines. True, it was a miserly offensive. Lawns are still generally off limits to children; but they did create fenced-off play areas, off limits to dogs.

Since then, the improvements have been massive. Children's theatres, festivals and playgrounds have sprung up all over. And while Vienna is still old and grumpy in many places, children are welcome precisely because they are cheerful.

*Vienna's best railway for kids? The **Liliput Bahn** in the Prater wins by a short head.*

That explains why there is something of a schizophrenic attitude towards children in the city. Anything that smacks of the beauty and innocence of childhood – mothers breastfeeding, toddlers singing, boys being helpful – is greeted with big smiles and nods of approval. Other aspects of childhood, like boisterous behaviour, aggression and loud giggling, will receive hard stares and diatribes. For now, at least, the old still define childhood.

So where does that leave you with your kids? First, it means the basics for babies and toddlers are easy. You can wheel a buggy on to any bus or U-Bahn (look for the blue signs telling you which door). Trams are still difficult, but the driver will get out and help if no one else does. You can also breastfeed in any café or on a park bench, at any time of day or night. There aren't many nappy-changing tables around, but people don't mind you improvising. And the city is generally very safe.

For people with older kids, it's a bit more difficult. Viennese children tend to be quiet and well behaved – that is the way to get ahead without any trouble. If yours are, you can go anywhere and do anything and no one will bat an eyelid. Normal kids on the other hand will have to put up with constant interference – so it really is worth seeking out the more relaxed, tolerant places and not provoking conflict.

The classic attractions for young tourists are the Prater funfair, the Spanish Riding School, the Butterfly House and the zoo (*see below*). All are worth a visit. Museums in Vienna are less geared to children than in many other cities. To make up, there are plenty of festivals – check out the Rathauspark, where there is usually something happening – and outdoor activities. And if all else fails, get on the tram 1 or 2 and ride round the Ring: great fun and you'll see half of Vienna's sites in an hour or so.

Emergencies

The best place to go if your child needs medical help is the Saint Anna Kinderspital. This specialist children's hospital has doctors on hand 24 hours a day to check out high fevers, odd rashes or worse. And the atmosphere is friendly and hectic, rather than clinical and scary.

Saint Anna Kinderspital

9, Kinderspitalgasse 6 (401 700). U6 Alser Straße/tram 43, 44.

Shopping

Nappies, wipes and baby food are found in every supermarket or, if you want more variety, in the chemist/generalist chains DM or **Bipa**. Vienna has a whole array of shops selling designer clothes and

shoes for kids at outrageous prices – nothing you won't find anywhere else. The real specialities are wooden toys and traditional *trachten* clothing.

Giesswein

1, Ringstraßengalerie, Kärntner Ring 5-7 (512 4597/fax 512 4597). U1, U2, U4 Karlsplatz/tram 1, 2, D, J. **Open** 10am-7pm Mon-Fri; 10am-5pm Sat. **Credit** AmEx, DC, MC, V.

Very cute and wearable versions of traditional trachten clothes.

Hennes & Mauritz

6, Mariahilfer Straße 53 (585 8550/fax 585 8550-30). U3 Neubaugasse/bus 13a. **Open** 10.30am-7pm Mon-Fri; 10.30am-5pm Sat. **Credit** AmEx, DC, MC, V.

Good for cheap and cheerful kids' clothes.
Website: www.hm.com

Pachisi

1, Ringstraßengalerie (top floor), Kärntner Ring 9-13 (512 7150/fax 512 7150-4). U1, U2, U4 Karlsplatz/tram 1, 2, D, J. **Open** 10am-7pm Mon-Fri; 10am-5pm Sat. **Credit** AmEx, DC, JCB, MC, V.

The place to find the kind of things you don't see in a normal toy shop. It specialises in wooden toys and has everything from trains to toadstools and a Noah's ark. But it also has huge cuddly animals and lots of beautiful, small gift ideas.

Babysitters

The best bet is to ask staff at your hotel if they can arrange babysitting. The only other service available is **Babysittingagentur Peter Pan** (616 9170), which can provide English-speaking babysitters with three to four hours notice. For weekends, you need to call by Friday morning.

Attractions

The **Prater** is a must. Forget the **Riesenrad** (Big Wheel) – it's very beautiful but boring. Walk straight past and up to the other end of the funfair, or take the Liliput Bahn steam train right up through the forest and back to the Hauptallee stop. Behind the **Schweizerhaus** (*see chapter* **Restaurants**) beer garden (fine for kids), there's an array of rides for younger children. And since Vienna is no place for modernity, the best of them are straight out of the 1950s and earlier – including racing-car rides, a pony-carousel from the nineteenth century, and pony rides. For the less nostalgic, there's a Kinderparadies, where you pay once for all the rides and games you can take. The Prater used to be an imperial hunting ground and there is still plenty of forest left. At Prater 113 behind the Schweizerhaus, you can hire bikes of all kinds by the day or hour – children's seats are thrown in for free.

In the 1st district the **Schmetterlinghaus** (Butterfly House), in a palm house at the bottom of the **Burggarten**, is a playground for hundreds

Options for kids at the zoo include feeding them to the bears and nicking their skateboard.

of huge, colourful tropical butterflies and a troop of dwarf quails. The atmosphere is rather weird – it's supposed to feel like a hot and steamy jungle, with gurgling streams, singing birds and luxuriant vegetation. The reality is a bit too plasticky to carry it off, but it's worth suspending disbelief just to see the butterflies close up. (Incidentally, just behind the palm house is part of the original city walls – and the restaurant next door is excellent.)

Also in the 1st district, the **Spanische Reitschule** is great for children want to see the dancing white Lipizzaner stallions, but going for an entire expensive performance is probably overdoing it. The horses train most mornings. And real fans can combine a visit with a trip to the **Lipizzaner Museum** across the road, which shows all the paraphernalia, paintings and stories associated with the horses and offers a tantalising glimpse into the Renaissance stables. *See chapters* **Museums** *and* **Sightseeing**.

Go to the **Tiergarten** (zoo) at **Schönbrunn** on a Sunday and you'll find a large portion of Viennese parents with kids in tow. It's not that the

zoo is so fantastic – it's actually one of the world's oldest and, as beautiful as the Baroque buildings are, they don't make the most suitable foundations for a modern zoo. But the place is very relaxed, with a great playground for smaller kids, horse-rides, a wood full of wolves and a Tirolean farmhouse with a range of organic food, plus your standard elephants, monkeys and hippos. Favourite slots: feeding the seals at 10.30am and 3.30pm, and feeding the wolves at 11am except Thursday and Sunday. *See chapter* **Sightseeing**.

Rathausplatz, the large square on the Ring outside the town hall, has become a year-round hive of activity, usually of interest to children. In January/February there's an outdoor ice-skating rink (no boot hire), plus food and trampolines. In summer there's an outdoor music and film festival with food from around the world. In December the whole park is turned into a truly magical Christmas market. The stalls are tacky, but the trees are beautifully decorated and there are pony rides and train rides around the park, and a baking/modelling workshop for 3-16-year-olds inside the city hall. At other times of year, there are circuses and concerts, which are always worth checking out. *See chapter* **By Season**.

The Danube Wetlands

Vienna boasts one of Europe's few intact wetlands – the original marshy forest found on riverbanks. Stretching down along the Danube to the Slovak border, it is called the **Lobau National Park** and falls within the city limits. The area is odd in many ways. In some parts it feels like a jungle, in others like scorching steppe lands; it's the haven for Vienna's numerous nudists, but it's also a favourite family outing spot; it's a nature-lover's dream, but has an oil terminal bang in the middle of it and was the site of some of the bloodiest of Napoleon's many battles.

For a walk through the woods, tracing Napoleon's steps, take bus 91a from the UN building to Panozza Lacke. Follow the path marked in green to Napoleon's HQ and past the French cemetery.

The best way to see the wetlands is by boat just east of Vienna. You can get a bus from Wien-Mitte bus station to Schönau, about an hour away, where guided boat trips take you through the Danube's many channels.

For information and reservations call Thomas Neumair at Nationalpark-Informationstelle (02214 233 518/t.neumair@oebf.at).

Museums

The best of Vienna's museums offer wonderful guided tours for children – but only in German. In **Schönbrunn**, for example, kids are taken through all the Habsburg children's rooms, nurseries and playrooms in a tour that is far more interesting than the standard one. But if you can't understand a word, there's little point.

So the best museums for English-speaking kids are those, like the Technical Museum, where doing and seeing take precedence over listening. The **Naturhistorisches Museum** is too dusty and dull to be of much interest.

History freaks might be interested in two specific exhibits. In the excellent **Museum der Stadt Wien** (Museum of the City of Vienna) there are two huge models of Vienna, one in the Middle Ages and the other before the city walls came down in the late nineteenth century. Both are fascinating for those obsessed by maps and city plans. The **Heeresgeschichtliches Museum** (Museum of Military History) is housed in nineteenth-century barracks. The museum is largely dull, except for the Turkish tents captured during the siege of Vienna in 1681. But what makes the place worth a quick visit is the re-creation of the assassination of Franz Ferdinand in Sarajevo – the event that sparked World War I. Everything is there, just like in the photos – the car with bullet holes, the blood-stained uniform and the feathered hat.

The Baroque Lobkowitz Palace that houses the **Österreichisches Theatermuseum** is truly stunning – and some of the exhibits will interest kids too. The museum also has a small children's collection, accessible by a steep slide from the main museum. Here you can see magical stage sets and marionettes up close, and play in a mini-theatre. If you can get a small group together, call Dr Dembski for a special tour.

The **Puppen- und Spielzeugmuseum** (Doll and Toy Museum) has a huge private collection of antique dolls and toys – but you can't help wondering whether it's not more interesting for parents than for their children.

The **Technisches Museum Wien** (Technical Museum) on Mariahilfer Straße has lots of levers to press and experiments to try, including a hamster wheel and a computer robot that imitates spectators. For older kids, there's the 1950s Silver Arrow racing car, a complicated water-driven, bell-ringing contraption and lots of musical instruments to try out. For under-threes, there's a mini-museum with playful experiments, all watched over by a qualified child-minder.

Marchenbuhne Der Apfelbaum

Fairy Tale Theatre
7, Kirchengasse 41 (off Burggasse) (523 1729-20/fax 523 1729-19). U2, U3 Volkstheater, then 10-minute walk/bus 48a Kellermanngasse. **Open** *Performances Sat, 2 Suns and 1 Wed a month.* **Admission** AS90. **No credit cards**.
For kids learning German at school, it might be worth trying a puppet theatre performance of a well-known fairytale. Der Apfelbaum plays classics such as *Hansel and Gretel* and *Snow White*, for children aged from four years upwards.

Marionetten Theater Schloß Schönbrunn

Puppet Theatre
13, Hofratstrakt, Schloss Schönbrunn (817 3247). U4 Schönbrunn (quickest to take Grunbergstraße exit to side entrance of Schönbrunn). **Open** Wed-Mon. **Admission** AS130-150; AS90-110 children. *Long performances* AS290-340; AS200-250 children. **Credit** DC, MC, V.
These exquisite puppet performances of *The Magic Flute, Aladdin*, or new stories like *Sisi's Secrets* or *Magic Strauss* rely on music and costume rather than language to keep kids' attention. Most performances last about an hour – but beware, *The Magic Flute* is over two hours.
Website: www.marionettentheater.at

Zoom Kindermuseum

Children's Museum
7, Museumsquartier, Museumsplatz 1 (522 6748/info@kindermuseum.at). U2, U3 Volkstheater/tram 46, 49/bus 2a. **Open** 8.30-10.30am, 1.30-3.30pm daily. **Admission** AS40; AS50 children; AS120 family. **No credit cards**.
Difficult for English-speaking tourists, but heaven for kids. Exhibitions here are for touching, playing

with and talking about. You need to call at least three days in advance to book a time – tours are for a limited number and start at 8.30am, 10.30am, 1.30pm and 3.30pm on weekdays; 10am, noon, 2pm and 4pm on weekends.
Website: www.kindermuseum.at (German only)

Activities

See also chapter **Sport & Fitness**.

Ice-skating
You can skate all over the place in Vienna, but if you're just visiting and so need to hire boots, the best outdoor rink is the Vienna Ice-Skating Association, by the Konzerthaus (Concert Hall):
3, Lothringerstraße 22 (713 6353). U4 Stadtpark/tram 1, 2. **Open** *22 Oct-15 Mar* 9am-8pm Sat-Mon; 9am-9pm Tue, Thur, Fri; 9am-10pm Wed. **Admission** *Mon-Fri* AS80; AS65 7-18s, over 65s; AS35 under-7s. *Sat, Sun* AS95; AS75 7-18s, over-65s; AS40 under-7s. Boot hire AS75.

Indoor swimming pools
Margaretenbad is not the kind of place you go to swim lengths. It's a mass of water-slides, wave machines and diving boards, seething with kids.
5, Strobachgasse 7-9 (587 0844/fax 587 0844-14). U4 Pilgramgasse/bus 59a. **Open** 10am-10pm Mon, Thur; 9am-11pm Tue, Wed, Fri-Sun. **Admission** *1*

Totally Orson: the **Third Man Walking Tour**.

hour AS68; AS42 concs. *3 hours* AS98; AS57 concs. *Daycard* AS123; AS82 concs. **No credit cards**.

Open-air swimming pools
Mix the interests of parents and kids, and the best open-air baths is the Schafbergbad. Like all the best baths, it's in the hills to the west of Vienna. But it offers everything from a quiet baby area to peaceful meadows and high diving boards.
17, Josef-Redlgasse 2 (479 1593). Bus 42b. **Open** *2 May-15 Sept* 9am-7.30pm daily **Admission** AS30; free children in school summer holidays.

Third Man Walking Tour
Meet at U4 Stadtpark exit. **Open** usually 4pm Mon-Fri, but call Dr Brigitte Timmermann (774 8901/fax 774 8933) to check times – or look in the monthly *Wiener Spaziergange* brochure, available from the Tourist Office. **Tickets** AS190; AS90 children. **No credit cards**.
This two-and-a-half-hour guided tour in English and German takes you down the canals and to all the places that featured in the Orson Welles film classic, *The Third Man*. If you watch the film before you come (or at the **Burgkino**), the tour will add a new dimension to shiny, imperial Vienna. Strong shoes required.

Parks & playgrounds

In the centre of town, there are beautiful parks but few really good playgrounds. The best combination is the **Stadtpark,** which stretches from the Ring to the Hilton Hotel, across the Wien River. The playground (Hilton side) is large and fenced in, and good for smaller children. Nearby is a fountain designed for kids to splash around in. The more beautiful area of the park is on the Ring side, where there's a duck pond and statues of everybody from Johann Strauß to Alma Mahler's father. *See also chapter* **Sightseeing**.

The **Burggarten**, the former imperial gardens between the Hofburg and the Opera, have many attractions, despite the lack of a playground: it's one of the few parks where lying around on the grass is tolerated, it has the best selection of trees around and the Butterfly House/Palm House is at the bottom.

If you're looking for a huge park with lots to do – and no history to mar the playing – you could head out for **Donaupark** in the 22nd district (U1 Alte Donau). At the main entrance it has Walkamals, large cuddly animals that wheel around with entranced toddlers on their backs (AS20 a go). There's a tiny train driving around the huge park; table tennis, minigolf and huge chess and draft games. There's a mini-zoo, with a bird house and a petting zoo. And there are three playgrounds, with enormous slides and creative rides.

The other good place for wild playgrounds (suitable for older children) and fields to play ball games is the **Jesuitenwiese**, which is part of the Prater area. Here there are enormous swings, mud pits, ropes – and picnic tables.

Might as well jump – the **Copa Cagrana** *is popular with young Viennese. See page 85.*

Restaurants

Eating out with children is no problem in summer – most restaurants have tables outside where the atmosphere is less smoky and more relaxed. But the best bet is to do what Viennese parents do on a hot evening and go to a *Heuriger* (wine tavern) in the hills. The worst are tourist traps, but the best are a grander version of a back garden picnic, with benches and tables dotted around under the trees, and a self-service buffet offering chicken, schnitzels and salads, with home-made wine or grape juice. Some Heurigen feature a swing or slide to give kids something to do, but most have plenty of room to run around. Zawodsky on Reinischgasse in the 19th district and Rath on Liebhartstalstraße in the 16th district are two of the more popular for children. *See also chapter* **Heurigen**.

If you have to eat inside, the Viennese will go out of their way to be nice to children – as long as they aren't too rowdy. If you're worried yours might be, there is always fast food. There are McDonald's restaurants at Schwarzenbergplatz, Mariahilfer Straße and Schwedenplatz. If you really want to go local, try a Wurstelstand (sausage stand) – the best are behind the Opera and on Schwarzenbergplatz.

Rosenberger on Maysedergasse in the 1st district does excellent self-service food on three floors. It isn't atmospheric, but it provides kids with crayons, balloons and cardboard crowns, has plenty of highchairs and even a changing table. *See also chapter* **Restaurants**.

Film

Beyond Arnie, Julie Andrews and Orson Welles...

Two of the most famous movies in film history were shot in Austria – *The Third Man* and *The Sound of Music* – although neither were well received by the Austrians. *The Third Man* was criticised by both film critics and the audience of the time for painting Vienna as a city full of shifty characters and potential murderers. Opinion has changed now, and the film is regularly shown at the **Burgkino**.

The Sound of Music was a total flop in Austria, and locals in Salzburg have little or no idea what tourists are talking about when they inquire about the home of the Von Trapp family. Other famous films shot in Austria include *Where Eagles Dare* (Richard Burton, Clint Eastwood), *Scorpio* (Alain Delon, Burt Lancaster), and, more recently, *The Living Daylights* and *Before Sunrise*.

This classic is still showing today.

Austria's film industry might not have the same worldwide reputation as its classical music, but actors such as Klaus-Maria Brandauer, Romy Schneider and Arnold Schwarzenegger have all made an impact internationally (although Arnie has never made a film in Austria). The last Austrian film to have any real success on the world stage was a trilogy on Empress Elisabeth, *Kaiserin Elisabeth* (played by Romy Schneider), made in the 1950s. The country has also made a small contribution to celluloid history – in 1930 Austrian actress Hedy Lamarr (*see page 210* **A Hedy cocktail**) appeared in the first nude scene in film history in *Ecstasy*.

The Austrian film industry produces about 15 films per year (many are partly state-funded), some of which do quite well in international film festivals. The most memorable and successful of recent times on the arthouse circuit was Michael Haneke's Austrian-produced *Funny Games*. Audiences during the 1998 film festival circuit were deeply shocked by, yet lauded Haneke's gut-wrenching treatment of violence – even though very little actually takes place on screen. Not only is *Funny Games* haunting and horrific, it also paints a darkly comic portrait of Austria's middleclass.

Many famous Hollywood directors from the golden age were of Austrian origin *(see page 208* **Out of Austria)**. They usually started their career in Germany (then one of Europe's film centres), but emigrated to the US when the Nazis came to power.

There are 45 cinemas and more than 100 screens in Vienna – these can be divided into Hollywood outlets and arthouse cinemas *(Programm-Kino)*. With the recent arrival of multiplexes there are now enough screens to show less commercial productions. Many of the theatres showing mainstream Hollywood fare only screen films in English – such as the **Haydn**, Burgkino and the **Artis Kino-Treff** – whereas the arthouse cinemas have films in original version with German subtitles (**Filmcasino, Votiv-Kino, Stadtkino**). In every cinema you will find at least a bar and sometimes, if you're lucky, a cosy café.

Film listings are in every newspaper, but for the best overview of foreign-language movies try *Der Standard*, which has a section for all films not in German. The most complete listings are in *Falter*, although they can be a little confusing. The small letters next to some films have the following meaning: *OV* or *OF* is original version; *OmU* is original version with German subtitles; and *OmE* is original version with English subtitles. Telephone reservations are standard procedure.

On Mondays, *Kino-Montag*, there's one price for all seats, the lowest of each cinema. Seats in Austrian cinemas are numbered – even if the cinema is half empty the audience tend to stick to the numbering, so you may be asked to move if you are not in the right seat.

In July and August the *Programm-Kinos* drop their regular programming and show a mixture of classics and cult films during their *Sommer-Kino* season. Check out the flyers in cafés around the city for listings.

In the summer Vienna also has two open-air cinemas: **Kino unter Sternen** in the Augarten park; and **Freiluftkino Krieau** in the Prater. Both have food stalls and restaurants next to them to complete a cinematic night out.

Vienna has a film festival – the Viennale – which starts in mid-October and lasts two weeks. It premieres films in Austria and also screens movies that have had difficulties being distributed – which usually results in an interesting mix of commercial and independent films by established directors and budding talents from all around the world. Although the festival has no own jury, FIPRESCI (Fédération Internationale de la Presse de Cinéma) give a prize – 1999's winner was *Nordrand*, by Barbara Albert.

Cinemas

Admiral

7, Burggasse 119 (523 3759). U6 Burggasse/tram 5/bus 48a. **Open** half hour before-11.30pm daily. **Tickets** AS75; AS65 Mon. **No credit cards**.
An old, neighbourhood cinema that looks Eastern Bloc in style from the outside but is cosy inside. Its long screening room (120 seats) resembles a large corridor. Its programming features less commercial films – often original version with subtitles.

Apollo

6, Gumperndorfer Straße 63 (587 9651). U3 Neubaugasse/bus 13a, 14a, 57a. **Open** 1.30-9pm Mon, Wed; 3-9pm Tue, Thur; 3-11pm Fri, Sat; late show 11pm Fri, Sat. **Tickets** AS85-110; AS70 Mon. **No credit cards**.
A pre-multiplex with impressive 1930s architecture, although it isn't quite so impressive inside. Its eight screens only show films in German, but every Tuesday there's a première in original version (90% of the time in English). Tickets are hard to get hold of, but can be bought a couple of weeks in advance.

Artis Kino-Treff

1, Schultergasse/Jordangasse (535 6570). U1, U3 Stephansplatz/bus 2a, 3a. **Open** half hour before show daily; late show 10.45pm Tue, Fri, Sat. **Tickets** AS85-120; AS70. **No credit cards**.
An inner-city cinema that only shows films in English in six rooms (848 seats altogether, the biggest has 316). The programming is mainstream Hollywood, and, of course, there is a bar.

Bellaria

7, Museumstraße 3 (523 7591). U2, U3 Volkstheater/tram 46, 49/bus 48a. **Open** 3.45-9pm daily. **Tickets** AS45-75. **No credit cards**.
As the original decoration (and the posters) show – time here seems to have stopped in the 1950s. The programming specialises in old German and Austrian light comedies from the 1930s to the 1960s, with some more recent films thrown in. The audience is elderly, and a couple of times a year the old stars of that era come here to sign autographs. If you're interested in Heimat films (cheesy Austrian-German film genre with lots of mountains and rosy cheeked young women) or in Germany's golden film age, Veit Harlan (popular German director of the 1930s) or Hans Moser (popular Austrian actor of the 1950s), this cinema will appeal. All films are in German.

Breitenseer Lichtspiele

14, Breitenseerstraße 21 (982 2173). U3 Hütteldorfer Straße/tram 49, 10. **Open** 6-10pm Wed-Thur, Sun; 6pm-midnight Fri, Sat. **Tickets** AS85. **No credit cards**.
Opened in 1909, and built in to an art nouveau house, this is possibly the oldest, still running cinema in the world. The 186 wooden seats, comfortable enough to sit through a film, haven't been changed in over 90 years and there is a *loge* (private box) for special guests. It normally screens English films with subtitles. Worth the detour.

Burgkino

1, Opernring 19 (587 8406). U1, U2, U4 Karlsplatz/tram 1, 2, D, J/bus 57a. **Open** half hour before show daily; late show 11pm Fri, Sat. **Tickets** AS80-100; AS70 Mon. **No credit cards**.
This centrally located, cosy cinema only shows only original version films. It has a small café downstairs. It's mainly commercial films in the bigger screening room (292 seats), whereas the smaller one (73 seats) concentrates on less mainstream or classic pictures, usually very late on Friday or Saturday. *The Third Man* has been shown here just about every other weekend since 1980. A stroll in the neighbourhood takes in many of the film's locations. Stanley Kubrick's *Dr Strangelove* is another perennial favourite.

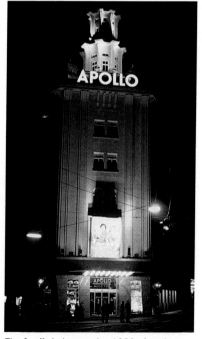

The **Apollo**'s impressive 1930s façade.

Out of Austria

Vienna and Austria produced some of the biggest names of Hollywood's golden age:

Billy Wilder

The director of *Some Like It Hot, Sunset Boulevard* and *The Apartment* was born in Austria in 1906 as Samuel Wilder. He went to school (*see chapter* **Sightseeing**) in Vienna before starting his career as a journalist. He became a succesful screenwriter in Berlin, but fled the Nazis to the US. There he worked on scripts for Ernst Lubitsch (*Bluebeard's Eighth Wife, Ninotchka*) and directed his first films, mainly war features, thrillers and social dramas. He surprised everyone by switching to comedy with *Sabrina* in 1954, followed by *The Seven Year Itch* and *Some Like It Hot.*

Otto Preminger

The director of such diverse films as *The River of No Return, Anatomy of a Murder, The Man With the Golden Arm* and *Laura* was born in Vienna in 1906 and started his career in theatre, where he became the protégé of Max Reinhardt. Of Jewish origin, he fled to the US in 1935 where, ironically, he rose to fame as an actor by playing Nazi officers. Although he had already directed a couple of films, his breakthrough came in 1944 with *Laura,* a film noir classic with Gene Tierney and Dana Andrews. In order to have more freedom, he distanced himself from the big studios and was one of the first to become an independent producer. After a series of great box-office successes (*Porgy & Bess, Exodus* and *The Cardinal,* which gave him his second Oscar nomination), his movies declined in quality and he stopped filming in 1979. He died in New York in 1986.

Fred Zinnemann

The director of *High Noon, Oklahoma* and *The Day of the Jackal* was born in Vienna in 1907 and started out as an assistant director in Berlin, then one of the centres of the European film industry. He left Germany in 1933, moving to Mexico and then the US, where he first made documentaries. He won the Oscar for Best Director with *From Here to Eternity* and *Man for All Seasons.*

Josef von Sternberg

Known for the movies that made Marlene Dietrich a world star *(Blonde Venus, The Shanghai Gesture, Dishonored)* to the point of being called MD's director, Sternberg was born in Vienna in 1894 and left for America at the age

of 14. Having worked as a laboratory assistant, projectionist, assistant director, cameraman, cutter and author, he first found fame with a privately funded film, *The Salvation Hunters,* in 1925. His *Blue Angel* (1929) is one of the rare German films of that time to achieve success on the world stage and marked his first encounter with Miss Dietrich.

Erich von Stroheim

Born in 1885 in Vienna, von Stroheim made a strong contribution to the development of silent film. Spotted as an actor by DW Griffith, who also made him his assistant, he became popular during World War I with his playing of ruthless German officers. He was given a chance to direct in 1918. His career as a director ended in 1933, but he continued to work as an actor (including *Sunset Boulevard*). He died in France in 1957.

Fritz Lang

A leading director in Germany in the 1920s and early 1930s, Lang (*pictured below*) was born in Vienna in 1890. He made such classics as *Dr Mabuse, Die Nibelungen, Metropolis* and *M.* Lang emigrated to the US in 1933 after being offered the job of 'grand-supervisor' of the German film industry by Goebbels, an unwanted admirer. When he pointed out to Goebbels that he was a Jew, the propaganda minister is said to have answered, 'I decide who is a Jew and who is not.' He continued his career in Hollywood mainly with action films, including *Fury, The Ministry of Fear* and *The Big Heat.* Lang returned to Germany in the 1950s, but did not produce films of the same quality. He died in Los Angeles in 1976.

Movies in English and plenty of leg space – you can bet on it at the **Filmcasino***.*

Filmcasino

*5, Margaretenstraße 78 (587 9062). U4
Pilgramgasse/bus 13a, 14a.* **Open** half hour before
show daily; late show 10pm Fri, Sat. **Tickets** AS70-
90; AS70 Mon. **No credit cards.**
Worth the detour to see original version films
within well-preserved 1950s décor. The 254-seat
projection room is unusually spacious – never mind
the film, feel the foot space. The programming is
centred on ambitious European films and also New
Asian cinema, especially films from Hong Kong.
Documentaries are sometimes shown, although
most of them are in German. Sommer-Kino in July
and August.

Filmhaus am Spittelberg

*7, Spittelberggasse 3 (522 4816). U2, U3
Volkstheater/tram 49/bus 48a.* **Open** 1 hour before
show. *Aug* closed. **Tickets** AS70-80. **No credit
cards.**
Opened in October 1994, this arthouse cinema (100
seats) in Spittelberg is surrounded by plenty of decent
bars and restaurants. It is linked (by ownership)
to the **Stadtkino** (*see below*) and has similar programming of original version films. It also has facilities for the disabled.

Filmhaus In Der Stöbergasse

*5, Stöbergasse 11-15 (546 66-0). U4
Kettenbrückengasse/bus 14a, 59a.* **Open** 6-9pm Wed.
Tickets AS80. **No credit cards.**
Films are shown every Wednesday, and every two
months there is a small film festival programmed
around a special theme: New York in film, films from
former East Germany, etc.

Filmmuseum

*1, Augustinerstraße 1 (533 7054). U1, U2, U4
Karlsplatz/tram 1, 2, D, J/bus 3a.* **Open** *Sept-May*
half hour before show daily. **Tickets** AS50

members; AS60; AS150 yearly membership; AS400
10 film card, valid for 1 year. **No credit cards.**
The austere look and the wooden seats of Vienna's
cinematheque serve to remind you that you are in a
sanctuary devoted to the adoration of film.
Everything is in original version, and almost never
subtitled. The programming centres on exhaustive
retrospectives of famous directors, early Russian
and German cinema, Japanese and Indian, as well as
all-time classics.

Flotten Kino

*6, Mariahilfer Straße 85 (586 5152). U3
Zieglergasse/bus 13a, 14a.* **Open** half hour before
show-10pm daily. **Tickets** AS70-110; AS70 Mon.
No credit cards.
This cinema features mainly Hollywood mainstream films in English, but also some European
films, dubbed in German. There are four screens
(384/178/134/66 seats) and a bar.

Haydn English Cinema

*6, Mariahilfer Straße 57 (587 2262). U3
Neubaugasse/bus 13a, 14a.* **Open** half hour before
show-10pm daily. **Tickets** AS70-100; AS70 Mon.
No credit cards.
Set on the city's main shopping street, Mariahilfer
Straße, this cinema puts on mainstream Hollywood
and British fare in its three rooms (376/144/84 seats).
It has a bar.

Schikaneder

*4, Margaretenstraße 24 (585 2867). U1, U2, U4
Karlsplatz/bus 59a.* **Open** half hour before show-
10pm daily. **Tickets** AS80; AS70 Mon. **No credit
cards.**
A popular, alternative cinema that puts on about
ten films a week, half of them in original version
with German subtitles. The programming ranges
from Manga-inspired Japanese action to French

A Hedy cocktail

The original idea and patent that led to cellular phone technology came from Hedy Lamarr.

Hedwig Eva Marie Kiesler was born in Vienna in 1913. She dropped out of school to find her fortune as an actress, making her film debut in 1931 in *Sturm Im Wasserglas*. Two years later she appeared in *Ecstasy*, the movie that catapulted her to fame because of her appearance in the first nude scene in film history (*see opposite*).

Lamarr soon married Fritz Mandl, a Nazi sympathiser, who attempted to buy up all the prints of *Ecstasy* he could lay his hands on. She learned a great deal about weaponry by listening to Mandl, an armament manufacturer. She left her husband when he became increasingly involved in deals with the Nazis and made her way to London, then on to Hollywood.

She'd kept her mind active on what she'd heard about the problems of radio controlled missiles and how easy it was to block the simple signal. She realised that if the signal jumped from frequency to frequency quickly and both sender and receiver changed in the same order, then the signal could never be blocked by someone 'listening in' who didn't know how the frequency was changing.

It was very difficult to design a way for this to be accomplished. Composer George Antheil thought of using something similar to piano rolls to keep both sides in synch. Together, he and Lamarr patented the Secret Communication System in 1942.

When the transistor became available the US Navy employed the idea in secure military communications and when transistors became really cheap the idea was used in cellular phone technology. By the time the Navy used the idea, the original patent had expired. Lamarr and Antheil never received royalty payments for their idea.

Hedy Lamarr did finally receive some recognition for her work with an award at the Computers, Freedom and Privacy conference in 1997 for 'blazing new trails on the electronic frontier'.

She died in Florida on 19 January 2000, aged 86.

---

auteur films. The screening room is small (80 seats) and has no seat numbering, except a couple of comfortable, cosy large sofas. There's also a modern, bar which hosts occasional poetry slams. Notice the vitrine at the entrance, the only clue that this was once a shop. The cinema is also open to a spot of redecoration – submit your idea to the owner and it might be accepted. One project in September 1999 had people living there for a week.

Stadtkino

3, Schwarzenbergplatz 7 (522 4814). U1, U2, U4 Karlsplatz/tram 71, D/bus 4a. **Open** 1 hour before show daily. *Aug* closed. **Tickets** AS85; AS650 10 film card, valid for 1 year. **No credit cards.**
An arthouse cinema showing original version films in its 172-seat projection room. It's run by cinephiles who publish informative, detailed brochures about the films on show. It has a little bar and is one of the few cinemas in Vienna which caters for the disabled. There's also a varied selection of some 1,000 videos (mainly documentaries and discussions) for viewing (AS15 per person, per hour). In June and July the regular programming is replaced by Sommer-Kino.

Top Kino

7, Rahlgasse 1 (587 5557). U2 Babenberger Straße/bus 59a. **Open** half hour before show-10pm daily. **Tickets** AS85-95; AS70 Mon. **No credit cards.**
Mainly German-dubbed films in the three small screening rooms (totalling 306 seats), but there are some films in English. You have to enter through the bar.

Votiv-Kino

9, Währinger Straße 12 (317 3571). U2 Schottentor/tram 1, 2, 37, 38, 40, 41, 42, D. **Open** half hour before show daily. **Tickets** AS70-95; AS70 Mon. **No credit cards.**
This cinema with a 1960s atmosphere shows films in original version on its three screens (174/88/74 seats). On Sundays there's a Film-Breakfast: AS125 buys breakfast and entrance to a film. Sommer-Kino runs from mid-July to August.

Multiplexes

UCI Lassallestraße

2, Lasallestraße 21 (21 100-0). U1 Praterstern or Vorgartenstraße/tram 5, 21, N. **Open** 10am-10.30pm Mon-Thur, Sun; 10pm-midnight Fri-Sat; late show midnight Fri, Sat. **Tickets** AS85-125. **No credit cards.**
Opened October 1999. Has 2,233 seats in nine screening rooms and shows three English films a week.

Kinepolis im Donau Plex

22, Wagramer Straße 67-71 (201 7171). U1 Kagran. **Open** 10am-10pm Mon-Thur, Sun; 10am-11.15pm Fri, Sat; late show 11pm Fri, Sat. **Tickets** AS80-120; AS80 Mon, Wed. **No credit cards.**
Opened in November 1999, this huge multiplex has 3,150 seats in 13 screening rooms. Predictably, the programming is mainstream, and some films are shown once a week in English (study the programme closely). It's set in the Donau Plex, a mall with plenty of restaurants and cafés.

Open-air cinemas

In July and August there are two open-air cinemas in Vienna:

Freiluftkino Krieau
2, Trabrennbahn Krieau (726 94-25). Tram N. **Open** July, Aug. **Tickets** AS90. **No credit cards.**
Set in the old Krieau racecourse in the Prater, and screening a mixture of classic and contemporary films. Films in English are the exception rather than the rule.

Kino unter Sternen
2, Augarten-Park (585 23 24 25). Tram 5 Wallensteinstraße, 31 Gaußplatz. **Open** mid-July-end Aug. **Tickets** AS90. **No credit cards.**
Six weeks of open-air cinema with classics in original version on a huge screen. Recent screening themes have included science fiction and blacks in American cinema. Many people who don't get tickets stay and listen to the film – there are enough tables and benches as well as stands with Indian, Greek and Austrian food nearby. Look out for programme booklets in cafés and cinemas.

Video stores

Alphaville
3, Schleifmühlgasse 5 (585 1966). U1, U2, U4 Karlsplatz/tram 62, 65 Paulanergasse/bus 59a. **Open** 10am-10pm Mon-Sat; 10am-7pm Sun. **No credit cards.**

Stocks 5,000 English-language movies and cult TV series such as *The Prisoner*. The Schikaneder (*see above*) is around the corner. Rental is AS30-50 per night, and you will need ID and police registration to become a member.

British Council
1, Schenkenstraße 4 (533 2616). Tram 1, 2, D Rathaus/Burgtheater. **Open** 11am-6pm Mon; 11am-5pm Tue-Thur; 11am-1pm Fri. *Aug* closed. **No credit cards.**
Has a variety of videos at a weekly rental fee of AS50. ID and police registration needed for membership.

Pickwicks
1, Marc-Aurel-Straße 10-12 (533 0182). U1, U4 Schwedenplatz/tram 1, 2, 21, N/bus 2a. **Open** 10am-10pm Mon-Sat; 4-8pm Sun. **No credit cards.**
The largest English-language video rental store in Vienna with over 7,000 movies, mainly English, but also French, Italian and Spanish. Rental is AS40-60 per night. ID and police registration needed to become a member.

Bookshop

Satyr Filmwelt
1, Marc-Aurel-Straße 5 (535 5326). U1, U4 Schwedenplatz/tram 1, 2, 21, N/bus 2a. **Open** 10am-7.30pm Mon-Fri; 9am-5pm Sat. **Credit** amEX, DC, MC, V.
Specialises in film and stocks biographies, posters, scripts and about 8,000 English videos, DVDs and soundtracks. Close to Pickwicks (*see above*).

Gay & Lesbian

Vienna's schwulen and lesben create a colourful and lively scene.

Bar stool boys at **Café Berg**.

The gay scene in Vienna became more prominent during the 1990s with the start of both the **Life Ball** and the **Rainbow Parade** and the opening of new bars and cafés. Queen bee and lesbian alike can generally feel safe and *gemütlich* in the city – cases of gay-bashing are rare and the integration of *schwulen* and *lesben* into Viennese life has met with little or no protest. In 1998 Alfons Haide, a popular Austrian actor and TV presenter fed up with leading a double life, succumbed to peer pressure and outed himself – probably causing many of the teenage girls and old women who 'adored' him to choke on their coffees – and as a result, donations to Aids charities tripled.

The first Rainbow (Gay Pride) Parade in 1996 was a way of 'increasing gay and lesbian visibility in Vienna' according to organiser Robert Kastl. Attendance at the 1999 parade came screamingly close to 100,000 and represented a cross-section of Austrian gays, lesbians, tourists and friends of the 'family'. *See page 215* **Colourful co-ordination**.

Likewise, 1999's grand fund-raising event for Aids – the Life Ball – was high profile. Started in 1992 by Gery Keszler, the annual ball attracts attention from all over Europe. In 1999 celebrities, politicians (including the Chancellor, Victor Klima), fashion gurus and the great and the good of Viennese society packed in to the plush chambers of the Hofburg Palace.

Vienna's options on gay-friendly restaurants, clubs, saunas and bars have improved over the last decade. The first port of call for visitors to the city is usually **Rosa Lila Villa**. The 'Villa' is an institution in Vienna's gay and lesbian community and, as well as having a restaurant and bar, offers information, advice, counselling, and group meetings.

Vienna has various cruising areas (*see below*) – one of which springs into action at the first hint of friendlier weather in the leafy Rathauspark directly in front of the **Rathaus** and right under the Mayor's nose.

A number of free publications including *Extra* (the best and most popular), *Bussi, Vienna Gay Guide* (the city map for gay tourists) and *Rainbow Life* appear monthly and are available at most gay venues around town. *See* **Media** *page 216.*

Under current legislation men are still imprisoned every year for offences relating to Article 209, whereby the age of consent for gay sex is 18 but only 14 for lesbians and heterosexuals. Austria's strongest party (the Socialists) has expressed the need for equality, so maybe changes in such antiquated laws are around the corner. The two other strong parties, however (Haider's Freedom Party and Schuessel's ÖVP Conservatives), are neither willing to abolish the law nor acknowledge any gay issues at all.

Advice & information

AIDS-Hilfe Wien

6, Mariahilfer Gürtel 4 (59937/fax 59916/wien@aidshilfe.or.at). U6 Gumpendorfer *Straße/tram 6, 18.* **Open** 4-8pm Mon, Wed; 9am-1pm Thur; 2-6pm Fri.
Aids tests, results and counselling.

HOSI

2, Novaragasse 40 (216 6604/office@hosiwien.at). *Tram N, 21.* **Open** 5-10pm. *Phone service* 6-8pm Tue; 7-9pm Wed, Thur.
Political meeting point for those interested in the fight against discrimination. Open house 5-10pm Tuesdays, lesbian group on Wednesdays at 7pm,

coming out groups on Thursdays from 6pm and an occasional dance night for women on Fridays at 7pm. *Website: www.hosiwien.at*

HUK
Homosexuals and the Church
1, PO Box 513 (tel/fax 983 3403/huk-wien@gay.at).
This Christian group meets every Tuesday at 7.30pm in the chapel of the Albert Schweizer Haus (9, Schwarzspanierstraße 13. Tram 37, 38, 40, 41, 42) or at 8pm in the Villa.
Website: www.huk.gay.at

Rosa Lila Tip
6, Linke Wienzeile 102 (585 4343/fax 587 1778/rosalila.tip@blackbox.at). U4 Pilgramgasse.
Lesbians should call 586 8150/fax 585 4159.
Counselling, discussion groups and advice for gays and lesbians (5-8pm Mon-Fri). English spoken.

Events

Life Ball
1, Grünangergasse 7 (512 6606/fax 512 6636). U1, U3 Stephansplatz.
This Aids fund-raising event is viewed as being elitist by members of Vienna's gay community. The annual ball usually takes place in the Rathaus in July and tickets (just under AS1,000 a pop) must be booked well in advance, or otherwise picked up in a special final issue for gays at Heaven (*see below*) on the final Thursday night prior to the ball.
Website: www.lifeball.at

*Sample some gilded glamour at **Café Savoy**.*

Accommodation

Pension Wild
8, Lange Gasse 10 (406 5174/fax 402 2168/info@pension-wild.com). U2 Lerchenfelder Straße. Rates *single* AS490-690; *double* AS590-990. **No credit cards.**
Well-located bed and breakfast with comfortable rooms, shower, toilet, minibar, cable TV, phone and latex mattresses. Breakfast buffet included.
Website: www.pension-wild.com

Hotel Urania
3, Obere Weissgerberstraße 7 (713 1711/fax 713 5694). Tram N, O. Rates *single* AS650-850; *double* AS890-1,550. Credit AmEx, DC, MC, V.
Apparently this hotel has been in existence since 1683. It has 36 rooms all with bathroom and TV.

Hotel Wimberger
7, Neubauguertel 34-36 (52 165-0). U6 Burggasse/tram 6, 18. Rates *single* AS1,200-2,100; *double* AS1,600-2,800. Credit AmEx, DC, MC, V.
Large, modern hotel located near Mariahilfer Straße, Vienna's main shopping street, but unfortunately right on the traffic-clogged Gürtel. Rooms have all mod-cons including cable television and minibars. Guests have free use of the fitness centre on the seventh floor. Solarium and massage, however, are extra. Breakfast buffet included. Jazz brunch every Sunday from 11am to 2pm, except in summer.
Website: www.arcotel.co.at

Cafés & bars

Café Berg/Löwenherz Bookshop
9, Berggasse 8. Café (319 5720). Bookshop (317 2982/fax 317 2983). Tram 37, 38, 40, 41, 42.
Open *Café* 10-1am daily. *Bookshop* 10am-7pm Mon-Fri; 11am-5pm Sat. **No credit cards.**
This cool and stylish café and bookstore (for mixed clientele) lies on the same street as Sigmund Freud's former residence and practice. Opened by Leo Kellerman in 1993, its friendly staff serve great breakfast/brunch combinations as well as cheap lunch specials and evening meals. A well-stocked gay bookstore adjoins the café and sells all kinds of gay literature, books, magazines and videos.

Café Savoy
6, Linke Wienzeile 36 (586 7348). U4 Kettenbrückengasse. **Open** 5pm-2am Mon-Fri; 9am-2am Sat. **No credit cards.**
One of the city's classic old cafés with a rather camped-up interior – chandeliers, feathers, the works. All ages and mostly only guys. Stop by on Saturdays on the way to the Naschmarkt. *See also chapter* **Cafés & Coffeehouses.**

Café Willendorf/Rosa Lila Villa
6, Linke Wienzeile 102 (587 1789). U4 Pilgramgasse. **Open** 6pm-2am daily. *Office and gay switchboard (586 8150).* **Open** 5-8pm Mon-Fri. **No credit cards.**
This prominent pink building has been a popular

Rosa Lila Villa – *the hub of Vienna's gay and lesbian community. See page 213.*

place for both gays and dykes for 16 years and is an ideal first point of call for tourists and locals. Owned and run by Andreas Pilz and Michael Rehrl since 1991, it houses a bar and restaurant with a pretty, ivy-covered courtyard (open during summer) and has a reasonably priced menu (until midnight) offering everything from snacks to full meals, local beer to imported wines. Saturday night parties are organised randomly throughout the year and are usually mixed but sometimes exclusively boys or girls. Discussion groups and counselling services for all age groups take place in the Villa and are listed in *Extra* (*see below*).

Eagle

6, Blümelgasse 1 (587 2661). Bus 57a. **Open** 9pm-4am daily. **No credit cards**.
Popular late-night spot with videos and an active darkroom. No entry charge.

Frauen Café

8, Lange Gasse 11 (406 3754). U2 Lerchenfelder Straße. **Open** *Café* 5pm-2am Tue-Sat. *Bookshop* 10am-6pm Mon-Fri; 10am-1pm Sat. **No credit cards**.
Small, cosy lesbian bar with reasonably priced drinks and friendly service. There's a disco three times a year for girls 'that wanna have fun'. Next door is the Frauen Buchhandlung, which specialises in women's literature.

Mango Bar

6, Laimgrubengasse 3 (587 4448). U4 Kettenbrückengasse/bus 57a. **Open** 9pm-4am daily. **No credit cards**.
This cruisy and crowded bar for gay men, opened

in 1992, has a door buzzer and spyhole entrance system. The staff are very friendly and it's always lively and popular (packed on Saturdays).

Orlando

6, Mollardgasse 3 (586 2327). U4 Margaretengürtel/bus 57a. **Open** 5pm-2am Mon-Sat; 10am-2am Sun (breakfast buffet 10am-4pm). **No credit cards**.
A predominantly lesbian bar/restaurant with an attractive summer garden that serves tasty Austrian dishes and offers an extensive selection of local and imported beers and wines. The prices are competitive and it's more spacious and much less smoky than other places. Guys (and canine friends) are always welcome.

Santo Spirito

1, Kumpfgasse 7 (512 9998). U1, U3 Stephansplatz/tram 1, 2. **Open** 11am-2am Sun-Thur; 11am-3am Fri, Sat. **No credit cards**.
This unique bar and restaurant (mixed gay and straight) with Spanish, Italian and Austrian cuisine is popular among artists and musicians and is known and loved for its early music recordings played at increasing decibels as the night progresses. Owners Hiro and Christian and their friendly staff offer an excellent selection of wines, reasonably priced food, and outdoor seating on a quiet cobble-stoned street in summer. A 'cultural breakfast' on selected Sundays (11am-3pm) features live Baroque music and pre-performance chat. There's no entrance fee, but keep some change for when the musicians pass the hat round. Table reservations are nearly always necessary. *See also chapter* **Restaurants**.

Stiefelknecht

5, Wimmergasse 20 (545 2301). Tram 62, 65.
Open 10pm-2am Sun-Thur; 10pm-4am Fri, Sat. **No credit cards.**
Vienna's only serious leather bar. The togs are required for entry.

Clubs

Arriba

6, Gumpendorfer Straße 9 (585 2726). Bus 57a.
Open from 6pm daily. **No credit cards.**
This new *lesbischwul* (mixed) club and cocktail bar is open every night from 6pm. Friday night is strictly for lesbians from 10pm.

Heaven in U4

12, Schönbrunner Straße 222 (815 8307/fax 812 1395). U4 Meidling Haupstraße. **Open** 10pm-5am daily. **Admission** AS70. **Credit** AmEx, DC, MC, V.
U4 hosts a mixed gay and lesbian disco every Thursday night (11pm-6am) with three bars, two dancefloors and a darkroom. Heaven is very popular with younger 'scene' gays and lesbians. *See also chapter* **Nightlife**.

Why Not?

1, Tiefer Graben 22 (535 1158). U1, U3 Stephansplatz. **Open** 10pm-4am Thur; 10pm-5am Fri, Sat. **Admission** AS100. **Credit** AmEx, DC, MC, V.
Popular bar/disco in the centre of town. The quieter upstairs bar has a lounge area, a darkroom and is open only on Thursdays (10pm-4am), Fridays and Saturdays (till 5am). Generally younger guys go here but dykes are also welcome.

Cruising areas

Cruising and loitering outside public facilities and park areas is mostly safe and police seem to turn a blind eye to activities. The Rathauspark is the most popular turf in spring and summer – on the left-hand side as you face the Rathaus, past the fountain. Just plonk yourself on a park bench or go for a wander – you'll see and hear the paths and bushes come to life.

Throughout the year, though, a number of U-Bahn passages are well visited from noon to early evening. The Babenburger passage on the U2 line (at Burgring), the Albertina passage crossing the

Colourful co-ordination

Small but successful, the first gay pride march in Vienna was held in June 1996 and drew some 25,000 people on to the streets. Since then the city's R e g e n b o g e n p a r a d e (Rainbow Parade) has increased in size, and in 1999 an estimated 100,000 people attended as 65 groups and 20 floats gathered together on a sunny afternoon in June outside Parliament.

Led by 'Dykes on Bikes', they set off at about 5pm around the Ring on a march of solidarity. Deliciously decorated floats, camp and colourful costumes, slogans and banners were on display all the way until the **Staatsoper**. Under the motto 'We're all in the same boat', Rainbow Life and Club Creativ (a gay and lesbian association) combined forces in launching a huge float aboard a ship on the Danube.

For the landlubbers, a selection of 'scene' venues provided food and refreshments at the Künstlerhaus near Karlsplatz. Here the raging

party, organised by employees of *Rainbow Life* magazine, Cosmos travel agency and Living Room restaurant, kicked on until the wee hours.

Meanwhile on Morzinplatz the *Monument to the Victims of Fascism* (1985) on the site of the old Hotel Metropole, Gestapo HQ during the war, was converted into a memorial for victims of Aids and homophobic violence and covered in flowers.

The stage at Karlsplatz featured alternating lesbian and gay shows, well-known local artists such as Dagmar Kollar (wife of the former Mayor of Vienna) singing 'I am what I am' and the great Jackie Clune singing her hits from the 1970s and 1980s. Enthusiasm was the word of the day – and so it continued into the night, the Rainbow Night, at the **Arena**. The 2000 Rainbow Parade is on 17 June.

Rainbow Parade

7, PO Box 143 (319 4472-33/rainbow@via.at). Website: www.pride.at

Santo Spirito – *staff compose themselves for more musical mayhem. See page 214.*

ring that connects the **Staatsoper** to Café Aida (funny mixture of old Viennese, tourists, and gay men on the prowl) and the front of the Staatsoper itself, are all well-known cruising grounds.

The Venediger Au near the Big Wheel at Prater and the Schweizer Garten next to Südbahnhof are less popular and, because of other mixed trade, fairly risky.

Media

Bussi
4, Graf Starhemberggasse 9/4 (505 0742/fax 505 4941-5).
Free monthly guide with addresses, book reviews and some useful listings including a daily what's-on guide. Also has a summary page in English.

Extra
PO Box 77, Vienna 1043 (0664 278 3161) extra@magnet.at.
The most established of Vienna's gay publications, this free monthly magazine has a calendar of events, classified ads, columns, bar listings and a more political leaning than its competitors. It's available at the Villa and most other gay venues.

Rainbow Life
12, Ratschkygasse 3/4 (812 3911/fax 8123 91130) rainbow-life@gmx.net.
This monthly colour magazine, started in April 1998, contains comprehensive listings of all groups, organisations and events in Austria's gay scene. It also features reports, articles and arts reviews.

Vienna Gay Guide
The city map for gay tourists produced by Pink Advertising indicating hotels/pensions, restaurants, bars, clubs, saunas, shops and cruising areas around town. Available in most venues.
Website: www.gayguide.at

Saunas

Kaiserbründl
1, Weihburggasse 18-20 (513 3293). U1, U3 Stephansplatz/tram 1, 2. **Open** 2pm-midnight Mon-

Thur; 2pm-2am Fri, Sat; noon-midnight Sun. **Admission** AS190 (daily ticket, includes locker); AS120 after 9pm Mon-Thur. **No credit cards**.
This beautiful men's baths was built in 1870 in Moorish-style architecture and is Vienna's biggest sauna. The painter Stefan Riedl (a young, gay artist who supervised the restoration of the baths) recently took on the task of adding wall paintings alongside the hand-finished mosaics from Istanbul. There are relaxation rooms, cabins, a darkroom, a Finnish sauna, massage, a solarium and a new bar area. Although it's not as popular as it once was, it's certainly worth a visit. Mostly older guys nowadays.

Sport Sauna
8, Lange Gasse 10 (406 7156). U2 Lerchenfelder Straße. **Open** 3pm-1am daily. **Admission** AS148; AS95 under-25s. **No credit cards**.
Popular sauna for the younger crowd with steam bath, bar, videos, cabins and fitness equipment.
Website: www.sportsauna.at

Sex shops

Love Bird Erotic Shop
7, Mariahilfer Straße 72/first floor (523 7507/fax 526 2512). U3 Neubaugasse. **Open** 10am-7pm Mon-Fri. **Credit** AmEx, DC, MC, V.
A huge range of videos for sale and rent (plus viewing cabins), lubricants, condoms, poppers (legal in Austria), and a discreet mail order service.
Website: www.gay-megashop.com

Man for Man
5, Hamburgerstraße 8 (585 2064). U4 Pilgramgasse. **Open** 11am-10pm Mon-Sat. **Credit** AmEx, DC, MC, V.
Lube, condoms, gay magazines and videos.

Tiberius
7, Lindengasse 2 (tel/fax 522 0474/leather@tiberius.at). U6 Gumpendorfer Straße. **Open** 3-6.30pm Mon-Fri; 10am-3pm Sat. **Credit** AmEx, DC, MC, V.
Vienna's foremost address for leather, rubber and S&M articles. *See also chapter* **Shopping & Services**.
Website: www.tiberius.at

Media

The state it's in.

We'll be watching you: journalists outside the Hofburg, February 2000.

Austria's media has its own idiosyncrasies: in a country where a state-run classical radio station attracts enough listeners to qualify it as a major success in the high-culture world, there is a tabloid that, measured by the percentage of the population who read it, is the world's most successful.

The daily press is highly concentrated with relatively few titles, even given the small market size. Almost all daily and weekly publications receive some government subsidy (unique in the EU). There is a handful of national publications aiming for quality and a strong regional press (particularly Styria/Carinthia's *Kleine Zeitung*). Austria's most popular newspaper, the tabloid *Neue Kronen Zeitung* – the name dates from post-1945, but retains the *Krone* (crown) in an attempt to keep the monarchic flame burning – is linked with the third-ranked daily *Kurier* on distribution, advertising and printing.

Although 'question authority' is not a bumper sticker you're ever likely to see in Austria, newspapers have become a bit more aggressive in recent years as younger, more internationally aware journalists have joined their staffs. At the same time, critics say some of the ills of modern journalism have spread here: a focus on people rather than issues, too many entertainment-based stories and a fondness for 'top 10' lists.

Some Austrian publishers and broadcasters complain of being dominated by companies from Germany – there hasn't been a major book publisher in Austria since 1982. Nevertheless, there's a broad special interest and general magazine market with many publications succeeding as Austrian copies of German titles. The weekly news magazines are the best places to look for the strongest investigative journalism.

Austrian television is in a unique situation – it's the last remaining state terrestrial TV monopoly in the EU. Austria has been taken to task for this by the EU, and although there has been discussion about change for almost a decade, no one expects the laws to change in the next year or two.

The law has been changed though to allow private cable and satellite stations, and in January 2000 ATV became Austria's first private, national station on cable and satellite. ATV hopes eventually to challenge state broadcaster ÖRF as a terrestrial station. ÖRF has already had to adjust to competition from new private radio stations in recent years.

Newspapers

Bazar
Classified ads paper that comes out on Tuesdays, Thursdays and Saturdays. Weekly magazines on housing and cars are also published. Copies go on sale at 2pm on the day before publication date. Information also goes up on *Bazar*'s website about the same time.
Website: www.bazar.at

Kurier
The third most popular daily. Tends towards the right in its coverage. A mid-market publication.

Neue Kronen Zeitung
National daily with the largest circulation, reaching some 42% of the population. Readers are loyal to its long-running columnists. Clever marketing also helps – the hanging newspaper honour bags that appear around Vienna on the weekends were a *Krone* idea in the 1960s. Reactionary tabloid that echoes the opinions of its publisher, Hans Dichand.

Die Presse
A 'Black' newspaper – ie supporter of the conservative People's Party (ÖVP). Successor to the venerable *Neue Freie Presse* of imperial times. *Der Standard*'s launch triggered a shake-up and revamp.

Täglich Alles
Barely enough words to be called a tabloid, but has the second largest circulation in Austria. Good if you like to keep up on the Pope and TV programmes.

Der Standard
Salmon-coloured, loss-making national daily that is 'Red' – favours the Social Democrats. Supported by a loan from Bank Austria. Launched in 1988 it intended to follow business and politics along the lines of the *Financial Times*, but has expanded its brief since then.

Wiener Zeitung
A Viennese daily founded in 1703 – making it the oldest in the world. The paper of record for court, government and other official notices that are required to be printed. One for those who are interested in learning bureaucratic German.

WirtschaftsBlatt
Daily business and economics paper.

Weeklies

Format
A Fellner brothers' publication. Aggressive marketing, but criticised for its fluffy approach to news.

News
A cheesy sister publication to *Format*, with more pictures and a real effort to include women's breasts on a weekly basis. It does include some serious journalism and aggressive reporting (it has always taken a strong anti-Haider stance) and is the second most-read weekly (behind the pictorial *Die Ganze Woche*).

Profil
The most serious of the weekly news magazines.

Listings magazines

City
Although *Falter* is bigger and better, at AS10 to the former's AS28, *City*'s less complete listings are fine

for the basics such as finding out which English-language movies are on where.

Falter

A breath of fresh air in the staid world of the Austrian press, *Falter* is a weekly paper dealing with politics from a left-leaning standpoint and the arts and entertainment – it carries the best listings in the city. It has a socially committed agenda and fearlessly denounces such ills as institutional racism.

Others

Augustin

A monthly sold by and partly produced by homeless people for their benefit with features, listings and fiction. Its circulation and presence are increasing.

Foreign press

International newspapers are widely available at kiosks and tobacco stores in the 1st district, other central sites and Vienna's train stations. Look for the logo of **Morawa** (*see also chapter* **Shopping & Services**), the main foreign press distributor at newsstands. There's an astonishing level of hardcore porn available at most newsstands, though not at Morawa's (it's resolutely Moslem-run).

English-language press

Austria Today

Weekly English-language newspaper. Some solid news interspersed with name misspellings, incomplete entertainment listings and fluff fillers mean it's really only relevant if you're desperate for news of Austrian politics, crime and business in English, or for coverage of the UN/embassy crowds.

Television

There are two state-run national channels – ÖRF1 and ÖRF2 – a selection of German channels and cable and satellite broadcasts. The 7.30pm news is on both state channels and some 66 per cent of households with cable and satellite still tune in to ÖRF's most popular programme. It's a tradition: first the news, followed by a brief sports bulletin on ÖRF1 or society news on ÖRF2. *Gemütlich.*

ÖRF1

Its more popular broadcasts include sports, the movies at night and US serials in the afternoon. The programming department seems to have a completion fetish, so if, for example, *Rocky I* is on, you know *Rocky II, III, IV* and so on will be airing soon.

ÖRF2

Tends towards more cultural programming than ÖRF1. Besides buxom women in *Dirndls* singing their hearts out in Alpine villages and an insuffer-

able talk show or two, you can catch an opera, some classical music, a play or a decent documentary.

Cable/satellite

Telekabel is the only cable television provider in Vienna, and about half the city's households have access. Nationwide 78 per cent of homes have cable or satellite television and there are plenty of stations available, mostly from Germany. Telekabel offers a few stations in English on its regular cable and separate movie service, including CNN, NBC, BET (Black Entertainment Television), BBC World, BBC Prime and MTV (90 per cent in German).

In January 2000, ATV became the first private national television station in Austria available on cable and satellite. It broadcasts its own news, magazine and talk shows, along with cartoons, including *Pokemon*, serials and, to fill the early morning hours, fashion show footage.

There's also TIV, an amateurish, slightly eccentric station, broadcast from 9pm to 11pm daily, featuring various doyennes of the Vienna club scene such as Amina Handke.

Radio

More than 50 regional and local private radio stations have sprung up in Austria since 1995, particularly since the law was liberalised in 1997. The changes and competition have spurred ÖRF to restructure its scheduling.

On 1 February 2000 ÖRF dropped what had been the best, locally produced source of news for English speakers, Blue Danube Radio – set up for the international community when the UN moved to Vienna in 1979.

FM4, the alternative music station that Blue Danube had shared a frequency with (103.8 FM), now goes out 24-hours daily. FM4 has been toned down and broadcasts more mainstream music than previously. The English-speaking hours are currently from 1am to 2pm with English-language news on the hour from 6am to 7pm.

ORF's station Österreich 1 (92.0 FM, 87.8 FM) offers a laboured and self-indulgent mixture of classical, jazz and opera music, including live concerts and other cultural programmes. Radio Wien (89.9 FM, 95.3 FM), one of ÖRF's regional stations, gears itself to local tastes with pop, news, weather and traffic. Ö3 (99.9 FM) is a slick, commercial station with lots of adverts.

Radio Austria International (in Europe 6,155 kHz, 5,945 kHz, 13,730 kHz) is ÖRF's short-wave station designed by the government to be the voice of Austria abroad, with news, information and an English, Spanish and Russian service.

Probably the best bet for more diverse programming is Orange (94 FM), which features soul, hip hop, jazz and African music.

Music: Classical & Opera

Viennese music comes bubble-wrapped in tradition, but its standards and the range on offer are still astonishing.

The very air of Vienna pulsates in three-quarter time and visitors to the city cannot help but be caught up in a musical heritage that is evident at every turn. The list of great composers connected with this city is long, and reads like a who's who of music: Beethoven, Schubert, Haydn, Mozart, the various Straußes (*see page 227* **Getting your Straußes straight**), Mahler, Lehár – it's no wonder that, even today, classical music lives and breathes here as nowhere else on the planet. The Viennese are rightly proud of their cultural heritage and the average citizen has a high level of knowledge of and involvement in the city's vast musical menu.

Of live performances, the choices on offer on any given evening in Vienna are daunting. For opera, you can choose between the **Staatsoper**, the **Volksoper**, the **Kammeroper** or one of four independent opera companies (*Freiegruppen*), which have allied together under the umbrella name **Wiener Opernszene**.

If you prefer an orchestral concert, the **Wiener Philharmoniker** or **Wiener Symphoniker** are likely to be performing, and if you're specifically interested in early and Baroque music, the **Concentus Musicus** conducted by Nikolaus Harnoncourt is at your service. High-calibre chamber ensembles such as the **Alban Berg Quartet** also call Vienna their home, and the city positively basks in solo recitals by top-notch instrumentalists and singers. Vienna also has a small but established musical comedy scene, with **Theater an der Wien, Raimund Theater, Etablissement Ronacher**, the **Metropol** and **Theater Akzent** all serving up original fare as well as German translations of Broadway and West End hits.

Despite the high quality and quantity of music available, who and what you actually see in Vienna are still sometimes outshone by where. Each of the city's major venues is in some way historically, architecturally or culturally significant – often all three. The **Musikverein**, for example, built by imperial decree during the great expansion of Vienna in the 1860s and 1870s, has perfect acoustics, and hosted the première of

Brahms' *Alto Rhapsody*. The **Konzerthaus**, **Schloßtheater Schönbrunn** and the **Palais Pálffy** are just a few of the other venues with similar pedigree.

This is not to say, however, that every performance is a gem. The downside to the historical awe accorded Vienna and its music is a certain complacency that sets in from time to time, a feeling of 'we are because we have always been'. Viennese complacency can also manifest itself in many other ways, from a lacklustre performance served up as 'good enough for the punters', to a feeling from the cloakroom staff that 'one should be grateful just for the experience'. Then again, maybe we should.

Tickets & information

Keep an eye out for the information columns scattered all over the city – they're covered with posters for upcoming events. Information on programmes is also available from tourist offices and in listings magazines such as *Falter*. Tickets can be bought in advance from the outlets listed below. The **Klangbogen** organisation, promoters of the Easter (**Osterklang**) and Summer (**Klangbogen**) festival programmes, also handles tickets through the year for a range of groups, especially **Wiener Opernszene** companies.

Vienna hosts festivals with classical music and opera throughout the year. *See chapter* **By Season**.

Österreichischer Bundestheaterkassen

State Theatre Booking Office
1, Hanuschgasse 3 (5144 42960/42959). U1, U2, U4 Karlsplatz/tram 1, 2, D, J. **Open** 8am-6pm Mon-Fri; 9am-2pm Sat; 9am-noon Sun. **Credit** AmEx, DC, JCB, MC, V

This official office has tickets to the Staatsoper, Volksoper, Burgtheater and Akademietheater. Tickets usually go on sale seven days before the date of performance. They can also be booked by telephone *(513 1513)*, with a credit card, from six days before a performance. The credit lines are open 10am-9pm daily and English is spoken. *Website: www.oebthv.gv.at/*

*The recently renovated **Konzerthaus**.*

Volksoper last-minute tickets

Tickets are available at 50% below the normal price from one hour before performances begin. They can be bought only from the Volksoper evening box office, *Währinger Straße 78 (51 444)*. **Credit** AmEx, DC, JCB, MC, V.

Wiener Staatsoper last-minute tickets

These can be bought only at the main ticket office, at *1, Hanuschgasse 3. U1, U2, U4 Karlsplatz/tram 1, 2, D, J* and from the information office in the arcades at the Staatsoper, from 9am-noon at a standard price of AS400, depending on availability. For information on last-minute ticket availability call *(5144 42950)*. **Credit** AmEx, DC, JCB, MC, V.

Wien-Ticket

6, Linke Wienzeile 6 (58 885). U1, U2, U4 Karlsplatz (exit Secession). **Open** 10am-7pm daily. *Credit cards* 3-6pm daily. **Credit** AmEx, DC, MC, V.
This office has tickets for the Theater an der Wien, Raimund Theater and Etablissement Ronacher.

Wien-Ticket Pavilion

U1, U2, U4 Karlsplatz/tram 1, 2, D, J. **Open** 10am-7pm daily. **Credit** AmEx, DC, MC, V.
This booth is located next to the Staatsoper. It supplies tickets for all venues.

Main venues
Orchestral, opera & operetta

Jugendstiltheater

14, Baumgartner Höhe 1 (911 2492-93/tickets through Klangbogen 42 717). Bus 48a. **Box office** *evening* from 1 hour before performance. **Tickets** AS180-480; AS150 students. **Credit** AmEx, DC, MC, V.
Located in the grounds of the city mental hospital, this Otto Wagner-designed masterpiece has fallen out of favour with most of the independent opera companies who use it, because of lack of facilities, amenities and just plain distance: a long and lonely bus ride plus a walk up a hill does not draw the crowds, and the seats are hard and squeaky. This is a pity, as the acoustics are magnificent.

Kammeroper

1, Fleischmarkt 24 (512 0100/box office 513 0100). U1, U4 Schwedenplatz/tram 1, 2. **Box office** noon-6pm Mon-Fri. **Tickets** AS120-380. **Credit** AmEx, DC, MC, V.
Ruled with an iron hand from its inception in 1953 by founder Hans Gabor, the Kammeroper, dedicated to smaller-scale opera productions, seems to have floundered a bit since his death in 1994. Production values and musical standards during the regular season range from fair to dreadful, rising sharply for the summer season, which is usually held amid the mock-Roman ruins in the park of Schönbrunn palace (owing to repair work expected to be completed in 2002, recent seasons have taken place indoors in the **Schloßtheater Schönbrunn**). More care is taken with casting these Mozart extravaganzas than is visible during the winter and the budget also seems beefier than normal (the performances regularly sell out and getting tickets can be difficult).
The permanent home of the Kammeroper is a tiny Jugendstil theatre on the Fleischmarkt in the heart of old Vienna, which is reached by way of what looks like a side alley and is easy to miss, so leave time for getting lost and asking directions. Architecturally speaking, the small space brings the action up close and personal and is, theoretically, the ideal venue for young up-and-comings to strut their stuff. Besides the Kammeroper itself, Gabor also instituted the Belvedere International Singing Competition, held every summer, usually in July. Recent years have seen a steady decline in the competition, reaching an all-time low in 1999 when participants and audiences alike were scandalised by low standards and the obviously biased attitude of the jury. So much for the future of opera.

Konzerthaus

3, Lothringerstraße 20 (712 1211/information 7124 6860/tickets 712 1211/fax 712 2872). U4 Stadtpark/tram D. **Box office** 9am-7.45pm Mon-Fri; 9am-1pm Sat. **Tickets** AS150-1,400. **Credit** AmEx, DC, JCB, MC, V.
As if the **Musikverein** were not enough, the Konzerthaus offers an additional three concert halls, the Großersaal, Mozartsaal and Schubertsaal, which will be joined in late 2000 by yet another hall which

has been built on the lower level of the building and will be used for avant-garde productions. This forms part of a AS20 million renovation of the Konzerthaus that has already included a much-needed and successful facelift for the main hall. The **Wiener Symphoniker** and **Concentus Musicus** both call this place home, but its offerings are not all classical music. Not as stuffy as the Musikverein, the Konzerthaus sometimes marches to a different drummer – even one with a definite rock rhythm.

Musikverein

1, Bösendorferstraße 12 (505 8190). U1, U2, U4 Karlsplatz/tram 1, 2, D, J. **Box office** *9am-7.30pm Mon-Fri; 9am-5pm Sat.* **Tickets** *AS150-1,400; standing room AS30-50.* **Credit** AmEx, DC, JCB, MC, V.

If you've ever joined the millions worldwide who watch the annual New Year's Day concert of the Vienna Philharmonic on TV, you've already seen their unofficial main home, the lavishly opulent Musikverein. The magnificent main hall of this building is more than just a pretty face, though: it's also an acoustical miracle. The ceiling above its 1,750 seats is not joined to the walls, but instead hangs freely to allow for better vibration; there is also an entire room underneath that polished wooden floor for the same reason. Concertgoers may wish to remember this if they're ever tempted to complain about the stifling heat on a summer's day – any modernisations that might interfere with that perfect sound are strictly prohibited. The smaller 600-seat Brahmssaal is no less ornate, and is used for chamber concerts and recitals. Tickets to one of the Saturday afternoon or Sunday morning Vienna Philharmonic concerts are among the hottest in town, and as for the famous 1 January event, you must have your written request for the next year in by 2 January. Like the **Staatsoper**, the Musikverein offers standing room tickets, but here you can buy them at the normal box office up to three weeks in advance. Seats that cost around AS150-200 have only a limited view.

Odeon

2, Taborstraße 10 (tickets through Osterklang & Klangbogen 42 717). U1, U4 Schwedenplatz/tram N, 21. **Box office** *10am-6pm Mon-Fri.* **Tickets** AS150-1,250. **Credit** AmEx, DC, JCB, MC, V.

Used for a whole variety of performances and events from classical concerts to raves, the Odeon is little more than an empty shell of a building, waiting for proper seating and a stage. Now the chosen site for performances of the Neue Oper Wien, part of the **Wiener Opernszene** independent opera group, it's not plush, but does the trick.

Radiokulturhaus

4, Argentinierstraße 30a (5017). U1 Taubstummengasse. **Box office** *10am-7pm Mon-Thur; 2-7pm Fri; 4pm, 5pm Sat, Sun.* **Café open** *8am-midnight daily.* **Tickets** AS40-390; student discounts. **Credit** AmEx, DC, MC, V.

Opulent surroundings and perfect acoustics: the magnificent **Musikverein**.

A three-part complex housing the Großer Sendesaal, home of the Vienna Radio Symphony Orchestra, the Radio Café and the Klangtheater Ganzohr ('all ears'). The last of these houses a permanent audio exhibit called *die Vier Jahreszeiten* (the Four Seasons), honouring Herbert von Karajan and Antonio Vivaldi and featuring the sounds of nature. There are 'performances' every hour on the hour, 10am-7pm Mon-Thur, 2-7pm Fri, 4pm, 5pm only Sat, Sun and holidays; tickets cost AS110 (AS95 students; group rates available) and reservations are required. The Großer Sendesaal hosts everything from classical, jazz and New Age music to cabaret, exhibitions and spoken theatre. The Radio Café, open every day, is badly designed and has neither old-world charm nor modern flair, but offers an eclectic mix of evening entertainment in a casual atmosphere.

Schloßtheater Schönbrunn

13, Schloß Schönbrunn (894 6690-51). U4 Schönbrunn. **Box office** *evening* from 1 hour before performance. **Tickets** AS120-380. **No credit cards.**

Opened in 1749 to entertain the court of Maria Theresia, this is the oldest working theatre in Vienna, and the closest you'll ever come to the inside of a gilded music box. It's used in summer for performances by the **Kammeroper**, when the open-air venue of the palace's fake-historic 'ruins' are not available, and also for a Johann Strauß dinner-theatre event titled 'A Soirée with Prince Orlovsky'. During the regular autumn-spring season it's rented out to a variety of ensembles and interested parties, including the nearby Hochschule für Musik und Darstellende Kunst (University for Music and the Performing Arts), which uses it for theme evenings and full productions.

Volksoper

9, Währingerstraße 78 (51 444). U6 Währingerstraße-Volksoper/tram 40, 41, 42. **Box office** *8am-6pm Mon-Fri; 9am-noon Sun.* **Tickets** AS50-900; *standing room* AS20-30. **Credit** AmEx, DC, JCB, MC, V.

The traditional role of the Volksoper (literally, people's opera) has been as Vienna's flagship operetta house. In 1996, however, it was merged under one administration with the august Staatsoper, an arrangement that had both advantages and drawbacks. The **Staatsoper** got a good place to try out fledgling stars without submitting them to the pressure of a 'Staatsoper' debut, while the Volksoper repertoire was expanded to include more opera and a few more star-studded evenings. The orchestras, however, remained strictly separate, which meant that the Volksoper got the short end of the stick musically, and the **Wiener Philharmoniker** did not have to go 'slumming'. They have now separated once again, but some changes for the better have remained. Rather than reverting to its straightforward former diet, the Volksoper has maintained its operatic bent, so that you're now as likely to find *Gianni Schicchi* or *La Bohème* on the bill as *Wiener Blut* or Franz Lehár's *Lustige Witwe* (*The Merry Widow*). It has come to specialise in modern productions of traditional operas, as well as interesting

*The **Staatsoper** – originally dubbed the 'stone turtle' by disgruntled locals.*

works from all eras that the Staatsoper for some reason can't or won't do. The Volksoper ensemble seems to have more rehearsal time and fewer 'stars for the evening' than their much grander colleagues across the city, which tends to add to rather than subtract from the final result. Then, of course, there is always the operetta, which is entrenched in the very stones of the building and is still the Volksoper's national and international calling card. Added to all that there is a healthy dose of musicals, topped off with a few dance evenings through the year.

The house itself is more impressive from outside than from within, and the red plush upholstery is belied by a stark, plain, almost astringent interior design. The acoustic is also somewhat dry, especially on the sides, and no one should think of sitting in the back row of a box – you'll hear little and see nothing. It is, though, more affordable than the Staatsoper and easier to get into, and the standard is generally high, even if the occasional evening disappoints. The 72 standing room tickets (balcony or stalls) are a real bargain.

Staatsoper

State Opera
1, Opernring 2 (5144 42960/2959). U1, U2, U4 Karlsplatz/tram 1, 2, D, J. **Box office** from 1 hour before performance. **Tickets** AS140-2,450 A (premières or star performances); AS120-2,150 B (regular performances); AS70-1,250 C (ballet). *Standing room* AS30-50. **Credit** AmEx, DC, JCB, MC, V.
The Viennese tend to view anything new with distrust and disapproval, which then turns into grudging acceptance. The State Opera House, or Staatsoper,

is no exception. Built in 1861-9 according to plans by the architects August Siccardsburg and Eduard van der Null, the finished, neo-Renaissance-style structure initially met with ferocious criticism from the local public, who called it the 'sunken crate' and the 'stone turtle'. Siccardsburg never designed again and died of a weakened heart; Van der Null, not to be outdone, killed himself. Neither lived to see the opera house officially opened, on 25 May 1869, with a performance of *Don Giovanni*. The building would eventually be taken to their hearts by the citizenry, however, to the extent that after 1945, when the Staatsoper had been almost completely destroyed, the Viennese painstakingly reconstructed it in work that took three years longer to complete than the original project of the 1860s. During the reconstruction, the Staatsoper company took up residence in the **Theater an der Wien**, where the legendary Vienna Mozart Ensemble came into being. As a sign of gratitude to the Theater an der Wien, where *Fidelio* had been premièred, the Staatsoper reopened on 5 November 1955 with a performance of that same opera, conducted by Karl Böhm.

Many men have overseen this pinnacle of musical and operatic achievement over the years – great conductors such as Richard Strauss, Karl Böhm, Clemens Krauss and Herbert von Karajan. It was, however, Gustav Mahler, director from 1897 to 1907, who left the greatest mark on the Staatsoper, and simultaneously changed opera itself in ways that are now taken for granted. Dimming the audience lighting during the performance, shortening intermissions to 15-20 minutes, and seating late arrivals only after the prologue or first intermission were all radical innovations brought in by Mahler in an attempt

introduced 'standing room pass', available for AS800 from the box office at Hanuschgasse 3, enables you to purchase standing room tickets through normal ticket sales, but not after noon on the day of a performance and only one per customer. For true aficionados and students who want to follow the action with a score, there are also specially designed desks with lights (ask for a *partiturplatz*). They cost AS140, but the view of the stage is limited.

TOURS
Tours of the Staatsoper building are provided daily, but for exact times, check the sign that is prominently displayed by the starting point for the tours – on the Herbert-von-Karajan-Platz side. Tours are available in six languages (English, French, German, Italian, Japanese and Spanish) and last about 35 minutes; tickets cost AS60 per person.

Other venues

Arnold Schönberg Center
3, Palais Fanto, Zaunergasse 1-3 (712 1888-50).
Tram D. Open 10am-5pm Mon-Wed, Fri; 10am-7.30pm Thur. **Tickets** AS180. **No credit cards**.
Opened in April 1998, the non-profit-making Schönberg Center encompasses an archive, a library, a concert hall, an exhibition hall and seminar rooms. Its mission is to promote interest in and knowledge of Arnold Schönberg and the Viennese school of the early twentieth century, and related contemporary music. The 204-seat hall is used for a whole plethora of events, with a standard entrance fee of AS180.

Bösendorfersaal
4, Graf Starhemberggasse 14 (504 6651). Tram 62, 65. **Box office** 9am-4.30pm concert days only.
Tickets free-AS270. **No credit cards**.
A permanent exhibition of pianos gives you something to do in the intermission at this small concert venue. The room has nice acoustics, but poorly placed columns and an oddly low ceiling make for unfortunate sight lines. It hosts a variety of small recitals by performers from students to professionals, which all have one thing in common – great pianos.

Herbert von Karajan Centrum
1, Kärntner Ring 4 (50 600-100/shop 50 600-200).
U1, U2, U4 Karlsplatz/tram 1, 2, D, J. **Open** 9am-5pm Mon-Fri; *shop* 10am-6pm Mon-Fri. **Tickets** free.
Credit AmEx, DC, JCB, MC, V.
Just across the Ring from the Staatsoper, the centre has an ultra-modern shop fitted with two high-tech research modules that allow you to sit in comfort while scrolling through all the audio and video clips ever made by Karajan; if you think you've missed something, ever-helpful archivists will point you in the right direction. In a slightly older style, the centre also boasts a concert hall that was built by Emperor Franz Josef for his mistress Katharina Schratt, part of the connecting Palais Königswarte, a protected national monument. A range of events is held there, from recitals and chamber concerts to discussions and book presentations. Admission to many events is free, but they are often for invited

to make the performance rather than the audience the centre of attention. A special concert is still performed in Mahler's honour in the Staatsoper every year on 18 May, the anniversary of his death.

The present-day Staatsoper has one of the largest opera repertoires in the world (some 70 different productions each year), achieved thanks to a combination of a long season (1 Sept-30 June) and a rotation system that calls for a different opera every day of the week. It hosts only opera and ballet, with a select few exceptions: Strauß Jr's *Die Fledermaus*, Léhar's *Merry Widow*, the 18 May Mahler memorial concert and the **Opernball**. The mammoth proportions of the Staatsoper output mean there are occasional performances that seem to go ahead under the motto, 'when in doubt, sing out – and for God's sake don't try to act, just die in the light'. Nevertheless, the Viennese public is nothing if not generous (or maybe they're all tourists), and almost every performance ends with bravos and extra curtain calls. The **Wiener Philharmoniker**, under the stage name *das Orchester der Wiener Staatsoper*, plays in the pit.

Good seats at the Staatsoper go quickly. Tickets and prices are divided into three categories (A, B, C), according to the type of performance. Quite often the only way to get a ticket is by buying one from the touts who hang around the box office. Try for one of the 567 bargain standing-room places. You can normally only get them from one hour before curtain, at the window marked *stehplätze*, and queues can be long. Once inside, tie your scarf around the rail to mark your place. The view from the standing room area at the back of the stalls is excellent, but it's worth the exhausting climb to the gallery for the best sights and sounds in the house. The recently guests only. The mix of state-of-the-art technology and old-world beauty is a fitting tribute to the man who to this day is still responsible for two-thirds of all classical CDs sold by Deutsche Grammaphon.

Sophiensäle

3, Marxergasse 17 (522 2770). U3, U4 Landstraße/Wien Mitte. **Box office** from 1 hour before performance. **Tickets** events are organised by different promoters, check local listings. **Credit** depends on promoter.
First constructed in 1838 as a Russian steam bath, this building was redesigned in 1845 as a combination swimming pool/dance hall by none other than Van der Nüll and Siccardsburg, who went on to design the **Staatsoper**. During the Nazi era the Sophiensäle was used as a collection-point for the deportation of Jews; post-war it was made into a ballroom, and is now under renovation and used for clubs, musicals, concerts and dance performances in the **Festwochen** summer festival. Its main hall is gorgeous, as is the smaller blue room, but the rest still needs a lot of work, and the exterior is downright ugly. Once again, acoustics are very good (probably thanks to the empty pool underneath).

Ensembles & associations

Alban Berg Quartet

1, Lothringerstraße 20 (in the Konzerthaus building) (712 1211).
In a city saturated with music of all kinds, an Alban Berg Quartet concert is still an event not to be missed. Günter Pichler, Gerhard Schulz, Thomas Kakuska and Valentin Erben have presented the string quartet repertoire, old and new, with an unsurpassable combination of intelligence and intuition, technical perfection and artistic freedom since the early 1970s, and are still going strong.

Concentus Musicus Wien

1, Lothringerstraße 20 (in the Konzerthaus buiding) (712 1211).
One of the world's première ensembles for *Altemusik*, early to Baroque music from the thirteenth to the eighteenth centuries. It's impossible to separate the Concentus Musicus from its founder and musical guru, Nikolaus Harnoncourt: together, the man and the group have succeeded in making once-dusty and apparently boring Baroque music come alive again, on original instruments. Harnoncourt turned 70 in 1999, and the Concentus 46, but their sound gets younger all the time.

Jeunesses Musicales Austria

1, Lothringerstraße 20 (in the Konzerthaus building) (710 3616/fax 710 3616-17). U4 Stadtpark/tram D. 1, Bösendorfer Straße 12 (in the Musikverein building) (710 3616/fax 710 3616-17). U1, U2, U4 Karlsplatz/tram 1, 2, D, J. **Open** 9am-7.30pm Mon-Fri. **Tickets** AS200-450 over-26s; AS65-300 under-26s. **Credit** DC, MC, V.
Celebrating its 50th anniversary season in 1999, this is Austria's only nationwide music promoter, organising about 300 concerts a year. Its initial aim was simply to provide music for young people, but its concert programmes, presented at the **Musikverein** or the **Konzerthaus**, are of exceptional quality. The only problem may be getting tickets – they tend to sell out quickly.

Radio Symphonieorchester Wien

Vienna Radio Symphony Orchestra
Radiokulturhaus, 4, Argentinier Straße 30a (5017 0377).
The Vienna RSO celebrated its 30th birthday in September 1999 with a programme chosen by present conductor-in-chief Dennis Russell Davies that included the Austrian première of Heinz Karl Gruber's new trumpet concerto, and Prokofiev's rarely played Sixth Symphony, from 1945-7. A penchant for the new, the unknown or the almost forgotten is the RSO's claim to fame and, at the same time, perhaps what keeps the orchestra from making a bigger name for itself. The RSO has performed the Vienna premières of works by the crème de la crème of contemporary composers such as Henze, Krenek, Ligeti, Penderecki, Rihm, Cerha and Martin. As with most radio orchestras, a high level of musicianship combined with a 'this is being taped' awareness makes for excellent performances. It can be found on its home turf in the **Radiokulturhaus** or in the **Musikverein** or **Konzerthaus**.

Wiener Opernszene

1, Klangbogen, Stadiongasse 9 (42 717/fax 400 099-8410). U2 Rathaus/tram D. **Open** 10am-6pm Mon-Fri. **Tickets** AS180-480; AS150 students. **Credit** AmEx, DC, JCB, MC, V.
Tired of fighting to stay afloat individually and having to vie against one another for their slice of the government-subsidised pie, several *Freiegruppen* or independent companies on Vienna's opera scene have banded together (loosely) in this association for more leverage. They maintain their individuality in terms of management and artistic integrity, but now share a common ticket service and mailing list (**Klangbogen**), which is also the organisational centre for Vienna's biggest summer music festival. Of the Opernszene companies, **Neue Oper Wien** gets the biggest chunk of subsidy, and spends it wisely, with an accent on opera theatre in the best sense of that concept. Its 1994 production of Berg's *Lulu* was exceptional, and it also managed to scoop the Staatsoper with the Austrian première of Benjamin Britten's *Billy Budd* in 1996. **NetZZeit** and **Musikwerkstatt Wien** are the new kids on the block, and are still working on long-term structures, which will move them away from their previous hand-to-mouth existence. NetZZeit showed promise with its offering of Ernst Krenek's *Der Glockenturm* in 1999. The smallest of the independent opera groups, **Taschenoper** (Pocket Opera), actually folded in 1996, but another group has started up with the same name. Their 1999 debut production of *Satyricon* by Bruno Maderna was well executed, but not particularly inventive. None of the companies has a permanent home but performs at various venues including the **Odeon**, **Jugendstiltheater** and **Sophiensäle**. Ticket prices are low enough to be a real bargain if a performance is good

Getting your Straußes straight

How well do you know your Straußes? The following is a brief guide to one of the most prolific names in music:

Johann Strauß Senior (1804-49) was well known in his time as a composer and conductor, but is now most famous for two things: having the title of *Hofballmusikdirektor* (director of the imperial dance orchestra) created especially for him, and fathering little Johann Junior. The best-known and, in Vienna, most beloved piece of his own music is the *Radetzky March*, which was written in celebration of one of the Habsburgs' most successful (and bloodthirsty) military commanders.

Johann Strauß, Sohn (or Junior, 1825-99, *pictured*), is the one you should go for when faced with any tricky Strauß question – he wrote 16 operettas, over 150 waltzes, and more than 300 other dances. This is the man who was known as 'The Waltz King' – the one whose picture has been painted on Austrian Airlines jets, the one who has a coffee named after him. His father forbade him to go into music, but with his mum's support Johann Jr did it anyway – and became the world's first modern musical superstar.

He made the dance music of Biedermeier Vienna universally popular, and his ten-year European tour (1856-66) produced 'Strauß hysteria', which was repeated on his American tour in 1872. Johann Jr is perhaps best commemorated by his masterpiece *Die Fledermaus*, but other important works are the operettas *Zigeunerbaron*, *Wiener Blut* and *Eine Nacht in Venedig*, as well as, of course, *An der schönen blauen Donau*, the Blue Danube Waltz, the unofficial Austrian national anthem.

There were two other Strauß boys: **Josef** (1827-70) was co-director with his brother Johann Jr of that Strauß touring orchestra, while **Eduard** (1835-1916) was the youngest Strauß son, which is his only claim to fame (this is the sort of family that got Freud started years later).

Richard Strauss (1864-1949) was born in Garmisch, Germany, and although not Austrian, had strong connections with both Vienna and Salzburg. He was one of the founders of the Salzburg Festival (with Hugo von Hofmannsthal and Max Reinhardt) and Vienna Staatsoper director from 1919 to 1924. His most recognisable tune is the main theme of *Also*

Sprach Zarathustra, inescapable ever since Stanley Kubrick's film *2001*, but aficionados would probably prefer to cite his operas, *Der Rosenkavalier*, *Elektra*, *Salome* or *Ariadne auf Naxos*, or his brilliant *Lieder* such as *Befreit* or *The Four Last Songs*. One of his favourite hangouts was Café Griensteidl, where he met his friends Hofmannsthal, Gustav and Alma Mahler, and Oscar Kokoschka.

Last but certainly not least is the silver-age operetta composer **Oscar Straus** (1870-1954). His biggest success came in 1907, with the operetta *Ein Walzertraum*, but his music is still very popular in Vienna today. Straus' 1908 operetta *Der Tapfere Soldat* was based on *Arms and the Man* by George Bernard Shaw; the translated version, *The Chocolate Soldier*, later became a hit on Broadway with its lovely song *My Hero*. Forced to emigrate to the USA in the 1930s, Oscar Straus returned to Austria at the end of World War II.

and not too painful a waste of money if you end up leaving in the intermission.

Wiener Philharmoniker

Musikverein, 1, Bösendorfer Straße 12 (505 5625).
Founded in 1842, the 140-member Vienna Philharmonic Orchestra has financed and managed itself since 1908. This is important, as it allows the orchestra the freedom to make decisions unmolested by pesky details such as civil rights or fashionable ideas of equality: it gave up AS2.5 million in state subsidies in order to retain its right to run things as it sees fit, including remaining virtually an all-boys club (so far, women have only been heard from in the Vienna Philharmonic as harpists). The distinctive sound and impeccable musicianship of this world-class ensemble certainly need no adjustment. As well as presenting a full season of concerts every year between September and mid-June at the **Musikverein**, including the traditional New Year's Day Concert, the Philharmonic performs each summer at the Salzburg Festival, tours widely, and is the house orchestra of the **Staatsoper**, under the alternative title of Orchester der Wiener Staatsoper. The logistics of these endeavours would stretch the resources of any orchestra, and conductors have been known to complain that they never have the same personnel in front of them from one rehearsal to the next. Still, especially when playing 'their' music (Mahler, Strauß, Mozart), the Vienna Philharmonic is unsurpassed.

Wiener Sängerknaben

The Vienna Boys' Choir
2, Obere Augartenstraße 1 (in the Augarten Palace) (216 3942).
These little cherubs in their blue and white sailor suits are the darlings of Austria, not to mention one of Vienna's most valuable exports. The boys' musicianship and general professionalism are at an indisputably high level, but at times they can seem a bit jaded – more red-eyed than rosy-cheeked. It's scarcely any wonder that, with their schedule: you can hear them at the **Burgkapelle** every Sunday and religious holiday at 9.15am, except between 10 July and mid-September, and at the **Konzerthaus** at 3.30pm on Fridays in May, June, September and October.

Wiener Symphoniker

6, Lehargasse 11 (589 7951).
Internationally somewhat in the shadow of the Philharmoniker, Vienna's 'second' orchestra nevertheless has a long and impressive history. It performed the world premières of Bruckner's Ninth Symphony (1903), Schönberg's *Gurrelieder* (1913), Ravel's piano concerto for the left hand (1932) and Richard Strauss' orchestral suite from *Der Rosenkavalier* (1946), to name but a few, and Leonard Bernstein and Lorin Maazel both made their Vienna debuts with this orchestra. The Vienna Symphony presents some 200 concerts per year, mostly in the **Konzerthaus** and the **Musikverein**, including three concert series of its own, a chamber music series and concerts organised by other promoters. It also tours extensively and serves as the festival and opera orchestra for the summer Bregenz Festival.

Wiener Tschuschenkapelle

22, Tamariskengasse 102 (283 5864).
The word *tschuschen* was originally a derogatory term used by the Viennese to describe people from the Balkans, which was expanded in true Viennese fashion to include just about anyone from an eastern country. The five-member Wiener Tschuschenkapelle turns this derogatory idea on its head with a mix of oriental, Slavic, gypsy, classical and Viennese music that celebrates a truly multicultural existence. It performs at a wide variety of venues.

Musical theatres

Etablissement Ronacher

1, Seilerstätte 9 (5141 1207). Tram 1, 2.
Box office from one hour before performance.
Tickets AS310-1,200. **Credit** AmEx, DC, MC, V.
Once upon a time this was Vienna's most glamorous theatre, and counted music-hall star Josephine Baker among its bevy of beauties. After a brief stint as a restaurant, the Ronacher jumped in as a stand-in for the **Burgtheater** when that building was destroyed in World War II. Recently given a much needed facelift, the Ronacher is still part of the Vereinigte Bühnen Wien, but is currently being rented out on an occasional basis for a variety of (mostly musical) events.

Metropol Theater

17, Hernalser Hauptstraße 55/Geblergasse 50 (4077 7407). U6 Alser Straße/tram 43. **Box office** 10am-8pm Mon-Fri and concert days. **Tickets** AS100-400.
Credit AmEx, DC, MC, V.
Various styles of entertainment are offered here, with one common trait – good value for money. A typical month might include gigs by New Age guru Gandalt, a musical gala featuring stars from the hit shows in town, evenings of Viennese cabaret and star-quality drag artistes on tour from Paris. A brilliant translation of *Guys and Dolls* into Viennese dialect was sold out every night. Also popular was the satirical show *Forbidden Musical*, spoofing Vienna-based musicals.

Raimund Theater

6, Wallgasse 18 (59 977). U6 Gumpendorfer Straße.
Box office 10am-1pm, 2-6pm, daily. **Tickets** AS310-1,200. **Credit** AmEx, DC, MC, V.
The Raimund opened in 1893 as a theatre for the middle classes in what was then an outer suburb of Vienna. Only spoken drama was presented until 1908, when director Wilhelm Karczag introduced opera and operetta. Its most popular and historic production was *das Dreimäderlhaus*, a compilation of works by Schubert. The Raimund had its heyday between 1948 and 1978, under the direction of Rudolf Marik. In 1987 it merged with **Etablissement Ronacher** and **Theater an der Wien** to form the *Vereinigte Bühnen Wien* or 'United Stages of Vienna', pooling the resources of these three musical-comedy theatres, and with a joint ticketing system and price structure.

Theater an der Wien

6, Linke Wienzeile 6 (58 830/tickets 5883 0265). U1, U2, U4 Karlsplatz. **Open** 10am-7pm daily; *box office*

*Opera for the people: the **Volksoper** specialises in modern productions of traditional operas.*

10am-1pm, 2-6pm, daily. **Tickets** AS310-1,200.
Credit AmEx, DC, MC, V.
This 1,200-seat treasure is most famous for hosting the premières of Beethoven's *Fidelio* (1805), Strauß Jr's *Die Fledermaus* (1874) and *Wiener Blut* (1899). Beethoven actually lived in the theatre during preparations for the presentation of his only opera. Since its opening in June 1801 the theater has also seen many performances of the *Magic Flute* (if not the première of that piece, as is often claimed), and it became the temporary home of the Vienna State Opera following World War II while the **Staatsoper** was being restored. Today it is part of the *Vereinigte Bühnen Wien*, the company that premièred the wildly popular German-language versions of *Cats, The Phantom of the Opera* and *Kiss of the Spider Woman*, which uses it mainly as a venue for big-scale musicals. Beginning with *Freudiana* in 1990, the company has also presented its own productions, including *Tanz der Vampire*, a musical version of Roman Polanski's film *Dance of the Vampires*, directed by Polanski himself to a score by Meatloaf-collaborator Jim Steinman. Star opera director Harry Kupfer of the Berlin Komische Oper has taken charge of two productions, *Elisabeth* and *Mozart*. The excellent natural acoustics of Theater an der Wien are wasted on the often over-amplified modern musical. The hall is still put to good use for at least some classical works when the **Festwochen** and **Klangbogen** festivals take over the theatre from May to September with a range of

opera and operetta productions. The cheapest seats in the house have only a limited view.

Traditional Vienna

If you're looking for the definitive performance of *Eine Kleine Nachtmusik*, don't bother with these shows, but they're a good opportunity to get off your aching feet for an hour and enjoy some nice tunes in beautiful surroundings. Their standard varies, but those listed here are the most popular.

Deutschordenskloster 'Sala Terrena'

1, Singerstraße 7 (tel/fax 911 9077). U1, U3 Stephansplatz. **Box office** 10am-9pm Thur, Sat, Sun. Concert times 7.30pm Thur, Sun; 5.30pm Sat. **Tickets** AS350-450; AS250 students. **Credit** MC, V.
Mozart concerts are performed here year round in concert dress rather than in period costumes, but this newly renovated 50-seat jewel, part of the church and cloister of the Order of the Teutonic Knights doesn't need other decoration.

Hofburg: Festsaal, Zeremoniensaal & Redoutensaal

1, Heldenplatz (Festsaal & Zeremoniensaal); Josefsplatz (Redoutensaal) (587 2552/fax 587 4397). U3 Herrengasse. **Concerts** May-Oct 8.30-10pm Tue, Thur, Sat. **Tickets** AS450. **Credit** MC, V.
By far the highest level of this sort of thing available – performers from the Staatsoper and

Having a ball – '*Alles Waltzer!*'

An ancient tribal ritual is re-enacted every year in Vienna to the pulsating rhythms of… Strauß. However old and steeped in tradition it may be, Vienna's ball season is an integral part of the city's social fabric. Each year there are over 300 balls to choose from between 11 November and late June.

For those actually going to a ball, a visit to dance school is de rigueur. Even in the Nintendo age, many Viennese teenagers attend one of the city's 30 odd schools to learn the basics. A beginners' course of ten lessons can be taken for as little as AS1,000.

Biggest, most expensive and most celebrated of these bashes is the **Opernball** (Opera Ball), held on the Thursday before Ash Wednesday at the Staatsoper. Also known as the *künstlerball* or artists' ball, this is the one that draws the stars – especially when they're guests of construction magnate and social climber Richard Lugner and his wife Christine, who have brought Sophia Loren, Faye Dunaway and Fergie to the Staatsoper floor. Entrance costs AS2,900, renting a table for six to eight people AS80,000, and a private box AS200,000. With around 5,000 people in attendance, you're sure to be poked, prodded and stepped on. The Viennese waltz to the left, and since few if any of the international guests even attempt this, chaos reigns on the floor. This is a snob fest, a 'see and be seen' extravaganza. Many believe the money raised goes to charity, but the AS30 million it generates goes into the Staatsoper's already heavily subsidised coffers. This is one reason for the demonstrations that take place outside every year in protest at this blatant display of recycled money and privilege.

Other particularly traditional balls include the **Philharmonikerball** at the Musikverein, the posh **Technikerball** at the Hofburg (invitation only), and the **Kaiserball** (Emperor's Ball) in the Hofburg on New Year's Eve and attended by the 'crème de la crème'. Less elite balls include the **Kaffesiederball** (Café Brewers' Ball), the **Zuckerbäckerball** (Confectioners' Ball), the **Jägerball** (Hunters' Ball), where revellers wear national costume rather than tail coats) and the **Bonbonball** (Candy Ball) at the Konzerthaus, when balloons filled with candies burst over the crowd at midnight.

There are also more socially conscious balls such as the **Regenbogenball** (Gay & Lesbian Rainbow Ball), the **Life Ball**, an event benefiting Aids charities, and the **Ball der Straßenzeitung Augustiner**, hosted by the *Augustiner* newspaper produced and sold by the homeless.

At traditional balls dress is formal, and the ticket price and the venue will give some indication of exactly how dressed up you need to be. Others tend to be much more laid-back. The **Mauerblümchenball** (Wallflower Ball) prides itself on a 'come as you are' dress code, suggesting beige and grey as best colours for 'blending in', while at the **Ball des schlechten Geschmacks** (Bad Taste Ball) just about any thing goes.

The dates of the individual balls vary from year to year. Many are dependent upon the start of Lent, others on the availability of halls. The City of Vienna puts out a brochure, *Wiener Ballkalendar,* with a complete listing of dates and locations. You can also call the city info number 52 550, or try the ball calendar webpage at www.ball.at.

Volksoper perform in the historic rooms of the Habsburgs' imperial palace. There are two box offices (one for each platz), which open one hour before each concert. It's best to reserve by phone or fax, but as none of the halls has numbered seating arrive early to get a good seat.

Orangerie in Schloß Schönbrunn

13, Schönbrunner Schloßstraße (812 5004). U4 Schönbrunn. **Box office** 9am-8pm daily. **Tickets** AS390-590. **Credit** AmEx, DC, JCB, MC, V.

A professional little group performs every day at 8.30pm in the Orangery of Schönbrunn Palace. Musicians are not in period costume, but the setting is magnificent nonetheless, and the concerts offer a full evening's entertainment of Mozart and Strauß,

with a pair of dancers, soprano and baritone accompanied by the Schönbrunner Schloßorchester.

Palais Eschenbach/Ferstel/Börse

1, Eschenbachgasse 9 (512 6263). Tram 1, 2, D, J. Palais Ferstel: 1, Strauchgasse 4, Freyung Passage (512 62632). U3 Herrengasse. Börse Palais: 1, Schottenring (512 6263). U2 Schottentor/tram 1, 2, D, J. **Box office** from 40 minutes before performance. Concert times *Nov-Feb* 8.30pm Sat; *Mar-Oct* 8.30pm Wed, Fri, Sat. **Tickets** AS350-650. **Credit** AmEx, DC, MC, V.

The Vienna Walzer Orchestra performs two to three times per week (usually Wed, Fri and Sat) year round, alternating between these three historic locations. The concerts are the standard Strauß and

At most balls a memento of the evening, the *Damenspende*, is presented to female guests. The Bonbonball gives everyone a little bag, to collect sweets during the dance. Almost every ball opens with a procession of debutantes in white, escorted by their partners, who then perform the opening dance. Then the Master of Ceremonies starts the real ball rolling with the traditional invitation *'Alles Waltzer!'* Another tradition is the *Einlage* (interlude), a short performance that at the Opernball might be a piece by the Staatsoper Ballet or a well-known singer. If you don't know how to dance the traditional quadrille at midnight (*Mitternachtsquadrille*), the MC usually calls it out, but few people seem sober enough by then to do it.

Mozart blend; dancers are costumed in Biedermeier style, while the singers and orchestra wear modern concert garb.

Palais Pálffy

1, Josefsplatz 6 (512 5681/tickets 726 5557). U3 Herrengasse. **Box office** 9am-10pm daily. **Tickets** AS390-550. **Credit** AmEx, DC, MC, V.

Imperial Concerts are offered in Baroque and Biedermeier costumes in the tiny *Figarosaal* (where Mozart first presented *The Marriage of Figaro* to a circle of friends) and the slightly larger Beethovensaal. Performance standards, if not exceptional, are good and the musicians enjoy themselves immensely, which is quite infectious. They're also extremely industrious, as from 2000 Imperial Concerts will be presented 365 days a year.

Sacred music

A visit to Sunday Mass is a good way to combine architectural, musical and possibly spiritual sight-seeing. As well as the **Burgkapelle,** in the 1st district, the **Augustinerkirche, Minoritenkirche, Karlskirche, Stephansdom** and **Michaelerkirche** are also all worth a visit.

Burgkapelle

1, Hofburg (533 9927). U3 Herrengasse/tram 1, 2, D, J. **Box office** 11am-1pm, 3-5pm, Fri. **Tickets** AS70-380. **No credit cards**.

The **Wiener Sängerknaben** (Vienna Boys Choir) performs here every Sunday and on religious holidays at 9.15am except during the summer, between 10 July and mid-September.

Music: Rock, Roots & Jazz

From smooth soundscapes to sonic self-indulgence.

During the late 1990s Vienna gained a reputation for being home to the new artisans of classy sound-scapes such as Kruder & Dorfmeister. Vienna's most-wanted DJ duo create original music of their own, remix for the likes of Depeche Mode and Madonna and still find time to DJ regularly in Vienna. Often the lush sounds they assemble reflect the city's opulence while at the same time pushing the melancholic note. The two also find time to work on solo projects such as Kruder's Peace Orchestra and Tosca, Dorfmeister's collaboration with school mate Rupert Huber.

Another DJ partnership whose reputation has gone global is Pulsinger & Tunakan. They have turned their hand to everything from driving funky techno (iO) to experimental electronic (Showroom Recordings) on their Cheap Records label. Both are often seen DJing in **Flex**, **WUK** and the **Meierei** (*see chapter* **Nightlife**).

Viennese clubbers seem to prefer lounging to gettin' down and events whose flyers appear to offer dance mayhem often turn out to be staid affairs. This is also reflected in the nature of some of the music produced in the city. Dub-influenced Sofa Surfers were described by one critic as crafting 'headmusic played with revolutionary zeal', while the Vienna Scientists, as the spliff-toting artwork of their albums suggests, continue in a similar vein. While the Surfers seem to have lost some of their initial momentum – they still DJ regularly but live appearances are rare – the Scientists, masterminded by DJ Jürgen Drimal, have been extremely active, touring throughout Austria and Germany and releasing two big-selling compilations of their varied mixture of dopey beats tinged with jazzy and Brazilian references.

If the city still has an avant-garde to match its glorious non-conformist past, it's the uncompromising experiments released on the Mego label. Artists such as Pita & Rehberg, Farmers Manual and Christian Fennesz have made a name for themselves on the international improv circuit, but are largely ignored at home. Admittedly, it's challenging stuff for the uninitiated – earsplitting frequency manipulations, fragments of machine noise and other aural detritus. Mego, however, is a

In the lab: Vienna Scientists.

broad church and its roster of artists includes DSL, considered by many in Vienna as Europe's finest hip hop DJ. Most nights of the week **rhiz** (*see chapter* **Nightlife**) offers a taste of this peculiarly Viennese form of sonic self-indulgence.

Vienna's conventional live music scene is not as dead as many locals would have you believe. You have a better chance of witnessing some memorable international action washed down with reasonably priced ale than in Paris, for instance. DJs draw crowds here. Nevertheless, venues such as **B72**, **Chelsea**, **Szene Wien** and **Arena** still have a full programme of geetar-toting bands, though the majority are not Austrian.

Few Austrian rock bands are worth the bother. However, Willi Resetarits, performing variously under the name Dr Kurt Ostbahn or Ostbahn Kurti, is a soul-of-the-city rocker who's been at it for years and deserves his following, especially for his uncompromising stance on racism in Austria. He's also translated Asterix into Viennese dialect!

At the more rootsy end of things is Roland Neuwirth and his *Extra-Schrammel* music, a frenetic reading of Vienna's traditional *Heurigen* music, performed with accordion, violin and guitars. While *Volksmusik* of this calibre commands respect, you are more likely to come across *Schlager* – slushy romantic crooning in an Alpine setting by singers such as the incredibly popular mullet-headed Hansi Hinterseer – which dominates the Austrian charts.

There is little in the way of Vienna-based world music apart from longstanding Brazilian resident Alegre Correa who regularly performs his smooth jazz 'n' bossa. **Reigen** and Szene Wien are two places which showcase roots music.

Jazz

Jazz has a long tradition in Vienna and it's not just due to the post-war gum and nylons euphoria for all things American. Long before World War II the stomping tunes of Storeyville were played here with gusto. Even during the Nazi period, the blanket ban on 'negro' music was waivered at the old Café de Europa opposite **Stephansdom** so that weary Wehrmacht officers could recharge their batteries by quaffing *Sekt* to the sound of Ragtime. Through the 1950s Vienna had its share of bandleaders such as Fatty George who brought a bit of life to a dour city under reconstruction.

A crucial figure was bandleader and mad improvisor Ützi Förster who owned the **Café Einhorn**, a favourite among Vienna's eccentric nightowls. A handful of internationally known names such as pianist Friedrich Gulda, multi-instrumentalist Michael Mantler and Miles Davis collaborator and grand daddy of jazz funk Joe Zawinul all emerged from the Vienna scene.

Zawinul and his associates plan to open a Vienna Birdland in the **Volksgarten** (*see chapter* **Nighlife**), much to the chagrin of the existing jazz clubs. Without the patronage of the illustrious, however, formations such as Matthias Rüegg's Vienna Art Orchestra have managed to galvanise local musicians into a durable, respected entity, performing with soloists such as John Surman and Art Farmer, the latter resident in Vienna until his death in 1999. Undisputedly classical music has had a great influence on jazz musicians in Vienna, creating an uneasy alliance between the two. This is evidenced by the use of the hallowed Mozartsaal of the **Konzerthaus** for appearances by key jazz and crossover artists. Buena Vista Social Club, Arto Lindsay, Kronos Quartet and John Zorn are among

the luminaries who have visited. *See also* **Wien Modern** *in chapter* **By Season**.

If you check the listings in *Falter* or other press in Vienna, you will notice that live music is divided between E-Musik (*Ernst* or serious music) and U-Musik (*Unterhaltungs* or entertainment music). This distinction makes the mind boggle when it comes to performers such as Fennesz. It also reduces royalty payments to the likes of the Three Tenors, who were furious to discover their recordings were considered U-Musik by the relevant authorities.

Two events worth looking out for are **JazzFest Wien** and **Wiesen**. *See chapter* **By Season**.

Venues

See also **B72**, **rhiz**, **Chelsea**, **Meieri** and **U4** in *chapter* **Nightlife**.

Arena

3, Baumgasse 80 (798 3339). U3 Erdberg.
Open *summer* 2pm-2am daily; *winter* 4pm-2am daily. **Admission** *concerts* up to AS300.
No credit cards.

Arena is an example of the bountiful state subsidies available for all kinds of counter-culture in Vienna. Located in deepest Erdberg in a former slaughter house, it holds concerts and raves on a fairly regular basis. In the summer, gigs are played outdoors

Arena: *a former slaughterhouse, now its for getting slaughtered and pogoing.*

in the courtyard and there used to be an eclectic mix of velvety 1990s acts such as Massive Attack and the raucous pogoing of the Green Day/Sepultra ilk. Recently the accent has been more on the latter. Open-air cinema in summer too. Reasonable bar prices and friendly laid-back staff.

Flex
1, Donaukanal (access from Augartenbrücke)
(533 7525). U2, U4 Schottenring. **Open** 8pm-4am daily. **Admission** AS40-200. **No credit cards**.
More subsidised fun and games on the banks of the Donaukanal. Flex has the most awesome sound system in the city and is regularly put to good use by K&D, Pulsinger & Tunakan, Sugar B, the Sofa Surfers and illustrious foreigners such as LTJ Bukem, Juan Atkins and Jeff Mills. Live music is also eclectic, with visits from Fugazi and Mouse on Mars in late 1999. Average age is very young and it has an admirable policy of cheap soft drinks. Even so, the whole place gets a lot of flak from cave-dwelling FPÖ councillors. Events in the main hall cost money, but you can hang in the narrow bar and stare at video art on numerous screens. Free Internet access and enormous terrace in summer with half-pipes and abundant graffiti. Not to be missed.
Website: www.flex.at

Jazzland
1, Franz-Josefs-Kai 29 (533 2575).
U1, U4 Schwedenplatz/tram 1, 2. **Open** 7pm-2am Mon-Sat *(summer* from 7.30pm). *Concerts* from 9pm. **Admission** from AS150. **No credit cards**.
Centrally located on Schwedenplatz, Jazzland is very much the oompah-oompah trad jazz night spot of

Vienna. That said it is worth checking the listings, but don't expect anything too ground-breaking. Drinks on the expensive side.

Libro Music Hall
2, Südportalstraße, Messegelände Halle 1
(726 5665/fax 726 5666). Tram 21. **Open** check posters and listings. **Admission** AS300-500.
No credit cards.
Great barn-like hangar located in the trade fair end of the Prater. Run by Libro, the WH Smith of Austria, this unpleasant venue holds around 5,000, but has abominable acoustics. A large K7 Records party with Kruder & Dorfmeister (who else?) and Thievery Corporation attempted to divide the place up into manageable sections without much success. It has attracted the likes of Lauryn Hill, the Beastie Boys and Nine Inch Nails.

Metropol
17, Hernalser Hauptstraße 55 (4077 7407). U6 Alserstraße/tram 43 Palffygasse. **Open** *Concerts* 8pm until midnight. *Bar* 10am-8pm Mon-Fri, concert days. **Admission** AS150-400. **Credit** AmEx, DC, MC, V.
An old music hall theatre and one of Vienna's most attractive venues. Events, however, are alarmingly irregular and quality control almost non-existent. Jazz nights used to be frequent but now tiresome old local rockers and international bores seem to dominate.

Miles Smiles
8, Langegasse 51 (405 9517). U2 Rathaus.
Open 8pm-2am Sun-Thurs; 8pm-4am Fri, Sat. **Admission** AS150 live acts. **No credit cards**.
Tiny jazz bar dedicated to the Lamborghini-driving

Fugazi at **Flex** *– a fine venue for top acts and a cool spot to chill by the Donaukanal.*

Men at **WUK**: *Cheap Records' Louis Austen croons to tunes from his* Consequences *CD*.

trumpeter. No regular performances, but things crop up from time to time, especially during the **JazzFest Wien** (*see chapter* **By Season**). Good snacks, much cosiness and decent prices.

Nachtasyl

6, Stumpergasse 53 (596 9977). U3 Zieglergasse. **Open** 8pm-4am daily. **Admission** AS50-100. **No credit cards**.

The Night Asylum is a wonderfully lugubrious cellar, attracting a clientèle which often lives up to its name. Run by Czech emigré Jiri Chmel, the early days of the Nachtasyl were a focus for Eastern European dissidence in exile, attracting actors, writers and politicians – Vaclav Havel even showed up. Fennesz occasionally attempted to win over the crowds with his ambient DJ sets. Now there are DJs every night and an irregular assortment of live acts, often bands from Jiri's homeland. If you are extremely lucky, you may coincide with the talented Iva Bittova, the sublime vocalist/violinist.

Planet Music

20, Adalbert-Stifter-Straße 73 (332 4641). Tram N **Open** check posters and listings. **Admission** AS100-300. **No credit cards**.

The latest reincarnation of one of Vienna's classic rock venues, the RockHaus, suffers from dull programming featuring a welter of has-beens. The recent appearance of the Tindersticks indicates a slight improvement. Located in a highly inhospitable part of the city with poor public transport connections, it is only for the committed fan.

Porgy & Bess

Temporary venue: Radiokulturhaus, 4, Argentinier Straße 30a (5017 0377). U1 Taubstummengasse. **Open** check listings. **Admission** AS100-250. **No credit cards**.

Currently without a permanent venue, these earnest jazz aficionados are awaiting the refurbishing of an old porno cinema in Riemergasse so that they can continue their programme of showcasing Vienna's local talent and the best of the more academic international scene. The new club is due to open in September 2000. In the meantime they are holding events at the Radiokulturhaus on Argentinier Straße. Heavily state subsidised, in case you were wondering.

Reigen

14, Hadikgasse 62 (894 0094/fax 982 1958). U4 Hietzing. **Open** 8pm-4am concert days. **Admission** AS80-250. **No credit cards**.

Far out of town in Hietzing, but easily reached with the U4, this 30-something dive, helped along with a bit of council largesse, showcases some of the best jazz/world music crossover to set foot in the city. It's a chairs and tables set-up with a raised gallery if you want a better view of the action. DJ nights are not Reigen's forte, but the live programme is unbeatable. Late 1999 saw appearances from Archie Shepp, James Blood Ulmer, Jorge Ben and Terry Callier. Drink prices are steeper than most and the staff are not the friendliest. Good food in a superb Jugendstil setting is available next door at the Café Wunderer.

Sargfabrik

14, Goldschlagstraße 169 (9889 8111/fax 9889 8114). U4 Hietzing/tram 52 Diesterweggasse. **Open** *café/restaurant* noon-3pm, 5.30pm-2am daily. **Admission** up to AS250. **No credit cards**.

The intriguingly named Coffin Factory is a part a housing association development, winner of the prestigious Adolf Loos architecture prize, which includes 70 flats, a steambath/pool/jacuzzi complex, a bar and restaurant and space for concerts, cabaret and performances of all types. Intended as a sort of urban village with homes tailor-made for special needs, the Sargfabrik enlivens the rather moribund Penzing district by offering superb vegetarian cooking and an interesting variety of performances of jazz, improv, world music, theatre and cabaret. With appearances by the likes of Marc Ribot and Uri Caine, the Sargfabrik seems to be on its way to becoming the Vienna branch of the Knitting Factory. Bar and restaurant prices are reasonable. The pool complex is usually residents only, but they have late-night sessions until 5am one Friday a month and monthly women only and gay men days. Call and check dates.

Stadthalle

15, Vogelweidplatz 14 (98 100-0/fax 9810 0395). U6 Burggasse. **Open** check posters and listings. **Admission** AS300-500. **No credit cards**.
The biggest hall for large-scale rock and pop events in Vienna with capacity for around 10,000 howling fans. Devotion to certain bands will be the main reason for attendance. Much more enjoyable are the record fairs that are regularly held in its ante-rooms. Look out for posters.

Szene Wien

11, Hauffgasse 26 (749 3341/fax 749 2206). Tram 71. **Open** check posters and listings. **Admission** up to AS250. **No credit cards**.

Miles out of town and only accessible with the snail-like tram 71. The Szene is, however, worth the trip as it is one of the few medium-sized auditoria in the city, consistently attracting interesting bands and spectacles. Like **Arena** (*see above*), the Szene has been subsidised by the council for many years now, keeping prices low and progressive thinking to the fore. Good cheap Middle-Eastern food is available and there's an overgrown garden in the summer.

WUK

9, Währinger Straße 59 (401 2110). U6 Währinger Straße/trams 40, 41, 42. **Open** check posters and listings. **Admission** AS80-100. **No credit cards**.
Long-standing arts centre with workshops, exhibition space, Kindergarten, coffeehouse and restaurant. The large hall is the scene of weekly DJ nights – Audioroom on Fridays is a popular night often featuring Kruder & Dorfmeister and international buddies such as Rockers Hi-Fi. Saturdays is H.A.P.P.Y, the regular house night. Performance art, dance and improvised music events throughout the year.

Sound selection: covers from Kruder & Dorfmeister, Waldeck, Vienna Scientists & more.

Sport & Fitness

Your sporting chances.

Vienna is a great city for outdoor activities. With the Alps running through the middle of the country, Austrians are major skiing and hiking enthusiasts and the Viennese share the enthusiasms of their country cousins. While moderate mountains and wooded nature are easily reachable by public transport – with *Lederhosen* optional – there are also plenty of good places in Vienna to walk, run, cycle or in-line skate.

Major stadia

Ernst-Happel-Stadion

2, Meiereistraße 7 (728 0854). U1 Praterstern, then tram 21.
The 49,000-seat Prater stadium – its renaming honours the Austrian international player and coach who died in 1992 – is Vienna's largest and the main venue for international football, big domestic and European fixtures, as well as some concerts.

Stadthalle

15, Vogelweidplatz 14 (981 000, but call event organisers for tickets). U6 Burggasse/Stadthalle.
Holds a variety of events including ice hockey and ice skating, dance, acrobatics and football, as well as concerts and other non-sports events.

Spectator sports

Football

Football is not a sport in which Austria excels at present. The national team's 9-0 humiliation by Spain in the Euro 2000 qualifiers in March 1999 led to the sacking of coach Herbert Prohaska. Spain have been drawn again in the qualifiers for the 2002 World Cup along with Israel, Bosnia and Liechtenstein. Austria have never made it to the final of a major tournament and no Austrian club has won a modern European trophy, although Austria did play an important role in the development of the European game. *See page 240* **Pass notes**.

Vienna's two Bundesliga teams, Austria Memphis and Rapid Vienna, have the heated rivalry of any teams sharing the same city. To stereotype: Austria's fans come from the bourgeoisie, Rapid's from the working class; Austria play a more technical, intellectual game, Rapid take a more traditional, fighting approach. In recent years Rapid have been the stronger club. Sold-out games are a rarity in Austria, so it's pretty easy to get tickets up to the last minute.

The national team play at the **Ernst-Happel-Stadion**. For tickets (around AS400) call the Austrian Football Federation (727 180).

Austria Memphis

Franz-Horr-Stadion. 10, Fischhofgasse 10-12 (27 788). U1 Reumannplatz, then tram 67. **Tickets** AS150-250. **Credit** MC, V only by e-mail sales: *fak@fk-austria.at*
The stadium has a 10,500 capacity.

Rapid Vienna

Gerhard-Hanappi-Stadion. 14, Keisslergasse 6 (tickets 544 544/info 910 010). U4 Hütteldorf.
Tickets average AS200. **Credit** AmEx, DC, MC, V.
Rapid are the biggest club in Austria and they play in a stadium named after their former player turned architect, Gerhard Hanappi, who designed it. The capacity is 19,600.

Horse racing

The Prater has both flat racing and trotting tracks:

Wiener Galopp-Rennverein

Viennese Galloping Race Association
2, Freudenau/Rennbahnstraße 65 (728 9535-0). U3 Schlachthausgasse, then bus 77a. **Open** *Mar-Nov* one weekend day (usually for afternoon racing) every other week. **Admission** AS50; bets start at AS20.
No credit cards.
The Freudenau racetrack is one of Europe's oldest, with splendid, more than 150-year-old stands that used to gather the upper crust of imperial Vienna.

Wiener Trabrenn-Verein

Viennese Trotting Association
2, Nordportalstraße 274 (728 0046). U3 Schlachthausgasse, then bus 83a, 84a; U1 Praterstern, then tram 21. **Open** *2pm most Sundays; closed July, Aug.* **Admission** AS40; bets start at AS10. **No credit cards.**
The Krieau track has Europe's first steel and concrete construction grandstand, built in 1912 by a student of architect Otto Wagner. The top part of the stands has been renovated and plans are to continue with the rest in 2000. The track also offers an all-you-can-eat brunch for AS350 where diners can watch races on TV and bet.

Activities

Boating

The Alte Donau is more popular for sailing; pedal and other boats can also be rented there and on the Neue Donau.

Have a ball on a bike...

Firma Ingeneur Wolfgang Irzl

22, Untere Alte Donau 29 (203 6743). U1 Alte Donau. **Open** *Apr, May-Sept* 9am-8pm daily. **Rates** AS150 per hour sailboat; AS80 per hour rowboat; AS120 per hour pedal boat; AS160 per hour motor boat; AS120 per hour windsurfer; AS80 per hour surfbike (new surfboard/bike combo). Offers both sailing and windsurfing classes.

Sailing School Hofbauer

22, An der oberen Alte Donau 185 (204 3435). U1 Kagran. **Open** *Apr-Oct* 9am-9pm daily. *22, Corner of Arbeiterstrandbadstraße and Wagramerstraße. U1 Alte Donau.* **Open** *Apr-Oct* 9am-11pm daily. **Rates** AS150 per hour sailboat; from AS120 per hour pedal boat, AS80 per hour rowboat, AS165 per hour motor boat, AS120 per hour windsurfer. **No credit cards.**
Photo ID needed as deposit. Sailing classes in English available at the Kagran location.

Bowling

Brunswick Bowling

2, Prater Hauptallee 124 (728 0709). Tram N. 17, Schumanngasse 107 (486 4361). Tram 9, 42. **Open** 10am-1am daily. **Rates** AS50 per person. Rental shoes AS20. **Credit** MC.
These alleys are good when you'd rather make like Fred and Barney than Franz Josef and Sissi. Both locations have 32 lanes.

Chess

Playing chess was a popular pastime during the heyday of Vienna's cafés. The city still has enough of a chess tradition to support the dozens of clubs that meet regularly in cafés today.

Café Museum is the best-known café for a pick-up chess game. There's almost always someone playing a match and games are often for money.

Chess clubs meet regularly, from about 6pm to 11pm, at **Café Sperlhof** (2, Grosse Sperlgasse 41; 214 5864; Tue, Fri); **Café Wilhelmshof** (3, Erdbergerstraße 27; 713 2701; Thur); and **Wiener Billardcenter** (4, Rechte Wienzeile 35; 587 1251; Thur). Newcomers are welcome and someone usually speaks English.

For more information, try:

Wiener Schachverband

Viennese Chess Federation
14, Penzingerstraße 72 (8972 1080). **Open** 4-8pm Mon; 4-7pm Wed.
Website: members.eunet.at/chess-vienna/

Climbing

Kletterwand am Flakturm

6, Esterházypark (585 4748). U3 Neubaugasse/bus 13a, 14a, 57a. **Open** *Apr-Oct* 10am-dusk Sat, Sun; 2pm-dusk Mon-Fri. **Fee** AS150 2 hours. **No credit cards.**
Pretend you're an Allied spy on a mission as you scale this imposing flak tower built by the Nazis during World War II. There are 25 climbing routes reaching up to 34m (111ft), with climbing difficulties ranging from 4 to 8. Inexperienced climbers can get instruction or a safety spotter, but should call first to make a reservation. *See pg 62* **Taking the Flak.**

Cycling

Generally flat and with more than 700km (435 miles) of bike paths in the city and its surroundings, Vienna is a good city to bike in. In town, bike lanes are pretty safe and convenient. Although Viennese drivers can be nuts, it's pedestrians who need to watch out for bicyclists. Particularly in the 1st district, some speed along on what they consider their inviolable turf, aggressively unconcerned about the confused tourist who might have strayed into a bike path.

Popular spots to bike include the Prater, along the Donaukanal and around the Alte and Neue Donau and on on the Donauinsel, with bike rental places in several spots near the river (*see also* **Strands** *below*). The Prater has hectares of green space and wooded areas beyond the amusement park. The Hauptallee boulevard through the Prater is popular for bicycling, skating and strolling. You can also circle the Ring on a bike path. Or, for a pleasant route out of town, follow the Danube heading west into the Wachau. *See also chapter* **The Wachau.**

Tourist offices have a pamphlet in German, *Tips für Radfahrer*, that lists rental places and provides a few routes. The pamphlet, *City Biking in Wien*, also in German, at the Rathaus information office, lists rental places and more extensive routes.

Bikes can be taken on the U-Bahn and local S-Bahn trains from 9am to 3pm and after 6.30pm Monday to Friday, after 9am on Saturday and all day Sunday and holidays. Bicycles must go in carriages marked with a bike symbol and require a half-price bike ticket. Bikes can only travel on trains that are marked with a bicycle symbol in their timetable; outside of Vienna's central transport *Kernzone* (Zone 100), which covers the entire of Vienna, bikes require a special ticket. Only folding bikes can be brought on trams and they aren't allowed at all on buses.

Fahrradverleih Skaterverleih Copa Cagrana

22, near the Reichsbrücke (bridge) on the east side of the banks of the Neue Donau in the Copa Cagrana (263 5242/0664 345 8585). U1 Donauinsel. **Open** *Mar-Oct* 9am-9pm daily; *Mar* closes 6pm. **Rates** from AS60 per hour-AS180 all day city bike; AS100 per hour-AS300 all day mountain bike; AS70 per hour-AS350 all day in-line skates. **No credit cards.**
This shop is centrally located for Donauinsel and river route exploration and rents all sorts of bikes including tandems, rickshaws, mopeds and bikes for the handicapped that can be pedalled with the hands. One hour free with four-hour rental. Photo ID and deposit required.
Website: www.fahrradverleih.at

Pedal Power Radverleih

2, Ausstellungsstraße 3 (729 7234). U1 Praterstern. **Open** *Mar-Oct* 8am-8pm daily; *Mar, Apr, Oct* closes

earlier. **Rates** from AS60 per hour-AS350 24 hours 21-gear bicycle. **Credit** AmEx, DC, MC, V.
Bikes come with locks and a map, and staff will provide advice on interesting routes. Store can drop off and pick up bikes from hotels. From May to September Pedal Power offers half-day bike tours of Vienna starting at 10am from the Prater for AS280.

Rent a Bike

Franz-Josefs-Bahnhof (580 0314-20). **Open** 6.30am-9pm daily.
Wien Nord (580 0348-17). **Open** 7.15am-10pm daily. *Wien Süd (580 0358-86).* **Open** 6am-midnight daily. *Wien West (580 0329-85).* **Open** 7am-midnight daily.
Wien Floridsdorf (580 0310-11). **Open** 6am-6pm Mon-Fri; 8am-6pm Sat, Sun.
Central number (0316 764 546/rentabike@aon.at). **Rates** AS120 half day; AS150 all day (discount with a train ticket for that day or the next morning). **Credit** *West* MC, V; *Floridsdorf* AmEx, MC, V.
Rent a Bike offers, yes, bike rentals at decent prices at train stations throughout Austria. There are five locations in Vienna renting 21 or seven-gear city bikes with locks. Children's seats also available for AS30 a day. Photo ID needed.

Golf

There are about 15 clubs in and around Vienna.

Golf Club Wien

2, Freudenau 65a (728 9564). U3 Erdberg, then bus 77a. **Open** during daylight hours, daily. **Fees** AS800 per person/game. **No credit cards.**
The Vienna club is Austria's oldest, founded in 1901, although the current course was built after World War II on the site of former polo grounds; the former course was used to grow food during the war. The 18-hole site cuts through the Freudenau horse racetrack. Non-members can play during the week, if they are members of another club and have a minimum 28 handicap. On weekends, visitors may only play as guests of members.

Golf Club Schloß Schönbrunn

2013, Schönbrunn 4 (02267 2863). By train: S-Bahn to Göllersdorf station. By car: take the A22 towards Stockerau – take the Obermallebran exit. **Open** 9am-dusk daily. **Fees** AS600 per person/game Mon-Fri; AS800 weekends. **No credit cards.**
This club, about 40km (25 miles) north of Vienna, has 27 holes spread over the grounds of a Baroque castle, which now holds the clubhouse. To play during the week, golfers must be a member of another club; on weekends they also need a minimum handicap: 28 for men and 36 for women.

Health & fitness

See also **Manhattan Fitness & Squash** *and* **Wellness Park Oberlaa** *pages 242 & 243.*

John Harris

1, Nibelungengasse 7 (587 3710). U1, U2, U4 Karlsplatz. **Open** 6.30am-10pm Mon-Fri; 9am-8pm

Pass notes

This may come as some surprise, but the English didn't invent football. The Scots invented football because the Scots invented passing. In having the wit to pass the thing to a man in a better position, the Scots switched the game entirely.

And what did they do with it? They took it to England, where the game was professional and where soon every major league club had a Scot in its engine room. English players heeded the lesson, and one man, later a coach, Jimmy Hogan, took it to Europe with him to expand the game's horizons there, shortly before World War I.

And where did he take it? Vienna. For 20 years between the wars, Vienna was at the cutting edge of the international game. Looking at the sorry state of Austrian football today, you may wonder how the game ever took root there at all. Walk into the small football museum in Vienna's **Ernst-Happel-Stadion** (Prater stadium), and you'll find the key. On display are photographs, match programmes, newspaper reports and artefacts belonging to two men: Hugo Meisl and Matthias Sindelar (*pictured*).

A Jew, Hugo Meisl was the force in developing the game in Vienna, where he worked at Bauer's Bank. It was he who brought Hogan over to teach local players the short passing game. All three major Viennese clubs were already in place by then: working-class Rapid; elegant Austria; and First Vienna, founded by gardeners at Baron Rothschild's estate.

Players were taught to keep the ball on the ground, to move into space and to use both ball and space intelligently. Meisl set up the Mitropa Cup, the forerunner of the European Cup, between Central Europe's major clubs. Austria Vienna

Sat, Sun. **Fee** AS250 one-day pass.
No credit cards.
Facilities include weights, cardiovascular machines, aerobics and dance classes, a solarium, massage, sauna, jacuzzi, Tai Chi classes and a swimming pool. If you belong to a club with IHRSA affiliation, the discounted pass is AS150. There's a smaller John Harris club in the **Radisson SAS Palais** (1, Parkring 16; 587 3710).

Hiking

Hiking is extremely popular among Austrians. For a touch of the woods and mountains (nothing more difficult than a moderate slope), the Wienerwald (*see chapter* **Wienerwald**) to the northwest of the city is a good place to explore. Trails are pretty well marked and the free tourist office map is

enough to orient you. For a detailed map of the Wienerwald with hiking and bike routes, **Freytag & Berndt** publishes the *Wienerwald Wanderatlas* for AS189.

Another place to try hiking is the Donau-Auen national park, created in 1996, which spreads east from the Danube near Vienna. To reach a 3km nature walk laid out in the park, take the U1 to Kagran, then bus 93a to the Danzergasse stop. Or try the Lainzer Tiergarten, former royal hunting grounds, open March to November. Take the U4 to Hietzing, then tram 60 to the Hermesstraße stop, then bus 60b. Brochures in German on the park and zoo should be available at the Rathaus information office; if not, try the municipal office MA49 at 1, Volksgartenstraße 3, 4th floor, from 8am to 3pm Monday to Friday.

won it twice, their star player was Matthias Sindelar, 'the Man of Paper'.

Thin, quick-witted and Jewish, Sindelar ghosted through defences with sheer wit and technique. Hogan, still coach and mentor, Meisl, Sindelar and the others would meet in the Wiener Ring-Café and talk tactics. In 1932, the Austrian national team, the Wunderteam, threatened England's invincibility at Wembley, losing narrowly 4-3. (Hogan was the guest of honour when England's record did fall, 6-3 to Hungary in 1953, the Magyars running over to their guest afterwards to acknowledge his coaching contribution in Budapest.)

The climax came in 1934, when Austria were co-favourites with hosts Italy in the first World Cup on European soil. Unfortunately, the soil on semi-final day was deep mud, and the game between the two took place in the drizzle of Milan. Sindelar lost his grip, and defensive error let in the only goal to the Italians, who went on to win the trophy.

Soon after came the *Anschluß*, Austria itself was no more, and, before all the Jews were rounded up, Sindelar killed himself, leaving a bizarre suicide note and a café, the Annahof, to his beloved wife. Meisl died soon after.

Austrian football, despite a mini-revival in the 1950s, never recovered. The audio-visual era, which came in with the European Cup, completely passed it by. Austria were also-rans. The great Viennese rivals, Rapid and Austria, continued to play out their derby games to eversmaller crowds. Admira, the team Meisl founded, foundered, their only claim to fame being their stadium's role as half-empty backdrop (*see above*) for the Wim Wenders film *The*

Goalkeeper's Fear of the Penalty. First Vienna, who featured in the first game on Austrian soil in 1894, sunk into the lower leagues. Worse, after not even being allowed to compete at league level against sides from the capital before the war, provincial sides sprang up, from Linz, Innsbruck, Graz and Salzburg.

These days, apart from hosting the occasional European final at the Prater, Viennese football is strictly low-profile, absurdly kept that way by the recent dictat of (German) SAT 1 TV forcing Rapid and Austria to play out their once-proud derby in the late afternoon. To find any kind of action at all, check out the Viennese local leagues, where Africans, Turks and ex-Yugoslavs of every stripe play out their own private World Cup – with Vienna as nothing but the empty stage.

Fußball Museum

Sector B, Prater (727 180). **Open** 9am-12.15pm, 1-4.30pm Tue-Fri; 2-6.30pm Sat, Sun. Closed until May/June 2000. **Admission** free.

Ice skating

Bring your sweetie to these outdoor skating rinks to get a feeling of Vienna as a winter wonderland. From late January to early March an outdoor ice skating rink opens in Rathausplatz. The Eistraum (Dream on Ice) festival (9am-11.30pm daily) has evening light shows and live music. Look for the German-language pamphlet *Wintersport in Wien*, available in the Rathaus information office; besides ice skating, it also lists places to ski and toboggan.

Wiener Eislaufverein

3, Lothringerstraße 22 (713 6353). U4 Stadtpark. **Open** *late Oct-5 Mar* 9am-8pm Mon, Sat, Sun; 9am-9pm Tue, Thur, Fri; 9am-10pm Wed. **Admission** AS80; AS95 Sun; AS35-75 under-19s; boot rental AS75. **No credit cards**.
This open-air rink also has a *Punsch* bar.

In-line skating

The outdoor sites listed for cycling are popular with in-line skaters too, though it's also not uncommon to see someone doing their grocery shopping on skates. There's a small ramp area for skaters in the Prater near the Riesenrad.

There are other skate rental places near the Danube, including at the Floridsdorfer Brücke on the Donauinsel.

See also above **Fahrradverleih Skaterverleih Copa Cagrana** *and below* **Freizeitparadies Weidinger.**

Skatelab

2, Engerthstraße (214 9565). U1 Vorgartenstraße/bus 11a. **Open** *Nov-May* 2-10pm Tue-Fri; 10am-8pm Sat, Sun. **Admission** AS90 over-19s; AS70 12-19s; AS45 under-12s; AS30 all-day

skate rental for over-12s; AS15 under-12s. **No credit cards.**
This indoor in-line-skating rink has a street course with obstacles, mini-ramps and videos for skaters who can't wait for good weather. It's popular with teenagers but older folks do skate here also.

Jogging

Jogging is a popular pastime in Vienna. Parks and other open spaces are good spots, of course, but it's common enough on the streets and Vienna has a safe enough feel that runners (in particular women) shouldn't feel conspicuous. For a pleasant run convenient to the centre, try the path along the Donaukanal. Joggers also like the Augarten in the 2nd district and the grounds of the Belvedere in the 3rd district. For those that fancy a competitive race there's the **Silversterlauf** on New Year's Eve and the **Vienna Marathon** in May. *See chapter* **By Season**.

Skiing

Austria says it's where modern alpine skiing developed – more than 60 per cent of the country's area is classified as 'alpine landscape'. Snow sports are hugely popular, with almost half the population practising either downhill, cross-country skiing or snowboarding. One-day package trips from Vienna are an easy way to sample this most Austrian of activities.

Many travel agencies offer one-day bus trips to ski slopes from December to March – try Columbus Reisebüro (1, Lueger Ring 8; 534 110). Austrian Railways also offers an all-inclusive day trip. *Dieters Schizug* ('Dieter's ski train') runs on weekends and holidays from early December to early March. The AS470 cost includes a round-trip train ride, transfers to the slopes and a one-day lift ticket at Semmering area sites. Check with travel agencies at Vienna train stations or telephone *(5800 34247). See also* **Skiing** *in* **Lower Austria**.

Also during the ski season, look for the *Snow & Fun* brochure in train stations. It lists a few one-day ski trips to Lower Austria from Vienna, with train, transfer to the ski site and lift ticket packages available for AS468-AS558.

Hohe Wand Wiese
14, Mauerbachstraße 174 (979 1057). U4 Hütteldorf, then bus 249, 449. **Open** *Dec-Mar* 9am-9.30pm Mon-Fri; 9am-10pm Sat, Sun. **Fees** AS40 10-ride lift ticket; AS160 day pass; AS120 half-day pass (from 1pm). **No credit cards**.
A good, local skiing site. It can make its own snow once there's a deep enough natural base, but season opening may be delayed until Mother Nature provides enough snow.

Squash

See also below **Wellness Park Oberlaa**.

Manhattan Fitness & Squash
19, Heiligenstädter Lände 17 (368 7311-0). U4/U6 Spittelau, tram D. **Open** 7am-midnight Mon-Fri; 9am-10pm Sat, Sun. **Rate** one-day pass AS300, includes squash. **Credit** AmEx.
A large club with 22 squash courts, as well as weights, sauna, steam room, pool, golf practice court, badminton court, restaurant, shop, aerobics and Tai Chi classes.

Swimming

Amalienbad
10, Reumannplatz 23 (607 4747). U1 Reumannplatz. **Open** 9am-5pm Tue; 9am-9.30pm Wed, Thur; 9am-7pm Fri; 7am-8pm Sat; 7am-6pm Sun. **Rates** AS150 4 hours saunas/pools; AS50 5 hours swimming; AS25 2 hours swimming. **No credit cards**.
Beautiful Jugendstil baths with solarium, massage, towel service, foot and cosmetic treatments and a restaurant, along with indoor pools. Men's, women's and mixed sessions in the two large sauna rooms.

Stadionbad
2, Prater-Krieau/Meiereistraße (720 2102). U3 Schlachthausgasse, then bus 81a, 80a. **Open** *July-Aug* 8am-8pm daily; *May, June, first half of Sept* 9am-7pm daily. **Rates** AS55 all day, AS60 with locker; AS45 half day. **No credit cards**.
One of Vienna's largest outdoor sites with six pools, kids' area, water slides and a swim-up bar.

Thermalbad Oberlaa
10, Kurbadstraße 14 (6800 99600). U1 Reumannplatz, then tram 76. **Open** 8.45am-6pm Mon, 6.30-10pm for nudists; 8.45am-10pm Tue-Sat; 7.15am-10pm Sun. **Rates** from AS105 2 hours-AS215 day pass. **No credit cards**.
This spa has five indoor and outdoor thermal pools, two children's pools, three whirlpools and men's, women's and mixed saunas, as well as services including a solarium, massage and herbal and eucalyptus rooms. It's part of a large complex; *see below* **Wellness Park Oberlaa**.

Strands

In the summer, the Viennese convert the banks of the Danube into a river beach. The Reichsbrücke is the centre of the (mild) honky tonk, with plenty of bars and restaurants, not to mention bike and skate rental and a jumping pen for kids. Take the U1 to Donauinsel; free swimming spots with grassy or concrete areas to lie out on are both north and south of the bridge on either side of the Neue Donau.

Topless sunbathing is generally acceptable, but head south for the nude spots (marked FKK on maps). The Alte Donau has for-fee beach clubs and is more family oriented.

A brochure, *Freizeitparadies Donauinsel*, at the Rathaus information office has a map of bathing sites, restaurants and rental shops around the Neue Donau.

...or have a fine time crossing the lines on your in-lines. See page 241.

Freizeitparadies Weidinger

*22, Raffineriestraße 42 (280 5065). U1
Kaisermühlen-Vienna International Centre, then bus
91a.* **Open** *Apr-Sept* 10am-2am Sun-Thur; 10am-4am
Fri, Sat. **Rates** AS90 per hour pedal boat; AS80 per
hour in-line skates; AS40 per hour bicycles. **Credit** V.
The 'Leisure Paradise' has just about everything you
need for the complete Donauinsel beach experience,
including the Villa Wahnsinn (crazy house) and
open-air disco. Besides boat, bike and skate rental,
there's a restaurant, sauna, steam room and solarium. The complex is on the east bank of the Neue
Donau, south of the Reichsbrücke.

Strandbad Alte Donau

*22, Arbeiterstrandbadstraße 91 (263 6538). U1 Alte
Donau.* **Open** *May-mid-Sept* 8am-8pm weekends;
slightly shorter hours Mon-Fri. **Admission** AS50.
No credit cards.
One of the many beach clubs along the Alte Donau
with three outdoor swimming pools, a volleyball
court, a children's play area and a small fitness course.

Tennis

Vienna has dozens of tennis courts, more indoor than
out. Check the *Gelbe Seiten* under *Tennishallen.* The
city also hosts the CA (Creditanstalt Bank) Trophy
tournament every October.

Tennis Point Vienna

*3, Corner of Baumgasse and Nottendorfergasse (799
9997). U3 Erdberg.* **Open** 7am-11pm daily. **Fees**
AS410 per hour tennis; AS140 per half hour squash.
No credit cards.
Has 11 indoor tennis courts and two squash courts.

Tennis Wien Leistungszentrum

*2, Wehlistraße 320 (726 2626-0). U1 Praterstern to
tram 21/bus 83a, 80b.* **Open** 7.30am-11pm daily.
Rates AS220-360 per hour. **No credit cards.**
Run by the Viennese Tennis Federation. The centre
has 11 indoor and outdoor courts. Phone for a reservation. There's also a restaurant, sauna, shop and
tennis classes are available.

Wellness Park Oberlaa

*10, Kurbadstraße 16 (6800 99700).
U1 Reumannplatz, then tram 76.*
Open *Racket sports* 7.30am-11pm Mon-Fri; 8am-
10pm Sat, Sun. *Fitness centre* 8am-10pm Mon-Fri;
8am-9pm Sat, Sun. **Rates** *racket sports* AS120-360
per hour; *fitness centre* AS210 day card.
No credit cards.
This park has 13 indoor and five outdoor tennis
courts, as well as 14 squash courts and 15 badminton courts. It also has a fitness centre with
weights and machines, aerobics and other classes, a
sauna and massage rooms.

Konzerte im Mozarthaus

The "Concerts im Mozarthouse" take place in the oldest concert hall in Vienna (18th century) where Mozart used to work and play for the Bishop Colloredo in 1781.

Come and enjoy one of the most beautiful works of classical music of Vienna: it will be just like in Mozart's time. We offer you concerts with a very high artistic performance in the heart of the capital and in the incomparable pleasant atmosphere of the "Sala Terrena".

Our musicians are internationally known and can be found among the best of Vienna. Works of Mozart, Haydn, Schubert and Beethoven will be in this context an unforgettable event in your life.

Book also individual performances for groups and special events.

Ticket reservation:
hotels, ticket offices, travelagencies,
tourist guides and box-office of the
"Deutsch Ordenshaus"
Vienna 1, Singerstraße 7
Tel: (+43-1) 911 90 77
Fax: (+43-1) 416 47 30
e-mail: konzerte.mozarthaus@netway.at

All Year:
Thursday - 19:30
Saturday - 17:00
Sunday - 19:30
Tickets:
Category A: ATS 450,-
Category B: ATS 350,-
Students: ATS 250,-

Theatre & Dance

All the city's a stage.

A panorama of drama: the nineteenth-century **Burgtheater**. *See page 246.*

Practically every district in Vienna has a stage offering some form of entertainment. Not all of this will be highly financed, but it will show you the spirit and humour of the Viennese. Theatre in the city ranges from amateur street action, month-long professional festivals to the pinnacle of the theatre in the German-speaking world, the **Burgtheater**.

Vienna's theatres are grouped into three main categories: *Grossbühnen*, *Mittelbühnen* and *Kleinbühnen* (large stages, middle stages and small stages respectively). The categories describe the position each holds in the Viennese theatre order more than their size. The big four among the Grossbühnen are the **Burgtheater**, the **Akadamietheater**, the **Theater in der Josefstadt** and the **Volkstheater**.

Near and dear to the Viennese theatre-goer is the Kabarett; an evening of comic satire, often including music, commenting on the current social and political scene. Unfortunately, this quintessentially Viennese experience is not suited to the casual observer – you not only need to understand German, but a number of Austrian dialects as well.

What is of interest to all theatre-goers is *Theater Dienstag* (Theatre Tuesday). This campaign was launched at the prompting of mayor Michael Häupl in March 1999 in order to keep the theatres active. The promotion runs at over 40 theatres where tickets are sold every Tuesday at two for the price of one (no half-price single tickets). In addition to buying from the individual box offices, tickets can be ordered via the Theatre Hotline (0699 77777).

Another theatre promotion that started in March 1999 is Die 7. Seven otherwise unconnected companies (**Schauspielhaus**, **dietheater Wien**, **Theater in der Drachengasse**, **Ensemble Theater**, **Gruppe 80**, **Odeon** and Theater mbH) came up with a promotional gimmick that works as follows: after visiting one of these seven participating theatres, keep your ticket. Present the ticket at the box office of any of the other theatres within four weeks, and you will be entitled to half-price entrance. This process can then be repeated with the last purchased ticket, and so on. The only catch is that the offer is not valid for premieres or for Theater Dienstag. In addition to this ticket promotion, the theatres release a new play listing every two months.

Visitors who do not speak German need not despair, there are two options for English-language theatre in the city – **Vienna's English Theatre** and the **International Theatre**.

Every month, the tourist information office puts out a booklet (*Program*) detailing what's on around the city. The English-language newspaper *Austria Today* also has some listings and reviews. During the summer months of July and August, most of the theatres close. The **Wiener Festwochen** (*see chapter* **By Season**) runs from 12 May to 18 July in many of the theatres around the city and offers a broad selection of premieres, contemporary productions and classics.

Theatre

Main venues

The Burgtheater, Akademietheater and Kasino am Schwarzenburgplatz are all under the Burgtheater's management and tickets may be obtained at its ticket office. Tickets can also be booked through the **Österreichischer Bundestheaterkassen** (*see chapter* **Music: Classical & Opera**).

Akadamietheater

1, Lisztstraße 1 (51444) U4 Stadtpark/tram D, 71. **Box office** 8am-6pm Mon-Fri; 9am-noon Sat, Sun. *Evening* from one hour before performance. **Credit** AmEx, DC, JCB, MC, V.

The 700-seat Akademie, the Burgtheater's second stage, was originally the training stage for the Academy for Music and Applied Arts. It was taken over in 1922 by the Burgtheater, at the request of the actors, for the staging smaller chamber works. It now tends toward contemporary fare – anything from Chekov and Ibsen to Albee, Tabori and Turini.

Visitors to the city often overlook the Akademietheater in favour of the more famous **Burgtheater**, but the Viennese themselves often prefer it for its more intimate atmosphere, which offers theatregoers the chance to see their favourite actors in a more personal environment.

Burgtheater

1, Dr-Karl-Lueger-Ring 2 (51444-4145/fax 51444-4147). U2, U3 Volkstheater or U2 Schottentor/tram 1, 2, D. **Box office** 8am-6pm Mon-Fri; 9am-noon Sat, Sun. Evening from one hour before performance. **Tickets** AS50-600; AS25 standing. **Credit** AmEx, DC, JCB, MC, V,.

Slightly dwarfed by the Rathaus opposite, the Burgtheater has been in the news due to the uncompromising programming of German director Klaus Peymann. Elfriede Jelinek's six-and-a-half hour *Sportstück* was more than most could handle and Peymann tendered his resignation, leaving in a blaze of glory by waving goodbye to his (many) admirers from the top of the theatre's cupola. His successor, Klaus Bachler quietly assumed the helm in September 1999, promising more premieres.

The Burgtheater is an imposing edifice by Gottfried Semper and Karl von Hasenauer composed of Renaissance and neo-Classical elements and finished in 1888. Like many Ringstraße buildings it was blighted by functional defects and had to be remodelled a few years after opening to improve its appalling acoustics and poor visibility. A joke at the time claimed that 'In the Parliament you can't hear anything, in the Rathaus you can't see anything and in the Burgtheater you can neither see nor hear anything'. The façade is a mishmash of busts of famous dramatists (an international selection), plus Apollo with the Muses of Comedy and Tragedy, and still bears the original lettering, k.k. Hofburgtheater (Imperial and Royal Palace Theatre). The two huge wings house the ornate gigantic staircases with ceiling paintings by Klimt and Franz Matsch. The latter fortunately survived the fire which destroyed the auditorium – another victim of the events of 1945.

The accent is very much on spoken drama so, if your German is not up to scratch, you may be lucky enough to catch a performance of the *Threepenny Opera* and at least be able to hum along to the tunes. There are no performances in July and August but guided tours are available all year round. The Burgtheater seats 1,350 with standing room for 150.

Website: www.burgtheater.at/

International Theater

9, Porzellangasse 8 (319 6272). Tram D Schlickplatz. **Box office** 10am-5pm Mon-Fri. *Evening* from 5pm. **Tickets** AS250-350. **Credit** MC, V.

This theatre for expatriates to put on plays is actually two venues: the main stage and a smaller performance area – the Fundus (the storeroom). The Fundus is in the cellar and is well suited to small, intimate theatre. Although well established (the company celebrated its 25th anniversary in 1999), the quality of the performances is more redolent of gung-ho community theatre than small professional team.

Kasino am Schwarzenbergplatz

3, Schwarzenbergplatz 1 (5144-44830). U4 Stadtpark/tram D, 71. **Box office** 8am-6pm Mon-Fri; 9am-noon Sat, Sun. *Evening* from one hour before performance. **Tickets** AS300. **No credit cards**.

For the anglophone angle, try **Vienna's English Theatre**. *See page 248.*

The Kasino was originally the Vienna residence of Franz Josef's brother, Erzherzog Ludwig Viktor. The theatre has been used by the Burgtheater since the 1970s as a rehearsal space and occasionally as a third stage. The auditorium has a maximum capacity of 200.

Theater Akzent

4, Theresianumgasse 16-18 (501 65 3306). Tram D. **Box office** *main office* (Argentinierstraße 37) 8am-6pm Mon-Fri. *Evening* from one hour before performance. **Tickets** up to AS600. **Credit** AmEx, DC, MC, V.

Aimed at the Viennese working class, this theatre offers entertainment and serves as a training ground for performers and stage technicians. Performances at the Akzent can include everything from a tribute to Mario Lanza to drag queens, cabaret and children's theatre. The quality of the productions and price of the tickets vary, as the place is rented out to different groups. One advantage is free parking in the theatre's underground garage.

Theater in der Josefstadt

8, Josefstädter Straße 26 (42 700-306). U2 Rathaus/ tram J. **Box office** 9am-6pm daily. *Evening* from one hour before performance. **Tickets** AS120-600; AS30 standing room. **Credit** AmEx, DC, JCB, MC, V.

Built in 1788 and remodelled in neo-Classical style by Josef Kornhäusel in 1822, it reached its apotheosis between the wars under Max Reinhardt's direction, before he fled to Hollywood. Apart from the **Burgtheater**, this nineteenth-century theatre is the oldest *Sprachbühne* (speech stage) in Vienna and one of its best-loved. The first time visitor will be impressed by the sight of the ornate chandeliers simultaneously rising towards the ceiling as the lights go down. The theatre continues to promote German-language plays under the direction of the former Burgtheater actor Helmuth Lohner. It is generally more accessible than the Burgtheater and has a reputation for staging quality productions of Austrian classics. It is featured in *The Third Man*.

Schauspielhaus

9, Porzellangasse 19 (317 0101/fax 3170 10122/ office@schauspielhause.at). U4 Roßauer Lände/ tram D. **Box office** 10am-5pm Mon-Fri. *Evening* from 6pm Tue-Sat (performance days only). **Tickets** AS150-300; AS100 Tue. **Credit** AmEx, DC, JCB, MC, V.

This small theatre in the 9th district focuses on new writing from German-language playwrights. The turnover of plays is relatively high. Not for mainstream audiences. *Website: www.schauspielhaus.at/*

Vienna's English Theatre

8, Josefsgasse 12 (4021 2600/fax 4021 26040). U2 Lerchenfelderstraße. **Box office** 10am-5pm Mon-Fri. *Evenings* from 5pm. **Tickets** AS190-490. **Credit** MC, V.

Founded in 1963, the English theatre has built up a reputation for quality performances in the anglophile and expat communities which it doesn't always live up to – especially when producing its own work. It hosts visiting groups from the UK and the US and has attracted the likes of Anthony Quinn, Larry Hagman and Leslie Nielsen to its boards. It has also premiered *The Red Devil Battery Sign* by Tennessee Williams and Edward Albee's *Three Tall Women*. The theatre also sometimes stages Italian and French plays.
Website: www.englishtheatre.at/

Volkstheater

7, Neustiftgasse 1 (524 7263/7264/fax 523 3501-282/ info@volkstheater.at/ticket@volkstheater.at). *U2 Volkstheater/bus 48a.* **Box office** 10am to performance daily. **Tickets** AS170-500. **Credit** AmEx, DC, MC, V.

Built in 1889 to a design by two experts in theatre architecture, Ferdinand Fellner and Hermann Helmer. One of its founding principals was to present German literature to a wider public than the Burgtheater. This principal continues, although it also puts on translated English plays such as *Who's Afraid of Virginia Wolf*. The Volkstheater is the first mainstream theatre in Vienna to have a female director – Emmy Werner.
Website: www.volkstheater.at/ge/

Smaller venues

For details of the **Odeon**, *see chapter* **Music: Classical & Opera.**

dietheater Konzerthaus

3, Lothringerstraße 20 (587 0504/tickets 712 1211/ fax 712 2872). U4 Stadtpark/tram D. **Box office** 4.30-7pm Mon-Sat. **Tickets** AS110-200. **Credit** AmEx, DC, JCB, MC, V.

Housed in what was once a restaurant in the cellar of the original Konzerthaus, this 50-seat theatre space shares only a front door with the rest of the Konzerthaus.

dietheater Wien

1, Karlsplatz 5 (587 0504). U1, U2, U4 Karlsplatz/ tram 1, 2, D, J. **Box office** 4.30-7pm Mon-Sat. **Tickets** AS110-200. **No credit cards.**

Two stages, dietheater Konzerthaus and dietheater Künstlerhaus, joined forces under the umbrella label dietheater Wien to present Vienna with even more experimental dance, theatre and interdisciplinary work, both Austrian and international.

Ensemble Theater

1, Petersplatz 1. U1, U3 Stephansplatz. **Box office** 9am-5pm Mon-Sat. *Evening* from one hour before performance. *Advance ticket sales* 1, Marc-Aurel-Straße 3-6 (535 3200). **Tickets** AS180-AS280. **No credit cards.**

Classical arches lend charm as does the large bar area which serves until 1am. The accent is on twentieth-century works with a political bent, lots of Brecht plus German-language versions of Pinter and O'Neill.

Gruppe 80

6, Gumpendorfer Straße 67 (586 5222/fax 5873 67211/gruppe80@netway.at). U3 Neubaugasse/bus 13a. **Box office** 10am-6pm Mon-Fri. *Evenings* 6-8pm Tue-Sat performance nights only. **Tickets** AS220. **Credit** V.

Since it was founded in 1980, Gruppe 80 has established itself as one of the leading ensemble theatres in Vienna. The group took over a pornographic cinema in 1983 and modified it to create their own performance space.
Website: www.gruppe80.nwy.at/

Theater in der Drachengasse

1, Drachengasse 2 (513 1444). U1, U4 Schwedenplatz. **Box office** 10am-5pm Tue-Sat. *Evening* 6pm-performance. **Tickets** AS150-300. **No credit cards.**

A tiny space that presents avant-garde chamber works in various languages, but mainly focuses on German and Austrian contemporary work. An English-language performance group, English for English Lovers, presents plays, readings, sketches and improvs on the last Friday of every month.

Dance

Vienna is not renowned for its dance scene – and this becomes obvious when looking through the limited number of dance performances in the weekly listings magazines. Ballet is limited to the Vienna State Opera Ballet which performs at the **Staatsoper** (only three to four times a month). Any other ballet is rare and more likely to be from visiting companies. Vienna does not have a stage which is devoted solely to dance, although some theatres do have a number of dance performances in their listings.

At **dietheater Konzerthaus** you can see modern dance choreographed by the likes of Saskia Hölbing, as well as visiting groups. **Theater des Augenblicks** schedules many performances of contemporary dance and also hosts visiting companies such as Compagnie Irene K.

As usual though, Vienna pulls out all the stops when it comes to its festivals. The **Wiener Festwochen** and **Im Puls Tanz** both turn the summer months into a dance frenzy. For details, *see chapter* **By Season.**

Theater des Augenblicks

18, Edelhofgasse 10 (479 6887). Tram 40, 41 Gertrudplatz. **Box office** 9.30am-2.30pm daily. *Evening* from one hour before performance. **Tickets** AS150-250. **No credit cards.**

A performance space which is mostly used by dance groups ranging from amateurs to some visiting professional groups.

Trips Out of Town

Getting Started

Viennese whirl too much for you? A plateful of stunning scenery lies just an hour away.

Vienna is located within an hour of all kinds of stunning scenery: vineyards, the Danube, the Vienna Woods, forests, marshlands and the Alps. Those with a yen for the east can explore Slovakia, Slovenia, Hungary and the Czech Republic; all no more than two hours' drive away.

The Austrian Tourist Board is so organised that even Austrians use it. Staff book hotels that often include extras such as a ski pass or wine tasting. The main office for the places below is the Lower Austria Tourist Information in Vienna, where phones are usually answered promptly, correct information is provided and English is spoken. The website also yields useful travel material. For detailed information about areas or tours, call the regional offices below.

Lower Austria Tourist Information
1, Walfischgasse 6 (513 8022-0). U1, U2, U4 Karlsplatz/tram 1, 2, D, J. **Open** 9am-6pm Mon-Fri. *Website: www.tiscover.com*

The Wachau
Wachau-Nibelungengau Tourist Information Undstraße, Krems (02732 85620). **Open** *mid-Oct-Easter* 9am-6pm Mon-Fri; *Easter-mid-Oct* 9am-7pm Mon-Fri; 10am-noon, 1-7pm Sat.

Lower Austria South Alpine Region/Semmering
Passhöhe, Semmering (0266 42539).

Tourist Region Vienna Woods
Hauptplatz 11, Purkersdorf (0223 1621 7612) tourismusregion.wienerwald@netway.at.

Thermal Baths Region Wienerwald
Kurdirektion, Baden by Vienna (0225 241206).

By boat

It is easy to travel by boat – they leave from Reichsbrücke on the Danube canal – to Bratislava, Budapest and the Wachau in the summer. Children aged 10-15 travel half price, under-10s free. Bicycles are allowed, but passengers should state their intention when calling to make a reservation. It takes longer to travel against the current (north) so cyclists often take the boat one way, and pedal back.

DDSG Blue Danube
(Booking and information)
1, Friedrichstraße 7 (58 880-0/fax 5888 0440). U1, U2, U4 Karlsplatz. **Open** 9am-6pm Mon-Fri.

Boats to Budapest
8-30 Apr, 4 Sept-29 Oct leaves 9am, returns 9am daily. *1 May-28 July* leaves 8am, returns 8am daily. *29 July-3 Sept* leaves 8am, 1pm, returns 8am, 1pm daily. Journey times *outwards* 5.5hrs; *return* 6hrs 20mins. **Tickets** AS780 one way; AS1,100 return.

Boats to Bratislava
19-30 Apr leaves 9am, returns 5pm Wed-Sun; *3 May-2 Sept* leaves 9.30am, returns 5.45pm Wed-Sun. *6 Sept-29 Oct* leaves Vienna 9am, returns 4pm Wed-Sun. Journey times *outwards* 1hr 30mins; *return* 1hr 45mins. **Tickets** AS240 one way; AS370 return.

The Wachau
14 May-1 Oct leaves Vienna Reichsbrücke 8.45am, arrives Krems 1.55pm, Dürnstein 2.30pm; leaves Dürnstein 4.30pm, Krems 4.50pm, arrives Vienna 8.45pm, every Sun. **Tickets** AS200 one way; AS270 return.

By bike

Vienna's excellent bike paths are well marked along most roads of the inner city. If you want to bike out of town, it is best to hit the Danube Bike Trail and either head south toward Budapest, or, even better, north toward Klosterneuberg and the Wachau. If you don't have a bike, Austrian Railways has a 'Rent a Bike' system for city cycles, mountain bikes and children's models, which operates from most railway stations. Bikes are rented for half days, whole days or by the week. Prices are reasonable, and machines can be returned to different railway stations for a minimal fee. Bicycles are also allowed on most trains at AS40 for an all-day ticket.

By train

Fast, reliable Austrian Railways is the main public transport system for travelling outside Vienna. There are four types of train: 'Schnellzug' are the fast trains with few stops, 'Eilzug' trains are slightly more ponderous, and the Intercity and Eurocity only travel between major conurbations. Only the Schnellzug, IC and EC take reservations. For short trips from Vienna, most trains leave every hour, so it is possible just to arrive at the station and take the next train. There are three train stations in Vienna, the Franz-Josefs-Bahnhof (trains travelling north), Westbahnhof (west) and Sudbahnhof (south and east). It is usually, but not always, fairly logical

which train station to choose based on the direction you want to travel. However, as the train schedules change frequently, check the times first with the ÖBB information service. The staff are easy to get hold of and speak English. You can buy your ticket either on the train or in the station. It is almost always cheaper to buy a train ticket in conjunction with public transport, so if you arrive by U-Bahn, tram or bus, show your ticket to the conductor.
ÖBB Austrian Railways Information (1717)
ÖBB Austrian Railways Booking (1700)

Wachau

To **Krems**: From Franz-Josefs-Bahnhof, trains leave every hour between 5am and 10pm; last train 8pm Sat. Journey time 1hr 10mins. **Tickets** AS133 one way.

Melk

To **Melk**: From Westbahnhof, direct trains leave every two hours from 6.28am-9.23pm. You can also travel to St Pölten and change – trains leave on the hour. Journey time 1hr 10mins. **Tickets** AS150 one way.

Klosterneuberg

To **Klosterneuberg**: From Franz-Josefs-Bahnhof, trains leave every half hour Mon-Fri; from 5.05am-23.38pm every hour Sat, Sun. Journey time 15mins. **Tickets** AS19 one way (one public transport ticket) in conjunction with a used public transport ticket. Bicycles AS40 for entire day.

Baden bei Wien

For **Baden**: From Sudbahnhof, trains leave every half hour from 5.10am-7.40pm. There are fewer trains in the evenings; the last train is at 11.15pm. Journey time 30mins. **Tickets** AS38 (two public transport tickets) in conjunction with a used public transport ticket, otherwise AS57 one way.

Semmering

For **Semmering**: From Sudbahnhof, trains leave every hour from 5.40am-11.15pm. The Schnellzug takes 1hr 15mins, the Eilzug takes 2hrs. As the train ride is particularly beautiful, take the slower train (sit on the left hand side of the train for better views) and enjoy the ride. **Tickets** AS160 one way.

Schneeberg

(spring, summer, autumn only)
For **Puchberg am Schneeberg**: From Sudbahnhof, trains leave every two hours from 6.58am-7.58pm. Change trains in Wiener Neustadt for Puchberg. Journey time 1hr 30mins. In winter the Wiener Neustadt-Puchberg part is closed. There are special steam trains that leave for Puchberg up the Schneeberg mountain. Check with the **Lower Austria Tourist Information** (*see above*) or any train station for times, and book it, as it fills up fast. **Tickets** AS350 return.

By bus

The Austrian railway infrastructure, especially out of Vienna, is so good that most people opt for the train when not using their car. Buses are main-

ly used by Vienna's Eastern European residents when revisiting homelands back across the borders. Because Austria's eastern borders form a gateway for the entire European Union, border control for buses tends to be particularly time consuming.

Eurolines Austria

Bus station
Landstraßer Hauptstraße 7 (712 0453). U3/bus 74a.
Open for reservations 12-9pm. **No credit cards**.

Vienna - Mikulov (Czech Republic)

Twice daily at 7.30am, 5.30pm. Journey 1hr 40mins. **Tickets** AS170 one way; AS340 return. If returning within four days AS264.

Bratislava

Ten times daily, first bus 8am; last bus 10.30pm. Journey time 1hr 30mins. **Tickets** AS120 one way; AS220 return.

Budapest

4 times a day, 7am, 11am, 5pm, 7pm; an extra bus at 3pm Sat. Journey time 3hrs 45mins. **Tickets** AS50 one way; AS490 return.

Postbus

In winter there is a bus service to some ski areas near Vienna. Call the Postbus information for details.
Information Bahn and Post (71 101).

By car

The Austrian motorways are mostly four lane and fast. Until recently they were also free. Heavy traffic from Eastern Europe has taken its toll on the roads, so now a 'Pickerl' road tax sticker is required for all cars using the motorways. Valid for one month or one year, the sticker can be bought at the borders and at most Traffik shops. Fines can be heavy if drivers are caught without their Pickerl.

Getting out of Vienna is easy, just follow the Ringstraße to find all roads and signposts you need. The A2 takes you south to Graz; the S6, a well-posted motorway, goes to **Semmering**. The Rax turnoff is at Gloggnitz, follow the route 27 to Reichenau and Payerbach. For **Schneeberg**, leave the A2 at Weiner Neustadt, following the route 26 to Puchberg.

The A4 is a new motorway all the way to **Budapest**, follow signs to Schwechat airport. Bratislava is also beyond the airport off the A4 on the route 7.

To **Mikulov** in the Czech Republic: follow the A7 north along the Danube canal in the direction of Brno; Mikulov is around 10km (6 miles) across the border.

To the **Wachau**: take the A1 to Melk, then drive down either side of the Danube to **Krems**, returning along the route 3 over Stockerau and **Klosterneuburg**.

Wienerwald

Just outside the city you can talk to the trees and come back with tales of the Vienna Woods.

The Wienerwald, or Vienna Woods, inspired Schubert, Beethoven, Mozart, Strauß and Schönberg, and still make Viennese hearts sing. The area is rather more user-friendly since Mozart's day, of course, but retains its wild beauty and charm. Few cities in the world have the luxury of such a large area of protected natural reserves close to the metropolis. The Woods, Vienna's green lungs, cover an enormous area of forests, hills and wilderness – 1,250sq km (483sq miles) in all – and encircle the northern, western and southern three-quarters of the city. Many parts of the Wienerwald can be reached by public transport in half an hour from the city centre.

The Wienerwald owes its existence to an early Austrian conservationist, Josef Schöffel, who launched a campaign in the *Wiener Tagblatt* newspaper to prevent the cutting down of the Woods to finance the government's heavy losses against the Prussians in the nineteenth century. After two years, the outraged citizens of Vienna put an end to this project. A century later, the Viennese are still congratulating themselves for their foresight.

Today many Viennese live in the small villages scattered throughout the Wienerwald, preferring the short commute to living in the city. Touring the Woods is an easy way to experience 'rustic' life without wandering far away from Vienna. If you only have a few hours, do what many Viennese do: ride to Leopoldsburg or Kahlenberg (Vienna's two local mountains) by bus or taxi for a short walk along the many well-marked trails, then afterwards ponder the view of Vienna over a cup of coffee in one of the small restaurants. However, in order to truly appreciate the Wienerwald and a few sights listed below, you'll need a full day.

Höhenstraße

This is for tourists with only an hour or two to spare, who want to see a little of the Vienna Woods. A short taxi or bus ride will take you along Vienna High Road, an old-fashioned cobblestone road that winds its way between the mountains of Kahlenberg and Leopoldsberg, before continuing on to Klosterneuburg. The 483m (1,585ft) summit

of Kahlenberg affords a magnificent view of the city of Vienna. Meander along to Cobenzl or to Leopoldsberg to drink a coffee and enjoy the scenery from the lovely tree-shaded terrace just behind the castle. *See also* **Grinzing & Kahlenberg** *in chapter* **Sightseeing**.

Klosterneuburg

The town of Klosterneuburg is dominated by the monastery of the same name. The imposing Augustinian monastery church, topped by a dome in the form of the Imperial Crown, speaks volumes about religious and imperial egos at the time. A walk inside the monastery, founded in 1108 by Margrave Leopold III of Babenberg, or Leopold the Pious, reveals some holy treasures. Among them, the stunning Verdun altarpiece, with two wings of gilded copper and 51 blue enamel plaques, created around 1181. The Collegiate Church nearby is in Romanesque style and dates from the early twelfth century. The present interior arrangement, with its high altar and organ, built in 1642 by Johann Freundt, is of seventeenth-century origin.

Klosterneuburg is a beautiful place to visit. The town is located on a pretty stretch of the Danube, and makes a great starting point to explore the Danube Bike Trail (*see below* **Mountain biking**). Only a 15-minute train ride

from Franz-Josefs-Bahnhof, Klosterneuburg is already in the deep countryside. Rent a bicycle at Klosterneuberg train station for a few hours, and ride along excellent marked trails that line the south bank of the Danube. If you get far enough, you can take a funny little wooden ferry, just big enough for a few cars and cyclists, to the Danube Island.

On a fine day a ride is very congenial, especially as you're never out of sight of a restaurant snuggled along the pathways. Ride as far as you wish, because it is always possible to catch a local train back to your starting point. You can even take the train to Vienna, where you can leave the bike at Franz-Josefs-Bahnhof. Good bikes are easy to rent, as long as prospective pedallers bring passport or photo ID, they're essential for the transaction (*see chapter* **Getting Started**).

Klosterneuburg Tourist Information
(02243 32038). **Open** *Feb-end Sept.*
Some English spoken.

Klosterneuburg Monastery
(02243 411-212). **Open** 10am-noon, 1.30-4.30pm daily; daily 45-min tour in German AS70; AS60 OAPs; AS40 students.

Baden & Bad Vöslau

Paddling in hot thermal pools is a popular diversion for Austrians, many of whom spend at least one weekend a year at one of the spas along the eastern border. Baden (the word means 'baths') is where generations of Habsburgs used to come to take the waters. Indeed the Habsburg court spent every summer here between 1803 and 1834. With its *Biedermeier* architecture, grandiose baths, spa park, quirky museums, theatre and casino, Baden still has a faded, turn-of-the-century charm. In the summer, operetta fans come here to enjoy performances at the theatre. The spa complex in Bad Vöslau is worth visiting just to ogle the architecture.

Both towns are easy to get to. Baden is 25km (16 miles) south of Vienna, Bad Vöslau only a few kilometres beyond Baden. Both can be easily reached by car, train, or bus (leaving from the **Staatsoper** on the hour). Baden makes an excellent starting point to tour the southern and western Vienna Woods. There are many hotels in both Baden and Bad Vöslau, so it may be worth staying overnight to enjoy the hot thermal waters one day, and tour the southern Vienna Woods on the second.

Bad Vöslau Information
Schlossplatz (02252 70743). **Open** 8am-noon, 1-4pm, Mon-Thur; 8am-noon Fri. English spoken.

Tourist Board Baden
Brusattiplatz 3 (02252 22600-600).
Open *1 May-31 Oct* 9am-6pm Mon-Sat;
9am-noon Sun; *1 Nov-31 Apr* 9am-5pm Mon-Fri.
English spoken.

Head to a Heuriger *in **Gumpoldskirchen**.*

Hotel Schloss Weikersdorf
Schlossgasse 9-11 (02252 483 010) **Rates** *single* AS1,340; *double* AS2,200; *suites* AS3,120. **Credit** AmEx, DC, MC, V.
Castle-like hotel with all mod cons, and a swimming pool and sauna for guests. Prices include breakfast, indoor swimming pool and sauna.

Gumpoldskirchen

This whimsically named community, just a few miles outside of Baden, is the most popular wine-growing village south of Vienna. Approach the village from any direction and you'll lose yourself deliciously in row upon row of undulating vineyards. Obviously, the main reason for stopping off in this town is a visit to a *Heuriger* (local wine restaurant) to try out some of the world-famous Gumpoldskirchner vintages. Stroll down the main street, choose from a number of Heurigen and do what Austrians do: spend hours consuming vast quantities of food and wine.

Mayerling & Heiligenkreuz

Driving from Baden to Heiligenkreuz will take you through the Helenental, the valley of St Helena, one of the most beautiful valleys in the Vienna Woods. Napoleon thought it so gorgeous he wanted to end his days here. The Helenental is more wild and woolly than the civilised rolling hills of the northern Wienerwald. On either side of the road rise steep rock faces, thick forests with overhanging branches and rushing rivers. Napoleon, of course, ended his days in a different St Helena.

Mayerling is famed for a tragic suicide pact immortalised in a 1935 film of the same name. Once the hunting lodge of Crown Prince Rudolf, Mayerling became a household word with the mysterious double suicide of the then heir to the throne Rudolf and his 17-year-old mistress, Baroness Maria Vetsera. Emperor Franz Josef converted the hunting lodge into a convent of atonement of the Carmelite nuns, so there's not much to see now, but it still is a popular place for tourists.

A few miles from Mayerling lies **Heiligenkreuz Abbey**, a romantic Cistercian abbey that harmoniously blends elements of the Romanesque, Gothic and Baroque periods.

Heiligenkreuz is set within the wilderness of the southern Vienna Woods, it feels peaceful and isolated. The abbey was founded in 1133 by Babenberg Margrave Leopold III. The first Cistercian monks came here from the Morimond Abbey in Burgundy.

The complex is an exquisite example of medieval architecture and houses a number of historical and artistic treasures. The basilica, begun in 1135, is the oldest example of ribbed vaulting in Austria; the chapterhouse, a Babenberg burial place, contains Austria's oldest ducal tomb. The tragic Maria Vetsera is buried here.

Stift Heiligenkreuz
Heiligenkreuz Monastery
(02258 8703-0). **Open** 10am-5pm daily.
Tours 10am, 11am daily.

Heiligenkreuz Tourist Office
Heiligenkreuz 15 (02258 8720). **Open** 8am-noon Mon-Fri. No English spoken.

Accommodation

The following are bed and breakfast lodgings in private homes.
Sattelbach contact: Hermine Wolf (02258 8367).
Schwechatbach contact: Grasel family (02258 2583).

Mountain biking

Austria has an enviable network of hiking and biking trails. Free maps of all descriptions, dozens of package-tour deals with hotels and restaurants with bike rental facilities, are all available at any tourist information centre.

A new mountain biking trail network throughout the Vienna Woods was inaugurated in June 1999. More than 40 cycle paths, all perfectly signposted, cover more than 900km (560 miles) of the Vienna Woods. There are 80 restaurants along the way, all geared for hungry cyclists. Mountain bikes and city bikes are available for hire from most train stations.

For bike trail maps, visit website: www.mtb-wienerwald.at or contact the tourist office for the Wienerwald (*see chapter* **Getting Started**).

Lower Austria

For summit completely different, try peak travel to Vienna's local mountain range.

Many people envisage Alpine scenery when they think of Austria, but in fact the Alps peter out before they hit Vienna. That is why the eastern Alpine region, only 90km (60 miles) outside the city, is so special to the Viennese. It is their little mountain range close to home, the last Alpine hiccup before the land flattens as it heads toward the Hungarian steppe lands.

Austrians love their mountains. A sunny day on the mountainside will magically transform the sedate Viennese into friendly rosy-cheeked nature buffs. Dressed in *Lederhosen,* and often sporting ski poles, the Viennese will happily jaunt up and down mountain trails for hours, chirping an informal 'grüss Gott' greeting to everyone they pass.

The most popular mountains close to Vienna are Rax, Schneeberg and Semmering. They are all within an hour's drive of the city. Semmering is the favourite port of call with day-and weekend-trippers from Vienna, and has its own tourists' railway built in 1854. Semmering also has the **Panhaus Grand Hotel** and many faded fairy-tale villas.

Rax, Schneeberg and Semmering are all easy mountains to *wandern,* the relaxed Austrian version of mountain hiking. All three have trains, gondolas or ski lifts working year round that will take you a fair way up the mountainside, so even exercise-phobes can experience a mountain view and the rustic charms of a mountain *Hütte.*

Adventurous hikers and climbers can follow well-marked trails covering the three mountains. Maps for the region are free, and there are plenty of *Hütte* for refreshments. For winter skiing, Semmering is well equipped for sporting day-trippers from Vienna, and Schneeberg and Rax also have their own cross-country slopes.

GETTING THERE

If you don't have a car, Semmering is the easiest place to get to, as there are direct trains leaving every two hours from Südbahnhof in Vienna. The train meanders along a series of 31 viaducts and tunnels amid beautiful Alpine scenery: it was the first railway to be entered in the registry of World Heritage Sites by UNESCO.

This mountain region is a favourite with retired people, which means plenty of skiing, walking, good hotels and cultural attractions all within walking distance of each other.

Travelling further afield to Rax or Schneeberg, taking in Reichenau and Semmering on the way back to Vienna, is easiest by car.

*The slopes of **Semmering** – the nearest skiing spot to Vienna.*

Semmering

Until 1854 Semmering was a relatively undisturbed mountain pass. Then Carl Ritter von Ghegas's first mountain railway succeeded in connecting this Alpine wilderness with Vienna. Never before was it so easy to get to the mountains.

Over the next 20 years Semmering, with its mild weather and its stunning views of the mountains Schneeberg and Rax, slowly gained in popularity. By 1882, the first villas were built on the edge of the mountain, and in 1889, the first Hotel Panhaus, with 44 rooms, was opened.

By 1900 Panhaus had become a massive Grand Hotel along the lines of the Palace in St Moritz. Semmering was the place to go, right up to World War II. The Panhaus guest book from 1900 to 1938 reads like a multicultural society register: Emperor Franz Josef, Austro-Hungarian aristocracy, writers, artists, actors and intellectuals from Europe and America all lived it up here (there is even a photograph of Josephine Baker riding a sled outside the hotel).

By 1913, Panhaus was a grand, spa hotel with 400 rooms, resident orchestra and facilities for hunting, fishing, riding, sledging, and bobsledding and winter skiing. Requisitioned by the Nazis during World War II, Panhaus was also popular with prominent Nazis Erwin Rommel and Field Marshall Göring. After the war, Semmering never regained its place in society, and Panhaus was closed in 1969.

However, in 1994 Panhaus was reopened in something close to its former glory. With the reopening, Semmering has blossomed again.

The modernised hotel has 113 rooms. Those in the modern wing, individually styled from cosy country to art nouveau, are the most expensive. Rooms in the original hotel are enormous with huge balconies, but some can be tatty.

Visitors who prefer a smaller hotel choose the **Panoramahotel Wagner**, which has wonderful views, Swedish-designed rooms and an excellent restaurant. Pure-air fanatics approve of its no-smoking policy (practically unheard of in Austria, a smoker's heaven).

Thousands of well-marked walks start from either of these hotels. For the best views, take the **Sonnwendstein chair lift** at Maria Schutz. Maps are available free from hotels and the **Tourismusregion Süd-alpin**. Semmering is also the best area close to Vienna for skiing.

Sonnwendstein chair lift

Maria Schutz (02663 8525). **Open** *during season* 9am-4pm daily. **Tickets** AS240 weekend day card; AS220 from 11am; AS190 half-day card; AS190 Mon-Fri day card.

Poet's corner

'On August mornings I can count the morning/glories, where to die has a meaning/and no engine can shift my perspective.'

One of England's finest poets, WH Auden, wrote this line in his 1969 poem *Moon Landing* about his garden in the town of Kirchstetten, about 25 kilometres west of Vienna.

Auden and his partner Chester Kallmann set up home in a small farmhouse in Kirchstetten in 1958. Auden wanted a 'Mediterranean life in a northern climate' in a German-speaking area that produced drinkable wine and give him access to an opera house of a high standard.

The house is at the top of the village, set against the woods. It's an impressive property with a large garden and a hanging roof.

Auden and his close friends would relax in the garden, doing crosswords and drinking Martinis. His *On Installing an American Kitchen* poem with it's 'grub first, then ethics' motto from Berthold Brecht, is about Kirchstetten.

Today the upstairs of the house, which during his lifetime was Auden's study, houses the Auden Museum with items such as his typewriter, his collection of (surprisingly modern) books and some Auden first editions. To arrange an appointment to visit you must call 2743 8206.

Auden was a well-liked figure in the village. He was known locally as 'Herr Dichter' (Mr Poet) and the locals were extremely proud of having a world-famous figure living among them. It seems the locals accepted Auden and Kallmann living together as a couple without much question. He was a regular worshipper at the local Catholic church (where he is buried in a modest grave, marked simply 'WH Auden, Man of Letters').

Austrian life and society became the subject of many of Auden's poems – *Glad*, the poem written for his young Austrian lover Hugerl, and *Whitsunday at Kirchstetten* are among his better-known later works.

Auden died in 1973 in Hotel Altenburgerhof, on Walfischgasse in Vienna – there's a memorial plaque for him on this rather drab building (the hotel has since closed) – after giving a reading at the Palais Palffy to members of the Austrian Society of Literature. Auden had achieved his wish to 'bugger off quickly'.

Panhaus Grand Hotel

Hochstraße 32, Semmering (02664 8181). **Rates** *double* AS660-960 per person; AS100 weekend supplement. **Credit** AmEx, DC, MC, V.
Four-star hotel with a swimming pool and sauna.

Panoramahotel Wagner

Hochstraße 267, Semmering (02664 25120). **Rates** AS735. **Credit** DC, MC.
Rates include breakfast.

Tourismusregion Süd-alpin

Hochstraße, Semmering (02664 2539-1). **Open** 8am-2pm Mon; 8am-4pm Tue-Fri. English spoken.
Staff at this regional tourist office can advise on daily excursions and provide hikers with maps.

Mount Rax

Mount Rax (2,007m/6,587ft) is a great place for someone wanting to experience the Alps without having to travel too far from Vienna. Like most Austrian tourist points, the mountain is well marked, so even the scattiest tourist shouldn't get lost. The Rax has an unusually large, 34km/21mile plateau dotted with eight mountain huts, all with superb views, which means there is always somewhere to stop and eat or drink.

You can get most of the way up Rax with very little effort. Following the signs to the *Rax-Seilbahn* in Hirschwang, you reach the **Rax Gondola**, which transports you 1,017m (3,338ft) in eight minutes. In an easy half hour you reach the Ottohaus (1,644m/5,395ft) for refreshment.

For a more vigorous hike, drive beyond the Rax Gondola toward Prainer Gscheid, where you can park the car and take the trail for a few hours toward Karl Ludwighaus (1,804m/5,920ft), then further up to the top of Rax.

Rax Gondola

Reichenau-Hirschwant (02665 2497/52450). **Open** 9am-4.30pm Mon-Fri; 8.30am-4.30pm Sat, Sun.

Schneeberg

Schneeberg is Vienna's 'local' mountain and at 2,075m (6,810ft) is the highest mountain in Lower Austria. It stands just outside Wiener Neustadt on the A2 motorway south, and can be reached by train. Consequently, Schneeberg tends to be more crowded than Rax.

Its popularity is compounded by having its own railway line: a steam engine and a train called the *Salamander* leave from the town of Puchberg am Schneeberg to carry visitors 9.5km (6 miles) to Hochschneeberg, near the summit.

Schneebergbahn Salamander Train

Hotline (02636 366120).
The trains operate from late April to early November, full ascents take 85 minutes and cost AS270 return.

Skiing

In the winter season many people descend on sedate Semmering for downhill and cross-country skiing. Semmering has two ski areas, Hirschenkogel and Stuhleck. Hirschenkogel, 1,318m high (4,326ft), is within walking distance of all Semmering hotels and has both artificial snow and a floodlit ski-piste.

In Spital am Semmering, 10km (6 miles) further on, is the less crowded Stuhleck with 20km (12 miles) of pistes and its own floodlit run open 6-9pm Monday to Saturday.

Semmering-Hirschenkogel

Semmering (02664 8038/snowline 02664 2575). 8 person gondola, 1 double ski lift, 1 T-bar, 1 help lift direct to Panhaus. **Pistes open** 8.30am-4pm daily. **Cost** AS315 day card, AS200 children; AS280 from 11am, AS175 children; AS245 half-day, AS140 children; AS335 day pass for all 3 local ski regions. *Website: www.semmering.hirschenkogel.at*

Stuhleck

Tourism information for Spital am Semmering (0385 3217/snowline 0385 333). **Open** 8.30am-4pm daily. *Website: www.spital-semmering.at*
Reichenau an der Rax has three different cross-country ski routes, including one that goes from the Bergstation to Ottohaus on the Rax plateau. Ask at the office for a map of the ski routes;.

Reichenau/Rax Tourism Office

65, Hauptstraße 63, Reichenau/Rax (02666 528 65/fax 02666 542 66/tourismus@reichenau.at). **Open** 9am-3pm Mon-Fri; 9am-5pm Sat.

Cross-country ski route

(02666 52450).

Living on the sledge.

The Wachau

As gorgeous as a sun-warmed apricot, the Lionheart's prison is travellers' heaven.

Stift Melk – *this beautiful Benedictine monastery overlooks Melk.*

Umberto Eco chose this lovely area as the setting for the beginning of his philosophical thriller *The Name of the Rose*. It's easy to see why. The exquisite Wachau section of the Danube, 80km (50 miles) north-west of Vienna, is dramatic scenery indeed. The landscape is punctuated by fortresses and monasteries whose defences bear witness to a turbulent history, when opposing armies fought for control over the river valley; even Richard the Lionheart was banged up in a fortress here for insulting Leopold V. Today, the area's historical importance is balanced with some of life's great pleasures – fine wines, outstanding restaurants and extraordinary views. It's not surprising people wax lyrical about the Wachau and flock to its villages in droves.

Although the name 'Wahowa' was first used around 830 AD to describe a few kilometres of the Danube banks in the area, it is now considered the 35km (22 miles) of the Danube between the towns of **Melk** and **Krems**. The Wachau begins as the Danube turns north past the Stift Melk, which overlooks the Danube bend. The river then flows into a magical landscape of rolling hills, monas-

teries, cloisters and castles harmoniously set among slope after slope of manicured vineyards that produce some of the best wines in Austria.

It is touristy, but not tacky. Along the banks are bicycle and hiking paths, sightseeing boats that make their way up and down the waters, beaches for swimming, as well as restaurants and wineries to attract food and wine-lovers from all over Austria. In the spring, when the apricot blossoms are in bloom, the Wachau looks achingly beautiful. Later on, the heavenly *Marillenknödeln* (apricot dumplings) are a delicious reason to head for a restaurant (*see* **Wine & food** *page 262*).

The Wachau is accessible and well organised for tourists. Both Melk and Krems are reached by train in just over an hour from Vienna; by boat in three hours. Although the Wachau makes a comfortable day trip for most travellers, those wishing to make the most of the prized countryside (in 1994 the European Council awarded the Wachau the European Diploma for Nature Conservation) may wish to stop for a night or two. There are many small hotels and restaurants with rooms to choose

The vineyards of the Wachau produce some fine wines.

from. During the high season, which is from April to October, bicycles can be rented at both Melk and Krems train stations and boats cruise up and down the Wachau between Melk and Krems three times a day. A great way to see a bit of everything is to ride a bicycle partway up the Wachau, then return to your hotel via boat or local train, all of which accept bicycles on board free of charge.

Melk

The town of Melk cowers in the shadow of its abbey, **Stift Melk**, perched on a cliff on two steep faces overlooking the Danube. The abbey is huge – 17,500sq m (188,370sq ft). Its side façade is an incredible 1,115m (3,695ft) long. Originally the residence of the Babenberg family, it has been a Benedictine monastery since the monks received possession of the monastery land in 1089. The Benedictine monks are still very active in the parishes, school (with 750 pupils), economy, culture and tourism of the entire area. The abbey was built in its present form in the eighteenth century by master builder Jakob Prandtauer. The marble hall and the library, with their high, tiered ceilings, are breathtaking.

Stift Melk
To book a guided tour (02752 52312-232/kultur.tourismus@stiftmelk.at). **Open** *Apr-Oct* 9am-5pm daily; *May-Sept* 9am-6pm daily.

Dürnstein

In 1192, Austrian Archduke Leopold V caused a sensation in Europe when he took Richard the Lionheart prisoner while the latter was on his way

back from the Crusades. Richard was accused of insulting Leopold. Locked in the Fortress of the Künrings in Dürnstein, many people thought the King of England was dead.

Legend has it that Richard's faithful minstrel Blondel took off, lute in hand, to find his master. Playing his master's favourite tune underneath the windows of Dürnstein Castle, Blondel was answered by Richard's voice.

Eventually, Richard was released upon the payment of a large ransom, which went towards the building of Wiener Neustadt. The ruins of the Künringerburg, the King's forced residence, stand on a hill above the picturesque village and offer fantastic views of the Danube.

The Chorherrenstift, part of a fifteenth-century Augustinan Monastery, has been restored and can be visited between April and October.

Dürnstein Town Hall
Dürnstein 25, 3601 (0271 1219).
Open 8.30am-noon, 1.30-4pm Mon-Fri.
Tourist information for the area is available here.

Willendorf

She isn't particularly pretty, but she's called Venus and admired the world over. Willendorf is the location where the 'Venus of Willendorf', a neolithic sandstone sculpture of a woman – one of the earliest in the world (current estimates say 26,000 years old) – was found. The sculpture excited a great deal of debate after it was discovered by archaeologist Josef Szombathy in 1908.

For years a replica was used, but now the original is on display in the **Naturhistorisches Museum** in Vienna (*see chapter* **Museums**).

*Oh **Krems**!*

Krems

The historical centre of Krems is more than 1,000 years old and is the eastern border to the Wachau. The town is made up of restored, clean, delightful pastel buildings. Wandering along its cobbled streets is the best way to appreciate the charm of the place. Krems is also a vinicultural centre: at the town's Kloster und Wine College, visitors can attend wine seminars and tasting sessions. Six kilometres (3.7 miles) south of Krems is its abbey, Stift Göttweig, founded in 1083. It can be visited daily between March and November and the restaurant in the grounds delights in spectacular views over the countryside.

Austropa Travel Office Krems

Undstrasse 6 (02732 82676). **Open** *30 Apr-1 Nov* 9am-7pm Mon-Fri; 10am-noon, 1-7pm Sat, Sun. *1 Nov-30 Apr* 9am-6pm Mon-Fri. *Closed weekends until mid-Apr.*

By bike, foot or boat

Bicycle paths run 1,300km (808 miles) along the Danube banks between Donaueschingen, Germany to Budapest, Hungary. They are well organised and it is very easy to hire a bike for a few hours or few days and pedal off into the sunset. *Wanderkarte*, detailed maps of the region, are provided for free by the Lower Austria Tourist Information. Bicycles can be rented from the train stations at both Melk and Krems, and can be transported on the trains and boats that plough up and down the Wachau. Many hotels and guesthouses accommodate hikers and cyclists in style, providing picnics, storage rooms and pick-up services for those who need it. The more adventurous trails can be found in the Waldviertel area along the south bank of the Danube, or in the Dunkelsteiner Wald. Less energetic potterers can enjoy sedate routes that stick to the banks of the river.

DDSG Blue Danube Boat Trips

Information (58 880-0)
From Krems: *1 Apr-29 Oct* 10.15am, 1pm, 3.45pm daily. From Melk: *1 Apr-29 Oct* 11am, 1.50pm, 4.15pm daily (stopping at Spitz, Dürnstein). **Tickets** AS200 one way; AS270 return (Krems-Melk-Krems). *In between stops* Melk-Spitz/Spitz-Krems AS110 one way; AS150 return.

Bike rentals

Krems Bahnhof (02732 82536-331). **Open** 7am-7pm daily; *winter* closed 11.15am-2pm Mon-Fri; 11.15am Sat, all day Sun. **Cost** AS150 full day, AS100 with train ticket; AS120 half day, AS80 with train ticket.
Spitz Bahnhof (02713 2220-350). **Open** 8am-7pm daily; *winter* closed as above. **Cost** as above.
Melk Bahnhof (02752 2321-350). **Open** 6am-6pm Mon-Sat; 7-8pm Sun; *winter* closed as above. **Cost** as above.

Wine & food

Austrian gastronauts drive to this productive region just to eat and drink. The origins of wine growing in the Wachau Valley date back to Celtic times, though the Romans were the first to cultivate it. The art of wine making died out during the medieval ages, but was rediscovered with a passion during the Renaissance.

The mild climate and rich soil of the Wachau were renowned for successful viniculture, so when Emperor Joseph II's 1784 decree permitted wine growers to serve their own wines, the Wachau, with its 31 monasteries and extensive vineyards, flourished. White wines such as Grüner Veltliner, Riesling and Burgundy are a speciality of the Wachau.

The **Weingut Jamek**, a small vineyard and restaurant along the northern bank of the Danube in Joching, is particularly lovely and looks more so when you've had a few free samples at the bar. Indulging in Wachau delicacies, washed down with a glass of Jamek's own Grüner Veltliner, while sitting on its sunlit terrace overlooking the river, is a heavenly experience.

Other excellent wines can be sampled at the Kloster und Wine College in Krems, Kellerschlößl of the Freie Weingärtner in Dürnstein, Winzer Krems in Krems and the WG Dinstlgut in Loiben.

One of Austria's best restaurants can be found in the town of Mautern, on the south side of the Danube across from Dürnstein. Top chef Lisl Wagner-Bacher, Austria's Delia Smith, presides over the **Bacher**. The restaurant has been awarded three Gault-Milleau stars. Lisl's sister Gerda Schickh runs her own restaurant with rooms, **Schickh**, in Klein-Wien at the foot of Göttweig Abbey, for those who prefer their food in a less formal setting.

Bacher Hotel & Restaurant

Südtiroler Platz 2, Mautern (02732 82937). **Open** 11.30am-2pm, 6.30-9pm Wed-Sun. **No credit cards**.

Restaurant Schickh

Klein-Wien (02736 7218). **Open** 11am-3pm, 6-10pm daily. **No credit cards**.

Weingut Jamek

Joching 45 (02715 2235). **Open** 11.30am-4pm Mon-Thur; 11.30am-11pm Fri, Sat. **Credit** DC, V.

Burgenland

Bird- and music-lovers, flocking to the region, only stop twitching to give themselves a good Haydn.

'The Rennweg is the gateway to Asia,' say the Viennese, declaring themselves to be the last outpost of European civilisation. The Rennweg is a road that leads out of the city towards the east. Politically speaking, this saying makes no sense, but biologically it is justified. To the east of Vienna there is a clear border to the habitats of many plants and animals found in Eastern Europe and Asia. This is particularly evident around the **Neusiedler See**, which can be reached within three-quarters of an hour from Vienna by car, rail or bus.

In the same way that the landscape, flora and fauna flow into one another in this region, many cultures meet here. Primarily there are both Austrians and Hungarians – up until 1921 the Burgenland region belonged to the Hungarian part of the Danube monarchy. Also there are Slovakian influences from the north: the Neusiedler See is visible from the towers of Bratislava Castle. Croatians who settled 500 years ago in Burgenland contribute southern Slavonic elements. The smallest ethnic group in Burgenland are the Roma, persecuted by the Nazis as cruelly as the Jews were.

Eisenstadt

Traces of this old European multiculturality can be discovered on a short tour of the area around the small provincial capital, Eisenstadt (in Hungarian: Kis Marton, in Croatian: Zeljezno). Eisenstadt's most famous resident, Josef Haydn, lived here for 31 years and, although he died in Vienna, his tomb is here, in the solemn Bergkirche. Standing above the town, **Schloß Esterházy** (the palace of the powerful Hungarian Esterházy family) is the reason Eisenstadt is provincial capital. The palace dates from the fourteenth century and houses Haydn Hall, a highly considered concert hall. In 1803 Central Europe's first steam engine was installed in the Orangery by David Watson. This technical innovation was not for industrial use, but served to lift water for an artificial waterfall.

Close to the palace and its gracious grounds, is the old Jewish ghetto. The lovingly arranged **Jüdisches Museum** tells of the history (and the extermination) of the Jews in Burgenland. It is no coincidence that it lies next to the palace. The Esterházys respected the Jewish community for their contribution to education and trade in this mainly agricultural region.

The family not only supported the economy, but also the arts. Haydn, as court music director, was the most famous artist in their service. His symphonies are performed in their original surroundings in the castle during the International Haydn Festival in September (02682 618 660).

Eisenstadt has few hotels, but the regional tourist office can help visitors find rooms in the town or a place to nest around the Neusiedler See. Eisenstadt's smarter hotels are listed below.

Regional Tourist Information
Burgenland Tourismus, Schloss Esterházy, A-7000 Eisenstadt (02682 633 8416). Some English spoken.

Gasthof Familie Ohr
Ruster Straße 51 (02682 624 60). **Rates** *single* AS650-680; *double* AS900-950. **Credit** DC, MC, V. Three-star hotel. Rooms have cable TV and shower.

Hotel Burgenland
Franz-Schubert-Platz 1 (02682 696). **Rates** *single* AS1170; *double* AS1,630; *suites* AS2,200. **Credit** AmEx, DC, MC, V. A four-star hotel with en suite rooms, an indoor swimming pool and sauna.

Schloss Esterházy
Eisenstadt (02682 719 3000). **Open** 9am-5pm daily; *1-31 Nov* closed weekends. **Admission** AS50; AS30 concs. **Credit** DC, MC, V.

Jüdisches Museum
Unterbergstraße 6 (02682 65145). **Open** *1 May-31 Oct* 10am-5pm Tue-Sun. **Admission** AS30; AS20 students. **Credit** MC, V.

Oslip & Rust

Leaving Eisenstadt in the direction of birdwatcher's paradise, the Neusiedler See, travellers are often charmed by Oslip. A small Croatian-speaking community, where the houses are arranged typically with their shorter sides along the street, Oslip is picturesque and villagey.

During the summer, many people bring out benches and tables and sit in front of their doors. They offer home-produced fruit and vegetables, wine and spirits for sale, while the children scramble around in the cherry trees.

On the edge of the village lies the **Cselley Mühle**, which provides a romantic setting for quality concerts of every type.

This other-worldly spirit is also present in the nearby Roman quarry of St Margareten. About 2,000 years ago the Romans began to extract the easily workable lime-sandstone for their camps along the *limes* (the fortified boundary of the Roman Empire). In the Middle Ages, the quarry supplied the building material for Vienna's **Stephansdom**. Over the centuries a huge, artificial crater landscape has taken shape here. But the quarry is not only a monument to the history of Austrian building; since 1959 it has provided a setting for one of the most important sculptors' symposia in the world. Artists from all over the world meet here in the summer to exchange information and to teach students – and leave the works they have produced standing here. This has resulted in one of the most vibrant land art projects on the Continent – because it is expanded every year.

A few kilometres further on is **Rust**, one of the smallest towns in Austria. The old architecture of its Renaissance and Baroque houses has been almost completely preserved. The wine trade made the community rich so quickly that Rust's citizens were able to bribe the advancing Turkish armies in the fifteenth and sixteenth centuries not to destroy the town. Hidden behind the mighty yard doors are beautiful inner courtyards where the regional wines are offered for tasting and sale.

Cselley Mühle

Cselley Mill
Cselley-Mühle Kultur, Aktionszentrum Sachsenweg 7064 Oslip (02684 2209/fax 06284 220914/info@cselley-muehle.at). Bus 556 from Landstraße, departs 5.40pm daily.
Website: *www.cselley-muehle.at*

Neusiedler See

This lake, like so many of the species of bird that visit it, is something of an exotic foreigner in the region. The westernmost lake of the Eurasian salt steppe region, its water is almost as salty as in the Mediterranean, but where the salt comes from is a scientific mystery. Climate-wise the lake is the interface between a variety of weather systems. Their conjunction brings long, hot summers, ideal for swimming, sailing or exploring the mostly flat shores on a bicycle – and long cold winters when the lake, only 1.8m (6ft) at its deepest, freezes into Europe's largest skating rink. The 230 sq km (89 sq mile) body of water is surrounded by a thick belt of reeds, sometimes up to 400m (1,313ft) wide, making it an ideal habitat for a variety of plants and animals that elsewhere are extinct or endangered. The lake is particularly important for birds; about 300 species breed or rest here on their transcontinental migratory flights, and therefore extremely interesting for birdwatchers.

One of the stars is the bee eater. This colourful relative of the kingfisher rivals the splendour of tropical hummingbirds. The spoonbills, stalking through one of the 40 or more shallow salty ponds to the east of the lake, are, by contrast, almost colourless. The avocet, with its upward-bending beak, trawls the water's surface for insects, dragonflies and other small creatures. Another special guest is the bittern. With its greenish-brown feathers it is hardly distinguishable from the reed stalks that are its preferred habitat.

There are daily guided tours during the summer months. They all start from the **National Park Centre** in Illmitz. This, the first trans-border national park in Central Europe, opened in 1993. With 95sq km (37 sq miles) lying in Austria and the rest (120 sq km/46sq miles) in Hungary it represents an optimistic political picture, after decades of forced separation by the Iron Curtain.

Three restaurants on the shores of the Neusiedler See illustrate the quality of food in this region. The **Taubenkobel** (Dovecote) in Schützen is one of Austria's best restaurants. Maitre Walter Eselböck uses ingredients almost exclusively from the region in dishes such as cold pea soup with avocado and mint; Wels (a freshwater fish of the catfish family) with veal brawn, cabbage and white asparagus; braised leg and rack of lamb, with garlic and wild spinach.

In Podersdorf on the eastern shore (the most popular tourist destination on the lake), there's a small restaurant called **Zur Dankbarkeit** (To Gratitude). It's run by the Lentsch family, who have created a simple menu from some forgotten treasures of Jewish cooking. In Weiden, on the lake's northern shore, the Weissberger family tend the **Blaue Gans** (Blue Goose) restaurant. This marks the eastern limit of haute cuisine from Alsace. Thomas Weissberger came here from France, and found his love on the Neusiedler See. A four-course meal in the restaurant garden on the lake shore is a blissful way to end a day. There is one native species, however, that al fresco diners could well do without. Punctually at 9pm the mosquitoes emerge from the reed beds.

National Park Centre

National Park Neusiedlersee-Seewinkel, Hauswiese, Illmitz (02175 3442). **Open** *Nov-Mar* 8am-4pm daily; *Apr-Oct* 9am-6pm Mon-Fri; 10am-5pm Sat, Sun. **Admission** free.

Taubenkobel

Haupstraße 33, Schützen am Gebirge (02684 2297). **Open** noon-2pm, 6-10pm, Wed-Sun. **Credit** AmEx, DC, MC, V.

Zur Dankbarkeit

Haupstraße 39, Podersdorf (02177 2223). **Open** *from Easter* Fri evenings, Sat, Sun. **Credit** MC, V.

Blaue Gans

Im Seepark, Weiden am See (02167 7510). **Open** *from 1 Apr.*

Moravia

Visit the land of Pils and say cheers to a Czech mate.

Only 65 miles (105km) north of Vienna, travellers are in for an extraordinary surprise. Cross the border into the Czech Republic and the clean order-liness of Austria gives away to ex-Communist grey drab prefab. Then out of nowhere appears an incredible castle with amazing follies, Roman arch-es and minarets and temples of Diana, all set like abandoned chess pieces in miles upon miles of landscaped parkland. It's somewhat run-down, but its rather shabby splendour makes it all the more bizarre and beautiful.

This is Valtice and Lednice, the estates of the fabulously rich Liechtenstein princes who lived in Moravia for 600 years. Right up until Communism took over, generations of Liechtensteins carried out major transformations on the two great castles of Valtice and Lednice, two of the 99 Czech homes the Liechtenstein family owned (they stopped short of 100 to avoid having a standing army). Between these two massive homes is an immense park covering some 200sq km (77sq miles), form-ing one of the oldest and most extensive designed landscapes in Europe.

Now, only 16km (10 miles) from the Austrian border, it stands in all its faded glory, unmod-ernised but intact. The Czechs didn't know what to do with this national heritage. Until recently, the beautiful land around Valtice/Lednice was going the way of many ex-Communist regions, destined to be covered by hamburger joints and supermar-kets. Then some American Czechs with money and know-how joined forces with some enterprising locals and decided to tempt tourists to the place. They created the Prague-Vienna Greenways, a network of 100-year-old hiking trails that connects cultural monuments, castles and historic towns through the little-discovered countryside along the Czech/Austrian border. You can travel the Greenways on foot, bicycle or horseback all the way from Vienna to Prague. Near the trail access points are certified hotels, pensions and restau-rants recently opened by Czech owners keen for a bite of the tourism cherry.

Moravia is the area of the Greenways that lies close to Vienna. Here many aristocratic Austro-Hungarians, like the Liechtensteins, maintained their great estates, for agriculture, forestry and wine. Now, with the help of the American Friends of Czech Greenways, many Moravians are learn-ing how to dish out Moravian wine and culture for the tourists to eagerly lap up. Charming hotels and a variety of restaurants have opened in the beau-tiful town of Mikulov, which is fast developing into a lively and worldly wise centre from which to start a Moravian tour.

Mikulov

In Mikulov, a small town where the Dietrichsteins' castle overlooks the Renaissance market square, wine cellars and restaurants are opening up apace, making for a congenial atmosphere for visitors. The ambitious Liechtenstein princes moved their family seat from Vienna to Mikulov in the thir-teenth century before moving to Valtice in the fifteenth century. Under the Dietrichsteins, whose castle dominates the hill town (and who owned it up to 1945), Mikulov thrived and became a cosmopolitan centre of commerce and culture on the trade route from Vienna to Brno and the north. Because the Dietrichsteins displayed an uncom-mon religious tolerance, Mikulov had the largest Jewish community in Moravia from the sixteenth to the nineteenth century.

Today Mikulov feels like an ex-Communist town on its way up in the world. Many of its Renaissance townhouses, some decorated in pictorial sgraffito, have been restored by incomers seduced by the town's lovely surroundings and cheap prices. Mikulov delights in an elaborate, pointed plague column, a Romanesque church and Baroque castle and an impressive mausoleum of the Dietrichstein family. Remnants of the town's once-large Jewish community include a fifteenth-century synagogue destroyed by the Nazis, but now restored and reopened as a museum; Mikulov also has one of the oldest Jewish cemeteries in Europe.

Valtice

In 1560 the Liechtensteins decided one castle just wasn't enough, they wanted to have a palace and grounds equal in splendour to the Viennese court. They sold their Mikulov headquarters and moved the family residence to Valtice, a huge castle with-in the town of the same name. In the beginning of the eighteenth century they began renovation, which continued for nearly 150 years. All the sur-viving parts of the earlier Gothic and Renaissance structures were destroyed and the garden was replaced by a more fashionable natural landscape park in the picturesque English style.

Today the Valtice castle is recognised as one of Moravia's most significant examples of Baroque architecture. From the marble chapel designed by Fischer von Erlach to the elegant stable buildings, all of its handsome features are in demand during the summer, when the castle is used for opera, music and dance festivals, notably the annual weekend of Baroque arts. The Valtice Gala Weekend is usually on the last weekend in August and features lots of different music from jazz to Moravian folk music. People who come here for the arts events enjoy strolling through the surrounding gardens, and making frequent visits to the famous wine cellar for a spot of tasting.

Lednice

Valtice apparently was not enough for the greedy Liechtensteins, and so, only 10km (6 miles) from Valtice, they created the summer residence of Lednice. This time they really went over the top. Outside it looks like an overgrown Scottish baronial pile; inside it's much the same story: there are stag horns on the walls, wooden cassette ceilings, parquet floors, and rooms full of mahogany furniture, all complemented by ornately coloured wallpaper from China and India. The most remarkable feature is the library's winding staircase, carved in the mid-nineteenth century from a single gigantic oak tree.

Bouncing along over Czech roads full of potholes on the way up to the castle, the formal romantic labyrinth garden, with hedges and trimmed lawns, which acts as a formal introduction to the estate, seems a bit out of place. The Dyje river meanders through the unique botanical garden, which includes a collection of North American trees and habitats for many bird and animal species. There is a long, narrow greenhouse that contains more than 250 species of tropical plant, an orangery and stables designed by Fischer von Erlach. Most extraordinary of all is a minaret standing in the distance behind a large pond dotted with 16 islands. Atop 302 steps at the spire's highest point, you can see the surrounding villages in the south Moravian wine region, the Palava limestone hills to the west, and on a clear day, the border regions of Austria.

Guided tours through the extravagantly furnished Lednice residence run every 45 minutes, and are given in English by eager tour guides.

Valtice-Lednice forest

The forest has thousands of miles of public footpaths, all clearly colour-coded with indications of distance, terrain and walking times. Just a little walking in the 200sq km (77sq miles) of parkland between Valtice and Lednice will do for a taste of what there is to offer. Along the way you can visit 15 of the surviving astonishing follies built

throughout the landscape. There is a classical Bordeaux chateau, a hunting lodge called the Temple of Diana, a tiny Gothic chapel dedicated to Hubert, the patron saint of hunters, a semicircular colonnade with statues of the Three Graces, and at the head of a lake, an impressive temple to Apollo. Outside the park there are the Palava Hills, a white limestone range designated a UNESCO Biosphere Reserve because of their unique flora and fauna.

Wine

Moravian wines are far cheaper than Austrian varieties. Their excellent wines, Vlassky Riesling, Rulandske and Frankovka, are available in every restaurant cellar. The Moravian wine growers have learned as much about the cultivation of tourism as about viniculture, so now tours of the wine trails can be arranged by bike, foot or car.

Information

Czech Greenways, a non-profit organisation, acts like a sophisticated tourist information agency arranging walks, bike rides, wine tasting, and access to the best Moravia has to offer.

Zelene Stezky

Czech Greenways
Panska 7/9, 602 00 Brno, CR (420 5422 18350/ greenways@ecn.cz). **Open** 9am-4pm Mon-Fri.
A Czech NGO that promotes the Greenways idea. An Austrian Greenways is being set up.

Friends of Czech Greenways

515 Avenue I, 1B, Brooklyn, New York 11230 (718 258 5468/friendsgw@aol.com).
US NGO with info on Moravia and the festivals.
Website: www.pragueviennagreenways.org

Accommodation

Rohaty Krokodyl

Husova 8, 69200 Mikulov (420 6255 11672). **Rates** CzK1,200-1,500. **Credit** AmEx, MC, V.
Small, pleasant hotel in the centre of Mikulov.

Hotel Drnholec

Namesti Svobody 8, 69183 Drnholec (420 6255 19307/hotel_drnholec@sol.cz). **Rates** CzK1,200. **Credit** AmEx, DC, MC, V
Small ten-room family hotel in Drnholec.
Website: www.pvnet.cz/www/hotel_drnholec

Hotel Apollon

P. Bezruce 720, 69142, Valtice (420 6273 52625/fax 420 6273 52009). **Rates** CzK1,200. **Credit** AmEx, DC, MC, V.
Smart little three-star hotel in a renovated building.

Vinarsky dvur Pension

Mala strana 198 691 42 ,Valtice (420 6273 52737). **Rates** CzK1,000. **Credit** AmEx, MC, V.
Small pension in Valtice with wine cellar and pool.

Bratislava

The quirky Slovak capital offers an entertaining few days.

With a population of 450,000, Bratislava, nestled between Budapest, Vienna and Prague, is the runt of the Habsburg urban litter; it's definitely a quieter town with less going on than its bigger sisters, but is a fascinating place to poke around for a couple of days – and escape the crowds at the height of the tourist season.

The people here seem to have a youthful feeling of possibility and post-Communist enthusiasm that is missing in the larger, more cynical capitals of Prague and Budapest – especially since the electorate's September 1998 rejection of Vladimir Meciar, who had ruled with a nostalgia for the Communist days and a penchant for strong-man tactics. More than anything, the youthful feeling comes because this really is a new capital. Slovakia gained independence on 1 January 1993, when Czechoslovakia became the Czech and Slovak republics, in one of the most amicable separations this region has seen. New Year's Day is therefore a double celebration.

Though settlements and fortifications at this site date back to the Iron Age, only in 1919, after independent Czechoslovakia was carved from the ruins of the Habsburg Empire, did Slovaks take over the city and name it Bratislava. Once it was the Roman town of Posonium, perched at the edge of empire. As Breszalauspurc in the ninth century it had been part of the Great Moravian Empire. For most of the rest of history it was an Austro-Hungarian city known as Pressburg to the Germans, who provided around half its inhabitants until 1945, and as Pozsony to the Hungarians, who used it as their capital for several centuries after the Turks occupied Buda in 1541. There are still around 700,000 ethnic Hungarians in Slovakia, and you'll often hear Hungarian spoken in Bratislava.

The Habsburg empire gave Bratislava a quaint old town and a castle that looks like a giant upturned bedstead. But the old town is not always the first thing a visitor will see. There's been a lot of more recent development and the result is a strange mixture of baroque and misguided Communist-era architecture, with some recent capitalist kitsch thrown in. Persevere, and you will be rewarded by getting to know a pleasant town.

There are two sights that can properly be described as unmissable – both in the sense of must-see and of can't-be-avoided. One is the castle, up on its hill, from where there's an excellent view of the Danube and the river plain to the south and the east. The other is the Most SNP – the Bridge of the Slovak National Uprising, also known as the Nový Most, or New Bridge. This splendid example of spacey, Communist design is a single-span suspension affair, sporting a café and restaurant resembling a flying saucer, high above the Danube on its one double pylon. Catch the lift up to the restaurant from mid-bridge – although the saucer no longer revolves, the view from most tables is fantastic, either north across the city centre to the vineyard-covered small Carpathian foothills, or south over the huddled high-rise housing of Petržalka, which looks almost pretty when lit up at night.

Petržalka was once a quiet, tree-lined suburb, but its oil facilities made it a target for American bombers in World War II. During the Stalinist era, planners decided to rebuild on a grand, Socialist scale. They put up endless rows of ugly blocks to

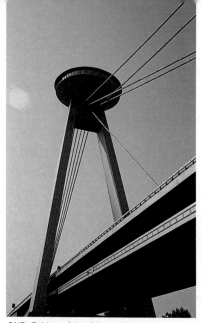

SNP: Bridge of the Slovak National Uprising.

create one of the largest housing estates in the world. These acres of concrete, home to 150,000 people – a third of the city's population – are so uniform that visitors sometimes get lost for hours, unable to distinguish one street from another.

Fortunately, all that is across the river from the worthwhile part of town, and easy enough to avoid. Other vestiges of Communism include hotel porters who offer to change money on the sly, the vast square called námestie Slobody with its Fountain of Friendship and the world's largest post office, and the extraordinary inverted pyramid, on the way out of town, that houses Slovak Radio.

Even downtown, the old and new vie for attention. Right at the centre of the city, in Kamenné námestie, there is a sprawling Tesco and adjacent modern towers that house the Hotel Kyjev and the Charlie's Pub disco. Eastwards and uphill past the námestie SNP, there's the Michalská veža (Michael Tower). Legend holds that you shouldn't speak while passing through the arch at the tower's base, because the city guards were once ambushed here while chattering away. On the other side is the old town, where it's possible to get lost for a while and forget that modern architecture exists. There are several small museums and exhibits as well as some nice quiet restaurants, cafés and bars.

Bratislava is a beer town, and some local brews are certainly worth trying. Zlatý Bažant (Golden Pheasant) is now brewed under licence in Hungary and elsewhere, but the domestic version is better. Smädny Mnich (Thirsty Monk) is another delicious local brew. And, of course, you can find most of the

popular Czech beers at a great price, plus Becherovka – the deceptively sweet and easy to swallow Czech herbal liqueur. Enjoy a glass or two, perhaps with a beer chaser, but before you have half a dozen, try to remember what your worst hangover was like.

Typical Slovak food is bog-standard central European – schnitzel and the like – and the Hungarian influence seems evident. In fact, many restaurants are staffed by members of the city's large ethnic Hungarian population. Some uniquely Slovak dishes include *strapatzka*, egg noodles and cheese; *parenica,* decoratively twisted smoked cheese; and *cesnakova polievka*, garlic soup, which can be truly delicious.

Most of the old town shuts down by midnight, but other places are open late and filled with a young, friendly, unpretentious crowd. One of the later spots inside the old town is Bar 17s on Hviezdoslavovo námestie, a small, congenial pub that sometimes tries to squeeze live music in the back. For a beer and bar food during the day, or a late nightcap when other places close, try KGB, a long cellar bar with a not-too-obvious entrance along Obchodná (look for the picture of a beer mug) that sometimes hosts rock bands. For underground (literally) techno there's the U-Club at NAG Ludvika Svobodu, an old air-raid shelter at the foot of the castle hill that draws a tattooed-and-pierced crew. For the full Bratislava nightlife experience, it has to be Charlie's Pub, at Špitálska 4, a large underground space with two big side rooms and a main dance floor animated by ancient pop and disco hits. Open until 4am, this is Bratislava's most popular nightspot, packed with revellers any night of the week.

There are several good hotels around the centre of town, some of which offer discounted rooms at weekends. The Perugia at Zeletná 5 (421 7 5443 1818) is the best looking of the posh new old town hotels. Fans of tatty Communist modernism will enjoy the skyrise Kyjev at Rajská 2 (421 7 361 082), just behind Tesco, with its delightfully dodgy nightclub and excellent views across the city. Some of the most affordable rooms in the heart of town are at the Gremium Penzion (421 7 544 306 53) at Gorkého 11, but it's small and often full. Most cheaper options tend to be a little out of town. BIS (below) can help in finding accommodation.

A handy pocket-sized guide and street atlas is available in various languages. The dreary local English-language paper, the fortnightly *Slovak Spectator*, is good for listings of venues and events.

BIS

Klobučnícka 2 (421 7 5443 3715). **Open** 8am-7pm Mon-Fri; 9am-2pm Sat, Sun. Some English spoken. Bratislava Information Service can help with accommodation, as well as providing information. Small selection of guidebooks on sale.
Branch: Hlavná stanica (main station) (421 7 5443 4370).

Budapest

Vienna's little sister.

Rail travellers to Budapest from Vienna used to steam to a less sophisticated, but exotic sister city at the fringe of the Dual Monarchy's mysterious east. More recently this line was a constricted artery running through the Iron Curtain and into the grey of Soviet communism. Today the Vienna-to-Budapest train is a three-hour scoot past white windmills and seas of sunflowers – with no interruption in mobile phone service. And almost without the Viennese noticing it's now become a journey from the somnolence of central Europe into a brash and adolescent city at once more tacky and charming than Vienna would ever dare to be.

Budapest is a city reinvented in the last decade. The visitor of 1990 might have smelled change in

the air, but that was a Budapest just awakening. Now, by comparison, it heaves with barely organised energy. There's a dizzying pace of construction, dirty new money, organised crime, ugly new poverty, Vietnamese food, French cafés, American sports bars, neon, sex and in-line skates. What the western European metropolis adopted over 50 years, Budapest has seized in ten.

Budapest still bears the shadows of imperial glory. The Habsburgs left their mark with a nineteenth-century building frenzy that lined broad boulevards in Pest with grand, sometimes graceful architecture. The construction craze also gave Budapest the glass-fronted Western (Nyugati) train station designed by the Eiffel company, as well as a glorious exercise in establishment kitsch, the parliament building sitting by the Danube.

Much of the Habsburg-era architecture is now shrouded under layers of soot. Inside, most buildings have long been looted of their statuettes, wrought iron railing work and brass carpet rods. Outside, their plaster flakes away in sometimes dangerous chunks. Many bear the scars of time. On the Pest side, strangely bland ground-level façades tell of the hasty repairs that followed the uprising of 1956, when Budapest exploded in anti-Soviet fury only to be brought to heel by Russian tanks and artillery. In Buda, bullet-holes ringing windows along the narrow, hilly streets date mostly from World War II when German and Russian soldiers fought house to house.

But the old scars and dirt are being steadily rubbed away in the more prosperous districts. Buildings are emerging from scaffolding, their mouldings repaired and their smudged faces suddenly yellow, orange or pink. In Buda there are garish new villas, while Pest is being peppered with modern office blocks, five-star hotels and, in unrealistic abundance, western-style shopping malls. Right next to Eiffel's elegant train station is the West End City Centre, a sprawling complex of cinemas, hotel rooms, offices and a cavernous shopping hall complete with a waterfall one-third the height of Niagara Falls (Canadians are responsible). Inside, thuggish security guards keep their eyes peeled for unwanted visitors while sullenly smoking beneath the no-smoking signs.

Also steaming ahead are public works projects. A new bridge has spanned the Danube, rebuilt tram lines criss-cross the city, the downtown pedestrian zone along Váci utca has doubled in length and a fourth metro line is planned.

So, too, does nightlife bubble. On a warm summer's night, a clutch of cafés on Liszt Ferenc tér flutter with the young and beautiful of Budapest, sipping whisky and energy drinks while solemnly keeping watch for new trends in footwear. Here, women put themselves on display in a manner that makes foreign jaws, male and female, drop.

For restoration and revival a different pack make for Budapest's baths – the best of these being the Rudas, where the oldest part of the complex was built by the Turks in the sixteenth century.

Another transformation is happening – a human transformation. Waiters still roll their eyes when asked to wait tables, and people still read newspapers as if they are tea leaves to decipher. Old women in housecoats still note carefully the hour of the night when the foreigner next door comes home, and thoughts of the future are still haunted by dim feelings of fear. But that Budapest is dying, however slowly. Pushing it into history are young people so different from their parents the term 'generation gap' fails miserably. Already there are stockbrokers, doctors and members of parliament who have no adult recollection of communism. And they, more than fresh paint and shopping malls, are making Budapest less and less recognisable to the visitor from 1990.

And yet, just when Budapest seems disappeared into Anycity and Everycity, there is a peaceful place to find. A place that is only Budapest. On a hot summer day, trudging up a bending road beneath Castle Hill, or on a grimy street in the old Jewish ghetto, follow a stream of cool air flowing from the doorway of a drab and peeling house.

Go past the soft stink of dust and trash in the hallway and you might find a nearly silent, arch-lined courtyard filled by the scent of lilacs, the only sound dribbling from a mossy wall fountain. A suspicious old woman in a housecoat will undoubtedly watch your every move. But if you asked kindly, she might tell you in bits of German and English about the day those bullet holes were made by her window.

It's possible to get to Budapest and back in a day, but scarcely worth the bother. We'd recommend two nights as the ideal short stay. Call in at an office of Tourinform on arrival, or buy our Budapest guide for a truly in-depth lowdown.

Tourinform

V. Sütő utca 2 (317 9800). **Open** 9am-7pm Mon-Fri; 9am-4pm Sat, Sun.
The English-speaking staff are helpful and have information on travel, sightseeing and entertainment.
Branches: Nyugati station, main hall (302 8580); VII. Király utca 93 (352 1433).

The Sopron shop stop

Sopron is way up in the north-west of Hungary, in a little Magyar nodule that extrudes into Austria. The location has had two effects on this fascinating small, old town. The first is that it escaped devastation by both Mongols and Turks and has managed to retain a medieval feel you won't find anywhere else in Hungary outside Budapest's Castle District. The second is that Austrians flood over the border to go shopping on the cheap.

The Várkerület, which encircles the Old Town, bustles with tiny shops selling bargain booze and cigarettes, budget salamis and household gadgets. Opticians proliferate. There are dentists, hairdressers and beauticians everywhere. Just about every business doubles as a money-changer.

Stepping from all this through one of the entrances into the Old Town is like cracking open a stone to find an extraordinary crystal formation within. Here cobbled, medieval-patterned streets are relaxed and traffic-free. Practically every building is listed: medieval dwellings rub gables with Gothic churches and

Baroque monuments. Commerce continues, but quietly, in discreet boutiques and jewellery shops nestling by small museums.

The Firewatch Tower, symbol of Sopron, sums up the town's history and offers a view that takes it all in. It's built on Roman foundations, with a twelfth-century base, a sixteenth-century column and balcony, a seventeenth-century spire, and a 'Fidelity Gate' installed in 1922 to mark the town's decision (they voted on it) to remain part of Hungary after Trianon. From the top you can see the streets and walls of the Old Town, following the lines of the previous Roman settlement, and the vine-covered hills beyond the outskirts.

Though there's plenty to look at in the daytime – the various old houses and museums around Fő tér and the Medieval Synagogue at Új utca 22 are particularly interesting – it's at night, after the day-trippers have all gone, when Sopron is at its most atmospheric. Wandering the medieval streets, quiet except for the chatter and clatter from restaurants and wine cellars, only a rare parked car intrudes between you and the illusion that you have stepped back several centuries.

Directory

Directory

Getting Around

Vienna has excellent public transport and is an easy city to get around. Many of the roads in the 1st district are pedestrianised and best negotiated on foot.

A public transport day ticket can be used on any of the trams, buses or U-Bahn lines that zig-zag and encircle the city centre. Forget taking a car into the 1st district as parking spaces are rare and garages are expensive.

Taxis aren't too expensive, but then again aren't really a necessity when there is such reliable public transport available.

Sooner or later, whether by foot, bus, train or tram, you end up at the Ringstraße, a broad road encircling the 1st district. Trams circle the Ringstraße both clockwise and anti-clockwise and can serve as a hop-on, hop-off city tour.

Arrival in Vienna

Vienna International Airport (Flughafen Wien-Schwechat) lies south-east of Vienna on the Ostautobahn (direction Budapest) and is the international airport for both Vienna and Bratislava. Because of the large international presence in Vienna, English is widely spoken and it is easy to get to and from the airport by public transport.

General Flight Information
(7007 22231/22232/22233).

Arrival Information
(7007 22197).

Departure Information
(7007 22184).

By public transport

Airport Shuttle Bus

Vienna International Airport is a 20-minute ride by bus or train from the centre of town. Buses operate two routes to/from the City Air Terminal (*Wien Mitte*) near the Vienna Hilton, and from Vienna's Westbahnhof, via Südbahnhof (it takes 35 minutes from Westbahnhof). The fare is AS70 one way, AS130 return per passenger, including luggage. Pay the bus driver as you board. Buses run about every half hour.

Vienna Airport Lines
(5800 2300). **Open** 4am-8.30pm Mon-Fri. **No credit cards.**

By train

The Schnellbahn 7 leaves from Wien Nord, via Wien Mitte, costing AS38 (two zones) one way. For more information call (051 717).

By taxi

When going to and from the airport it is better to take an airport taxi rather than a normal taxi as they charge a cheaper flat rate. Most Viennese use C+K Airport Service (1731), which charges a flat rate of AS270 one way. Upon arrival in the airport, go to its stand directly to the left of the exit hall; drivers are usually immediately available.

By limousine

Limousines and selection of large and small vans are available from Airport Service Mazur (7007 36422), but need to be reserved in advance.

Airlines

Austrian Airlines
1, Kärntner Ring 18 (1789/1766 7630/fax 1766 7699). U1, U2, U4 Karlsplatz/tram 1, 2, D, J. **Open** 9am-6.30pm Mon-Fri. **Credit** AmEx, DC, MC, V.
Website: www.aua.com

Aeroflot
1, Parkring 10 (5121 5010/fax 5121 50178). U3 Stubentor/tram 1, 2. **Open** 8am-1pm, 2-5pm Mon-Thur; 8am-1pm, 2-4pm Fri. **Credit** DC, MC, V.

British Airways
1, Kärntner Ring 10 (50 660/ fax 504 2084/reservations 7956 7567). U1, U2, U4 Karlsplatz/tram 1, 2, D, J. **Open** 9am-5pm Mon-Fri. Reservations 8am-8pm Mon-Fri. **Credit** AmEx, DC, MC, V.

Delta Airlines
1, Kärntner Ring 17 (5126 6460). U1, U2, U4 Karlsplatz/tram 1, 2, D, J. **Open** 9am-7pm Mon-Fri; 9am-5pm Sat, Sun. **Credit** AmEx, DC, MC, V.

KLM
1, Kärntner Ring 2 (7007 35388/ fax 7007 35569/reservations 5892 45090/24-hour reservation hotline 0031 2047 47747). U1, U2, U4 Karlsplatz/tram 1, 2, D, J. **Open** Reservations 9am-6pm Mon-Fri; 9am-1pm Sat. **Credit** AmEx, DC, MC, V.
Website: www.klm.com

Alitalia
Airport (7007 32643/fax 7007 35237/reservations 505 1707/24-hour reservation hotline 00390 665642). **Open** 6.30am-5.30pm daily. Reservations 9am-6pm Mon-Fri. **Credit** AmEx, DC, JCB, MC, V.

Lauda Air
1, Opernring 6 (7000 76730/fax 7000 576730). U1, U2, U4 Karlsplatz/tram 1, 2, D, J. **Open** 8.30am-5pm Mon-Fri. **Credit** AmEx, DC, MC, V.
Website: www.laudaair.at

Lufthansa
Airport (reservations 599 110/ fax 599 1190/24-hour reservation hotline 0800 900800).

Open 8.30am-5pm Mon-Fri.
Credit AmEx, DC, MC, V.
Website: www.lufthansa.at

Swissair
*1, Rotenturmstraße 5-9 (1789/7007
62510/fax 1766 4230). U1, U3
Stephansplatz.* **Open** 8am-7.30pm
daily. **Credit** AmEx, DC, MC, V.

Tyrolean Airways
*1, Opernring 1/R/third floor (586
3674/fax 587 1799). U1, U2, U4
Karlsplatz/tram 1, 2, D, J.* **Open**
9am-noon, 2-4pm Mon-Fri. **Credit**
AmEx, DC, MC, V.
Website: www.tyrolean.at

Public transport

Public transport is safe,
reliable, fast, easy to
understand and goes almost
everywhere. The Eastern
Region Transportation
Association (VOR) is a
network of eight zones
covering a huge area that
includes Vienna and
surrounding towns. The
central zone is known as the
Kernzone (zone 100). There
are trams, buses and five U-
Bahn metro lines that run
till midnight, with nightline
bus services running
overnight. Maps of Vienna's
transport system as well as
timetables (yes, the lines are
that reliable) can be bought at
any U-Bahn station.

Tickets & passes

Tickets can be bought at any
U-Bahn station as well as the
many little Tabak newsstands
sprinkled all over Vienna. Most
U-Bahn stations have automat
machines that sell tickets and
dispense change. If you don't
speak German, buy your
tickets from a person rather
than a machine, as they can
help you choose the ticket and
explain how to validate it. A
ticket needs to be validated
upon starting a journey. You
can use as many forms of
transport as you want for one
ticket, as long as it is within
one hour of its validation.
The validation machines are
relatively small and

inconspicuous boxes at the
entrance of each U-Bahn
station, and within all buses
and trams. Take the ticket and
slide it into the mouth of the
blue box (until you hear the
punching sound and a bell),
which will imprint the card
with the time and relevant
travel information.

It is an honour system, but
guards do wander on and off
the buses, trams and U-Bahn.
A fine costs AS560, and take
note that the dumb-tourist
routine doesn't work. The
important thing to remember is
that once you validate your
ticket, keep it with you in case
you get checked.

Transport Information Offices
*Vorverkaufsstellen der Wiener
Located at U-Bahn stations
Stephansplatz, Karlsplatz,
Westbahnhof, Landstraße
(Wien Mitte) (for all offices 790
9105).* **Open** 6.30am-6.30pm
Mon-Fri; 8.30am-4pm Sat, Sun
(except Landstraße). **Credit** AmEx,
DC, MC, V.
Information plus tickets for the bus,
tram and U-Bahn networks.

Prices

If you are going to be in
Vienna for more than a day,
public transport costs can be
reduced by purchasing either
monthly, weekly, three-day or
daily cards on the U-Bahn,
buses and tram. Tickets come
in either a multi-strip or single
form. The strip tickets
(*Streifenkarten*) are valid for
four or eight trips, one punch
per journey. You can also
purchase a Vienna Shopping
ticket, valid in zone 100 for one
day 8am-8pm, or the Vienna
24-hour ticket or 72-hour
ticket, valid in zone 100 for 24
or 72 hours after it is punched.
Another option is the Vienna
Card, which will set you back
AS210. It's valid for 72 hours
and carries the added bonus of
claiming discounts at
museums, galleries and
restaurants. Tickets can also
be bought on trams, but they

are more expensive and you
must have the correct change.

Children up to the age of six
can travel free all year round,
and children up to the age of
15 can travel free on Sundays,
public holidays and Austrian
school holidays. Senior citizens
(who must travel with ID
proving their age) can travel
with Pensionisten tickets, which
can be bought in advance.

Prices
Monthly card – AS560
Weekly card – AS155
3-day ticket (72 hours from when it is
validated) – AS150
Umweltkarte – AS300 for 8 non-
consecutive days
Pensionisten ticket for women over
60 and men over 65 – AS26 return
Daily card (8am-8pm) – AS50
Daily card (24 hours from when it is
validated) – AS60
Shopping card – AS50
Vienna Card – AS210

Single public transport tickets
from a newsstand or at the U-
Bahn station cost AS19 for an
adult, AS10 for children. They
are valid for one hour.

Tickets purchased on the
trams are more expensive (you
can't buy tickets in U-Bahns
and buses) and cost AS22 for
an adult and AS11 for children.

If you only plan to travel
two to three stops on public
transport, buy a ticket called a
Kurzstreckenfahrschein
(AS38), which will allow you
four trips: two to three stops
on the tram or two stops on
buses and U-Bahns.

Dogs also need a ticket and
are charged the same price as a
child. Nightlines cost AS15 for
one way or a four-way ticket
costs AS45.

U-Bahn

The U-Bahn is reliable, quick
and comfortable. Routes are
self-explanatory, and you'll
find pamphlets in English
available in most information
offices in the U-Bahns. Routes
on maps are colour-coded (U1
is red, U2 is purple, U3 is
orange, U4 is green and U6 is

Directory

brown) with all station signs in the same colours. Doors don't automatically open on the U-Bahn, so pull the handle sharply or press the lighted button. Don't be shocked by a peculiar statue of a red-haired person with an elephant trunk standing at the entrance of some U-Bahn stations; it is meant to remind passengers to throw their cigarettes away before entering (most people ignore it).

Local trains

The S-Bahn and Lokalbahn are the local and fast railways that can be used in Vienna and further afield. The Badner Bahn connects Vienna and the town of Baden (*see chapter* **Getting Started**).

If you are taking an S-Bahn within Vienna, you probably don't have to buy another ticket, but if you travel outside zone 100, you will need to buy an additional ticket according to how many zones you are travelling in. You can find this out by looking at the bull's eye zone map posted in all stations.

Tram

Vienna has a great system of trams, or *Straßenbahnen*, that will take you everywhere within the city and its outskirts. All trams are clearly marked with stops and timetables listed on white placards on one of the windows outside. Every stop is announced by name, with corresponding connecting lines, which probably doesn't help if you don't speak German, but at least if you know which stop you need to get off at you'll be able to recognise it. Tram doors don't automatically open, so press the lighted button by the entrance and exit doors. Tram line numbers or letters stand alone, for example 2, J, D.

Bus

Buses go to all the places that trams can't. Their stops look just like the tram stops and also have maps and timetables clearly displayed. Bus lines are identified by numbers ending with an 'a' or by three-digit numbers, for example 3a, 149, 234.

Bus Information
(71101).

Useful bus, tram & U-Bahn routes

Tram 1 circles the 1st district clockwise along the Ringstraße, and tram 2 circles the same road anti-clockwise. Hop on either tram and ride it in a full circle, which is probably the easiest and cheapest way to have a look at some of Vienna's most beautiful buildings. Trams D and J also run along the Ringstraße, but leave it eventually.

Bus lines 1a, 2a and 3a are the only public transport possible within the 1st district. The stops are clearly marked and have maps posted on them. The routes zig-zag their way through the 1st district, but as everywhere is really within walking distance, you can't go too far wrong.

The U-Bahn line U2 runs along the Ringstraße, and the U1 and U3 stop at **Stephansdom**.

Nightline

Vienna rolls up its pavements at midnight, however, Nightline buses run from 12.30am to 5am on the half hour on 22 routes. Like everything else in Vienna, the lines are pretty safe. Tickets have to be bought on the bus.

Train

Trains are used for most domestic travel within Austria, and travelling on them is a

very pleasant experience. Timetables can be picked up from the information office at any train station.

There are all sorts of special services available, such as a pick-up service for customers with confirmed reservations, where a reserved taxi or hotel representative meets you at the train station or accommodation (usually free); or the Haus zu Haus luggage service, which picks up and delivers your bags, charging AS180 for 40kg. It is especially useful for skiers not wanting to lug their skis around.

If travelling west towards Salzburg or Tirol, try to take a Panorama compartment, a first-class car with huge windows that are perfect for viewing the fabulous scenery. There are three main train stations: Westbahnhof for trains to the west, to locations such as Salzburg, Frankfurt, London and Paris; Südbahnhof for trains to Bratislava, Budapest, Prague, Venice and Rome; and Franz-Josefs-Bahnhof for north-western Austria and Prague. For all reservations and information call the numbers below.

ÖBB

Austrian Railways Information (24 hours *1717*/24-hour booking *1700*).

Taxis

Vienna's taxis are reliable and not that expensive. Most taxi drivers can speak a smattering of English. You can't hail them on the street, however, but will find them at clearly marked taxi stands. Calling a taxi often takes less than three minutes' waiting time. A small tip or 'rounding off' of the fee is expected. There is a basic rate on weekdays (AS22) plus a per-kilometre charge and a small transport fee. On Sundays, public holidays and at night (1-6am) both the basic fare and per-kilometre rate go up. There is also a waiting charge. Most taxis don't take credit cards, and a receipt is available upon request. The highly regulated taxi market has just been opened so expect changes to occur to the taxi services.

Taxi phone numbers
(31 330/40 100/60 160/81 400/ 91 091)

Taxi ranks in 1st district with telephones
Babenbergerstraße/Burgring (523 2355).
Hoher Markt/Marc-Aurel-Straße (533 0498).
Opernring/Operngasse (586 5205).
Rotenturmstraße/Franz-Josefs-Kai (532 1080).
Schottentor/Schottengasse (533 1260).
Schwarzenbergplatz/Kärntner Ring/Hotel Imperial (505 4163).

On the road

Like everything else in Austria, driving is highly regulated and relatively safe. It is required by law to have all documents and driving licences on you in case you are stopped. Austrians are aggressive drivers, but not as bad as their German neighbours. Speed limits are 30-50km per hour in residential areas, 100km per hour on country roads and 130km per hour on motorways. Be advised that spot checks are normal in Austria, and so is the breath test.

Car rental

Renting a car is fairly standard in Austria, but do specify if you plan to drive into Eastern Europe as there are a high number of car thefts and you want to make sure your insurance covers you.
Check for special rates and weekend fares.

Autoverleih Flott
6, Mollardgasse 44 (597 3402/fax 596 7429). U4 Margaretengürtel.

Open *7am-8pm Mon-Fri; 7am-12am Sat.* **Credit** *AmEx, DC, MC, V.*
Website: www.flott.at

Avis
1, Opernring 5 (587 6241/fax 587 4900/24-hour reservation hotline 0800 0800 8757). U1, U2, U4 Karlsplatz/tram 1, 2, J, D. **Open** *7am-6pm Mon-Fri; 8am-2pm Sat; 8am-1pm Sun.* **Credit** *AmEx, DC, JCB, MC, V.*

Europcar
3, Erdbergstraße 202 (799 6176/ fax 796 4295/airport 7007 33316/fax 7007 33716). U3 Erdbergstraße. **Open** *7am-7pm Mon-Fri; 8am-4pm Sat; 8am-1pm Sun.* **Open** *Airport 7.30am-11pm Mon-Fri; 8am-7pm Sat; 8am-11pm Sun.* **Credit** *AmEx, DC, JCB, MC, V.*
Website: www.europcar.com

Hertz
1, Kärntner Ring 17 (512 8677/fax 512 5034). U1, U2, U4 Karlsplatz/tram 1, 2, D, J. **Open** *7.30am-6pm Mon-Fri; 9am-3pm Sat, Sun.* **Credit** *AmEx, DC, JCB, MC, V.*

Breakdown services

Austria has two 24-hour major breakdown services that operate rather like England's RAC. The service is free for members; however, non-members can call on their services and pay by cash or credit card. Funds can be reimbursed at a later stage if you have motor insurance that covers you for Austria.

ARBÖ
15, Mariahilfer Straße 180 (891 210/fax 8912 1236). Tram 52, 58. **Credit** *AmEx, DC, MC, V.*
24-hour emergency hotline (123).
24-hour information hotline (891 217).
Website: www.arboe.at

ÖAMTC
1, Schubertring 1-3 (711 990/ fax 7119 91482/24-hour hotline 120). Tram 1, 2, D, J. **Open** *8am-5.30pm Mon-Fri.* **Credit** *AmEx, DC, JCB, MC, V.*
An extra fee of AS1,600 will be charged to non-members on top of other costs if you use this service. The cost of towing a car within Vienna is AS1,600.
Website: www.oeamtc.at

24-hour petrol stations

All international petrol stations take credit cards, but the local stations may not.

Aral
10, Am Wienerberg 68 (667 6173);
19, Heiligenstädterstraße 46-48 (368 2380).

BP
3, Erdberger Lände 30 (715 4826);
13, Hietzinger Kai 133-135 (877 1451).

Mobil
1, Morzinplatz 1 (Franz-Josefs-Kai/Schwedenplatz) (533 7398).

Shell
22, Wagramerstraße 12-14 (263 3691).

Parking

Parking in most areas of the 1st district is a nightmare, so avoid it whenever possible. You can never be sure where you can or cannot park, and the police are quick to ticket and tow, which can cost anywhere from AS300 to AS2,000.

Districts 1-9 have blue zones, which means that you have to purchase parking vouchers, available at newsstands. In the 1st district you can park for up to an hour and a half, 9am-7am Mon-Fri and Sat as marked. In other districts you can park for up to two hours, 9am-8am Mon-Fri and Saturday as marked. Look for designated parking spaces marked with blue lines. Vouchers come in 30, 60 and 90 minute increments. Cross-off the appropriate date, time and hour to the closest 15 minutes, and display it on your windshield. In the 1st or 7th district it might be simpler to park in a parking garage, marked with a blue P.

When driving on the Ringstraße, parking garages, plus the number of parking spaces available, are marked in lit signs on the road. Remember to pay the ticket at the Automat machines that are placed at the entrances before you get into the car.

Cycling

Vienna is a great city for bicyclists as long as you avoid main roads and tram lines, which any biker worth his salt would do anyway. The 7km (4-mile) bike path around the Ringstraße is a lovely way to tour the city without getting lost. The Danube also has bike paths to south Hundertwasser Haus and to the Prater, which is filled with bike paths, children and dogs. You can easily bike further north to Klosterneuburg for the day, or even further to the Wachau (*see chapter* **The Wachau**). A booklet in German called *Rad Wege* shows Vienna's cycle routes and is available at book stores. City cycle tours from May to September are available from Radverleih

Salztorbrücke under the Salztor bridge (535 3422). *For bike rental see chapter* **Sport & Fitness**.

Walking

Vienna is a very walkable city. In the 1st district, with its pedestrian zones and narrow one-way streets, walking is the best way to get around. The trams on the Ringstraße run against the traffic, so look both ways when you cross the street. Jaywalking is frowned upon by locals, and could even result in a fine if the police feel so inclined. For all their orderliness, Austrians become aggressive, Lauda-like drivers when they get behind the wheel, so be careful when crossing the street – zebra crossings are often ignored

and many cars won't stop for jaywalkers.

A monthly multi-language brochure can be found at the **Vienna Tourist Office** (*see below*) called *Walks in Vienna* (*Wiener Spaziergänge*).

The office also provides walking tours. No need to book in advance, just show up at the designated meeting point. Tours last about one and a half hours.

Vienna Tourist Information

Wiener Fremdenverkehrsamt
*1, Kärntner Straße 38 (513 8892).
From June 2000: 1, Albertinaplatz 1
(same telephone number). U1, U2,
U4 Karlsplatz/tram 1, 2, D, J.*
Open 9am-7pm daily.
Call the tourist office to learn more about the 50 or so guided walking tours in and around Vienna, exploring themes such as Baroque or *Biedermeier* Vienna.

Resources A-Z

Accommodation

The best way to find a flat in Vienna is to buy the *Kurier*, *Standard* or *Presse* on Saturdays and look under the section *WohnungsMarkt*, where flats are listed by district. *Bazaar* also publishes a housing magazine on Wednesdays. *See also chapter* **Media**.

Flats are rent controlled in Vienna, which means that many families have enormous flats for 40 or 50 years and are paying practically nothing for them, while smaller flats are going for 100 times the price. Because of that, large flats are sometimes cheap, but in need of serious investment. Many Viennese rent a flat and pay lots of money to modernise it, knowing they may never receive their investment back, but as they plan to spend their lives there, the controlled rent soon becomes cheaper as the years go by. Foreigners only wanting to spend a short few

years here will want to rent a modernised flat with conveniences and kitchen included. Estate agents usually take two to three months' rent as their commission, but it varies so always check.

Consumer

If you have questions about your rights as a consumer, contact the organisation below, which has English speakers:

Consumer Information Association (VKI)

*6, Mariahilfer Straße 81 (58 877-0).
U3 Neubaugasse.* **Open** 9am-3pm Mon-Fri.

Crime

Vienna is one of the safest cities in Europe. Many people, including women, don't think twice about walking alone in most districts even at night. Public transport is generally safe day and night. The opening up of the borders with Eastern Europe, however, has

begun to take an effect. An increasing amount of pickpocketing and petty crime is occurring in tourist places, so it is wise to take precautions, especially in crowded places such as the Naschmarkt. There are very few places to steer clear of in Vienna – Karlsplatz station is renowned as a drug centre; the Prater at night is known for pickpocketing.

Customs

As Austria is part of the EU, it abides by EU rules, which means you can bring the following into the country duty free, provided you paid taxes in your EU country of origin: 800 cigarettes, 400 cigarillos, 200 cigars, 1 kilogram smoking tobacco; 100 litres spirits, 20 litres alcoholic beverages containing no more than 22% volume; 90 litres wine (or 60 litres sparkling wine) and 110 litres of beer.

Duty free purchases in
Austria are as follows: 200
cigarettes or 100 cigarillos or
50 cigars or 250 grams
smoking tobacco; 2 litres wine
and 1 litre spirits; or 2 litres
spirits or 2 litres champagne;
and 50 grams perfume and 250
millilitres eau de toilette and
500 grams coffee and 100
grams tea.

There are VAT refunds for
travellers with destinations in
non-EU countries. You can get
the necessary forms from
stores where you bought the
items. Allow an extra 15
minutes at the airport to go to
the special tax free line and
process your refund.

Embassies

Australian Embassy
*4, Mattiellistraße 2-4 (5128 5800/fax
513 1656). U2, U3 Karlsplatz/bus
4a.* **Open** 9am-1pm, 2-5pm Mon-
Thur; 9am-1pm Fri.

British Consulate
*3, Jaurèsgasse 12 (7161 35338).
Tram 71.* **Open** 9.15-noon, 2-4pm
Mon-Fri.
British passport holders only in the
afternoon.

British Embassy
*3, Jaurèsgasse 12 (716 130). Tram
71.* **Open** 9am-5pm Mon-Fri.

Canadian Embassy
*1, Laurenzerberg 2 (5313 83000).
U3 Schwedenplatz/tram 1, 2.*
Open 8.30am-12.30pm, 1.30-3.30pm
Mon-Fri.

Indian Embassy
*15, Kärntner Ring 2 (505 8666/fax
505 9219). U1, U2, U4
Karlsplatz/tram 1, 2, D, J.* **Open**
9am-noon Mon-Fri.

Irish Embassy
*3, Landstraßer Hauptstraße (Hilton
Centre 16th floor) (7154 2460/
fax 713 6004). U3, U4 Landstraße.*
Open 9.30-11.30am, 1.30-4pm
Mon-Fri.

South African Embassy
*19, Sandgasse 33 (3206 4930/
fax 3264 9318). U6 Nussdorf.*
Open 8.30am-noon Mon-Fri.

US Consulate
*1, Gartenbaupromenade 2 (31
339/3005). U3 Stubentor/tram 1, 2.*
Open hours vary. *Visas* 8.30-10am
Mon, Tue, Thur, Fri.

US Embassy
*9, Boltzmanngasse 16 (31 339/fax
310 0628). Bus 40a.* **Open** 8.30am-
5pm Mon-Fri.

Disabled travellers

In general, Vienna is an easy
city to get around; however,
the public transport is not well
set up for disabled travellers
on their own. Trams and buses
don't have wheelchair lifts,
although most U-Bahn stations
do. It is assumed that disabled
travellers will be accompanied.

That said, there are
organisations that can give
specific details for anything
you want to see or do in the
city. The train station has an
entire magazine available for
disabled travellers called
Behindertenführer der ÖBB.
You can also pick up a guide
for handicapped people,
available in English, from
the **Vienna Tourist
Information** or call City
Information for a guide to
public accessibility on
(525 500).

Bizeps
(5238 92123).
A multilingual support group run by
and for the disabled.

Fahrtendienst Haas
(27 700). **Open** 6am-9pm Mon-Fri;
8am-9pm Sat-Sun.
Taxis equipped to transport
wheelchairs. Flat rates to
destinations within Vienna and
airport.

Information on the
U-Bahn for the blind
(7909 41301).

Landesjugendreferat
der Magistratsabteilung
(MA) 13
(400 0843-55).
For AS100 you can order
Behindertenatlas Ämter, Soziales and
Kultur und Freizeit für Jugendliche,
which are brochures full of
information in German about social
services and government agencies
that serve the disabled.

Social & Disability
Department of Vienna
*1, Schottenring 24/1 (53 114-853
74). U2 Schottentor/tram 1, 2, D.*
Open 3.30-6.30pm Mon, Thur.

If you are a resident in Vienna, this
department offers information on
accessible transport, worker's
protection and schools.

Drugs

Vienna is a city of contrasts
when it comes to drugs.
Although no drugs, either soft
or hard, are allowed in Austria,
the possession of marijuana
seeds is not illegal. Hence
shops such as **Bush Planet**
(*see chapter* **Shopping &
Services**) in the 7th district
offer seeds and kits for grow-
your-own marijuana plants.
On the other hand, prescription
drugs such as sleeping pills,
sedatives and Prozac are
considered illegal in large
quantities. If you bring any of
these drugs into Austria, it is
recommended to bring your
prescription with you so that
they will not be confiscated.

Vienna has an open drug
scene where drug dealers,
often under police surveillance,
concentrate in well-known
places such as at the
Kettenbrückengasse U4
station, the tunnels leading to
Karlsplatz and certain stations
on the U6 U-Bahn. For the past
ten years, the Austrian drug
authorities have been fighting
a problem of drug dealers,
mainly immigrants from ex-
Yugoslavia, Albania and
Africa, who are pushing hard
drugs such as morphine and
heroin in Vienna. In 1999 over
100 drug dealers from West
Africa were arrested in a
highly controversial drug raid.

Because of its strong social
system, Vienna isn't a bad
place for drug addicts. There is
a strong network of social
workers, doctors and
psychologists working to help
those with a drug problem.
Three-quarters of its addicts
are in drug therapy, and strict
rent control means most drug
users aren't homeless.

Drug laws are officially the
same for Austrians and

foreigners; however, if you are from the EU you will probably have fewer problems than if you are Eastern European or African. The rules are complicated, but basically if you are caught with a small amount of drugs you will receive a slap-on-the-wrist notification, or *Anzeige*, from the police, but probably nothing more. Punishment can vary but can include obligatory therapy to coach you on how not to become an addict, submission to medical tests, and if you are Austrian, you can lose your driver's licence. In 1999 drug-related deaths jumped to 130, from 80 in 1998. The new government is likely to introduce more draconian measures to deal with any perceived problems as their electoral campaigns clearly announced.

Drogenberatungstelle
6, Gumpendorferstraße 64 (586 0438-0). Bus 13a, 14a. **Open** 4-8pm Mon; 2-8pm Tue-Sun.
Advice and help for drug addiction.

Drug hotline
(405 2244).

Education

State schooling is very good, and since so many citizens are paying huge amounts of taxes for a social welfare system that includes education, most parents end up sending their children to state schools. Compulsory schooling in Austria lasts nine years. The four-year elementary school for ages 6-10 is followed by secondary education in either *Hauptschule,* or for brighter pupils, an *Allgemein Bildende Höhere Schule,* which provides a general education in the arts and sciences. Pupils who leave school at 14 who don't want to pursue further education can enrol at a technical school to learn various trades. Apprenticeships are required to attend a vocational school. A graduation certificate is

required to enrol in university. State schools are free, as is the university, although there are discussions about bringing in sorely lacking funds to the university via the introduction of some sort of fee system.

Electricity

The current used in Austria is 220v, which works fine with British 240v appliances. If you have US 110v gadgets, it is best to bring the appropriate transformers. Plugs have two pins, so bring an adapter.

Emergencies

A useful tip to know is that the German word *Ambulanz* means emergency room or outpatient clinic, and *Rettung* means ambulance. So if you need an ambulance, say Rettung or the emergency service might think you are going to the emergency room on your own.

Fire
Feuerwehr *(122).*

Police
Polizei *(133).*

Ambulance
Rettung *(144).*

Vienna Medical Association Service Department for Foreign Patients
1, Weihburggasse 10/12 (5150 1213). U1, U3 Stephansplatz. **Open** 8am-4pm daily.

Fachärzte Lugeck
(512 1818).
A group of English-speaking doctors and nurses on call seven days a week, 24 hours a day.

Health & medical

Most doctors in the Austrian Health Service (KK) speak English. Hospital care is divided between general care *(allgemeine Klasse)* or Special *(Sonderklasse),* which is like BUPA. Treatment is available for all countries with special

treaties with the Austrian KK, which includes most European countries. Britain has a reciprocal arrangement with Austria so that emergency hospital treatment is free when you show a British passport. Technically, seeing doctors, dentists or outpatient departments is also free. However, in reality, receiving free medical treatment can involve lots of bureaucracy, so it is best to take out full health insurance. Almost no hospitals take credit cards for payment.

Hospitals

There are a number of private clinics and hospitals, but the largest and most comprehensive hospital is the Vienna General Hospital (AKH) in the 9th district. There are many Accident hospitals *(Unfallspitäler)* listed under Hospitals *(Krankenhäuser)* in the white pages of the phone book. The following are a few hospitals that accept emergencies 24 hours a day, seven days a week.

Allgemeines Krankenhaus (AKH)
9, Währinger Gürtel 18-20 (40 400-1964). U6 AKH.
The largest hospital in Europe, the AKH is affiliated with the University of Vienna. It is probably your best option if you are in central Vienna.

Lorenz Böhler Unfall Krankenhaus
20, Donaueschingenstraße 13 (33 110). U6 Dresdnerstraße.

Poison Antidote Service
Vergiftungsinformationszentrale *(406 4343).*
This is a 24-hour service, seven days a week, staffed by English-speaking physicians.

Unfall Krankenhaus Meidling (UKH Meidling)
12, Kundratstraße 37 (60 150). U4 Meidling, then bus 7a.

Dentists

Austrians have good dental care, but only some dental costs are covered by the state system. Many Austrians skip across the border to Hungary, where they can usually get the same treatment for a third of the cost.

On-duty dentists

(512 2078). **Open** 8am-1am Mon-Fri; 9am-6pm Sat, Sun.
This recording in German gives the names and telephone numbers of dentists on emergency call in Vienna. You can also look in the weekend newspapers under 'Emergency Services' *(Notdienst).*

University Dental Clinic

9, Währinger Straße 25a (outpatient 40 181-0/dental prosthesis 40 181-2001). U2 Schottentor, then tram 37, 38, 40, 41, 42. **No credit cards.**
The university emergency dental clinic is open Mon-Fri, but only for a few hours. Check to confirm times.

Pharmacies

Pharmacies *(Apotheken)* are found in all districts in Vienna and are normally open 8am-noon, 2-6pm Mon-Fri; 8am-noon Saturdays, although many chemists in the 1st district are also open Saturday afternoons and weekdays during lunchtime. They can be easily spotted by a cursive 'A' sign posted prominently outside. Some chemists are beautiful, such as the 1901 *Jugendstil* Engel Apotheke in the 1st district (Bognergasse 9). Many over-the-counter drugs can be found in local **Bipa** (*see chapter* **Shopping & Services**) stores.
Pharmacies take turns as to which are open 24 hours, and always hang a sign showing which pharmacy nearby will be the closest one open. You can also find them in the phone book under *Apotheken.*

Medicine Delivery Service

Medikamentenzustelldienst *(89 144).*
For AS170 this 24-hour service will pick up and deliver medicines from pharmacies.

Pharmacy Information

Apotheken-Bereitschaftsdienst *(1550).*
A tape recording in German listing pharmacies open after normal business hours and on weekends.

Alternative medicine

Austria has a well-organised system of professional organisations and doctors' councils in alternative and complementary medicine. Choose any of the organisations below and they will be able to suggest a specialist. Be prepared to bring cash. You can also pick up a copy of the magazines *Wellness* or *Gesundheit for General Health and Fitness* or the more esoteric magazine *Pulsar* for other tips.

Austrian Society of Homeopathic Medicine

7, Mariahilfer Straße 110 (526 7575).
A list of homeopathic doctors is available from this English-speaking group.

Austrian Scientific Council in Acupuncture

4, Schwindgasse 3/9 (505 8594).

Beers Health Club

1, Neutorgasse 16 (535 1234). U2, U4 Schottenring/tram 1, 2, D. **Open** 9am-11pm Mon-Fri; 9am-9pm Sat, Sun. **Credit** AmEx, DC, MC, V.
This chic sport club offers Reiki, Shiatsu, Chinese acu-pressure massage, reflexology and Thai massage. Cost AS580-670 per hour.

International Academy for Alternative & Complementary Medicine

10, Kuradstraße 8, Wien Oberlaa (688 5070).
Will supply information on all types of complementary and alternative medicine in Vienna.

Internationale Apotheke

1, Kärntner Ring 17 (512 2825). U1, U2, U4 Karlsplatz/tram 1, 2, D, J. **Open** 8am-6pm Mon-Fri; 8am-noon Sat. **Credit** AmEx, DC, MC, V.
This pharmacy specialises in all types of homeopathic medicine and can also orient you to any alternative treatment you require.

Vienna School of Osteopathy

13, Frimbergergasse 6-8 (879 3836).

General medical

Austrian Red Cross Blood Donor Centre

4, Wiedner Hauptstraße 30-40 (5890 0251). Tram 62, 65.

Open 8am-5.30pm Mon, Tue, Thur, Fri; 8am-8pm Wed.

Outpatient Clinic for Pregnancy Help

1, Fleischmarkt 26 (512 9631). U1, U4 Schwedenplatz/tram 1, 2. **Open** 8am-5pm Mon-Fri; 8am-noon Sat.
Pregnancy tests, birth control advice and confidential abortion counselling is available from this group. English spoken.

Pollen Alert Service

(1529).
Invaluable, up-to-date information service in German about pollen levels in Vienna.

Aids Help

Aids hilfe
8, Wickenburggasse 14 (408 6186). U2 Rathaus. **Open** 4-7pm Mon, Wed; 9am-noon Thur; 2-5pm Fri.
Information, testing and all-round care for HIV-positive people. English spoken.

AIDS-Hilfe Wien

6, Mariahilfer Gürtel 4 (59937/fax 59916/wien@aidshilfe.or.at). U6 Gumpendorfer Straße/tram 6, 18. **Open** 4-8pm Mon, Wed; 9am-1pm Thur; 2-6pm Fri.
Aids tests, results and counselling.

Alcohol abuse

Alcoholics Anonymous

3, Barthgasse 7 (English speakers 317 8876/German speakers 799 5599). U3 Schlachthofgasse. **Open** 6-9pm, or call Dolores at the above number anytime.
A number of English-speaking groups meet regularly, two evenings and two days a week.

Child abuse

Viennese Children & Youth Protection

Wiener Kinder- und Jugendanwaltschaft
9, Sobiestkigasse 31 (1708 85905). U6 Nußdorferstraße/tram 37, 38. **Open** 9am-5pm Mon-Fri.

Domestic violence

House for Threatened & Battered Women

Frauenhaus
(545 4800/408 3880/202 5500/ 485 3030).
All of these three shelters answer calls 24 hours a day. English spoken.

Family crisis

Crisis and Stress
9, Spitalgasse 11 (406 9595-0/406 9966-0). Tram 5, 43, 44/bus 13a.
Open 10am-5pm Mon-Fri.

Psychiatric/suicide

Befriender's Crisis Intervention
(713 3374). **Open** 9.30am-1pm, 6.30-10pm daily.
Hotline answered by English speakers.

Rape

Women's Emergency Centre
Frauen Notruf der Staft Wien *(71 719).*
If you have been raped, call this number and an English speaker will help you.

Veterinary

Viennese Animal Protection Society/ Animal Rescue
Wiener Tierschutzverein/Tierrettung *(804 7744).*

Insurance

Britain, Norway, Finland, Sweden and the former Warsaw Pact countries have reciprocal agreements guaranteeing free emergency treatment to their citizens. Although the Austrian state medical programme is very good, it is still best to take out comprehensive travel insurance because non-emergency treatment is not covered, and it avoids long queues and bureaucracy at state hospitals.

Internet

For such a traditional city, Vienna is up to date when it comes to the Internet and e-commerce. For example, Post Telekom has just launched the newest Internet lines, ADSL, throughout Austria. Internet access for tourists, however, is limited to the venues listed below. The AOL access

number from Vienna is (07189 15052), EUnet is (07189 18999) and Compuserve is (07189 15160/07189 15161).

Websites

There are many websites provided by the Austrian government about Vienna, but most are in German. Websites in English: *www.wien.gv.at* has a list of events in Vienna up to 2002 and general info on Austria. *www.info.wien/at,* the Vienna Tourist Information site, has coverage of tourist events and other info about the city. *www.tiscover.com* has features on sports, leisure activities (including live cams at ski resorts) and holidays in Austria. *www.austria.org* is an Austrian press and information service based in Washington DC.

Internet cafés

For free Internet access head for one of the three branches of **Amadeus** (*see chapter* **Shopping & Services**). Each branch has at least six touchscreen terminals. The paying option isn't particularly attractive as there isn't a 'cyber-café' as such in the city. **Café Stein** (*see chapter* **Nightlife**) has four terminals, but sets you back a whopping AS65 per half hour. Much cheaper are **Das Möbel** (*see chapter* **Cafés & Coffeehouses**) and **rhiz** (*see chapter* **Nightlife**) at AS20 per hour, but there's only one terminal in each. If you happen to find yourself in the main hall of **Flex** and can hear yourself think, there are two free terminals.
Einstein at Rathausplatz 4 has access and Café Schottenring has an Internet café for over-50s on Tuesdays from 2pm to 4pm. Cafè Nanubar at Schleifmühlgasse 11 (587 2987) has four terminals (AS50 per hour).

Language schools

Berlitz
main office: 1, Graben 13 (512 8286). U1, U3 Stephansplatz/bus 1a. 6, Mariahilfer Straße 27 (586 5693). U2 Babenbergerstraße. 1, Rotenturmstraße 1-3 (535 6120). U1, U3 Stephansplatz, bus 1a. 10, Troststraße 50 (604 3913). U1 Reumannplatz, then bus 66a, 67a. **Open** 8am-8pm Mon-Fri. **No credit cards.**
Individual, intensive and evening courses in German taught in the Berlitz method.

Cultura Wien
1, Bauernmarkt 18 (533 2493). U4 Schwedenplatz/bus 1a, 3a. **Open** 9am-6pm Mon-Fri. **No credit cards.**
Intensive four-hour classes taught daily and evening courses two days a week in courses lasting four and eight weeks. Good summer programme for younger students.

Inlingua Sprachschule
1, Neuer Markt 1 (512 2225). U1, U3 Stephansplatz/tram 1, 2, D, J. **Open** 9am-6pm Mon-Fri. **No credit cards.**
Four hours a day intensive courses in sessions lasting two weeks or longer, as well as twice a week evening courses in business German. Classes are limited to four to eight students.

Talk Partners
1, Fischerstiege 10/16 (535 9695). U4 Schwedenplatz/tram 1, 2. **Open** 8am-5pm Mon-Thur; 8am-2.30pm Fri. **No credit cards.**
Individually designed programmes by the students who choose content, time, place, duration and intensity of course.

University of Vienna
1, Ebendorferstraße 10/4 (405 1254). U2 Schottentor/tram 1, 2, D. **Open** 9am-5pm Mon, Tue, Wed, Fri; 9am-5.30pm Thur. **No credit cards.**
Nine-week German courses for 10-18 students a class and for 12 weeks for 14-20 students a class. Probably the most inexpensive courses around.

Left luggage

You will find left luggage facilities in the airport and all the larger train stations. Look for the sign that reads *Gepäckaufbewahrung.* In the airport, left luggage is in the entrance hall across from the rental cars and costs AS35-80 per day, depending on the size of luggage. All credit cards are accepted. The large train stations in Vienna also have left luggage, open 5am to midnight, costing AS30-50 a day, but they do not accept credit cards.

Libraries

American International School Secondary Library
19, Salmannsdorfer Straße 47 (4013 2220). U1 Kagran. **Open** 8am-4pm Mon-Fri.
A good selection of American magazines, newspapers and journals are available, if you like school libraries. Books may be borrowed for up to two weeks. Closed during school holidays.

Austrian National Library
1, Josefsplatz 1 (53 410). Bus 2a, 3a. **Open** 9am-7pm Mon-Fri; 9am-12.45pm Sat.
More than a library, this is an experience. Browse the card catalogue, select what you want, pick the books up the next day to take to the reading room. A good selection of English titles.

British Council Library
1, Schenkenstraße 4 (5332 61682/fax 5332 61685). Tram 1, 2, D. **Open** 11am-6pm Mon; 11am-5pm Tue; 11am-5pm Wed, Thur; 11am-1pm Fri.
Over 21,000 volumes of literature from all English-speaking Commonwealth countries. Films can be rented for a fee. Library is open to the public, but membership is required (annual membership is AS400 plus a new-member registration fee of AS50 paid in cash). Proof of identity is required for registration.

Bruno-Kreisky-Forum
19, Armbrustergasse 15 (318 8260). U4 Heiligenstadt/bus 83a. **Open** 9am-3pm Mon-Fri.
Comprehensive reference library for international politics, East-West relations, Islamic and Jewish studies in English, French and German. In addition, internationally recognised politicians, business people and academics are invited to Vienna to participate in discussions and seminars.

Städtische Büchereien
8, Skodagasse 20 (4000 84550). U6 Josefstädter Straße/tram 5, J. **Open** 10am-7.30pm Mon, Thur; 2-7.30pm Tue, Fri.
Vienna's public libraries have an excellent collection of books, tapes,

CDs and records, mostly in German, but they do stock about 20,000 non-German works. To find the nearest branch call the main library above.

University of Vienna Libraries
Hauptbibliothek (Main Library)
1, Dr Karl-Lueger-Ring 1 (4277-0). U2 Schottentor/tram 1, 2, D. **Open** 9am-7.45pm Mon-Fri; 9am-12.45pm Sat.
An extensive network of books in business, economics, literature and music, some in English.

Lost property

If you've left something behind on public transport, there's a good chance you will get it back again. If you lost something on a tram or bus, call the **General Information Office** (790 943-500); on a train call **Südbahnhof** (5800 35656) 7am-5pm Mon-Fri. Each bus and tram has a station where found articles are taken. After one week, however, everything is stored at the central police lost and found office. Go in person and have patience, it might be there but there'll be a lot of looking to do. Bring a German speaker with you.

Central Lost & Found
Zentrales Fundamt
9, Wasagasse 22 (313 4492-11). Bus 40a. **Open** 8am-noon Mon-Fri.

Maps

City centre maps and U-Bahn maps are included at the back of this guide. Free maps with enlarged city centres are available from most hotels and from the Vienna Tourist Information. All U-Bahn stations have detailed system and street maps at the entrance, and trams and buses have maps showing their routes attached to their stops.

Vienna Tourist Board
Main office: 1, Kärntner Straße 38 (513 8892). From June 2000: 1, Albertinaplatz 1 (same telephone number). U1, U2, U4 Karlsplatz/tram 1, 2, D, J. **Open** 9am-7pm daily.

2, Obere Augartenstraße 40 (211 140). Tram 31. **Open** 8am-4pm Mon-Fri.

Money

The unit of currency is the Austrian Schilling, usually abbreviated as ÖS, ATS or AS, the convention we have used in this guide. One Schilling equals 100 Groschen, which come in featherweight coins of 10 Groschen and 50 Groschen. Coins come in denominations of AS1, AS5, AS10 and AS20. Notes start at AS20. The notes feature prominent Austrians such as Karl Landsteiner, Nobel prize winner for medicine in 1930, or the-turn-of the-century women's rights leader Rosa Mayreder. Austrian banknotes come in denominations of AS20, AS50, AS100, AS500, AS1,000 and AS5,000.

ATMs
Automat machines are dotted throughout Vienna and will display a lit sign with two parallel horizontal green and blue stripes. Most take foreign credit cards and Eurocheque cards with PIN codes, so check the machine for the credit card symbols.

Many machines also offer the service in different languages. *Bestätigung*, the green button, means 'confirm'. Note that none of the machines gives receipts.

There are also a few automatic currency-converting machines, stating 'Change/Cambio' with instructions in English, that will accept foreign bank notes. A few central ATMs in the 1st district are:

Die Erste Bank
Graben 21/Wollzeile 15.

Creditanstalt
Kärntner Straße 7/Mariahilfer Straße 54.

Bank Austria
Stephansplatz 2/Am Hof 2.

Banks

The best place to exchange money is in a bank, as it will give you a better rate. It is also better to exchange a larger sum in one go, as there is often a minimum commission charge. Eurocheques are acceptable at many restaurants, shops and hotels as long as you present a valid Eurocheque card. Most banks stay open 8am-12.30pm and 1.30-3pm, and on Thursdays until 5.30pm. A few banks, such as the main **Creditanstalt** bank on Schottengasse and the **Die Erste Bank** on Graben 21, do not close for lunch. Some banks, generally at main railway stations and airports, stay open longer than usual. Be aware that opening times are changing and it soon might be that some banks stay open during lunch hours. *See also* **Business**.

Bureaux de change

City Air Terminal
U3, U4, Schnellbahn Wien Mitte.
Open 8am-12.30pm, 2-6.30pm daily.

Opera/Karlsplatz
U1, U2, U3, U4/tram 1, 2, D, J.
Open 8am-7pm daily.

Schwechat Airport Shuttle
Open 6.30am-11pm daily.

Südbahnhof
Tram D. **Open** 6.30am-10pm daily.

Westbahnhof U3
Tram 5, 6. **Open** 7am-10pm daily.

Credit cards

Compared to Western Europe, Budapest and Prague, Vienna is not a credit card friendly town. Many of the smaller hotels and restaurants do not take credit cards, mainly because the retail credit card percentages are some of the highest in Europe. Normally that isn't a problem as there are so many ATMs in town that in a pinch you can hop around the corner to the nearest ATM to get money to pay the bill.

Opening times are currently going through a revolution in Vienna. A few years ago times were reminiscent of Britain in the 1950s, with Thursday being the late shopping day and all shops closing for lunch and at noon on Saturdays. Now everything is changing, so it is wise to check opening times before you go out. Generally shops open at 8.30am or 9am and close at 6pm. Many smaller shops, especially outside the 1st district, close for lunch. Some larger shops, especially in the 1st district, are now open on Saturdays until 5pm. All stores in Vienna close on Sunday and public holidays. After hours you can buy groceries, flowers, books and newspapers at all major railway stations. The supermarket at the airport and the **Billa** supermarket at Franz-Josefs-Bahnhof are open seven days a week.

Until recently post offices opened and closed at different hours and closed for lunch. The introduction of competition has given the monopolistic Post Telekom Austria a kick up the backside, so currently everything is going the customer's way – post offices are opening throughout the entire day, telephone prices are becoming cheaper and even the staff seem to be becoming nicer. Actually the post service works extremely well throughout Austria, and posting a letter is easy. Every post office has a window marked *Fremdsprache* (Foreign Language) although most workers speak English anyway. Postboxes are bright yellow little boxes sporting a two-ended horn and are often mounted on buildings. An orange stripe denotes the box will be emptied Saturday, Sunday and holidays. Pick-up times are posted on the box.

Look in the telephone directory's white pages under *Post- und Telegraphenverwaltung* for locations of post offices and their opening times. All post offices offer express mail and faxing services.

Post codes

Post codes in Austria consist of four numbers. The first number denotes the region, the next two denote the city location, and the last should be ignored. All Vienna codes start with 1. The middle numbers will indicate which district, so 1010 is the 1st district, 1100 the tenth district, 1190 the nineteenth and so on.

Prices

To post a letter within Austria or Europe Priority class will cost AS7. Worldwide airmail costs AS13. To have the receiver sign for a letter will cost AS25. There are also next-day and two-day services available. These cost AS95 for up to 5kg, AS170 for up to 10kg, AS300 for up to 15kg, AS520 for up to 31.5kg. To send a package inland costs AS42 for 2kg; to send the same package in the EU will cost AS135. For more information call the Post Office 24-hour hotline (08100 10100).

24-hour post offices

Main Post Office
1, Fleischmarkt 19. U1, U4 Schwedenplatz/tram 1, 2.

Franz-Josefs-Bahnhof
9, Althanstraße 10. Tram D.

Post Office Information
(51 551-0). **Open** 8am-5pm Mon-Fri.

Südbahnhof
10, Wiedner Gürtel 1b. Tram D.

Westbahnhof
15, Europlatz. Westbahnhof U3.

Police

Police have a lot to do with life in Austria. If you are planning on staying for more than 60 days (*see also* **Visas**), you'll need to register yourself with the police to obtain a *Meldezettel*, or residence permit. Meldezettels are requested for everything from renting a flat to applying for a library card. Buy the forms at any newsstand and locate the police station in your area (in the phone book under *Polizei*). Then, look for your district's police headquarters under *Bezirkspolizeikommissariate und Wachzimmer*. File the form any time between 8am-1pm Mon-Fri. Bring your passport. If you don't want to disclose what may seem like private information under the Religion blank, make sure to put ORB (not admitting religion) or you'll be automatically registered as some religion and will get calls demanding tithes from the Evangelical church, for example, if you are registered as Protestant. Religion is taken very seriously here, so shrugging the call off won't work, and the orders have the right to a percentage of your salary unless you are registered as ORB. If you change address, you'll need to deregister yourself in your current police station and reregister yourself in the new one. The police are generally straightforward, speak English and are polite – as long as you do what they say.

Public holidays

Austria has one of the highest amounts of public holidays in Europe (*see chapter* **By Season**). Stores are usually open half the day on 24 December and 31 December,

otherwise make sure you stock up on food as shops take their holidays very seriously.

Public toilets

There are 330 public toilets in Vienna and these are easy to spot by a large WC sign. They are open from 9am to 7pm. You will have to have a AS1 or AS5 coin to use them, but at least they are clean. Many public toilets still have attendants. The art nouveau WC on the Graben was designed by Adolf Loos and is worth a visit. Other usefully located WCs are in the Opernpassage and Rathauspark, opposite the **Burgtheater**. All underground stations have toilets, but not all are open all the time.

Religion

Because of Vienna's musical importance, many people attend church for their fantastic musical repertoire. Look out particularly for details of Sunday Mass at the **Augustinerkirche, Minoritenkirche, Karlskirche, Stephansdom** and **Michaelerkirche**. The acclaimed Vienna Boys' Choir can be heard during Mass at the Burgkapelle every Sunday and religious holiday at 9.15am except from July to mid-September, but be aware that you have to pay both a concert fee and will still have a bag thrust under your nose for church donations, which can be rather off-putting for some people. If you can't arrange tickets in the chapel ground, don't bother with the balconies because you'll be crammed into an uncomfortable room without a view and will watch the whole concert on a television monitor.

Anglican
Christ Church
3, Jaurèsgasse 17-19 (720 7973). Tram 71.
Holy Communion 8am Sunday; Sung Eucharist & Sunday School 10am Sunday; Morning Service 10am third Sunday. Many singers from Viennese choirs are often invited as guest singers.

Protestant
Church of Jesus Christ & Latter Day Saints
2, Böcklinstraße 55 (367 5674). Tram N/bus 80a.
Sacrament meeting 9.30am Sunday.
International Baptist Church
6, Mollardgasse 35 (804 9259). U4 Margaretengürtel.
Worship service 12.30pm Sunday.
United Methodist Church
15, Sechshauser Straße 56 (893 6989). Bus 57a.
Worship service 11am Sunday.

Roman Catholic
St Augustin
1, Augustinerstraße 3 (533 7099). U1, U2, U4 Karlsplatz/bus 3a.
Occasional English services.
Stephansdom
1, Stephansplatz (5152 2530). U1, U3 Stephansplatz.
Occasional English services.
Votivkirche
9, Rooseveltplatz 8 (4085 05014). U2 Schottentor/tram 1, 2, D.
Mass 11am Sunday.

Jewish
City Synagogue
1, Seitenstettengasse 2 (531 040). U4 Schwedenplatz/tram 1, 2, D.
Worship Service 9am Friday; 9pm Saturday. In order to be admitted, you must bring your passport.

Smoking

It's curious that in a city so environmentally friendly and obsessed with cleanliness, Austrians are some of the heaviest smokers in Western Europe. Smoking is banned on public transport but most people ignore it, especially in U-Bahn stations. No-smoking areas in restaurants didn't exist a few years ago, but recently some coffeehouses such as Oberlaa, **Café Griensteidl** and **Café Central** have begun to set a few tables aside for non-smokers.

Club International Universitaire (CIU)

1, Schottengasse 1/Mezzanine (533 6533/fax 533 6533-9). U2 Schottentor/tram 1, 2, D. **Open** 9am-8pm Mon-Fri.
Lectures, debates, social events, courses and trips are organised by this focal point of international student activity in Vienna.

Institute of European Studies

1, Johannesgasse 7 (512 2601/ fax 512 9060). U1, U3 Stephansplatz/tram 1, 2. **Open** 9am-5pm Mon-Fri.
A semester or academic year abroad for college juniors and seniors. Most classes are taught in English. Subjects offered include East-West studies, humanities, German and international business. The total enrolment is about 100 students.

International Christian University

3, Rennweg 1 (718 5068-13/ fax 7185 0689). Tram 71.
A small American university offering undergraduate and graduate degrees and certificates in marketing, management, accounting, economics, computers, English and German.

Open University

1, Fischerstiege 10, 16 (533 2390/fax 533 2396). U1, U4 Schwedenplatz.
A complete English curriculum is offered in the humanities and social sciences, as well as a selection of masters degrees and postgraduate programmes in management and business.

Webster University

22, Berchtoldgasse 1 (269 9293/ fax 209 9293-13). U1 Vienna International Centre/tram 90, 91/ bus 92a.
A fully accredited American university fully recognised in Austria with BA, MA and MBA programmes in English in a range of subjects including international relations, management, computer science and psychology.

Until recently Post und Telekom Austria, the state communications monopoly, had some of the most expensive tariffs in Europe. The recent deregulation has been a godsend to Austrians and tourists alike.

Now there is a plentiful amount of public telephones sprinkled through the city. However, if you are staying in a hotel you might want to follow an Austrian custom and use the local post office, where the tariffs are much cheaper to make any long-distance call.

Every post office has a phone cabin for telephone calls. Go to the post office counter and say you want to make a call and you will be directed to a numbered cabin. You pay at the counter after you have finished. Business telephone hours are 8am-6pm Mon-Fri; cheaper hours are evenings, weekends and holidays.

Telekom Information

(0800 100 160). **Open** 7am-6pm Mon-Fri.
This number will tell you about the wide range of current telephone tariffs in Austria.

Directory Enquiries

Austria (11 811).
Germany (11 812).
Europe (11 813).
World (11 814).
Foreign Language (11 815).
Conference Calls (11 816).
Credit Card Calls (free 0802 3456) or (0800 287 421).
Mobile Telephones (0800 664 664).
Telegrams (0800 100 190).

Recently companies that offer cheap rates for long-distance calls have been set up in Austria, with rates significantly cheaper than Austria Telekom. You can register yourself and calls will automatically be charged to your credit card.

Econophone

(478 2000).

Public telephones

Newly designed smart glass public telephone booths are popping up all over Vienna. A few single schillings are enough for a quick local call, and have a few extra one and five schilling pieces on hand if you need them.

Information Operator

(11 811).

Making calls

To make an international call, dial 00, then the country code, city code and telephone number. A few country codes are Australia 61, Germany 41, Hungary 36, India 91, Ireland 35, Japan 81, New Zealand 64, South Africa 27, UK 44, USA/Canada 1.

All telephone numbers in Austria have prefixes, which are usually printed in parentheses. To make a call to Vienna from outside the city, dial 0, then the number. Vienna's code is now 01, but it used to be 0222 so if the number doesn't work, try dialing 01 and then the number.

To call Vienna from abroad, dial 43, followed by 1 and then the number. To dial a mobile phone (usually 0676 or 0664 numbers) dial 43, then the number without the 0.

Don't be concerned if the telephone number you want to call has only four digits or ten. Many general city numbers, such as the train station or post office, only have four digits. Austrian telephones have direct-dial extensions that are often placed at the end of the telephone number, preceded by a hyphen. Usually an 0 after the hyphen gives you the main operator.

Mobile telephones

A mobile telephone is called a Handy, a nifty English word that Austrians are disappointed to learn isn't used in Britain. As there is plenty of competition, you can get your mobile free and pay for your calls plus your monthly telephone rate. The best going rate for a Handy and line rental is about AS200 per month at present.

Max.mobil
3, Kelsenstraße 5-7 (0676 2000).

Mobilkom
(0800 664664).

One
19, Heiligenstädter Straße 215 (370 7070).

Telekom Information Office
1, Fleischmarkt 19 (535 3801). U1, U4 Schwedenplatz/tram 1, 2. 3, Erdberger Lände 36-48 (715 2514). U3 Rochusgasse. **Open** 8am-5pm Mon-Fri.

Time & dates

Austria is on Central European Time, which means it is one hour ahead of Britain, except for two brief periods at either end of the summer.

Tipping

There are no fixed rules about tipping, but it is customary to either give 10 per cent of your bill or to round up the bill in a restaurant. Announce the total sum to the waiter as he or she takes your money. He or she will probably acknowledge the tip with a *Danke Schön*, pocket the tip and return your change. Taxis normally receive an extra 10 per cent over the metered fare, and AS10 per bag is normal for porters and bellhops. Tipping is common in Austria, so an extra AS10 or AS20 for workers, hairdressers or any services will never hurt.

Tourist information

Vienna is almost like an open-air museum, therefore it isn't a surprise that its tourism agencies are so well organised. Simply call or drop by any of

the following information offices and smiling Austrians will hand you brochures in English on just about anything you could possibly want to do in Vienna. There is a lot of crossover between agencies, but the best is the Vienna Tourist Board.

Austrian Promotions
4, Margaretenstraße 1 (587 2000). U1, U2, U4 Karlsplatz/tram 1, 2, D, J. **Open** 10am-5pm Mon-Wed, Fri; 10am-6pm Thur.
This agency has information on skiing and other attractions in Austria.

Information at City Hall
1, Friedrich-Schmidt-Platz 1 (Rathaus) (52 550-0). U2 Rathaus/tram 1, 2, D. **Open** 8am-6pm Mon-Fri, 8am-4pm Sat-Sun.
This isn't a tourist office but it does provide a number of maps and brochures in English. Call for opera performances, ticket sales and museum hours.

Lower Austria Tourist Information
1, Walfischgasse 6 (513 8022/fax 513 8022-30). U1, U2, U4 Karlsplatz/tram 1, 2, D, J. **Open** 9am-6pm Mon-Fri.
This centre has a number of brochures in English on trips to the Vienna Woods.

Vienna Tourist Board
1, Kärntner Straße 38 (513 8892). From June 2000: 1, Albertinaplatz 1 (same telephone number). U1, U2, U4 Karlsplatz/tram 1, 2, D, J. **Open** 9am-7pm daily.
2, Obere Augartenstraße 40 (211 140). Tram 31. **Open** 8am-4pm Mon-Fri.

Youth Information Vienna
1, Bellaria Passage (17992 39148). U2, U3 Volkstheater. **Open** noon-7pm Mon-Fri; 10am-7pm Sat.

Visas

Austria joined the EU in 1995, and therefore abides by the rules of all European countries. Citizens of other EU countries have the right to enter Austria and remain for an indefinite period of time. As Austria borders Eastern Europe, the road and train borders are particularly fierce if you are holding an Eastern European

passport. A visa is not required for US citizens for up to three-month periods; at the end of a six-month stay you must leave the country if you do not have a residence permit. Anyone staying in Austria in a private house or apartment for more than 60 days is technically required to register with the police, although it is not enforced (*see* **Police**).

Vocabulary

High German *(hoch Deutsch)* is the official language, but Austrians speak German with a softer, more lilting accent filled with their own particular colloquialisms. The Viennese speak *Wienerisch*, a twangy and curious dialect of German littered with Czech, Hungarian and Yiddish words and distorted vowel sounds. Some shopkeepers find it easier to speak English than high German.

Austrians greet each other not with the German *Guten tag* (good day) but with *Grüss Gott*, which means Greetings to God. It's considered bad form not to greet someone in a lift or in a shop when you meet eyes, so when in doubt a Grüss Gott will never go wrong. Ingratiate yourself to the Viennese by greeting them with a hearty *Servus* and seeing them off with the slightly ridiculous *Baba* (stress on the first 'ba').

The Würstelstand is the ideal location to hear dialect first hand. Order a Bratwurst (in Vienna the subtleties of the German indefinite article are conveniently reduced to a simple Anglo-Saxon 'a') and you will be asked 'Schoaf od'r sues', referring to the type of mustard you require – hot or sweet. If you're not happy with your sausage, you could always complain with a highly provocative 'Dis is a Schass' (it's crap).

Directory

Grüss Gott Frau Doktor!

Nowhere is the Austrian's nostalgia for the Empire so clearly seen as in their dogged persistence in using titles, especially the academic variety.

Open a bank account here or have your electricity bill put in your name and the relevant form will require your academic title. Degree holders fill in Mag. (Magister) and those with a PhD, Dr (Doktor).

The ubiquity of the latter gives the impression there's a GP on every corner, but inquiring after the state of your health to Dr Jörg Haider is unlikely to be helpful, especially if you're not Caucasian.

The vast numbers of ferocious ladies who answer to the title of Frau Doktor is not an indication of women playing an inordinately important role in the life of the country – it's just by dint of marriage, though the process does not work the other way round.

Other common titles include Herr or Frau Diplom-Ingenieur or the utterly pathetic practice of a bloke with an equivalent HND in business studies calling himself Herr Diplom-Kaufmann. The wife of an engineer is Frau dipl. engineer Kaufmann (Mrs Diploma Engineer Kaufmann).

The advantages of sporting your title are still substantial in the more reactionary corners of Austrian society – the banks, certain coffeehouses and balls – and ensure the fawning attentions of many a minion.

Directory

Here is a basic survival vocabulary:
Closed *Geschlossen/Gesperrt*
Danger *Gefahr*
Entrance *Eingang*
Info *Auskunft*
No vacancies *Besetzt*
Out of order *Ausser Betrieb*
Please/you're welcome *Bitte*
Pull *Ziehen*
Push *Drücken*
Signature *Unterschrift*
Thank you *Danke, Danke Schön*
Exit *Ausgang*
WC *Toiletten, WC*
Working *In Betrieb*

Water

Viennese tap water is one of the highest qualities in all of Europe. Most districts in Vienna receive clear, clean mountain water which comes directly from the Styrian mountains and it tastes wonderful. Why most Viennese pay to drink bottled soda water is a mystery. In a restaurant order *Leitungswasser* to receive quality mineral water for free.

Women

Austrian women have a reputation for their free thinking and socialist tendencies. Rosa Mayreder, an early writer and pioneer of the feminist movement in the late 1800s, was recently commemorated when her portrait was placed on the new Austrian 500 Schilling note. Another well-known woman, who died in January 2000 was the architect Margarete Schütte-Lihotzky, whose architecture in many ways pioneered social council flats and improved social housing standards in the severely overcrowded working-class quarters in Vienna.

Because Austria has a judiciously planned social security and welfare system, in general women are well taken care of, as long as they are holding jobs.

Mothers may not work eight weeks before and after birth, and either she or her partner may take one year and six months maternity leave (down from two years) from the day of birth. During this time, parents may not be dismissed from their jobs. A state benefit is payable on the birth of a child.

There are a number of women's initiatives, both private and government sponsored, that are available for Austrian women. As there is also a large number of wives and working women in the international community in Vienna, there are many organisations to help settle you in the city as well as improve career possibilities for women living in Vienna.

Austrian organisations

Feministisches Magazin für Politik, Arbeit und Kultur
3, Hetzgasse 42/1 (715 9889/13).
This magazine comes out once a month.

Frauen-Kommunikations-und Kulturzentrum
*6, Windmühlgasse 26 (58 980).
U3 Neubaugasse/U4 Kettenbrückengasse.* **Open** 9am-4pm Mon-Wed; noon-7pm Thur.

Frauencafe
*8, Lange Gasse 11 (406 3754).
U2 Lerchenfelder Straße.* **Open** 5pm-2am Tue-Sat. **No credit cards.**

Frauenhaus Wien
16, Maroltingergasse 19-23 (54 54800). U2 Lerchenfelder Straße. **Open** 5pm-2am Tue-Sat.

Die Möwe
(532 1515). **Open** for telephone calls 9am-1pm Mon, Thur, Fri; 9am-1pm, 2-6pm Tue. 9am-1pm Fri. Support group for those with mentally and sexually disturbed children.

For English speakers

American Women's Association (AWA)

19, Sieveringer Straße 22a/1 (320 1495/fax 328 2534). Tram 38 from Schottentor. **Open** 9am-3pm Mon-Thurs.
A non-profit organisation to help American women and other English-speaking women living in Vienna.

Work

Austria is part of the EU, so citizens of the European Economic Area are exempt from the bureaucratic requirements of obtaining work permits. If you're not a citizen of the EEA, then it's a hassle, because Austrians are already struggling to manage the large number of Eastern Europeans entering the country (legally and not). You'll need a work permit (*Arbeitsgenehmigung*) unless you are specifically exempt according to the Law Governing the Employment of Foreigners (*Ausländerbeschäftigungsgeset z*). If you marry an Austrian life becomes easier, however in order to work you must have a residence permit (*Aufenhaltsbewilligung*) and a written confirmation from the regional Labour Office (*Arbeigsmarktservice*) which certifies your work permit exemption. Look in the phone book 'white pages' under *Aarbeitsmarktservice* to find the closest office to you.

Business

The last few years have seen a lot of change in the business world. After much humming and hawing, Austria finally decided to become a full member of the European Community in 1995. This, together with the opening up of Eastern Europe in 1989 has had a profound effect on the economy. Until then, the small Austrian market had been an independent capitalistic island surrounded by Eastern Europe.

With its well-functioning information and services network and solid economic foundation, Vienna was the base from which many westerners ran their Eastern European interests. So long as you had the right political connections – everything from media to medicine is still dependent upon government patronage – things ran smoothly. The EU introduced competition, and with that, a certain level of uncertainty.

Politicians such as Jörg Haider have taken advantage of the uneasiness Austrians feel about all these changes, which is why his fundamentalist, kick-the-foreigner-out-of-Austria approach is so popular. Many think that their government-sponsored high social living standards might start to drop as they are forced to agree to many European standards. For example, opening and closing hours, which were highly regulated, have now become lax, with Saturday shopping extended to 5pm rather than the mandatory noon closing time.

European integration in 1995 at first created a bubble of expectation. The speed with which international investors reacted became apparent after the referendum in 1994. Many new investors, mainly from the US, Germany and Switzerland, actively expanded their activities in Austria.

Foreign investment has increased by 70% since 1994. Some 40% of all direct foreign investments in Eastern Europe came from Austria. Housing prices, especially in Vienna, boomed. These high expectations began to run into problems such as the non-competitive Austrian attitude to business and the high fees incurred to maintain a bloated social system.

By 1997 Austria's direct foreign investments declined from 40% to 5.3%. Austrian exports and imports with Eastern Europe continue to climb, its partners mainly being Hungary, the Czech Republic and Poland. An important branch of Austria's foreign trade is transit trade in conjunction with the mediation of East-West trading transactions.

Austria ranks tenth among the OECD countries, well above the EU average, and is one of the wealthiest economies in the EU. It took part in the stage three of the Economic and Monetary Union which has cemented its sometimes uncomfortable relationship with the EU.

It is a highly developed industrialised nation predominantly dealing in foodstuffs and luxury commodities, mechanical engineering and steel construction, chemicals and vehicle manufacturing.

Accountants

Arthur Andersen
1, Teinfaltstraße 8 (53 133-0). Tram 1, 2, D/bus 1a.

Coopers & Lybrand
9, Berggasse 10 (31 377-0). Tram D/bus 40a.

Deloitte & Touche
1, Friedrichstraße 10 (58 854-0). U1, U2, U4 Karlsplatz.

ISOB Wirtschaftstreuhand-und Steuerberatungsges
9, Georg Sigl Gasse 12 (310 6010/fax 310 6010-6). U3 Rossauer Lände.

Directory

Naked lunch boxes

If you forget to pack your bikini or trunks and the temperature is in the 80s, fret not. Getting your kit off in public is an activity which Austrians young and old unanimously enjoy. Nudism, both informal and organised goes under the moniker of FKK (Freie Körper Kultur) – Strength Through Joy unavoidably comes to mind.

Virtually all Vienna's excellent public swimming baths have nudist areas and vast tracts of the Donauinsel are given over to nude bathers.

Add to this the other great summer pastime, barbeques, and you are often confronted with the comical sight of a weeny hanging over the sizzling wieners.

The Gänsehäufel section (*see chapter* **Sightseeing**) of the Alte Donau is also a great favourite but the number one nudist area is definitely the Lobau, a natural park located in the most overgrown jungle-like tributaries of the Danube (take S80 from Südbahnhof).

FKK is taken very seriously all over the German-speaking world and aficionados are often paid-up affiliated members of nudist associations, connected internationally by newsletters and websites.

Banks

It is not widely known that Austria offers facilities for confidential bank accounts similar to the Swiss bank account. Many Austrians and foreign nationals have anonymous bank savings and securities accounts which are accessed by a password. Nowadays if you have piles of cash to deposit you might have to identify yourself, as Austrian authorities have begun to crack down on international money laundering. Then again, the interest rate for savings accounts is around 2%, so it might be better to deposit it where you'll get a better rate of interest. All large Austrian banks in the 1st district do all the banking services you need. Rates are high, especially with foreign transactions.

American Express
1, Kärntner Straße 21-23 (51 567-0). U1, U3 Stephansplatz/tram 1, 2, D, J. **Open** 9am-5.30pm Mon-Fri; 9am-noon Sat.

Bank Austria
1, Am Hof 2 (71 191-0). U1, U3 Stephansplatz. **Open** 8am-3pm Mon, Tues, Wed, Fri; 8am-5.30pm Thur.

Creditanstalt
1, Stephansplatz 7a (53 425-0). U1, U3 Stephansplatz. **Open** 8.30am-2.30pm Mon; 8.30am-5.30pm Tues; 8.30am-2.30pm Wed; 8.30am-5.30pm Thur; 8.30am-2pm Fri.

Erste Bank
1, Graben 21 (53 100-0). U1, U3 Stephansplatz/bus 1a. **Open** 8am-3pm Mon, Tues, Wed, Fri; 8am-5.30pm Thur.

Raiffeisenlandesbank
1, Kärntner Straße 51 (512 9182-0). Tram 1, 2, D, J. **Open** 8am-3.30pm Mon-Thur; 8am-5.30pm Thur.

Convention centres

Hofburg Congress Centre
1, Heldenplatz (5873 6660). Tram 1, 2, D, J. **Open** by arrangement.

Messe Wien Congress Centre
2, Messestraße, Tor 1 (7272 0208/fax 7272 0195). U1 PraterStern. **Open** 7am-8pm Mon-Fri. **Credit** AmEx, DC, JCB, MC, V. *Website: www.messe.at*

World Trade Centre
Vienna Airport (7007 36000). Airport Shuttle. **Open** 24 hours daily. **Credit** AmEx, DC, MC, V.

Couriers

DHL
3, Steingasse 6-8 (71 181). Tram 71. **Open** 8am-7.45pm Mon-Fri; 8am-12.30pm Sat. **Credit** AmEx, DC, MC, V.

Mail Boxes Etc
3, Landstraße Hauptstraße 99-101 (512 4515). U3 Rochusgasse. **Open** 9am-7pm Mon-Fri; 9am-2pm Sat. **Credit** AmEx, DC, MC, V. *Web site: www.at.mbe.com*

UPS
Express Counter 1, K (0660/6630/0711/336 630). U2 Oper/tram 1, 2, D, J. **Open** 10am-8pm Mon-Fri. **Credit** AmEx, MC, V.

Gov't organisations

Federal Chancellory
1, Ballhausplatz 2 (5311 52443). Tram 1, 2/bus 2a, 3a.

Ministry for Business Affairs
1, Stubenring 1 (71 100/5555). U3 Stubentor/tram 1, 2/bus 1a.

Ministry for Culture & Education
1, Freyung 1 (53 120/2242). U2 Schottentor/bus 1a.

Ministry of Defense
7, Mariahilfer Straße 24 (5200/21 180). U3 Neubaugasse/tram 5, 6.

Ministry for the Environment, Youth and Family
13, Franz-Josefs-Kai 51 (families 53 475/180/children and youth 0660 6076). U1, U3 Schwedenplatz/ tram 1, 2.

Ministry of Finance
15, Himmelpfortgasse 4, Parterre, Zimmer 2 (513 1353/5143 31779). U1, U3 Stephansplatz/bus 1a.

Ministry of the Interior
14, Minoritenplatz 9 (53 126/3110). Tram 1, 2, D/bus 3a.

Ministry of Justice
7, Museumstraße 7 (526 3686).
U2 Volkstheater/bus 2a.

Ministry for Work, Health and Social Affairs
1, Stubenring 1 (712 6349/71 100).
U3 Stubentor/tram 1, 2/bus 1a.

Libraries

Amerika Haus Information Resource Center (AHIRC)
1, Friedrich-Schmidt-Platz 2
(405 3033/fax 406 5260). U2
Rathaus. **Open** 2-5pm Tue, Thur.
By appointment only.
For serious researchers only. The
AHIRC provides current information
resources about US government and
public policy, economic and social
issues.

Webster University Library
22, Berchtoldgasse 1 (2699 29320).
U1 Vienna International Centre/
tram 90, 91/bus 92a. **Open** 10am-
8pm Mon-Thur; 10am-6pm Fri;
2-6pm Sat.
Library focuses on management,
international relations, computer
science and psychology. Only a
reference library, books can't be
checked out.

Networks

Women's Career Network
19, Sieveringer Straße 22a/1 (320
1495/fax 328 2534). U4

Heiligenstadt, then bus 39a.
Open 9am-3pm Mon-Tue; 9am-noon
Wed; 9am-noon Thur.
Affiliated with the American
Womens Association, this network
offers bi-monthly meetings in the
Marriott hotel, a newsletter and
member directory for women
living and working in Vienna.

US Chamber of Commerce
9, Porzellangasse 35 (319 5751).
Tram D. **Open** 9am-noon Mon-Fri.

US List
(Fax 310 6910)
A directory of US firms, subsidiaries,
affiliates and licensees in Austria
is available for members for AS400
and non-members for AS500. It can
be ordered directly by fax.

British Trade Council
1, Laurenzerberg 2 (533 1594).
U1, U4 Schwedenplatz/tram 1, 2.
Open *by appointment.*
A British equivalent of the above can
be found here.

Office services

McCollum Business Services
Marriott Hotel: 1, Weihburggasse 29
(513 1023). Tram 1, 2. **Open**
8.15am-noon, 1-6pm Mon-Fri.
Credit AmEx, DC, JCB, MC, V.
Extremely useful for those starting
their own business. Offers virtual
office facilities, shared offices,
user addresses, work spaces,
computers, copying, printing,

communications services,
translating.

Regus Business Centre
1, Schottenring 16 (53 712-0).
U2 Schottentor/tram 1, 2, D. 1,
Parkring 10 (599 99-0). Tram 1, 2. 6,
Mariahilfer Straße 123 (59 999-0).
U3 Neubaugasse.
Open 8am-6pm Mon-Fri.
Credit AmEx, DC, JCB, MC, V.
Virtual office space and related
business services.

Relocation services

The following companies
have English speakers
available.

Interdean International Movers
23, Eitnergasse 5 (865 4706).
Open 8am-5pm Mon, Tue, Wed,
Fri; 8am-2.30pm Thur. **No credit
cards.**

Kühner & Son
19, Muthgasse 19 (369 1601/fax 368
2949). **Open** 8am-noon, 1-4.30pm
Mon-Fri. **No credit cards.**

Relocation Service Erika Strohmayer
Schwechat, Am Concorde-Park 1/b1
(70 177-440/mobile 0664 100 4038).
Open varies. No credit cards.
Sobolak International Removals
Leobendorf, Stockerauer Straße 161
(0226 2691). **Open** 8am-5pm
Mon-Fri; 8am-2.30pm Thur.
No credit cards.

Further Reading

Thomas Bernhardt *Cutting Timber*
Vituperative novel portraying
contemporary Viennese artistic and
literary circles. Bernhard at his
trademark maniacal and
misanthropic best (he was even sued
by one of the characters).
Bill Bryson *Neither Here Nor There*
Flippant but often perspicacious
account of his Vienna sojourn as he
retraces his teenage backpacking trip
through Europe.
Elias Canetti *Auto-da-Fé*
Perhaps the best-known work of
fiction by the Nobel Prize winner. A
misanthropic sinologist living in
Vienna at the turn of the century finds
his life falling apart after he falls for
the machinations of the coarse,
scheming cleaning woman he marries.
Elias Canetti *The Tongue Set Free*
The author spent his formative
school days in Vienna in the years
leading up to World War II. Fond
memories of the Tunnel of Fun at the

Prater, and a family friend who
spoke of Bahr and Schnitzler and
was 'Viennese if for no other reason
than because she always knew,
without great effort, what was
happening in the world of the
intellect.'
Lilian Faschinger *Magdalena the
Sinner*
A leather-clad woman on a
motorbike kidnaps a priest and ties
him to a tree in order to confess her
sins. Enjoyable and blasphemous
antidote to Viennese Catholicism.
Patrick Leigh Fermor *A Time of
Gifts*
Contains a lengthy amusing chapter
on the Vienna stage of his walk from
London to Constantinople in 1933-4.
Brigitte Harman *Hitler's Vienna*
Grim, fascinating and essential
reading about pre-war Vienna. 'A
prologue to the inhuman.'
John Irving *Setting Free the Bears*
High jinks in Schönbrunn – the story

concerns a plot to liberate all the
animals from Vienna Zoo. Kurt
Vonnegut Jr called it 'the most
nourishing, satisfying novel I have
read in years.'
Louis James *The Xenophobes
Guide to the Austrians*
A quirky look at Austrians.
Allan Janik & Stephen Toulmin
Wittgenstein's Vienna
Dense but fascinating book that sets
the aesthetic and literary scene of
Wittgenstein's life.
**John Lehmann and Richard
Bassett** *Vienna, A Travellers'
Companion*
Eye witness accounts, letters, stories
of Vienna through the centuries.
Claudio Magris *Danube*
Brief but to the point on Vienna,
packed with literary landmarks and
coffeehouse visits. Visiting Joseph
Roth's house in Rembrandtstraße, he
observes, 'living in this building it

Vienna by numbers

Population of Vienna **1.61 million**
Population of Vienna plus surroundings
1.87 million
Global ranking of Vienna for city size:
  in 1900 **5**
  in 2000 **190**
Area of Vienna in square km **414.95**
Radius in km **133**
Population of Austria **8.06 million**
Area of Austria in sq km **83,859**
Inhabitants per sq km **96**

Number of tourist overnight stays in Vienna
in 1998 **7,669,421**
Average duration of stay **2.5 days**
Number of hotels and other
accommodation **347**
Number of beds **39,930**

Number of university/college students in
Vienna in 1999 **140,000**

Number of foreigners in Vienna: **263,470**
coming from:
  Yugoslavia **83,772**
  Turkey **45,708**
  Poland **17,501**
  Bosnia **17,301**
  Croatia **16,159**
  UK **2,362**

Religions (1991): Roman Catholic **899,903**
Protestant **82,414**
Muslim **62,305**
Jewish **6,554**
Other confessions **83,437**

Life expectancy:
in 1970 men **66.4** years; women **73.3** years
in 1998 men **74.6** years; women **80.8** years

Average age of retirement in Austria:
in 1970 men **61.9** years; women **60.4** years
in 1998 men **58.2** years; women **56.7** years

Number of museum visitors **7,066,619**
Number of theatre-goers **2,759,000**
Number of balls during the Fasching **382**

Global ranking of Austria for:
Least hours of strikes per capita **3**
Suicide **4**

Number of Olympic medals won by Austrian
skiers: **78** (Gold **24**)
Places of Austria's male skiing team at the
Super G in Innsbruck 1998:
  1, 2, 3, 4, 5, 6, 7, 8, 9
Result of Euro 2000 qualification football
match Spain-Austria in 1999: **9-0**

State budget revenues: **AS6,944 billion**
State budget expenditures: **AS7,676 billion**
Growth rate 1999: **2.2%**
Expected growth rate in 2000: **2.8%**
Claimant unemployment in Austria 1999:
  4.4%
Average net monthly earnings of full-time
employees (1999):
  men: **AS39,086**;
  women **AS22,960**

Price of a modest two-room flat in Vienna,
districts 2-9 (1999): **AS1,600,000**

cannot have been difficult to become
a specialist in melancholy.'
Franz Maier-Bruck *Das Große
Sacher Kochbuch*
A great collection of Austrian recipes
and grand cuisine.
Robert Musil *The Man Without
Qualities*
Impressive in size and reputation: the
kind of book you really should read,
but never quite get round to (you
could just read chapter 15, for its
account of the intellectual
revolution). Set in the years leading
up to the outbreak of World War I.
Frederick Morton *A Nervous
Splendour*
The events before the fall of the
Habsburg empire.
Christoph Ransmayr *The Dog
King*
An absurd, beautifully written tale
about the horrors of war. Set in a

fictional Alpine town controlled by
American troops just after World
War II.
Joseph Roth *The String of Pearls*
The Shah of Persia visits Vienna,
demands the services of a countess,
and gets a look-alike whore instead.
Lots of melancholic doomed
characters and scenes in coffeehouses.
Arthur Schnitzler *Dream Story*
Read the book before you see the
film, and don't imagine Tom and
Nicole as Fridolin and Albertine
while you do so.
Carl Schorske *Fin de Siècle Vienna*
Seven scholarly studies on the artistic,
intellectual and political shockwaves
which emanated from turn-of-the-
century Vienna and rocked the world.
Paul Strathern *Wittgenstein in 90
Minutes*
Summary of Wittgenstein's life
and philosophy ('if people did not

sometimes do silly things, nothing
intelligent would ever get done').
Georg Trakl *Selected Poems*
For serious and professional
melancholics.
Plachutta Wagner
Die gute Küche
One of Vienna's great chefs.
Traditional recipes with quirky
touches.
Stefan Zweig *The World of
Yesterday*
Fascinating explanation of the key
role the Jews played in the artistic
development of Vienna, and of how,
'hospitable and endowed with a
particular talent for receptivity, the
city drew the most diverse forces to
it, loosened, propitiated, and pacified
them.'
Stefan Zweig *The Royal Game*
The influence of Freud and the early
psychoanalysts is impossible to miss.

Index

Page numbers in **bold** indicate section giving key information on topic; *italics* indicate illustrations.

Advertisers' Index

Maps

A Cozy Stay At A
Comfortable Price®

- 4-Star (****) hotel in the cozy style of a country estate, with open fireplace and spacious rooms
- All 86 rooms with airconditioning, minibar, cable/pay TV, in-room coffee-maker, fax/modem connection, some rooms with kitchenette
- Free coffee, cookies, candies and newspapers in the lobby
- Good location opposite the Vienna International Centre/UN building, the Austria Center Vienna, 10 minutes to city center
- Non-smoking rooms, rooms for disabled guests
- Free parking in our garage
- Seminar facilities
- Cozy Bar "Country Lounge"
- Garden
- Fitness facilities

Hotel Country Inn & Suites
Wagramer Straße 16
A-1220 Vienna
Tel.: +43-1-260 40-0, Fax.:+43-1-260 40 699
http://www.country-inn-europe.com

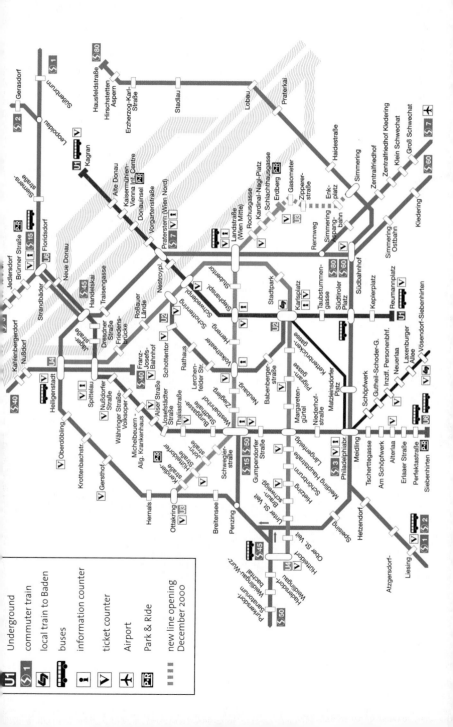

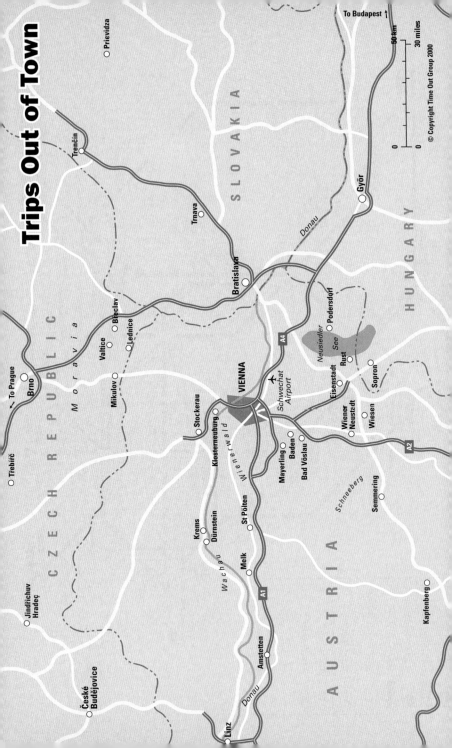

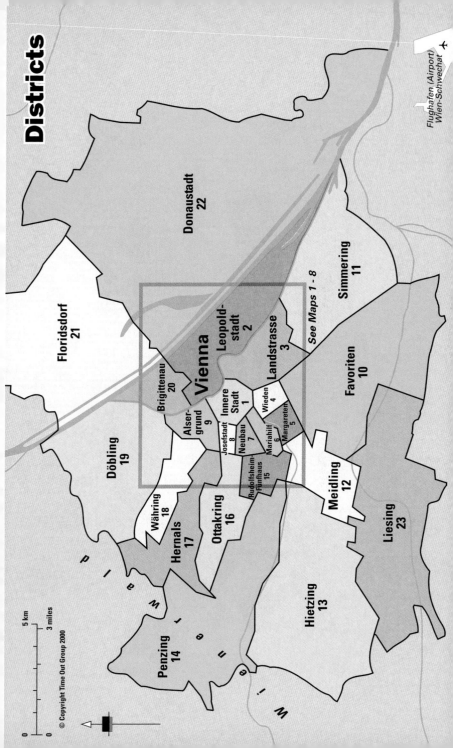

Districts

Floridsdorf 21

Donaustadt 22

Döbling 19

Brigittenau 20

Alser- grund 9

Vienna

Leopold- stadt 2

Landstrasse 3

Simmering 11

See Maps 1 - 8

Innere Stadt 1

Josefstadt 8

Neubau 7

Wieden 4

Margareten 5

Mariahilf 6

Favoriten 10

Währing 18

Rudolfsheim- Fünfhaus 15

Hernals 17

Ottakring 16

Meidling 12

Penzing 14

Hietzing 13

Liesing 23

W i e n e r W a l d

Flughafen (Airport) Wien-Schwechat

5 km

3 miles

© Copyright Time Out Group 2000

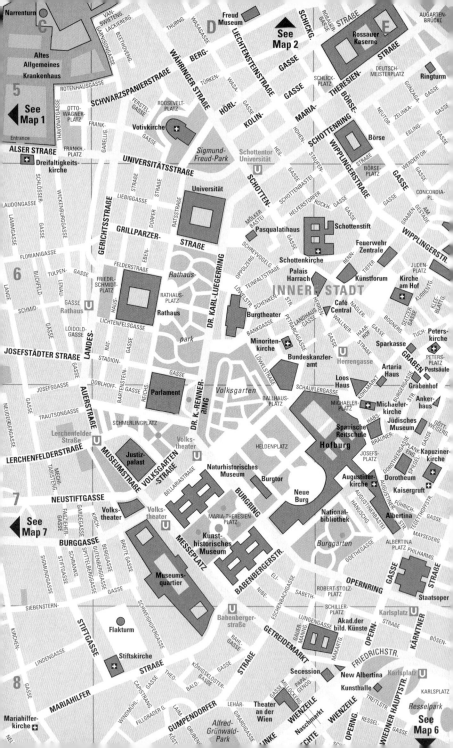

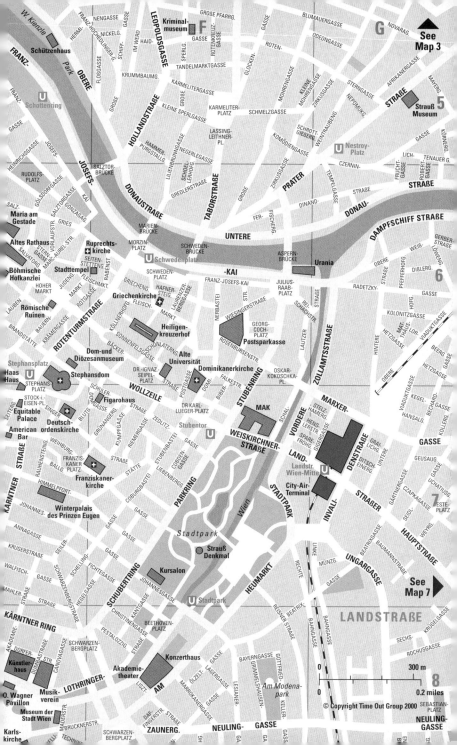

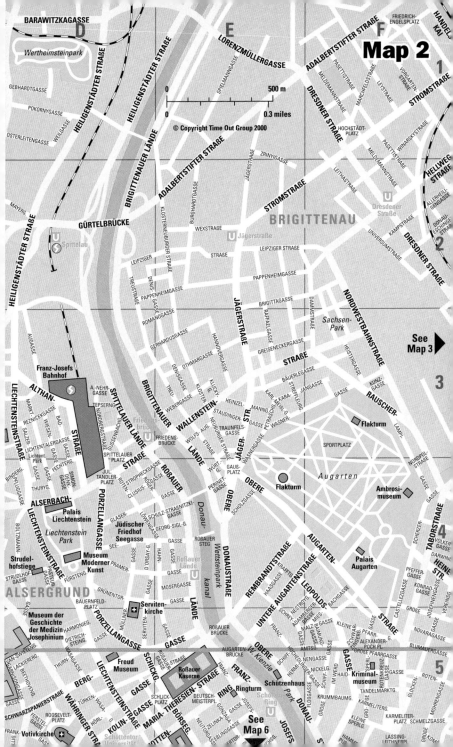

Map 3

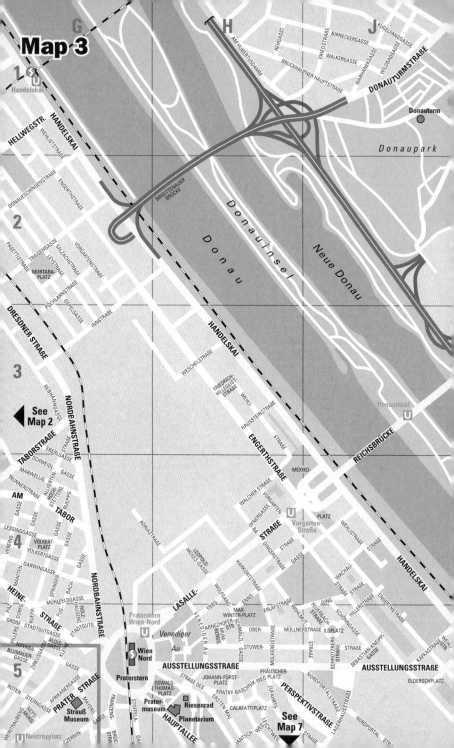

G

H

J

1 Handelskai

HELLWEGSTR.

HANDELSKAI

WEHLISTRASSE

DONAUESCHINGENSTRASSE

ENGERTHSTRASSE

2

PASETTISTRASSE

TRAISENGASSE

SALZACHSTRASSE

LEYSTRASSE

VORGARTENSTRASSE

MORTARA-PLATZ

PÖCHLARNSTRASSE

OSPELGASSE

INNSTRASSE

DRESDNER STRASSE

3

REBHANNGASSE

NORDBAHNSTRASSE

See Map 2

TABORSTRASSE

EBERLGASSE

SCHWEIDL-

ALLIIERTEN-

STETTERS

MARINELLIG.

GASSE

TRUNNERSTRASSE

AM

RUEPPG.

LESSINGGASSE

TABOR

VERENS-

GASSE

GASSE

GASSE

STETTERS

GASSE

4

VOLKERT-PLATZ

VOLKERTGASSE

DARWINGASSE

SPRINGER

BACH-

MANITENG.

HOLZ

HAUSERG.

MÜHLFELDGASSE

HEINE-

PAZ.

FORG.

TORG.

GROBE

STADTGUTGASSE

STRASSE

PILERS

STADTGUTG.

NORDBAHNSTRASSE

NOVARA-

ALOIS-

GASSE

BLUMAUER-

KLEIN

ZIRKUSGASSE

GASSE

GASSE

5

ROTEN-

STERNGASSE

AFRIKANERGASSE

PRATER

NFD.

WENTRAUBENG.

STRASSE

STRASSE

MAYRG.

NOVA

MAILING.

GASSE

Strauß Museum

FRANZENS.

CZERNIN

STOFFELA

BRÜC

GAS

STRA.

Nestroyplatz

BRIGITTENAUER BRÜCKE

Donau

Donauinsel

Donau

Donauinsel

Neue Donau

Donaupark

Donauturm

DONAUTURMSTRASSE

KUGELFANGGASSE

BIRNECKERGASSE

REHGASSE

FRIEDSTRASSE

WALKERGASSE

WARHANERGASSE

WILDBADGASSE

AM HUBERTUSDAMM

BRUCKHAUFNER HAUPTSTRASSE

HANDELSKAI

WESCHELSTRASSE

FRIEDRICH-HILLEGEIST-STRASSE

WEHL-

HAUSTEINSTRASSE

ENGERTHSTRASSE

STRASSE

Donauinsel

REICHSBRÜCKE

MEXIKO-

WALCHER STRASSE

VORGARTEN-

OPNERGASSE

PLATZ

STRASSE

Vorgarten-Straße

WEHLISTRASSE

HANDELSKAI

DINGERSTRASSE

STRASSE

GASSE

WACHAU-

STRASSE

STRASSE

ENGERTHSTRASSE

ADRIASTRASSE

LEDPOLD-MOSES-GASSE

HARKORTSTRASSE

JUNG-

FEUERBACH-

SCHÖNNGASSE

HILLERSTRASSE

SEBASTIAN-KNEIPP-

STRASSE

KAFKASTRASSE

WEHL.

LASALLE-

VENEDIGER AU

YBBS-

WOLFGANG-

MAX-WINTER-PLATZ

SCHMALZ-

ARNEZHOFER-STR.

MUM

BERGG.

OBER-

MÜLLNERSTRASSE

ILGPLATZ

SCHROTZBERG

NORDPORTALSTRASSE

NORDPORTAL STR.

Praterstern Wien-Nord

Wien Nord

ENNS-

ERLAFSTRASSE

WOHLMUT-

STUWER-

MÖLKERSTRASSE

STRASSE

Praterstern

OSWALD-THOMAS-PLATZ

AUSSTELLUNGSSTRASSE

JOHANN-FÜRST-PLATZ

PRÄUSCHER-

PLATZ

ELDERSCHPLATZ

AUSSTELLUNGSSTRASSE

Prater-museum

Riesenrad

Planetarium

HAUPTALLEE

KRATKY-BASCHNIK-WEG

ERSTEN MAI

CALAFATTIPLATZ

ZUFAHTS.

PERSPEKTIVSTRASSE

JANTSCH-WEG

LEICHTWEG

See Map 7

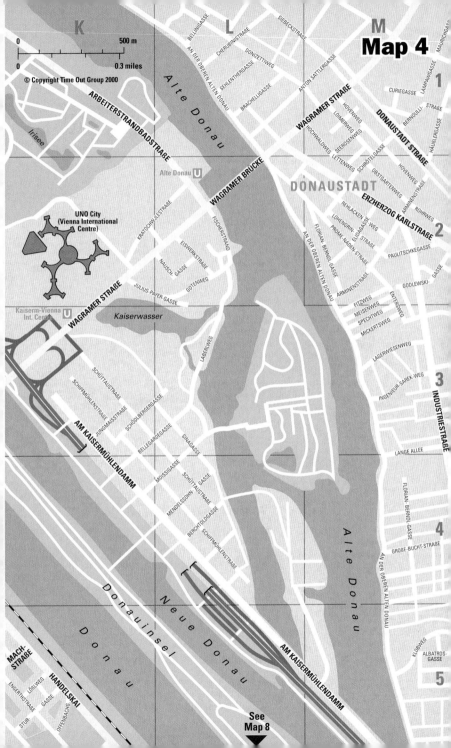

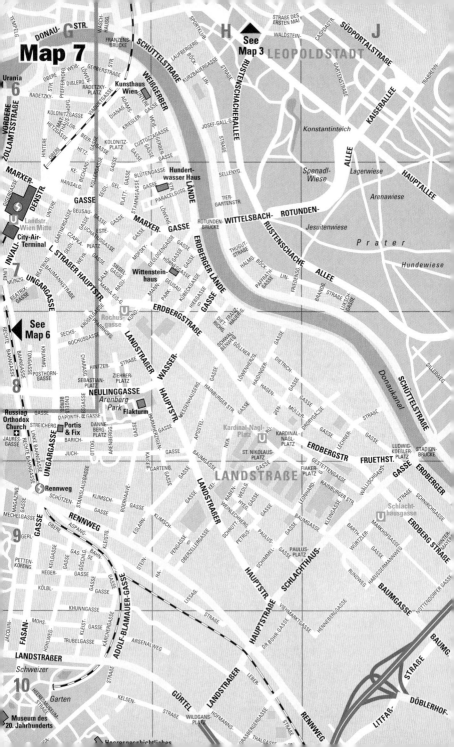

Map 8

See
Map 4

K

L

M

0   500 m

0   0.3 miles

Donauinsel

STRAßE

VORGARTENSTRAßE

HANDELSKAI

ENGERTHSTRAßE

WEHLISTRAßE

ICHMANNGASSE

STRAßE

Ernst-Happel-
Stadion

6

7

MEIEREI-

MARATHONWEG

HANDELSKAI

RUSTENSCHACHERALLEE

LUST

ALLEE

HAUS-

Oberes Heustadelwasser

HAUPTALLEE

WEHLISTRAßE

8

STADION-

STRAßE

KLASCHKAWEG

Unteres Heustadelwasser

HAUPTALLEE

Unterer Prater

Lusthaus

9

LÄNDE

ERDBERGERBRÜCKE

U Erdberg

SCHNIRCHGASSE

GÄRTNERSTRAßE

FRANZOSEN-

MITTLERER

GRABEN

WEG

STRAßE

GUGL-

ERDBERG STRAßE

PARAGONSTRAßE

KAPPGASSE

GASSE

OSTAUTOBAHN

SIMMERZINGER LÄNDE

U NN

GASSE

CENTER-

STRAßE

10

Street Index

Seidengasse - B8
Seidlgasse - G6, 7
Seilerstätte - E7, F7
Seippgasse - H10
Seisgasse - E10
Seitenstettengasse - E6, F6
Seitergasse - E7
Seitzergasse - E6
Sellenygasse - H7
Semperstraße - C3, 4
Sensengasse - C5
Servitengasse- D4, 5
Seumegasse - B10
Severin-Schreiber-Gassee - A2,3
Severingasse - C4
Siebeckstraße - L1, M1
Siebenbrunnengasse - C10, D10
Siebenbrunnenplatz - C10
Siebensterngasse - C7, 8, D7
Siebertgasse - B10
Siegelgasse - G7
Sigmundgasse - C7
Sillerweg - J8
Simmerzinger Lände - L10
Simon-Denk-Gasse - D4
Sinagasse - L3, 4
Singerstraße - E7, F7
Skodagasse - B6, C5, 6
Slezakgasse - B5
Sobieskigasse - C3
Sobieskiplatz - C3
Sollingergasse - A1
Sonnenfelsgasse - F6
Sonnenuhrgasse - B9
Sorbaitgasse - A7
Spalowskygasse - B9
Sparefrohgasse - F7, G7
Sparkassaplatz - A10
Spechtweg - M3
Spengergasse - C10, D10
Sperrgasse - A9
Spiegelgasse - E7
Spielmanngasse - E1
Spitalgasse - C4, 5
Spittelauer Lände - D2, 3
Spittelauer Platz - D3
Spittelberggasse - C7
Spörlinggasse - C9
Sportklubstraße - H6
Springergasse - G4
St. Johann-Gasse - B10
St. Nikolaus-Platz - H8
St. Ulrichs-Platz - C7
Stadion-Allee - K7, 8
Stadionbrücke - J8
Stadiongasse - D6
Stadtpark - F7
Staglgasse - A9
Stammgasse - G7
Stanislausgasse - G9
Stättermayergasse - A8
Staudgasse - A3, 4, B4
Staudingergasse - E3
Steggasse - D9
Steinergasse - A5
Steingasse - G9, H9
Steinhagegasse - B10
Stelzhamergasse - F7, G7
Stephansplatz - E6, 7
Sterngasse - E6
Sternwartestraße - A2,3, B3, C3
Stiegengasse - D8
Stiegergasse - A10
Stiftgasse - C7, 8, D8
Stöbergasse - D10

Stock-i.-Eisen-Platz - E7
Stoffelagasse - G5
Stolberggasse - D10
Stollgasse - B8
Stolzenthalergasse - B6
Straße des Ersten Mai - H5, 6
Streffleurgasse - E3
Streichergasse - G8
Strobachgasse - D9
Strohgasse - F8
Strohmgasse - B9
Stromstraße- E2, F1, 2
Stropheckgasse - D4
Strozzigasse - C6, 7
Strudlhofgasse- D4
Stubenbastei - F7
Stubenring - F6, 7
Stuckgasse - C7
Stumpergasse - B9, C9
Sturgasse - K5
Stuwer-Straße - J5
Südportalstraße - J6
Syringgasse - B5

Taborstraße – F4, 5, 6, G3, 4
Talgasse - A9
Tandelmarktgasse - F5
Tannengasse - A8
Taubstummengasse - E9
Technikerstraße - E8
Tegetthoffstraße - E7
Teinfaltstraße - D6
Tellgasse - A8
Tempelgasse - G6
Tendlergasse - C4
Tepserngasse - D3
Teschnergasse - B3, 4
Thaliastraße - A6
Thavonatgasse - C5
Thelemanngasse - B6
Theobaldgasse - D8
Theresianumgasse - E9, F9
Thorooicngasse - B5
Thugutstraße - H7
Thurngasse - D5
Thurygasse- D4
Tiefergarben - E6
Tiergartenstraße - H7
Tigergasse - B6, 7
Tilgnergasse - E9
Tongasse - G8
Trabrennstraße - J6, K6
Traisengasse - G2
Trappelgasse - E10
Traunfelsgasse - E3
Traungasse - F8
Traußengasse - D9
Trautsongasse - C7
Treitlstraße - E8
Treustraße - D2, 3, E3, 4
Trubelgasse - G10
Trunnerstraße - G4
Tuchlauben - E6
Tulpengasse - C6
Türkenschanz Platz - A2
Türkenschanz-Straße- A3
Türkenstraße - D5, E5
Turmburggasse - C9
Turnergasse - A9

Uchatiusgasse - G7
Uhlplatz - B6
Ullmannstraße - A10
Ungargasse - G7-9
Universitätsstraße - D5, 6
Universumstraße - F2
Untere Augartenstraße - E4, 5, F4

Untere Donaustraße - F6, G6
Untere Viaduktgasse - G6, 7
Untere Weiß-Gerber-Straße - G6, H6, 7
Urban-Loritz-Platz - B8

Van-Swieten-Gasse - D5
Vedikstraße - A9
Vegagasse - C2
Veithgasse - F8
Veithgasse - F8
Venediger Au - H5
Vereinsgasse - F4, 5, G4
Veronikagasse - B5, 6
Viehmarktgasse - H9, 10, J10
Viktor-Christ-Gasse - D10
Viktorgasse - E9, 10, F10
Viktoriagasse - A9
Vinzenzgasse - A3, 4
Viriotgasse - C3
Vogelsanggasse - D10
Vogelweidplatz - A7, 8
Volkertgasse - F4, G4
Volkertplatz - G4
Volksgarten Straße - D7
Vordere Zollamtsstraße - F7, G6
Vorgartenstraße - F1
Vorgartenstraße - F1, G2, H4, J4, 5, K6
Vorlaufstraße - E6
Vormosergasse - C1

Waaggasse - D9, E9
Wachaustraße - J4
Wagramer Brücke - L2
Wagramer Straße - K2, 3, L1, 2, M1
Währinger Gürtel - B5, C3, 4
Währinger Straße - A3, B3, C4, D5
Walcher Straße - H4
Waldsteincasrdstraße - H6, J6
Walfischgasse - E7
Walkergasse - H1, J1
Wallensteinstraße - E3, F3
Wallgasse - B9, 10
Wällischgasse - J9
Wallnerstraße - E6
Waltergasse - E9
Warhanekgasse - J1
Wasagasse - D5
Waschhausgasse - G6
Wasnergasse - E3
Wassergasse - H7, 8
Webergasse - E3
Webgasse - B9, C9
Wedlgasse - H9
Wehlistraße - G1, 2, H3, J4, 5, L6, 7, M7, 8
Wehrgasse - D9
Weidmanngasse - A4, 5
Weihburggasse - E7, F7
Weilgasse - D1
Weimarer Straße - B2-4
Weinberggasse - A1, B1
Weinlechnergasse - H9
Weintraubengasse - G5
Weiskirchnerstraße - F7
Weißgasse - A5
Weiß-Gerber-Lände - G6, H6, 7
Werdertorgasse - E5
Weschelstraße - H3
Westbahnstraße - B8, C8
Wexstraße - E2
Weyprechtgasse - A6

Weyrgasse - G7
Weyringergasse - E10, F10
Wickenburggasse - C6
Widerhofergasse - C4
Widerhoferplatz - C4
Wiedner Gürtel - E10, F10
Wiedner Hauptstraße - D10, E8-10
Wiesengasse - D3, 4
Wiesingerstraße - F6
Wildbadgasse - J1
Wildgansplatz - H10
Wimbergergasse - B7, 8
Wimmergasse - D10
Winarskystraße - F1
Windmühlgasse - D8
Wipplingerstraße - E5, 6
Wittelsbach-Rotunden-Allee - H7, J6, 7
Wohllebengasse - E8, 9, F8
Wohlmut-Straße - H4, 5, J5
Wolfgang-Schmälzl-Gasse - H4, 5
Wolfsaugasse - E3
Wollzeile - F6, 7
Worellstraße - C9
Würtgasse - E4
Würthgasse - C1
Würtzlerstraße - J9
Wurzbachgasse - A7, 8

Ybbsstraße - H4
Yppengasse - A6
Yppenplatz - A6

Zaunergasse - F8
Zedlitzgasse - F7
Zeinlhofergasse - D9
Zelinkagasse - E5
Zeltgasse - C7
Zentagasse - D10
Zentaplatz - D10
Zeuggasse - D9
Ziegelhofengasse - D9, 10
Zieglergasse - B7, 8
Ziehrerplatz - G8
Zimmermannplatz - B5
Zinckgasse - A8
Zirkusgasse - F5, 6, G5
Zollergasse - C8
Zrinyigasse - E1, 2
Zufahrtsstraße - H5
Zwölfergasse - A9